For here we are not afraid to follow the truth wherever it may lead—nor to tolerate any error so long as reason is free to combat it.

Th: Jefferson

RICHARD HOWLETT CARLTON

LAND OF THE SCOTS

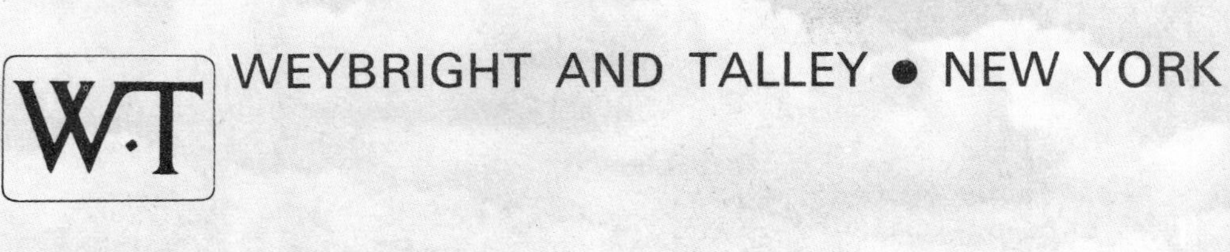
WEYBRIGHT AND TALLEY • NEW YORK

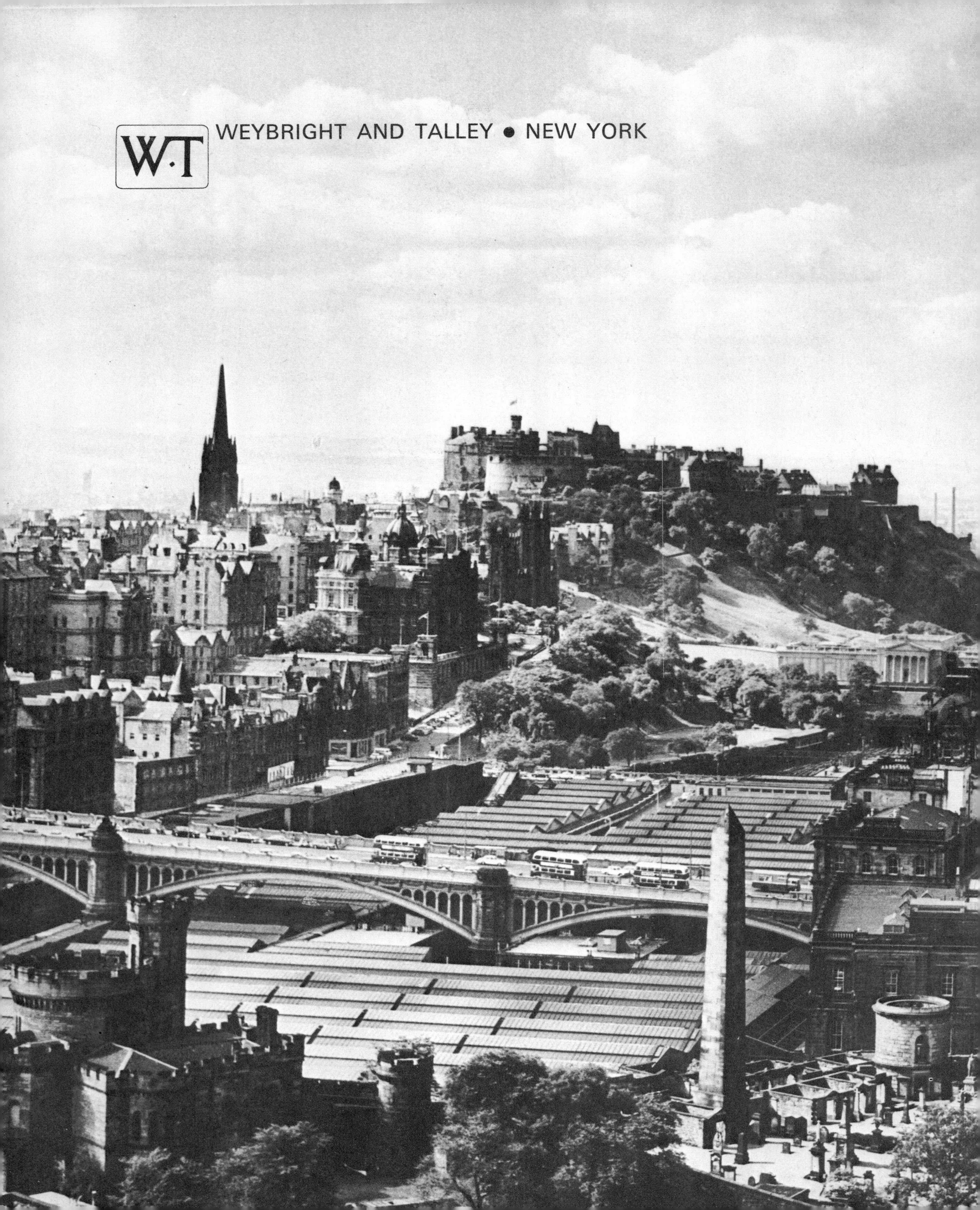

LAND OF THE SCOTS

NIGEL TRANTER

Library of Congress Catalog Card No.
69-13497

Designed by Drummond Chapman

Text set in Ehrhardt 12 pt series 453
captions set in Univers 9 pt series 689
by C. Tinling & Co. Ltd, Prescot and London

Four colour and black and white plates
made and printed in Great Britain,
by Lowe & Brydone (Printers) Ltd, London

Printed on Hi-speed blade-coated
supplied by W. Rowlandson & Co. Ltd, London

Jacket reproduced and printed litho
by Gilmour and Dean Ltd, Glasgow

Bound by Nevett, Key & Whiting Limited, London

Published in the United States by
Weybright and Talley, Inc.
3 East 54th Street,
New York, N.Y. 10022.

CONTENTS

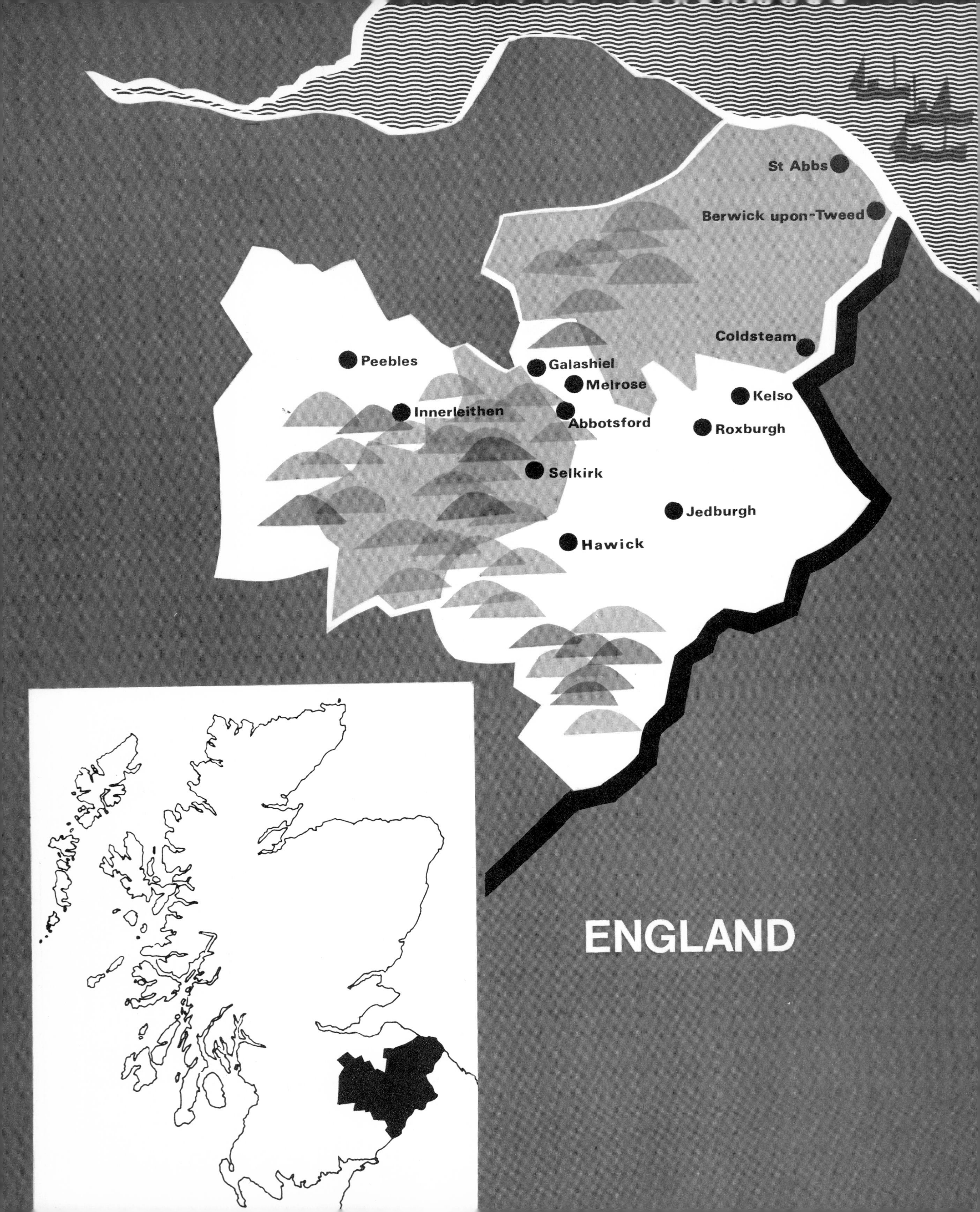

St Abbs
Berwick upon-Tweed
Coldsteam
Peebles
Galashiel
Melrose
Kelso
Innerleithen
Abbotsford
Roxburgh
Selkirk
Jedburgh
Hawick
ENGLAND

CHAPTER 1
THE BORDERS

Whatever other reaction strikes the visitor at first sight of Scotland, the fact that it is *different* must surely be the most immediate and vivid - and this however the traveller arrives; by air, over the green Southern Uplands or the Hebridean seaboard of the Western Approaches; by sea, up the spectacular painted reaches of the Firth of Clyde; by train, through the hills by either East Coast or Midland route; or by road over the Border. In the last, perhaps, is the impact greatest, the transition so strangely sudden. More so on the east than the west, probably. After the long miles of the worthy but somewhat unexciting English North and the levels of the Northumberland plain, the sight of the deep dip of the Tweed estuary, with its three great bridges, and the climbing huddle of Berwick's grey walls and red roofs rising beyond, backed by the thronging green hills and thrusting cliff-girt coastline of Berwickshire, is something to stir even the least perceptive - even though Berwick town itself, by one of those historical nonsenses, has been technically part of England, on the wrong side of Tweed, since the fifteenth century. Thus early does the past start to make itself felt on the Scottish scene.

But even more dramatic than this is the approach over the Cheviots by the A.68 road. I defy anyone however down-to-earth, to emerge from the high barren constrictions of the pass at Carter Bar, to gaze northwards over

8 THE BORDERS

Scotland, and not to be moved. There, spread out abruptly, delectably, is a whole province, the Merse and the East March of the Border, a rolling fair upland of broad farmlands and green sheep-strewn ridges, of rich valleys watered by fine rivers, of compact small towns and castle-crested heights, reaching to the far heathery line of Lammermuir, to Lothian itself. There is 150 square miles of lovely and challenging introduction to Scotland, with names that sing a song—Rulewater, Jedwater, Kalewater, Teviotdale, Tweeddale, the Blackadder, the Whitadder and Coldinghamshire.

For better or for worse, this is another land.

Down the long winding hill, the first little town to be reached, nestling deep in its narrow valley, is Jedburgh, an ancient and royal burgh, and county town of Roxburghshire, which is as good a start as any to a survey of present-day Scotland. For here is a small community of only 4,000 souls, steeped, almost drowned in a history as bloodcurdling and colourful as any in the land, and proud of it—but no sleepy hollow dreaming of the past. As much a fighting community today as ever it was, indeed, though grievously hit by the harsh economics of centralisation, its main mills closed down, its railway link arbitrarily closed—yet hitting back from its quiet valley, with self-help its watchword. After seeking in vain to entice industry to come to employ its folk left idle by the 'rationalising' closure of its mills, its former Provost, James Elliot, went personally all the way to the United States—and in due course came back triumphantly with the promise of an American precision-tools factory for Jedburgh. So now,

BERWICK-ON-TWEED, gateway to Scotland. Oldest of the three bridges, built by James VI. Looking down on it from the two modern bridges that carry the railway and the busy A.1 highway, it vividly assures the traveller that here he enters a *different* land.

beyond the noble ruins of the great abbey, pillaged so often as first stop for English invaders, rises the ultra-modern premises of the most advanced technological progress. It is perhaps as typical as it is amusing that the great trans-Atlantic firm dragooned to the rescue—and finding the process to its taste—should be called Starrett. For these very valleys were once much upset by a Borderer named Starrett, or Starhead, who with two others was outlawed for the assassination of the Scots Warden of the Marches, just before Flodden. The Warden was named Kerr—still the main landowning family around Jedburgh. As ever, the crowding past remains just around the corner for even the most go-ahead Scots.

Starretts, and Jedburgh, are still having their battles to fight, largely against bureaucratic red-tape—but at least fewer Jethart folk have to board the fleet of buses every day to carry them to work a dozen miles and more away.

It is down Jedwater and up fair Teviotdale that most of those buses have to run. By lovely reaches of the river, by ancient battlefields and ballad-haunted slopes, under proud Minto Tower soaring on its crag, and beneath the shapely cone of Ruberslaw where the Covenanters defied state control three centuries ago, the buses come to Hawick—Queen o' a' the Borders, according to Hawick folk.

That is one of the most important aspects of all this area, which will be forgotten by the planners, politicians and everybody else at their peril—the intense local patriotism of the Borderers. It permeates their attitude to life, and is expressed in their work, their interests and their play—most

JEDBURGH ABBEY. One of the lovely abbeys of the Borderland, in the county town of Roxburghshire. In the town, Mary Queen of Scots lay ill, after riding half across Scotland to see Bothwell, and later was to grieve, in an English prison, "would that I had died at Jedworth!"

notably in trade competition and in the friendly rivalry of the hard-fought rugby fields. Above all, in those exciting and splendid manifestations of Border high spirits, the Common Ridings and Festivals.

At a Common Riding, here or elsewhere in the Borderland, those unfortunates born elsewhere will nevertheless enjoy themselves to the full. That is, provided they have the necessary stamina. For the pace is hot, the programme full-blooded and the engagement long. It can last a whole week; indeed preliminary canters, rides-out to various historic points on the boundaries of the former commonlands—often many miles away—go on for weeks before the final climax. Then all the mills and shops shut, the burgh goes on holiday, plumbers and butchers'-boys suddenly become horsemen, the town's colours are worn in every buttonhole, and provosts and town councillors prepare to earn their titles the hard way. Up at dewy dawn, to welcome the sunrise at some mound or stone which can go back to Druidical times, the day is old and throats are hoarse with singing even before the Provost's breakfast—where the visitor learns to take public oratory with his porridge, and the teetotaller finds himself at distinct disadvantage. Then to horse—and even though, of course, the majority of the townsfolk do not actually find themselves in the saddle, an astonishing number do; which is one reason why Border fields are still so hearteningly full of horseflesh. Then the Cornet, a young unmarried stalwart chosen by vote to be the burgh's standard-bearer—the greatest honour perhaps open to any Borderer—receives the banner, and the chase is on. No two Common Ridings are held in the same week, so that riders can come from all the other burghs to support—or to decry and outride—the local talent. And not only in cross-country riding and racing, but in band-playing, oratory, song-singing, story-telling, banqueting, dancing, and—whisper it—drinking. Three days—and three nights—of this, and it is a remarkable visitor who can still remember what life was like before the Common Riding.

Exiles, Border folk who have emigrated, come back from the ends of the earth for these affairs—and long may they do so.

Hawick, five times the size of Jedburgh, can claim to earn probably more foreign exchange for the economy than any other town of its size in the United Kingdom. In every corner of the world, wherever top quality knitwear and hosiery is appreciated, Hawick and the names of its famous firms are household words. Here the finest jumpers, sweaters, twin-sets and the like are produced, imitated all over but never rivalled in quality, design or style. In this highly competitive modern industry, the mills of the Borders lead the way.

Hawick is not alone in the quality woollen trade, of course. Galashiels, Selkirk, Peebles, Innerleithen, to mention only the best-known, are likewise involved; and Langholm, just over into Dumfriesshire, where the famous Reid and Taylor proudly advertise the most expensive twist suitings cloths in the world and combine a modern art gallery with their worker's canteen. The baaing of sheep, long the background music of the Borderland, with the people's competitive spirit, has brought this about. Fine cloths and worsteds, as well as knitwear and underwear, spun yarns and just plain wool for knitting and carpet-making, come in some form from every valley. The word tweed speaks for itself.

Galashiels, in the midst of the lovely Scott country, whose rivalry with Hawick is intense in almost every sphere, is a lively place that by no means takes Queen-o'-a'-the-Borders sort of talk lying down. Approximately of similar size, it boasts the Scottish Woollen Technical College, necessarily one of the most advanced of such establishments in being, and a Mecca for aspiring textile leaders. Also, amongst its many renowned firms one is deservedly proud of having broken into the charmed circles of the Paris haute couture market—Ebenezer Y. Johnston and Hunter and Co., whose fashion fabrics lead the field.

But it must not be supposed that Border initiative is confined to this traditional industry. Diversification is a growing and healthy preoccupation, for the woollen trade employs a preponderance of female labour. Some of the new projects are adventurous indeed. For instance, in Galashiels also there has grown up in recent years a firm called Royal Scot Bows—the largest bowmakers in Europe. This is the saga of George Birnie, a Gala boy apprenticed to a Melrose bowmaker, forced to emigrate to America—where he taught Commanche Indians the use of the bow and arrow—but who returned to his native town and, with the current revival of archery as a sport, makes bows by the thousand, and has turned his attention to water-skis.

The belated decision to declare the Borders a Development Area has sparked off considerable controversy—not because the Borderers are against development but because certain high-level government planners decided in their

12 THE BORDERS

(Below) THE CORNET'S CHASE, at Hawick Common Riding. These march-riding festivals, held by all the Border burghs, however small, are one of the most exhilarating and authentic manifestations of the independent Border spirit. (Right) TIBBIE SHIELS INN, St. Mary's Loch, set in the lonely hills between Selkirk and Moffat.

wisdom that the development should take place just east of Galashiels. A glance at the map would have shown these experts that Sir Walter Scott's famed home, Abbotsford, lies just east of Galashiels; and a word with one or two ordinary Border folk would have informed them that not only are the people hereabouts inordinately proud of their Sir Walter and everything connected with him, but that they would infinitely prefer their development spread over the existing burghs. The least awareness of the vigorous Border mentality would have indicated caution, here. But no; far-away authority made its decision—and the balefires started to blaze again in the Borders.

That is also Scotland today.

Selkirk, possibly the most proudly ancient of all the Border towns, a royal burgh since the twelfth century and with a vested interest in Sir Walter—whose sheriffship was seated here—sits quietly by and watches, prepared to join in when necessary. Unlike most of its neighbours, which are set deep in their valleys, Selkirk is built on a hillside, climbing high above the Ettrick, with glorious views down Tweed and up to the wild hills of Ettrick and Yarrow. Despite its setting, however, this is a busy manufacturing place also, with mills and dyeworks as renowned as any, and it, not nearby Galashiels, is the county seat. Once, there were two Selkirks. Selkirk Regis clustered round the royal castle which formerly crowned a hill here; and Selkirk Abbatis, the town beside the abbey. For those who do not connect an abbey with Selkirk, it should be explained that David I founded one here in 1113, actually before he was king. This, believe it or not, is the well-known Kelso Abbey. For reasons not explained, after thirteen years of existence the establishment was removed lock, stock and barrel, over twenty miles eastwards to Kelso on the edge of the coastal plain of the Merse, 'for convenience'. Selkirk has a common riding tradition second to none.

The high round green hills everywhere dominate the Borderland. But at Selkirk the sense of being on the very edge of the wilderness is more vivid than elsewhere. Not only because of the wider panoramas, but because in fact it *is* the last outpost. South and West of it the great hills march range after range, almost empty save for the remote small village, the lonely peel tower, the occasional sheep-farm. Deep amongst these upland fastnesses lie the tranquil St. Mary's Loch, the largest sheet of inland water in South Scotland, and the smaller Loch o' the Lowes, beloved of Scott, Wordsworth, Hogg the Ettrick Shepherd and lesser folk—'fifteen miles from anywhere'. It is in fact exactly fifteen and a half miles south-west of Selkirk, and fifteen and a half miles north-east of Moffat in Dumfriesshire—and nothing larger than the merest hamlet between either. Such is this corner of our crowded isle, still.

The Tweed itself does not quite reach Selkirk, but swings away north-westwards through close-crowding hillsides on its lovely way, by Yair and Fairnilee, Caddon-

(Below) THE TWEED VALLEY near Elibank, looking west towards Peebles. (Right) THE EILDON HILLS, on the Berwickshire-Roxburghshire border. Near here was Sir Walter Scott's favourite view. On the flank of the right hand peak is Thomas the Rhymer's Glen and Tree.

foot and Elibank, to Innerleithen and Peebles. This reach is for me the finest, and because the nudging hills insist, the road keeps it close company for twenty famed and enchanting miles that, in name at least, Scott has made familiar to millions. Not unnaturally so, for apart from the loveliness it was here that he made his first Border home, at Ashiestiel. It is the custom to picture Sir Walter doing most of his writing at Abbotsford, but much was written here, including most of *Marmion*. He lived for eight happy and productive years at Ashiestiel and it is believed that had he been able to buy the property instead of only renting it, there would have been no Abbotsford.

By Traquair's ancient laird's house, where one laird used to fish out of his bedroom window, another found this too watery altogether and diverted Tweed to run a quarter-mile further back, and their present-day descendant marches with the times and takes a lively part in the stately-homes business, even brewing and selling his own beer from the tower brewhouse—by Traquair we come to Peebles.

Peebles is somehow different from all other Border burghs, gentler, more relaxed, a comfortable matronly town of fine hotels, modern shops and substantial housing, spreading itself in a widening of the valley. Its position is in fact magnificent, and best appreciated by climbing one of its adjacent heights. Here the hills draw back somewhat, and though high, lose something of their austerity, with slantwise fields and hanging woodlands. There is industry at Peebles, of course—the name of Ballantyne ranks high amongst the knitwear and woollen firms—but the impression given is not of any manufacturing town. I have the impression that Peebles prefers to be looked on as a 'literary' place. And with reason. For, apart from Scott and Wordsworth, Christopher North, James Hogg, Robert Louis Stevenson and Samuel Crockett were all lovers of the town, the brothers Robert and William Chambers were born here; and in more recent times the connection of John Buchan and his sister O. Douglas with Peebles is well known.

Innerleithen, six miles downstream, is an unlikely sort of place to find in this country, a compact, businesslike, douce little town giving no impression of age and looking as though it had been planned rather than having grown. As indeed is the case, for until 1790, when the first woollen mill was established here, the place was only a hamlet and a kirk. So Innerleithen is something of a 'new boy' in this land of age-old communities—though the parish of that name was

ancient enough. Its transformation came about in two ways. First, a Traquair blacksmith named Brodie was an early example of that enduring species, the Scots lad o' pairts, who went down to London and made a fortune; in due course to return to his native valley and establish this mill at Innerleithen, which, with others following, throve mightily. Then the excellent Sir Walter publicised its mineral spring, St. Ronan's Well, so effectively that the place became a spa, with pumproom and recreation rooms. It even spawned a satellite village of Walkerburn, with another mill, in 1855—altogether a rather extraordinary development for the Borderland.

As for the rest of Peebles-shire, the Upper Tweed basin, few areas of Lowland Scotland can have so little of industry about them—save only Berwickshire to the east. It is a highly attractive area, scenically, an angler's paradise with sparkling waters everywhere, old estates, hill farms and small villages. There are no other towns. It is strange that an area so close to industrial Central Scotland should have remained so undeveloped, for the county boundary is only about seventeen miles form Edinburgh G.P.O., and Peebles itself twenty-two. The important highways pass it by. I have heard no complaints.

Back down Tweed into Roxburghshire again, the valley widens and the hills draw back as the great river flows in more stately fashion, by Melrose, St. Boswells and Dryburgh, to the Merse. Melrose, lying snugly between the spectacular triple peaks of Thomas the Rhymer's Eildons and the hanging orchards of Gattonside, might be thought of as one of Scotland's most sheltered communities. Peace and beauty seem to lap it, and the mellow red-stone ruins of the famous abbey preside benignly over all. It is not to be wondered at, therefore, that the area has become a notable haven for retired colonels and ex-empire-builders. Yet Melrose is not so withdrawn from affairs as it may seem. Perhaps one of the ancient abbey sculptures, of a pig blowing the bagpipes, may hint at a different character. Some of the liveliest public meetings of the Borders have been held here; it was the focal point of protest against the long-range planners; and the vigour of its rugby seven-a-sides are famous throughout the land. It would be strange indeed if spirit was lacking in Melrose for here, in the abbey, was buried the heart of the great Bruce, at his own request.

And to those other Borderers who rather look down well-doing noses at Melrose on account of lack of industry and commercial initiative, it should be remembered that

16 THE BORDERS

this is in fact one of the great tourist centres of the land—and tourism is today one of Scotland's most rewarding industries, whether the Scots admit it or not.

Nearby is an amusing example of the triumph of fiction over fact, amongst an allegedly hard-headed people—allegedly, for of course, despite their own vigorous assertions to the contrary, the Scots are one of the most romantically-minded races on earth. Up the Allan Water, north of Tweed, is a group of three ruined tower-houses. Ask anyone about these, and they will tell you that the name of the best-preserved is Glendearg. In fact most will refer to the whole area as Glendearg. If this strikes you as a very Highland-sounding name for a Border peel and valley you will be right. For Glendearg is not its true name at all. We come back to Walter Scott, as is so often the case in the Borderland. For purposes of his own, Scott used this location in *The Monastery*, and chose, for some reason unspecified, to call the Cairncross's tower of Hillslap, Glendearg. What was wrong with Hillslap—a good Border-sounding name? But Glendearg it gradually became, so that now even locals cannot point the way to Hillslap, and the maps themselves print only the novelist's word for it. There is a lesson here, somewhere.

It is one of the unexplained oddities of Scotland that, out of no vast number of abbeys, four of the greatest of them should have been erected within a few miles of each other—and in such dangerous proximity to the English border. Which makes it all the more strange that Selkirk's establishment should have been shifted down here, to Kelso, to add to the clutter. Dryburgh is only three miles from Melrose—not as the Tweed bends but as the crow flies—and though its ruins are more fragmentary than those of its neighbours, they are unsurpassed in beauty. Here lies Sir Walter himself, in the company of the first Earl Haig from nearby Bemersyde, and other illustrious Borderers.

When you refer to St. Boswells, most people today tend to think of the rather unlovely and utilitarian community, Newtown, which has grown up around the railway junction, and which has developed, because of ease of communication and a central position—plus its great livestock market—into too much of a power-in-the-land for most of the other independent-minded Border towns. But nearby, on a side-road to the south-east, is the original and attractive village of St. Boswells itself, backing on to Tweed and facing south over a very lovely prospect to the Cheviots. With its enormous village green, and the fine old sixteenth century fortalice of Lessudden rising just behind it, here is a spot deserving to be better known than just as the headquarters of the Duke of Buccleuch's Foxhounds.

For sheer modest excellence of appearance Kelso, at the junction of Tweed and Teviot, beats all other Border towns—indeed rivals any in Scotland. And that despite some modern blemishes—though I am glad to say that the great new high school handsomely set in spacious greensward on the northern environs does not come into that category. Looking almost Flemish with its colour-washed eighteenth century houses, its wide market square and riverside lanes, all in a delightful setting of spreading parkland, gentle slopes and water meadows, it has a mellow spaciousness and urbanity not usually associated with Scottish urban areas, which is the more surprising in that it lies only a few miles from the Borderline, and has a record rather greater than average of strife and pillage.

Kelso, essentially the market town for a rich agricultural area, has become involved in the Eastern Borders Development Association. Whether this will eventually alter the basic character of the place remains to be seen.

Small Duns, away up in the southern lap of the Lammermuirs, since Berwick's defection, is all that Berwickshire has for a county seat. This is not to belittle Duns as a town, for it is an attractive place in its remote rural setting, with its burghal architecture set down in picturesque disarray. But with a population of only 2,000, no railway and no main highway within miles, it is hardly a suitable metropolis for the county—where all roads lead inevitably to stolen Berwick-on-Tweed. But Duns does its best—and at least its great and handsome public park is worthy of a town ten times its size. The Duns annual Summer Festival, too, a week's Common Riding and allied excitements, is as spirited an affair as any in the Borders—a challenge and reproach to communities infinitely larger the land over. 'Duns Dings A' is the town's motto—and it is not the Duns folk's fault if it does not.

If Duns is a paragon in the scale of its annual celebrations, what of Lauder in the hills twenty miles to the west, one of the three other burghs of Berwickshire—and its only royal burgh at that, though with only about 650 of a population? For this tiny but ancient municipality mounts its own Common Riding on a scale with the rest—a heroic yearly effort indeed, though admittedly for the remainder of the year Lauder may give the casual visitor the impression of lying back in recuperative slumber. The busy A.68

IN THE LYNE VALLEY, Peebles-shire, a tributary of Tweed.
Typical Border country.

THE SAVAGE YET MAGNIFICENT SEABOARD of Berwickshire, one of the most dramatic in the kingdom. North of St. Abb's Head, with the ruins of Fast Castle in the background. Lifeboat Stations, 3 Coastguard Stations and a Signal Station within 25 miles. They were not enough for the *SS Nyon.*

highway to the south threads it—and it is perhaps typical of Lauder that it makes the road circuit its quaint town-house, plumped right in the middle of the street. A street which, it might be added, can boast two subsidiaries respectively entitled Upper and Under Backsides.

It has been indicated that there are only four burghs in Berwickshire, a county of nearly 300,000 acres. But this is not to imply that it is any sort of upland desert. Some magnificent farming land is to be found here, and the rolling green countryside of the Merse is richly scattered with large 'farm-touns'. The system has developed of each farm becoming almost a self-contained community, with its row of sturdy cottages, and often a smiddy and a little shop as well—sometimes even a small school. Though burghs and villages are few and far between, the land gives no impression of impoverishment.

This was the traditional stamping-ground of the warlike Border clan of Home—and much of the land is still in the hands of Home lairds, with Sir Alec, lately fourteenth Earl of Home, only one of many. Scotland is a great country for the old families clinging to their lands—however ill-gotten in the first place. Some of the tales of Home doings in the Merse could make Messrs. Bond & Company look very small beer indeed.

Sir Alec Douglas-Home's house, The Hirsel, lies close to Coldstream, the third of the burghs. The little town, though famous to the Southron only as the founding-place of the Coldstream Guards, has in fact been a very important place in Scotland's past, for here was the first ford and crossing-place of Tweed above the heavily-guarded bridge at Berwick. Consequently armies and raiders innumerable, from both sides, have used Coldstream. It is fitting that it is this small community which should each year mount an ambitious cavalcade to Flodden Field, some five miles into England, to pay ceremonious respect 'to the dead of both nations'. Equally, it is perhaps indicative of the different attitudes of the two peoples that very little reaction tends to be manifested on the English side towards these ceremonies.

And so we come to the last and least typical area of the Borderland—the coastal strip which stretches northwards from Berwick to Dunbar in Lothian. Here is one of the wildest and most spectacular seaboards in these islands, surprisingly little known, even by Lowland Scots folk—partly because there is no lateral road to serve it. There are some twenty-five miles of it, fierce cliffs reaching as high as 300 feet at St. Abb's Head, thrusting reefs, rocky coves and towering pinnacles, where the North Sea wages ceaseless war with the land. Something of its style may be gauged from the fact that there are three Lifeboat Stations, four Coastguard Stations and a Signal Station within twenty-five miles.

Yet here, cowering under the cliffs, are small fishing villages of great character and charm. And half-way up the coast, where the cliffs draw back and the Eye waters flows into a small bay, is the county's largest burgh, Eyemouth. At one time famous as a smuggling centre, and even now not entirely at one with authority over the out-dated and inequitable salmon-fishing laws at sea, Eyemouth is today one of the most important fishing ports of the Scottish East Coast, however modest in size. It has recently tackled a most ambitious harbour improvement scheme, amounting almost to a re-making; it is in the forefront of the new lobster-fishing and exporting trade; its fine school is said to produce more navigators than any other in Scotland; and it is a busy place with its fish-market, boat-building yards and tourist accommodation.

The main East Coast highway, A.1., a few miles north of Berwick, strikes off up the valley of the Eye westwards, cutting off a strange corner of land where the Lammermuir Hills come down to the sea as in a clenched fist. It seems that this has always been a separated and distinct area, of about forty square miles, anciently known as Coldinghamshire—though that was an ecclesiastical jurisdiction stemming from the great Priory of Coldingham, princely once, the much truncated ruins of which still dominate the attractive village of that name. Why more people do not visit and appreciate this exciting land, I do not know—although perhaps the Coldinghamshire folk are well content to have it so.

Looking back over the Borderland from the crests of Lammermuir, then, we see a territory of great beauty, challenge and diversity, fiercely individual and independent, steeped in history—but on the march, now as it has ever been. That it is steadily losing its sturdy folk by eroding depopulation is a tragedy, an indictment of central government and a grave loss to Scotland. The Borderers do not want help from anyone; just to be allowed to gang their ain gait. But perhaps that is too much to ask in the twentieth century?

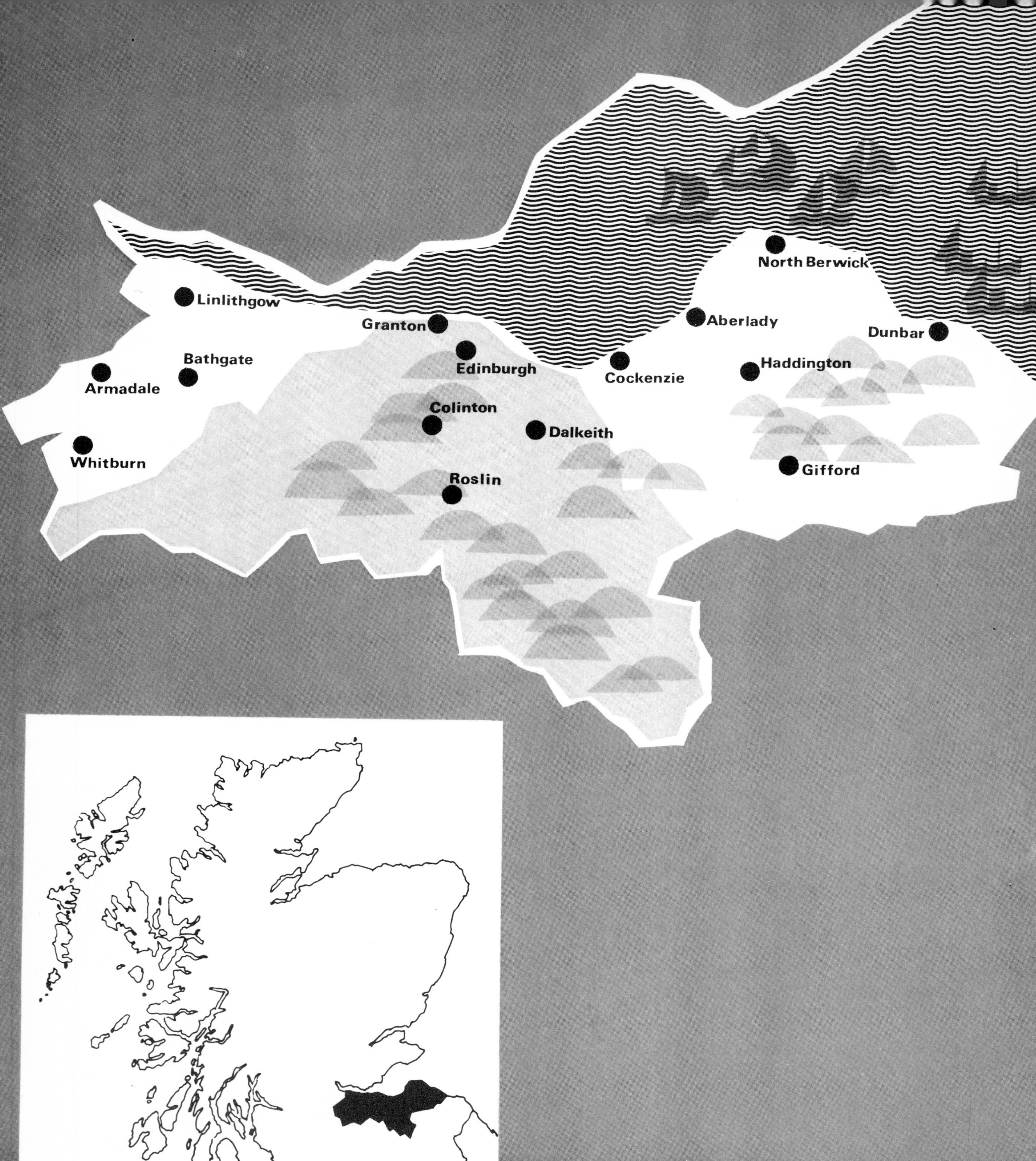

Linlithgow
Granton
Edinburgh
Bathgate
Armadale
Colinton
Dalkeith
Whitburn
Roslin
North Berwick
Aberlady
Dunbar
Haddington
Cockenzie
Gifford

CHAPTER 2
EDINBURGH AND LOTHIAN

There are some who will tell you that the Lothians are the least Scottish part of Scotland, now and always have been. Though these experts will almost assuredly come from Glasgow and the West, there is perhaps a grain of truth in the assertion. This may seem strange, with Edinburgh, the capital city dominating the area. Of course, it is declared that London is not England, nor Paris France, but this is rather a different claim. It is not the big-city aspect that is referred to - for Glasgow, much larger, is never suggested to be anything but sufficiently Scottish; nor is it any appearance of the countryside, which is in the main highly attractive and authentic enough - not to be mistaken for any part of England, certainly. It is against the character and attitude of the people that this charge is apt to be levelled - though, some, of course, might term it a compliment. I shall not press the matter. But at least let us remember that the rest of Scotland tends to look with some slight suspicion on Edinburgh and Lothian, with or without reason, and seems always to have done so. It is something of a joke, of course - but such age-old jokes often have their roots in something more than humour.

Once, to be sure, most of Lothian was not reckoned by the rest of the country to be part of its polity at all, but merely an outlying part of Northumbria. There was even a theory advanced that its people were purely Anglo-Saxon as to stock. This is sheer nonsense, for the very name is thought to derive from Loth, sixth

22 EDINBURGH AND LOTHIAN

century king of the Southern Picts, whose capital was on the noted landmark of Traprain Law in the midst of East Lothian—and the Picts were a Celtic people. Innumerable of the place-names of the Lothians give the lie to any purely Anglo-Saxon origin. Dunbar, Dunsappie and Dundas, to pick out one of hundreds from each of the three Lothians, are typically Scoto-Celtic.

The area, consisting of the three modern counties of East, Mid and West Lothian, plus the city of Edinburgh, lies along the south side of the great estuary of the Firth of Forth for some fifty miles, with an average depth of one-third of that—say 750 square miles altogether. Not a great slice of Scotland, as mileages go—less than half of the Border area, for instance—but an entity enormously important in the land, historically, politically, industrially, and every other way. Here, for better or for worse, a major part of Scotland's story has been spelt out; that, even the most violent denigrator will not deny.

The Lammermuir Hills form the boundary between the Borders and Lothian, to the east. Were it not for these, East Lothian could mainly have been included in the Merse—for there is a Border aspect to this county. It was, of course, on the direct invasion route from the South, via Berwick. In fact Dunbar Castle, now nothing more than a red fang jutting from an equally red rock above the attractive fishing harbour, was always reckoned to be a Border fortress.

East Lothian falls naturally into four main divisions: the coastal plain; the very lovely vale of Tyne, parallel to it but separated by the long whaleback of the low, green Garleton Hills; the rolling foothill country of Lammermuir to the south; and westwards, apart and distinct, the mining and industrial area—which in fact is much more typical of Midlothian than East.

The estuary of the Forth has been uncomplimentarily compared with its sister estuary of Clyde at the other side of Scotland—though not so far away, for the two salt-waters come within a mere thirty miles of each other. Admittedly the Forth lacks the magnificent backcloth of the Highland hills and islands which come down practically to Glasgow's doorstep and throng the Clyde; but it is a noble firth in its own right, and it has finer and much more extensive sandy strands to flank it, on both sides, than has the painted Clyde. Few great cities can have the like on their thresholds.

The forty-odd miles of scalloped coastline, from the Esk at Musselburgh to the Cockburnspath coves, quickly become one of the most pleasing and distinctive littorals in the two kingdoms, not spectacular and wild like the Berwickshire cliffs, but characterful, varied, and sun-soaked under great skies—for East Lothian is one of the sunniest parts of the British Isles. Extraodinarily remote-seeming, too, to be so close to Edinburgh. It is a seaboard of golden strands backed by steep, tall sand-dunes, range after range, where the marram-grasses and buckthorns rustle; of bays great and small, where the wildfowl and waders flight at dusk and dawn; of thrusting small rocky headlands decked with wild-flowers, salt-sprayed; of vast empty tidelands and salt-marsh where a myriad pools reflect the great light, and sunsets are a glory; of little rock-girt fishing harbours with red-pantiled, crowstepped-gabled villages and ancient square-towered churches; of off-shore islands, haunted by the seals, the gannets, the cormorants and the terns, culminating in the mighty stack of the Bass Rock that stands guard over the entire estuary.

As well as all this, the coastline is bordered by a resounding and famous series of splendid, wind-swept golf-links—Longniddry, Kilspindie, Luffness, Gullane, Muirfield, North Berwick. For this, rather than St. Andrews, is where the game originated. It is recounted of a Prime Minister of Denmark, on a visit to Scotland, that as a rest from formalities in the capital he was taken for a drive down the Lothian coast to North Berwick—where the Provost asked him how he liked what he had seen.

'Magnificent!' the Dane replied. 'I note that all the land totally unfitted for golf-courses is given over to agriculture!'

This, of course, is less than fair. If the visitor had been taken by one of the inland roads, by the wide Vale of Peffer—which is so gentle a vale as to be almost a plain—or through the great Vale of Tyne, by Haddington the county town, he would have spoken differently. For here is some of the finest grain-land in all Europe, farmed with such expertise as to prove it to the hilt, with yields of wheat and barley, potatoes and roots unmatched anywhere else in the world. The great farms of East Lothian are in a class by themselves—as their enormous rents proclaim—and farmers come from far and near to see and admire. The rich red soil is so fertile, stone-free and easily worked that even Cromwell's soldiers declared 300 years ago that here was 'the greatest plenty of corn they ever saw, not one of the fields fallow.' Since then the standard has continued to rise, and out of East Lothian have come a long and distinguished line of land improvers, who have enriched not only their own broad acres but the agriculture of the world—names such as

DUNBAR, East Lothian, looking south towards the Berwickshire cliffs. Skateraw Lighthouse in middle distance. Fang guarding outer harbour is all that remains of ancient castle of Earls of Dunbar, one of 'the keys of the Kingdom'. Dunbar is probably the driest, sunniest spot in Scotland, and a favourite holiday resort and fishing port.

EDINBURGH, from Calton Hill area. The raised arm of the Old Town rises to the clenched fist of the Castle, on left. Prospect of Princes Street, one of the most famous thoroughfares on earth, reaches westwards, with New Town on right. Behind is the wooded ridge of Corstorphine Hill, with the Pentlands hazy in the distance.

(Below) NEAR NORTH BERWICK. Typical stretch of East Lothian coastline. Mile upon mile of such sands flank the Firth of Forth, backed by dunes, frequently transformed into some of the finest golf courses in the world. (Right) LOTHIAN FIELD-WORKER. These bonnets are still worn, and made, by the farm-workers, as protection against the sun.

Lord Belhaven, Fletcher of Saltoun, Cockburn of Ormiston, Hunter, Meikle, Wight, Hope and many another.

The huge expansive fields make a sea of purple-red or rippling gold, depending on the season, islanding the green demesnes, castles and mansions of age-old lairdships, which in such numbers eloquently testify to the richness of the land. Here are some of the finest examples of Scotland's authentic native architecture, tall mellow stone tower-houses such as Lennoxlove, Winton, Fountainhall and Pilmuir; and later noble mansions of the calibre of Tyninghame, Whittinghame, Colstoun, Gosford and the like.

To the south the fields begin to rise to sheep-strewn uplands—but there is still mile upon mile of splendid farming country, interspersed with magnificent woodland and rich pasture. These foothill lands are amongst the most attractive, in a pastoral, unspoiled, settled fashion, of all Lowland Scotland. The views northwards from their braes over the spread of Lothian to the silver plain of the Forth can be quite breathtaking. There are no towns here, only small and delightful villages tucked away in sheltered valleys and hollows—Gifford, Bolton, Garvald, Stenton, Oldhamstocks and others. There is one called Spott—and believe it or not, there is a Little Spott. The villages of Scotland are, by and large, not her most attractive feature—certainly not to be compared with many in England; but here they are a sturdy delight.

East Lothian is not however a wholly agricultural entity. Its western section has long been fairly highly industrialised—though much that is scenic survives, largely because of the abundance of trees and the undulating nature of the land. But even in the characteristically rural parts a go-ahead spirit is in evidence, with new ventures meeting the challenge of the mid-twentieth century; so that we find a modern electronics factory perched on the cliff-top just across from the tremendous ruins of Tantallon Castle, the Douglas stronghold near North Berwick; a great cement-making complex on the rich coastal plain east of Dunbar; and a brand-new abbey built amongst the Lammermuir foothills at Garvald.

Perhaps typical of the Scots' notable fondness for being both forward-looking and backward-looking at the same time is the highly successful and exciting facelift that Haddington, the county town, has applied to its burghal aspect. Sponsored by the Civic Trust and the Town Council, but paid for by the individual owners, the ancient town by the Tyne has spruced up its street frontages in a

comprehensive scheme of repainting, harling and colour-washing. Always a notable example of the excellent and dignified Scots burgh architecture, Haddington has now restored much of the colour and gaiety of former days to its exterior street scenes, at the same time as modernising the interiors, in a most worth-while lead to civic communities everywhere.

Coal and salt were the foundations of the industrial development in East Lothian, to which fishing and pottery-making were added. The salt-pans of Preston and the coal-mines of Tranent were both famous from an early period—although notorious might better describe the latter, for some of the most terrible excesses in the employment of female and child labour underground occurred here, even though it was the monks who first won coal under Tranent. But those days are gone, and now Tranent, though still the largest burgh in the county, with a population of over 6,000, has diversified its industry, and there is an industrial estate to the east, at Macmerry. Prestonpans now produces neither coal nor salt, but nearby, at Cockenzie, is the great new power-station, the largest in Europe at time of writing, sited on land largely reclaimed from the sea. Though this monster, with its network of cables and pylons marching off in all directions, hardly adds to the amenity of the area, at least its lines are clean and functional—and beneath it the fishing harbours of Cockenzie and Port Seton still go about their traditional business unconcerned. And to the other side, in the centre of modern Preston, is one of the most distinguished groups of fine architecture in the country—the tall tower of Preston itself, the seventeenth century lairds' houses of Northfield and Hamilton, with their doocots, and the delightful market cross, also of the seventeenth century; all of which should be better known. The new Roman Catholic church erected nearby, in the most advanced modern style, at least is in striking contrast.

Prestonpans is only a few miles from Edinburgh's outskirts. But it is no suburb of the capital—Musselburgh sees to that. For between them, on the banks of the Esk, lies this most sturdy and independent of communities, the largest burgh of Midlothian, and known as the Honest Toun for over 600 years. Musselburgh's main preoccupation for most of that time seems to have been to keep great Edinburgh at bay.

'Musselburgh was a burgh when Edinburgh was nane,
And Musselburgh'll be a burgh when Edinburgh's gane!'

(Left) DUDDINGSTON VILLAGE AND LOCH. Looking out over Midlothian from Arthur's Seat. Few cities can have so distinctive and unspoiled a village within their boundaries. The loch is a wild-bird sanctuary. (Below) VAST NEW COCKENZIE POWER-STATION, built on reclaimed foreshore beside the ancient fishing-harbour. Prestonpans and Musselburgh beyond.

(Below) OLD EDINBURGH. The Canongate, near the Palace of Holyroodhouse, with effective street lighting. Many of these ancient houses and tall 'lands' have been restored in an ambitious municipal programme. (Right) WHITEHOUSE CLOSE, one of the major restoration works of sixteenth century Edinburgh, now converted into modern flats.

runs the jingle that is shouted vehemently from every throat at each annual Honest Toun's Festival—a Common Riding affair to rival any in the Borders. A busy, bustling place of wire-works, prefabricated-housing-works and the famed Inveresk paper-mills, and unfortunately threaded, all but choked, by the main A.1 highway, Musselburgh has no great distinction of appearance; though its late sixteenth century tolbooth is attractive with a Dutch look, and the handsome fortified mansion of Pinkie now part of the well known Loretto boys' school, adds dignity to the town. But what it lacks in beauty it makes up for in history and spirits. For this, the only crossing-place of the Esk for miles, was inevitably a major strategic location as far back as Roman times. And even Glasgow cannot hold a candle to Musselburgh in its attitude to Edinburgh. Poor Edinburgh!

Perhaps it is as well that the capital has to suffer this age-old attitude of criticism and suspicion from the rest of Scotland—otherwise it might well become too intolerably puffed-up, conceited and self-satisfied altogether. For this, the Athens of the North, the Dun-Edin of the Celtic kings, the Capital on the Seven Hills, the Cradle of the Golden Age and home of culture, the Festival City of today—this of course is one of the most famous and beautiful cities in all the world. Many cities outdo Edinburgh in population, but only Rio de Janeiro, that I know, vies with Edinburgh in beauty and location, and cannot compare with it in character and architecture.

Most visitors undoubtedly gain their first impressions of the capital from famed Princes Street—that is, if they have not had the misfortune to arrive by train, in daylight, and so been introduced via the back premises of endless dingy but highly durable stone tenements; but to view Edinburgh adequately it is necessary to get up on high. The choice of vantage points is legion, the best-known, no doubt, being the Castle battlements, or that other artificial height, the top of the Scott Monument in Princes Street. The really energetic get at least some way up Arthur's Seat, that extraordinary lion-shaped hill mass which rears its proud head amongst its surrounding crags in the very centre of the city, to dominate all. But these give only limited vistas, since all are central. From the far ridge of the Pentland Hills the panorama, of course, is superb, but just a little too distant for fullest detail. The prospect from the Braid or Blackford Hills, to the south, is delectable—even that from the top of Liberton Brae; while from various points on Corstorphine Hill to the west, Edinburgh is a sight to

uplift the heart. And there are many others. One little known, from the ridge at Fawside Castle behind Musselburgh, is an excitement. The modern city is built in a vast enclave between the Lammermuir, Moorfoot and Pentland Hill ranges, and the Firth of Forth. This enclave itself, however, is no hollow, but actually a great slantwise shelf which slopes down in waves and rolls to the sea, and out of which rise unnumbered lesser heights, abrupt, rocky, tree-clad, or merely gently green. Round these islands the great, grey city eddies and swirls, and surges quite high up not a few, crowning some, like the Calton and Blackford and Craigmillar Hills, with castles and monuments from the sublime to the ridiculous. Edinburgh, like other large communities, has not escaped the more painful follies and petty vandalisms of the improver and the desecrator both; but the scale of it all, the magnificence of the total picture, backed either by the lofty enduring hills or the blue sparkling waters of the Forth and the green Fife heights beyond, dwarfs follies and criticisms together.

Reams have been written about Edinburgh, its romantic Old Town, its splendid New Town, its noble architecture, its problems, its culture, its present decadence. I have neither the space nor the need to seek to rival any of all this. But this matter of standing back, standing high, and just looking at Edinburgh as an entity, is one which seems to me to have been insufficiently stressed, advised and extolled. It can be almost the most rewarding exercise that the capital offers.

The Old Town, from which it all grew, is islanded on the mile-long hogback of rock which rises from the foot of Arthur's Seat, where lies the ancient bloodsoaked seat of the Stewart kings, the Palace of Holyroodhouse, right up to the mighty precipices crowned by Edinburgh Castle, 300 feet above Princes Street's promenade. This restricted spine of rock used indeed to be islanded, for the Nor'Loch —now drained to form Princes Street Gardens—hemmed it in to the north, and the steep trough of the royal demesne land of Arthur's Seat did so on the south and east. Consequently space was scarce, and as the old Edinburgh grew, it had to do so upwards. As a result we have one of the most stimulating skylines on earth, a rearing, soaring extravaganza of thrusting, jostling towers, spires, pinnacles, gables and turrets that pile dizzily above the narrow streets and ancient wynds, sixteenth and seventeenth century architecture at its most exciting. It would be unsuitable to call these housing flourishes tenements; that

HOY, ORKNEY, where cliffs rise over 1,000 feet sheer from the Atlantic. The green but deserted grazings of the second largest of the Orkneys. This island has a population now of only 700, although a century ago it had three times as many.

gives quite a wrong impression. Lands is the old Scots word, presumably from the many landings or flats incorporated. Six, seven and more storeys they reach, often corbelled and overhanging in ingenious and picturesque stonework—for Edinburgh is a stone city—and decorated with the coats-of-arms and mottoes of a proud people. These were once the town houses of the Scots nobility and gentry. I have sometimes wondered where the commonality dwelt? Presumably in the topmost garrets, the vaulted cellars or down the closes and pends which slant on either side of the central spine—though here too heraldry and carved work proliferate. Perhaps there were really no commonality in old Scotland—the Scots having always been a blood-proud and clan-conscious race, all in cousinship to the laird.

Strangely enough, though long deserted by the quality and intelligentsia for the spreading splendours of the New Town, this ancient quarter is once again becoming a desirable neighbourhood and acceptable address for folk of taste and discrimination. The time may yet come when it will again be the 'best' people who live in Edinburgh's Royal Mile, with the smells, the wifies and the urchins banished to the suburbs.

This transformation—for the historic Old Town where so much of Scotland's colourful story has been written had become little better than a mile-long slum—has come about through an enlightened programme of rehabilitation and restoration of the ancient buildings, a moving out of the tenants to new housing areas, and a wonderful freshening-up in paint and colour-wash. It is a costly and admirably sustained effort, like Haddington's on a vastly larger and more comprehensive scale, which reflects great credit on the city fathers. Though the same gentlemen have much need of the credit, for they are by no means guiltless of official vandalism elsewhere within their borders, having of recent years pulled down not a few precious and irreplaceable examples of our heritage in stone, including the ancient mansion of Niddrie Marischal and the seventeenth century tower-house of Craigentinny. Still, credit where credit is due. A walk down the Royal Mile today, with glances in behind, down the wynds and pends, at the rear views which are frequently the finest, will do a lot for the Town Council's esteem. And the same walk, by night, in the imaginative new lighting there installed, will leave the visitor with an impression not readily forgotten.

The New Town, the very acme and model for the science of town-planning, has long been Edinburgh's pride—and worthily so. Its classic frontages, symmetrical design,

NUNGATE BRIDGE, HADDINGTON, over the East Lothian Tyne. A peaceful scene in the thriving county town. But this river can rise alarmingly, fed from the Lammermuir Hills in the background. The warm red pantiles are a feature of the East Lothian landscape.

broad streets, handsome squares and landscaped gardens make it one of the most brilliant examples of the eighteenth century golden age of building, and on a huge scale. The names of Craig, the brothers Adam, Drummond, and later, Gillespie Graham, Playfair, are imperishably enshrined here.

Though perhaps imperishably is not quite accurate. The New Town was designed for the Golden Age, not for the Motor Age. Almost daily the pressure grows. Even the university, old enough to know better—even if, born in only 1583, it is the youngest in Scotland before the new batch—is not blameless, having taken over and destroyed the lovely George Square with determined ruthlessness. Edinburgh has such a plethora of riches, architecturally, that the struggle between preservation and destruction in the name of advancement is continuous.

This is sad indeed, in a city so famed for its educational excellencies. The great boys' schools of Heriot's, Watson's, Daniel Stewart's, the Royal High, Fettes', Merchiston and many another are renowned—not forgetting the equivalent Merchant Company's establishments for girls. Perhaps as famous should be the equally great Education Authority secondary schools such as Boroughmuir, Broughton, Gillespie's and Leith Academy, which have led the world in the education which used to be Scotland's boast. Heriot-Watt, long a name to conjure with in technological advancement, is now one of the universities, and Napier College a vast answer to the challenge of the scientific age, built round the old castle of Napier of Merchiston, inventor of Logarithms.

Edinburgh is also full of lawyers, being the seat of the law of Scotland—which is so different from English law—and the site of the High Courts with all their satellites. Full of civil servants too, for here is St. Andrew's House, the much derided, enormously overgrown establishment from which Scotland is administered—at the behest of Whitehall, of course, so that all the best windows naturally face south. Full of clergymen, likewise, since here is the headquarters of the Church of Scotland, that stout, strong Kirk which for so long has had to be the authentic voice of Scotland, even when it was wrong; and here muster annually, for the General Assembly, the ministers and elders from 1500 parishes. All this everyone knows, and it is what tends to give Edinburgh its reputation amongst other Scots as a pompous, pretentious, east-windy and west-endy place, a sham capital deprived of a government or a royal court.

But, of course, that is laughably inaccurate—or, at least

34 EDINBURGH AND LOTHIAN

THE GEORGIAN NEW TOWN OF EDINBURGH. The architectural splendour of Randolph Crescent, Ainslie Place, Moray Place, etc., at the West End, with the leafy gardens and dignified frontages which make this a model for town-planners the world over. The valley of the Water of Leith, Edinburgh's own river, on the left.

inadequate. For Edinburgh is, in fact, a great, modern commercial city, with the vast majority of its nearly half-million population employed in industry and trade. Here are the headquarters of, for instance, brewing, distilling, paper-making, printing, banking, insurance and finance.

Industry in the capital is diversified. There is not Glasgow's dangerous dependence on heavy industry, such as ship-building and steel-making. The progress into the scientific era has been marked and swift, and some of the most advanced and delicate electronic work in the United Kingdom is carried out at establishments like Ferranti's great factory at Pilton, and Nuclear Enterprises, at Sighthill. Those who look on Edinburgh as a kind of semi-stagnant backwater of pride and spurious culture should acquaint themselves with all this.

This culture taunt is a dire one, and difficult to rebut. For the fact is that, whatever it was in the illustrious past, Edinburgh today is not truly a city of culture at all. Almost certainly there is more true appreciation of and support for things cultural in Glasgow than in the capital—and that is not necessarily saying a great deal. Yet Edinburgh stages its annual Festival of Music and Drama and the Arts, and thereby calls all the cultural world to its doorstep. This is an extraordinary situation, for the Festival has been established only at great effort and expense on the part of Edinburgh's civic leadership—if not of her citizenry, who in the main ignore it, except insofar as they have to help to pay for its annual losses, and grumble accordingly. Yet it is a tremendous conception. Perhaps, indeed, it does typify Edinburgh—that strange two-faced city of beauty and shabbiness, the educational Mecca that can act the vandal, the capital which is without what makes a capital?

'Edinburgh is a lovely, a magnificent, whited sepulchre!' someone once said to me. That is unfair—but I know what he meant.

If Edinburgh is a capital without a government, Midlothian is a county without a capital. Of the three Lothians, this is the most difficult to describe, the most difficult to comprehend as an entity—just as it might be the most difficult to run as an autonomous unit. And all because of Edinburgh. For the city, of course, *was* the county town of Midlothian—and still is, in that the county administration is mainly carried on from there. Yet the City of Edinburgh is now a county of its own, and Midlothian is left truncated, a long and gangling body lacking a head.

A glance at the map will show Midlothian to be a very odd-shaped area indeed, with two great sprawling legs running south-east and south-west, and not a lot of body in between—and out of that body a huge bite taken, the City of Edinburgh, which has stolen Midlothian's coastline save for the tiny toe-hold at Musselburgh. Ask most Scots about Midlothian and they will declare it to be a fairly highly industrialised and not terribly attractive area on the outskirts of Edinburgh; some may expand on that and say that it is largely the coalfield valley of the Esk, with appendages. It has both these aspects, of course, but how much more. For in acreage it is much the largest of the Lothians, with the highest population—yet it contains more unoccupied land than any other county in Central Scotland, its two legs comprising most of the Moorfoot and Pentland Hills, hundreds of square miles of heather and bracken and deer-hair grass. Not everyone even in Midlothian itself, I have discovered, realises how far down into the Borderland the county reaches. It extends in fact almost as far south as Galashiels, and further south than the town of Peebles. And on the other south-west leg, it drives a salient deep into Lanarkshire, so that its most westerly point is nearer to Glasgow than to Edinburgh, up in the high barren moorlands into which the Pentlands tail, as desolate an area as Scotland has to show, littered with the relics of played-out mining.

Yet Midlothian has, scattered over its farflung extent, some of the loveliest beauty-spots and most exciting places of pilgrimage in all the Lowlands. To name a few at random: Newbattle, the sequestered village deep in the sheltered leafy vale of the Esk, near the busy town of Dalkeith; here, in tranquil setting, the former ancient abbey has become the well-known residential college of adult education, the only one of its kind in Scotland, where is pursued the splendid experiment in liberal studies for those who may have had to leave school before their true talents had chance to blossom. Further up the Esk, on the very lip of the deep gorge of Roslin, all beetling cliffs and hanging woods, clings the castle of the 'lordly line of high St. Clair', where the Sinclair Earls of Orkney held fabulous court to rival their monarchs, in the days when lords were lords and seventy-five gentlewomen were said to be in constant attendance on the Countess—and where William, third Earl, built the quite fantastically romantic and beautiful Roslin Chapel in the year 1401. And nearby, Hawthornden, where the poet Drummond tacked his seventeenth century mansion on to the stern walls of another ancient castle, to cling like an

(Below) MIDLOTHIAN LANDSCAPE. The Pentland Hills, from Flotterstone. Trees planted on Turnhouse Hill mark the situation of government dragoons and Covenanters, at the Battle of Rullion Green, 1666. These hills form a wonderful 'lung' for Edinburgh. (Right) HAWTHORNDEN CASTLE, near Roslin, in the wooded valley of the North Esk, seventeenth century home of the poet William Drummond. Here visited Ben Johnson in 1618.

eagle's nest high on the cave-riddled cliffs where Bruce once found refuge. And yet still further up the same river, near its genesis in a Pentland glen, Habbie's Howe, allegedly the verdant scene of Allan Ramsay's *Gentle Shepherd*.

But all the beauty is not confined to this North Esk—nor indeed to its sister-stream to the south; for the river divides in the great ducal policies of Dalkeith Palace, and the South Esk has its own quieter loveliness, especially around the most attractive and unspoiled village of Carrington, and in the valley of Temple. In both there is an air of settled peace less than typical perhaps of this vigorous land.

The twin valleys of Borthwick and Crichton, with their magnificent but so different castles, both haunted by the enduring presence of lovely, hapless Mary Queen of Scots, are now quiet sanctuaries, and downstream from Crichton a few miles, Ford Village, with its entrancing late seventeenth century manor-house, crouches deep in a noble dean and turns its serene back on the great modern highway where traffic rumbles high above.

That is the key to this peculiar and incoherent county of Midlothian—the jumbled mixture of ancient and modern, of beauty and ugliness, of teeming population and empty vastness, of enduring peace and the jangling effects of man's heedless exploitation.

This area had the dubious advantage of being situated on a rich coalfield, but the coal deposits were patchy and scattered and the land naturally broken and diversified, so that pockets of unspoiled terrain remained. Elsewhere the great bings—as the pit refuse heaps are called—rose to spoil the landscape. But not to dominate, for here the ever-present outlines of the enclosing hills do that, heaven be praised. And now that the coal industry is being largely run down, the remaining unsightliness is not even to be excused on grounds of profit or national need. The last few generations, all over these islands, have much to answer for in this heritage they have left behind, surely.

Midlothian has turned with some vigour, however, to improving the situation. New industries have replaced old, light tending to replace heavy. But paper-making, long the staple of the Esk valley, remains and flourishes, for today's demand for paper ever increases, and the mills of Penicuik, Auchendinny, Polton, Lasswade and of course Inveresk, are famous. Nor are they confined to the Esk and this side of the county, for out westwards, on the other leg, the mills of the winding and comely Water of Leith, from Colinton to Balerno, add their reams to the mighty flood of paper.

Another traditional industry, perhaps strange in a land noted for stone building, is brick-making, and this still continues, with tile and pipe-making ancillaries, particularly on the outskirts of the coalfield. Less fortunate has been the shale-oil production of the Calders area to the west, even though out of it grew the once-mighty Scottish Oils, part of the colossus of British Petroleum. Alas for Midlothian, the natural crude oil of the Middle East proved a much simpler proposition to tap and transport. So we are left with the red shale bings here, like the black coal ones elsewhere. All that can be said is that they are very slightly less unsightly, and vegetation seems to grow on them a little more readily.

Oddly enough an elementary Midlothian natural pro-

duct, that has not been overtaken by events, is water. The county's great areas of hill-land are productive of an enormous volume of water, and innumerable are the lochs and reservoirs, natural and artificial—but almost consistently attractive assets scenically—which dot the uplands and help to supply Edinburgh and the rest of the low country with an unrivalled supply of excellent drinking water. It so happens that paper-making, brewing and distilling are industries particularly requiring a great deal of high-quality water, and the Pentland and Moorfoot reservoirs contribute their essential part of all the prosperity.

Apart from Musselburgh, the largest, there are only three other burghs in the county—Dalkeith, an old-style country town which sprang up under the lordly benevolence of its ducal palace; Bonnyrigg and Lasswade, of the paper, carpets and coal; and Penicuik, paper-maker since even the Darien Scheme of the late seventeenth century, but with literary overtones linked with Allan Ramsay, Henry Mackenzie, the *Man of Feeling*, Drummond, and sundry talented Clerks, long lairds of the place. There used to be two other burghs, Leith and Portobello—but Edinburgh has swallowed these; just as she has swallowed the many formerly attractive villages belonging to the county, such as Colinton, Cramond, Corstorphine and Swanston—the latter tiny place almost unbelievably picturesque and quaint, preserved as something of a museum-piece to Robert Louis Stevenson, under his beloved Hills of Home.

This swallowing-up process by the city does not stop at the county boundaries, of course. Inexorably the built-up area spreads into the countryside, here as elsewhere, despite all the planners' exercises; and though the vast suburban sprawl, reaching out to engulf ancient communities like Currie and Balerno and Hermiston, may help the county's rating finances, it tends to be the kiss of death, for sooner or later the metropolis will seek to digest what it has swallowed. This is a problem that grows ever more acute the world over. Let us be thankful that, by and large, Scotland suffers less than most therefrom.

Livingston is a good point to leave Midlothian. For here, straddling the border with West Lothian, is perhaps the most ambitious piece of community planning ever projected in Scotland, a completely new town on a vast scale, still in its birth-pangs but planned to be eventually of one the greatest centres of population in the land, with possibly as many as 100,000 inhabitants. What will be the effect on Edinburgh and the adjacent countryside of this great and wholly modern city remains to be seen. It will find employment for its thousands mainly in the burgeoning and go-ahead industrial expansion of West Lothian, but the challenge to the capital and to Midlothian cannot fail to be great.

West Lothian, formerly called Linlithgowshire, is the third smallest county in Scotland in area, though far from so in population. And though it has also had its problems due to the decline in the coal and shale industries, it has been able to overcome them of late in truly extraordinary fashion—indeed to be in the very forefront of Scottish industrial expansion. Just why this has come about may not be very obvious at first glance—and not so long ago it might have seemed improbable. But its situation is central, mid-way between Edinburgh and Glasgow, with good rail, road and sea communications—and the tremendous new Forth Road Bridge, so long agitated for in Scotland and at last erected, revolutionises the transport position of the county. Here has been sited the vast new British Motor Corporation's factory at Bathgate, with ancillary establishments springing up around. And perhaps almost equally important is the nearness of Grangemouth, the oil boom port of Scotland, on the upper Forth, which though just over the border into Stirlingshire nevertheless spreads its stimulating effects in housing, labour and commercial morale into the adjoining county.

What ever the reason, West Lothian surges ahead.

The county, of course, suffers from few of the geographical and administrative problems which affect Midlothian. It is compact, more or less oblong in shape, bounded by the Rivers Almond and Avon, with no great and unproductive hill areas. It has some high moorland to the south-west, but not enough to be a handicap. And its county town, Linlithgow, lies approximately central to all.

Linlithglow is a strange town, famous in history, notably picturesque as to situation beside a loch amongst low green hills, with outstanding architectural gems—yet it is not very attractive of appearance and gives little impression of its quality. The great A.9 highway to the north runs through its not very prepossessing main street—and most travellers tend to run through with it. They should stop.

Linlithgow always seems to have been an important place. The Romans had a station here, and it is claimed that the semi-legendary King Achaius, in the eighth century, founded the burgh, leaving a stone cross known as King Cay's Stane, now disappeared. David I had a royal castle

LINLITHGOW, county town of West Lothian. In the handsome ruined palace beside the loch, favourite seat of the Scottish kings, Mary Queen of Scots was born. St. Michael's Church is one of the finest in the land. The modern town, threaded by the A.9 highway to the North, is less attractive. The visitor hurries through, to his loss.

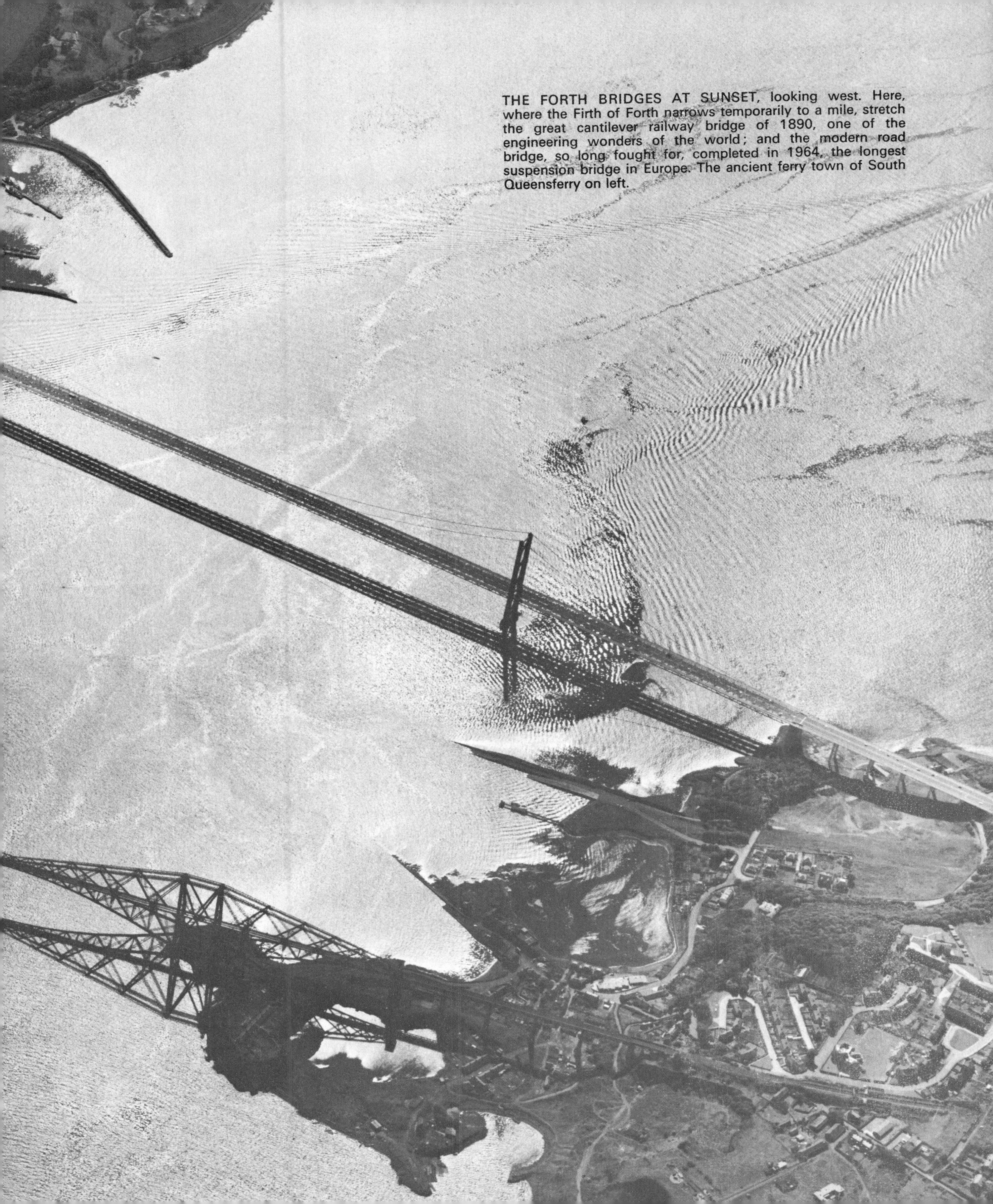

THE FORTH BRIDGES AT SUNSET, looking west. Here, where the Firth of Forth narrows temporarily to a mile, stretch the great cantilever railway bridge of 1890, one of the engineering wonders of the world; and the modern road bridge, so long fought for, completed in 1964, the longest suspension bridge in Europe. The ancient ferry town of South Queensferry on left.

(Below) BATHGATE, West Lothian, showing some of the output from the large BMC factory. The busy industrial burgh is, however, ancient. Here was born Sir John Y. Simpson, inventor of chloroform, in 1811. (Right) THE PRECEPTORY OF THE KNIGHTS OF ST. JOHN, in the village of Torphichen, built in the thirteenth and fifteenth centuries, with the sixteenth century and later post-Reformation parish church.

here, and much demesne land; and the invading Edward of England in 1301 made Linlithgow his headquarters for the attempted subjugation of Scotland—indeed the remains of the new castle he erected 'mekill and stark' are incorporated in the north-east corner of the present palace.

The great ruined Palace of Linlithgow is one of the glories of Scotland. Standing proudly on its grassy mound above the town on one side and its loch on the other, it gives a notable appearance of unity and homogenity of construction. But this is an illusion, for it was built over long stages, with most of the Stewart kings having a hand in it, though James IV and V added the greatest magnificence—the latter especially, for here he brought his French bride, Mary of Guise, to be impressed by it, and through it by the rest of her new country. Impressed she was, naming Linlithgow the most princely dwelling she had ever seen, and in fact she made it her favourite seat during her long widowhood. Here was born her daughter, in 1542, who within a few days was Mary Queen of Scots, on her father's death, and from here, during the unruly years of her minority, Scotland was largely governed. Suitably perhaps, its destruction as a palace was effected by the same agency that destroyed the last hopes of the royal line that built it—for the Hanoverian troops on their way south after Culloden, bedded here and burned down the palace when they burned their bedding straw.

Nearby stands St. Michaels' Kirk, declared by Billings to be 'assuredly the most important specimen of an ancient parochial church now existing in Scotland. Founded in the twelfth century, most of it dates from the fifteenth, though it suffered grievously from the reforming zeal of the Lords of the Congregation in 1559. It lost its great open stonework crown which topped its square tower, after the fashion of Edinburgh's St. Giles; but this has of recent years been replaced by a modern finial, tall and somewhat spiky, and painted gold, which attracts much speculation from uninformed passengers on the Glasgow trains which pass close by.

There are only three other burghs—though the village of Broxburn is larger than two or three Border burghs put together. Bo'ness, or Boroughstoneness to give it its full title, has suffered declension for some time, without the resurgence which has revitalised much of the county. It was the port of Linlithgow—but Grangemouth rather stole its thunder. A harbour for the export of coal and the import of pit-prop timber, the mining run-down hit it hard. Nevertheless it fights back and will no doubt win again its share of the general prosperity—for it has been existing since Roman times also, with the end of the Antonine Wall based here. Bathgate and Armadale, close together on the wide inland plain of the Almond, are in the forefront of expansion—but cannot lay any claims to beauty; though Bathgate once boasted a great castle, belonging to the High Steward of Scotland, no less, whence the Stewarts descend. Armadale, a small mining and industrial town of 6,500, though unfavoured by major outside development, is a model of enterprising self-help. It has devised and financed its own development plan, costing nearly £2,000,000, with an ambitious new town centre, traffic-free precinct, and entertainments area, and aims to increase its population to 10,000. Nearby, to the north, is the imposing fifteenth century preceptory of the Knights of St. John, at Torphichen, an Order once so powerful in Scotland that its Masters were automatically made Lords of Parliament as Lords Saint John.

West Lothian, despite all its industry and bustle, has a great deal of highly attractive country surviving, especially in this high ground between Bathgate and Linlithgow. Here are three modest summits; Cairnpapple, where have been excavated perhaps the most ancient relics known to Scotland, a burial place and religious centre of our misty ancestors of 4,000 years ago; Cockleroy, which is said to be a corruption of Cuckold-le-Roi, and commemorates the marital humiliation of some monarch, variously and unconvincingly identified; and Glower-o'er-'em, a hill which speaks for itself.

If the county is not particularly rich in charming villages—though Ecclesmachen, hidden amongst these little green hills, and Abercorn lost amongst the Forth-side woods, rank high—it *is* rich in ancient castles and mansions, from such a royal fortress as Blackness on its rock in the Firth to Hopetoun, probably the most palatial private residence in the land, seat of the Marquesses of Linlithgow.

West Lothian, then, is not just a county to do business in, or to hurry through. The character is there; it is the reward for only a little seeking.

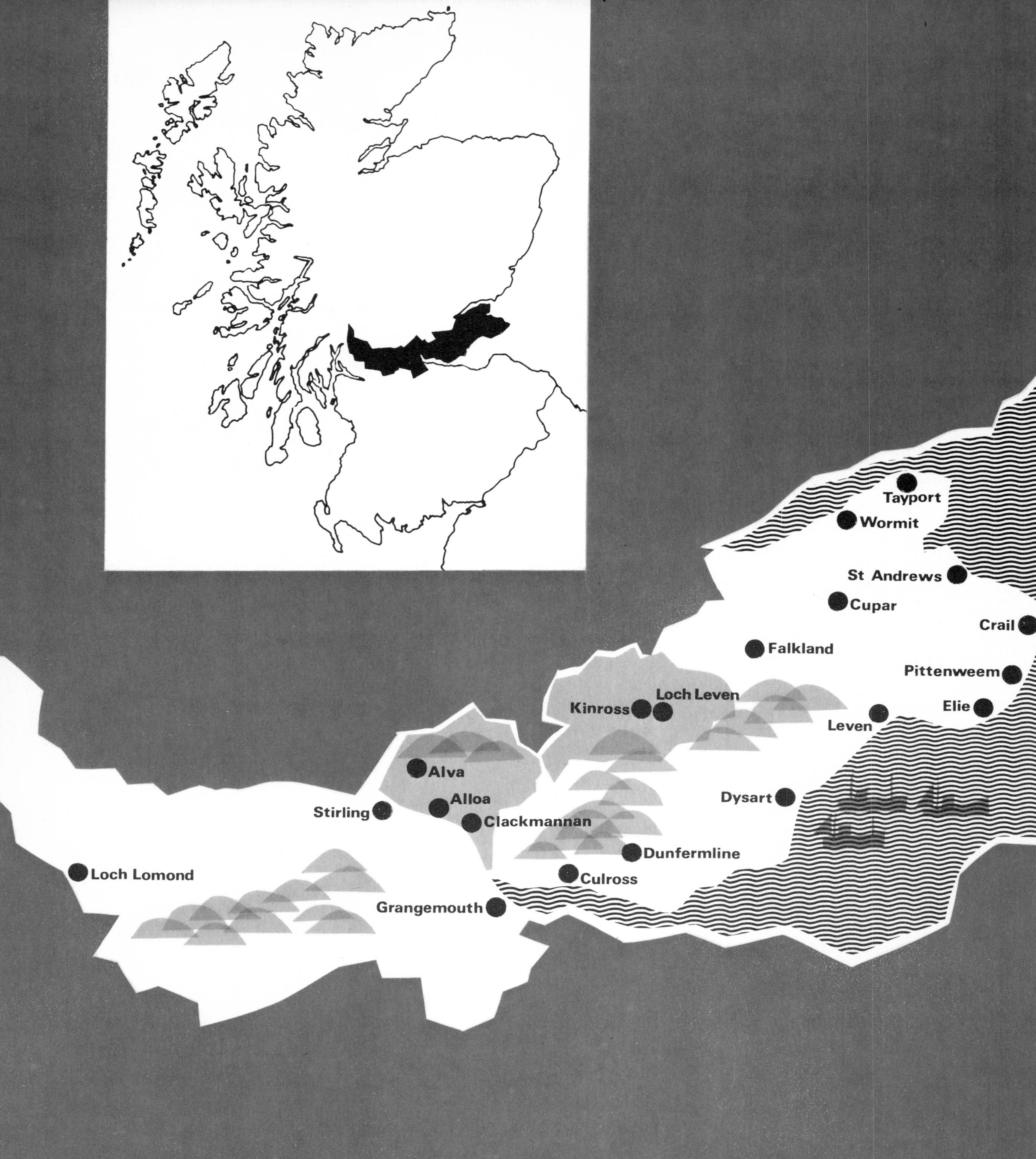

Tayport
Wormit
St Andrews
Cupar
Crail
Falkland
Pittenweem
Loch Leven
Kinross
Elie
Leven
Alva
Alloa
Stirling
Clackmannan
Dysart
Dunfermline
Loch Lomond
Culross
Grangemouth

CHAPTER 3
STIRLING, CLACKMANNAN, KINROSS AND FIFE

Scotland has always been a great country for battles. There are battlefields galore in every area - but Stirlingshire beats them all; even the Borders. A glance at the map will show two reasons why. Here, before the days of big modern bridges, was the first possible crossing of the long Forth estuary; and here, to the north, is the mighty bastion of the Highland Line, the junction of Lowlands and Highlands. But there is a third geographical feature, not so obvious from the map. The great wide valley of the winding Forth, west of Stirling, is notably level, flat, for Scotland, where really flat land is almost unknown. The entire flood-plain of the Forth, some twenty miles long by five broad, was once almost under water, one of the largest areas of bog and marshland in Scotland, possibly in all Britain. Nine-tenths of it is drained now, and makes splendid cornland; but the west end is still a waterlogged wilderness, and over it the mallard flight and the wild-geese honk their high challenge. It is called the Flanders Moss, and it is the strange secretive heart of Stirlingshire and one of the most important factors in its stirring history and development, little as this may be appreciated.

This vast quaking barrier could not be crossed, by individuals or by armies, but only by certain of the fierce and proscribed clan of MacGregor - who preserved its secrets jealously, to their own advantage. The great estuary to the east might be crossed, with difficulty, by boat - but not the Flanders Moss. And

just where the one meets the other, and fresh water becomes salt, a huge rock rears itself abruptly out of the watery levels, to dominate this one possible crossing-place—and on its summit, in due course, was built Stirling Castle, quite the most powerful and strategic position in the land. Below it, the one slender link between north and south, between Highlands and Lowlands, arched across the suddenly narrowed river. This was the key to Scotland—not Edinburgh Castle, equally powerful as it looks; nor Dumbarton, guarding the Clyde. Hold Stirling and its bridge, and you split Scotland in two—for the country is oddly shaped, and this is the curiously narrow waist of it, with only some thirty odd miles separating North Sea from Atlantic salt water.

Small wonder then that this, as well as being the principal seat of the Scots kings, was also the cockpit of Scotland, where all must stand or fall, where Wallace triumphed at Stirling Bridge, Bruce at Bannockburn, the Old Pretender failed at Sheriffmuir and his son Charles Edward won at Falkirk—to name but a few of the major encounters. The bloodshed in the Borderland fighting and the Highland clan feuding tended to be continuous but, as it were, retail; here it was wholesale.

Stirlingshire, therefore, has always been a place of stress and change, of the ebb and flow of more tides than the Forth's. And still it is. For it is as strategic an area today as ever is was, plumb in the centre of Central Scotland, yet with ocean-going ships able to approach it on either side, from the Old World or the New. This, coinciding with the coming of oil and oil-products to be the arbiter of nation's fates, has ensured that Stirlingshire should be the boom-area of Scotland. For not only do the huge tankers from the Middle East come fifty miles up the Forth to unload at Grangemouth, in sight of Stirling's proud castle, but those from the Western Hemisphere come up the Clyde, to a great oil-terminal at Finnart, not so very far away, and from there the oil is pumped through a pipeline eastwards. So at Grangemouth rise the refineries, the storage-tanks, pumping installations, cracking-plants, with their contorted miles of piping, their fantastic nightmares of futuristic construction, their clustered cooling-towers and their lofty flaming phallic-symbols of the new industrial fertility, where the unpronounceable and polysyllabic progeny of the scientist wedded to petroleum products are born—polypropylene, polyvinylchloride, polystyrene and the like—and turned into plastics and plasticisers, detergents, solvents, dyes and

(Left) GRANGEMOUTH, Stirlingshire, in the upper Forth plain; the dramatic industrial spread against the background of the Ochil Hills and the Highland Line. The great petrochemical development and oil refining centre, with its docks and cracking plants. (Right) WHERE HIGHLANDS AND LOWLANDS MEET, The Carse of Stirling, from the Touch Hills, looking across the reclaimed corn-lands that once were the marshes of Flanders Moss.

synthetic fibres. Out from Grangemouth the plants spread and proliferate, with their ancillary industries and the housing, scholastic and entertainment needs in a chain-reaction of development, exciting, invigorating.

Falkirk, just inland, has long been an industrial nexus. Here, at the famous, many-chimneyed Carron Ironworks, were forged the carronades that thundered at Waterloo. In due course swords were beaten into ploughshares and Falkirk became the centre of that part of the iron industry known as light-castings, turning out baths and stoves and grates for our grandparents. But here too pace has been kept with this developing age, and in this era of refrigerators, washing-machines and steel sinks, the casting shops of Falkirk have remained in the forefront of progress.

So, with the surrounding towns and villages, such as Camelon, Denny, Larbert, Bonnybridge and Lauriston, the entire Falkirk-Grangemouth area of East Stirlingshire has become one vast complex of manufacturing development. Yet despite the far spread of it, the grim blight of a wholly industrialised landscape is largely absent. This is because of Scotland's enduring and unfailing gift of hills and mountains, great and small. Seldom indeed are the eyes not to be uplifted and solaced by the sight of green braesides, hanging woods or blue distant ranges. All Stirlingshire lies embosomed in hills, the Ochils, the Gargunnock, Fintry and Kilsyth Hills and the Campsie Fells, with nearer at hand the lesser heights of Torwood, Touch, Bannockburn and Stirling Rock itself, all under the lofty regard of the Highland giants.

Stirling town itself, though a busy modern spreading place also, indeed inevitably a traffic maelstrom, is unusual in that it looks almost as romantic as it is—at least, from a distance and most angles. From close up, or within, there may be disenchantment. But seen from almost any approach, in especial the southern ones, the grey town climbing steeply from the plain up the great rock towards the towering battlements of the castle is a sight to stir the imagination. Stirling, to my mind, should have been the capital of Scotland, not only on account of its central position and magnificent transport availability, but because of its history. For Stirling's history is the basic history of Scotland, in a way that Edinburgh's never was. Edinburgh and its castle was almost as often in rebel, usurping or enemy as in Crown hands; not so Stirling. The realm stood or fell with Stirling.

Why Stirling was not the capital is too large a question to

RIVER BROOM, WESTER ROSS, emerging from the Corrieshalloch Gorge and flowing west into the sea-loch of Broom. Ullapool lies on its north shore, out of sight.

go into here, but I have a shrewd suspicion that the answer may be found, as in so much of Scotland's story, in the voracious ambitions and power-hunger of the House of Douglas, which for long centuries made it its business to keep the throne and kingdom weak, to its own advantage. Douglas lands surrounded Edinburgh, but they had little land or influence in the Stirling area. It may have been almost as simple as that. When it is remembered that few of the Stewart monarchs reached middle age, and that for a large proportion of her time Scotland was governed by regents on behalf of babes or juveniles—and the Douglases had usually a major hand in the appointment of such regents—something of it all may become clearer.

At any rate, Stirling has never had her due in the Scottish polity. It is belated justice, and an excellent choice, that the decision to site one of Scotland's new universities there was taken.

But there is more to this county than the busy east and the great farmlands of the Carse of Stirling that was once the Flanders Moss. There is West Stirlingshire, an area entirely different, almost detached, that belongs in character to the West and indeed contains within it a wholly detached portion of the Clyde county of Dunbarton. From purely Highland—how many realise that Ben Lomond itself and much of Rob Roy's country of glen and loch is in Stirlingshire?—it graduates to almost purely residential; but everywhere it is hilly, from the great rock and heather mountains where Glasgow's water comes from, to the green sheep-dotted slopes of the Campsie Fells, into the deans and lowermost valleys of which villa-dom creeps inexorably. Save for the one rather depressed-looking burgh of Kilsyth on its most southerly fringe, there are no towns—and the villages look as though they never forget that Glasgow is just around the corner, whither the roads all run. It must seem a far cry to the county town of Stirling.

But there is much beauty here, in nooks and corners, in leafy dells and curlew-haunted moors. And there is an enormous forest, in the lonely loch-dotted Carron valley, midway between Glasgow and Stirling—not perhaps what might be expected in highly developed Central Scotland.

Across the Forth from Stirling we are at once in different territory—for both Perthshire and Clackmannanshire come to within a mile or so of Stirling's Rock. Clackmannanshire has one of the biggest names but the smallest area of any county in Scotland—a mere 35,000 acres. Indeed it is difficult to know why it was erected into a separate

EILEAN DONAN CASTLE, WESTER ROSS. MacRae stronghold, restored, much-photographed but unfailingly challenging, where Lochs Duich, Long and Alsh meet, in Kintail. Here passes the road to Kyle and Skye.

county at all, for it was only a parish at one time. And, strangely enough, its county town is not Clackmannan, but Alloa.

At least its shape is readily comprehended, roughly a square with seven mile sides, based on the Forth where it narrows drastically from an estuary to a river. Half its area is empty hilltops, the remainder the flat and highly populated littoral across which meander two rivers, both called Devon —though one has the prefix Black to distinguish it.

Though small, Clackmannanshire is still very much on the map of Scotland. In fact it is an intensely developed and prosperous community, gaining all the economic advantages of centrality and compactness, highly industrialised yet with no major burdens of roads and services to maintain over long distances. In consequence the tiny county is more advanced in local government and scholastic matters than some of its larger neighbours.

Leaving aside the hill mass but not forgetting it, we can consider the place in two divisions, parallel approximately and not far apart, each served with a main axial road—the coastal levels and the Hillfoots. Note that the name is hillfoots and not foothills. It is well described, and there is a world of difference. Never, I think, have I come across a more sudden and definite transition from flat plain to steeply rising hillside than here, where the tall frowning Ochils drop to the Forth. Here are no foothills at all. You either tread completely level ground, or you climb sharply —too sharply for roads or even tracks. So these Ochils remain an extraordinarily abrupt and complete barrier to the north, dictating the entire character and atmosphere of Clackmannanshire.

Along these hillfoots are strung the villages and little towns of Menstrie, Alva, Tillicoultry and Dollar, each with its claim to attention. It is as well, though, that the sun does not circle north-about, or these would be dull places indeed, so steep are the overhanging heights.

Distilling and textiles are the main industries here—though there is a quality printing-works at Alva, with a national reputation. And Dollar is more famous for its great Academy, one of the few early co-educational foundations in Scotland. High above Dollar, in the lap of the hills where the burns of Sorrow and Care meet in deep ravines—all this emphasis on melancholy in a far from sorrowful area is peculiar, Dollar allegedly itself being formerly Dolour—rears the notably fine Castle Campbell, originally called The Gloume, built by the fifteenth

century MacCailean Mor, First Earl of Argyll, Chief of Clan Campbell who became Chancellor, or chief minister, of Scotland, and requiring an establishment nearer the seat of government at Stirling than was far Inverary. It is perhaps interesting that he brought with him out of the Campbell country one of his lesser Highland chieftains, head of the MacAlisters, who settled at nearby Menstrie, and in due course his descendants anglicised their name to Alexander. It was the seventeenth century Sir William Alexander, poet, statesman and coloniser who, in fulness of time, conceived the brilliant idea of King James VI of Scotland, and I of the United Kingdom, raising much-needed money for the colonising of New Scotland, or Nova Scotia, by the creation, at a suitable price, of hereditary knighthoods of a sort, called baronetcies—and himself became first Earl of Stirling in consequence. Menstrie Castle, his delightful fortalice, was scheduled to be demolished, until public protest saved it—with the help of the Prime Minister of Nova Scotia—and it is now restored, the showpiece of the county, centre of a housing development and containing a museum for the Order of the Baronets of Nova Scotia. If only other local authorities with such attractive buildings in their care—as a great many have, in this land of castles—would take note of what assets such can become.

The Forth-side strip of the county has only the one real town, Alloa—but it is larger than all the rest put together and in fact dominates Clackmannanshire to an unusual extent. A bustling, thriving place of 14,000 inhabitants, it was once a port, but the river became so silted up as to preclude navigation. Alloa, however, did not allow itself to decline with its harbour, and it has become one of the most happily diversified industrial developments in the land—brewing, glass-making and engineering predominating. It is not a town of great architectural pretensions, but there are relics of the past surviving, in especial Alloa Tower, a great square keep which has been the home of the Erskines, Earls of Mar and Kellie, hereditary keepers of Stirling Castle, for long centuries.

More readily discerned than Alloa Tower, because it crowns a green hill above the small, ancient town of Clackmannan itself, is the fine double tower of that name, dating from the fifteenth century, and formerly the seat of a senior branch of the great family of Bruce. This upper Forth basin was Bruce country, and it is said that a beacon lit on the topmost parapet of Clackmannan Tower could be seen and acted upon from a round dozen Bruce castles

(Left) OLD TOLBOOTH, market cross, and STONE OF MANNAN, Clackmannan. These ancient tolbooths are a notable feature of Scots burgh architecture, and used to house municipal offices, court-room and jail. (Below) SUNSET ACROSS THE FORTH, TO ALLOA, the thriving county town of Scotland's smallest county, Clackmannanshire. The Ochil Hills rise behind, with the Wallace Monument, Stirling Castle, and in the left distance, Ben Lomond.

dotted over the area, both sides of Forth. The last of the Clackmannan Bruces was a notable lady, worthy representative of the line of the hero-king, who knighted the poet Robert Burns here with the sword of King Robert.

If Clackmannanshire is almost over-industrialised, Kinross-shire is the reverse. Although larger in area it has only the two small towns, sited so close together as to be almost one. Neither is a hive of industry—although the knitwear mill at Kinross not long ago achieved the spectacular feat of taking over an old-established competitor at Hawick. The county town has a population of only 2,300, Milnathort almost exactly half that. The shire therefore is almost wholly rural, and must find its finances quite the most difficult of all non-Highland Scotland, for though there is good agricultural land here too, the greater part is either water or pasture and hill; for as well as the Ochils Kinross-shire comprehends the Cleish and part of the Benarty and Lomond Hills—no connection with Loch Lomond.

As to the water, Kinross-shire is really little more than just the basin of the great Loch Leven, undoubtedly its best-known feature. Perhaps six square miles of water, it has many claims to renown. Scenic beauty, for one. Its fishing, for another—its trout are legendary, and here each year is held the great fly-fishing international competition which draws contestants and devotees from far and near.

Less regular a venue, but rather more stirring to watch, is the bonspiel, or huge curling match, which takes place here when the loch is frozen over—a game rather like bowls in theory but not in the least in practice, played with beautifully turned and polished stones and a maximum of vocal encouragement to both contestants and stones, calling inevitably for continual liquid refreshment of a sort calcula-

ted to keep out the cold. Such a bonspiel is one more vivid proof of the fallacy of the odd idea, so prevalent in the south, that the Scots are a dour, stolid and unemotional people.

But of course it is history which makes this loch perhaps the most romantic in all Scotland. Mary Queen of Scots had the extraordinary quality of glamourising everything that she touched—for posterity, if not always for her contemporaries, who were surely a pretty hard-headed lot. But the glamour of her connection with Loch Leven is authentic and not to be questioned even by the most determined Mary-debunker. For here she was brought, the prisoner of her own subjects—or at least of some powerful few of them—in 1567, and confined in the square Douglas castle that still rises uncompromisingly from its little island at the north-west end of the loch. Mary had the misfortune to be a young, beautiful and spirited girl, and worse still a Catholic, at a moment in time when Scotland had just turned violently and Calvinistically Protestant—or most of her nobility and gentry had done so, which came to the same thing politically. So Mary could do no right, lest her popularity might send the pendulum swinging back to the Old Religion, as would indeed have been very easy, but disastrous, not only for Knox, Buchanan and the other new Kirk leaders, but for the lords as well—the Lords of the Congregation, they called themselves collectively, with a certain grim humour. For the former vast church lands, more than half of the best land in all Scotland, had been expropriated and parcelled out amongst the said lords and gentry. So Mary must either change her faith, or be proved a danger and a liability to all good and respectable folk. The Douglases, long experts in keeping the throne in its place, provided Loch Leven Castle, and Sir Robert Douglas as gaoler.

But they reckoned without another aspect of human nature; indeed they reckoned without Mary herself, the effect of her royal beauty, charm and hapless state on even young Douglas hearts. For those who decry Mary-worship as a modern sentimental nonsense—and the issue is still hotly debated; Scotland is like that—here is the answer. After eleven months in the castle Mary had so won over the affections of the two Douglas sons that they were her willing and adoring slaves. One night Willie escorted her out by a postern-gate, to where he had a boat waiting, and rowed her across the dark waters of the loch to where George waited with horses. Enlightened self-interest for once took a beating.

(Below) BONSPIEL AT LOCH LEVEN, Kinross-shire. The wide shallow loch freezes fairly readily, and is famous for its curling matches. Here also, in different weather, are held equally famous angling contests. In the castle here Mary Queen of Scots was held prisoner by some of her own lords in 1567, and forced to sign a deed of abdication.

I have ofter wondered what happened to Willie and George Dougals, on account of this escapade.

Kinross-shire is rich in other small and sturdily attractive castles, one of the most distinctive and delightful aspects of the Scottish scene. I use the adjective delightful advisedly, although it is not the one many would normally apply to castles. But the Scottish castle is something unique, and there have been literally some thousands of them. Even yet there are between 600 and 700 still remaining, of which the main features survive, perhaps half still occupied as family homes. These are not fortresses but fortified houses, often as small as to contain only half a dozen rooms—usually one on top of the other. But they have, by and large, an architectural excellence and rightness of appearance, such as no other country can display, that makes them a joy to behold and a heritage to treasure.

Oddly enough, it was that same sordid land-grab at the Reformation which was largely responsible for all the excellence. For one of the conditions for a grant of the newly dismembered church lands was that a fortalice or tower of defence should be erected on such property—theoretically for the better maintaining of law and order, though in fact the reverse was more apt to result, with each laird thereof tending to cock a snook at all and sundry from the safety of the said little strongholds.

The reason for the architectural delight is also to be found in the same historical context. Mary succeeded to the throne at the age of one week, and was sent off to France for safety at the age of five—for Henry VIII would have had her, otherwise, and Scotland with her. She came back nineteen years old, more French than Scots, to reign. In the long interim, her talented French mother, Queen Mary of Guise, had had an enormous influence on Scotland, both as Regent and as a fount of patronage and culture. So throughout the entire Reformation period of twenty-odd years, the French influence in Scotland was stronger than ever before, or since—and that is saying something, for the Auld Alliance between the two countries, based on the containment of aggressive England on either side, had endured for many centuries. It was the lively and more lightsome French ideas of castle, or chateau, building, so very different from that of England, which, allied to the sturdy, plain Scots vernacular style, blossomed out into what is undoubtedly the most attractive and exciting castellated architecture of all Europe.

In small castles like Tullibole, near Fossaway; Cleish, on

the north flank of the Cleish Hills; and the restored Aldie, not far away, Kinross-shire can vie with any county in Scotland. Their strong white-harled walls, pepper-pot angle-turrets, slender stair-towers, crowstepped gables and dormer windows, all enhanced with heraldic stonework amongst a wealth of shot-holes, are a joy to behold.

To move over the county boundary eastwards, into Fife, is to be confronted with a radical change—the more strange in that these three shires of Clackmannan, Kinross and West Fife used together to form a separate semi-province known as Fothrif, an entity which has disappeared from the Scottish scene so completely that not a single individual approached by myself on the subject had so much as heard of it. Yet, pre-Reformation, it was important enough seldom to be left out when Fife was mentioned. That is why I called it a half-province; Fife and Fothrif went in harness, and one was little less important than the other. Now the title is only preserved in ancient charters and in the corrupted name of a stretch of moorland behind Dunfermline.

West Fife is as rich in industry as Kinross-shire is lacking. It is sited on a coalfield, but it was an important area before ever coal was worked. Both Church and State saw to that. For Dunfermline Abbey here was the greatest and richest monastic establishment in all the land, a principality in itself, with vast lands and parishes, and formed probably the foremost centre of mediaeval development in Scotland. And twenty miles away, over on the other side of the Lomond Hills, is Falkland, seat of the original Mormaors and Earls of Fife, principal nobles of the early kingdom, and in due course judiciously taken over by the royal house as favourite place of relaxation. Between the two, with good sea harbours and the first comparatively sheltered crossing place of the Forth by boat, at Queensferry, West Fife could not fail to loom large in Scotland. And even though the mitred abbots, the kings and the coal today no longer dictate the pattern, geography still does, and here are based the northern ends of the two great Forth Bridges, rail and road, mighty engineering feats that mean so much in Scots development, as well as bringing admirers to view them from all over the world.

Dunfermline today is a large and busy town and shopping-centre, of nearly 50,000 people—which puts it amongst the 'top ten' of Scotland. It is set quite high, three or four miles back from the Forth, on the sweeping south-facing slopes—for Fife is another county of low, green hills. Since

(Left) DUNFERMLINE ABBEY and PALACE, Fife. A seat of Scots kings and one of the richest abbeys. Bruce's body (less his heart which lies at Melrose) rests here. His name is picked out on the abbey's east tower. (Below) TULLIBOLE CASTLE, Kinross-shire, home of the Lord Moncrieff, a good example of the attractive Scottish fortified house of the sixteenth-seventeenth centuries, so distinctive a feature of Scotland. Many hundreds of these little castles survive.

the road bridge was opened it has become much better known to the rest of Scotland, to the advantage of all. Strangely, Dunfermline was possibly the one place in the land that feared the coming of the long-awaited bridge, her tradespeople and shop-keepers dreading that to be within half an hour's car-run of Edinburgh would spell their ruin. This fear has proved largely groundless.

For Dunfermline has much to show—even though its burghal aspect is scarcely entrancing. I do not know whether it is more proud of its abbey—where Bruce's body, as distinct from his heart, is laid—or its magnificent Pittencrieff Glen park, a beautiful estate and an old mansion which its honoured son Andrew Carnegie presented to the town of his birth. Carnegie, son of poor linen-weavers here—the linen trade has long been Dunfermline's staple—cut a wide swathe in the world and left his mark in many places; but nowhere quite so intimately and notably as here, where the little dynamo of energy and shrewdness, prototype of all self-made multi-millionaires, made a start in life in a back-street cottage, in 1835.

No coalfield area is apt to draw gasps of admiration, and the West Fife coal towns of Cowdenbeath, Kelty, Lochgelly and the like are no urban Edens. But the sight of wooded hills and green ridges and the pervasive feeling of the sea's nearness, ensure that one is never quite submerged in man's grey flood.

An ever-present awareness of the sea is something not to be escaped in all Fife, as the county is almost an island, bounded by the North Sea and the Firths of Forth and Tay—with, moreover, the Ochil Hills forming a major barrier on its fourth side. Because its slopes and terraces sweep up to fairly high central ridges all round, blue water has a way of getting into most vistas. Even in the Howe of Fife, the wide central strath flanked by the summit ridges, the salt winds and sea mists and seagulls remain, and one is never unaware of being less than ten miles from the coast. It is a long and fertile valley, twenty miles of rich farmlands, fine estates and prosperous townships, Falkland of the kings at one end, and St. Andrews of the archbishops and the professors at the other. And plumb in the centre, Cupar, the couthy county town, capital for the canny Fifers. The Fife folk have a reputation for canniness, not so much of the monetary Aberdonian variety but of a cautiously self-preserving sort all their own. 'Wha to Cupar maun to Cupar' the old saying goes, referring to the ultimate journey to the Sheriff of Fife's pit and gallows in the royal burgh,

CASTLE CAMPBELL, Clackmannanshire. Set high on the hillside above the little town of Dollar, famous for its Academy, this fine stronghold was formerly called The Gloume, and dates from the fourteenth century. The name was changed when it came into the possession of the chief of the Campbells, the Earl of Argyll, in the fifteenth century. John Knox dispensed the Lord's Supper here on a great occasion in 1556.

which seems to have had a more daunting effect here than elsewhere—possibly because their renowned self-interest led more Fifers thitherwards than was normal in other parts. At any rate, today more non-Fifers maun to Cupar than ever before, for the royal burgh with its great sugar-beet factory is on the way between the new Forth and Tay road bridges, and no longer something of an island capital.

Kirkcaldy is ten times the size of Cupar, its county town, with over 50,000 inhabitants, and the largest community of Fife. Although a manufacturing town on the coast it is not a port, and though it has more or less engulfed the once busy port of Dysart, no ship-handling harbour survives. Port facilities are available a few miles away on either side, at Methil and Buckhaven to the east, and Burntisland to the west—the latter a shipbuilding centre on a modest but specialised scale, as well as an importing place for the ore to feed the great aluminium works sited here. At Burntisland Castle, now called Rossend and in danger of demolition by an unappreciative Town Council, Mary the Queen had the privacy of her bed-chamber invaded for the second time by the love-besotted French poet Chatelard—who paid for the attempt with his life, at St. Andrews. Further to the west still, beyond the pleasant little resort of Aberdour, with its silver sands and off-shore island Abbey of Inchcolm, is the interesting modern dual development of industrial estate at Donibristle and ambitious executive-type housing area of Dalgetty Bay, on the Douglas Earl of Morton's former estate—all further examples of the opening-up process speeded by the Forth Road Bridge.

Kirkcaldy used to have almost all its eggs in one basket—linoleum. Many were the tall and unlovely mills, and loud the scarcely more attractive smell that identified Kirkcaldy even on the darkest night. With the decline in this trade, the town might have declined also, but a forward-looking policy has saved it. Now Kirkcaldy, with its serried ranks of skyscraper flats, its mile-long esplanade, its modern factories, splendid new high school and fine parks, is a model of civic enterprise. But its past is not wholly forgotten, and excellent restoration work is going on amongst the fine traditional architecture of old Dysart.

In the hinterland here industry flourishes in many directions—paper-making at Leslie, Haig's great whisky distillery at Markinch, engineering at Leven, coal-mining all around. And at Glenrothes nearby is one of the foremost new-town enterprises in the country, where the planners have had a free hand and all is according to the most

(Left) THE PALACE, CULROSS, Fife. A seventeenth century laird's town-house in the little royal burgh by the Forth, noted for the wealth of its architectural heritage. (Below) A CORNER OF FALKLAND, Fife, clustering around the royal hunting palace beneath the Lomond Hills, in the central vale of the county. But there is industry here also.

advanced theories. How successful these great outspread modern experiments will prove, socially and economically, compared with tighter-knit communities that have grown naturally, remains to be seen; but with Cumbernauld and East Kilbride in the west, and Livingston and Glenrothes in the east, Scotland will find out in due course. Electronics and components factories are here amongst the most outstanding.

The East Neuk of Fife has long represented delight and freedom to many generations of Scots families, for this seaward tip of the peninsula vies with the Clyde coast as the largest holiday playground in the land. And deservedly. Here, starting at Leven, on Largo Bay, and strung out for almost forty miles, right round the point of Fife Ness and on to St. Andrews, is a splendid succession of small, characterful havens, fishing villages and modest resorts, each with its golden sands, boat-harbour, typical sturdy cottage architecture, golf-links and ancient church. Fife is particularly rich in handsome old churches, the East Neuk in especial—no doubt from having as it were grown up under the shadow of St. Andrews, the great metropolitan see of Scotland. There is scarcely a parish whose church is not worth visiting, though this is not, perhaps, what the coastal resorts would advertise as their main attractions—despite the fact that here are none of the promenades, bright lights, shooting-galleries and kindred enticements of what frequently go by the name of seaside resorts elsewhere. Lundin Links, Largo, Elie, St. Monans, Pittenweem, Anstruther, Crail and Kingsbarns entice by their own distinctive charms and native facilities, their beaches, sea-fishing, cliff-walks, golf and so on. And their devotees come back and back.

St. Andrews, of course, deserves a book to itself. Undoubtedly it is one of the most attractive, distinguished and rewarding towns in all Scotland—this clean, sparkling, age-old little city, that was ancient when its university, the first in Scotland, was founded in the early fifteenth century, that treasures all the experience of men in its mellow stones, noble halls and soaring towers, and yet is always young, with each year a fresh tide of red-robed students. Here barefoot pilgrimages were made, kings were wed, martyrs burned, archbishops assassinated, pageantry performed, highest revelry resounded and blackest treachery was plotted. Surely no town of fewer than 10,000 souls ever packed more into its story. Come here for that, or for learning, or for the celebrated golf, or just for a seaside holiday—but come.

The north flank of Fife is the least typical and the least

(Left) PITTENWEEM, FIFE. The harbour of one of the series of attractive and characterful fishing burghs and seaside resorts which string the picturesque Fife coast of the Forth, from Largo to Fife Ness. (Below) ST. ANDREWS, the old metropolitan see of Scotland, steeped in history, seat of its first university (1412) with its cathedral, castle, colleges and handsome town wall and gates.

known—indeed I suppose it has been one of the quietest backwaters of Lowland Scotland—*has* been, because now that the Tay Road Bridge has been built, all this will change and a hitherto secluded area become almost the back door of the city of Dundee. The cluster of coastal communities directly opposite Dundee, of course, because served by ferries, have always been to some extent suburban to the city—Tayport, Newport and Wormit. It is the long stretch of country westwards that is due for an awakening.

The inner estuary of the Tay is very different to that of the Forth, shorter, shallower and much less navigable. On the southern shore there are none of the harbours and villages that gem the Forth coast; just long reaches of flat tidelands and saltings, of shallow creeks and mudflats, a great place for wildfowl but not for habitation. Inland there is much green and level country, tilth and pasture, wood and demesne land, but no industry other than agriculture, no towns and few villages. Yet the area has its own quiet and withdrawn attraction. And it was more important to Scotland once, for here were the large abbeys of Balmerino and Lindores, playing their part in the development of the land; and on the fall of the abbeys the castles rose, as usual. The ruins of both still dot the green plain.

At the extreme western end of this preoccupied territory, on the borders of Perthshire, stands Newburgh, now little more than a village but once an important place with a harbour, and still a royal burgh. Auchtermuchty a few miles inland, renowned for its long name used to confound the poor English—I have heard one gallant attempt at pronunciation make it Ockerty-mockerty—but less well known in fact, despite an old world attraction and a good Tolbooth, was also once a royal burgh. In the old days, when Falkland represented government and the abbeys trade and progress, these two were significant and privileged towns. Today the tide of events has receded for them. But who knows—the new bridges, and that other tide which flows in Scotland, a national stirring, may bring them to the fore again.

I cannot leave Fife without mentioning Ceres—although many another worth-while place must be overlooked. Here, in mid-county, is one of the most picturesque and fascinating villages in the land, a scattered, leafy, mellow place with greens on either side of a river and an ancient bridge. Here in June each year is celebrated by games a historical event that predates even the earliest of the Border Common Ridings—the return from Bruce's victorious Bannockburn of a band of Ceres men in 1314.

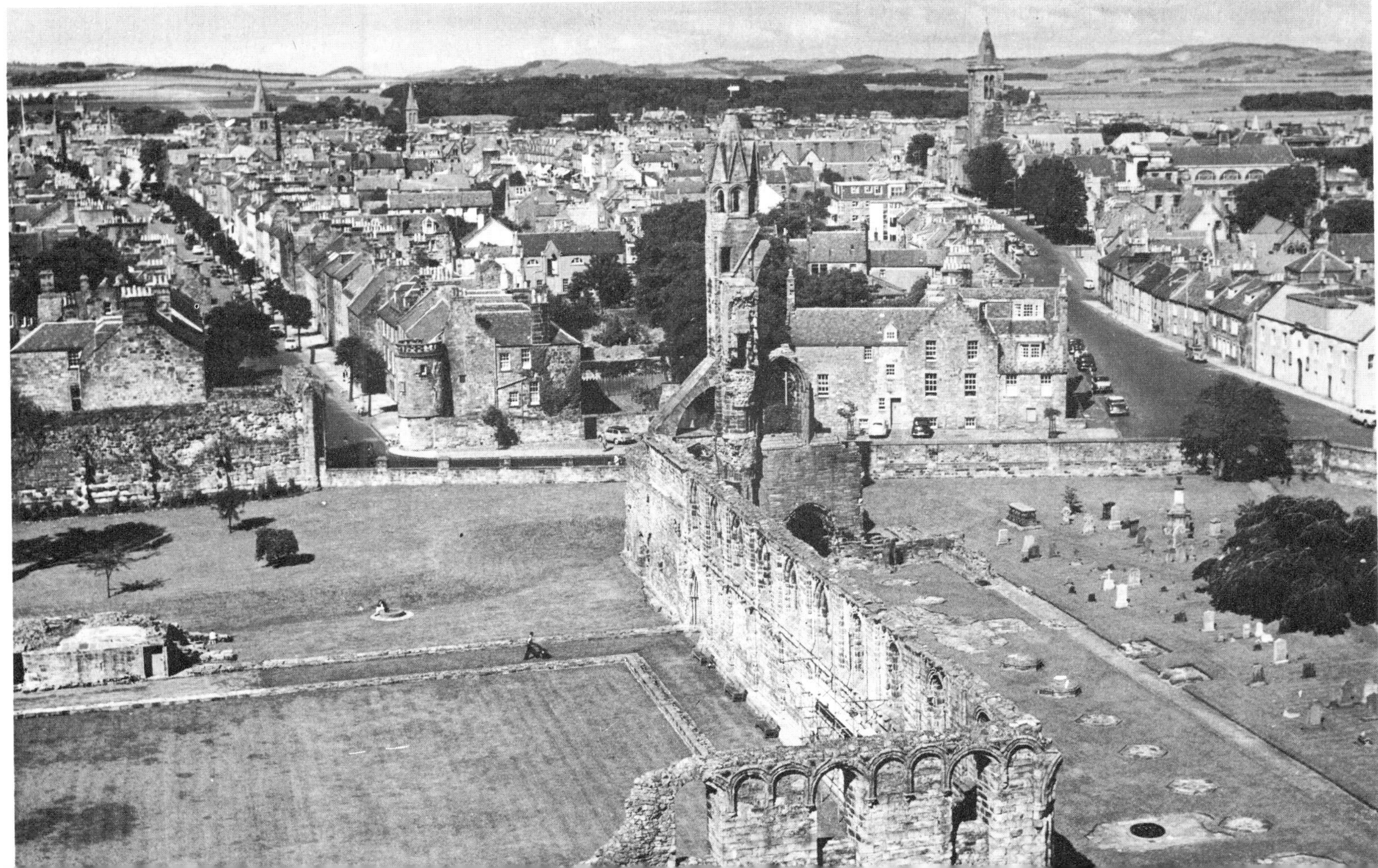

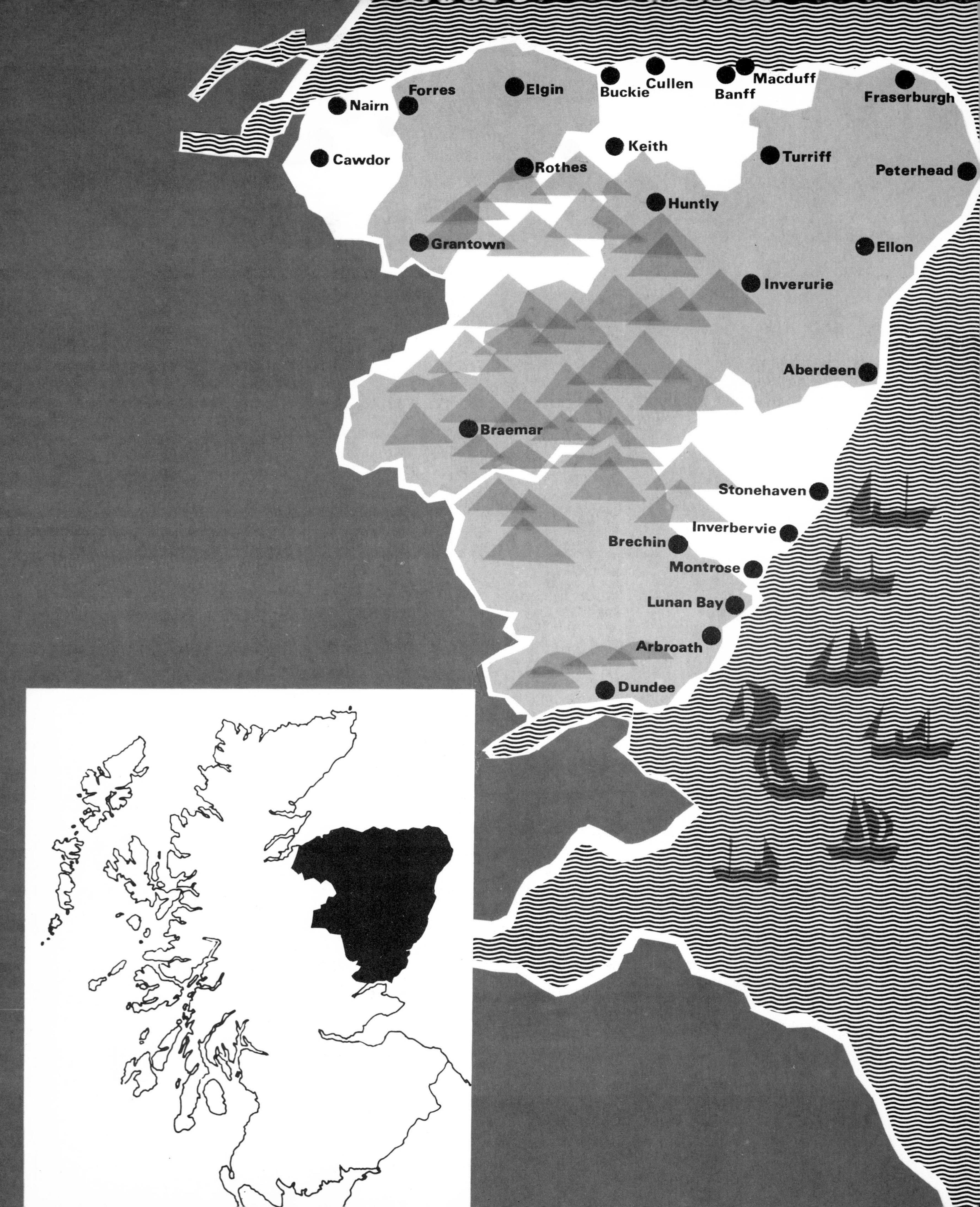

Nairn
Forres
Elgin
Buckie
Cullen
Banff
Macduff
Fraserburgh
Cawdor
Keith
Turriff
Peterhead
Rothes
Huntly
Grantown
Ellon
Inverurie
Aberdeen
Braemar
Stonehaven
Inverbervie
Brechin
Montrose
Lunan Bay
Arbroath
Dundee

CHAPTER 4
THE NORTH-EAST

The Tay Road Bridge disgorges its traffic directly into the centre of Dundee. A north-south traffic flow is something new for this city of 180,000 inhabitants, Scotland's fourth largest, which hitherto has been somewhat out on a limb in relation to the rest of the country. Whether its basic character of almost aggressive self-containment, strangely friendly however detached, will survive, remains to be seen. Certainly it is already the most swiftly developing of our cities.

Though its situation is highly attractive, on land slanting fairly sharply up the Sidlaw Hills where the Tay estuary meets the sea, no one could really claim Dundee to be a beautiful city. Nor, despite its long and stirring history - it was a royal burgh as early as the twelfth century, and Wallace attended its grammar school - can it be described as either an antiquarian or an architectural Mecca. But it is a cheerful, bustling, practical no-nonsense sort of place, with its own attractions and claims to fame, now as in the past. It used, of course, to be renowned for its three Js - jute, jam and journalists - with whales and shipbuilding thrown in. The whaling has been replaced by the manufacture of computers, accounting-machines and electronics - but the others survive, if no longer in quite the same proportions.

Some would say that Dundee's golden age was the second half of the nineteenth century, when it was the jute metropolis of the world, and reckoned

Calcutta practically its own private colony. Why this enormous and world wide jute trade should have become so concentrated at Dundee is something of a mystery. Assuredly vast fortunes were made for some, and the great and not always tasteful palaces of these nabobs sprang up by the score all along this seaboard; but as well as these sprang up the endless lines of dingy stone tenements and unsightly slums that disfigured so much of these Tayside braesides, where the less fortunate but infinitely more numerous citizens of Jute-opolis subsisted in the glorious reign of great Victoria. Much of the ancient town was swept away then, in the production of the sacking, sailcloth, waxcloth and other jute products which that world wanted —a lot of which has now been swept away in its turn. But by no means all, of either. The nabobs' mansions are now mainly hotels or institutions, or have been demolished, and great new housing areas and tall flats rise from their grounds. But the grimy heritage of the earlier exploiters is not so easily disposed of, and the relics of a more gracious age are few and far between. The large and ancient cruciform church, now islanded in the city centre and known as the Old Steeple—which is in fact three parish churches under one roof—the massive many-towered Dudhope Castle, former seat of the Scrymgeours, Hereditary Constables of Dundee; and the Ionic-pilastered town hall, built in 1734 to the designs of the elder Adam—these are the most notable.

It is to the future, therefore, that Dundee turns. Everywhere the skyscrapers go up; the great, clean-lined, grass-islanded modern factories proliferate; the new-style shopping precincts spread; the glass and concrete cliffs of new office buildings, colleges and hotels challenge the eye.

Development, modernisation, diversion, progress—these are the watchwords of the city, to an extent unusual in Scotland. The great white bridge is only one symbol of it all, long fought for. The East Tidal Harbour and Fish Dock was recently reconstructed. The former Queen's College extension of ancient St. Andrew's University is now at last Dundee's own independent university, and the College of Art, the College of Education and the Technical College advance in step—for Dundee is a great place for education, with no fewer than seventy schools. Although the housing development is already the most costly and ambitious in the country, the Town Council intend to build no fewer than another 10,000 in the years between 1967-72, with private housing estimated to increase by a third of that. The city

DUNDEE, at the mouth of the Tay, with its new road bridge, the older railway bridge just out of the picture. This is the fourth city of Scotland, ancient even in Wallace's day, but expanding and developing even faster than Glasgow. Once famous for jute, jam and journalists, it has diversified itself into the forefront of the 'technological revolution'. It now has its own university. Although not a beautiful place in itself, its setting is attractive.

centre has been entirely reshaped. The city's industrial estate continually expands, and brings in an interesting tide of technicians and experts from America and elsewhere. A new hospital rises at Ninewells, incorporating a new medical school. And so on. Dundee positively vibrates with initiative today.

But all this preoccupation with modernity has by no means extinguished Dundee's three Js, even though jam-making, originally started here because of the proximity of the great fruit-growing lands of the Carse of Gowrie and Strathmore, no longer bulks so large as it did. Jute Industries, a great combine originally formed out of six foremost Dundee firms, still leads the world in this trade. And as for journalists, the extensive complex of newspapers and magazines of the D. C. Thomson Group, training-ground for so many notable publicists, still produces such a number and variety of publications, from the *Sunday Post* to the *Scots Magazine*, and the *People's Friend* to *The Beano*, that their combined circulation must make even Fleet Street look thoughtful.

Dundee is in the very right-hand bottom corner of the county of Angus, an area which in the past generally made infinitely more impact on Scottish affairs than did the city. Always it was important, partly because of the rich farmlands of Strathmore, partly on account of the power here of the ancient Church, but also in that this was the homeland of some of the most potent families in the land—in especial the Red Douglases, Earls of Angus; the Lindsays, Earls of Crawford; the Ogilvys, Earls of Airlie; and the Lyons, Lords Glamis. Around these, and others like them, history was built.

Angus falls naturally into three more or less parallel belts—the coastal plain; the great central Vale of Strathmore, thirty-two miles long by an average of five wide; and the Braes of Angus, the foothill country lifting to the mighty heather breasts of the Grampians.

The seaboard area, sandy and flat to the south, rocky and cliff-girt to the north, is a pleasing one, dotted with little towns and resorts—although Arbroath, half-way up, is more than that, a thriving manufacturing place that sprang up round the princely abbey of Aberbrothack, from which Cardinal David Beaton once ruled the land—the impressive ruins of which huge establishment are one of Scotland's most precious heritages. Here, in 1320, was signed by the assembled barons of Scotland the Declaration of Independence, one of the most splendid affirmations of liberty extant.

Arbroath today, with its engineering, textile and boat-building industries, a five million pound housing programme, its own industrial estate and over-spill agreement with Glasgow, is an inspiring place.

Broughty Ferry, Monifieth and Carnoustie are sufficiently near to Dundee to act as playgrounds for that city, as well as residential areas, and their attractions of sands, golf-courses and good hotels bring many visitors. But north of Arbroath, the great cliffs of Red Head, leading down to the wide and lovely bay of Lunan, provide an exciting away-from-it-all region which deserves to be better appreciated in other parts of Scotland. Despite Scott's pin-pointing of the area in *The Antiquary*, the villages of Auchmithie, Ethiehaven, Redcastle, Lunan and Inverkeilor remain but little known to most of the population, to its loss.

Montrose, up near the county boundary, is justly renowned for its good looks and its popularity as a holiday resort. But, it has an increasing industrial production also of jute, chemicals and precast concrete. Its great land-locked tidal basin is unique in Scotland, imparting to the town an atmosphere all its own.

Strathmore starts in East Perthshire, and ends in The Mearns but the great bulk of it belongs to Angus. It is a splendid wide and fertile vale, flanked by the green Sidlaws and their extensions on one hand and the purple-brown ramparts of the Highlands on the other, some 200 square miles of tilth and pasture, plantation and estate-land, interspersed with gentle eminencies. It is very much an entity on its own, a little province by itself, with a galaxy of modest but characterful towns and villages and a wealth of castles, towers and churches, a settled ages-old territory.

Blairgowrie, Scotland's foremost fruit town, is over the Perthshire border, as is Alyth—although it looks as though it should be part and parcel of Angus, and indeed part of its parish is. Oddly enough, despite its name, Coupar Angus is just over into Perthshire also, by the loops and links of winding Isla, an ancient place whose once-rich abbey formerly spoke with a loud voice.

Forfar, in the middle of the great strath, is the county town of Angus—indeed for some time the county was known as Forfarshire. Although one of the most ancient royal burghs in the land, and a favourite seat of Malcolm Canmore, who held a parliament here in 1057 and conferred its first charter, there is a notable lack of ancient building to be seen today. As befits the capital of Strathmore, Forfar —or Farfar, as its natives pronounce it—is a town of

(Left) BRECHIN CATHEDRAL AND ROUND TOWER, Angus. Pleasant town in the famed Vale of Strathmore. The cathedral dates from the twelfth century, but the Round Tower—one of only two on the Scottish mainland—is probably two centuries earlier. (Below) STRATHMORE, Angus. The great central vale which runs for 30 miles, from Coupar Angus to the Howe o' the Mearns, and flanked on the west by the mighty barrier of

sturdy and independent character, reminiscent of one of the Border burghs. Typical of its attitude is the story of the Forfar man who at Euston Station approached the bookstall for a copy of the *Dispatch*. When asked which Dispatch he meant, he answered *Farfar Dispatch* of course. When told that unfortunately they didn't stock this he sighed and remarked that he'd just have to take their local paper, picking up *The Times*.

With 10,000 of a population, it is another go-ahead place, its textile mills spinning not only jute but flax, fine cottons, wool and man-made fibres. A firm formerly manufacturing reeds and cambs for jute mills, seeing that market shrinking turned to the entirely new field of ladder-making, and now exports both wood and metal ladders all over the world. Agricultural engineers have grown out of blacksmith's shops to make farm machinery, feeding trays, lifters and harvesters. Joiners have developed into prefabricated-buildings makers, and so on. Yet with it all there is still the more gentle rhythm of a farming and market town.

Brechin, ten miles up the strath, though smaller by a third, likes to be called a city because it has a cathedral, even though of modest proportions, with its bishop domiciled in Broughty Ferry! Amongst all its well-doing and up-and-coming neighbours, perhaps Brechin has a little of the poor-but-proud preoccupation such as Edinburgh has for Glasgow, for the town has seen better days, its population having actually fallen from 13,000 to 7,000. Nevertheless it is seeking to redress this and to attract industry and capital —and it has much to offer, for it is an attractively sited place, with much more natural beauty than Forfar. Its famed Round Tower, attached to the cathedral, is over 100 feet high to its conical top, and is believed to date from the tenth century.

Kirriemuir, up amongst the Angus braes, looks out over a splendid prospect of the strath. Famous as the birthplace of J. M. Barrie, it was a weaving town whose weavers were permanently at feud with the souters or shoemakers of Forfar. Drummond of Hawthornden used to recount that when he travelled here in 1648 he was refused shelter in Forfar because he was a poet and a royalist; but though these two failings were equally deplored when he went to Kirriemuir, he was warmly welcomed merely because Forfar had rejected him. Today it is a neat, douce town, though less distinguished than its setting.

(Below) GLEN DOLL, one of the many fine Angus glens, where the high Grampians open on to Strathmore. (Right) RED CASTLE, AND LUNAN BAY, Angus. Red Head, nearby, is a magnificent promontory guarding one of the finest and largest sandy bays in East Scotland.

At the very north-east tip of the county, Edzell, a village rather than a town, sits in the lap of the great hills, at the mouth of Glen Esk beside its handsome castle. The feel of the heather and the scent of the pines are strong here, so that, in a way, this little place represents that greatest and almost empty quarter of Angus where the grouse and the curlew reign, hundreds of square miles of mountain and moor and glen. Quiet those uplands may be—but no one, even in lushest Strathmore, is ever allowed to forget them for long.

The Angus castles are a joy. Glamis, of course, the Queen Mother's early home, is known to all; but there are a great many more, of like worth if lesser size. Airlie, on the brow of its ravine, Cortachy in its green haugh, and Inverquharity, tall amongst its hillocks, are all Ogilvy strongholds; Edzell and Finavon, Lindsay seats; Ethie and Melgund linked with Cardinal Beaton. The latter's lovely rose-red pile was built by that controversial Prince of the Church for the lady whom the Reformers referred to as his 'chief Lewd', Marion Ogilvy, daughter of the Lord Ogilvy of Airlie, but who was probably in fact his wife, unacknowleged for state reasons, yet to whom he remained faithful after his fashion. His is one of the most execrated names in Scots history—but the lovingly conjoined initials D. B. and M. O. in the mellow masonry of Melgund Castle, perhaps whisper a different story.

Kincardineshire, or The Mearns, although geographically little more than a north-easterly extension of Angus, has indeed a very different character. It is altogether a barer, sterner county, dominated by great skies, its bones as it were nearer to the surface. Contained between the north Esk, and the Dee, with the sea on one flank and the high hills on the other, it is a compact triangle of a quarter-million acres, most of them mountainous or lofty plateau-land. The name confuses many, for there are no fewer than seven Kincardines in Scotland, and almost all of them more important than the place which gives its name to this county—though it was a highly important royal castle once. Now, near Fettercairn, there is just a name on the Ordnance Sheet, and a field marked King's Park, where once a monarch ruled, and one was murdered.

Again the area falls naturally into three sections—only this time, although most of the population is concentrated along the seaboard, there is no coastal plain, the land rising fairly steeply from a largely cliff-girt and rocky shore, dotted with caves, coves and the remains of castles. Inland

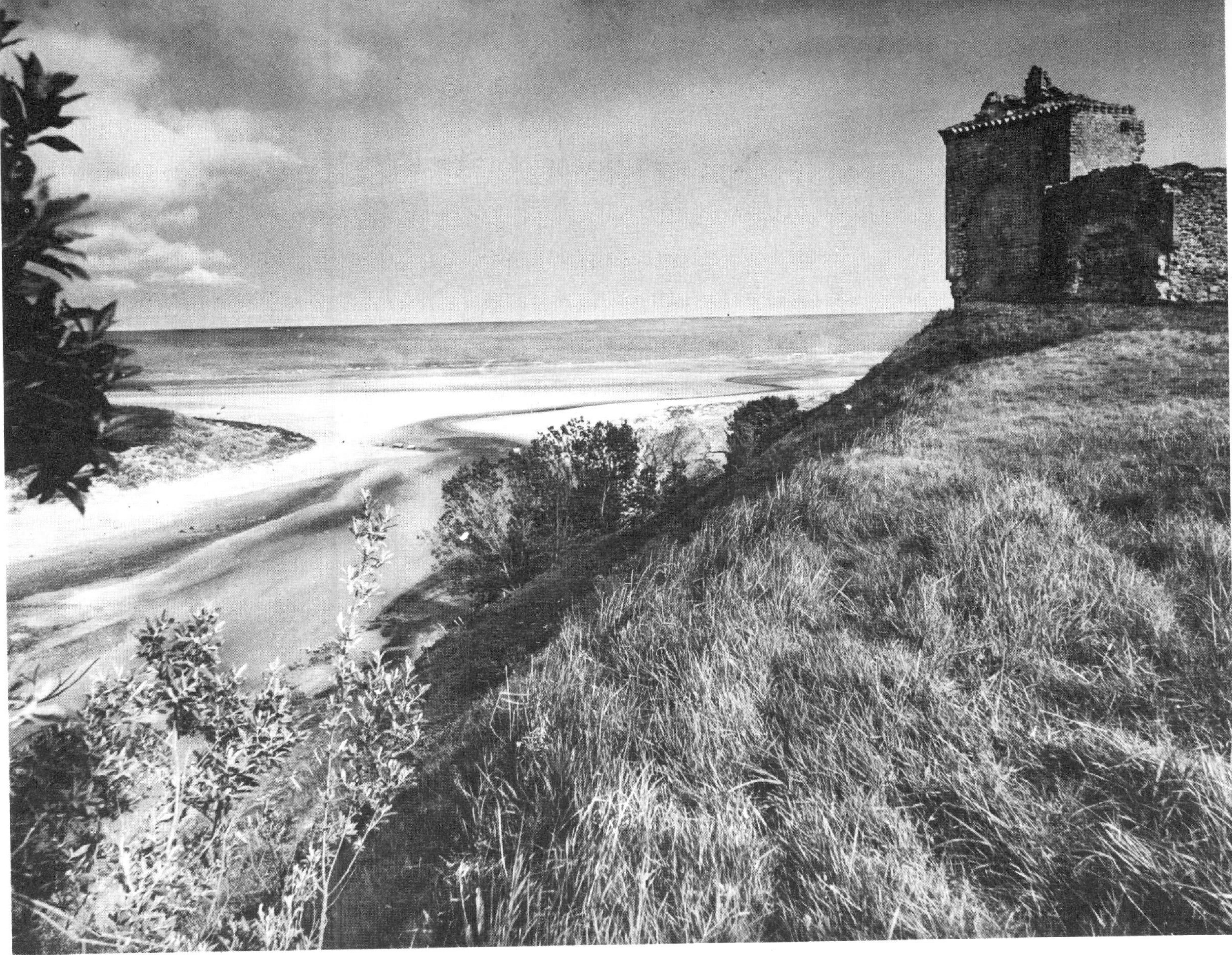

there is the Strathmore extension, the Howe of the Mearns, famed in literature for the quality of its farming folk equally with that of its red-soil land. Then there are the uplands and the mountains, comprising half of the county area, most of it typical empty Grampian country, pierced by long and twisting glens.

Kincardineshire is short on towns—there being in fact only three, and all small. Stonehaven, or Stanehive as its people pronounce it, is the county seat, sited in a deep hollow where the Cowie and Carron Waters reach the sea at a rocky bay, all roads descending to it by long and steep hills. Although of only 4,500 population, it is a busy little place, a holiday town, with a distillery, sundry lesser industries and a large harbour. This was extended from the old fishing haven, and the sea-wall built, from designs by the famous engineer, Robert Stevenson, grandfather of the still more famous R. L. S. I find that it is not always known, even by the local folk, that the town got its name from a large rock which projected from the sea to the south, and which was removed during those extension operations.

Inverbervie, or just Bervie, as it is more frequently called, ten miles to the south, is very much just a smaller edition of Stonehaven, with less than 1,000 inhabitants, though a royal burgh. But it considers itself superior to the comparatively modern county town, for it has held its charter since 1341, when David II and his young English Queen Joanna were shipwrecked here, at Craig David, at the base of Bervie Brow, the bold headland to the north. There are other relics of antiquity. A Carmelite Friary stood at what is now known as Friars' Dubb, near the bridge; and overlooking the little town from the south is Hallgreen Castle, a mainly sixteenth century stronghold of the Raits, still occupied. An even more interesting castle is Allardyce, a mile inland up the Bervie Water, where the peculiarly Scottish art of elaborate label-corbelling, part functional, part ornamental, reaches perhaps its apogee, on the multi-turreted stair-tower.

This county is again rich in castles, and while Dunnottar, crowning its great thrusting sea-girt rock, is one of the most famous in Scotland, others such as Benholm nearby, Balbegno at Fettercairn, Fiddes on the heights of Bruxie Hill, Inglismaldie on the North Esk, and Thornton in the Howe, deserve greater appreciation. Muchalls, to the north of Stonehaven, is indeed one of the most notable seventeenth century houses in the land, with quite magnificent heraldic plaster ceilings.

(Below) MUCHALLS CASTLE, Kincardineshire. An unspoiled seventeenth century laird's house, with splendid heraldic plaster ceilings. Note the triple shot-holes protecting the courtyard gate. (Right) STONEHAVEN, county town of Kincardineshire, locally called Stanehive, its harbour and sea-wall built by Robert Stevenson, grandfather of R.L.S.

Laurencekirk, once called Conveth, is the capital of the Howe, but though a douce, well-doing place stretching for a mile along the main Aberdeen highway, no one could call it an exciting centre for so storied a neighbourhood. It serves the agricultural needs of a wide area, and once was a great place for making snuff-boxes and Mearns Linen. The folk hereabouts were noted for their prowess, skills and strength, so much so that the proverb says—'I can dae fat I dow; the men o' the Mearns can dae nae mair!' It is said that the Howe took its name from Mernia, a brother of King Kenneth II whose castle of Kincardine stood nearby.

A feature of the Kincardineshire scene not to be overlooked is the series of small fishing villages which crouch and cling under the cliffs of this rock-bound coast—Johnshaven, Gourdon, Catterline, Cowie, Muchalls, Skateraw, Portlethen and Cove, places of a stark but doughty character that speaks eloquently of the age-old battle with the North Sea at its sternest.

It may not always be realised that this county extends northwards right to the very gates of Aberdeen itself, and not only is one side of the famed River Dee in Kincardineshire but that the county actually crosses to the north side for quite a stretch, so that the little town of Banchory is in fact in this county, not Aberdeenshire. This riparian section, almost detached from the rest by low hills, is of a quite distinct nature. But because this riverside strip is very narrow, though long, there is little population and no villages—save at the two ends. Torry, to the east, has developed from a fishing harbour to being a suburb of Aberdeen, and so incorporated in that city; and twenty miles to the west, the Banchory enclave into the northern shire belongs in all else but boundary to the pine-forested upper Deeside polity.

The situation of Aberdeen, the third of Scotland's four great cities, has not the same scenic advantages of Edinburgh and Dundee. But it is a much more handsome city, nevertheless, than the latter. Occupying a knuckle of levelish land between the mouths of the Rivers Dee and Don, it is a notably large community to find so far north in these islands, the most northerly city of the Commonwealth,—nearly 200,000 people. And it is most obviously and definitely a very civilised city—in a fashion Dundee does not aspire to, a planned, self-contained and individual place of great character. Comparisons with Dundee, of course, are unfair—but almost inevitable, for the two, only seventy miles apart but each far from any other large community,

are much of a size. They are, indeed, great rivals. But while Dundee may be outstripping Aberdeen in its striding into the new age, the latter has a dignity and assurance which the former lacks—even though Dundee claims to be the more ancient city.

Aberdeen in reality is composed of two towns, the modern commercial city at the mouth of the Dee, largely an early nineteenth century creation of fine planning on an older base; and the ancient cathedral and university town to the north, which might more properly be named Aberdon, now called Old Aberdeen. The two, of course, are conjoined, but remain more distinct entities than, say, the Old and New Towns of Edinburgh, where the one merely grew out of the other.

Every visitor to Aberdeen is struck at once by the clean, airy, sparkling freshness of the place—not the usual impact of cities. This is, of course, largely because of the glistening white local granite of which almost every building is constructed, a hard, straight-edged stone which never seems to grow dirty or rounded—or, for that matter, mellow. Normally it is a simple matter to tell which is ancient stonework and which modern in a church or castle; not so in Aberdeen granite, which defies weathering. But the climate also has something to do with the clean appearance, for the city's position is exposed in a fashion unusual for a great urban mass, seeming almost to thrust out into the North Sea, a place of sunshine and cold winds. It rains of course in Aberdeen, too.

Union Street ranks with Edinburgh's Princes Street as one of the great thoroughfares of Britain—and with more reason, for it is the position and open southerly prospect of Princes Street, and by no means its architecture, which is so deservedly renowned. Union Street, stately, spacious and straight, and with its extensions almost a mile long, has been described as one of the finest of any city in the world; flanked by consistently good building and excellent shops, and incorporating Telford's Union Bridge, it is a homogeneous whole, planned and built in 1800 by master architects and far-seeing city fathers—who yet bankrupted themselves in the process—clearing away a hill and vast amount of what was alleged to be 'undistinguished hovels' to do so, though no doubt destroying something of the city's ancient heritage likewise. Union Street, though the most famous of Aberdeen's thoroughfares, has of course a great many neighbours almost equally fine, King Street and George Street being notable, as on another scale is Rubislaw

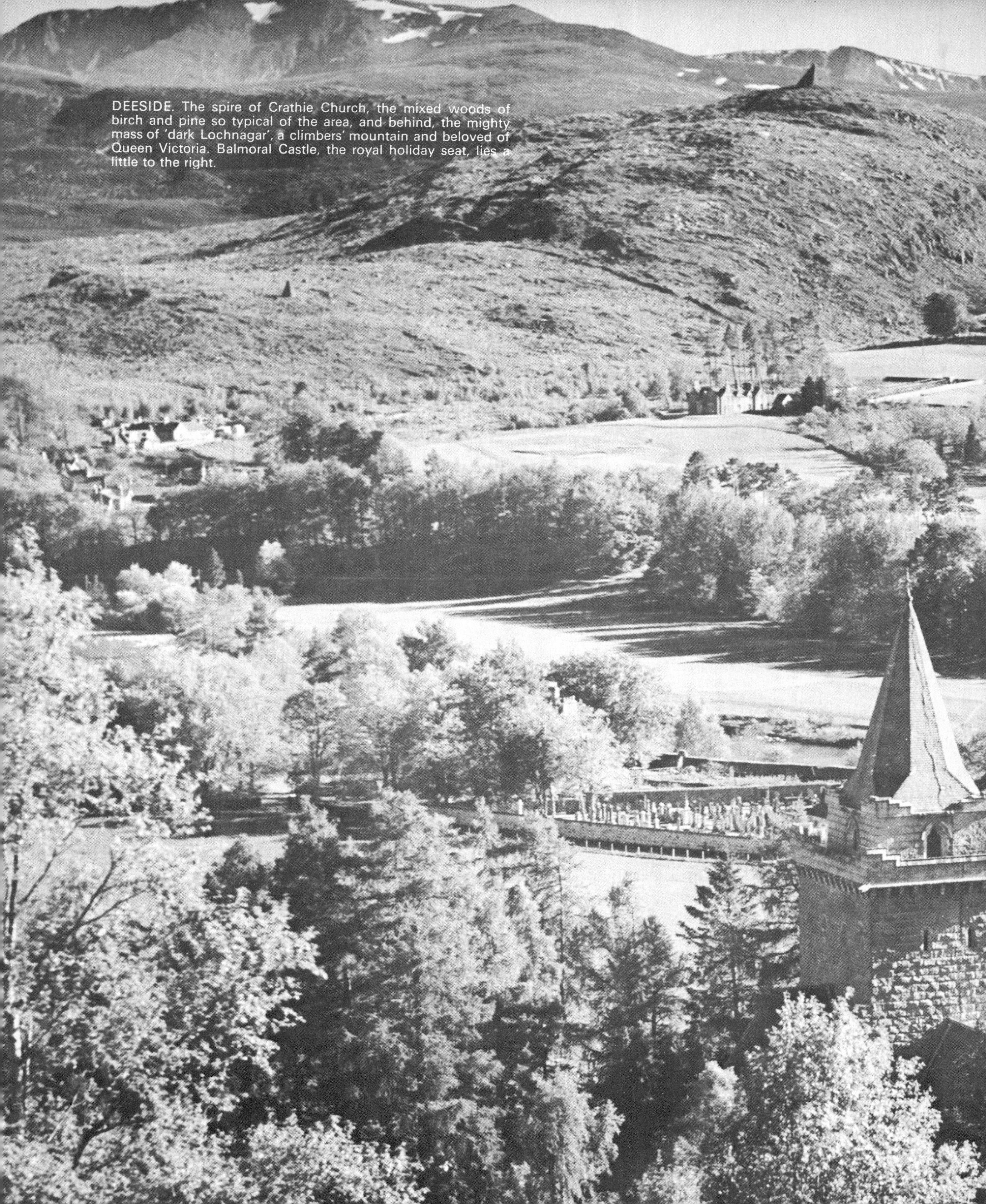

DEESIDE. The spire of Crathie Church, the mixed woods of birch and pine so typical of the area, and behind, the mighty mass of 'dark Lochnagar', a climbers' mountain and beloved of Queen Victoria. Balmoral Castle, the royal holiday seat, lies a little to the right.

(Left) ABERDEEN PANORAMA IN GRANITE. Union Street, one of the great streets of Britain, crosses the picture diagonally. Marischal College can be distinguished in the centre background. (Below) FISH-MARKET, ABERDEEN, famous feature of this, one of the world's biggest fishing-ports.

Terrace. To one side of Union Street lies the dock area, very close; to the other, in slowly rising waves, spreads modern Aberdeen, from Georgian squares and crescents to present-day functional building and high housing.

Nevertheless, it is at the far north end of the city, Old Aberdeen, that the true architectural treasures cluster. Here is St. Machar's Cathedral, the only granite cathedral in the world. Though partially destroyed by the Reforming mob in 1560 and now represented only by the nave and western towers, it is still a most handsome structure, with a great western window divided by six long shafts of stone. Here is the Chanonry, or ancient cathedral precinct. Here is King's College, dating from 1500 and added to throughout the centuries, with its great lantern tower. Bishop Elphinstone, Chancellor of the Realm, who founded the university in 1494, is buried here. Another college, founded by Keith, Earl Marischal in 1593, in New Aberdeen, was re-built in 1844, though its very well known Broad Street frontage of thrusting spires and soaring buttressess was added in 1906. Marischal and King's Colleges were united in 1860 to form the university of Aberdeen as we know it now.

Aberdeen is proud of its university, in a way that Edinburgh and Glasgow are not, for it makes a greater impact on the life of the city and adds to its lustre. It has long served as the university not only of the North-East but of much of the Highlands and Islands area also, and today it is still in the forefront of academic advance.

The city's enduring prosperity has always been founded securely on the two basic elements which flank and nourish it—the land and the sea. The sea, and proximity to the great North Sea fishing grounds, made Aberdeen into one of the largest fishing ports of the world—and the advent of the long-range trawler era, with its exploitation of the far northern and semi-Arctic fishings, ensured that this most northerly great port was strategically placed for major development. So here is the white-fish metropolis, where are based the great trawler fleets. Aberdeen's fish market is world-famous, and an early morning visit thereto one of the sights of these islands. From here the long fish-trains rumble, day and night, on the long haul to all the cities of the south, not least to London. Around the docks arise the kippering-sheds, the fish-meal and processing mills, the fertiliser-works, while ship and boat-building yards, fish-box factories and ice plants are natural adjuncts.

Aberdeen is not only a fishing-port, of course; its general shipping trade is large, with good dock-handling facilities.

(Below) ST. MACHAR'S CATHEDRAL, ABERDEEN, the only granite cathedral in the world. This handsome city is almost entirely built of white sparkling granite, which, aided by the weather, makes it seem one of the cleanest places on earth. (Right) MARISCHAL COLLEGE. Now part of Aberdeen University, deservedly renowned as a more modern example of granite architecture.

The other great basic element is the land, the vast agricultural hinterland of Aberdeenshire. Just how vast this is will be brought out hereafter—but it demands an enormous service base and comprehensive marketing facilities—and these Aberdeen provides. For instance, between 4,000 and 5,000 cattle pass through its markets each week.

There has always been a healthy diversification of industry here, with engineering, implement-making, tweed-milling, linen-weaving, paper-making, meat-processing, not to mention distilling. The Scottish hosiery trade might be said to have originated here, not in the Borders, with woollen stocking-making strong as early as the seventeenth century, of a quality to bring all Europe here for clothing shapely legs. In 1771, for instance, no fewer than 69,333 dozen pairs of stockings were produced, chiefly for export. Added to the traditional trades are the up-to-the-minute radio, electronics, chemicals, plastics and fibre-glass works, so that Aberdeen is well equipped to face the challenge of the future, especially as the city has an advantage which Dundee and Edinburgh have not, its own commercial television service, in Grampian T.V.

In conversation with others I have frequently noted how little understood are the dimensions of the rural area backing Aberdeen. Admittedly this is only the sixth county in Scotland in size—but whereas the other five giants are Highland, with the vast proportion of their area empty mountains, Aberdeen, though it has its mountains also, is preponderantly Lowland. Though there is much hilly land, it is by and large a farming county. A glance at the map will show that this is the largest and most solid lump of sheer territory in all Scotland, and if the wider farming areas of the Mearns and Banff, Moray and Nairn are included in the natural entity, then here are well over 2,000 square miles of farm land, at least 1,500,000 acres, possibly the largest single stretch of unbroken agricultural land in the British Isles. There have been said to be 10,000 farms in Aberdeenshire alone, and I well believe it—for in 1879 there were 7,472 actual landowners in the county, tenant-farmers excluded.

This, of course, is the home of the most famous beef-cattle breed, the black, stocky, short-legged Aberdeen-Angus, which takes second place to none amongst the world's stock-breeders, and which, with the great shorthorn herds, produce the original prime Scotch beef beloved of butchers. It is on this most solid foundation, and the forage

BRIG O' DEE, Aberdeenshire. Near Braemar, where the Dee issues, amongst beautiful pine forests, from the mighty Cairngorm Mountains.

crops to feed it, that the enormous farming community of the North East has developed. Only sheer travel through the length and breadth of this vast clenched fist of Scotland will bring about a true appreciation of how important and enduring, if little publicised, is this huge part of our polity and economy—a major but rewarding activity.

Briefly to describe this great countryside, it may be divided conveniently into the traditional earldoms of early Scotland—Mar, Buchan and Strathbogie.

Mar, the old southerly division, formed of Braemar, Midmar and Cromar, could be said to extend up into the central area once known as Formartine, and so include both the Dee and Don basins. This is a region of great natural beauty, with the high hills here coming closer to the sea than further north. Deeside, though possibly the best known, by reputation, is the least typical area of the county, a territory where social, sporting and tourist influences overlay the more solid worth of the rest, but a place of magnificent mountain views, salmon-rich rivers, forests, pine-scented air and fine estates. Its attractive and dignified centres of Aboyne, Ballater and Braemar feature in all the pictorial calendars, and make good places to visit, with excellent hotels, picturesque walks and an aura of royal favour. The Dee rises in the mighty Cairngorm Mountains, and its upper reaches provide splendid attractions for the mountaineer, the hill-walker and hiker, the naturalist and the photographer.

Donside is quite different—which is strange, for the Don has its own scenic beauties. This huge basin is much more down-to-earth, with better farming land, larger townships, if less exciting mountain prospects. It is Aberdeenshire's own domestic peak, Benachie, which dominates Strathdon—though the upper river does rise deep in the Grampians. Here are the busy small granite-built towns of Kintore, Inverurie, Kenmay and Alford, dotted along the great river; and standing further back, Oldmeldrum, Old Rayne, Insch and Rhynie, with villages, churches, milltons and little schools innumerable, all catering for the widespread farming community. The age-old nature of this land-based population is witnessed to by the plethora of castles—thicker on Donside perhaps than anywhere else in the land, and reaching heights of excellence unsurpassed. There are twenty-five or more surviving in the Kintore-Strathdon area alone.

Buchan is the eastern division of the county, and scenically the least attractive—though some of its coastal

THE WIDE, WIDE FARMLANDS OF CENTRAL ABERDEENSHIRE, near Lumphannan, the greatest single spread of agricultural land in all Scotland, possibly in the British Isles. All may not realise the vastness of it. There are said to be 10,000 farms in Aberdeenshire.

prospects can be very fine. Here are no high hills, though it is far from flat, a great undulating terrain, a whole province of green knowes and knolls, endless fields, squat low-browed farmhouses and long grey villages. There is little that is soft or gentle about Buchan—but it is strong and vital country, and its folk are friendly. Indeed this is a notable feature of all the shire—the sheer good-hearted friendliness of the people.

Buchan has two large burghs, both on the north coast—Peterhead and Fraserburgh; but elsewhere its towns are small and wide-scattered—Rosehearty, a fishing place, and Ellon, Strichen and Turiff inland. Villages there are by the score.

Peterhead, perhaps unfortunately linked in most outsiders' minds with the large prison sited there, is a town of 12,000 inhabitants, occupying an isolated position forty-four miles north of Aberdeen, at the mouth of the River Ugie—indeed its parish was formerly called Peter-Ugie. Sternly built of its own granite, and a town obviously with no nonsense about it, Peterhead seems the last place to associate with the supernatural. Yet it was the scene, in 1642, of an ominous and other-worldly manifestation.

> 'About the 5th of November, in ane seamanis house of Peterheid, there was hard, upone the night, beatting of drums, uther tymes sounding of trumpetis, playing on pifferis, and ringing of bellis, to the astonishment of the heareris. Trubles follouit.'

The said troubles were occasioned by the dynastic and religious wars of Charles I, wherein the district did not escape. Later, indeed, with the forfeiture of the dominant Keith Marischal family after the Jacobite Rising of 1715, Peterhead was actually sold as a whole to the infamous York Buildings Company, who later retailed it to the Edinburgh Merchant Company. The harbour of Peterhead has long been important, not only as a fishing and granite-export place but because it was the first haven of shelter for vessels approaching Scotland from Northern Europe, in seas notable for storms.

Fraserburgh, another eighteen miles along the coast, is only a little smaller, a quite attractive town occupying the rocky promontory of Kinnaird's Head (the Promontorium Taexalium of Ptolemy). Neatly and regularly built, by various members of the Fraser family, latterly Lords Saltoun, Fraserburgh is entitled to have its own university, a charter having been granted to that effect to Alexander

SUN, SHADOW AND STORM-CLOUDS OVER GRUINARD BAY, Wester Ross, near Mellon Udrigle. The mountains of Coigach tower beyond the mouths of the two Lochs Broom, in the background. None who visit here will ever quite escape its spell.

Fraser of Philorth, the real founder of the town, in 1592—and never cancelled. The nearest it ever got towards university status, however, was in 1647 when an outbreak of plague in Aberdeen brought King's College here temporarily. Fishing, fish-curing and other allied trades are still the principal industries.

Strathbogie, the north-westerly division of the county was, of course, the ancient domain of the proud Gordon lords, Earls of Huntly and hereditary Lieutenants of the North. There is still a Presbytery, comprising a dozen parishes, but the old Lordship of Strathbogie was larger, extending north into Banffshire, and comprising all the Bogie and Deveron basins, from Ryhnie in the south to Keith in the north, Dufftown in the west to Turriff in the east. This great stretch is mainly foothill country, though it runs up into the mountains, a land of stock-rearing and distilleries—but almost more famous for battles and feuding as becomes the stamping-ground of the Gordons, Cocks o' the North. Huntly itself is the only town, the handsome Gordon capital, with a much more ambitious and dignified aspect than its mere 4,000 population would lead the visitor to expect. Situated in attractive hill country, its wide market square and well-built streets are dominated by the great and stately ruined castle which has played so large a part in Scottish history—and which James VI once took part in trying to pull down with his own royal hands.

The Deveron, a great salmon river, pursues a winding and consistently picturesque course from the high Grampians to the sea, over sixty miles, for a part of the way marking the border between Aberdeenshire and Banffshire. It is notable for the number of fine and ancient estates which line its banks.

The three counties of Banff, Moray and Nairn complete the vast land-mass known as the North-East. They could be considered conveniently as a whole, as the old province of Moray, a great territorial and ecclesiastical entity, with its capital at Elgin. With an eighty-mile base along the shore of the Moray Firth, it makes a massive triangle between Aberdeenshire and Inverness-shire, reaching back to the very summit ridge of the Cairngorms and comprising the basins of the magnificent rivers of Spey, Lossie, Findhorn and Nairn. The wide and fairly flat coastal plain here is one of the most fertile and productive of all Scotland, known as the Laigh of Moray; the havens of Macduff, Portsoy, Cullen, Portnockie, Findochty, Buckie, Lossiemouth, Hopeman and Burghead, between them constitute one of

(Below) CAWDOR CASTLE, near Nairn. One of the most romantic and unaltered great castles of Scotland, seat of Earl Cawdor, with its fifteenth century keep towering above seventeenth century courtyard buildings. (Right) ELGIN CATHEDRAL, showing the groin-vaulted South Aisle, with recumbent effigies. Elgin and its cathedral, once the finest in the land, was burned in 1390 by the notorious Wolf of Badenoch, son of Robert II. It was repaired, but the Reformers destroyed it in their turn.

the greatest concentrations of fishing-ports in these islands; and the upland area, supplied by the splendid water from the mountains, and the barley-crops of the Laigh, is the prime whisky-producing area of the world, with more distilleries crammed into these glens than anywhere else on earth—famous names like Glenlivet, Longmorn, Balvenie, Mortlach, Knockando and Glenmorangie.

Elgin is one of Scotland's most renowned towns—or cities, for it has claimed this title for long, and calls its chief magistrate *Lord* Provost, though its population is only 12,000. History and antiquity jostle with progress everywhere here, and its old-world narrow streets and traditional architecture contrast vividly with the ambitious new housing areas and highly modern suburbs. The presence of two great naval and military air stations at Lossiemouth and Kinloss nearby helps to keep Elgin in a stir—but it has its own native vigour and liveliness. The ruined cathedral was one of the glories of the kingdom, the most splendid example of ecclesiastical architecture in the land. Tragic that it should have suffered so—and not only at the hands of the infamous Alexander Stewart, Earl of Buchan. The son of Robert II, nicknamed the Wolf of Badenoch, he burned it in 1390 as reprisal for being excommunicated by its bishop. But others have been equally destructive since, the Reformers making their usual efforts to destroy a beauty which they equated with 'popishness', and even the Privy Council, in 1568, authorising the stripping of all lead from the roof, to sell for the maintenance of the godly Regent Moray's troops. The ship taking the lead to be sold in Holland, incidentally, got only as far as outside Aberdeen Harbour when it foundered and sank. From that day until modern times, the splendid cathedral was exposed to wind and weather, and what was not ruined thus was pillaged and pulled down, even the fine carved woodwork and

(Below) CULBIN SANDS AND FOREST, Moray. This formerly fertile area was overwhelmed with blown sand in the seventeenth century, so deeply as to bury even the barony's church steeple. It is now planted with millions of pine trees, to hold the sand. (Right) STACK-BUILDING AT BALLINDALLOCH, Speyside, Banffshire. Here the farmlands reach up into the hills, amongst the greatest concentration of distilleries on earth.

screens used to keep the parish minister's fire alight. In 1711 the great central tower, 198 feet high, collapsed, bringing down much that was left.

I have heard it alleged that the Scots are philistines, unappreciative of beauty. This is nonsense, for in the past they raised monuments of the greatest beauty and delicacy, and today in almost every sphere of the arts such beauty is again fostered. But admittedly there was a period following upon the Reformation when the stern doctrines of Calvanism were misinterpreted to see beauty, gaiety, music and art as sinful, and the power of the Kirk imposed this upon the people, however totally against their natural character.

Banff, a royal burgh since before 1165, of only 3,000 inhabitants, is attractively placed at the mouth of the Deveron, at one side of Banff Bay, with the more busy and workaday and modern town of Macduff at the other. Banff rises steeply up a hillside above its harbour, its characterful streets terraced one above another, with some good old houses remaining. The fine park of Duff House, belonging now to the town, is conspicuous to the south.

Keith, twenty miles inland, is only slightly larger, a thriving place set amongst green braes, with links with the great Montrose. Rothes, Dufftown and Aberlour are small but famous Speyside distilling towns to the west, not in themselves beautiful, but pleasingly set. And Grantown-on-Spey, isolated twenty miles further up the great river, is a deservedly popular holiday resort for the discriminating, amongst the pine-forests of a lovely valley, where hotels are almost as prevalent as private houses.

Forres and Nairn, only ten miles apart, almost identical in size, and with other similarities, are set well to the west in the coastal plain, pleasant, bright, non-industrial towns in one of the driest and most salubrious situations in the land. The Forres area is richly wooded, with the ancient and formerly royal Forest of Darnaway to the south and the new vast plantations of Culbin to the north, pine-planted to hold fast the huge sand-blown tracts overwhelmed in the late seventeenth century when an entire barony was blotted out, higher than its church steeple—a disaster famous in Scotland's story. Today the walks through the dozen square miles of pine forest are a delight.

Nairn, on the coast, is a famous holiday resort, with notable golf-courses, sands and fine hotels. Nearby are the splendid castles of Brodie, Kilravock and Cawdor, all still in the hands of the families who have owned them for centuries, the last one of the most magnificent and unspoiled strongholds in Scotland.

Ahead lies Inverness.

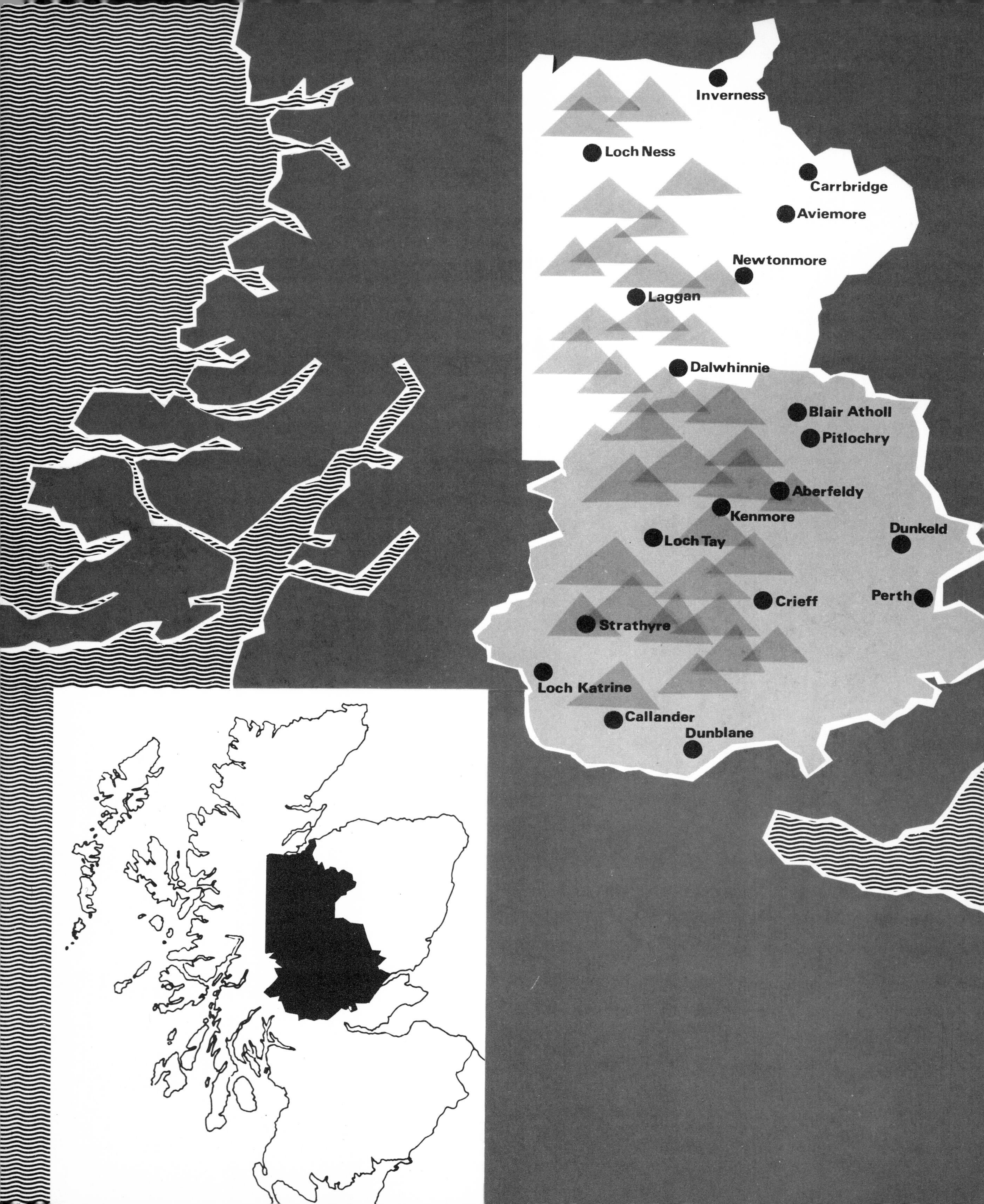
Inverness
Loch Ness
Carrbridge
Aviemore
Newtonmore
Laggan
Dalwhinnie
Blair Atholl
Pitlochry
Aberfeldy
Kenmore
Dunkeld
Loch Tay
Crieff
Perth
Strathyre
Loch Katrine
Callander
Dunblane

CHAPTER 5

PERTH, INVERNESS AND THE CENTRAL HIGHLANDS

Nothing is so vague a geographical entity as the Grampian Mountains. Nobody, however erudite, could tell you just where they start or end, what they include – nor even why so much of upland Scotland ever was given the name. Yet they are one of the schoolboy's first facts of life – though few but the educationalists ever refer to them in factual fashion thereafter.

It seems to have been the sixteenth century Aberdeen scholar and historian, Hector Boece, who gave this name to the huge mass of the Central Highland area – oddly enough, taking it as a library-bound academic might, from Tacitus' *Agricola*. That Roman defeated, in A.D. 86, the Caledonians' leader Galgacus, at a place called Mons Graupious – equally vague on the map, but apparently somewhere north of Tay. If this was a scanty reason for so naming so large a part of Scotland, it must be remembered that in Boece's day respectable Lowlanders looked on all such mountainous parts as *terra incognita*, a barbarous and alarming wilderness of unknown dimensions, peopled by uncouth savages who spoke a strange language and were little better than vermin to be ignored if they could not be exterminated. Scotland has progressed some distance since then, but the name Grampians still sticks – at least scholastically – and perhaps some slight relics of the attitude remain to be eradicated also.

At any rate, from just north of Stirling for over 100 miles, to Inverness, and

THE MOOR OF RANNOCH, from the air. This great water-logged desolation, on the Perthshire-Argyll border, must be one of the wildest places in these islands, something like 75 square miles. One corner is crossed by the A.82 road to Glencoe, the other by the railway to Fort William. This view looks south-west across Loch Tulla to the far Western Sea.

from the Braes of Angus west to the head of the sea-lochs of Argyll, Lochaber and the Great Glen, another 100 miles, is a vast conglomeration of mountain ranges, plateaux and individual peaks, valleys and glens wide and narrow, lochs great and small, rolling high moors and rushing, foaming rivers, which together make up the Central Highlands, comprising perhaps one-fifth of Scotland's total area, a mighty conception by any standards.

It may puzzle the reader as to why the Scottish mountain country should be split up into the Central Highlands and the Western Highlands. Sometimes the area north and west of Inverness is referred to as the Northern Highlands. But where are the Southern and Eastern Highlands? The fact is, the Central and the Western Highlands have become the accepted terms used to cover practically all of Scotland north of a line from the Clyde estuary to the upper Tay, with heights north-east of Inverness, in Easter Ross, Sutherland and Caithness having no inclusive appellation.

What is still more strange is the distinct difference in character, in scenery, history and to some extent in people, between the Central and Western Highlands. This is a little difficult to explain, but the difference is there. The hills themselves are different, in the first instance. The Central Highland mountains, though perhaps less spectacularly formed, less jagged and abrupt, are on the whole higher, heather-covered where the others are grassier, greener; and more rich in natural—as distinct from modern plantation—forest. Yet it is the West that draws the greater rhapsodies, that is considered to be the more romantic, the more attractive to visitors—if not the grouse-shooter, the deer-stalker or the salmon-angler. Today, however, the Central mountains are strongly drawing a new kind of devotee—the skiers and winter-sports enthusiasts. For they attract and retain infinitely more snow than do the sea-board hills to the west. Moreover the longer smoother-flowing slopes suit the skiers.

This is the clan country. A great deal of nonsense has been spoken and written about the Scottish clans, and one of the biggest misconceptions is that they were confined to the Highlands. Clanship was a basic element in the Celtic way of life, and practically all of Scotland came under the Celtic polity—even Lothian, which though often described as the least Celtic part of the land is yet full of purely Celtic place-names, such as Aberlady, Ballencrieff and Kilspindie, witness to Celtic inhabitation. It is a fact that quite the largest-scale and most ruthless clan-fights and

(Left) BEN VENUE IN THE TROSSACHS, WITH LOCH KATRINE, Perthshire. Readily accessible tourist ground, but with a beauty unspoiled. Rob Roy MacGregor's country. (Below) THE RIVER TEITH, at Callander, gateway to the Trossachs. Ben Ledi and the entrance to the Pass of Leny, in the background.

feuding in all Scotland took place, not in the Highland North but in the Lowland South-West; one pitched battle between Maxwells and Annandale Johnstones, in 1593, resulted in the loss of 700 out of the 2,000 Maxwells engaged, including their chief, the Lord Maxwell.

Nevertheless, it was in the Highlands undoubtedly that the clan system reached its greatest development. And there is a recognisable difference between the clans of the Central and West Highlands, however difficult it is to pin-point. The valleys and straths of this central area are wider, with more tillable land, and so the people were on the whole more settled. Some of the largest clans here, indeed, such as the Murrays, Drummonds and Grants, were really only half-Highland, and their ennobled chiefs most certainly considered themselves a cut above the picturesque and warlike chieftains of the West. Though some of the truly Highland clans of these parts were very large, Mackintoshes, Macphersons, Frasers and the like, by and large the units were smaller, and the Central area was the home of many of resounding fame but comparatively modest numbers—the MacGregors, MacLarens, MacNabs, Menzies, Robertsons, Buchanans, MacFarlanes and so on.

North of Stirling two main valleys probe into the enormous mass of the hills—the straths of the Allan and the Teith, thrusting north-east and north-west, from a hub around Dunblane. This is a pleasant old town on the edge of Sheriffmuir—where was fought the indecisive but fatal battle of the Jacobite Rising of 1715. The cathedral here is a fairly plain but impressive building of the thirteenth century, with a partly eleventh century Norman tower and a fine west front. Here are buried Margaret Drummond, the gallant James IV's true love (whom some say he married secretly, before Margaret Tudor), and her two sisters, all poisoned at their home of Drummond Castle, probably at the instigation of Henry VIII so that nothing should come between the marriage of his sister to the King of Scots.

To the west of Dunblane is an area which was once highly important on the Scottish scene, and which, like Fothrif to the east, has faded away almost entirely as an entity—Monteith, the mounth or watershed of the River Teith. This was a powerful earldom once, and comprised a large area, with its capital at Doune, the picturesque little town famous for the making of fine pistols, where the great castle of its earls still stands majestically above the river. The fading of Monteith, or *Men*teith as it has become more commonly spelt, is not so difficult to explain as that of

Fothrif—for it was deliberately suppressed as an earldom by the Scottish crown for dynastic reasons, when the Albany branch of the Royal house of Stewart grew too powerful for safety. An earlier stronghold of the Menteith earls stood on an island in the Lake of Menteith—often described as the only lake in Scotland, though there is another at Pressmennan in East Lothian; but there is no real significance in this nomenclature, for the lovely waters were described as a loch, like the rest, until comparatively recent times. A little further to the west is the attractive village of Aberfoyle, rich in history and one of the most accessible gateways to the Highland scenery around the Lochs Ard, Arklet and Katrine. Here we are in the renowned Trossachs area, whose sylvan beauties combined with loch and mountain to send the Victorians into rhapsodies. The Duke's Road, from Aberfoyle northwards over the hills to the Trossachs, is well worth crossing.

Callander, another of the recognised entrances to the Highlands, pleasantly situated where the handsome Pass of Leny opens out on to the wider strath of the Teith, is one of the most popular tourist centres, being so readily accessible and with quite major mountains like Bens Ledi and Vorlich close at hand. Recently Callander has gained a new sort of fame, as the filmic location of the Dr. Finlay television town of Tannochbrae.

North of Callander, up the wooded winding shores of Loch Lubnaig, lies Strathyre, bonny in song and bonny in fact, under Ben Ledi's towering bulk, now the centre of vast forestry operations. Opening to the west, beyond, is Balquhidder, the very beautiful cul-de-sac glen—never called *Glen* Balquhidder—which embossoms the Lochs Voil and Doine, and where every stick and stone speaks of Rob Roy MacGregor, who here started his independent career—and here ended it, oddly enough, in his bed.

These Central Highland glens nearly all run east and west, in a wrinkled pattern of range and valley, the latter usually at least partly loch-filled. Reaching eastwards from the head of Strathyre is Strathearn, with gentle Loch Earn at its head, where an enterprising hotel proprietor has pioneered the sport of water-skiing and dinghy-sailing on inland waters. At the other end of the loch is delightfully situated St. Fillans, and further down the valley is the little resort of Comrie, where Glen Artney from the south and Glen Lednoch from the north join the Earn.

(Left) ST. FILLANS, at the foot of Loch Earn, Perthshire, looking towards the Balquhidder area, where Rob Roy is buried. (Below) LOCH LUBNAIG, from high on Ben Ledi. Forestry Commission plantations clothe much of the hillsides. A Commission tree-nursery is located in Strathyre, round the bend of the loch. More Rob Roy country.

Where the strath begins to open out, on a hill above the river, stands Crieff, another of Scotland's deservedly well-known holiday resorts, and an excellent centre for exploring the southern parts of this ancient and storied province of Breadalbane. Crieff is comparatively large for a Highland town with a population of over 5,000. But it is an attractive place, and its hilly site ensures that at all times its surroundings of wood and vale and mountain strike the eye. Here, in the Clan Drummond's capital, Rob Roy proclaimed King James VIII; here Prince Charles Edward held a stormy council-of-war; and here was established in 1859 Morison's Academy, one of Scotland's famous schools. It so happens that another, Trinity College, Glenalmond, is not far away, only ten miles or so over the hills to the north, near the mouth of the dramatic if prosaically-named Sma' Glen.

Lower Strathearn is a magnificent, wide and fertile vale, dotted with ancient lairdships and fine farms, where names like Innerpeffray, Inchaffray, Madderty, Gask and Muthill sing loud in the age-old song of Scotland. Always important, the Romans established themselves here; it became an early royal earldom and stewardship; and the ancient Church found it to its taste.

Just north of where the Earn meets Tay stands Perth, the Fair City, once known as St. Johnstoun, and by any standards one of the most significant towns in Scotland. Whether indeed it is now fair of aspect is a matter of opinion, but its situation certainly is, encircled by hills great and small, where the Tay narrows in to its first possible bridging-point prior to recent engineering developments. This ensured Perth's importance, like Stirling on the Forth; but as well, nearby was ancient Scone, capital first of Pictavia, then of the united kingdoms of the Picts and the Dalriadic Scots, which became Scotland. Here, in Scone Abbey, was kept Scotland's most precious talisman, the Stone of Destiny, on which her monarchs were crowned—and which English Edward I came to steal and take south to Westminster, and which seven centuries later figured in the sensational rescue of 1950. There is good reason to believe, however, that the true Stone, of very different quality from the shapeless lump of red sandstone hallowed for so long by later royal posteriors, never actually left Scotland, having been secreted away by the Abbot of Scone before Edward could lay hands on it.

Perth, with 40,000 people, is the largest town from Tay northwards, excluding the cities of Dundee and Aberdeen. It is a thriving place, attractive along its riversides and

(Left) THE TAY, AND FERTILE CARSE OF GOWRIE, east of Perth from Kinnoull Hill. The background here is North-West Fife. (Below) VIEW OF THE FAIR CITY OF PERTH, from very near the same position as last picture, looking west. Perth itself is not a Highland town, though it makes an excellent approach. Behind stretches green Strathearn, with Crieff its 'capital', and the Highland giants.

CASTLE VARRICH AND THE KYLE OF TONGUE, on the North Sutherland coast, near Tongue village. This far northern seaboard has a quiet loveliness all its own. Mackay country, it is a land of hundreds of lochs and splendid fishing.

around its splendid spreading parklands of the North and South Inch, but elsewhere less fine than its setting, with narrow crowded streets and sprawling suburbs, and surprisingly few ancient buildings remaining, considering its renown and antiquity. The excellent and restored Church of St. John, which formerly gave its name to the town, dates from the fourteenth and fifteenth centuries—a period when the Blackfriars Monastery here was one of the favourite residences of the Scottish kings. In this handsome establishment, now completely disappeared, was murdered James I, the poet and warrior king, in front of his Queen and her ladies—one of whom, Catherine Douglas, made the famous if unsuccessful gesture of using her arm in the sockets of the stolen door-bar, to hold it against the assassins. Nearby was Gowrie House, where the murdered monarch's descendant, James VI, 163 years later arranged a dual murder of his own, of the Ruthven brothers, in the murky business known as the Gowrie Conspiracy.

Today Perth is a great road and rail junction and an industrial town where distilling, brewing, linen-making and dyeing is carried on, with ancillary trades, certain of the blends of whisky emanating from here being very famous indeed. It is the marketing centre for a great area, and one of Britain's largest insurance companies, General Accident, was founded and has its headquarters here.

Perth, although the capital of a great, mainly Highland county, has itself no aspect of the Highlands. But north of it the big hills begin to close in, and by the time that Dunkeld is reached, still in the Tay valley, the entire character of the land has changed, and from here onwards the mountains prevail. Dunkeld itself, with its companion place Birnam, across one of Telford's famous bridges, is little more than a village by population standards, but is an ancient burgh of barony, never having availed itself of Queen Anne's charter erecting it into a royal burgh in 1704. It has nevertheless a handsome fifteenth century cathedral, wherein, oddly enough, is a gigantic stone effigy, in coat-of-mail, memorial to the same Alexander Stewart, Wolf of Badenoch, who played such havoc with the greater cathedral of Elgin. A hill where the militant Bishops of Dunkeld used to hang many a Highland cateran rises close by.

Eight miles north of Dunkeld the Tay swings away to the west, at Ballinluig, the strath narrowing notably. Aberfeldy nestles in mid-valley, where a fine bridge, one of the best built by General Wade, spans the river; his military roads did much to open up, and therefore to make possible the

KILCHURN CASTLE, ARGYLL. Former seat of the Campbells of Glenorchy, later Earls of Breadalbane, at the foot of Loch Awe, a spur of Cruachan, the Campbell mountain, behind. Nearby is the Pass of Brander, on the road to Oban, and the great new hydro-electric pump-storage station inside the mountain.

subjection of, the Highlands after the Jacobite Rising of 1745. Nearby is the handsome Castle Menzies, long empty and semi-ruinous, but now being taken in hand by the Menzies clan society—a worth-while activity which many another clan society might emulate.

Loch Tay is one of the larger fresh-water lochs, a magnificent sheet of water over fourteen miles long, flanked by fairly smooth-sloping mountains including the lofty Ben Lawers, only sixteen feet short of 4,000 and the highest summit in Perthshire. At the east end of the loch is the attractive village of Kenmore, formerly little more than an adjunct to the princely castle of Taymouth, seat of the Earls and Marquesses of Breadalbane, a branch of Clan Campbell, whose lands once stretched almost from the Atlantic to the North Sea. At the other end is Killin, where the River Dochart falls in picturesque rapids down to the loch, and where the Campbell chiefs, at ruined Finlarig Castle, had a beheading pit. The burial ground of the chiefs of Clan Macnab is on a small island in the river here.

Parallel to Loch Tay to the north lies Glen Lyon, one of the most lovely glens in Scotland, with the pretty village of Fortingall at its mouth—which, strange to say, claims to be the birthplace of Pontious Pilate, this having been a Roman outpost. Glen Lyon twists and turns in consistent beauty for twenty-five miles westwards, to its own Loch Lyon and beyond, to end amongst the great westland mountains on the edge of Argyll.

The next of these parallel east-west Central Highland straths is that of the Tummel and Rannoch, reached from Pitlochry, or up from Fortingall by the Strath of Appin. It is dominated by the stately conical peak of Schiehallion, and peters out into the vast waterlogged wilderness of Rannoch Moor, to the west, possibly the most spectacularly desolate and savage expanse in all Scotland. This enormous morass of peat-bog and outcrop, pitted by little lochans innumerable, covering over fifty square miles at above 1,000 feet, is not to be crossed from east to west, its only road traversing its west end from south to north. Loch Rannoch, however, is not on the Moor, but some miles to the east, served by good roads both north and south. On the latter side of it is the Black Wood of Rannoch, one of the few remaining sizeable remnants of the ancient Caledonian Forest, which once clothed all this mountain country. Loch Tummel is still further east in the same valley, celebrated for the prospect from its north shore which so delighted Queen Victoria and is still known as the Queen's View.

Millions of people know the words of the song, *The Road to the Isles*—'By Tummel and Loch Rannoch and Lochaber I will go . . .'; but in fact this is no practical route, save for the most determined walker, for Rannoch Moor's quagmires, or great mountain masses, bar the way. The real road to the Isles, for those who want to get there, rather than just sing about it, we shall come to later, in Lochaber.

The River Tummel, short though it is, is spectacular in its wooded gorge, the Linn of Tummel. Below it, where Tummel and Garry join, is Pitlochry, another favourite resort and tourist centre, noted for its fine hotels—and also for its Festival Theatre, the Theatre in the Hills, one of the most bold and successful cultural ventures of recent years. The area, richly wooded and scenically lovely, has been the location of large hydro-electric developments; but despite forebodings this has by no means spoiled the amenity. In fact, many will assert now that the new Loch Faskally which the engineers of the Tummel-Garry Scheme have formed just west of Pitlochry, amongst hanging woods, is an enhancement to the scene; while the salmon ladder, constructed to permit the great fish to surmount the fifty-foot barrier of the dam, is an unfailing source of fascination to visitors. At Faskally also is a training school for foresters.

North of Pitlochry lies the celebrated Pass of Killiecrankie, the dramatic rocky defile of the River Garry where Graham of Claverhouse, Viscount Dundee, in 1689 won his famous battle against the forces of William of Orange—and lost his own life.

(Left) LOCH TUMMEL, Perthshire, looking into the sunset behind Schiehallion. Beyond the gap in the distance lies the Moor of Rannoch and the Glencoe mountains. (Below) THE PASS OF KILLIECRANKIE, Perthshire. An unusual view from on high, with Atholl opening beyond. The famous Battle was fought on the right of the picture, when Graham of Claverhouse, Bonnie Dundee, was slain in the moment of victory.

(Left) FARM-BUILDINGS AND LOCHAN AT INSHRIACH, in Strathspey, Inverness-shire, on the 'back road' to Rothiemurchus, so much more attractive than the parallel busy A.9. The Monadh Liath Mountains in the background. This is rich tree-growing land.

We are in Atholl now, another of Scotland's age-old divisions, long a Stewart earldom and still a Stewart-Murray dukedom. Blair Atholl, a few miles on, is the capital of a vast domain, reckoned to cover some 450 square miles, a mighty heritage indeed, as the well-known song makes one of its earlier lords declare:

'Blair in Atholl's mine, Jeanie; Little Dunkeld is mine, Jeanie;
St. Johnstoun's Bower and Huntingtower (Perth)—
and all that's mine is thine, Jeanie!'

Blair Castle, much altered by many generations of powerful chiefs, each of whom played his part in Scottish history, is still the Duke of Atholl's seat, and open to the admiring public.

On Atholl are some of the vastest grouse-moors and deer-forests of the country, for the hundreds of thousands of its northern acres are all but empty of habitation. Whether this country could support more people is a moot point—though once it did, when the clan system prevailed and the glens were full of folk, whatever their standards of living. It may be that those days are gone for good, and better gone, and that such tracts are only fit to be the playground of the rich and the delight of the tourist and visitor; but it might be thought that in these overcrowded islands there was still a more fruitful use for such comparatively accessible, very lovely, and far from desert territory.

North of Blair Atholl the long, long glen of the Tilt reaches up towards the Cairngorm Mountains, through scores of miles of completely roadless and uninhabited country, known only to a few shepherds, stalkers and some of the hardier long-distance hill-walkers. The road continues westwards up the Garry.

There are no more towns now, no more villages really, until we reach upper Strathspey, almost forty miles on; just great rolling heather-clad hills, rushing, foaming amber rivers, blue lochs, brown peat-bogs and outcropping quartz-shot granite, with water gleaming everywhere. It is too high here for forests in the accepted sense of the word, and such trees as there are are stunted and small, or are hidden deep in ravines. It is the land of the deer, the grouse, the ptarmigan and the buzzard—and occasionally of the eagle and the wild-cat.

Over the bleak Pass of Drumochter, where road and railway rise together to over 1500 feet, the highest point reached by the latter in these islands, we leave Atholl for another great upland territory, Badenoch, and two massive mountains, the Boar of Badenoch and the Sow of Atholl, glower at each other out of the mists. This is also the Perthshire-Inverness-shire border. To right and left of the road, here seeming slender and insignificant indeed, stretch such endless and trackless wastes as to challenge the imagination; there are few places in Britain where it is possible to look thirty miles to the right and more than that to the left, and know that there is no other road in all that compass.

However fond the traveller may be of solitude, it may well be something of a relief to arrive at Dalwhinnie, at the head of Loch Ericht, one of Scotland's lonely communities where nevertheless there is a distillery, a railway station and hotels. Here a road forks left for Laggan and the north-west, often blocked with snow in winter. Loch Ericht stretches fifteen miles south-westwards into the wilderness. Above its far end towers great Ben Alder, 3,757 feet, on the side of which is the remote cave where Prince Charlie lay concealed in 1746, tended by the loyal Macphersons, whose clan territory this is.

Near Newtonmore the Truim, down which the road runs, reaches the Spey, and the character of the land again alters entirely. The mountains draw back to flank a wide and lovely strath at the same time growing more rugged and attractive in their outlines. Those to the west are called the Monadh Liath, or Grey Mountains; those to the east the Monadh Ruadh, or Red Mountains. This is allegedly because of the prevailing colours of their respective granites—though I personally have seen just as much grey and pink granite in the one as in the other. The Monadh Ruadh are seldom called that now, the name having changed to the Cairngorm Mountains. This a strange case of the widespread acceptance of error, for of course Cairngorm, meaning the blue peak, refers properly to only the one mountain in a great range, and that by no means the highest—although it is the most accessible, certainly now that the ski access-road and chair-lift rise more than half-way up its swelling flank. I understand this change of name to have come about gradually because of an early mountaineering club in Aberdeen adopting the title of Cairngorm, and in time all its stamping-ground in the Monadh Ruadh became labelled thus.

This tremendous range is in fact the highest land mass in Britain—for though Ben Nevis, at 4,406 feet and fifty miles to the south-west, is higher than Ben MacDhui by 110 feet, that is one isolated peak whereas here we have what is in effect a vast Alpine plateau at nearly the 4,000 feet level, covering many square miles, a unique semi-arctic tract out of which rear the four mighty summits of MacDhui, Braeriach, Cairn Toul and Cairngorm, all over the 4,000, with a great many more just a little below it. I have heard new visitors complain, at first sight, that the Cairngorms are in fact less spectacular in appearance than they had expected. This is accounted for, firstly, in that these are not pointed peaks but humped summits in a vast plateau; and secondly in that few viewers realise just how far away they are, and indeed the scale of all the distances and features involved. No one who penetrates these exciting fastnesses is ever left in any doubt as to their dimensions, their magnificence, or their rigours—for the Cairngorms generate a climate all their own, often quite at odds with conditions prevailing elsewhere, the severity of which has been the death of many an unprepared or too casual climber or walker. Today, with the increasing appreciation of mountaineering, hill-walking, and the strenuous outdoor activities, the Monadh Ruadh are becoming one of the most noted and challenging playgrounds of the land, their delights no longer known only to the comparatively few. This is fine—so long as the hazards are recognised.

Newtonmore is the first of a series of deservedly famous small Badenoch and Strathspey resorts, long established, but which have of recent years accepted the challenge of their splendid situation and siezed with both hands the opportunities of developing the area into an all-the-year-round paradise for the energetic and scenery-loving holiday-maker. Newtonmore was one of the pioneers of pony-trekking, as well it might be, with its surrounding wealth of climbing glens, pine forests, heather tracks and by-roads through the hills. This is the cradle of Clan Macpherson, with Cluny, the former seat of its renowned chiefs, nearby. At Newtonmore is the clan museum, and above rears the hogback of Craig Dhu, which provides the clan's slogan.

Kingussie, a few miles on, is slightly larger, a burgh with a name apt to be mispronounced by the uninitiated—King-*you*-sie being correct. This is a fine centre for both Monadh Liath and Southern Cairngorm exploration. Across the wide water-meadows of Spey from here rise the imposing ruins of Ruthven Barracks on their green mound, famous from the '45 days, and themselves constructed on the site of one of the Wolf of Badenoch's castles. On this back road—which incidentally is one of the loveliest in

(Left) CHAIR-LIFT at the ski slopes on Cairngorm, looking north. Below is Loch Morlich and the huge Forest of Rothiemurchus and Glenmore. (Below) AVIEMORE, AMONGST THE BIRCH WOODS, with the new winter-sports development, looking across Spey to Rothiemurchus, Coylum Bridge and the Cairngorm Mountains. In the centre background is the great cleft of the Lairig Ghru Pass to Deeside.

Scotland, winding all the way to Rothiemurchus through the birch woods, and infinitely to be preferred to the busy and more humdrum A.9 for those not in a tearing hurry—on this road is Tromie Bridge, where that rushing river comes foaming through rocky jaws out of its remote glen, and the attractive villages of Drumguish and Insh.

Kincraig, on the shores of comely Loch Insh—which is just a great widening of the Spey—reveals little of itself to the main highway, but down its hill, amongst the birches, it presents a vista eastwards towards the Cairngorm bastions that is very notable. This is the access to the splendid Glen Feshie, one of the finest in the land, that probes deep into the empty wilderness where the great rivers are born, Tilt and Dee as well as Eidart, Geldie, Tromie and Feshie. Feshie Bridge, on the aforementioned back road, is a place to linger in the memory, where the pine forest muffles the roar of the spectacular peat-brown torrent.

Strathspey is probably the best region in all these islands for the growing of conifers, and this is the true home of the most handsome of all such, the great, spreading, indigenous Scots Pine of the ancient Caledonian Forest, which here, as nowhere else, proliferates in heartening natural regeneration. Rothiemurchus is the acme and monarch of all Scotland's forests, the huge, undulating, pine-clad basin of the western Cairngorms where scores of square miles of scattered open woodland embosoms the lovely Lochs an Eilean and Morlich, where forest paths branch and entice, the air is resin-scented, and the trees are sufficiently far apart, growing out of heather, seldom to obscure the mighty dominant mountains that enclose all.

GREAT HERD OF RED DEER—all stags, be it noted—alarmed by aeroplane in the Forest of Atholl (a deer-forest need have no trees). The wild red deer of the Highlands tend to increase in numbers under present economic conditions, which militate against deer-stalking as a sport. There is large-scale deer-poaching, unfortunately. In the old clan days the hills used to carry cattle in large numbers.

Aviemore, Rothiemurchus and Coylum Bridge are, of course, the centres of the most dramatic winter-sports development north of the Alps, catering for the northern Cairngorm slopes at the head of Glen More. Here, amongst the pine forests, rise the hotels, guest-houses, chalets and ski-schools, the ice-rinks and cinemas and sports emporia, and all the colourful bustle and excitement that goes with it. Not everybody likes it, but nevertheless, the development can mean much-needed new life to the Central Highlands, for the impact spreads far and wide, and lower Strathspey shares in the prosperity, with places like Carrbridge, Dulnan Bridge, Boat of Garten, Nethy Bridge and even Grantown itself participating. Not only ski-ing, curling and other winter sports are catered for, but pony-trekking, climbing, fishing, shooting, sailing and canoeing, golf and ornithology—for the vast pine forests have their own distinctive bird-life, and this is the area to which the ospreys have made their dramatic return, after long absence.

One by-product of all this is that, at last, there is talk of official interest in the long-advocated project of building a road from Deeside through the sub-Cairngorm wilderness, via Glen Feshie; and though once again this will not please everyone who loves the lonely and magnificent glen, it is something that ought to have been done generations ago—even General Wade contemplated it. For a glance at the map will show that there is, in fact, no transverse road across Scotland in this area, and such a highway would bring Aberdeen and the North-East fifty and more miles nearer to the western seaboard—an advantage not only to the motorist and visitor, but a matter of vital importance, for instance, to the fishing industry, whose boats have to follow the herring-shoals from east to west coast waters, and

(Left) OSPREYS, or fish-hawks, are nesting again in the forests of Strathspey, after long absence from the British Isles, drawing large numbers of observers. (Below) INVERNESS, 'capital' of the Highlands. On the left is the Episcopal Cathedral (modern) and on the right, also modern, the castle built on the site of the original fortress so important in Scots history.

whose crews and catches have to ferry back and forth across the mountainous land at week-ends.

North of Carrbridge the land changes once more, as the road lifts up out of the pine country, through more desolate hills, towards the high and grim pass of the Slochd Mor, or Great Throat, where one of the last wolves in Scotland was shot. Beyond, on the high tableland where the Findhorn headstreams rise, we are into Clan Mackintosh country, with Moy, still their chief's home, beside its loch. But soon we are in mixed clan territory, for the Grants, though now centred in Strathspey, originally came from Strathnairn and Stratherrick, the wide valleys that strike off westwards from Daviot, the Frasers moving in after them. Moreover, this is the home of the smaller Clan Macgillivray.

After Daviot's northern ridge, the land sweeps down in a vast prospect quite breathtaking after the constrictions of 100 miles of hills. We are faced with that tremendous natural divide, the Great Glen of Scotland, that cuts the Highlands in two, its west end sunk in the Atlantic waters of the Firth of Lorne almost another 100 miles away, its east in the blue depths of the Inverness and Moray Firths. To the right, now, the moors sink away towards fatal Culloden, where the clans died in hopeless gallantry for the last of the Stewarts; and beyond to the sea. To the left long Loch Ness reaches twenty-five miles south-westwards down the great rift-valley, backed by a thousand mountain peaks. And in front, where the shelving land dwindles to the short River Ness, between loch and sea, Inverness itself lies, grey amongst the greens and blues, backed by rising layers of sepia-brown hills until the snow-streaked bulk of giant Ben Wyvis bars all further view.

Inverness, acknowledged capital of all the Highlands, is a stirring and exciting royal burgh of 29,000 inhabitants, where all roads converge, with an important railway centre and an airport at Dalcross to the east. King Brude of the Northern Picts, to whom St. Columba preached in the sixth century, had his capital here, and ever since it has been a place of vital moment to Scotland, at the only crossing place between the long barrier of Loch Ness and the sea. Fought over, harried and sacked and rebuilt times innumerable, by Highlander and Lowlander alike, Inverness always survived and rose to flourish again, because of the essential prominence of its strategic position. Stirling and Perth, somewhat similarly sited, may be partly by-passed by the wonders of modern bridge-building; but nobody is going to build a bridge across the Inverness or Moray Firths.

(Left) THE CAIRNGORM MOUNTAINS, the highest land mass in Britain (Ben Nevis being an isolated peak) a vast Alpine plateau on the 4,000 feet contour, a skier's and hill-walkers' paradise—but with its own dangers. Seen across Loch Morlich and the Rothiemurchus Forest.

Its bloody past has ensured that not a great deal of old Inverness has survived. There is still a public building called The Castle, on its handsome mound above the river, but it is quite modern, as is the episcopal cathedral on the north bank, a nineteenth century erection. But the fine Dunbar's Hospital, of 1668, remains, and Abertarff House, restored by the National Trust, is a delightful example of a sixteenth century laird's townhouse, in Church Street. In contrast, nearby are the ultra-modern municipal library and museum buildings.

Inverness is fortunate in the quality of its suburbs; contrary to the usual pattern they are on the whole more attractive than the town centre, spacious, leafy and with the beauty of the surroundings more apparent. The riverside park, utilising islands in the River Ness, is notable.

Industry and development have by no means by-passed the town, even though its harbour is less important than once it was. This is the northern entry to the famous Caledonian Canal, which links the lochs of the Great Glen, and boat-building has burgeoned here encouragingly. But it is as a shopping and marketing centre, probably, that Inverness is more renowned, and in this respect, it is unrivalled, with a hinterland of something like a quarter of Scotland's area to draw upon and supply. Market-days in Inverness are stirring occasions indeed, with more Harris tweed and tartan to be seen, both worn and for sale, than anywhere else on earth, amongst scores of different soft Highland accents, the lowing of cattle and the clink of glasses. Unfortunately, also, the revving of engines and fumes of petrol nowadays, for in common with other bridge towns, Inverness's narrow streets have become a proverbial traffic bottleneck.

If I may be forgiven, I shall not leave Inverness without a word on that intriguing phenomenon, the Loch Ness Monster. Although sceptics have dismissed this as a modern fabrication designed to attract gullible tourists, the fact is that there have been reports of strange creatures in Loch Ness for as long as there have been reports on anything at all in Britain. St. Adamnan, Abbot of Iona in the seventh century, refers to the 'aquatilis bestia' in the loch, and all down the centuries credible witnesses have made similar reports of large monsters, not to be identified with any known species. The Great Glen is a geological fault, and the waters of the loch are enormously deep. That creatures dwell in it which are beyond our present knowledge is, I think, beyond dispute—and I use the plural, for all indications and probabilities point to more than one. No doubt one day patience and scientific methods will solve this mystery—and leave the world possibly the poorer for one less intriguing enigma.

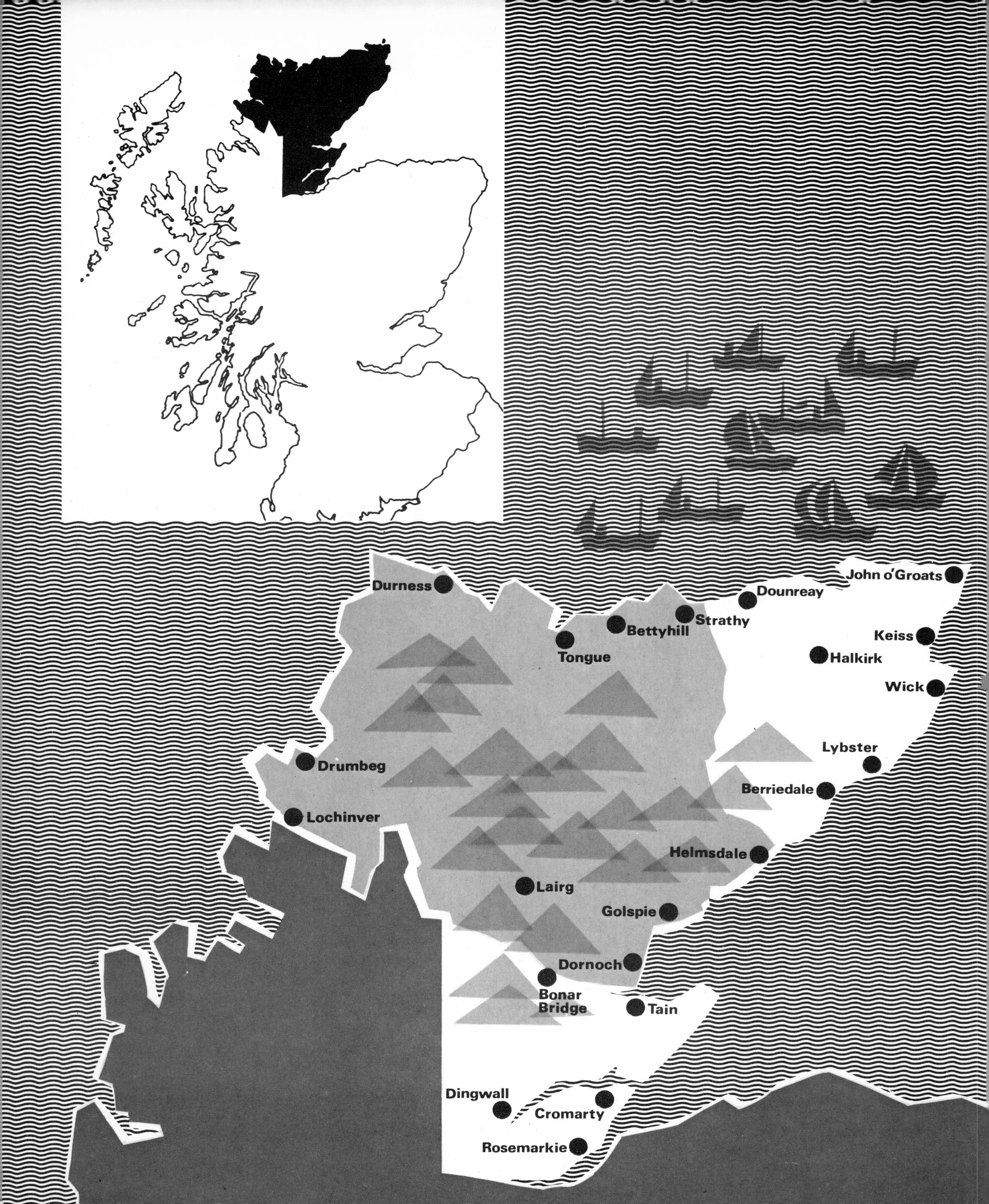
Durness
John o'Groats
Dounreay
Strathy
Bettyhill
Tongue
Keiss
Halkirk
Wick
Lybster
Drumbeg
Berriedale
Lochinver
Helmsdale
Lairg
Golspie
Dornoch
Bonar Bridge
Tain
Dingwall
Cromarty
Rosemarkie

CHAPTER 6
THE FAR NORTH

There is a great deal more of Scotland north of Inverness than probably most people realise, even excluding the Orkney and Shetland Islands. It is about 160 miles further to Thurso, up on the Pentland Firth as far as from London to Doncaster or Sheffield. And it is a great deal more to far Cape Wrath, the final north-western snout of the mainland. By any standards there is a lot of territory up here.

Also contrary to common belief much of the east side of it all is no *ultima Thule*, no remote and barren tract, but a fairly populous, advanced and often fertile land, entering quite dramatically into the new era of challenge.

This applies to Easter Ross, in especial. Ross-shire, which now includes the former county of Cromarty, starts ten miles north of Inverness, just beyond the little town of Beauly, at the head of the Firth of that name, a pleasant wide-streeted place with a ruined priory, and nearby is the modern seat of Lord Lovat, the Fraser Chief, Beaufort Castle. There is nothing in the least Highland-seeming about this area, but the big hills are not far away, and this is the starting-off point for Strath Glass, the Chisholm country, and the very lovely glens of Affric, Cannich and Farrar, which some will say are the most beautiful in the land.

Ross, with approximately 2,000,000 acres, ties with Argyll for the place of second largest county in Scotland - and therefore in Britain. It will be convenient,

(Below) SALMON-NETS AND COBLE AT CROMARTY, in the Black Isle of Easter Ross. (Right) SALMON ANGLING ON THE OYKELL, Easter Ross. One of the major sports of the Highlands.

however, to deal here only with Easter Ross, which is a fairly consistently recognised division, leaving Wester Ross for inclusion in the later chapter dealing with the Western Highlands—of which it is so important a part.

Easter Ross is the populous part of the county, with many small towns and villages. There is not a single centre of population with more than 1,600 inhabitants in the western sector. The nature of the land, as well as the difference in accessibility, accounts for this. There is just no comparison between the fertile lowlands of much of the east and the dramatic but largely barren magnificence of the west.

Muir of Ord, the first centre of population to be reached, cannot claim outstanding natural beauty, the moor being more obvious than attractive. But it is an important centre and road junction, noted for its cattle fairs in the past—and now with a newer fame as the headquarters of the Logan contracting organisation which has made such an impact on Scotland, the builders, amongst other things, of the Tay Road Bridge. From here roads branch off to east and west—the latter up Strathconan to Contin and Garve, and so through the mountains to Ullapool and the western seaboard; the former eastwards into the Black Isle.

This Black Isle area is of great importance in Ross. It is not of course a true island but a twenty mile long peninsula between the Beauly, Inverness and Moray Firths on the south, and the Cromarty Firth on the north, connected to the mainland by only a comparatively narrow isthmus. A ridge of high ground called Millbuie—properly *meall buidhe*, the yellow, rounded ridge—runs down the centre as a spine, dividing it into two distinctive areas. That to the south is much more sheltered, fertile and populous, with handsome estates, fine farms, and many communities, all on the coast—North Kessock, where there is a ferry from Inverness, Munlochy, Avoch, Fortrose, Rosemarkie and Cromarty itself, once the capital of its own county. An inconvenient county town Cromarty must have been, however attractive, out at the very tip of the long peninsula, where the Cromarty Firth narrows in to a dramatic entrance between the bold bluffs known as the Sutors. These little towns and villages are interesting and often picturesque places—Rosemarkie is a royal burgh of 500 people, and Fortrose boasts the ruined fourteenth and fifteenth century cathedral of the Bishops of Ross, some of the stones of which Cromwell carted across the firth to help build his fort at Inverness. Hereabouts there are sandy beaches, caves, cliff scenery and fishing havens for the visitor.

The north side, being more exposed and unsuited for harbours, is less well populated and tree-clad. But it has fine views to the north and west. Strangely enough it was here, at Castlecraig, a lonely gaunt fifteenth century tower perched inconveniently on a cliff overhanging the firth, that the Bishop of Ross had his principal seat, not beside his much more comfortably-placed cathedral. It is improbable that this was for reasons of pious contemplation, but rather a preoccupation with security.

Back to the mainland at Conon Bridge, the A.9 highway heads north for Dingwall, the county town of Ross, whilst another road goes westwards over high ground to Strathpeffer, the famous spa amongst the wooded hills. This is a favourite holiday resort and touring centre, with the Earl of Cromartie's splendid sixteenth century castle nearby and the great and isolated peak of Ben Wyvis towering to the north—a mountain from whose top both the North Sea and the Atlantic may be seen, in suitable conditions.

Dingwall is a busy royal burgh, with a harbour constructed by the great Telford, and a star-fish as the town's coat-of-arms. These links with the sea are scarcely obvious to the casual visitor, the mile-long main street and environs giving little impression of the nearness of salt-water. Actually the harbour is almost a mile away. This is the administrative centre for a vast area (even the Isle of Lewis, in the Outer Hebrides, is in Ross), a market town and railway junction, for here the line for Achnasheen, Kyle of Lochalsh and Skye branches off, though under threat of closure by far-away authority. Once the ancient Earls of Ross here held semi-royal sway, but today the site of their castle is barely to be discerned.

The main road follows the rather quiet and unspectacular north shore of the Cromarty Firth for more than twenty miles thereafter, passing the oddly Dutch-looking seat of the Munro chiefs, Foulis Castle, the village of Evanton and the larger distilling centre of Alness, to the thriving burgh of Invergordon. This town has had a somewhat chequered career, first the railway killing its important seaport trade;

then the Admiralty discovering the tremendous natural harbour facilities of the sheltered Cromarty Firth, where a whole fleet could lie hidden, and turning Invergordon into a naval base—only to abandon it when a large navy was no longer policy. But today the place is again humming with more private development and industrial initiative, which bids fair to make of it the boom-town of the North. Anything may happen at Invergordon.

Nigg Bay, a vast indentation of the Cromarty Firth, and the Dornoch Firth to the north, together make another great peninsula, hammer-shaped this time and not so large as the Black Isle, but some fifteen miles long nevertheless. It is a sandy, mainly low-lying tract of old demesnes, good farms and fishing-havens, making up the ancient abbey-lands of Fearn, a rich jewel of the Ross bishopric once. The fifteenth Abbot of Fearn was Patrick Hamilton, proto-martyr of the Reformation, burned at St. Andrews in 1528—although it is to be doubted if he ever so much as visited his remote northern abbey, for he was a young man of lofty lineage more concerned with the court than the cloister, and his martyrdom more political than religious. Fearn is approximately in the middle of this interesting peninsula, with the fishing village of Balintore nearby, Portmahomack and Tarbat Ness to the north, and the Hill of Nigg to the south—an impressive feature of high cliffs, bold bluffs and two lochs, which was the hunting-ground of the semi-legendary Fionns, who used to leap across the Cromarty Firth on their hunting-spears.

Tain, at the mouth of the Dornoch Firth, the last of these great east coast fiords, is the second largest town of Ross—but even so has only 1,700 inhabitants. It is a neat little place of much character, one of the most ancient of royal burghs, claiming that Malcolm Canmore made it so in 1057. Indeed, remotely sited as it is, Tain has played a surprisingly large part in Scottish history, largely on account of the Chapel of St. Duthac here, which was a notable place of pilgrimage. St. Duthac, born here about the year 1,000, was known as The Confessor of Ireland and Scotland, in the ancient Celtic Church. Here fled the wife and daughter of Robert the Bruce, hunted by Edward of England—and here, to his shame, the then Earl of Ross seized them in the sanctuary of the chapel, and handed them over to the English and to shocking barbarities. Many of the Scots monarchs came here on pilgrimage—but it was James IV who made a regular habit of it, probably so that he could visit his mistress Flaming Janet Kennedy at Darnaway, en route. His son, James V, actually made at least part of the pilgrimage barefoot, his route across the moorland to it still being called the King's Causeway. Tain's seventeenth century Tolbooth has a fine peal of bells.

We now leave Ross. If only the coastal areas seem to have been described, this is because inland stretch only the great immensity of the empty mountains, the vast deer-forests of Wyvis, Strathvaich, Kildermorie, Diebidale, Glencalvie and the like—magnificent scenery, but roadless, hundreds of square miles of it. One road does drive straight north through the hills from Novar, by Struie, to the upper Dornoch Firth—but that is all, a mere drop in the bucket.

Sutherland is another vast county, in area 1,300,000 acres in population only 13,000—one person per 100 acres, the most sparsely inhabited county in the British Isles. With only 2.9 of its area tillable land, it could not possibly carry a large population; nevertheless it held many more people once. This was the scene of the worst of the shameful Highland evictions of the early nineteenth century, the Sutherland Clearances, when the clansmen and crofters were driven out to make way for sheep—profitable then, for mutton and wool, in the period of semi-blockade during the Napoleonic Wars. Between 1811 and 1820, no fewer than 15,000 inhabitants were forcibly ejected from their inland holdings in this county. Most settled along the coasts, to try to make a living from fishing; but a great many emigrated to the new World, and many more went south. Even so, the population in 1845 was 21,784.

Sutherland is a comparatively simply-shaped area, comprising all the top fifth of Scotland above a line drawn westwards from the Dornoch Firth—with the exception of the jutting easternmost snout, which is the county of Caithness. So it has North Sea, Pentland Firth and Atlantic seaboards. That it is called Sutherland, rather than Northerland as one might expect, is because it was so named by the Norsemen of the Orkney and Shetland Islands—an indication that we are here passing from the Celtic to the Scandinavian area.

Dornoch is just across the firth from Tain—but to reach it the road must make a twenty-eight mile detour via Bonar Bridge—where the routes to Strathoykell, Lochinver, Lairg and the north-west branch off. Then on round the north shore of the firth, by Creich, Spinningdale and Skibo, Andrew Carnegie's palatial modern castle, to the ancient royal burgh, county town, golfing and holiday resort, population 1,000.

(Below) THE DORNOCH FIRTH, where Easter Ross and Sutherland join, looking west. The little town of Bonar Bridge can be seen **in the distance.**

(Right) SUILVEN, the Sugar-Loaf mountain of West Sutherland, towering over the road to Lochinver. The mountains of Sutherland are unique in Scotland, isolated and strangely-shaped peaks, not ranges, rising out of a primeval wilderness of outcropping stone and standing water.

Here was the cathedral of the one-time see of Caithness, with its dean, precentor, chancellor, treasurer, archdeacon and ten canons, a great establishment, in First Pointed style, with a massive central tower—of which little more than the last remains to form the parish church. In the southern transept, sixteen Earls of Sutherland lie buried. Nearby, Dornoch Castle still dominates the main street, a sixteenth century portion of the former Bishop's Palace.

Northwards, round the basin of Loch Fleet, we come to Golspie, a large village, with Dunrobin Castle, the great seat of the Earls and Dukes of Sutherland, towering on its hill above. Here, as at Brora five miles further on, is some of the very scanty good arable land of Sutherland, as well as sandy beaches, fishing harbours and golf-courses. The Brora River is particularly notable for its salmon, and Loch Brora, inland, is picturesque. At Brora, too, is Scotland's most northerly coal mine, which was functioning as early as 1573. Here is a distillery, a wool-mill, and a brick-works saved from extinction by the Highland Fund in 1961. Inland from Golspie is the crofting area of Rogart.

The mountains now come almost as close to the sea here on the east coast as they do on the west, although the hills themselves are less dramatic in outline. The empty wastes preoccupy the land, and the deer and the grouse reign supreme. The insignificant haunts of man seem very much to crouch beneath it all.

At Helmsdale, another of this series of small fishing places and resorts, the roads fork again, the main A.9 highway to continue up the coast and into Caithness, the other, narrower and more adventurous, to follow the Helmsdale River up long Strathullie, making its lonely and challenging way into the wilderness, first west, then due north, forty twisting switchback miles to the top of the map, to Strath Halladale, and Melvich on the Pentland Firth.

Deep towards the centre of the county, reached by the Bonar Bridge road, is Lairg, at the foot of the seventeen-mile long and rather featureless Loch Shin—surely one of the most necessarily independent and self-sufficient communities of 1,000 souls in our land. Lairg is a great place for little roads radiating north and west into the remoter fastnesses, a bus centre and sheep market. Here, inevitably, is something of the atmosphere of the frontier.

The west coast of Sutherland I have not chosen to deal with under the Western Highlands, for reasons that are a little difficult to explain—but which are obvious enough to those who know the area. West Sutherland is certainly Highland enough and west-coast enough—but it is different. Blindfolded and then given your sight, in Wester Ross or Knoydart it is always possible that at first you might think you are in Lochaber or Moidart or Argyll. But here there could be no doubt that but you are in Sutherland. Is it all in the land structure. Nowhere else is there such prevailing barrenness; nowhere else does naked stone and standing water contribute by far the major proportion of the landscape; nowhere else are the mountains bare abrupt giants, rising like leviathans out of the grey-brown seas of gneiss and heather, fierce isolated peaks, not ranges, with strange shapes and stranger names—Stac Polly, Cul Mor, Quinag, Canisp, Suilven and so on. I suppose the sides of these monsters are the steepest in the land—and the views from their summits might be of another world, much more strange and outlandish than anything the moon has been able to show us.

In this fantastic terrain it seems improbable that there should be any place for men at all, much less quite sizeable communities. Yet, though they are by no means thick on the ground, there are such, mainly on the shattered coast—and places of charm and much character at that, old and settled-seeming, with nothing of the air of transient shackery which so often goes with outposts in the wilderness.

Lochinver is the queen of these, a delightful village in an exciting setting at the head of its sea-loch, under the sugar-loaf tower of Suilven, where the short but salmon-rich River Inver comes in from long and lonely Loch Assynt. Lochinver makes a fine centre to explore this dramatic and little-known corner of Scotland; and for those who prefer to stay put and are less interested in fishing, boating and climbing, there are some of the most delicious bathing beaches in these islands to picnic on, of white cockle-shell sand between multi-coloured weed-hung rocks, with Hebridean views—places like Achmelvich, Enard Bay, Clachtoll, Stoer and Clashnessie.

Assynt lies inland, with Ben More Assynt, the highest peak in Sutherland rearing to 3,273 feet. Beneath it lies Inchnadamph, meaning the Island of the Stag, an anglers' paradise with even its own species of trout, named gilaroo. Along the shores of Loch Assynt are the two ruined castles of Ardvreck and Calda, at the former of which the great Montrose, one of the noblest Scotsmen ever to grace our land, finally lost his freedom at the hands of Macleod of Assynt, to be taken the long, long road to the south, treated with every ignominy, to die on the scaffold in Edinburgh.

North of Assynt, on the shores of lovely, isle-dotted Eddrachillis Bay, is Drumbeg, a delightful little resort amongst some of the most challenging road gradients in the British Isles. Nearby is Kylescu Ferry, where the traveller northwards must cross the narrows at the yawning mouths of the fiord-like Lochs Glendhu and Glencoul—at the head of which latter is the little-known but highest waterfall in the land, the 600-foot cataract, Eas-coul-aulin.

Onward through the rugged gneiss-and-water chaos of Eddrachillis, the road twists amongst a myriad of lochans, to Badcall and Scourie, a crofting village where growing palm trees astonish the eye—for the climate here, thanks to the Gulf Stream, is by no means so extreme as the scenery. Seawards, amongst a multitude of islets, is the larger island of Handa, a seabird-sanctuary with cliffs 400 feet high.

Under the tall cone of Ben Stack, the famous salmon river of Laxford runs down into Loch Laxford, with a by-road alongside that has come gallantly across the hills from Lairg, to join the west-coast road at Laxford Bridge. We are in the Mackay country now, its mountainous interior going by the name of Lord Reay's Forest—this being the title of the clan chief. So desolate and grandly fierce is the landscape here that the area between Lochs Laxford and Inchard, even in the undemonstrative Gaelic, is known as *Ceathramh Garbh*, the Rough Territory.

The highway does not penetrate much farther north, on this west coast. At Rhiconich at the head of Loch Inchard, the slender passing-bay road swings away north-eastwards, to Strath Dionard and the long winding narrows of the Kyle of Durness, to Durness itself, fifteen miles on, and the exposed northern shores of the Pentland Firth. Though the tip of Cape Wrath is still many miles away due north, a small side road goes only a short way towards it, to Kinlochbervie, a fishing station, stopping for good a little way beyond, at the crofting place of Sheigra. After that, the north-western extremity of the British mainland is roadless in its unvisited beauty.

The Sutherland north coast is almost as greatly indented with sea-lochs and fiords as is the west, a spectacular seaboard round which it is impossible to hurry. Lochs Eriboll and Hope, and the Kyles of Durness and Tongue, bite deep into the mountainous land, and there are innumerable smaller inlets and bays. The villages of Durness (the most northerly of the mainland) Tongue, Bettyhill, Strathy and Melvich, all have their attractions of sandy beaches, cliff scenery and caves, with

(Left) RUINED ARDVRECK CASTLE, on the shore of Loch Assynt, Sutherland. Here the great Marquis of Montrose, one of Scotland's noblest characters, finally lost his freedom at the hands of MacLeod of Assynt. (Below) TYPICAL CAITHNESS SCENE, so different from neighbouring West Sutherland. The ribbon of road unrolls across the treeless but far from barren landscape of the Ord of Caithness, with the sea always in evidence.

exciting hinterlands up the straths of Dionard, More, Naver and Halladale, which pierce the remote heart of upland Sutherland, where Foinaven, Ben Hee, Ben Hope and Ben Loyal keep their proud and lonely watch.

Such, briefly, is Sutherland, the county where the ultimate is reached in emptiness, barren-ness and wildness. But in some notable forms of beauty also, as in a great, almost over-whelming sense of freedom, of space, of eternity. It is a place which, once visited, will draw the visitor back and back.

Caithness is utterly different. It is only one-third of the size, yet has four times the population—and its numbers are tending to grow, not decline. It has a mountainous inland area, but this is all to the south-west and takes up less than half the total. Yet no one would call it a low-lying county. The majority of the land is a sort of undulating plateau, bare, vast and rolling, seeming almost to be pressed to a pervading flatness under enormous skies. In Caithness one is more aware of the skies than almost anywhere else I know, a land of far, almost featureless horizons, of endless unbroken moorland, of sheer distance, a land where great winds blow and trees are almost non-existant. Unlike its neighbour, the bare bones of rocks do not thrust through but are clad in smooth thick layers of peat and heather. There is plenty of stone, of course,—but the most obvious sign of it is in the endless lines of upended flagstones which everywhere score the land instead of dykes and hedges, a feature unique to Caithness.

The underlying stone, too, is very evident everywhere along the coastline, for this county has probably the most consistently cliff-girt and rockbound shoreline in Scotland. Indeed Caithness could be said to be dominated by its coast in a way unknown elsewhere. One thinks of Caithness as a maritime county almost exclusively—although it has vast inland areas too; for though only one-third the size of Sutherland it is still a large county, larger than twenty others.

By far the greater proportion of the population live along the coastline—and this population is different also. For we are now definitely in the land of mainly Scandinavian heritage and background, with more affinity with the Orkney and Shetland Islands than with the Celtic Highlands of the mainland. This is a Nordic place—and if it seems strange at first that its dominating clan is that of Sinclair, or St. Clair, a Norman name if ever there was one—then let it be recollected that the Normans were Norsemen also once—a point that is often forgotten. The first of the line came

LOCH HOPE AND BEN HOPE, in North Sutherland, in the country which suffered so terribly in the Highland Clearances of the early nineteenth century.

over the Channel with William, the Conquerer, and his descendants found their way up to Scotland, where they settled at Roslin in Midlothian. Henry St. Clair, great-grandson of one of Bruce's supporters, became, through his mother, heir of the Norse Jarls of Orkney, and was recognised as a scion of the Scandinavian blood-royal—so that the term Princes of Orkney was no empty one. This Henry became Lord High Admiral of Scotland, and incidentally discovered Greenland. His grandson, William, third Prince and Earl of Orkney, was Chancellor of Scotland, and he it was who founded the splendid Chapel at Roslin with its famous pillar. James II compelled him to resign his island principality in 1455 and instead created him Earl of Caithness. Oddly enough he settled this earldom on his second son, the elder being the progenitor of the Lords Sinclair of Ravenscraig, in Fife, chiefs of the name until the late eighteenth century, when this line died out. So, though the Sinclairs came to the North via Normandy, they found themselves amongst people of their own ethnic background. There were Mackays and Gunns here, of course, before the Sinclairs—but the latter were also of Norse blood, hereditary Coroners of Caithness. The Sinclairs however took the dominant role, and retain it to this day.

Unlike Sutherland, Caithness has towns, real towns, larger than anything since Inverness—Wick and Thurso. Typical of the ethnic and historical situation, Wick and Thurso are right up at the top of Caithness, looking towards the Norse Isles. After all, the Sinclair Earls of Caithness were junior to their Orkney predecessors, in the 'lordly line of high St. Clair'.

Wick is the county town, though Thurso, with 10,000 inhabitants, is now the larger as well as the more attractive place, a clean, tidy, windswept town of character on the edge of the Pentland Firth, and a thriving, fast-growing place today. For nearby, (as far away as is possible from the populous south-eastern corner of England, as the cynics point out), has been sited the great Dounreay atomic centre, the first fast reactor prototype in the world, and the forerunner of the power-stations of the 1980's, the most advanced piece of public investment in Britain. It is almost inconceivable that this futuristic development could have been set down and accepted amongst the traditional-minded Celtic folk of the Highlands; but amongst the harder-headed Caithnessians, the thing is feasible and is working, socially at least—whatever the top-secret results of what goes on inside the great science-fictional premises at Dounreay.

(Left) DOUNREAY ATOMIC POWER ESTABLISHMENT, with the first Fast Reactor prototype in the world, set down on the far northern Caithness shore of the Pentland Firth, with the Sutherland mountains in background. (Right) THE DRAMATIC EASTERN SEABOARD OF CAITHNESS, north of Helmsdale. A fairly populous land, by Northern Scottish standards.

The 'atomics', as they are called, have of course made a big impact on Thurso and district—and it would probably be fair to say that Thurso and Caithness have come to make almost as great an impact on the atomics. It is one of the most drastic implantations of modern times, the setting down of a large and intricate company of scientists, technicians and boffins, mainly from the crowded urban society of Southern England, in this utterly remote and northwards-looking community—not as a mere temporary arrangement, for a spell of duty, but to live and settle there. Difficulties, failures, problems, frustrations there have been, of course; but by and large the newcomers seem to have found themselves to be pleasantly surprised, have learned much, and have come to appreciate new values and unanticipated fulfillments—while the local people, doubtful at first, have been stirred up, enlivened and enriched in more than their pockets.

There have inevitably been subsidiary developments, industrially, in the area, opening up new avenues of initiative and employment. But one heartening project, at Wick, is of purely local inspiration—the Caithness Glass enterprise, in which the Hon. Robin Sinclair, son of Viscount Thurso, is prominent, turning out quality decorative glassware of a high order. If the royal burgh of Wick, twenty-one miles to the south-east, cannot claim to equal Thurso's recent advances, it is nevertheless a busy, active place, with an airport and large tidal harbour, designed by Telford and improved by Stevenson. It was an important place even in Viking days—and the need for a sheltered haven on this wild coast is emphasised by the fact that only a few miles to the south the waves have quarried great masses of rock from the base of the cliffs and piled them up on top, sixty to 100 feet above high-water-mark. Some of these blocks of stone are of such size that they have been estimated to weigh as much as 500 tons.

Fishing, fish-curing and the shellfish industry, with ancillary trades such as rope, ice and net making flourish, and Wick's streets are frequently full of visiting fishermen from far and near. Here is a meteorological and radio station, serving shipping. There is a great rivalry with Thurso, as is inevitable and the latter's folk are apt to talk loftily of an 'ancient and fishlike smell' emanating from Wick. The ruined castles of Sinclair and Girnigoe are nearby, spectacularly sited on the edge of a cliff. In the latter the Master of Caithness was imprisoned for six years by his father, the fourth Earl, eventually starving to death

—but in the meantime managing to strangle the brother who visited him in his dungeon; the sort of thing, I suppose which might happen in any high-spirited family. These cliff-top castles are, in fact, an integral part of the Caithness scene—although one, which has become well-known of late, the Queen-Mother's Castle of Mey, formerly called Barrogill, stands back from the shoreline near Mey Bay between the thrusting capes of Dunnet and Duncansby.

There is only one sizeable centre of population inland—Halkirk, a large village of 1,400 inhabitants, on the road between Wick and Thurso and about eight miles south of the latter, a great place for angling, with fully fifty lochs and lochans nearby, to say nothing of fine streams noted for their trout. Halkirk now boasts a plastics factory.

Other large villages are Reay, Lybster, Castleton and Dunnet—the latter's fourteenth century church having been the charge, from 1601-08, of Timothy Pont the famous cartographer. Its mighty headland is the most northerly point of the British mainland. For some reason, John o' Groats, a tiny village seventeen miles north of Wick is usually taken to represent the ultimate north, although there are many houses further north than this—including the aforementioned Castle of Mey. The place got its name from an early sixteenth century Dutchman, John de Groot, about whom many tales are told. Why the term 'Land's End to John o' Groats' has developed, I do not know. 'Land's End to Dunnet Head' would have more point; or even Duncansby Head, the extreme north-eastern tip, would make more sense.

'Over the Ord of Caithness,' the 1,000-feet-high granite buttress between Helmsdale and Berriedale, over which travellers have had to cross for untold centuries, has meant something of adventure, even terror to the southron, and exile to the Caithness folk—the demarcation of a different land, a land where names like Staxigoe, Gote o' Tram, Occumster, Keiss, Toftcarl, Weydal and the like speak of Norway (which, indeed, is nearer than Manchester and Hull). Caithness, then, is a far cry from even Berwick and the Merse—almost as far from there as to London, a point which strangers to Scotland often overlook. But we are by no means at the top of Scotland yet. Though only islands lie beyond, these are many, populous and highly individual. The true 'top of the map', the tip of Shetland, is 200 miles more still.

Shetland
Orkney
Lewis
Harris
Uist
Uist
Skye
Mull
Jura
Islay
Bute
Arran

CHAPTER 7
THE ISLANDS

Although it is convenient, for present purposes, to deal with all the major island groups of Scotland together, this must not be taken as an indication that there is any real similarity, or indeed any essential sympathy, between the Orkneys and Shetlands on the one hand, and the Inner and Outer Hebrides on the other. Apart from the fact that they both comprise large numbers of islands, great and small, at a fair distance from the mainland, they have little else in common. Their appearance, their climate, their history, their people, their whole character, outlook and problems, are so different as to be quite extraordinary considering that only 100 miles of sea separate the Old Man of Hoy from the Butt of Lewis.

Physically the northern islands resemble the Caithness mainland as against the Sutherland west - they are not mountainous but nor are they flat, with rolling low hills cut off short at great cliffs and pierced by innumerable voes, creeks and arms of the sea. In fact these islands compare with the mainly mountainous and colourful Hebrides in very much the same way as do the east and west sides of mainland Scotland. The people being largely of Scandinavian origin are in contrast to the very Celtic Hebrideans in appearance, tradition and attitude to life.

To deal with the Orkneys first, the Orcades of the Romans, we must realise

that we are here considering no minor group of rocky atolls but a highly complex system, fifty miles long and thirty wide, comprising some fifty-six major islands and innumerable lesser islets, eighteen of the former inhabited, with the others largely used for grazing. There is a total land area of 240,000 acres, and the population, at 18,000, is not so large as Caithness but much larger than Sutherland. It is important to appreciate, therefore, that this is no remote unpopulated backwater, dreaming in a sort of twilight— whatever the fame for its 'simmerdim', its nightless, summertime half-light—but a vital, well-doing and forward looking community of farming, fishing and what might be called cottage industries, a county of which there are six others in Scotland with lower population and ten others with smaller area.

By far the largest of the islands, extraordinarily irregular as is its outline, is Pomona, usually called the Mainland, roughly central in the complex and on which Orkney's two largest towns are sited, Kirkwall and Stromness.

Kirkwall, the capital, has been a royal burgh since 1486 —fourteen years after the Orkneys were ceded finally to the Scottish crown, as an unredeemed pledge by King Christian of Denmark and Norway for part of the unpaid dowry of his daughter, the Princess Margaret, on her marriage to James III in 1468. Shetland came to Scotland at the same time—a somewhat mercenary arrangement between spirited peoples. But Kirkwall was ancient then, having long been a vital link in the Viking chain, even though its harbour is much less useful than that of Stromness. King James, in his charter, referred to the 'great and old antiquity of our said city.' A fine town of old buildings and very narrow paved streets, with some 4,000 inhabitants, it is famous for its great and handsome cathedral of St. Magnus founded in 1137 but developed in five different styles of architecture; indeed, owing to its size and position it fairly dominates the town—it is 234 feet long, nearly thirty feet longer than St. Giles in Edinburgh. It had a more lofty and graceful spire once, but this was struck by lightning in 1671, and replaced by the present less shapely one.

This is not the only handsome ancient building here. Nearby stands the remains of the thirteenth century Bishops' Palace, where King Hakon, after the battle of Largs, took up his winter quarters, and where wounded and broken-hearted he died—though the surviving portions of this palace are mainly of the great Bishop Reid's mid-sixteenth century work. There is also the more architec-

(Left) STREET SCENE IN STROMNESS, Orkney Islands. The best harbour of the Orkneys is here, with the steamer-link to Scrabster in Caithness. (Below) SCAPA FLOW, the great sheltered anchorage surrounded by the Orkney Isles, wherein lay the battle fleets of two world wars, and where the surrendered German High Seas Fleet scuttled itself in 1918. Note the treeless state of the islands.

turally exciting Earl's Palace—though this is an early seventeenth century building in the typical and ornate castellated style of that period, erected by the Earl Patrick Stewart, who inherited the Orkney earldom from his father, the Earl Robert, formerly Bishop thereof, and one of the many illegitimate sons of James V. Despite their fine buildings, these late Stewart overlords were a sore blight on Orkney.

But not all of Kirkwall is of the past. There are excellent shops, an airport, two distilleries nearby, and 200 miles of good motoring roads radiating from the town. Even so, Kirkwall claims the oldest public library in Scotland.

Easily reached from here are two very different places of interest, with very similar names—Skara and Scapa. The first, Skara Brae, is the famous prehistoric village, believed to date from at least 2,000 B.C., one of the most renowned excavated sites in Britain. The other is the great, sheltered anchorage of Scapa Flow, enclosed within the clustered isles, used by the Royal Navy as a base in two world wars. The Admiralty have gone—but they have left more than just the usual litter of broken-down buildings, for four long causeways were constructed here, joining the mainland to Burray and South Ronaldshay, for tactical reasons. This was when, in the last war, the battleship Royal Oak was torpedoed in the anchorage by a daring U-boat, with the loss of 800 lives. These causeways were to seal entrances to Scapa—but happily they now provide valuable road links with these two other southern isles. They are known as the Churchill Barriers. It was in Scapa Flow, of course, that the great surrendered German High Seas Fleet scuttled itself in 1920.

Stromness is situated attractively on a fine bay at the south-west corner of Pomona. Its harbour is the best of the islands, and it has the mail-steamer link with Scrabster, the Thurso port, thirty-five miles away across the turbulent waters of the Pentland Firth—which, by the way, should really be called the Pictland Firth. The paved streets of Stromness, population 1,500, are of a narrowness which has to be seen to be believed, demanding a high degree of patience and courtesy from all concerned. Nearby is Login's Well, notable as a source of water for shipping before or after braving the long North Atlantic voyages. Captain Cook's ships watered here in 1780 on their way home, and the Hudson's Bay vessels constantly used it.

LIATHACH FROM ALLIGIN, Upper Loch Torridon, Wester Ross. One of a spectacular group of mountains built of the oldest stone on earth, in an area of almost unsurpassable beauty.

Strangely enough, although feuds between neighbouring towns are common enough, that between Stromness and Kirkwall not only reached a stage of bitterness and spleen seldom rivalled, but actually reached the House of Lords, in 1758, when a battle by the Stromness folk against exactions and taxes imposed upon them by the neighbouring royal burgh passed through all the courts of the land, finally to end up by freeing all the villages and small towns of Scotland from this municipal overlordship by the privileged royal burghs.

Birsay, a large village lying to the north-west amongst some of the most fertile land in the islands, has a ruined palace of the Orkney earls. This was indeed the principal residence of the old Jarls, largely because of the excellent hunting available in this vicinity, and the fishing on six lochs. The name of Birsay in fact is a corruption of *Bergish-crad*, or hunting territory. The later Stewart earls re-modelled the palace on Holyroodhouse in Edinburgh, but it is now much delapidated.

Finstown, north-west of Kirkwall, on the Bay of Firth, is one of the most attractive villages of Orkney, notable for the mature trees which grow here—unusual indeed for the islands. Nearby is the celebrated prehistoric Pictish burial mound of Maeshowe, thirty-six feet high. Everywhere on the islands such relics of the distant past are frequent, in standing-stones, tumuli, hut-circles etc.; also, of course, the brochs, or circular stone forts of later days.

Hoy, south-west of Pomona, is undoubtedly the most spectacular of the Orkney isles, as well as the second largest. It perhaps is apt to give many visitors a wrong impression, for it is the first seen from the steamer from Scrabster. It could be called mountainous, with its northern end formed by a triangle of three large bluff hills, the highest, Ward Hill, reaching 1,565 feet, the most elevated point in all Orkney. But still more impressive are the enormous cliffs with which Hoy confronts the Atlantic waves, cliffs which dwarf all others in Britain save those of Foula and St. Kilda, rising to the fantastic sheer height of 1,160 feet, providing quite stupendous rock scenery. Famous is the isolated stack known as the Old Man of Hoy, standing out from one of the cliffs to tower to a height of 450 feet—formerly deemed to be unclimbable but recently scaled by intrepid and ingenious climbers. The island extends to about 40,000 acres but though there is much good level ground to the south, it has a population of only 700—a century ago it was almost three times as much.

SUNSET OVER SKYE. When the sun dips into the isle-dotted Hebridean Sea, it can be in sublime enchantment or in breath-taking splendour.

The other islands all have their claims to fame. South Ronaldshay, the most southerly, probably presents a more cultivated appearance than any other, and here it was that Margaret, the Maid of Norway, died aboard her ship on her way to her Scots kingdom in 1290—a death which was to precipitate the disaster of the long Wars of Independence with the throne vacant. Rousay has more magnificent rock scenery and is a paradise for bird-watchers. Egilsay is smaller, but has one of the three round towers of Scotland, attached to its roofless Norman church. Stronsay, a weirdly shaped island that seems to throw out arms in all directions, comprises 16,000 acres yet no part of it is more than a mile from the sea—and even so there are eleven inland lochs, which with its medicinal wells make it a watering-place indeed. Westray is large, with over 1,000 inhabitants, good soil, and boasting a cavern called the Gentleman's Cave where a number of Orkney Jacobites hid successfully in 1746, after Culloden, although they were searched for daily by government troops; and also boasts the handsome ruined sixteenth century fortalice of Noltland Castle. North Ronaldshay is the most northerly of the Orkneys, separated by a firth highly dangerous to navigation, and is noted for its indigenous breed of sheep. Oddly, these animals live mainly on seaweed, and indeed a wall twelve miles round has been built to keep them from the arable land.

These are but a few of Orkney's islands, serving only to illustrate the character and aspect of this age-old archipelagic community that has produced one of the most sturdy breeds of men on earth, great figures of the arts, administrators, thinkers and sea-captains by the thousand. It will be tragic for more than Orkney if the population decrease continues, and more of these Viking isles revert to the seafowl, the wild flowers and the seals, after forty fruitful and vigorous centuries.

Some sixty rough sea miles north of Orkney lies Shetland; but in between is the notable small outpost of Fair Isle, three miles long by two broad and accessible only at one point, another place of cliffs and promontories and voes. In 1948 a Bird Observatory was established there, now run by the Scottish Ornithological Club, though the island is owned by the National Trust. It is a great staging point on the bird migratory routes. Here was wrecked, in 1588, the flagship of Admiral the Duke of Medina, of the Spanish Armada—and it is alleged that it was the 200 surviving Spanish sailors who taught the islanders the designs which

(Left) LERWICK, CAPITAL OF ZETLAND, the most northerly town in Britain, with a population of nearly 6,000. Note the style of the boats, little changed since the Viking days. (Right) STANDING STONES of the Ring of Brogar, Orkney, in the sunset. These islands were heavily populated in prehistoric times.

have become renowned as one of the best-known knitwear patterns of the world.

There are, of course, inevitably great similarities between the isles of Shetland and those of Orkney. But there are differences too—and nobody more determined to point them out than the Orkneymen and Shetlanders. The Shetlands are more compactly grouped than the others, consisting of about 100 islands of which twenty are inhabited, and cover a greater acreage—350,000. But the population is very slightly less, at 17,800—although there were 31,000 a century ago. Nevertheless, save for the cliffs and voes and sounds, the general aspect of the islands is domestic, rather than spectacular—except in their sunsets and the beauties of the summer nights. George Buchanan may perhaps be forgiven for declaring in 1582 that it is 'so uncouth a place that no creature can live there in except such as are born there.' But how can we excuse the Dictionary published in 1800 which asserts that 'in Shetland the sun does not set for two months in summer nor rises for two months in winter'? Or the Commissioners of Customs who in 1810 refused to pay a bounty on herring caught at Shetland in winter, on the grounds that fish could not have been caught there since the islands are surrounded in ice during that season? The fact is that the climate of these islands is more equable than in most parts of southern Britain, with the average range in temperature sixteen degrees, against twenty-five degrees in London, the atmosphere being humid, with very little frost and snow. Admittedly there are storms, when spume from the great seas covers much of the land—but where else can you hear the larks singing at one in the morning? Or read your newspaper out of doors at midnight? The springs are late and cold, but the rate of growth in summer is phenomenal.

Lerwick, the present capital, and the most northerly town in Britain, is an interesting, indeed an exciting place of 6,000 inhabitants, situated on a sound of the east coast which is protected by the island of Bressay, thus providing one of the finest achorages in the country. It is a busy fishing port, and its excellent harbour was important even before King Hakon put in here on his way to defeat at Largs, in 1263. Some of the houses of the town are actually built with their foundations in the sea, in highly picturesque and Scandinavian fashion. Although larger, Lerwick cannot rival Kirkwall as a county town, for not only does it have nothing like St. Magnus' Cathedral but it is not even a royal burgh. Indeed, although it has an appearance of

antiquity, the oldest part of the town dates only from the seventeenth century. There presumably was a village attached to the harbour before that, but in 1625 we read of an Act of the Scottish Parliament 'anent the demolishing of the houssis of Lerwick.' This was allegedly in consequence of the notorious wickedness going on between the inhabitants and the Dutch fishermen who used to make this their base. The sheriff of the day intimated that in his opinion there was no need for a town here! Be that as it may, Lerwick today certainly and cheerfully supplies the needs of a large area, and its narrow paved streets are busy. In these same streets, each January, is enacted the picturesque festival of Up Helly A, supposed to celebrate the return of the sun—although this would seem to be somewhat anticipatory in January. In it a Viking ship is trundled and escorted round the town, accompanied by torch-bearers, who eventually set the whole thing on fire amid scenes of great enthusiasm. The Norse feeling is very strong here—for after all, Bergen is only 220 miles away, whereas Edinburgh is 300.

The old capital of Shetland is Scalloway, formerly a burgh though now only a village, but nevertheless the only other sizeable centre of population in the islands, which go in for farming and crofting townships rather than villages. It lies seven miles to the west of Lerwick, on the Atlantic side, clustered around the imposing ruins of another of Earl Patrick Stewart's castles—which the said tyrant forced the locals to build for him, even to supply their own materials and provisions. With an excellent harbour, formerly most of the Shetland land-owners had town houses here. The Ting, or island parliament, met on an islet in the Tingwall Loch nearby.

At Sumburgh, the extreme southerly tip of the mainland, is to be seen the phenomenon known as the Sumburgh Roost, a tidal upheaval rather similar to the famous Corrievreckan whirlpool of the Inner Hebrides, caused by fierce currents meeting and being forced upwards by submarine ridges around the islands. This can be dangerous at any time, and shattering in a storm. There are many similar if less famous 'jangles' around the Orkneys and Shetlands. Near Sumburgh is the Shetland airport, and the notable archaeological site of Jarlshof. The island of Noss is now a nature reserve, its great cliffs being the haunt of vast numbers of seabirds.

Although there are not many villages of any size in Shetland, there are many centres of farming and fishing

(Left) CROFTER WOMEN, at Trebister, Shetland, using their peculiarly-shaped spades. (Below) THE UP HELLYA FESTIVAL, at Lerwick, an ancient Norse celebration of the return of the sun. On the last Tuesday in January a model of a Viking ship is escorted round the town by torch-bearers, and thereafter burned, amid vigorous proceedings.

communities. Walls, to the west, where the mailboat for Foula docks, and Voe and Hillswick to the north, are mainland villages. Near the last, Ronas Hill, at 1,475 feet, is the highest in the islands, from which magnificent views may be obtained.

Across the sound from here is the island of Yell, the second largest, but almost two islands, so narrow is the neck linking south to north at Whalefirth and Reafirth. Over 1,000 people live on this isle, the northern section of which boasts fiord-like scenery. To the east is Fetlar, famous for its Shetland ponies. And to the north, Unst, the ultimate isle, with its fishing-port of Baltasound, the nature reserve of Hermaness to the west and the noted caves of Burrafirth nearby. On a rock beyond is Muckle Flugga lighthouse, the final most northerly point of Britain, halfway from Edinburgh to the Arctic Circle.

As well as crofting and fishing, and the production of the gossamer-fine Shetland knitwear, renowned the world over, these isles are celebrated for the great number of prehistoric remains, and for trout-fishing, free in many places. It seems extraordinary that when King Christian handed over Shetland to the Scots, he did so for the paltry sum of 8,000 florins.

We cannot leave the far north without a glance at the most lonely isle of all—Foula, sixteen miles out to the west, and notable for more than its remoteness. For here are cliffs that make even Hoy's look moderate, soaring 1,220 feet sheer, half as high again as the top of Edinburgh's Arthur's Seat. This was the scene of the film, *Edge of the World.* A small isle, three miles long by half that in breadth, it consists mainly of five conical hills, absolutely cliff-girt save for the one landing-place—the fishing-station of Ham.

Although it is almost as far from Kirkwall to Lerwick as it is to the Outer Hebrides, off the west coast of Highland Scotland, the voyage might be not only to a different world but almost to a different century. It would be unfair to say that the Hebrides look backwards where the North Isles look forward—but something of that atmosphere prevails. This is the land where time does not matter, where reality is not quite as in other places, where the people, thin on the ground as they are, are kindly, musically-voiced, polite to a degree and pathologically resistent to change. It is also in my opinion the most beautiful land on the face of the entire globe, where blue mountains rise dreaming from painted seas, and everything is coloured delight.

The Hebrides, or Western Isles of Scotland, are divided fairly distinctly into Inner and Outer Isles, with a belt of skerry-strewn sea averaging perhaps twenty-five miles wide between them. But while it is simple to treat the Outer Isles as a separate entity, it is difficult, if not almost ridiculous, to try to deal with much of the Inner Isles as separate and distinct from the West Highland mainland. Almost all the seaboard of the mainland is in fact Hebridean in character, and many parts of it are actually more so than are certain east-facing parts of the islands. So fretted and cut up by sea-lochs, sounds, kyles and channels is the whole coastline that what happens to be island and what promontory and peninsula of the mainland is quite fortuitous. For instance, the long and magnificent peninsula of Ardnamurchan and Sunart projecting thirty miles out into the Atlantic to form the most westerly point of the whole British mainland is distinctly more Hebridean in every respect save the insular than is, say, the eastern flank of the great Isle of Mull nearby.

important, and hydro-electric development was early here. Forestry also is becoming an increasingly vital industry, as in Mull, though not all the islands are suitable for tree-growing. Skye has a population of almost 8,000, and an area of over 600 square miles.

Between north Skye and the mainland is the long narrow island of Raasay, with its lofty flat-topped summit of Dun Caan and ruined Brochel Castle, of the Macleods. The laird here was one of Prince Charlie's faithful followers in adversity, unlike his chief.

Rum, just south of Skye, is the most dramatic in appearance of all the Hebridean isles, being in fact little more than a mountain range thrusting up out of the sea, its shapely rock peaks providing one of the most photographed skylines in Scotland—although mainly photographed from a distance. Under private ownership, this island was as hard to enter as a fortress, and now, the nation's property, the Nature Conservancy still limits visiting strictly by permit, in the furtherance of their red deer and other studies—quite a thought for an island of 30,000 acres, about the size of the county of Clackmannan. Rum is notable for its so-called 'parasitical clouds', which its mountains manufacture and which usually sit above its summits like puffs of cotton-wool, however cloudless the sky may be elsewhere. It is perhaps of interest that the four young Scots who comprised the Scottish Hindu Kush Expedition of 1965, exploring and mapping in unknown Afghan mountains, saw such similarity between the shape and outline of a group of these and the Rum mountains at home, that they gave them the same names—so that now there are Hebridean Askival, Ainshval, Trollval and so on, far away and infinitely higher, on the Roof of the World.

IN GLENCOE, ARGYLL, a place of superlatives and dramatic contrasts, the thread of the main road lost in the scale of its grandeur.

Eigg, south of Rum, is quite a different sort of island, populated and with considerable levelish ground, though having a notable projecting snout, the Sguirr of Eigg, forming a well-known landmark. The recent decision of Eigg's wealthy southern proprietors to sell the island, with the resultant uncertainty for the local population, has highlighted the problem of sole private ownership in these days when social security is accepted as vital elsewhere. It was on Eigg, in the sixteenth century, that one of the most terrible incidents of clan warfare took place, when Macleod raiders from Skye suffocated all the Eigg MacDonalds, with their wives and children, to the number of 200, in a cavern of the island.

The low-lying isle of Muck, a corruption of the Gaelic word *muic* for swine—Buchanan called it 'insula porcorum' —lies to the south, and Canna, another small and non-mountainous island though with a hill rising to 630 feet, gives magnificent views of Rum, five miles northwest.

The great thrusting mainland peninsula of Ardnamurchan separates the northern group of the Inner Hebrides from the southern, and from its shores and headlands some of the most exciting and delightful prospects of both may be seen. To the immediate south is the very large island of Mull, second only to Skye in size, being some thirty miles long, almost as broad and containing 350 square miles of land. Formerly fairly populous, there were 7,500 people here a century ago but today only 1,670—which is tragic, for there is much good land to support a population on Mull, and its accessibility and attractiveness for the visitor are great.

The east coast, served by the daily steamer from Oban, is the best known but least scenically exciting. The fine restored castle of Duart on its guardian rock, seat of the Maclean chief, and the little ports of Craignure and Salen make good starting points for exploration. Tobermory, up at the north-east tip, is famous as the spot where the treasure-ship of the Spanish Armada sank, and has been sought for ever since—but it is a delightful little town in its own right, crescent-shaped round its sheltered bay, and well served with hotels. Here the Scottish Council of Physical Recreation yachting scheme is based.

The long and greatly indented west coast of Mull is varied and continuously interesting. Dervaig, at the head of its sea-loch, is one of the most attractive island villages. The splendid silver sands of Calgary Bay are celebrated. A great bight then cuts into Mull from the west, and in it

NEWARK CASTLE, SELKIRKSHIRE. Former principal stronghold of the great Ettrick Forest, seems almost to sink back into the green Vale of Yarrow from which it rose. Held successively by the Crown, Douglases and Scotts, Walter Scott's Last Minstrel here sang his Lay to the sorrowing Duchess of Buccleuch and Monmouth after her royal husband's execution.

are the lesser isles of Ulva and Gometra. This bight becomes long Loch na Keal, which almost cuts Mull in half, reaching to within three miles of Salen again. On its south side is the massive range of grand mountains, culminating in Ben More of Mull, 3,169 feet, and these sweep down to the spectacular coastal cliffs of Gribun under which the switchback road creeps.

The south-west of Mull thrusts out in a long, knobbly and low-lying peninsula known as the Ross, and at the tip of this is the renowned island of Iona, reached by ferry from the little haven of Fionnphort. Iona, with its cathedral and monastery, shrine of St. Columba who from here campaigned in the sixth century to Christianise Scotland, is today also famous as the headquarters of the notable religious and social experiment of the Iona Community. It is a beautiful little island, with exhilarating prospects on all hands.

Westwards lies Coll, a crofting island of little high ground ten miles long, with the township of Arinagour; and nearby is Tiree, somewhat larger, a flat place with quite a sizeable population, known as the Granary of the Isles because of its much fertile land and which, surprisingly perhaps, holds the record for possibly the finest weather in the British Isles, an almost sub-tropical isle in the Gulf Stream, with no hills to break the Atlantic rainclouds. Its beaches are well-known, it exports variegated coloured marble, and it has an airport.

South and west of Mull there is a great welter of islands: Seil, Shuna, Luing and their satellites, more exciting for their seaward views than for themselves perhaps; further out, the Garvellochs, or Isles of the Sea, and the Treshnish with their strange geological formations which produce odd outlines like that called the Dutchman's Cap. There is Colonsay and Oronsay, the former's mansionhouse having a fine sub-tropical garden, and the latter the remains of a fourteenth century priory. There is Staffa, famous for its columnar basaltic cliffs and caverns, the inspiration for Mendelssohn's 'Hebridean Overture'. And there are the larger and major islands of Jura and Islay, flanked by smaller Scarba and Gigha respectively.

Between Scarba and Jura lies the notorious Strait of Corrievreckan, the tidal maelstrom where the fierce Atlantic currents surge in and out of the Sound of Jura over submarine cliffs. Even on a calm day the roar of Corrievreckan may be heard from the mainland, many miles away.

(Below) IONA, St. Columba's small isle, showing the restored cathedral, with the large Isle of Mull in the background. The Iona Community, which draws its inspiration from here, is a notable experiment in practical Christianity. (Right) THE SOUTH CHOIR OF THE CATHEDRAL, Iona. From here Columba missionarised the mainland and islands in the sixth century. Here are the graves of many early kings, including Duncan alleged to have been murdered by Macbeth.

Jura, with its shapely peaks, frankly named the Paps—though there are in fact three of them—is a long, long island, presenting a fairly unbroken coastline. Despite its size—nearly thirty miles long—it is largely a private deer-forest, with a very small population mainly concentrated at the southern tip, where at the little port of Craighouse there is a distillery. Roads and accommodation are not Jura's strong points. Islay, on the other hand, just across the sound, is a populous and tourist-conscious island, forward-looking and welcoming, with many townships such as Port Askaig, Port Ellen, Bowmore and Bridgend, many hotels and guest-houses and an airport. Nearly 4,000 people live here, and there are a number of famous distilleries, so that this, the most southerly of the Inner Hebrides, is also the most active and busy. It was always a place of importance, partly on account of its considerable agricultural land, and partly in that it was one of the main centres of the ancient Lordship of the Isles, the ruins of its castles being notable.

Gigha, between Islay and the mainland, though quite a small place of crofts and creeks and coves, is comparatively populous, with good anchorages favoured by yachtsmen. At the south-west tip it is pierced by a long natural tunnel in which the tide spouts and booms. The gardens of Achamore House are famous.

We can leave the islands here, though we have been able to touch on only a tiny proportion of the whole. Here is a wonderland which increasing leisure will undoubtedly open up to an ever-growing number of people from the crowded south and overseas. The problem of seeing that it is not spoiled in the process is no light one—but it must be tackled.

Though, when you come to think of it, it would be difficult really to spoil the Hebrides.

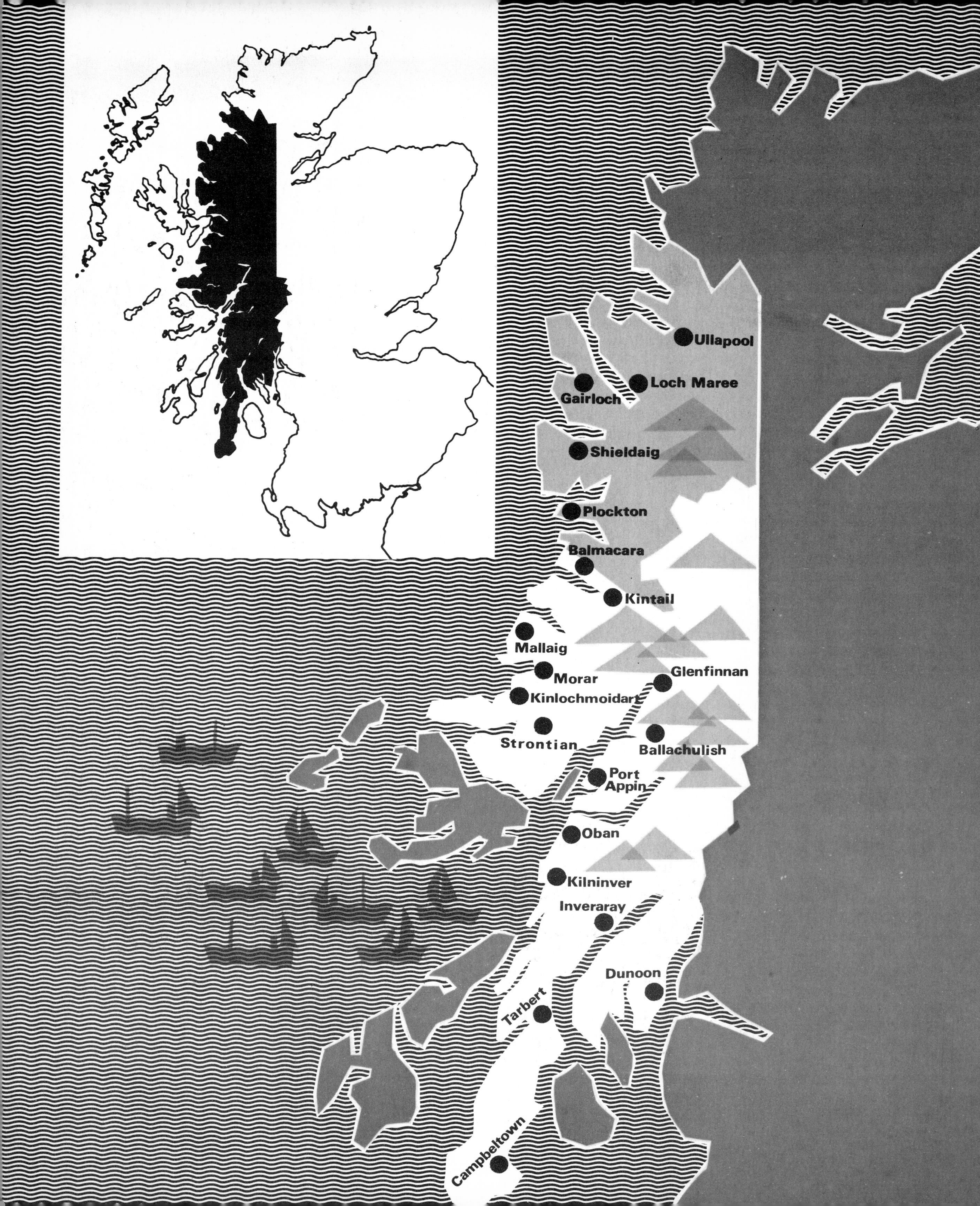

Ullapool
Loch Maree
Gairloch
Shieldaig
Plockton
Balmacara
Kintail
Mallaig
Morar
Glenfinnan
Kinlochmoidart
Strontian
Ballachulish
Port Appin
Oban
Kilninver
Inveraray
Dunoon
Tarbert
Campbeltown

CHAPTER 8

THE WESTERN HIGHLANDS

The reader cannot but be already conditioned to and informed about the Western Highlands, from general knowledge, books innumerable, tourist literature, and even from references in earlier chapters of this book - for surely no part of Britain outside London itself has been so greatly written about, photographed, painted, sung and romanticised. Here is the land that, had it a better climate, would almost certainly be the playground of Europe - which, I suppose, may be a matter for congratulation towards the much maligned weather.

But there are innumerable misconceptions about the Western Highlands, nevertheless - one, this very matter of climate. It does not rain nearly so much as is usually suggested. The trouble is that the rainiest periods happen to coincide with the popular holiday months of July, August and September, and until this pattern is changed, the great mass of visitors will continue to moan. Spring in the Highlands is usually the driest time of the year, often with actual shortage of precipitation, and late autumn can often rival it - while the winters in the west are much more equable and open than in the east and south. This seaboard - and nearly all the Western Highlands are seaboard, with sea-lochs penetrating twenty miles and more inland - in May, with cloudless skies and ultramarine isle-dotted seas, the hillsides ablaze with golden broom and crackling gorse, and cuckoos calling in the sun-filled valleys, is of the stuff of dreams.

Although it is frequently declared that this land is age-old and changeless, the fact is that there have been great changes all through the centuries, with regard to the land itself, as well as the people on it—who here, of course, have suffered grievously from political hostility and neglect, evictions, absentee-landlords and lack of communications. But the great present-day changes are topographical—the alteration of the landscape in a big way by forestry and hydro-electric programmes.

These are on a very great scale—so much so that the Forestry Commission is now much the largest landowner in Scotland. While undoubtedly there are drawbacks and problems connected with these two modern developments, by and large I think that there are few who know and love the Highlands who can honestly declare that they are not better off for them. Although pylons striding hugely across lonely hills and moors may not please every aesthetic sense, they do speak vividly of power on leash and linkage with the world without; and though the dark green mantle which now covers the shoulders of so many of our mountainsides may represent too radical a change from the heather, the bracken and the deer-hair grass, and therefore the ecology, atmosphere, and even drainage of vast areas, yet there is satisfaction in seeing the hillsides providing trees, and it must not be forgotten that once almost all Highland Scotland was covered by the great Caledonian forest. But more important than all this, the forestry in especial has brought and is bringing people to live in the glens again. Communities are springing up in remote places. And little schools are being re-opened which closed down for lack of pupils. It is surely a good thing to hear children's laughter once more in the Highlands.

The trouble, of course, is when the hydro-electric developers flood good bottom land which was needed to grow winter feed for stock—and might be needed again—and so turn into useless wilderness the higher pastures of the hillsides where the cattle and sheep can no longer subsist through the winter. Or where the foresters plant up whole estates, leaving the arable patches uneconomically isolated, so that no farmer or crofter can effectively work them. These things have happened; but in the main the development has been much to the good, and all Britain is the richer. For a lot of it, too, we have to thank one man—the late Tom Johnston, who, as the best Secretary of State Scotland has produced for long years, saw the need and the opportunity, and staked his career for his country's benefit.

These two great and widespread developments have helped, and will continue to help, to expedite another—the improvement of the road system. This is an enormous problem, and distinctly less near solution in the Highland area than even elsewhere in Scotland; nevertheless, certain steps have been taken of late, sometimes necessitated by hydro-electric schemes flooding existing narrow roads and requiring their replacement as was the case with the Glen Garry-Glen Moriston road. Moreover, the rapidly growing forests are going to require infinitely better roads for the extraction and marketing of the timber. So we have, for instance, the road from Cluanie Inn being widened and straightened all the way to Kyle of Lochalsh; the real road to the isles, from Glenfinnan right to Mallaig, is finished and vastly improved; the Ardgour-Sunart road is being tackled; and the two brand-new roads, scenically magnificent, through Moidart and bridging the Balgy Gap south of Torridon, are open. This is excellent—but it is only the beginning. There are still thousands of miles of single-track, passing-bay, yet allegedly A-class main roads in the Highlands, a menace and weariness, and a grave social and economic handicap to locals and visitors alike; innumerable long detours round narrow but endless sea-lochs, where quite modest bridges would save hours; and far too many expensive and time-wasting ferries, in force since the horse-and-cart days, which in this mobile motor age would be comic were they not little short of tragic.

Continuing with our brief north-to-south survey, I shall not attempt to stick to the county delineation, so odd and arbitrary are the boundaries. Instead I shall deal with the districts by the ancient names, one after the other. These names largely date from the days of clan supremacy, and most of them are still in everyday use, even though they may no longer have administrative entities or clearly defined boundaries.

Just south of Sutherland, and similar to it in character, is Coigeach, a spectacular but little populated area, dominated by another Ben More, or great mountain, and extending into an attractive and comparatively low-lying peninsula wherein lies the seacoast resort of Achiltibuie, looking out to the picturesque Summer Isles. Inland the great mountain masses of Cromalt and Rhidorrach stretch across the watershed of Scotland, embosoming some of the wildest country in the land, for no road crosses this area for scores of miles. Deep in its lonely heart is Corriemulzie, beloved of mountaineers who do not mind a dozen-mile

LOCHALSH, Wester Ross, home of the Clan Matheson looking across the narrows of Kyle to the Red Hills of Skye. The sunsets of this seaboard are legendary.

LOCH BROOM, Wester Ross. Fishing-boats off Ullapool, looking south-eastwards towards the Fannich Mountains.

(Left) LOCH MAREE, Wester Ross, probably one of the loveliest lochs in all Scotland, with the magnificent isolated peak of Slioch behind. Maree is noted for its fine trout-fishing. (Right) THE GORGE OF CORRIESHALLOCH, Braemore, near Ullapool, a Scottish National Trust property in which are the lofty Falls of Measach, some of the finest in the land.

tramp, with heavy packs, before they start their climbing.

Next is the district of Lochbroom, just as mountainous but more accessible, for here at least there are two good roads—good by Highland standards—one coming from the south via the fretted coast, by lovely and famous Gruinard Bay and Little Loch Broom, and the other across the mountains from the east, by Garve from Inverness. Here, on the shores of greater Loch Broom, is Ullapool, a well-known little fishing town and holiday place which makes a good centre for visiting a huge range of attractive country. The village did not grow naturally but was founded by the British Fishery Society in 1788, and was intended to be a fairly large town—an early example of planning, both as to location and layout. The views to the east and south especially, towards the Ben Dearg group of peaks, is very fine; and in the nearby valley of Strath More, near Braemore, is the exciting Corrieshalloch Gorge, a tremendous deep ravine spanned by a dizzy fragile-seeming bridge, beloved of photographers. In this gorge are the Falls of Measach, very fine. At Braemore, a road grimly named Destitution Road because it was made as a relief project during the famine of 1851, swings away westwards across the Dundonnell Forest. From it are magnificent views of the mighty isolated mountain mass of An Teallach, or The Forge. South by east lie the remote Fannich Mountains, rising to 3,637 feet.

Gairloch is the next district southwards, Mackenzie country, comprising three peninsulas separated by Gruinard Bay, Loch Ewe and Gair Loch itself, and backed by high, barren and tremendous mountains known only to those who can walk long distances, since again they are entirely roadless, the wilderness between Fionn Loch and Loch Fannich. Gairloch itself has hotels, sandy beaches and fine vistas, and nearby is the large crofting township of Strath. Poolewe, at the head of Loch Ewe, is renowned for the sub-tropical gardens of Inverewe House, National Trust property; and inland is long and lovely Loch Maree, island-dotted, dominated by the mighty mass of Slioch, and undoubtedly one of the most beautiful of all Scotland's lochs, and celebrated for its trout-fishing. Strangely, although no one would associate Loch Maree with industry, on its north shore, at Letterewe, iron used to be smelted for cannon, using charcoal from the ample surrounding woodlands. Loch Maree seems once to have been a sea-loch, though there is now a narrow intervening neck traversed by the short River Ewe separating it from Loch Ewe. It is interesting to note that the little village

(Left) STORM-CLOUDS over Alligin, Upper Loch Torridon, Wester Ross. (Below) BEALACH NAM BO, or Pass of the Cattle, on the Applecross Peninsula, Wester Ross, looking eastwards across Loch Kishorn to the mountains of Cannich and Affrick. This famous route, the only road to Applecross, with its fierce gradients and hairpin bends, is perhaps the most exciting Alpine road in Great Britain, rising over 2,000 feet in less than 5 miles.

of Kinlochewe is not at the head of Loch Ewe, but twelve miles away at the head of Loch Maree. To the south of Gairloch is the most attractive coastal area of Badachro and Shieldaig, Port Henderson and strangely named Opinaan, reaching to the fine sands of Red Point, all backed by the splendid prospect of the hills of Flowerdale Forest—a country of superlatives.

This brings us to Torridon, an area famous for giving the name to one of the most ancient geological formations in the world, Torridonian Sandstone. The mountains flanking Torridon's sea-loch on the north are most individual in character and unforgettable in their proud beauty—Ben Alligin, Ben Dearg, Liathach and Ben Eighe. 10,000 acres of the pine and birch clad slopes of the last constitute a National Nature Reserve, rich in wild life, where the eagle the wild-cat and deer may be hopefully looked for if not always seen. These Torridon peaks are unique in the stepped formation of their steep and rocky sides, and their tops are strikingly streaked with white quartzite. Remotely situated along the north shore of Outer Loch Torridon is the extraordinarily-placed little township of Diabaig, enclosed within a steep horseshoe of hillsides and cliffs, now reachable by an adventurous road which had to be well fought for.

Another road which took a deal of winning is now open on the south side of the loch—for formerly there was no through road south from here. This Balgy Gap, as it was called, has now been closed and it is possible to motor right down to Strome Ferry and, providing the ferry is running, to Kyle of Lochalsh. And a most excellent scenic route it makes. Shieldaig—not to be confused with the smaller Shieldaig near Gairloch—is a splendidly placed fishing and crofting village at an inlet between Outer and Upper Loch Torridon, and from here it is possible for the determined walker to tramp round the roadless Applecross peninsula to the township of that name which faces across the Inner Sound to Raasay and Skye. Cars desiring to reach Applecross must surmount the tremendous and daunting Bealach nam Bo, the Pass of the Cattle, which strikes off the Shieldaig road at Loch Kishorn, and with its soaring gradients, up to one-in-four, its hairpin bends and breathtaking prospects of one kind or another, rising over 2,000 feet in six miles, is probably the most challenging stretch of road in Britain—but a challenge well worth accepting.

We are now in the area of Loch Carron, where are the

(Left) PLOCKTON, Wester Ross, a delightful village on an inlet of the sea-loch of Carron, near Kyle of Lochalsh, a favourite anchorage for yachtsmen. (Below) FROM THE NEW SHIELDAIG-TORRIDON ROAD, which closed the 'Balgy Gap', looking across to the famous Torridon Mountains. The forests of Scots pine are notable.

pleasant villages of Lochcarron itself, sometimes prosaically called Jeantown, and the even less magnetically-named fishing haven of Slumbay, with the long Glen Carron stretching north by east, by attractive Achnashellach all the way to the lonely and distinctly bleak railway outpost of Achnasheen, where passengers for Gairloch and the north-west must alight—indeed the most north-westerly point reached by the railway in Scotland. Incidentally, should storm or other trouble close the Strome Ferry across the narrows of Loch Carron, the south-bound motorist has no option but to drive north all the way to Achnasheen, then right across the roof of the country to Inverness itself, and back down the Great Glen to Glen Moriston, through this to Glen Shiel in Kintail, and so by Loch Duich and Dornie and Balmacara back to South Strome, a distance of 157 miles, in order to circumnavigate half a mile of water. There have long been agonised agitations to bridge or otherwise ameliorate this crazy situation, and a new road is now to be built round the head of Loch Carron.

Near South Strome is the delightful village of Plockton, a sanctuary for yachtsmen, artists and indeed all who appreciate natural beauty, peace and unspoiled Community living. Less well-known, but also attractive, is the village of Duirinish nearby.

Kyle of Lochalsh is the railway terminal and ferry port for Skye, indeed the largest place north of Fort William on the mainland west, with 1,650 people. It is a busy little port in a fine situation, and the shopping centre for a great area—although centre is perhaps a misnomer in the geographical circumstances.

We are now in the famous district of Kintail, headquarters of the great Clan Kenneth, or MacKenzie, a country renowned for its scenery in a land where practically every scene is magnificent. Lochalsh, separated from Skye only by the narrows of Kyle Rhea opens east-

(Below) KINTAIL, Wester Ross, with Loch Duich, and the topmost tip of Eilean Donan Castle just visible, seen from above the road to Kyle and Skye. Heart of the Mackenzie country, now National Trust property. (Right) THE FAMED FIVE SISTERS OF KINTAIL, seen from the Mam Ratagan Pass to Glenelg. Glen Shiel enters on the right.

wards into lovely Loch Duich, with the splendidly sited Eilean Donan Castle—surely one of the most photographed buildings in the world—seat of the MacRaes, hereditary standard-bearers of Clan Kenneth, standing guard on its rock at the mouth. The Five Sisters of Kintail, a handsome group of pointed mountains at the head of Loch Duich, flanking Glen Shiel, are as deservedly photogenic, and here was fought, in 1719, the Battle of Glenshiel, an indeterminate skirmish, between the Risings of 1715 and 1745, wherein the Jacobites were aided, not very effectively, by a Spanish contingent from ships in Loch Duich. One of the Five Sisters is still named Sgurr nan Spainteach, the Point of the Spaniards, in memory. Dr. Johnson, in his tour of the Hebrides, was much impressed with the scenery of Glen Shiel—as well he might be—and a boulder is still pointed out as Clach Johnson, where he rested.

To the south of Kintail the steeply rising pass of Mam Ratagan carries a cul-de-sac road, 1,116 feet over into the area of Glen Elg, with its picturesque village on the shore of the Sound of Sleat, where the currents are fierce and there is a summer-time ferry over to South Skye. By this extraordinary route came the great droves of Highland cattle from Skye to the ancient trysts or fairs at Falkirk on the Forth. A small glen, Glen Beg, strikes eastwards from here, a pleasant green place notable for waterfalls and the two fine Pictish brochs, or round towers.

Below Kintail are the great empty tracts of Knoydart, to all intents roadless and accessible only by boat. This is a vast territory to be all in private hands, a deer forest, formerly known as the Rough Bounds and the home country of the MacDonnells of Glengarry, a branch of the great Clan Donald. It lies around the long sea-lochs of Hourn and Nevis—Hell and Heaven—on the shores of the latter standing Inverie, the only village, where is the mansionhouse of this vast estate. The area covers roughly

(Left) RAIL VIADUCT AT GLENFINNAN, on the scenic route from Fort William to Mallaig. (Below) THE SILVER SANDS OF MORAR. This coastline, with its cockle-shell sands, skerries, islets and magnificent views of Eigg, Rum and Muck, is one of the most beautiful in the land. The Ardnamurchan Peninsula in the background.

eighty-five square miles, and must be one of the least populated on the mainland—although the clansmen dwelt here once in large numbers. The scenery is grand rather than beautiful, in the main, and the mountains of Sgurr na Ciche and Ladhar Beinn, or Larven, very fine. A road of sorts connects little, isolated Arnisdale on the north side of dark Loch Hourn with Glenelg; and Kinlochhourn, at the head, is reachable by the determined from the Glen Garry road that passes the hydro-electric project of Loch Quoich.

Morar, next to the south, and the ancient territory of another branch of Clan Donald, Clanranald, is very different—an open, fair and lovely place of low green hills and promontories, with some of the finest beaches and coves in all Scotland, of white Hebridean sand, and with glorious views to the Inner Isles, accessible by both the railway and the greatly improved road from Fort William and Glenfinnan—the road to the isles indeed, by Ailort and by Morar to the sea, ending at the pier at Mallaig.

Morar is a holiday-maker's paradise, although in some danger of being spoiled by that very fact, as the caravans proliferate along the delightful coastline from Arisaig, by Back of Keppoch and Camusdarrach to Morar itself. Here surely the shortest river in all the land, the Morar River, spills in a half-mile cascade out of long Loch Morar into salt water, now tamed to turn a hydro-electric turbine—for Morar is a fresh-water loch, and said to be the deepest of any water in all Europe, going down to over 1,000 feet; it is well beyond Rockall, over 300 miles out into the Atlantic, before even the sea-bed reaches such a depth. On an island in the loch, the famous and elusive Lord Lovat of the '45 was eventually captured, humiliatingly, hiding in a hollow tree, and taken to London and execution. At the head of the loch is a wild and picturesque mountain country, through which very rough tracks give access to Arkaig and Lochaber.

All this country is linked with Prince Charlie. It was at Mallaigbeg, at the mouth of Loch Nevis, that he landed on the mainland after his Hebridean wanderings in 1746, before he finally embarked for France at Loch nam Uamh near Arisaig—where he had also landed in 1745, to raise his standard some way to the east, at Glenfinnan. Modern Mallaig is a thriving fishing port, where the steamers leave for the isles, handsomely set but not beautiful in itself, where road and railway end. It is an enlivening experience to watch the fishing-fleet come into

CY.65
CY.65
CY.44

(Left) BUSY FISHING PORT OF MALLAIG, where the road ends beyond Morar. At Mallaigbeg, round the headland, Prince Charles Edward landed from his Hebridean wanderings after Culloden. (Below) PRINCE CHARLIE'S MONUMENT AT GLENFINNAN, where he raised his standard at the start of the ill-fated Rising of 1745. Ben Nevis in the background.

Mallaig for the week-end, and see the bustle of fish-unloading and marketing prior to being sent south by road or rail.

Loch nam Uamh, meaning the loch of the caves—in one of which Prince Charlie sheltered—is island-dotted and most picturesque. This Arisaig area where the delectable road reaches the sea, after coming by Loch Eil and Loch Ailort, is richly sub-tropical in its vegetation, and the banked rhododendrons through which the road passes for miles are magnificent in late spring.

Moidart, the land south of Morar, used to be almost as inaccessible as was Knoydart to the north. But recently this has been to some extent altered by the opening of over twelve miles of completely new road—the largest new road to be constructed in the Highlands for over 150 years—linking Loch Ailort in the north with Lochmoidart and Acharacle in the south. This will of course make a great difference to the area—but even so it can hardly do much to open up the interior of Moidart, since it follows the coastline most of the way. And a splendid coastline it is, by the sheer rocky shores of Ailort, under the high regard of Roshven, 2,876 feet, by Glenuig Bay, to turn south and cut the corner of the evocatively-named peninsula of Samalaman and Smearisary, to reach the narrow North Channel of Loch Moidart opposite wooded Eilean Shona, and so to the existing road at Kinlochmoidart. Not only does this make a wonderful scenic highway, with fine views seawards to the Hebrides, but it makes the Sunart-Acharacle road from Ardgour no longer a dead-end, so that a truly lovely round trip may be made from the Fort William area, something that has long been required.

Slantwise up through the lonely centre of Moidart, from Acharacle, strikes the eighteen-mile long Loch Shiel, a fresh-water loch of great beauty beside which no roads run, so that a trip up it by boat is a rewarding experience. At its head is Glenfinnan, where a monument marks the spot where the West Highland clans assembled and Charles Edward raised his standard for the ill-fated last Jacobite Rising. Acharacle itself is an anglers' resort and a good centre for the Sunart, Ardnamurchan and Moidart area, with hotels. Nearby is the delightful little series of sandy coves at Ardtoe, and to the north, in the narrows of Loch Moidart, the finely situated ruined Castle Tioram on its islanded rock, the former dramatic fortress of Clanranald.

The great peninsula of Ardnamurchan has already been

(Below) EVENING AT INVERARAY, on Loch Fyne, Argyll. This is the Campbell 'capital', a delightful little town of mainly late eighteenth century architecture, with much dignity. (Right) HUGE NEW PULP MILL AT ANNAT, at the mouth of Loch Eil, with Fort William in the middle distance, and Ben Nevis, highest mountain in Britain behind. This area has become the most highly developed in the West Highlands.

remarked on. It is an individual and lovely place by itself, almost an island, with its base at attractive Salen on Loch Sunart. Mingary Castle, out near its 'capital' of Kilchoan, was the fortalice of its ancient lords, the MacIans of Ardnamurchan, part of the great Clan Donald Federation, who played a vivid role in the eventful history of the Lordship of the Isles. Ardnamurchan should not be missed —the more so that in visiting it it will be necessary to follow the lovely and winding shores of the very long sea-loch of Sunart, with its attractive little communities of Glen Borrodale, Salen and Strontian.

To the south of the loch is the great hill area of Morvern, about 150 square miles of rough and almost empty territory, facing across the Sound of Mull, and again in the main more remote than most of the Hebridean islands. A road does cross this, adventurously, from the head of Sunart down to the little silica-sand port of Lochaline, where the steamers from Oban call on their way to Tobermory. The road then winds along the coast westwards, by Fiunary, to finish in a dead-end facing Ardnamurchan and the Western Sea once more.

Ardgour, east of Sunart, after all this wildness, is comparatively gentle and populous, facing across Loch Linnhe to Lochaber, Appin and Lismore. A car-ferry at the Corran Narrows takes travellers across conveniently to the main north-south highway between Ballachulish and Fort William; but for those who are in no hurry and enjoy scenery, it is possible to carry on right round Ardgour and by the shores of Loch Eil and the Cameron country, and so to Fort William by Corpach and Banavie.

We are now in Lochaber, a populous and dynamic area, and the site of much industrial development centred round Fort William. It is an area that has always been important in the history of Scotland, controlling the western end of the Great Glen, and in a position to cut off the north-west Highlands from the south. Fort William is magnificently placed, where Loch Eil joins Loch Linnhe, under the frowning bulk of mighty Ben Nevis, the highest mountain in Britain—but from the town itself this is hardly apparent. Indeed, it is a rather disappointing place to look at—though seen from across the loch it is quite different. Its long, narrow, traffic-filled main street is a famous bottleneck—but an equally famous shopping-centre. There is a great feeling of life and bustle about this fast-growing town, untypical of the Highland West.

Industry has long been established here, of course. There are distilleries, and the aluminium works with their early hydro-electric development—indeed Fort William was lit by electricity as early as 1896. It is also the southern end of the great Caledonian Canal, a steamer port and rail junction. But the most exciting forward step has been the siting at Corpach nearby of the huge new pulp-mill, the first in Britain, where the produce of the enormous Highland forestry schemes will come to be rendered into paper

THE PAP OF GLENCOE, Argyll. Evening on Loch Leven, from the Inverness-shire side. Nearby, a surprise to many visitors, are the big aluminium works at Kinlochleven, using hydro-electric power from the Moor of Rannoch catchment.

products. This is a vast conception, and must inevitably be of great advantage to a very large area. All roads will increasingly lead to Fort William.

The town has had a strange diversity of names since Cromwell's General Monk founded a fort here, at Inverlochy in 1655. General Mackay replaced it by a larger fort in 1690, and changed the name to Fort William, after his master, William of Orange. But the town itself was called Gordonsburgh, because it was built on Gordon land, and this was changed to Maryburgh, after King William's consort. Like Stirling, this was a great strategic area for battles. Of the many fought here, Montrose's notable victory of Inverlochy, after forced marches through the Lochaber mountains, is the most famous.

Once over Ballachulish Ferry across the mouth of another Loch Leven—where a bridge ought to have been built long since—the road south splits left and right. Left takes us eastwards along the shores of the loch, with the conical Pap of Glencoe ahead, to turn southwards into the yawning mouth of that great and awesome valley, grand in its scenery, notable for its climbing—and nowadays its ski-ing—and terrible in its history. Thereafter the road leads on across the vast desolation of the Moor of Rannoch.

Turning right at Ballachulish brings us into Appin, a Stewart area flanking the south shores of Loch Linnhe, under towering peaks. No roads lead inland. We pass Duror, where in 1752 was committed the famous, political Appin Murder, for which James Stewart, of nearby Acharn, was unjustly hanged—a relic of the clan animosities following the Jacobite troubles. Port Appin itself is the centre of quite a populous district, from which a ferry gives access to the ten-mile long green and fertile island of Lismore—which means the great garden—splendidly situated where Loch Linnhe opens into the Firth of Lorne and the Sound of Mull; here the views and the sunsets are exceptional. Lismore was formerly the seat of the bishopric of Argyll, and had its own tiny cathedral, now the parish church. Seen from the main road, near Port Appin, is Castle Stalker, picturesque fortalice of the Appin Stewarts on its rock in the bay, now being restored.

The long sea-loch of Creran separates Appin from Benderloch and although the railway used to bridge it, the road does not, entailing a lengthy though very scenic circular drive. Happily the railway-bridge over the narrows of the next sea-loch, Etive, does now carry the road, at Connel Ferry. Loch Etive's upper reaches are magnificent,

(Left) OBAN, Argyll, and its R.C. cathedral, from McCaig's Folly, above the town. The island of Kerrera is on the left, and across the Firth of Lorne is Lismore and the hills of Morvern. (Below) THE NEW CRUACHAN DAM, high above the Pass of Brander and Loch Awe. Deep underground in the heart of the mountain is the mighty pump storage station, a wonder of modern engineering.

probing towards Glencoe and the Moor of Rannoch, and are steeped in the lore of early Celtic Scotland.

Now we are into Lorne, the northern part of Argyll, mixed MacDougall and Campbell country, where again the road splits. To the east a branch follows Loch Etive-side to Taynuilt—from where Robert Burns' ancestors are thought to have come—and then turns into the stark mouth of the narrow Pass of Brander, right under the bulk of Ben Cruachan, Argyll's greatest and multi-peaked mountain from which Clan Campbell takes its war-cry. Here is the great Cruachan hydro-electric scheme, with its high-level reservoir scooped dramatically up in a corrie of the mountain, its shaft boring straight down through the living rock to the vast turbine-house hollowed out of the heart of Cruachan itself, to work a pump-storage generating system that is one of the wonders of modern civil engineering. Beyond, the pass opens out to twenty-three mile long Loch Awe, with the impressive ruined Campbell castle of Kilchurn at its head. Thereafter is the district of Glenorchy, with attractive Dalmally as its centre, a fine base for exploring the Campbell country.

Back at Connel Ferry the right-hand road leads due south five miles to Oban, the largest town on the west side of Scotland north of the Clyde estuary, with 6,700 people. It is a delightfully situated place on an inlet of the Firth of Lorne, sheltered behind the picturesque island of Kerrera, a place full of varied attractions and character, deservedly famous as a holiday resort. But it is also a highly important port for the Inner Hebrides and south-west Highlands, a railway terminal and the focal point of a well-populated farming and crofting country. It is a great place for hotels, boat-trips to the isles, golf, castles—Dunollie, Dunstaff-

(Left) THE BRIDGE OVER THE ATLANTIC. The road to Easdale, Argyll, crosses the narrow sound here, to the island of Seil. The higher island in the background is Luing, becoming famous for its new breed of cattle. (Below) GALLANACH, south of Oban, on the Sound of Kerrera.

nage, Gylen, Barcaldine, Carnasserie, Kilmartin, Duntrune and others are all reachable from here—and of course sandy bays and fine walks, while the sheltered waters of the bay and sounds are a yachtsman's paradise. Oban—*ob-ban*, the white or fair land-locked bay—is still locally called *The* Oban, and correctly of course. It may not have played so large a part in national history as some other localities, despite all its castles, but its off-shore island of Kerrera makes up for it. Here Alexander the Second died of a fever when assembling an expedition against the Hebrides in 1249; and fourteen years later King Haakon of Norway held a meeting of island chiefs here prior to his disastrous defeat at Largs further south.

The territory south of Oban is very attractive and comparatively populous, with strong links with the early Celtic Church—as the names of Kilmorie, Kilbryde, Kilninver, Kilmelford, Kilchrenan and Kilmartin indicate, *kil* meaning the cell or religious centre of one or other of the missionary saints. There are a series of islands here, some quite large—Seil, Torsay, Luing and Shona—but so close to the mainland that they are scarcely to be reckoned as Hebridean; indeed Seil is reached by a fine, single-arched bridge, known as 'The Bridge over the Atlantic', where the sound is only fifty or sixty yards wide and looks like a river—although the tides surge through it at times with great velocity. Slate used to be worked on these islands, but now their accessibility makes them ever more favoured by holiday-makers. The island of Luing is now notable for a new breed of cattle developed by an enterprising farming family there.

The Craignish peninsula, further south, has a delightful six-mile road out to its point, from which splendid Hebridean views may be obtained. Thereafter the main highway climbs abruptly inland through a high pass amongst the

rocky green hills that throng the head—not the foot, be it noted—of Loch Awe and so down, past dramatically sited Carnasserie Castle, to the flat and fertile lands around the head of Loch Crinan, old indeed in Scotland's story. For this is the territory of Dalriada, and the capital of the first Kings of the Scots, Dunadd, is represented by a fort-crowned rock rising out of the level flood-plain. Here traditionally first came the Stone of Destiny, from Ireland—whence also of course came the Scots—before being moved to the next capital of Dunstaffnage, nearer Oban, and thence to Scone, on the union of the Scots and the Picts, to form Scotland. The little village of Kilmartin is pleasingly situated, with notable Celtic sculptures in the kirkyard.

Nearby is the north end of the Crinan Canal, a short but important waterway which allows small craft to sail by sheltered lochs and sounds all the way from the Clyde to the Inner Hebrides, instead of having to brave the dangers and long haul of rounding the Mull of Kintyre. It is here that that great and lengthy peninsula has its roots, almost cut off from the mainland by Loch Fyne. It thrusts south by west for almost sixty miles, and at its end is only a dozen miles from the Northern Irish coast. Not unnaturally Kintyre was accepted as part of the Hebrides, and under the dominion of the Lords of the Isles. At its northern end is the almost detached area known as Knapdale, richly wooded and highly scenic, penetrated by Loch Sween and cradling the delightful village of Tayvallich with its sheltered anchorage.

Knapdale is joined to Kintyre proper only by the

(Left) DUNSTAFFNAGE CASTLE, near Oban, ancient seat of early kings—indeed once the capital of the Scots, where the Stone of Destiny was taken, from Dunadd farther south. Later a Campbell stronghold. (Below) TARBERT, LOCH FYNE, with West Loch Tarbert and the Isle of Gigha beyond. This cuts off the peninsula of Kintyre. Here Bruce built a castle, and other monarchs used it in their warfare with the Lords of the Isles.

narrow isthmus of another Tarbert, a highly strategic spot where Bruce built a castle, and which James IV later used as base for his successful campaign to bring the Lordship of the Isles to order. Soon after Tarbert the road splits, one arm going down either side of the long, long peninsula, both joining again, about forty miles on, at Campbeltown. This is an extraordinarily placed royal burgh of nearly 6,500 people, a fishing-port and holiday resort, with distilleries and an airport at Machrihanish, six miles to the west—not what might be expected to be found in so out-of-the-way a position. But it must be remembered that Campbeltown is comparatively accessible from Glasgow, by sea, and a favoured sail it makes. It is still ten miles more to the foot of the peninsula, at Southend, where Columba is said first to have set foot on Scottish soil, another popular resort of Glasgow folk. The long stretches of Kintyre between Tarbert and this south end hold their own attractions on both sides, and many are the old Campbell lairdships, with their castles and mansions, dotted thereon.

Fyne is, I suppose, quite the longest sea-loch in all Scotland, being over forty miles long, and reaching from the Sound of Bute deep into Argyllshire. Inveraray, the Campbell capital, is its most renowned community, but this is near its head, and both Lochgilphead and Ardrishaig, on the small side-loch of Gilp, are larger, the former being a seat of local government and the latter the little steamer port at the southern end of the Crinan Canal. Inveraray itself is a most handsome little royal burgh, of whitewashed buildings largely of late eighteenth and early

SHETLAND FERRY. A common scene in the islands, when the mail-steamer arrives, and stock, goods and post—also passengers—are transferred to or from the shore by tender.

nineteenth century construction, dignified in character as befits its history and the headquarters of the most consistently powerful—if by no means most popular—clan in Scotland. The Duke of Argyll's castle, nearby in a park that was formerly thirty miles in circumference, is not ancient, but pleasantly situated and a great attraction for visitors. Not far away, however, on a little promontory in the loch, is a much more authentic though restored example of the true Scottish castle—Dunderave.

The area of Argyll south of Loch Fyne is called Cowal, a land of modest mountains penetrated by many sea-lochs from the south, which make magnificent sheltered sailing for yachtsmen since they all open off the Firth of Clyde—Ridden, Striven, Holy Loch, Long and Gare Loch—and enclosing one large freshwater loch of Eck. This extensive district of some 500 square miles is fairly well served with roads, considering its highly broken-up state—the main through highway being famous for its high pass on the watershed below the Arrochar Alps, Rest and be Thankful. But its water communications are almost more important, since these link it speedily with Glasgow and the Clyde basin. Scattered over it are many little resorts and steamer piers, the innumerable great mansions of the former Clyde nabobs, and the one large town of Dunoon. This famous holiday place for Glasgow citizens has nearly 10,000 of population. Its delights are necessarily broadly-based, but it is enchantingly situated and with fine vistas. Here is held each August the Cowal Highland Gathering, a great and spirited social event; and in July the Clyde Yachting Fortnight is important, based on the nearby village of Hunter's Quay. With Kirn and Innellan close at hand, this corner of Cowal is highly developed indeed. Elsewhere the resorts of Kilmun, on the Holy Loch; Lochgoilhead on that loch; Arrochar, Cove and Kilcreggan on Loch Long; Garelochhead and Rhu on the Gare Loch; and Strachur on Loch Fyne itself, with the Kyles of Bute villages of Tighnabruaich and Colintraive, to name but a few, all cater handsomely for the holiday needs of Scotland's industrial West. Few great urban areas can have such a glorious hinterland for their recreation as have Glasgow and the Clyde.

But all here is not geared to recreation. These Cowal lochs are important in many aspects of the nation's life. Best-known probably is the Polaris base on the Holy Loch. Loch Goil is also used by the Navy. At Faslane, on Gare Loch, is a great ship-breaking yard, where many a

SILVER SANDS OF LUSKENTYRE, OUTER HEBRIDES. In South Harris, near Tarbert. These brilliant white strands, so common in the North-West, are formed from ground-down cockle-shells, and are a great factor in colour-staining the clear waters of this seaboard.

famous vessel has finally cast anchor. And on Loch Long is the Finnart Ocean Oil Terminal, where the big tankers disgorge their cargoes, to be pumped through the pipeline to Grangemouth's refineries.

Only the narrow but picturesque channels known as the Kyles separate Cowal from the island of Bute, fifty square miles, a county of its own and a celebrated place in history as the main seat of the Lord High Stewards of Scotland, who duly became the Stewart kings. Rothesay on its splendid bay, renowned in song:

'The great black hills, like sleepin' kings
Sit grand roun' Rothesay Bay.'

being their principal castle and still giving the heir to the throne his senior Scottish title of Duke of Rothesay. The castle, a restored ruin, is still there—though strangely it has not a particularly imposing nor strongly-sited appearance. It was captured and retaken times without number, by the Norsemen, the Islesmen, the English, and the Covenanters; in it died of a broken heart Robert III after the murder of his eldest son, David, Duke of Rothesay, and the capture by the English of his other son, later James I; Oliver Cromwell partly destroyed it. For long it has been in the hereditary keepership of another branch of the Stewart family, the Crichton-Stuarts, whose head is the Marquis of Bute, still the main landowner. Rothesay town is a royal burgh of 7,000 inhabitants, and as famous a holiday resort as Dunoon. Port Bannatyne, Ascog and Kilchattan are small resorts. There are many ruined chapels on Bute, and the two castles of Kames and Wester Kames are notable.

Buteshire consists of six other islands—Arran, Big and Little Cumbrae, Holy Isle, Pladda and Inchmarnock. Arran, comprising 165 square miles, is three times the size of the rest put together. In appearance it is one of the noblest islands of all Scotland, with a great central range of mountains crowned by shapely Goat Fell (2,866 feet), and dominating all the Firth of Clyde. Although so near to Glasgow Arran is truly Highland and Hebridean in most of its character, and a favourite haunt both of artistic residents and discriminating visitors. It is readily accessible by steamer from the mainland. A perimeter road fifty-six miles long circles the island, and two cut across it, one in the centre known as the String Road, and one more difficult to the south, through Glen Scorrodale. The principal centres are Brodick, the steamer port, with its

(Left) BRODICK CASTLE, ISLE OF ARRAN, now a National Trust property. Arran is a spectacular holiday island, now suffering from the draining away of young people. (Right) CLOUD SEA FILLING THE TROUGH OF LOCH LOMOND, Ben Lomond standing out like an island on the left. Climbers on Ben Dubh Chraig, Argyll.

fine castle nearby, now National Trust property and a former seat of the Dukes of Hamilton; Lamlash, with fine bathing, and the spectacular Holy Isle rising abruptly in its splendid sheltered bay; Whiting Bay, with Kingscross Point nearby where Bruce left for his final desperate campaign to free Scotland; Blackwaterfoot, facing west across Kilbrannan Sound; Lochranza on its attractive bay with its ruined castle; Sannox, at the mouth of its fine glen into the high hills; and Corrie, under Goat Fell.

The Cumbraes, Great and Small are of course not in the least Highland or Hebridean in character, but they are part of Bute county, though nearer to the Ayrshire coast. Big Cumbrae comprises some 3,000 acres of green low hills and mild cliffs above flat beaches, with some good fertile farmland. The island was once a possession of the Stewarts and famous for a special royal strain of hawks bred there. Millport is quite an ambitious little town for so small an island, with 1,300 of population, good sands, bathing and golf. Oddly enough it has a modern Collegiate church which was in 1876 consecrated as the Episcopal Cathedral of Argyll and the Isles—a somewhat off-centre establishment, undoubtedly. Also at this south end is the Marine Biological Station. Little Cumbrae lies less than two miles to the south-west, and has only 700 acres with little population. It had the second-earliest lighthouse in all Scotland, and a castle on a tiny off-shore isle.

Back on the mainland, to the east of Cowal lies the final strip of West Highland territory—which by its situation as well as its renown in song and story, is probably the best-known of all. This is the area from Strathfillan and Crianlarich southwards, which encloses the lovely reaches of long Loch Lomond. This indeed is as much as many visitors to Scotland ever see of the Highland West—which is of course a pity, for it is hackneyed, crowded at times and in places, and untypical. Yet much better that the hurried traveller should see the Bonnie Banks of Loch Lomond than nothing at all of the Highlands, for nothing can obliterate its beauty, island-dotted, mountain-girt and queened over by the mighty Ben Lomond. The loch is twenty-four miles long, and the twisting, coiling road up its west side, though a delight for the sight-seeing visitor with lots of time, can be a frustration indeed for the urgent traveller heading northwards—for this is the main north-west road from Glasgow. A new highway is mooted. It is strange that there is no road up the east side—a provision which seems elementary, both for the tourist and the

(Left) LOCH LOMOND, Dunbartonshire. Although so well-known and much-visited, and only a few miles from Glasgow, Loch Lomond has a beauty nothing can spoil.

ordinary traveller; which brings about the extraordinary situation that only some fifteen miles from Glasgow there is a vast stretch of inaccessible mountain country reachable only by those prepared to clamber over rough steeply-sloping foothills. Though this may have its advantages, too.

At the foot of the loch, Balloch, an unlovely sprawl in a lovely setting, has seen 'development' run rife. There is a road to Balmaha and Rowardennan on the east side, which latterly is attractive, but which does not go any further. On the west the highway holds back from the loch-shore for some miles till past the Colquhoun chief's property of Rossdhu where it rejoins the waterside and thereafter continues all the way to Ardlui at the loch-head, by a scalloped shore of little bays, green headlands, wooded islands and entrancing vistas. At one more Tarbet, nineteen miles up, the road splits, the left fork to cross the narrow isthmus westwards to the head of Loch Long and salt-water—and so to Rest and Be Thankful and the long reaches of Loch Fyne. It was across this isthmus that Norse Magnus, King of Man, dragged his war-galleys in 1263 to aid his father-in-law King Haakon by creating enormous havoc in the inland Loch Lomond area of Lennox.

The Lomond-side road continues up past the great power-station at Inveruglas, where the Loch Sloy hydro-electric scheme turbines are housed. Directly across the loch, on the east side, is highly attractive Inversnaid, Rob Roy MacGregor's one-time lairdship, which may be reached by a scenically splendid road from Aberfoyle, or by boat across the water. The upper reaches of the loch penetrate close under that dramatic group of mountains, beloved of Glasgow climbers, Bens Vorlich, Vane, Ime and Arthur, often called the Arrocher Alps, and best seen from over on the Inversnaid side.

The Loch Lomond area, providing climbing, walking, sailing, bathing, fishing and scenic beauty, all within a few miles of Glasgow, is a very wonderful heritage—although its delights undoubtedly could be more effectively and attractively utilised. Even so, it is a notable gateway to the Highland West.

When we leave Balloch, southwards, into the Vale of Leven—that was once Levenax or Lennox—we have reached the Lowlands again.

Ahead lies Glasgow and the Clyde.

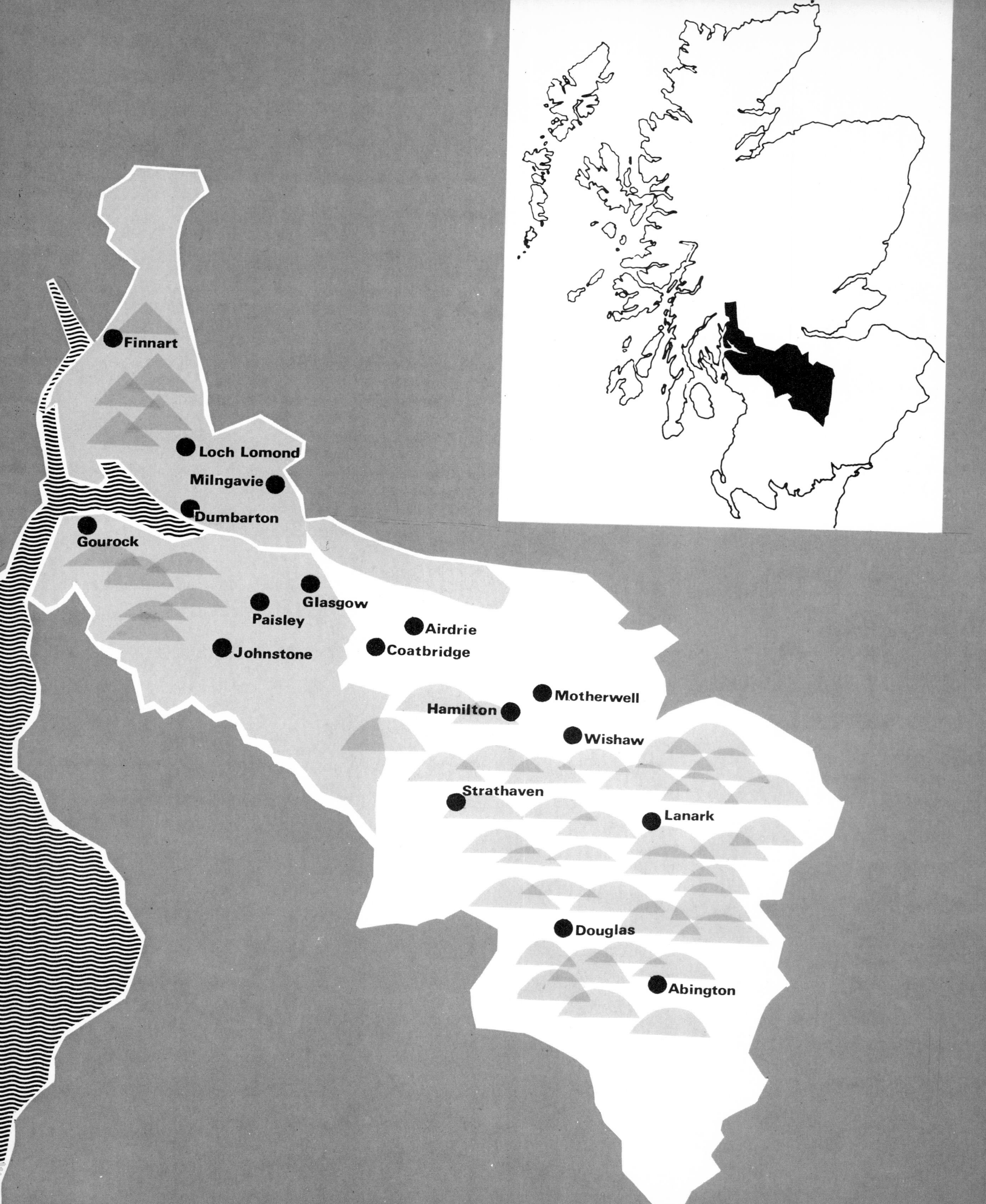

Finnart
Loch Lomond
Milngavie
Dumbarton
Gourock
Glasgow
Paisley
Johnstone
Airdrie
Coatbridge
Motherwell
Hamilton
Wishaw
Strathaven
Lanark
Douglas
Abington

CHAPTER 9

GLASGOW AND THE CLYDE

Scotland has a population of some five millions, and more than half of it is crammed into the Clyde basin, that wedge of low-lying land from Dumbarton on the north-west to Cumbernauld on the north-east, and Lanark on the south-east to Greenock on the south-west, with the city of Glasgow at its centre - perhaps 250 square miles, less than half the size of the Isle of Skye, and one of the most densely populated and industrialised areas on the face of the globe. A lot could be said about it all, reams have been written regarding its dirt and drabness, its undistinguished, endless sprawl, its teeming, unpolished and 'unrefined' people, and its labour troubles - for the Red Clydeside myth dies hard. But while there is truth in some of all this, such a general picture is not only inaccurate but quite false. Nobody who really knows Glasgow and the Clyde can fail to have a great affection and admiration for it and its warm-hearted people - which is not, for instance, 100 per cent true about Edinburgh. Inevitably the two great cities and their environs are compared - their own citizens indeed never cease to do so - and comparisons here are not only odious but quite inapplicable. It is as profitable to compare Glasgow with Edinburgh as a dynamic, shrewd, go-getting, youngish businessman of somewhat untidy appearance with a mature but still beautiful lady of title; although such can and often do make a most profitable match together.

DUMBARTON FROM ITS CASTLE ROCK. Where the Highlands reach the Lowlands again, and town and country meet. The River Leven, flowing out of Loch Lomond, joins the Clyde estuary. Behind, in the Vale of Leven, is Alexandria, bleaching and manufacturing town, and beyond are the mountains of Rob Roy's country, Ben Lomond dominant.

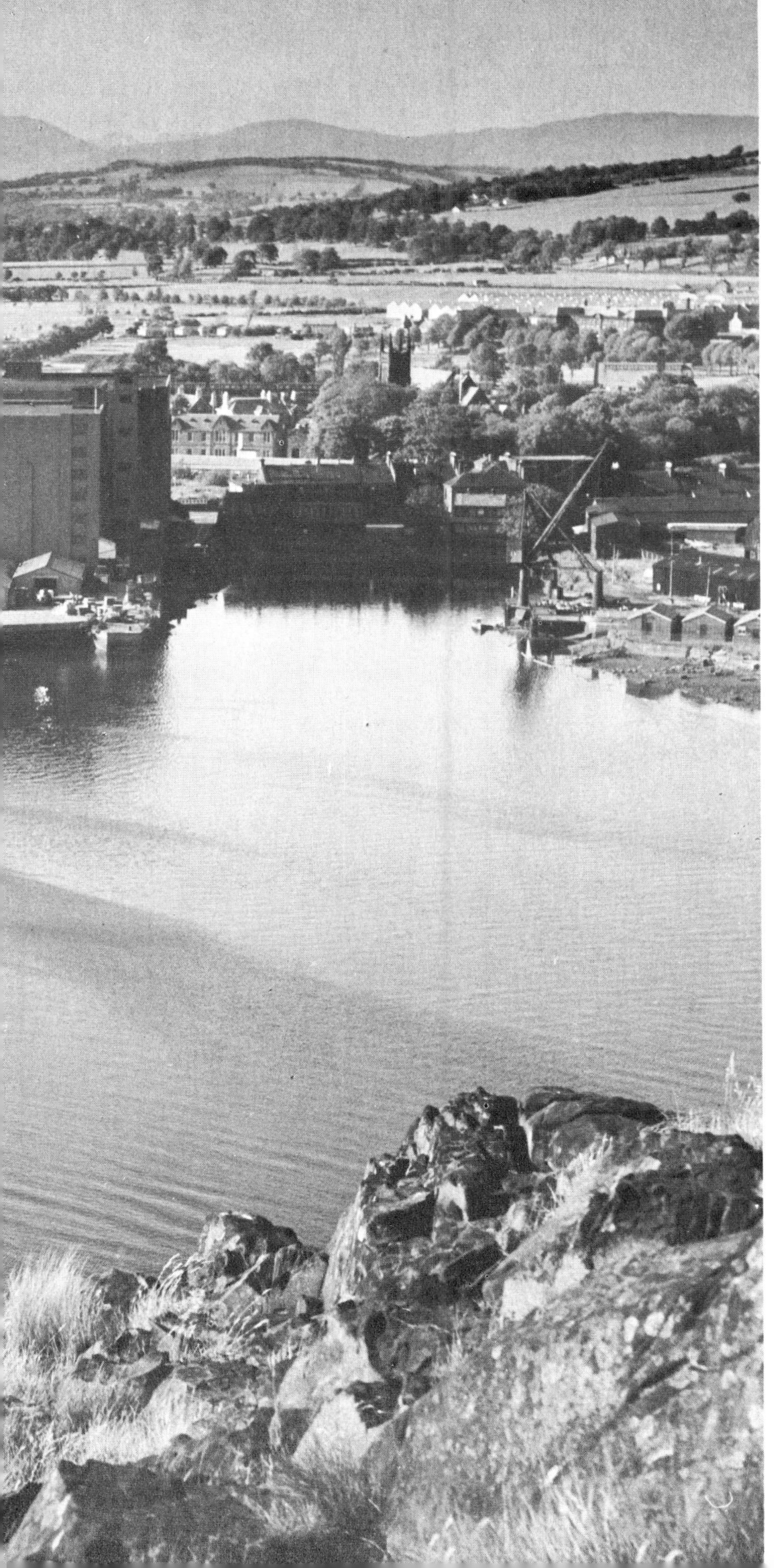

But it is well to remember that this area is not just Greater Glasgow. There are a host of other and highly individual communities all around, lesser places in relation to the city's millions but compared with the rest of Scotland large and important towns in their own right; places like Airdrie, Bearsden, Clydebank, Coatbridge, Dumbarton, Greenock, Hamilton, Lanark, Motherwell and Wishaw, Paisley, Port Glasgow, Renfrew and Rutherglen and many another, in no sense adjuncts, much less suburbs of Glasgow. Some of these burghs have populations as high as 70,000 and even 95,000 at Paisley, and so as large as Stirling, Perth and Inverness put together. And there are the completely new towns of East Kilbride and Cumbernauld, social-industrial experiments on a great scale.

To deal with Glasgow first, it is as well to recollect that as an important centre of population and commerce, the city is comparatively modern—new and brash, as age-old Edinburgh likes to suggest. It was Dumbarton that was the important place on the Clyde, because of its finely defensive castle-rock, throughout the Middle Ages. Glasgow, defensively unpromising, owed its origin and indeed existence to the Church, from the time of its semi-legendary founding by Saint Mungo or Kentigern, in the sixth century, right down to Reformation times, and its history was little more than the annals of its bishopric. At the end of the fifteenth century it was considered necessary, politically rather than ecclesiastically, to counter the enormous power and hegemony of the Archbishops of St. Andrews, Primates of Scotland; and Glasgow, which had just obtained the second university in Scotland, founded in 1450 by Bishop Turnbull, was the obvious see to raise up, to play York to Scotland's Canterbury, in 1488. But even so, Glasgow town remained little more, for some considerable time, than a bishop's burgh, a large ecclesiastical and salmon-fishing village where the Molendinar joined the Clyde, clinging to the skirts of the university and the great cathedral of St. Mungo—which still dominates the old part of the city. It is interesting to note that Glasgow arms and motto are still a tree, a salmon and an episcopal ring, with the legend LET GLASGOW FLOURISH BY THE PREACHING OF THE WORD—even though the last six words are frequently missed out!

It was not, in fact, until after the Union of the Parliaments in 1707, and the rise of the American trade, that Glasgow, facing the Atlantic to the north of Ireland, and with splendid harbour facilities, began to become really important as a trading community. The spectacular rise of the tobacco and sugar merchant princes of Glasgow is one of the romances of Scotland's commercial history, much antedating the jute nabobs of Dundee. Then the onset of the Industrial Revolution, and the development of the great coalfields of Lanarkshire, with the shipping and ship-building opportunities of the Clyde, did the rest. Glasgow grew at a phenomenal rate—and not unnaturally, she did not grow mellowly. So to Glasgow, as the Highland glens were being emptied by eviction, streamed the dispossessed clansmen; and across the North Channel, with the contemporary famines, streamed in vast numbers the hungry Catholic Irish, to fill the vacuum, as well as to create great problems which are still with the city—but also to help create that tingling vitality and vigour and humour so much a feature of the place.

It has by no means been all a success story. Largely because of the unlimited coal and the ship-building, Glasgow came to depend too greatly on the heavy industries of iron and steel—and in times of recession these are the first to feel the cold blast. Nowhere was worse hit during the lean years. If the workers of Glasgow led the way in vigorously seeking to change a system which jeopardised their livelihoods at the caprice of every economic wind that blew, it was only in keeping with their sturdy independence of character—the same character which makes the bulk of them the finest artisans and industrial craftsmen available.

Today Glasgow is surging ahead again, her industries greatly diversified, her initiative and restless energy driving her into every aspect of the new age. On all sides the industrial estates spring up and new factories arise, to manufacture electronics, computers, components, plastics, chemicals, synthetics, solvents, detergents, machine tools, adding and sewing machines and the like. These have not, however, replaced the old heavier industries, only complemented them. The great ironworks still thunder and clang, the blast-furnaces roar and glow, the shipyards resound to the rivetter's challenge, the dockland cranes creak and swing and ships' sirens wail. But all these are taking on a new look likewise, with modern methods—indeed modern products—as the huge steel strip-mills pour out the materials for car-bodies and domestic hardware, and the pressing-shops stamp them into the shapes of steel sinks, washing machines and refrigerator-casings

(Left) CLYDE-BUILT. John Brown's world renowned shipyard where some of the most famous vessels afloat have been constructed. The spread of Glasgow behind, and the Campsie Fells and Kilsyth Hills as back-cloth. (Right) ST. MUNGO'S CATHEDRAL, GLASGOW, the oldest part of which dates from 1197, though the tower and choir are of the thirteenth century. The vaulted crypt, Blackader's Aisle, is notable.

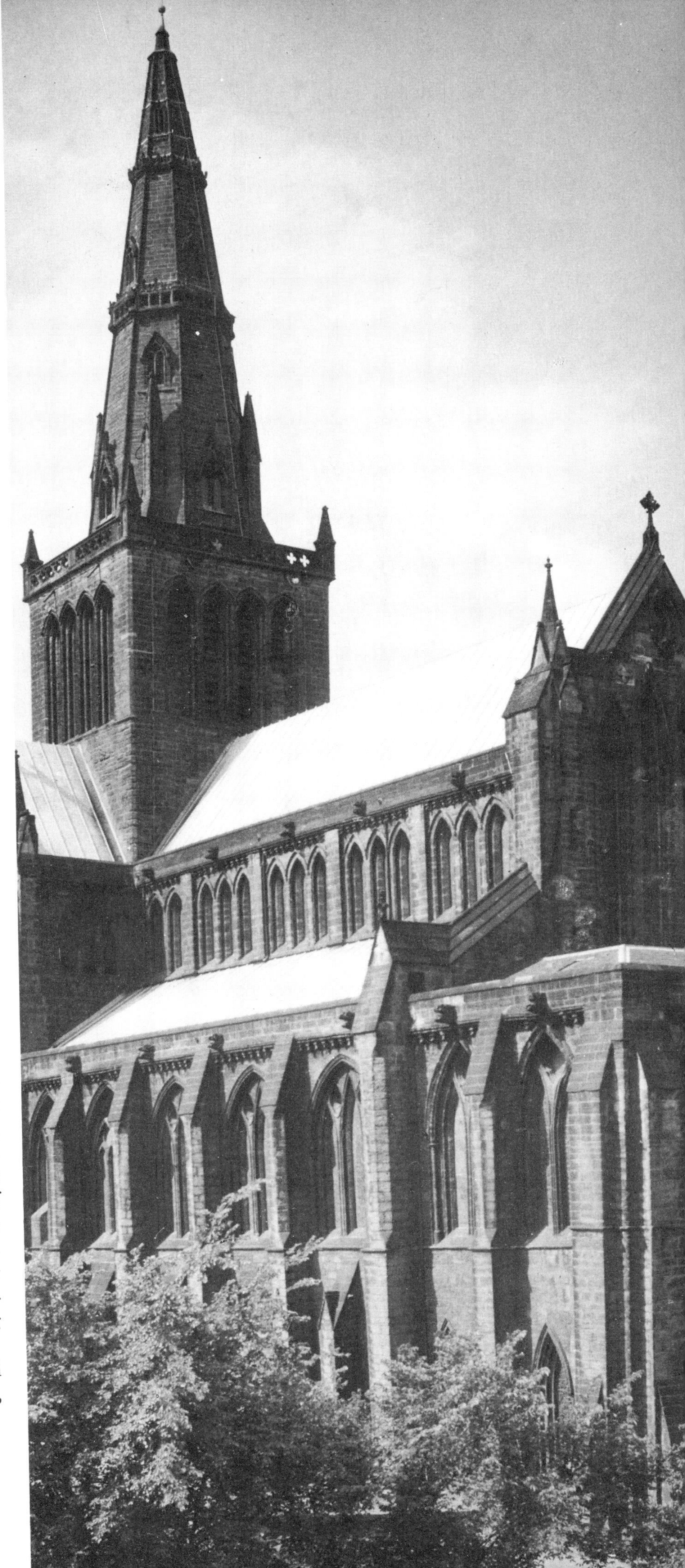

while the aero-engines jostle those of the ships. New projects, new techniques, new ideas, mergers, and experiments proliferate—and not only in processes and products. The heartening experiment in management-labour relations at Fairfields shipyard, and the slackening of rigid trade-union demarcation lines, could be a lead to the entire United Kingdom. From Hillington to Linwood, from Newhouse to Cardonald, from East Kilbride to Ravenscraig, industry watches and debates. Another great experiment on the shipbuilding front is John Brown's scheme to alter the course of the Clyde itself, to facilitate launchings, straighten the channel and gain space. This same firm pioneers further by building the new off-shore drilling-rigs for gas.

All the giant strides are not being taken on the industrial front, however. The municipality of Glasgow has undertaken the largest redevelopment programme, with no less than twenty-nine major urban areas redeveloped in two decades, to sweep away the slum detritus of the Victorian era at its most ruthless exploitation. Here are skyscrapers arising innumerable, with the tallest flats in all Europe. Here is the first decked industrial area to be designed for any British city. Here is Britain's newest airport, and first municipally-owned educational television system for schools. Glasgow aims to be a smoke-controlled area by 1970.

This has seldom been called a beautiful city, although Daniel Defoe did declare it to be 'the beautifullest little city in Europe.' There is, nevertheless, more fine building in Glasgow than is usually credited. The works of Charles Rennie Mackintosh are of especial merit. Of fine parks, too, there are many—and from many an otherwise drab area the distant views of the Campsie Fells and the Highland hills bring a lift to the heart.

As a business and professional city Glasgow's importance is sometimes overlooked—for here is centred enormous wealth, and it is the headquarters of huge banking, insurance, stockbroking and merchandising enterprises. Its Trades House is famous, with its incorporated guilds and deaconaries, second only to those of the City of London. It has now two universities, with Strathclyde additional to the ancient establishment on Gilmorehill. And colleges of art, technology, seamanship, and further education generally, with great new secondary and comprehensive schools, spring up all around with bewildering rapidity.

To glance even cursorily at all the thriving industrial towns which encircle Glasgow is quite impossible here,

(Left) TOWN CENTRE, EAST KILBRIDE NEW TOWN. This imaginative and ambitious project established a new concept in Scotland, with industry and its related housing given space and light and colour. (Below) RAVENSCRAIG. The huge Steel Strip Mill at Motherwell and Wishaw; showing through the shaven turf of the golf course fairway are the drainage lines between the riggs of age-old strip-cultivation.

but brief mention of some few must be made. Paisley is the largest of all, the fifth largest community in Scotland. It is an ancient town, set in the plain of the Cart Rivers only seven miles west of Glasgow, in Renfrewshire, and the greatest thread-manufacturing centre in the world, the headquarters of the famous firm of Coats. It has an Abbey Church of the fifteenth century, with a restored Commendator-Abbot's house alongside. Paisley shawls were famous—as was the political advice 'Keep your eye on Paisley!' Next in size comes Greenock, also in Renfrewshire, fifteen miles further west and near the great bend in the Clyde estuary, with offshore the well-known roadstead for shipping known as the Tail of the Bank. It is a port and ship-building centre and the birthplace of the great engineer James Watt. It is built on fairly steeply rising ground, terraced, and although scarcely beautiful in itself, its views across the Clyde to the Highland hills and the Kyles of Bute are memorable. This is the great sugar-refining town of Scotland, but there are numerous other industries, many of them connected with seafaring. Here is the dramatic Cross of Lorraine memorial to the Free French seamen who gave their lives in the Battle of the Atlantic, set on a viewpoint above the estuary.

Almost as large is Motherwell, in Lanarkshire, famous for its great Colville's steelworks. Probably no town in Scotland has grown quite so fast as this, for in 1841 its population was 726, a century ago it was 3,000, and today it is 73,483. Jerviston House, a late sixteenth century fortalice of the Baillie family, and the fifteenth-seventeenth century castellated pile of Dalziel, are worth visiting. Just across the wide haugh of Clyde from here is Hamilton, once the seat of great ducal power, with its palace and vast parks, now a manufacturing but still royal burgh. The fourth Hamilton Earl of Arran assisted in procuring Mary Queen of Scots' release from Loch Leven Castle, and it was to here that she fled, to shelter at a spot in the town still called the Queenzie Neuk, before the Battle of Langside not far away. Coatbridge, seven miles to the north, is another large ironworks town, in the midst of the Lanarkshire coalfield; with nearby Airdrie it once had no fewer than twenty-one collieries grouped around—yet it also had a theatre to seat 2,000, and its main monument, a twenty-foot high granite fountain, was erected in memory of a humble local poetess named Janet Hamilton.

I must restrict myself to mention of only two more of this great urban complex—Bearsden and Dumbarton, both

(Left) SAUCHIEHALL STREET, GLASGOW. The old, the not-so-old and the new. Glasgow did not have the chance to grow so gradually or so gracefully as Edinburgh. Its population is now well over a million. (Right) NEW TOWN OF CUMBERNAULD, where the 5,000th new house was opened recently. Commenced in 1958, in ten years its population reached 20,000, with jobs for over 4,000 provided.

in the latter's shire. The former is notable because it is so different from all the others. Although it has a population of over 18,000, it has only fairly recently, after considerable struggle, managed to shake off the county fetters and become a burgh, and so control its own local affairs. And it is no manufacturing town but a highly select residential area, a prosperous commuters' dormitory for Glasgow; yet with a strong, almost militant sense of individuality—a *rara avis* indeed. Dumbarton itself, of course, is as old as history. On its great rock, as early as 519, St. Modwena is said to have founded one of her seven Scottish churches, but its military possibilities soon substituted soldiers for priests, and right down the ages, to modern times, Dumbarton Castle has been a garrison and fort for the Clyde estuary area, commanding with its guns the river passage. Here, indeed, was the capital of the ancient kingdom of Strathclyde. Around the rock the royal burgh grew, where the River Leven, out of Loch Lomond, reached salt water. And here, only a stone's throw, as it were, from the mountains, grew up a busy port, shipbuilding and manufacturing town—probably the burgh with the longest pedigree in the West of Scotland, whatever Whithorn may say.

Two other places must have special consideration—the new towns of Cumbernauld and East Kilbride. Set up to deal with Glasgow's overspill of labour, they represent an ambitious and imaginative rise to a great challenge, settling large numbers of people in a hitherto underdeveloped area, with all—or at least most—of the facilities and amenities townsfolk should expect, with industries and trades to employ them, all brand new. Such projects, needless to say offer both enormous problems and enormous opportunities. With four such new towns developing, Scotland cannot be accused of being backward on this adventurous road.

Something of the dimensions of these new town projects may be gauged from a recent ceremony at Cumbernauld to open the 5,000th house built there since 1958. There is now a population of 20,000, and jobs for over 4,300 have been provided, with another 1,700 or so in prospect. The local development corporation is building standard factories for incoming firms to occupy, and completing 1,000 more houses each year. Forty-seven industrial companies have already established themselves here. Figures like these may rattle off glibly—but a little thought brings out the size of the effort, in planning, work, skills and sheer

faith, on the part of the instigators, the manufacturers and the incoming families, the educators, the churches, the shopkeepers and so on. Even in terms of cash, the housing alone represents an investment of over twenty million pounds to date.

East Kilbride, as well as attracting much new industry and manufacturers, has become the location of extensive research laboratories, a heartening matter for Scotland. One very important aspect of this new town development which should not be overlooked is the banishing of the old concept of industrial ugliness, of the idea that dirt and squalor and harshness are inseparable from industry. The clean, bright, spacious grass-surrounded character of these new-town factories and works is something very significant and gratifying.

It is not only in actual new towns and development corporations that this challenging spirit is evidenced. Take Bishopbriggs, for instance. Here is Scotland's newest burgh of all, a status attained only in 1964, with a population today of nearly 19,000, although only two or three years ago it was given as 11,000. Bishopbriggs plans its services and municipal programme on a population of 32,000. This is no amorphous attachment to Glasgow's major conurbation, to use the planners' sorry phrase, but a vital and go-ahead community with its own individuality—yet set in the midst of the vast industrialised area only five miles north-east of Glasgow's centre. Nor is it a dormitory, as Bearsden and Milngavie tend to be, for it actually draws in labour from outwith the burgh to staff its no fewer than fifty-seven commercial concerns, which range from engineering to publishing, from brick-making to wire-rope manufacture. It has a new shopping centre with pedestrian precinct; a recently built High School for 800; three primary schools have all come into being within the last ten years, a fourth is to be built and a fifth reconstructed at a cost of £150,000. It is to be emphasised that this is no authoritatively-planned project from above, but local initiative that had indeed to fight something of a battle with the said authority to gain its freedom. Nor had it the advantage of a clean start on undeveloped ground, but had a vast field of neglect and industrial detritus to clear away. How far Bishopbriggs has come may be gauged from the relevant item in the Ordnance Gazetteer, published in 1882. 'A village in Cadder parish, Lanarkshire . . . it presents a somewhat unprepossessing appearance and is inhabited chiefly by poor Irish families . . . has a

GALLOWAY LANDSCAPE, near Gatehouse of Fleet, in the Stewartry of Kirkcudbright, typical of that green and pleasant land of grey castles and abbeys and red-and-white Ayrshire cattle.

Church of Scotland mission station, a Free Church and a public school with accommodation for 74 children . . . and a population of 782.'

Here is something of the spirit of Scotland's industrial West.

But there is another Lanarkshire. Fully half of the county area is high moorland, the catchment region of the River Clyde and its tributaries. The county was formerly divided into an Upper and Nether Ward. Lanark town itself was the head burgh of the Upper, and Rutherglen that of the Nether Ward. Lanark, a royal burgh since 1140, is situated where the Clyde drops quite dramatically from what may be called Clydesdale into the lovely and fertile Vale of Clyde. It is an ancient grey town with something of the character of a Border burgh; indeed it runs an age-old annual Common Riding festival, called Lanimer Day, with a Lord Cornet and mounted followers. It is the marketing centre for a large farming area, and its live-stock sales are famous, as are its races, held at the race-course on Lanark Moor nearby. Although there is an artificial mound here representing a Roman fortified camp, and the patriot Wallace lived and did great things in Lanark, there are not a great many relics remaining of that stirring past. There is a street called Castlegate—but nothing left of the royal castle where the Scots Parliament met on occasion. The Clydesdale Hotel stands on the site of the Greyfriars monastery, and there are only a few fragments left of the fine twelfth and thirteenth century church of St. Kentigern. But the past is not forgotten—one of the most individual manifestations of which is another local festival held each March, for the children this time, and known as Whuppity Scoorie, partly religious and partly mock-battle, which is alleged to represent Wallace's castigation of the English garrison of Lanark in 1297, but almost certainly has still more ancient origins in probably pagan rites, whuppity scoorie seeming to denote whipping and scourging.

New Lanark, a mile to the south, was the scene of a notable social and industrial experiment, when in 1784 David Dale, a Glasgow merchant-prince, and his son-in-law Robert Owen, founded cotton-mills here, run on socialist-philanthropic lines, with model houses, and a factory school—the new-town planners' forerunner.

The famous Falls of Clyde near Lanark—Corra Linn, Stonebyres Linn and Bonnington Linn, picturesque in their wooded gorges—carry the river down into that ten-

NORTH OF LOCH MAREE, WESTER ROSS, looking into one of the finest and greatest roadless and empty tracts remaining in these islands, the deer forests of Letterewe, Dundonnell and Fannich.

mile stretch so renowned for its fruit-growing fairness. Nothing could be more of a delightful contrast than to drive out from the industrial complex of the lower Clyde valley only a little way up-river into this land of hillside orchards and ranked fruit-bushes, green meadows, old mansions and fine trees. In blossom-time, especially, the Vale of Clyde is a heart-lifting sight indeed—for here is not only quiet and peaceful beauty but the ingenious use of land and natural resources developed to a high order. Crossford village is at the centre of this, and nearby is the most splendid restored ruin of Craignethan Castle, Scott's *Tillietudlem*, built in the sixteenth century by one of Scotland's most talented and scoundrelly nobles, Sir James Hamilton of Finnart, the Bastard of Arran, assassin, traitor, King's Master of Works and man of taste.

Upper Lanarkshire, to south and east, is largely high sheep country divided by fertile valleys such as those of the Douglas and Nethan Waters, the Mouse, and the upper Clyde itself, with major hills like Tinto and Culter Fell rising over 2,000 feet. Biggar, a small burgh on the very edge of Peebles-shire, seems much more to belong to the Borders than to the West; but Douglas, four times as large, is more typical of Lanarkshire, that strange mixture of the pleasingly rural and the sternly industrial, with collieries and the housing apt to go with them amid the green rolling scenery of Douglasdale. Here was Douglas Castle, undermined by the coal-winners, and still there is the chancel of St. Bride's Church and the tombs of so many of the great race of Douglas. Amongst the relics are caskets containing the hearts of the eighth Earl of Douglas, Lord-Lieutenant of the Kingdom, who once attended a tournament to celebrate the marriage of the Princess of Gueldres to James II, with a 'suite' of 5,000 men; and the famous Archibald-Bell-the-Cat, fifth Earl of Angus, who made private treaties with Henry VIII.

Strathaven, between here and East Kilbride, is another compound of the grim and the attractive, a grey place on the edge of the moors, with narrow streets and old houses amongst undistinguished later development. A ruined castle dominates the centre of the town, built by an illegitimate Stewart of the royal line in the fifteenth century; but more famous today is the house Sir Harry Lauder built here to make his home.

The moors stretch on westwards into Renfrewshire. It may tend to be forgotten that this county, synonymous with Glasgow's westerly sprawl, is still more than half

(Left) CLYDESDALE, Lanarkshire, a few miles from Motherwell, Wishaw and the rest. One of the great fruit-growing and horticultural areas, with orchards decking the slopes mile after mile, and glasshouses by the hundred-acre. (Below) THE ANCIENT TOWN OF LANARK. Facing up the street is a statue of the hero Wallace, on the parish church, who here commenced active warfare against the English invader.

upland pasture and moorland, rising to hills as high as 1,700 feet. This north-westerly portion, in especial, is almost all upland—the Strathgryfe of olden days—a bare and lofty plateau of heather and bog and tufted grassland, remarkable for the paucity of roads that cross it, so that we have a large area of seventy or eighty square miles partly in this county and partly in North Ayrshire, but only a short distance from Glasgow's spread, almost inaccessible save to the shepherd and the energetic walker.

Around the perimeter of this moorland mass are sited several communities of diverse character—Kilmacolm, a select and substantial residential neighbourhood, in the Gryfe valley, notable for the refinement of its inhabitants and the 'foul, gross and palpable' ghost which is supposed to haunt the nearby castle of Duchal; Houston with its mercat cross, modern church with fifteenth century effigies, and the Barochan Celtic cross nearby; Bridge of Weir, famous for leather and hide products, with the great children's village of the Quarrier Homes, founded by a poor Greenock boy who made a fortune in Glasgow; Kilbarchan, a village where 1,000 looms once wove silk and Paisley shawls, and where now the Linwood motor-car and pressed steel works cater for different days; Johnstone, a large and more modern engineering and milling burgh of 19,000; Lochwinnoch beneath the high hills of Misty Law and Hill of Stake and at the edge of its loch which, averaging only five feet in depth, freezes over very easily and provides the townsfolk with the best curling in the land; and Wemyss Bay, a popular seaside and golfing resort on the Clyde coast whence the steamers ply to Arran and Bute. This western coastline is narrow indeed, with the hills coming steeply down to the estuary, and the scenic road clinging to the braesides.

So we come back to the Clyde, the river that has meant so much to Scotland, one of the great commercial waterways of the world. It rises 1,550 feet above sea-level amongst the hills where Lanark, Peebles and Dumfries shires meet. Two other great rivers rise there also so that the rhyme runs:

> 'Annan, Tweed and Clyde rise a' oot o' ae hillside;
> Tweed ran, Annan wan—Clyde fell and broke its
> neck ower Corra Linn.'

It winds and sweeps and falls, gaining beauty and strength, for 106 miles until, at Dumbarton, it loses itself in the salt waters of its Firth. Probably no other populous area in Britain is so much bound up with its river. Certainly in no city that I have ever visited is one so aware of the presence and importance of the river as in Glasgow. Clyde is just the old Celtic word *clwyd*, meaning strong. The river has lived up to its name.

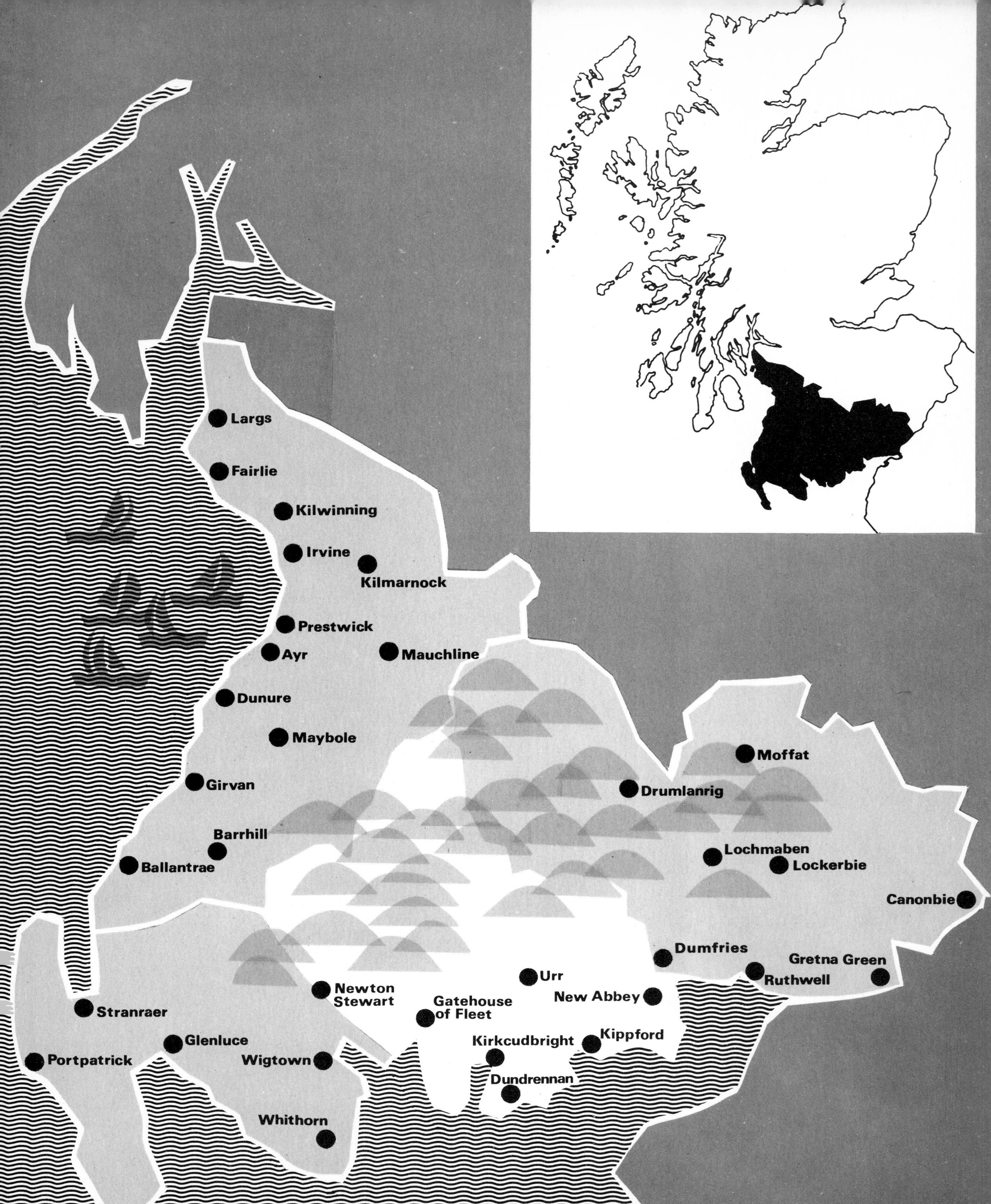

Largs
Fairlie
Kilwinning
Irvine
Kilmarnock
Prestwick
Ayr
Mauchline
Dunure
Maybole
Girvan
Barrhill
Ballantrae
Moffat
Drumlanrig
Lochmaben
Lockerbie
Canonbie
Dumfries
Gretna Green
Ruthwell
Urr
New Abbey
Newton Stewart
Gatehouse of Fleet
Stranraer
Glenluce
Portpatrick
Wigtown
Kirkcudbright
Kippford
Dundrennan
Whithorn

LARGS, Ayrshire, a favourite West Coast holiday resort and centre for cruises on the Firth of Clyde. Yachting is popular.

199

AYR. Evening light at the harbour of one of the most important and pleasing towns in Scotland, a seaport, resort and industrial centre in one, with exciting historical associations—and, of course, the closest links with Robert Burns.

King Cole, or Coil, a Pictish king buried in the vicinity. Certainly there is a Coilsfield estate—whereat, incidentally, Robert Burns' Highland Mary was employed as a dairymaid. Kyle is really the basin of the River Ayr, which divides it into King's Kyle to the south and Kyle Stewart to the north—although today it might more truly be called Burns' Kyle, for here was born Scotland's renowned bard;

'There was a lad was born in Kyle . . .'

and few are the scenes therein which he has not enshrined for all the world in his deathless verses.

Ayr itself:

'Auld Ayr, wham ne'er a town surpasses
For honest men and bonnie lasses,'

is by any count one of the country's most important and at the same time pleasing towns, set finely on the shores of its great bay and looking across to the peaks of Arran and Argyll. A royal burgh with a population of 46,000, it incorporates in its arms the date 1202 when it received a charter from William the Lyon who had built his 'new castle of Ayr' ten years before. It has never failed to take its major part in Scotland's vigorous story, for the Romans were here, and the Norsemen after them. It was a vital point in the Wars of Independence. Wallace surprised an English garrison here and burned 500 to death in their barracks. Bruce—whose own castle of Turnberry stood not far away, for he was Earl of Carrick—burned the town itself to prevent it becoming an enemy strongpoint. It was the scene of violent affrays during the feuding days of the Kennedys, Campbells of Loudon and the Crawfords. Oliver Cromwell erected a citadel, at so great a cost that he complained that it might as well have been built of gold. In Covenanting times Ayr was in a constant turmoil. Today it is a thriving county seat, shopping-centre, busy port, renowned holiday place, something of a cultural oasis, and yet an important industrial community, its diverse products including carpets, iron-castings, fertilisers, electrical equipment, agricultural machinery, leather goods, furnishing fabrics, woollens, and the well-known Ayrshire bacon. Ayr Academy is a notable school, and the new Craigie College of Education is an ambitious establishment, with further hostel accommodation planned for no fewer than 600 female student teachers. There is a new Technical College also. There is a famous racecourse, no fewer than three golf-courses, and other sporting amenities on the same scale—plus the only Butlin's Holiday Camp in

Scotland. Moreover it boasts two theatres, one a civic venture. And, of course, there are everywhere reminders of Robert Burns' life hereabouts—the parish church where he was baptised, the Tam o' Shanter Inn where he spent so many evenings, the kirkyard with the graves of many of his characters, friends and patrons, the Auld Brig, so narrow that 'Two wheelbarrows tremble when they meet', but that yet has carried 'a' ye douce folk I've borne aboon the broo'. Another equally famous, Auld Brig o' Doon, crosses that river at Alloway nearby to the south, where is Burns' birthplace cottage and museum and elaborate monument, his father's grave, and Alloway's roofless 'auld haunted kirk'.

To Alloway stream thousands each year from all over the world—and just to the other northern side of Ayr stream similar thousands, to Prestwick Airport, one of the most important international air terminals in Europe, the most fog-free in Britain, and long the U.S. Air Force's main staging-post. Prestwick however is quite a town in its own right, with a famous golf-course, and a magnificent swimming-pool.

Kyle's other large town, just slightly bigger than Ayr indeed, is Kilmarnock, twelve miles inland to the north-east. Auld Killie is a vital, bustling, practical sort of place, heavily industrialised and noted for its Johnnie Walker whisky, carpets, boots and shoes, steel and marine engines, amongst other things. But despite this brisk aura of trade and commerce, like so many other Scots manufacturing towns, it is ancient at heart, and with an innate character which redeems it from mere brashness. There are still the wynds and closes of earlier days. The place was mentioned in Barbour's *Bruce*, regarding the flight of the Good Sir James Douglas in 1306:

'Tharfor furth the wayis tuk he then,
To Kylmarnock and Kylwynnyne
And till Ardrossane eftre syne.'

In those days Killie was but a village belonging to the great castle of Dean, which still stands in double-towered majesty in a fine park north of the town. It was a Boyd stronghold, that Ayrshire family at one time being great in the land, marrying into the royal house and for a while wielding supreme power. The fifth Lord Boyd it was who had James VI erect Kilmarnock into a burgh in 1592, the place being then famous for the manufacture of Scots bonnets—a trade that still survives. Steel-making also is of long-standing, for in 1658 it was declared '. . . for their

DUNURE CASTLE, Ayrshire. This coastline, highly attractive in itself, is enhanced by the number of ruined castles which crown its many headlands. Dunure, like so many others, was a Kennedv stronghold.

temper of metals they are without compeer—Scotland has not better; and as they are artisans in dirks, so are they artists in fuddling, as if...art and ale were inseparable companions.' Perhaps this facility was what made John Walker set up his distillery here in the mid-nineteenth century.

Up the wooded valley of the River Irvine from Kilmarnock, there is a string of little towns—Hurlford, Galston, Newmilns and Darvel. Galston has in its vicinity the famous Loudon Castle and Kirk, seat of the once so powerful Campbell earldom of Loudon. Newmilns and Darvel are lace-making towns; but the former is renowned for its sturdy support of Abraham Lincoln in the American Civil War, which brought about the presentation of a Stars and Stripes flag by the President, since renewed by Congress; while the latter was the birthplace of Sir Alexander Fleming, discoverer of penicillin. The pass under the isolated cone of Loudon Hill, at the head of the valley, was a great place for battles. Here the Romans had a fort, Wallace had a skirmish, Bruce defeated a five-times larger English force, and the Covenanters fought the Battle of Drumclog.

Dundonald, to the south, was an important place in old Scotland, its ruined castle being one of the principal seats of the royal Stewarts, here dying the first Stewart king, Robert II, in 1390. Tarbolton is quite a sizeable town, wherein Burns founded the Bachelor's Club in 1780, the house involved being now National Trust property; while at Mauchline there is now a museum where he set up house with Jean Armour. The farm of Mossgiel, which he leased for four grim years, is a short distance off. Auchinleck, further south still, is linked with another literary figure, James Boswell thereof, the biographer, but though the mansion and estate are very fine, the mining town of that name is less so. Cumnock, Old and New—and a surprising distance apart—are also mining places amongst the hills. The great Lugar Ironworks were established nearby in 1845. Keir Hardie came from Old Cumnock. Near New Cumnock is the delightful Glen Afton about which Burns wrote the haunting song *Flow gently sweet Afton.* Dalmellington, on the very edge of Kyle, is one more coal and iron town, in sheltered hills, though it dates from the eleventh century. Loch Doon and the northern section of the great Glen Trool National Forest Park lie directly to the south.

But here we are in Carrick, the southern and largest area of Ayrshire, a green and highly attractive countryside,

(Below) 'YE BANKS AND BRAES O' BONNIE DOON'. The upper valley of the River Doon, immortalised by Burns. (Right) GIRVAN, South Ayrshire, at the mouth of a very lovely valley. The hills come close to the sea as we reach down towards Galloway.

where industry tends to be left behind. This is the Kennedy country. They were the Kings of Carrick, and their castles dot the entire region and crown the headlands that thrust into the Firth—Greenan, Dunure, Culzean, Ardmillan, Cassillis, Baltersan, Dalquharran, Kirkhill, Newark of Bargany, Maybole, and so on. This land has suffered perhaps some of the grimmest scenes of clan warfare and feudal savageries. The Kennedys are still strong here, under their chief, the Marquis of Ailsa. Their capital was at Maybole, a charming and peaceable-seeming town today, in pleasant rural country, manufacturing leather goods and farm machinery. But it was once otherwise, for no fewer than twenty-eight Kennedy lairds had their town houses here, and they were as awkward and troublesome a bunch as history has thrown up. Their chief's own town castle of Maybole still stands proudly dominating the main street—although it seems strange that such a place was necessary when his great stronghold of Cassillis is less than four miles away. John Knox and the Abbot of Crossraguel once held a marathon and vigorous public debate here, for three solid days. Culzean Castle, another famous Kennedy seat on a cliff-edge a few miles to the west, was remodelled in the eighteenth century by Robert Adam to make one of the most palatial mansions in Scotland, and is now one of the National Trust's show-pieces, with a flat reserved for the use of General Eisenhower as a token of appreciation for war-time services.

The only town of any size in Carrick is Girvan, at the mouth of the long and attractive valley of the Girvan Water. A resort of 6,000 people, with a fishing harbour and thriving modern boat-building yard, it has good beaches and other amenities and a fine stretch of coast scenery. Ten miles offshore, but looking closer because of its great bulk, is Ailsa Craig, the massive conical island which rears out of the sea to a height of 1,114 feet, and is known as Paddy's Milestone from the fact that it lies half-way on the steamer route between Glasgow and Belfast. There are many castles, ruined or still occupied, reachable from Girvan. Killochan, three miles up-river, is a particularly handsome and interesting example of the tall old turreted Scots tower-house, standing in seventeenth century terraced gardens, open to the public. The inland villages of Dailly, Crosshill, Kirkmichael, Straiton, Barr and Barrhill are all set in the pleasing valleys of the Girvan, Stinchar and Duisk Waters, none of them large, although

the quiet anglers' resort of Barr has of recent years greatly expanded to become a forestry community in connection with the great Glen Trool National Trust Forest Park nearby, where tree-planting has developed on a vast scale.

From Girvan southwards the road makes one of the finest coastal drives in South Scotland, by cliffs and coves and caves and ruined towers, by Kennedy's Pass, thirteen miles to the little seaside place of Ballantrae, its name famous from the Stevenson novel—though this was not actually set here at all, the author choosing the name purely for its euphony. There are other notably euphonious place-names hereabouts, such as Colmonell, Knockdolian, Pinwherry and Trochrague, names with a Galloway ring about them, for that great province has as distinctive a nomenclature as it has character. We are now at its northern edge.

Galloway is very much an island community to the rest of Scotland, for high and trackless hill ranges insulate it from the north and east, while the sea and the great Solway Firth do the same to south and west. Because of the ins and outs of its huge bays of Loch Ryan, Luce, Wigtown, Fleet, Kirkcudbright, Auchencairn, Rough Firth and Carse, it must have a longer coastline than any other two counties in Lowland Scotland. And not only has it this geographical separateness; it has an ethnological one also—for its name of Gallgaidhel means the land of the stranger. Gaels, and certainly the Celtic people here are of a different brand to most of the rest of Scotland, perhaps more Irish in character. Because of inaccessibility, and the fact that this is an almost wholly farming and pastoral country with little to attract industry, the Galloway folk have preserved their individuality. To the rest of the Scots their names tend to raise a smile indeed. Galloway has been called the Land of the Uncouth Macs—and surnames like MacAdoo, MacClumpha, MacClung, MacGuffog, MacHaffie, MacSkimming and MacWhirr, are common.

Galloway, under its almost independent lords, has tended to hold aloof from much of what exercised the remainder of the country, though it was to Galloway that Christianity first came to Scotland, when in 397 St. Ninian, a native princeling, started his mission at Whithorn; since when there have always been strong religious currents—though these by no means always made for peace. The Reformation took much longer to establish itself here, for the Auld Kirk was very strong—indeed some of its churchmen were the most competent and

(Left) RUINED CASTLE KENNEDY, Wigtownshire, burned in 1715. (Below) BALLANTRAE, at the very south of Ayrshire, with the ruined Ardstinchar Castle on the right. Ailsa Craig, out to sea, rising to 1,114 feet, is one of the best-known landmarks of the Firth of Clyde, known as Paddy's Milestone, owing to its position midway between Belfast and Glasgow.

formidable of the Reformers' opponents. Abbot Gilbert Brown of Carsluith, in especial, the last and wiliest Abbot of Sweetheart Abbey, the Privy Council were complaining about as late as 1596; he managed to defy the Protestant authorities until his arrest in 1605. Once Galloway did turn Calvinist, however, it did so wholeheartedly, and it was here that the most determined fight was put up by the Covenanters against compulsary episcopacy, with much bloodshed. The abbeys and priories of Galloway were more numerous than anywhere else—even the Borders—Sweetheart, Lincluden, Dundrennan, Glenluce, Candida Casa or Whithorn, Glenlochar, Soulseat and Tongland.

This reference to the Borders may strike the uninitiated as strange, for geographically Galloway might itself be supposed to be a Border province, with England just across Solway. But strangely enough, the Gallowegians have never considered themselves as Borderers, and still do not. Dumfriesshire, yes—but not Kirkcudbright and Wigtown.

I have always held that the time *par excellence* to visit Galloway is in May—bluebell time. And not only bluebells, for everywhere the cattle-dotted knowes and knolls in which the province abounds are ablaze with golden gorse and broom. Summer seems to come early to this territory. It is frequently not realised just how far south and west this is. The Mull of Galloway is in fact further south than the Yorkshire border, and further west than the Isle of Man, Anglesey or three-quarters of Cornwall. This canting of the map can cause surprise. For instance, Edinburgh is not only west of Carlisle but west likewise of Liverpool and even Cardiff. There is no part of Scotland so far east as Manchester.

Wigtownshire is the western section of the province. The Moors are the northerly part, the high and more or less empty uplands and their greener skirts which run down well into the great central peninsula of which the Machars are the southern two-thirds. Machar is a Gaelic word meaning a low-lying coastal area, and the part here so called extends southwards from Wigtown itself down to Whithorn. Rhinns is another Gaelic word meaning a point or promontory, and refers to that curious semi-detached portion, thirty miles long by perhaps five wide, projecting into the Irish Sea and linked to the rest only by the flat isthmus wherein stands Stranraer.

This is the largest town in Galloway, a port for the mail-steamers to Northern Island, a railway terminus—

(Below) GLEN TROOL AND LOCH TROOL, in the Galloway Highlands, a haunt of Robert Bruce during his days as a hunted wanderer. (Right) NEWTON STEWART, Wigtownshire, a pleasant town near the mouth of the salmon-rich River Cree.

British Rail permitting—and an airfield. It was Graham of Claverhouse's headquarters when, as both military commander and Sheriff of Galloway, he was charged with the grim duty of making the independent South-West conform to governmental ideas on prelacy. His base was Stranraer Castle, which still stands, somewhat altered and neglected, amongst back streets. There is another building called the North-West Castle here, but it is no real castle—the home of the famous Arctic explorer Sir John Ross. The great military port of Cairn Ryan, to the north, has been something of an embarrassment to Stranraer, enormously important in wartime but otherwise left to stagnate. Many have been the schemes and attempts to utilise this huge dockyard area in an out-of-the-way spot, so far with little success.

The Rhinns peninsula, almost an island, has a long and exposed seaboard to the west, which the road only touches at two points—Port Patrick half-way down, and Port Logan away to the south. The former is a delightful place, with something of a Cornish look about it, on a hilly site; houses and hotels on terraces, above a winding main street that runs down a valley to the exposed harbour amongst the rocks and reefs of the savage coastline which has a grim record for shipwrecks. But there are sandy bays and coves too, and this is a popular holiday resort. Port Logan is only a tiny fishing-village, but a great place for producing sea-captains. The gardens of Logan House are notable for their exotic and sub-tropical plants, including palms and even bamboos. The east shores of the Rhinns are more sheltered, populous and better served with roads. Kirkmaiden, with the Mull of Galloway nearby, is the most southerly parish of Scotland.

The Machars are fine dairy-farming country, flanked by a less exciting coast, with the huge indentation of Luce Bay separating them from the Rhinns. Glenluce at the head of the bay, with the vast Sands of Luce close by, was the site of the important abbey of that name, of which the vaulted chapter-house remains intact. Thomas Hay, who got the lands at the Reformation, used stones from the Abbey to build the handsome nearby Castle of Park in 1590. He did not manage to hang on to all the abbey property, for he had to compete with the infamous fourth Earl of Cassillis, he who roasted the similarly placed Commendator of Crossraguel for a transfer of the lease. In this case we read that the Earl 'dealt with a monk to forge the late Abbot's signature, then hired a carle called Carnochan to

stick the monk, next wrought on his uncle, Bargany, to hang the carle and so had conqueist the landis of Glenluce'. Thus one aspect of the Reformation in Scotland.

At the other, eastern, root of the great Machars peninsula is Newton Stewart, a most attractive little town, on the banks of the salmon-rich River Cree, many of its houses seeming almost to rise out of the waters. As well as for angling this is an excellent centre for exploring much of Galloway, for the Cree valley leads up into the mountainous area of Glen Trool Forest Park, and also gives access to the Moors district.

Wigtown Bay, as deep but much narrower than that of Luce, hems in the Machars on the east, and seven miles south from Newton Stewart is Wigtown itself, the little royal burgh high on its hill, a quiet place for a county town, with only 1,200 inhabitants. But it was not always quiet. Here were executed, in the barbarous 'Killing Times', the victims of shameful governmental policy, known as the Wigtown Martyrs. Whithorn, another royal burgh near the tip of the wide peninsula, has more signs of its age-old importance. Its religious foundation of Candida Casa, later the Priory of Whithorn, founded by Fergus, Lord of Galloway in 1126, made it a famous place of pilgrimage—so much so, indeed, that after the Reformation its popularity did not diminish, and Parliament itself had to make the practice illegal in 1581. The archway to the Priory, itself in ruins, still opens as a pend from the main street—though this is a fifteenth century gateway with the royal arms of Scotland emblazoned above. Not only was there a bishopric of Whithorn once, but it was the richest see in Scotland after the archbishoprics of St. Andrews and Glasgow.

At Newton Stewart we cross over into the Stewartry. This is what the eastern section of Galloway prefers to the

humdrum terms of county or shire—the Stewartry of Kirkcudbright, emphasising the fact that it had as its lord a royally-appointed Steward. Stewart is still the surname of the Earls of Galloway. There is a distinct difference between the Stewartry and Wigtownshire in more than history and nomenclature—even though it also consists of a mountainous central core with peninsulas projecting down into the Solway Firth. Its hills are higher and come closer to the sea; it is more heavily wooded and diversified as to scenery, with more rivers; its bays and inlets are much smaller and narrower though more numerous; and it is itself much larger, almost twice the acreage, though with slightly smaller population.

The Stewartry consists of the great upland northern area known as the Glenkens, empty moorland, lochs and reservoirs, and forestry plantations, with some very high hills, the monarch of which is Merrick, 2,764 feet, up near the Ayrshire border; and a more populous and lower-lying southern area, split into sections by a series of fast south-flowing rivers that rise in the mountains and run into Solway—the Fleets, Big and Little, the Tarff, the Dee, the Urr and the Cluden. But this southern portion has its high hills too, some of them rising impressively close to the shoreline; for instance, Cairnsmore of Fleet, 2,331 feet is less than four miles from salt-water, and Criffel away to the east rises 1,866 feet in little more than a mile from the shore. As a consequence of all this, there is less of the green whin-clad knolls and slantwise cattle-dotted fields so typical of Wigtownshire, and more of a dramatic scenery of contrasts.

Creetown is quite a pretty village on the coast some seven miles from Newton Stewart, with some of the most famous granite quarries in the land nearby, from which came the stone for the Thames Embankment and Liverpool docks. This is a great granite country. On the delightful, winding coast road from here to Gatehouse of Fleet, there are three strikingly-sited castles; Carsluith, of the former Abbot Brown of Sweetheart; Barholm, which John Knox used as a hiding-place in his early days; and Cardoness, of the bloodthirsty lairds. Dirk Hatterick's Cave a renowned smuggler's hide-out is hereabouts, but hard to locate. Gatehouse is one of the most attractive little towns in all Scotland, both in its position at the head of picturesque Fleet Bay and in its douce burghal appearance. Burns wrote his famous and stirring *Scots Wha Hae*, almost the national anthem of Scotland, in the Murray Arms Hotel here, and

changed the course of history, for it was here, in 1306, in the former Greyfriars monastery church—another of the public-spirited Devorgilla's foundations—that he stabbed to death John Comyn, Lord of Badenoch, the other principal claimant to the Scots throne, and thereafter captured the castle, thus rekindling the War of Independence to its eventual successful conclusion. Bruce's brother-in-law, Sir Christopher Seton, was hanged by the English here. Nevertheless, despite long centuries of warfare and burning, it is to the pen that Dumfries owes its greatest renown, for the town has almost as notable links with Robert Burns as has Ayr. Here he lived the last five years of his life; here he unhappily played the gauger—and did much of his most popular work, including the writing of a great number of his Scots songs, such as *Ye Banks and Braes o' Bonny Doon*, *My Love is Like a Red Red Rose*, *Auld Robin Gray*, and *Auld Lang Syne*. And here in 1796 he died, worn out with living, at the early age of 37, and is buried in St. Michael's churchyard, his wife Jean Armour and many of his children likewise. The houses in which he lived, and died, the pew in which he worshipped, and the inns where he drank and wrote, are visited each year by thousands.

Less well known is the fact that Sir J. M. Barrie was a pupil at the famous Dumfries Academy. Thomas Carlyle, of course, was often here, the Sage's birthplace being only a dozen miles away, at Ecclefechan.

Dumfries's annual March Riding, known as the Guid Nychburris Week, or Good Neighbour's Festival, is a lively and inspiriting affair, with the Cornet as usual carrying the burgh flag and supported by a large mounted cavalcade, with all the citizenry on holiday. The good neighbourliness originates from a custom whereby quarrelsome citizens were at such time brought before the magistrates and required on oath in future to keep Guid Nychburhude.

A few miles to the east of Dumfries is the village of Ruthwell, famous for the remarkable eighteen-foot-high Ruthwell Cross, of the eighth century. Less well-known is that this little place was the home of the savings-bank movement, where in 1810 the Rev. Henry Duncan set up the first such bank—the little cottage premises for which were purchased in 1953, by the Scottish Trustee Savings Banks, as a lasting memorial.

Annan, six miles further to the east, near the mouth of its own river, is the only other largish town, with a popula-

(Left) ROBERT BURNS' STATUE, DUMFRIES. Here the poet spent the last five years of his life, and wrote much which became world-famous. Here his body lies. (Below) DRY-STONE DIKERS at work in the valley of the Nith.

THE GREY MARE'S TAIL, a famous waterfall in the wild hills of the watershed between the East and West borders, near Moffat.

tion of 5,700, a red-stone royal burgh in a green countryside, with fine prospects across the Solway to the Lakeland hills. It has a broad High Street but few marks of antiquity—yet its history was sufficiently stirring, with the Border less than ten miles off. Here, at the Academy's predecessor, Thomas Carlyle went unwillingly to school—and later returned to teach. This is Irvine country, and here he met Edward Irving, the famous preacher, who charmed all hearers, even Queen Victoria, and helped to found the Catholic Apostolic Church—often, to his pain, called the sect of Irvingites—and was deposed by the local Presbytery for so doing, though in the end his fellow-townsfolk erected a statue in his memory. Nearby is the huge Chapelcross nuclear power station. And at the Border itself is Gretna, with its famous—or notorious—smithy at the Green, where runaway couples for so long have come, from England and abroad, to contract their hurried marriages. Just why this village should have become the one Mecca for such elopers is hard to understand—for, of course, it has no particular advantage over any other place in Scotland, where a marriage by declaration is legal, provided the three-weeks' residential qualification is complied with. Gretna's fame is not one of which most Scots are particularly proud.

In considering the Dumfriesshire dales, it is worth recognising that they were not, and are not, mere hinterland for the Solway plain. In fact, they were historically probably the most important part of the county, because they were the territories of the powerful and numerous clans which dominated the West March and found greater security in these hill-girt valleys—the Maxwells and Douglases of Nithsdale, the Jardines of Dryfesdale, the Johnstones of Annandale, the Armstrongs of Eskdale and the Elliots of Liddesdale. These clans' chiefs became the most important men of the area. From their ranks were appointed the Wardens of the West March. And great of course, was the internecine strife between them all.

Nithsdale, of the Maxwells to the south and Douglases to the north, is the greatest and most populous, rich in red-soiled agricultural land, in villages and estates, about twenty-five miles long from its emergence from the close clasp of the hills to its junction with Solway. It was long claimed that one plough in Nithsdale would turn up as much ground as two elsewhere. Thornhill, in the upper or Douglas stretch, is a quietly dignified and attractive little town of broad tree-lined streets, very much the ducal bailiwick—for the great late-seventeenth century castle of Drumlanrig, seat first of the Douglas Dukes of Queensberry and now of Buccleuch, stands amidst enormous parkland to the north. Penpont, Tynron and Moniave, three picturesque villages, lie to the west, near the second of which is Maxwelton House, amongst its braes, the home of Annie Laurie. Closeburn, a few miles down from Thornhill, is famous for its massive early-fourteenth century castle, probably one of the oldest inhabited houses in Scotland, whose Kirkpatrick laird aided Bruce to 'mak siccar' of the Red Comyn at Dumfries in 1306. There are many castles in this vale, two small examples, Fourmerkland and Isle, being particularly pleasing. Also the site of the little-known Maxwell-founded Abbey of Holywood, and Burns' last farm, Ellisland, lie to the south of the comely village of Auldgirth, with its handsome bridge which Carlyle's mason father helped to build. Maxwelltown—not to be confused with Maxwelton of the Lauries—is now just a suburb of Dumfries across the river, but once was a burgh on its own. Down amongst the estuary levels are the romantic ruins of the huge fortress-castle of Caerlaverock, the Maxwell lords' chief seat, an almost impregnable strength set in a swamp.

Annandale, whose Johnstone chiefs rose to become marquises thereof, reaches northwards parallel with Nith, and across it now runs the great new A.74 dual-carriageway highway en route for Glasgow. Up near its head, lying snugly amongst high green hills, is Moffat, one of the most entrancingly placed and winsome little towns in Scotland, with a fine wide High Street and some good architecture, much of it dating from the heyday of the town when it was a spa and the resort of the great and celebrated. Nearby, to the north-west, is the famous Devil's Beef Tub, rimmed dramatically by the climbing road, a vast hollow wherein the Annandale cattle-reivers hid their spoils; and to the north-east, on the attractive road which winds through the hills to St. Mary's Loch and Selkirk, is the equally renowned waterfall of the Grey Mare's Tail, 200 feet high.

Lochmaben, in mid-dale, is a quiet and charmingly situated royal burgh, beside its lochs, which once was one of the most important places in the kingdom, for here was the great castle of the Bruces, Lords of Annandale, where some hold that the hero-king was born, and where at least he spent much of his youth. It was a huge and powerful stronghold, covering as much as fifteen acres, and with four moats to defend it. The chronicler Bellenden declares

that, amongst other idiosyncrasies, 'the pepill . . . quhais cruelteis wes sa gret that thay abhorrit nocht to eit the flesche of yolding prisoneris. The wyuis vsit to slay thair husbands quhen thay wer found cowartis, or discomfist be thair ennymes, to give occasioun to otheris to be more bald & hardy'.

Below Lochmaben, the Dryfe Water and the amusingly-named Water of Milk, come in from the east, out of their own lesser vales, and between them stands the busy road-junction and market town of Lockerbie, just where the hills begin to steepen. That two of these nearby heights should be called Lamb Hill and Whitewoollen Hill is significant, for Lockerbie is most famous for its great August Lamb Sales, at which astronomical numbers of Border lambs are sold, largely to English dealers. Thirty thousand to 50,000 was commonplace, numbers having been known to reach 70,000. This trade has made Lockerbie a prosperous place.

Eskdale lies further to the east; indeed its mouth is in England, an untidy arrangement. The busy woollen-mill burgh of Langholm half-way up has already been mentioned, in the early Borders chapter, for it belongs in

MOFFAT, a little town of great charm at the head of Annandale.
A scene typical of North Dumfriesshire.

character to that countryside. Higher up the Esk, remote amongst the hills, is Westerkirk, the village where Thomas Telford was born, the great bridge-builder, engineer, and designer of the Ellesmere and Caledonian Canals. Incidentally from here also came the forebears of Lord Thomson of Fleet. Canonbie, further down the dales, is a sizeable and prepossessing village, with an air of settled peace—which is wholly denied by its past, for this was on the very edge of the Debatable Land where lawlessness was endemic, neither Scotland nor England being certain whose territory it was and making little attempt to enforce law and order. Moreover, this was also the land of the Armstrongs, probably the most ungovernable of all the Border clans, whose depredations and insolences are proverbial. One of their leaders, in the sixteenth century, Johnnie Armstrong of Gilnockie, whose fortalice of Hollows Tower still stands sturdily at the roadside north of Canonbie, once bargained arrogantly for his life with young James V, offering the King the produce of twenty-four mills, twenty-four men-at-arms, horsed and equipped at all times permanently at the royal service, and the rents of every man and house between Liddesdale and Newcastle-on-Tyne. Lest this be taken as mere braggadocio, it falls to be recorded that the said Johnnie was reputed to have burned no fewer than fifty-two churches and held all the English North, as far south as Newcastle, under terror and blackmail. Wisely, probably, King James turned a deaf ear, and hanged Johnnie, with thirty-six other Armstrong lairds—a bold decision when it is realised that the clan could field 3,000 to 5,000 armed mosstroopers.

So now we have reached Liddesdale, last of the dales and final strip of Scots territory. For many miles the River Liddel forms the Borderline. *March, march, Eskdale and Liddesdale, all the blue bonnets are over the Border!* runs the well-known and stirring song. And indeed this valley, renowned in ballad and story, has seen more reiving, raiding, plundering and counter-marching than any other in the land. Not more actual slaughter perhaps, for these difficult hills were not the routes for invading armies, and here was no fertile Merse lying open for large-scale ravishing. In Liddesdale it was private enterprise rather than state control which prevailed. For all that it is a fair and often beautiful vale in its lower and mid reaches, with stretches of cataracts and rapids in rocky gorges, though bare and bleak towards its head, deep in the Cheviots; but here the Forestry Commission have planted vast acreages of the hillsides, as part of the Border Forest Park. Newcastleton, in Roxburghshire, is the only large village, a community of 1,000 people remotely situated and founded as late as 1793 by the third Duke of Buccleuch as a weaving centre. Liddesdale once sported between thirty and forty Elliot peel-towers, but the heavy hand of authority eventually triumphed, and of these relics of an independence that was almost anarchy, only a few mossgrown stones remain. However, Hermitage Castle, which at least did represent authority, however savage, still rears itself majestically in a side valley, a tremendous place that has played a notable part in history, frequently as the advance base of the Wardens of the West March. Built by the treacherous and cruel de Soulis, Lord of Liddesdale back in the thirteenth century, it quickly became noted for its terrors and excesses—until the independent-minded folk of these parts took matters into their own hands, in the person of de Soulis, rolled him up in lead—no doubt from his own roof—and boiled him in a great copper cauldron, melting him, lead, bones and all. This may not be strictly true—the official story is that he died a prisoner in Dumbarton Castle—but it has been believed by countless generations of Borderers, and accounted to be meet and just, and so is indication of the sort of folk we are dealing with. Thereafter Hermitage came to the great family of Douglas, who knew well how to maintain the character of the place. Here came Mary Queen of Scots, making her highly dramatic ride across the rough hills from Jedburgh, to the sick Bothwell's bedside, and back, in one day—one of the most extraordinary feats of Mary's extraordinary reign. Today Hermitage Castle still scowls out over the fair green countryside, typifying in itself and its setting something of the theme and substance of Scotland's story, of strength and beauty, harshness and romance, sentiment and a great practicality.

Perhaps it is no bad place to leave this land of the Scots. We have made the circuit of it, and seen that it is a great and splendid country, nourishing a vigorous, forceful nation of five million people, almost too full of character and individuality for their own good, with a colourful past and an enormous sense of history—yet a practical self-reliant folk who are marching ahead into the new age with a growing impatience at the bureaucratic shackles of far-away authority.

PHOTOGRAPHIC CREDITS

G. F. ALLEN — 11, 206, 210, 213

BY COURTESY OF THE ATOMIC ENERGY AUTHORITY, DOUNREAY — 122

THE BRITISH TRAVEL ASSOCIATION — 178, 188

BY COURTESY OF JOHN BROWN & COMPANY — 186

J. ALLAN CASH, F.I.B.P., F.R.P.S. — 100, 127, 130, 141

COURIER AND ADVERTISER, DUNDEE — 8, 9, 64, 70, 82, 95

BEN DARBY — 77

JOHN DEWAR, PLANAIR, EDINBURGH —
23, 34, 39, 40, 41, 74, 88, 89, 104, 105, 123, 167, 171, 175

NOEL HABGOOD, F.R.P.S. —
71, 92, 108, 120, 121, 156, 161, 162, 166, 168, 169, 170, 180, 202, 203, 215

HAWICK NEWS — 12

A. F. KERSTING, A.I.B.P., F.R.P.S. — 75, 83, 152, 153, 155

JOHN MACKAY — 28, 59, 67, 98, 204, 211

A. D. S. MACPHERSON —
42, 43, 46, 47, 54, 55, 56, 57, 61, 72, 73, 90, 93, 94, 99, 117, 136,
137, 139, 163, 172, 173, 179, 184, 185, 187, 189, 190,
191, 194, 195, 200, 201, 205, 209, 212, 216, 217, 218, 219

P. K. McLAREN — 66

R. NISBET — 18

THE NATIONAL TRUST OF SCOTLAND — 134, 160

L. S. PATERSON — 119, 199

J. PETERSON — 133

PICTUREPOINT LIMITED — 24, 25, 106, 131

J. L. RODGER, A.R.P.S., STORNOWAY — 135

SCOTLAND'S MAGAZINE — 52, 221

THE SCOTSMAN PUBLICATIONS LIMITED — 29, 30, 31, 37, 68

THE SCOTTISH TOURIST BOARD — 13, 26, 36, 102, 115, 142, 208

KENNETH SCOWEN, F.I.B.P., F.R.P.S. — 15, 58, 79, 91, 118, 151, 154

W. A. SHARP — 14, 17, 50, 51, 69, 76, 84, 126, 143, 157,
158, 159, 164, 165, 174, 207, 222

JOHN TARLTON, A.I.B.P., A.R.P.S. — 85, 113

E. W. TATTERSALL — 60, 107, 132, 146, 147

JOHN TOPHAM LIMITED — 27, 112

TOM WEIR — 103

ROCKHURST UNIVERSITY

The First 100 Years

SHIRL KASPER

Special appreciation to
Joseph T. Fahey, '70,
J. M. Fahey Construction Company,
and the Fahey Family Foundation
for underwriting
the printing of this book.

ISBN 978-1-886761-31-5

Manufactured in the United States of America
Printing by Greystone Graphics
Kansas City, Kansas

10 54321

Rockhurst University Press
1110 Rockhurst Road
Kansas City, Missouri 64110
www.rockhurstpress.org

Contents

Foreword

As a university, we embrace a commitment to be timeless. This allows us to celebrate the past, to be accountable in the present moment, and look optimistically towards the future. As a Jesuit university, we participate in a worldwide network of shared values, stellar reputations, and unique histories.

The history of Rockhurst is a story of successes, modest and significant, contrasted with periods of challenges and uncertainty. Most of all, it's a story of an institution being faithful to its mission as a Jesuit and Catholic university intent on transforming lives in a learning community through the ebbs and flows of time.

As with many Jesuit institutions, the foundation of Rockhurst was based upon a community need and a link to an existing Jesuit institution. The need was for Catholic higher education, at the beginning of the twentieth century, in Kansas City, a growing urban community in the Midwest. The link was with Creighton University through Father Michael Dowling, S.J., who twice served as Creighton's president.

In 1909, Fr. Dowling, the first president of Rockhurst, purchased 25 acres at the corner of 53rd and Troost. In 1910, a charter was granted by the state of Missouri enabling the institution to award degrees. Four years later, high school students were admitted. And in 1917, the first collegians began their classes.

In these pages, you will encounter photos, stories, artifacts, ideas, and anecdotes. All speak to the notion of "companions on the journey" in the Ignatian tradition. The Rockhurst story is truly one of Jesuits and their lay colleagues attempting to find God in all things. This Jesuit core value is the dominant thread found in the garment worn in the first 100 years of Rockhurst.

Finding God in all things begins with engaging the world in which we find ourselves. It places each of us in the unique position of seeing the world as good but also capable of improvement. We neither reject the world as evil nor do we try to obliterate it. Rather, we fully engage it as the gift of creation and accept our role as co-creators in faithfully trying to make it better. When success comes, we celebrate it and give thanks to God, the source of the blessing. Even when success eludes us, we must remain faithful. This will ensure that we are committed to being timeless—responsive to the transcendent.

This is the legacy of Rockhurst University in its first 100 years. Today, we continue this timeless journey.

Rev. Thomas B. Curran, O.S.F.S.
14th President of Rockhurst University

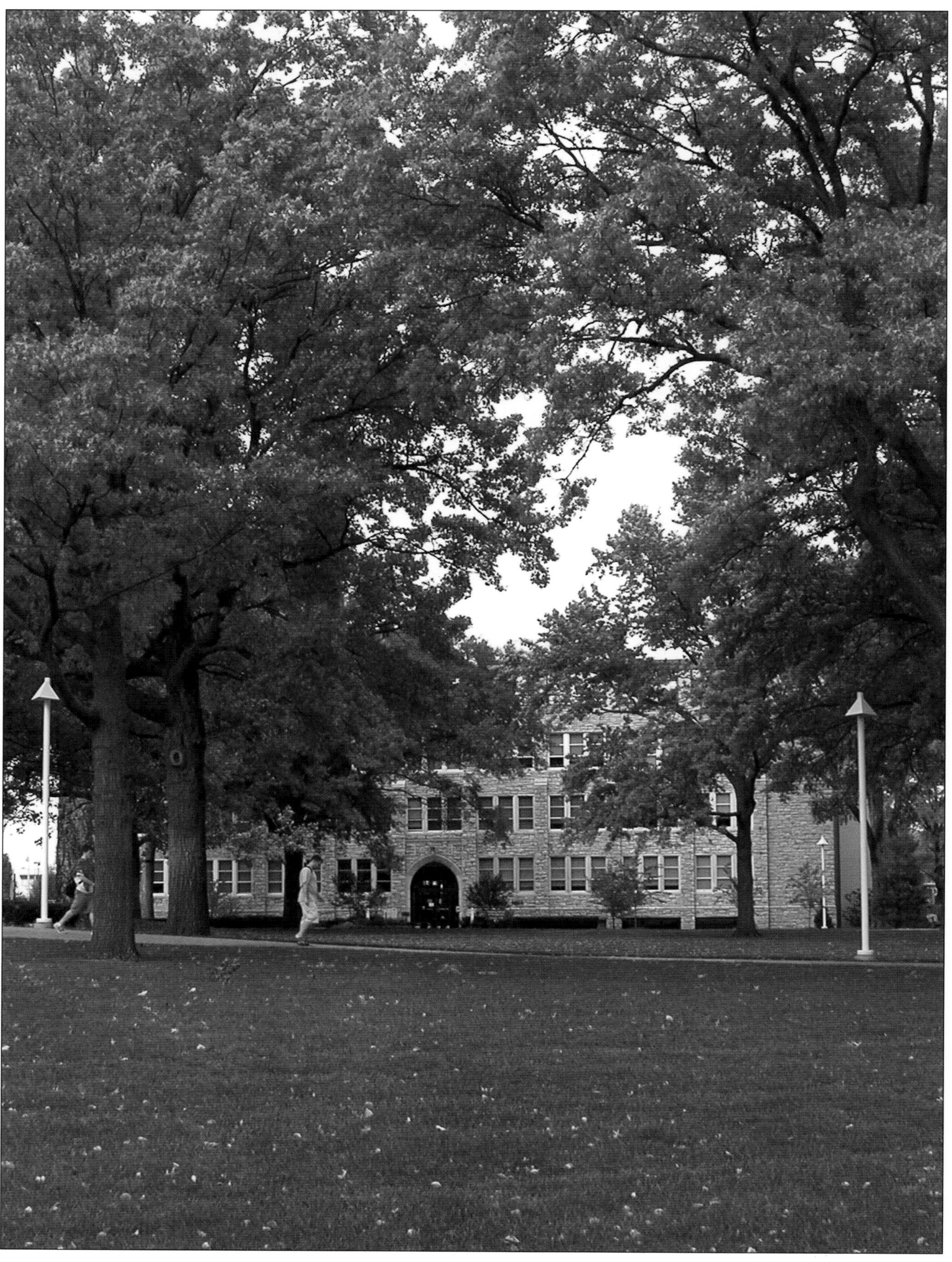

Preface

When my telephone rang a few years ago and it was Rockhurst's Bill Stancil on the line, inviting me to write a centennial history of the university, there simply was no way I could turn him down. Never mind that I was just then getting some traction on my dissertation at the University of Colorado, and the idea of taking on another large project was downright silly. But I couldn't turn Bill down, because I knew learning more about Rockhurst meant learning more about Kansas City and would keep me connected to a city I loved. And so the struggle began, two big projects, two towns, trips back and forth, Kansas City-Denver, Denver-Kansas City.

From an office in Greenlease Library, I soon discovered that the story of Rockhurst University was a story of struggle, as well. When Rockhurst founder Michael Dowling, S.J., arrived in Kansas City in the spring of 1908, he had no building, no money, and a city with relatively few Catholics. There was prejudice to overcome, convincing to do, and competition to be faced from the new De La Salle Academy at 15th and The Paseo. Struggle would become the overarching theme in the history of Rockhurst University: a struggle to establish itself, a struggle to build, a struggle to gain accreditation, a struggle to attract students.

Rockhurst's ability to adapt, then and now, has been the key to its survival and its success. To overcome prejudice, Rockhurst adopted a secular name; to weather the harsh years of the Great Depression, it opened a business school; to address the turbulent issues of the 1960s, it agreed to let students sit on its administrative and faculty committees, and, of course, it opened its doors to women. When the Rockhurst neighborhood showed signs of decline in the 1970s, the university stepped in to help reverse the trend. Over the years, Rockhurst revised and modified its curriculum, but the university never lost sight of its Jesuit tradition, which looked to the centuries-old *Ratio Studiorum* and St. Ignatius of Loyola's belief that the development of the intellect went hand in hand with the development of faith. Rockhurst, in other words, was a blend of the pragmatic and the ideal.

Above all, Rockhurst's history is the story of its people and the relationship it has maintained with Kansas City and Catholicism. In special moments or the everyday—be it the 1964 basketball championship, the 1996 dedication of the Science Center, or another of its many gallery openings—the university has brought honor and enrichment to the city around it. And in the university's hour of need, the community has given back, be it the women of the Rockhurst Circle, the businessmen of the Honorary Directors, the generous layman Lee Sedgwick, the devoted Catholic Henry J. Massman, or the faithful Virginia Greenlease. This reciprocity has taken root on campus, where Rockhurst's reputation as a caring place for students has molded students who likewise show concern for others, which they express through university service projects. Rockhurst's ever increasing caliber of students, who live in dormitories with iPhones and laptops, contrasts sharply with the self-described Boonville rube Robert Murray Davis, a 1956 graduate who was the first in his family to go to college. Though he lived in a tar-papered barracks salvaged from a World War II military base and slept on a surplus Army cot, Robert Davis, as students still do, found at Rockhurst a home and a place to grow.

Rockhurst's caring attitude has extended to this historian, who was blessed to have the professional and genteel Bill Stancil as editor and guide. He was always kind, always patient, always there to help, and always a scholar of the first magnitude. It was Bill who took me down to the basement of Greenlease Library, where Rockhurst archivist Ed Kos was busy identifying pertinent material. Over the intermittent 4 years it took to research and write this history, Ed would pull box after box from his shelves and cart them upstairs, where I would find them waiting on my next trip to Kansas City. Just next door to my office on the library's mezzanine, history professor and Catholic scholar Rick Janet read a draft of the manuscript, offered suggestions and, because I had little background in Catholic studies, provided valuable insight. It was Rick who sat down one day and, just like that, listed the overarching themes as he saw them in the manuscript. These themes, which I have mentioned above—the struggle at the core of Rockhurst's history, the university's blend of the pragmatic and the ideal, the story of its people and its relationship to Kansas City and Catholicism—are Rick's insights and reflect the broad perspective that he brought to the project.

As in the writing of any history, those who go before lay the foundations for those of us who follow. Special thanks go to the late Patrick F. Harvey, S.J., who not only was Rockhurst's first faculty member, but its first historian. His undated *History of Rockhurst College* offers rich insights into the university's early days when it wasn't a university at all, but still a high school. Former Rockhurst student John Jennings contributed to our understanding of Rockhurst with his 1938 Ph.B. thesis, *History of Rockhurst College*, followed in 1939 by the soon-to-be World War II GI Hugh M. Owens' excellent *History of Rockhurst College: The First Quarter Century (1914-1939).* On the occasion of Rockhurst's 75th anniversary, Sandra Scott Wilks brought the story up-to-date with her *Rockhurst College: 75 Years of Jesuit Education in Kansas City, 1910-1985.* Following their lead, this centennial project approached Rockhurst's history chronologically.

Historians would be at a loss without the assistance of archivists and their library staffs. At the Midwest Jesuit Archives in St. Louis, Nancy Merz, David Miros, and Mary Struckel were particularly helpful, pointing me, for example, to the *Woodstock Letters* and files containing Father Dowling's correspondence with Provincial Rudolph Meyer as he worked so tirelessly to establish Rockhurst College. At the Community of Christ archives in Independence, Ronald E. Romig graciously shared his research on the fascinating history of the Morman Church in Jackson County and how it was people of the Mormon faith who originally purchased the land where Rockhurst now stands. Librarians in the Missouri Valley Room at the Kansas City Public Library, who had been so helpful as I worked in the late 1990s on a history of Kansas City, came to my rescue again, directing me to census records, Sanborn maps, and Catholic histories of Kansas City, including Dorothy Brandt Marra's *This Far By Faith* and the Rev. William F. Dalton's *Historical Sketches of Kansas City.* It was in the Kansas City Public Library's extensive newspaper collection that I found back issues of *The Kansas City Star* and *Times,* and in its collection of Kansas City *Directories* that I was able to ferret out the railroad background of Lee Sedgwick's father and learn, among other details, that Rockhurst's great benefactor lived "in well-appointed hotels," a detail that seemed to tell so much about the elusive Mr. Sedgwick. Robert Murray Davis' reminiscences of life at Rockhurst in the 1950s, Pat O'Neil's work on the Irish in Kansas City, Sherry Lamb Schirmer's on the city's ethnic communities, and the meticulous Jesuit scholarship of the late Gilbert J. Garraghan, S.J., were important, as was research into Jackson County land deeds compiled by O.B. and Joanne Chiles Eakin and Pearl Wilcox.

Not to be overlooked is the staff at Greenlease Library, who stood at the ready for anything from fielding a question to queuing up the microfilm reader. The staff pointed me to past issues of *The Rockhurst Sentinel* and *The Rockhurst Hawk*, as well as newspaper clippings that some unheralded person had pasted into scrapbooks over the years. Rockhurst University catalogs, *The Province News-letter*, *The Jesuit Bulletin*, *The Catholic Register* and, especially in later years, publications such as *Rockhurst* magazine, the various *President's Reports* and the campus newsletter, *Rockhurst Community*, were invaluable.

It has been a privilege—and not so much of a struggle after all—to write this centennial history of Rockhurst University. Thank you for making me a part of your community.

Shirl Kasper

Chapter One

Catholic Beginnings

The morning of September 15, 1914, could not have been more miserable in Kansas City. A downpour had started in the middle of the night and did not let up for hours, dumping so much rain that torrents of water washed down 23rd Street, upending the asphalt paving and strewing a pile of wood blocks that were stacked along the curb, waiting to be installed in the street. The heavy, creosoted blocks floated away, leaving in their wake an obstacle course to be negotiated by passengers stranded on the stalled cars of the Metropolitan Street Railway Company, who had no choice but to disembark, then "slipped and slid and stumbled," *The Kansas City Star* reported, "from one foot wetting to another."[1]

Rain poured down from the bluffs into the West Bottoms, flooding old Union Depot and forcing waiting passengers upstairs. On Southwest Boulevard the water was 3 feet deep, and the residents of Rosedale were preparing to evacuate. Farther south, where Kansas City was only beginning to grow, Brush Creek was out of its bank, and nearby Federal League Baseball Park at 47th Street and Tracy Avenue had turned into a lake. Just up the Troost Avenue hill, in the doorway of a brand new academy slated to open its doors on this very miserable morning, stood Father Michael Dowling, S.J., the founder of Rockhurst.

In what has become a story rooted in Rockhurst legend and tradition, the thunder and lightning were terrifying that morning as a worried Father Dowling looked out. He'd been hoping and praying for good weather—but now this! Would any students show up? How possibly could they with the Troost Avenue hill covered in mud and streetcar passengers stranded downtown? "The college was supposed to open at 9 a.m., but at 8:30 the rain was still pouring down in torrents without any sign of ceasing," re-

Sedgwick Hall under construction, June 28, 1914. When classes began on September 15, 1914, the exterior structure was complete but the upper two floors were unfinished. "The college was supposed to open at 9 a.m., but at 8:30 the rain was still pouring down in torrents without any sign of ceasing," recalled Patrick F. Harvey, S.J., the school's first faculty member. Harvey had spent the morning with Father Dowling sweeping water out of the building. Courtesy of Rockhurst University Public Relations and Marketing.

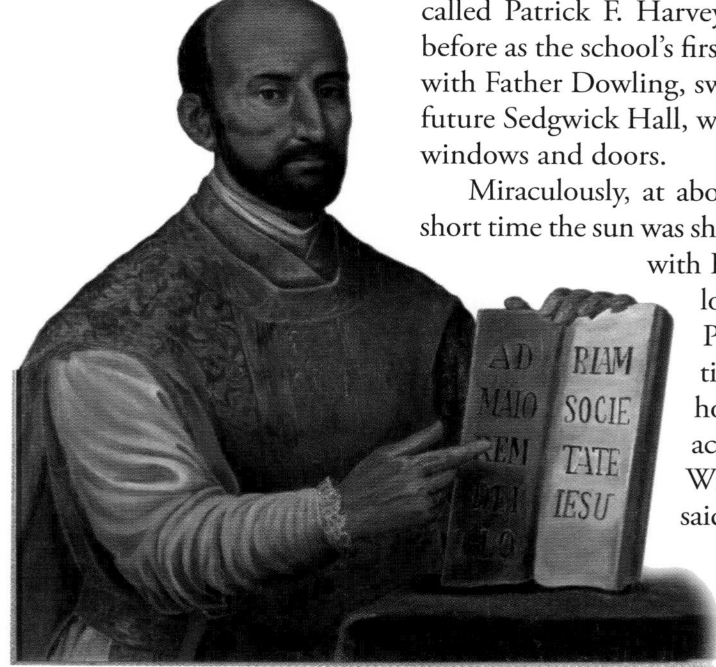

Portrait of St. Ignatius Loyola, nineteenth century. The Society of Jesus was founded in 1540 by St. Ignatius of Loyola. Within a few years the Society was receiving requests from various parts of Europe to establish colleges and universities for young men. Courtesy of Saint Joseph's University.

called Patrick F. Harvey, S.J., who had arrived at Rockhurst just weeks before as the school's first faculty member.[2] Harvey had spent the morning with Father Dowling, sweeping water out of the school's one building, the future Sedgwick Hall, which stood only half finished and still lacked all its windows and doors.

Miraculously, at about 9 o'clock "the clouds began to break and in a short time the sun was shining brightly," Harvey remembered. He stood then with Father Dowling at the back door of Sedgwick Hall, looking hopefully across the empty fields toward The Paseo, where the Marlborough streetcar line ran. In time, a car stopped at 53rd Street, and, lo and behold, a procession of boys disembarked and marched across the muddy field to the new Rockhurst College. When the first bell rang at 9:30 that morning, Harvey said, he "took down the names of forty-two boys who had braved the storm to come to Rockhurst."

For all the drama, the announcement of Rockhurst's beginnings received the driest of accolades in the newsletter of the Society of Jesus, the *Woodstock Letters*: "With the beginning of the scholastic year, the new Jesuit classical school, known as Rockhurst Academy, situated at Troost Avenue and 53rd Street, Kansas City, was opened to receive students. Two classes were organized, numbering in all, about forty boys, a number that will undoubtedly be increased as the year progresses."[3] No announcement made the Kansas City newspapers. Perhaps the press was too busy covering the big downpour, or perhaps the silence told much about Rockhurst's humble standings in Kansas City. It was only in later years, as the story of Rockhurst's founding was told, that that first, rainy Tuesday morning became a fitting symbol for the college's many long struggles. Nothing would come easily for Rockhurst's pioneers, but it seemed, just as the sun had broken through that first morning, it would again and again whenever the future seemed most dreary.

— THE JESUIT COLLEGES —

Rockhurst, of course, was a Jesuit college, the twenty-seventh[4] established in the United States since 1789, when America's first Catholic bishop, John Carroll, located the young nation's first Catholic college on Georgetown Heights, overlooking the Potomac River and the brand new capital of Washington, D.C. It was that same year that Congress adopted the country's new Constitution with its Bill of Rights, guaranteeing freedom of religion, an important point in a nation where only one percent of the population was Catholic. Carroll intended Georgetown primarily as a place to educate candidates for the priesthood, but, gradually, that changed as the Roman Catholic Church turned the work of advanced education over to the various religious orders, be they Jesuit, Redemptorist, or Christian Brother. In the process, writes church historian David J. O'Brien, Catholic colleges came to reflect the aspirations of the Catholic middle class and the traditions of their founding religious orders.[5]

Jesuit schools like Georgetown embraced the *Ratio Studiorum*, a handbook of educational methods first published by the Society of Jesus in Europe in 1599 and touted as the first educational system the world had ever seen. The *Ratio Studiorum*, or "Plan of Studies," stressed 4 things: the humanities; an orderly system of pursuing successive branches of knowledge; repetition of material; and the active involvement of students in their own education through argumentation, discussion, and competition.[6] Immersed in the methods of the *Ratio Studiorum*, it was no wonder that boys educated at Jesuit colleges gained an edge when it came to debate or writing competitions. They had learned to express themselves confidently—be it spoken or on paper.

Other Jesuit colleges followed in Georgetown's footsteps: Saint Louis University in 1818, Cincinnati's St. Xavier in 1831, New York City's Fordham in 1841, and Philadelphia's Saint Joseph's, which opened in cramped quarters in Willing's Alley in 1851. Philadelphia and its surrounding county had mushroomed to more than 400,000 people by then as famine-starved Irishmen and political refugees from Germany sought refuge in America. When St. Joseph's opened its doors, nearly one-third of the area population in Philadelphia was Roman Catholic.[7]

How different the story was in Kansas City. By 1851, though recently incorporated as the Town of Kansas, the future city was little more than a frontier outpost abutting the Indian Territory to the west. There was no state of Kansas yet, just the reservations of more than a dozen Indian nations, their lands stretching for 150 miles along the future border of Kansas and Missouri. The Shawnee, the Delaware, and the Wyandot lived within a few dozen miles of Westport, and the Kickapoo had settled near Fort Leavenworth. The Potawatomi, many of whom had historic ties to seventeenth-century Jesuit missionaries in the Great Lakes region, had recently relocated to a new reservation at St. Marys, 20 miles west of Topeka.

Portrait of John Carroll, America's first Catholic bishop, c. 1804, painted by Gilbert Stuart, famous portrait painter of George Washington and other political figures. Courtesy of Collection of Georgetown University Library, Special Collections Research Center, Washington, D.C.

It was to evangelize these Indian tribes that the first Catholic missionaries traveled to western Missouri. They were men like the young and zealous Joseph Anthony Lutz, who begged and begged his superiors in St. Louis—as well as Indian Superintendent William Clark—to allow him to go west to open a mission to the indigenous Kansa, who lived in villages 125 miles up the Kansas River near today's Manhattan. Lutz was only 26 years old, a German born in Baden on June 9, 1801, two years before President Thomas Jefferson purchased the great expanse of Louisiana. Lutz studied with the Jesuits at Brieg, in Switzerland, was ordained in Paris, and then sent to St. Louis, where he was assigned to the Cathedral as an assistant to Father Edmond Saulnier. Though he had studied with the Jesuits, Lutz was a diocesan priest and one so full of youthful zeal and romantic ideas that those who knew him described him as a man with a lively disposition, but one who acted on the spur-of-the-moment without much prudence. When his wishes at last were granted, Lutz, accompanied by the Indian agent Baronet Vasquez, set out for the mouth of the Kansas River, quite underestimating, in the words of historian Gilbert Garraghan, "the difficulties he would have to encounter."[8]

Before embarking up the Kansas River that August of 1828, Lutz stopped at the future site of Kansas City, where he found a tiny settlement of fur traders—French-Canadian *voyageurs* and *engages*, rough men, who had come down from the Rocky Mountains and settled with their Indian wives and mixed-blood children in the sandy river bottoms where the Kaw emptied into the Missouri—a place called Kawsmouth. The *voyageurs* had cleared the thick trees and divided the rich bottomland into arpents, where they grew onions, turnips, and potatoes.[9] Nearby was the home of the Indian agent Baronet Vasquez, who lived on the banks of the Missouri with his wife, Emilie, and their children. The son of a Spanish officer, Baronet was Catholic, as were his wife and the French-Canadian *voyageurs*. Spain and France were Catholic countries, unlike Great Britain, where the Protestant Reformation had spawned sects like the Puritans and their descendants, the Presbyterians and the Congregationalists, who built their steepled churches in New England and laid America's foundation as a Protestant country.

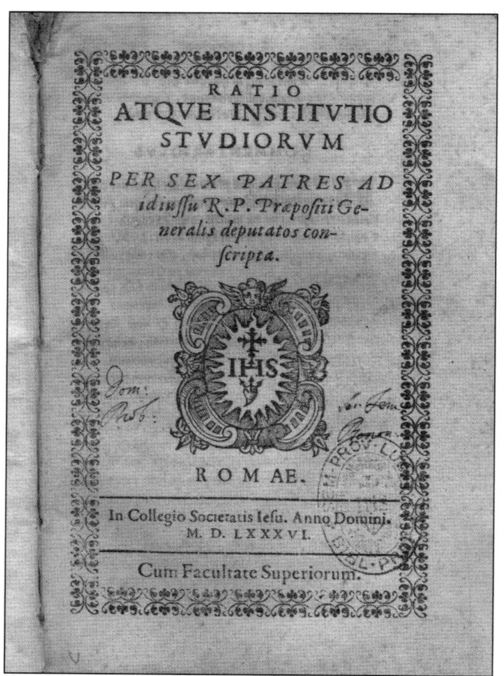

RATIO
ATQVE INSTITVTIO
STVDIORVM
PER SEX PATRES AD
iussu R.P. Præpositi Generalis deputatos conscripta.

ROMAE.

In Collegio Societatis Iesu. Anno Domini. M. D. LXXXVI.

Cum Facultate Superiorum.

The Ratio Studiorum (Rule of Studies), *officially published in 1599, provided Jesuits with standards and goals for the education of lay students as well as Jesuits. The* Ratio *made provisions for instruction in the humanities as well as philosophy and theology, stressing intellectual, spiritual, and moral development. Courtesy of Collection of Georgetown University Library, Special Collections Division, Washington, D.C.*

But beyond the 13 colonies, in the St. Lawrence River Valley, the French had established Quebec in 1608 and Montreal in 1642, and had sent Jesuit missionaries to convert the Algonquian-speaking peoples there, including the Potawatomi, Ottawa, Fox, Sauk, Kickapoo, and Miami. As early as 1673, the French Jesuit Jacques Marquette had explored the Mississippi River as far south as Arkansas, and the Frenchman Robert de La Salle, seeking to buy all the furs and skins he could, reached the Gulf of Mexico in 1681 and named the place Louisiana in honor of the French monarch, King Louis XIV.[10] The Roman Catholic faith held sway in French-Canadian strongholds, just as it did in Mesoamerica, where Spanish conquistadors had conquered the native Incas and Aztecs and the Pueblo people who lived in the valleys of the Rio Grande.

The Potawatomi, many of whom had historic ties to seventeenth century Jesuit missionaries in the Great Lakes region, relocated to a new reservation at St. Marys, Kansas, 90 miles west of Kansas City. St. Mary's mission and school served the Potawatomi people until they moved to a new reservation in Oklahoma. After that, St. Mary's grew into a thriving college—the first in Kansas, attended by many Kansas City boys over the years and used as a retreat center for Kansas City Jesuits. St. Mary's College would later figure prominently in the Rockhurst story. Courtesy of the Kansas State Historical Society.

It was the Spanish Catholic Baronet Vasquez who escorted Father Lutz to the Kansa villages, though his guidance was short-lived. Tragically, Vasquez contracted cholera on the way and died. Perhaps it was Father Lutz who broke the news to Emilie Vasquez because on his return from the Indian villages in the fall of 1828, it was at the widow's house he stayed and, while there, prepared a number of mixed-blood little girls for their first Holy Communion. He also visited the just-built Fort Leavenworth, where he heard the confessions of 2 soldiers—one Irish, the other German—and baptized the infants of 6 officers. Then Father Lutz crossed over the Missouri and went looking for Catholics in the town of Liberty, the oldest in western Missouri, founded just 6 years before by American pioneers, mostly from the South. They were so overwhelmingly Protestant that Father Lutz sounded a bit taken aback when he wrote to Bishop Rosati: "I found there only one Catholic soul," he reported, "the wife of Mr. Curtis, and a native of St. Louis."[11]

Lutz had better luck at Kawsmouth, where he told how the Catholic Chouteau brothers, Francois, Cyprian, and Frederick—grandsons of St. Louis founder Pierre Laclede and members of the wealthy Chouteau fur trading family—were in the midst of putting up "a grand edifice" on the Kansas River that would serve as a "a sort of emporium" for the sale and exchange of goods with the nearby Shawnee and Kansa. If the settlement at Kawsmouth had a patriarch, it was the oldest of the Chouteau brothers, Francois, whose wife, Berenice Thérèse Menard, was the daughter of the prominent Pierre Menard, of Kaskaskia, the first lieutenant governor of Illinois (1818-1822). Like her husband and father, Berenice was a devout French Catholic.

Despite his zeal and the kindness he received from the Chouteaus, Father Lutz spent only 6 months in the Kansas mission field, writing his last letter from Kawsmouth on November 12, 1828. He had grown frustrated with the Kansa, who had failed to return from their hunt and were nowhere to be found, though the weather had turned harsh and the Missouri River already was jammed with ice. Fearing he would be stuck all winter in this "alien land," Father Lutz boarded a "public coach" bound for St. Louis on December 2, 1828, never to return.[12]

The Head of the Virgin, a signed marble relief by Guiseppi Mazza of the School of Bologna, ca. 1700. Courtesy of Greenlease Gallery.

— A French Village —

Father Lutz was the first of a succession of Catholic priests who would visit the tiny settlement at the mouth of the Kansas River.[13] On November 14, 1833, 5 years after Lutz's departure, the priest Benedict Roux arrived at what he called "the French Village." Roux, a Frenchman himself, had come to America only 2 years before, sent by the Association of the Propagation of the Faith and zealous to evangelize the Indians on the Missouri frontier. Roux set to work at once to learn English, receiving his first lessons from Bishop Rosati in St. Louis and then taking up residence with the Spencer family of Dardenne, Missouri, 9 miles west of St. Charles, where he was given a small room, and devoted himself to his exercises.

"I say Mass here twice a week, with the family assisting," he wrote to Bishop Rosati. "Mr. Spencer is perfectly well able to teach me English ... But he has too great an inclination to speak French; I have to tell him often, very often, to speak English, an embarrassing thing for me to do as I am afraid of giving him offence."[14]

By April, Father Roux had relocated to the home of a Mr. and Mrs. Kelly of St. Charles, where he was still trying to master "the difficulties of the language" and begging the bishop to send him on his Indian mission "as soon as possible." By November his wish was granted, and he was dispatched from St. Louis to minister to the pioneer settlement at Kawsmouth. Father Roux arrived with big plans to build a church and to secure at least 2 nuns to establish a school—one nun to teach in French, the other in English—for it was plain to see that English was being heard more and more at Kawsmouth as American pioneers began to flood the region after Jackson County was created in 1827. English-speaking Americans bought up land on the river bluffs, in the wooded valley of the Big Blue, and on the prairie beyond. It was, in fact, in a house made available by an American Protestant that Father Roux on Christmas Day 1833 held his first Catholic services, probably near the Chouteau trading post, about 10 miles up the Kansas River in today's Johnson County, Kansas.

"There, vested in my soutane, surplice and stole I preached first in French, for the Catholics of the neighborhood had eagerly gathered at the place; then, would you believe it, I was presumptuous enough to preach in English and to start off with a subject really beyond my capacity." But, he wrote, "God was indeed pleased to bless my efforts" for all the American Protestants "listened to me with interest and with the greatest attention."[15]

But the winter was bitterly cold, and Father Roux felt "pitilessly confined" without even the "least little house where we can meet and celebrate the Holy Mysteries." He didn't dare take up the American Protestant's offer to continue to use his house for services because he "is a lover of balls and took advantage of our Christmas meeting to give one in the evening and another the day after." Father Roux seems to have quarreled with Berenice Chouteau, who found nothing wrong with the joyful dances and the plentitude of food. But he got along well with her husband and told him of his high hopes of building a church.

Immediately, Roux said, Francois Chouteau "called a meeting of the Catholics of the locality to discuss means towards getting a church and supporting a priest." By February 1, 1834, Roux's French parishioners succeeded in leasing for a year a house to serve as a church, probably near today's 2nd and Cherry streets. Two smaller, attached houses served as a presbytery, where Roux, once described as "a little smooth-shaven Frenchman, slight of build and delicate," spent miserable Saturday nights sleeping uncomfortably on an old mattress "raised on a large wooden support." He apparently spent the rest of the week at the Chouteau trading post farther up the Kaw in Indian Territory and came down to Kawsmouth every Sunday for services, the first of which he held on February 2, 1834.[16]

"I have the pleasure of seeing many Americans present," he wrote to Bishop Rosati that March. "They listen with the greatest patience to my poor English. I preach in French and English every Sunday." Though there was not one American Catholic in all of Kawsmouth, Roux smiled at the Protestants' curiosity and believed that before long that would change. It was with that in mind that Roux baptized 12 children on February 23, making sure to do it "with all the pomp and solemnity possible, so as to inspire the Protestants" and "draw them by such attractions to our Holy Religion."

For all his high hopes, when Father Roux left Kawsmouth for an assignment in Kaskaskia, Illinois, in the spring of 1835, he counted only 20 Catholic families in the entire vicinity. In all of Liberty and Independence, the area's leading towns, he'd found only 4 Catholic families and concluded that it would be impossible to establish a Catholic church in either town because the "prejudice is too strong there against our religion."[17]

— MORMON LAND —

But even the prejudice against Roman Catholics could not compare to that levied against members of The Church of Jesus Christ of Latter-day Saints, the Mormons, who, like the Jesuits, felt called to minister to the Indians living just over the Missouri border.[18] As early as 1830, a handful of Mormons were in the Indian Territory trying to establish a mission to the Delaware. But the U.S. government ordered the Mormons to leave. Undeterred, they turned their focus then to buying up as much land as possible as close to the forbidden Indian country as they could get—which meant in the newly established town of Independence and the surrounding Blues Country, so-called for the Big and Little Blue rivers, which flowed through the heart of the newly formed Jackson County.[19]

Edward Partridge, first bishop of The Church of Jesus Christ of Latter-day Saints, today referred to as Mormons. During their residence in Jackson County, Missouri, Partridge and other Mormons acquired almost 2,000 acres of land on behalf of the church. Partridge distributed this land to church members as spiritual and temporal "inheritances" in "Zion," in anticipation of the envisioned establishment of God's kingdom upon earth. Part of the land that Partridge purchased embraces today's Country Club Plaza, the Crestwood and Sunset Hill neighborhoods, and Brookside Boulevard. It was from these old Mormon lands that in 1909 Father Michael Dowling, S.J., purchased 25 acres for the future Rockhurst College. Courtesy of Community of Christ Archives, Independence, Missouri, H636.1.

The government had wasted no time in surveying and platting the land into a grid of ranges and townships. Sections were numbered, each containing 640 acres, further divided into half sections, quarter sections, and on down to one-quarter of a quarter section—or 80 acres. In this way, the land was offered for sale—at a minimum price of $1.25 an acre, an amount that enticed ordinary farmers of limited means. Settlers surged west, mostly from Virginia, North Carolina, Kentucky, and Tennessee, swelling Missouri's population 19 times over in just 30 years—from 20,000 in 1810 to 383,702 by 1840. The population of Jackson County more than doubled, from 2,822 in 1830 to 7,612 in 1840.[20]

Settlers went to the government land office in Lexington, where they put down their money in cash—$100 for an 80-acre parcel, $200 for a 160-acre quarter-section. That was a lot of money, especially in a time when the average farmer was self-sufficient and did not generally deal in much cash. The Mormons made a collective effort to raise money from their members in the East by instructing everyone who could to throw cash into a pot. With the money in hand, the church's first bishop, 37-year-old Edward Partridge, went on ahead as a kind of scout to buy up as much private and public land as he could.[21] It was on July 26, 1831, at the land office in Lexington, that Partridge laid his cash on the counter and purchased 80 acres on the rolling prairie west of the Big Blue and just south of Brush Creek. A year later Partridge bought an adjoining 80 acres, giving the Mormons 160 acres in the northwest quadrant of Section 33, Township 49, Range 33 of Jackson County, Missouri—land that, in time, would become the home of Rockhurst University.[22]

Edward Partridge was a New Englander by birth, born in Pittsfield, Massachusetts, on August 27, 1793, during the opening years of the Second Great Awakening, when religious revivals—fanned by ministers who traveled the countryside—swept across America. It was during these years that the Baptist and Methodist faiths burgeoned as circuit riders spread the gospel by holding emotional "camp meetings" in frontier villages all the way to Kentucky. Partridge learned the hatter's trade and joined the sweeping tide west, where the religious fires of revivalism burned bright in America, especially along the new Erie Canal and in what came to be called the "burned over" district of western New York. The great evangelist Charles Finney prayed for sinners by name and encouraged women

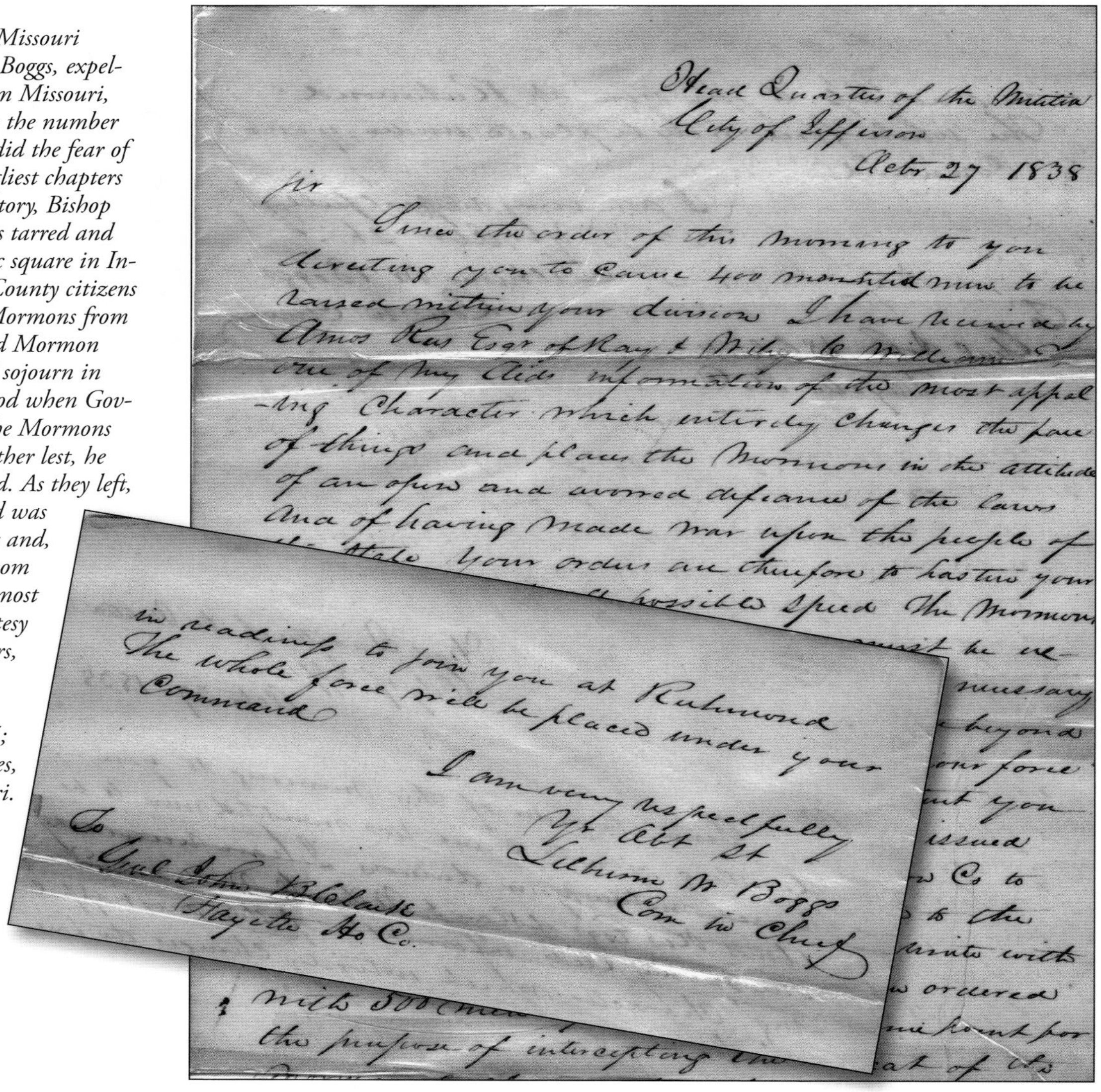
Head Quarters of the Militia
City of Jefferson
Octr 27 1838

Sir

Since the order of this morning to you directing you to cause 400 mounted men to be raised within your division I have received by Amos Rees Esqr of Ray & Wiley C. Williams one of my Aids information of the most appalling character which entirely changes the face of things and places the Mormons in the attitude of an open and avowed defiance of the laws and of having made war upon the people of the State. Your orders are therefore to hasten your ... possible speed the Mormons ...

in readiness to join you at Richmond
The whole force will be placed under your
Command

I am very respectfully
Yr Obt St
Lilburn W Boggs
Com in Chief

To
Genl John B Clark
Fayette Ho Co.

Executive order from Missouri Governor Lilburn W. Boggs, expelling the Mormons from Missouri, October 27, 1838. As the number of Mormons grew, so did the fear of them. In one of the ugliest chapters in Jackson County history, Bishop Edward Partridge was tarred and feathered in the public square in Independence. Jackson County citizens forcibly expelled the Mormons from the county and burned Mormon homes. The Mormons' sojourn in Missouri ended for good when Governor Boggs ordered the Mormons out of Missouri altogether lest, he said, they be massacred. As they left, much of their old land was offered at sheriff's sales and, over time, would blossom into some of the city's most coveted acreage. Courtesy of Mormon War Papers, 1837-1841; Office of Secretary of State, Record Group 5; Missouri State Archives, Jefferson City, Missouri.

to testify at public gatherings, a suggestion that went decidedly against nineteenth-century gender norms.

By the 1820s, Protestants were shunning Calvinist doctrines of predestination in favor of free will and the idea that anyone could be saved. If individuals could become perfect, in the image of God, then, some believed that society could, too. Utopian movements sprung up, from the Shakers and John Humphrey Noyes' Oneida Community to the new Church of Jesus Christ of Latter-day Saints—the Mormons—founded in 1827 by Joseph Smith,[23] the son of a poor farmer in western New York. Smith announced that he had discovered a set of golden tablets on which was written the *Book of Mormon.* The book told the story of how God led individuals of Israeli descent to the Western hemisphere. Christ appeared to their posterity upon this continent. Unfortunately, a cruel civil war followed. Survivors of this war, unrighteous Lamanites, are the ancestors of modern day Native Americans. Smith proclaimed that he had a mission to restore God's ancient church.

The first contingent of saints—known as the Colesville Branch, originally from Colesville, New York area—arrived in Jackson County, disembarking near the mouth of the Big Blue River, then up the river to the Blue River Ferry, where they wound their way to Joshua Lewis', near Troost Lake Park. They spent a few weeks in this area, until moving onto the lands secured by Edward Partridge for a new Mormon settlement near the prairie, embracing today's 51st to 55th streets, between Troost Avenue and The Paseo.

Here the Knight family founded the Colesville Settlement. That fall and winter, 10 related Knight families moved into a single unfinished log cabin, the frozen ground serving as floor. Also, that same season, 14 elders and 31 members of the church held their first conference in Missouri, at the home of Joshua Lewis. Later, another conference was held in the home of Newel Knight, surely within sight of today's Rockhurst.[24]

In addition to the 80 acres that someday would include the site of Rockhurst, Partridge bought land embracing today's Country Club Plaza, the Crestwood and Sunset Hill neighborhoods, and Brookside Boulevard. He bought 200 acres between 27th and 31st streets, overlooking Troost Lake, and 80 acres between 35th and 39th streets on what would become The Paseo. In just over 2 years, Partridge, as well as individual saints, purchased as much as 1,985 acres in Jackson County.[25] Old settlers watched with increasing alarm, not only as parcels were snapped up, but as the Mormon population swelled—from 538 people in November 1831 to 1,200 just 2 years later—representing one-third of the county's population.[26]

As the number of Mormons grew, so did the fear of them. In one of the ugliest chapters in Jackson County history, the old settlers got together in July 1833 and destroyed the church's printing office in Independence where *The Evening and Morning Star* was being printed. Edward Partridge, the man who had purchased so much of the county land to be distributed to the saints, was taken from his house and escorted to the public square in Independence, where he was stripped of his hat, coat, and vest, and daubed with tar and feathers from head to foot.[27] In November 1833, Jackson citizens forcibly expelled the Mormons from the county and burned Mormon homes. As explained by historian Joseph A. Geddes, the old settlers, most of whom were Southerners, feared the Mormons for a number of reasons: Mormons were Northerners who did not own slaves, and worse, the church had admitted a handful of free blacks and mulattos. Mormons also were sympathetic to the nearby Indians, whom settlers tended to fear or despise. But probably, Geddes argues, the most important reason was the Mormons' stated intent to buy up all the lands in Jackson County and force the old settlers out.[28]

Bishop Peter Richard Kenrick. Bishop Kenrick oversaw the huge Diocese of St. Louis, which stretched from the Mississippi north to the Canadian border, south to Louisiana, and west to the Rocky Mountains. With the population of western Missouri growing, Bishop Kenrick himself paid a visit to St. Joseph and declared the Catholic population there the greatest of most any town along the Missouri River. He soon dispatched diocesan priest Bernard Donnelly to serve Catholics farther south in Independence and the little Town of Kansas, the locus of the future metropolis of Kansas City. Courtesy of Archdiocese of St. Louis.

Of course, events turned out just the opposite, as it was the old settlers who expelled the saints from Jackson County. Expelled, the Mormons took refuge across the Missouri River in Clay County—until the saints agreed to withdraw into newly created Caldwell County, where they found temporary asylum. By 1836, the bulk of the saints had established their headquarters at Far West, Caldwell County. While living there, on March 2, 1839, Edward Partridge appointed David W. Rogers, of Quincy, Adams County, Illinois, as his attorney and signed over 16 parcels of land that he had purchased in Jackson County for the ill-fated Zion.[29] The Mormons' sad sojourn in Missouri ended for good when Missouri Governor Lilburn W. Boggs, in the winter of 1838-39, ordered the Mormons out of Missouri altogether, lest, he said, they be massacred. As they left, much of their old land was offered at sheriff's sales and, over time, quietly would blossom into some of the city's most coveted acreage.

It was from the old Mormon lands that *The Kansas City Star's* William Rockhill Nelson would carve his beautiful Rockhill District, and that developers Fred P. Schell, Robert W. Cary—and, in time, J.C. Nichols—would plat housing developments along 53rd and 55th streets as Kansas City grew southward at the dawn of the twentieth century. It was from these old Mormon lands, as well, that Father Michael Dowling would find a home for Rockhurst College.

— CATHOLIC GROWTH —

The land that Edward Partridge lost when the Mormons were expelled from Jackson County passed through a number of hands before Father Michael Dowling purchased 25 acres for Rockhurst College in 1909. The flow of deeds is recorded at the Jackson County Courthouse, where, on September 4, 1840, we find a 36-year-old farmer, Jesse Thomas, who had lived in the county for at least a decade, purchasing 35 acres turned over by Partridge just a year before. Jesse Thomas' 35 acres, purchased at sheriff's sale, were in the south half of the west half of the northwest quarter of Section 33, Township 49, Range 33—the exact acreage that Father Dowling would, in time, buy.[30]

We find Jesse Thomas present at another sheriff's sale of the old Mormon lands, this time on September 5, 1844, when he bought 5 acres—for $1—from Sheriff Thomas Pitcher. That same day, Jesse Thomas also purchased, probably again for back taxes, another 45 acres—giving him the entire 160-acre quarter section that today embraces the area from 55th to 51st streets and Troost to Woodland avenues.

Like the great majority of Jackson County's early settlers, Jesse Thomas was a Southerner, and, like most Southerners, a non-Catholic. He was born in Virginia, migrated west to Kentucky, and got married in Henry County, Missouri, to another Southerner, the Kentuckian Elizabeth Brummett, 13 years his junior.[31] They would farm the old Mormon lands, buy more acres over the years, and by 1860 were doing well, with 10 horses, 9 mules, and 7 cows. When he was 63 years old, in 1867, Jesse Thomas sold the future Rockhurst land—the south 25 acres of the northwest quarter of the northwest quadrant of Section 33—to a 41-year-old blacksmith, Thomas C. Peers,[32] a New York native who was living in Westport Township with his wife, Lurinda, a Kentuckian by birth.

Living with the Peers were 2 young men who helped them in the blacksmith shop, 21-year-old Thomas Conway and 21-year-old Theodore Hanley, both of whom were born in Ireland, as were their parents. The census taker did not say whether the young immigrants Thomas and Theodore were Catholic, but they probably were, as were the great majority of Irish immigrants who fled to America as economic conditions deteriorated in Europe. A potato blight in 1846 caused widespread starvation in Ireland and forced almost a fifth of the country's 9 million people to seek new lives elsewhere. Two-thirds of the Irish went to America, which saw its immigrant population mushroom by 2.6 million in the decade before the Civil War. Germans and Irishmen composed the bulk of the surge, each contrib-

Father Nicholas Point, S.J., arrived at Kawsmouth in the winter of 1840 and counted 23 Catholic families. By spring 1841, he had left to join Father DeSmet in their expeditions to the Rockies to establish Indian missions. Father Point was an artist and left a large body of paintings, watercolors, and drawings, including this image of wagons heading south to Westport past the first Catholic church building in the settlement that would become Kansas City. Courtesy of Pierre Jean DeSmet Papers, 1764-1970, Cage 537, Manuscripts, Archives, and Special Collections, Washington State University Libraries.

uting more than 900,000 people to a young, industrializing nation sorely in need of laborers to build its railroads and work in its factories.[33]

Looking on from afar was Bishop Peter Richard Kenrick, who oversaw the huge Diocese of St. Louis, which stretched from the Mississippi north to the Canadian border, south to Louisiana, and west to the Rocky Mountains. With the influx of Irish Catholics, Bishop Kenrick dispatched diocesan priest Thomas Scanlan, an Irishman from Tipperary, to serve the growing German and Irish Catholic population in St. Joseph, Missouri, a town whose storied history dated to 1827 when the fur trader Joseph Robidoux established a trading post at Blacksnake Hills, named by the Indians who had long powwowed there. Joseph Robidoux had prospered and, like the Chouteaus at Kawsmouth, employed French-Canadian *voyageurs* and *engages*—Catholics all. And just as the pioneer priests Lutz and Roux visited the French and mixed-blood peoples at Kawsmouth, so Catholic priests did at Blacksnake Hills. The Jesuit Charles Van Quickenborne had visited as early as January 1837, when he baptized 14 Potawatomi children. Christian Hoecken, S.J., had visited from his station at Council Bluffs, Iowa, and Anthony Eysvogels, S.J., a missionary to the nearby Kickapoo, often visited Blacksnake Hills, celebrating Mass in Robidoux's house.

The missionary Peter DeSmet, S.J., had a pleasant visit there on his way up the Missouri to missionize Indian people in 1838, writing that he "had a long talk with Joseph Robidoux, who keeps a store and runs his father's fine farm." Robidoux had talked of building a little chapel and noted the fine location for a town.[34] Eight years later, when Father DeSmet returned from his famous journeys to the Rocky Mountains, he paid another visit to Blacksnake Hills, on November 23, 1846, and found it with the new name of St. Joseph and boasting a population of 3,500 residents, 350 houses, 2 churches, a city hall, and jail. "Its population is composed of Americans, French Creoles, Irish and Germans," DeSmet reported. Plans were being laid for a Catholic church, and Father Eysvogels was paying visits not only to Catholics in St. Joseph, but also in nearby Irish Grove and Weston, and in the new Platte Country, opened to non-Indian settlement in 1837. It was the Rev. Eysvogels who officiated at the marriage of Sophie Hickman and John Byrne O'Toole, whose father, James, was one of the earliest Irishmen to settle in the Platte Purchase.[35]

— A Visit from the Bishop —

With the population of western Missouri growing, Bishop Kenrick himself paid a visit to St. Joseph, noting in his travels along the way that he had found not a single Catholic family in all of Clinton County, Missouri, and only a few at the bustling steamboat landing of Lexington. He was far more pleased with what he found at St. Joseph, declaring the Catholic population there the greatest of most any town along the Missouri River. In addition to the Rev. Scanlan, he dispatched another Irishman, diocesan priest Bernard Donnelly, to serve Catholics farther south in Independence, Missouri, and the little Town of Kansas. The town had been platted only a decade before by a company of 14 men who purchased Gabriel Prudhomme's 271-acre farm, which lay on the south side of the Missouri River, from

St. Francis Regis, the first Catholic church building of Kansas City. The church and rectory (here shown) were log structures constructed in 1838 and stood near the intersection of Pennsylvania Avenue and 11th Street. Here Jesuit missionary Nicholas Point celebrated Mass in the winter of 1840 and spring of 1841, before joining Jesuit Father Peter DeSmet on his journeys west. After Fr. Point's departure, it would be another 40 years before a Jesuit returned to live at Kawsmouth. Courtesy of Missouri Valley Special Collections, Kansas City Public Library, Kansas City, Missouri.

today's Broadway, to Holmes, and south to 5th Street. The land rose from the river in sheer bluffs, but at its base the mighty Missouri had gouged a natural stone landing where boats could dock.[36] The town company divided the land into lots so steep that their backs curled up the bluffs. The men named the place the Town of Kansas, though it was so overgrown with brush and so laced with ravines that the local wits suggested that Rabbitsville or Possumtrot would have been more appropriate.

When Jesuit missionary Nicholas Point arrived in the winter of 1840-41, he counted a grand total of 23 Catholic families in the town, each "comprising a Frenchman with his Indian wife and half-breed children." They were poor, he said, but "had somehow contrived to build themselves a church." Father Point set to work in the little church, though it was so cold inside that at times the chalice froze. But nothing, he said, could keep the Catholic Creoles from attending his services.[37] It was Nicholas Point who drew the only map extant of the early French and Indian settlement at Kawsmouth, which he called *Plan de Westport*. He labeled the location of every Creole family—among whom were mixed-blood people of French, Iroquois, Sioux, Kickapoo, Potawatomi, and Gros Ventre descent.

Like Gabriel Prudhomme, the Creole Peter Laliberté had purchased land and recorded his name in the earliest of Jackson County deed books. On October 22, 1832, Peter Laliberté staked claim to 82 acres in Section 6, Township 49, Range 33, on the high bluffs overlooking the Kansas River Valley. Less than 2 years later, on April 5, 1834, Laliberté and his wife, Eleonora Chalifoux, conveyed 40 acres of the tract to Father Benedict Roux for $6. Father Roux later sold the tract—except for 10 acres on which, by the fall of 1838, stood the log church where Father Point celebrated Mass. That log church, writes historian Gilbert Garraghan, S.J., "is the historic pioneer church-structure of Kansas City." It stood, until its demolition, at the intersection of Pennsylvania Avenue and 11th Street, a block away from the present Cathedral of the Immaculate Conception.[38]

Although the Town of Kansas would become the locus of the future metropolis of Kansas City, at the time only a single crude road cut up a gully from the river landing and meandered over the hills to the prospering town of Westport, 4 miles to the south.[39] Father Point had seen the vast herds of oxen grazing on the prairie in the spring, waiting to be muscled into service for some caravan or other to Santa Fe. Westport, he noted, "was the gathering point for all expeditions to Mexico, California and the Rocky Mountains." It was from Westport that a vast assortment of manufactured goods from Missouri and around the world headed down the trail for Santa Fe after trade with Mexico was opened in 1821—cotton cloth, silks, and velvets; French wines and champagne; pianos; pins and needles; canned oysters; and strawberry jam. Traders, both American and Mexican, returned to Missouri with long teams of wagons carrying silver coins, mules, beaver pelts, and wool. The "commerce of the prairies," as it was called, was an extremely profitable venture that made a fortune for men like Jackson County's Alexander Majors, who in time would found the Pony Express. Westport was a prosperous town that by the mid-1850s would count 13 merchandise stores, 5 wagon shops, 3 hotels, one slaughterhouse, several schools, and an abundance of saloons. Westport was alive with merchants and traders and so many traveling men waiting to set out for Santa Fe in the spring that Father Point imagined "the great feast" of souls that could be had if Easter "could be properly celebrated."[40] It was soon after the Easter season of 1841, however, that Father Point said goodbye to Westport and joined Father DeSmet on his journeys west. It would be another 40 years before a Jesuit returned to live at the mouth of the Kaw.

Bernard Donnelly. Father Donnelly, a diocesan priest, was born in 1810 in Ireland and ordained in 1845 in St. Louis. His first appointment was "for the Missions of Westport Landing, Independence, Westport, Liberty, Clay Co., and about a hundred other places." Donnelly was pastor of the old log church, St. Francis Regis, and was largely responsible for bringing the first wave of Irish Catholics to Kansas City. Courtesy of Diocese of Kansas City-St. Joseph. Quotation cited in Dorothy Brandt Marra, This Far by Faith: A Popular History of the Catholic People of West and Northwest Missouri, *vol. 1 (Kansas City, Mo.: Diocese of Kansas City-St. Joseph, 1992), p. 331.*

— THE IRISH FIND WORK —

It was not a Jesuit, but diocesan priest Bernard Donnelly whose name appears prominently in Kansas City history. Father Donnelly, who arrived in 1846, gets credit for bringing the first wave of Irish Catholics to Kansas City. Looking for men to work in a quarry he opened near 12th Street, between Pennsylvania and Jefferson, he advertised for laborers in newspapers popular with Irish readers in the East, such as the *Boston Pilot* and the New York *Freeman's Journal*. Father Donnelly offered steamboat passage to Kansas City and promised jobs at his quarry, named "Rocky Point." Irishmen took Donnelly up on his offer and went to work making bricks and lime, digging streets through the steep river bluffs, and cutting stone to riprap the banks of the Missouri.[41]

Steep river bluffs are visible in this early view of 2nd Street looking east between Delaware and Main. Father Bernard Donnelly, who arrived in Kansas City in 1846, advertised for laborers in newspapers popular with Irish readers in the East, and offered steamboat passage to Kansas City to work a quarry he opened near 12th Street. Irishmen took Donnelly up on his offer and went to work making bricks and lime, digging streets through the steep river bluffs, and cutting stone to riprap the banks of the Missouri. Courtesy of Missouri Valley Special Collections, Kansas City Public Library, Kansas City, Missouri.

The immigrants were men like Peter Soden, who arrived in Kansas City in 1855 and, to earn a living, began digging basements and cisterns. Kansas City author Pat O'Neill writes that Soden saved enough money to send back home for his sister, Margaret, and brothers Patrick and Michael. With Patrick's help, Peter built up a contracting business and set to work on the initial grading of Kansas City's Main, Delaware, and Wyandotte streets.[42] In time, the Soden family became one of the city's first wealthy Irish families, and Henry P. Soden would be among the first students at Rockhurst College. By 1860, the Kansas City directory "was packed with Irish names," O'Neill writes, most identified as laborers with addresses in lower-class neighborhoods such as "Stringtown," next to the levee, or as renters in the boarding houses lining either side of Broadway, and along 6th and 7th streets.[43]

The old German Catholic church, St. Peter and Paul, partially funded with money from Father Donnelly's brickyard, had stood on the southwest corner of 9th and McGee streets since 1866. As more and more Irish

St. Patrick Church, 1890. By 1870, almost 9 percent of Kansas City's population was Irish born, composing the city's largest ethnic group. As more and more Irish Catholics arrived in the city, plans were laid for an Irish parish, St. Patrick, established in 1868. Within a few years it would locate at 8th and Cherry streets, where the church still stands, today named "Old St. Patrick." By 1880, St. Patrick Church had grown to nearly 400 families. Among congregants was the elderly Berenice Chouteau, a woman now almost 80 years old and a living link to the early settlement of Catholics at Kawsmouth. Courtesy of Missouri Valley Special Collections, Kansas City Public Library, Kansas City, Missouri.

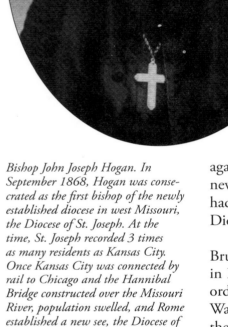

Bishop John Joseph Hogan. In September 1868, Hogan was consecrated as the first bishop of the newly established diocese in west Missouri, the Diocese of St. Joseph. At the time, St. Joseph recorded 3 times as many residents as Kansas City. Once Kansas City was connected by rail to Chicago and the Hannibal Bridge constructed over the Missouri River, population swelled, and Rome established a new see, the Diocese of Kansas City. In 1880 Bishop Hogan was ordered to move from St. Joseph to Kansas City, where he set to work planning the copper-domed Cathedral of the Immaculate Conception, a testament to Kansas City's new status as a diocesan city. Courtesy of Diocese of Kansas City-St. Joseph.

Catholics arrived in the city, plans were laid for an Irish parish, St. Patrick, established in 1868. Within a few years it would locate at 8th and Cherry streets, where the church still stands, today named "Old St. Patrick." While Catholics at St. Peter and Paul listened to the German-speaking Father Reusse, St. Patrick drew English-speaking Catholics living east of Main Street—about 200 families.[44]

— The Diocese of St. Joseph —

Although Kansas City would grow after the Civil War, St. Joseph had long outpaced it, especially with the arrival in 1859 of the St. Joseph and Hannibal Railroad, which linked St. Joseph to markets in Chicago.[45] By 1860, St. Joseph recorded 8,900 residents—3 times as many as Kansas City. Bishop Kenrick had recognized St. Joseph early on when, on June 17, 1847, he had been on hand to dedicate the city's first Catholic church, a small brick building at 5th and Felix streets.[46] Over the next several years, sisters of the Sacred Heart established a school for girls, and the Christian Brothers opened an academy for boys. In 1868, St. Patrick Church was under construction, and in 1869 Kenrick came again from St. Louis, this time to lay the cornerstone on St. Joseph's grand new Immaculate Conception Cathedral. St. Joseph—not Kansas City—had been selected to be the see for a new diocese in western Missouri—the Diocese of St. Joseph, established March 3, 1868.

That September, John Joseph Hogan, a 39-year-old Irishman born in Bruff, County Limerick, was consecrated as bishop.[47] Hogan had studied in Ireland, then entered the diocesan seminary at St. Louis, where he was ordained a priest on April 10, 1852, in those tense years before the Civil War. Times were especially ugly in Missouri, where rural slaveholders in the river valleys of "Little Dixie" vied for power with the state's large, antislavery German population, centered in St. Louis. In Jackson County, citizens feared for their lives as they traveled the country roads, on the watch for both the murderous Missouri bushwhackers and raiding Jayhawkers from Kansas. It was after the war that Father Hogan attracted widespread public notice when he openly repudiated the test oath of loyalty required under Missouri's new Constitution, adopted in June 1865. The oath required all voters, public officials, teachers, lawyers, jurors, clergymen, and trustees of church property to declare that they had never sympathized with or aided the South during the war. The test oath had met with widespread opposition by Protestants and Catholics alike. In fact, no Catholic priest in the state subscribed to it, and 3 priests had been put on trial and fined for preaching without taking the oath.[48]

Hogan moved from his post in Chillicothe and took up residence in St. Joseph, where he estimated that—despite all the excitement attached to the new see—he had only 3,000 Catholics in all of his new diocese, though it encompassed the entire state of Missouri north of the Missouri River and west of the Chariton.[49] And even as the new Cathedral rose, it was becoming apparent that the bitter, 4-way rivalry—between St. Joseph, Leavenworth, Atchison, and Kansas City—to become the next great city of the future was shaking out not in St. Joe's favor, but to that upstart Kansas City. The turning point came when Kansas City struck a deal with the St. Joseph and Hannibal Railroad to build a spur line from Cameron, thus connecting Kansas City to Chicago and all the markets of the East. But even more importantly, the deal called for construction of the first bridge over the Missouri River—the Hannibal Bridge, which would link Kansas City not only to markets in Chicago, but also to those in the great hinterlands of the West.

— A PARISH IN THE WEST BOTTOMS —

The Hannibal Bridge opened to great fanfare on July 3, 1869, near the foot of Broadway, heralding a new day for the old Town of Kansas. Over the next decade, Kansas City mushroomed from a muddy canyon of streets cut from the river bluffs to the principal city of the region. The 1870 U.S. Census pegged Kansas City's population at 32,260, surpassing that of St. Joseph, at 19,565, and every other city or town nearby: Leavenworth (17,873), Atchison (7,054), Lexington (6,336), Richmond (5,581), Liberty (4,831), Independence (3,184), Weston (2,453), and Westport (1,051).

As railroad tracks snaked into the West Bottoms, the French *voyageurs* and *engages* moved on. "The growth of Kansas City for the five years previous to 1872 was so rapid that it had a startling effect upon (their) quiet, pastoral natures," wrote Father William Dalton, a diocesan priest who arrived in Kansas City in the summer of 1872 to lead the new Annunciation Parish. Father Dalton, a St. Louis native born of Irish parents, came to

The Hannibal Bridge under construction, 1868. When the bridge opened on July 3, 1869, it became the first bridge to span the Missouri River and secured Kansas City's place as the principal city of the region. Courtesy of Missouri Valley Special Collections, Kansas City Public Library, Kansas City, Missouri.

Kansas City when he was 25 years old and would remain his entire life.[50] He watched an era fade as the old farms of the original French and Indian people gave way to the railroads, packinghouses, and flour mills that came to dominate the West Bottoms. In just 10 years, Dalton's parish swelled to 1,200 families, though there were only 25 when he said his first Mass in an empty storefront at 14th and Wyoming streets, on June 30, 1872.[51]

It was near the end of the Civil War, Dalton said, that farms in the West Bottoms were sold and platted into additions. By 1870, the Kansas Pacific, Missouri Pacific, and Fort Scott & Gulf railroads were pushing their tracks through the old farm fields, and, on April 7, 1878, Kansas City's new Union Depot, a monster of a building, 384 feet long with a maze of crooks and corners, towers and steeples, rose out of the sandy plain of the Kansas

— A PARISH IN THE WEST BOTTOMS —

Father William J. Dalton standing in front of Annunciation Church with first Communion class. Fr. Dalton, a diocesan priest who arrived in Kansas City in the summer of 1872 to lead the new Annunciation Parish, would witness the boom of railroads, packinghouses, and flour mills that came to dominate the West Bottoms. In just 10 years, Dalton's parish swelled to 1,200 families, though there were only 25 when he said his first Mass in an empty storefront at 14th and Wyoming streets.

"They were hard drinking days. Men had to drink to keep up with the work," recalled Father Dalton, who told how he carried a big stick and was not averse to going into a saloon to force a wayward Irishman home to his family. The importance of home and family was central to the message Dalton brought to Kansas City's Irish immigrants. "I used to preach each Sunday for ten minutes on the Gospel of the day and twenty minutes on real estate," he once said. "I urged my people to marry young and have their families, and I dogged them until they bought a little home." Though the homes all were small, each was fenced in, with flowers blooming.

Photo courtesy of Missouri Valley Special Collections, Kansas City Public Library, Kansas City, Missouri. Quotations from Missouri Democrat, *February 23, 1927.*

Union Depot opened on April 7, 1878. Located in the sandy plain of the Kansas River bottoms, the building was 384 feet long with a maze of crooks and corners, towers and steeples. As passengers by the thousands hurried through its doors, Kansas City seemed to grow up overnight. Courtesy of Missouri Valley Special Collections, Kansas City Public Library, Kansas City, Missouri.

River bottoms. With its new depot, the old Town of Kansas came of age. The city, as America itself, changed in the last decades of the nineteenth century from a predominantly rural society to a place where mass production and time-clock efficiency prevailed. Perhaps that explained the 4-sided clock tower, 125 feet high, that loomed over the entrance to the city's new depot. As passengers by the thousands hurried through its doors, Kansas City seemed to grow up overnight.[52] Switch tracks, freight depots, and machine shops followed, along with boarding houses, hotels, and saloons to serve the clerks and porters, and the men working in the switchyards and in the machine shops.

The stockyards took root along Genessee Street, and by 1889, the Rock Island added its tracks to the mishmash of industry that was turning the West Bottoms into Kansas City's industrial hub. When reporter Charles Dudley Warner stepped off the train in the fall of 1888, he was struck by the number of warehouses and marveled at the city's new elevated railway, which ran right over the top of the Wabash freight house and across the West Bottoms to Kansas. Warner, who wrote for *Harper's New Monthly Magazine*, said he doubted that a town ever had built up "so solidly" as Kansas City—or grown "more substantially." It was growing faster than St. Louis, if figures from the city's Board of Trade were to be trusted: from 41,786 people in 1877 to 165,924 in 1887.[53] Warner laid out the statistics: 4,054 houses built in the year ending June 30, 1886, another 5,889 by June 30, 1887, and a total of 4,565 miles of railway facilities "stretching out in every direction."

Even with Kansas City's steep hills, Warner had no trouble getting around. Kansas City had 35 miles of cable road, more than any city in the country except San Francisco and Chicago. Most impressive was the wrought iron 9th Street Incline, which linked downtown to the industrial West Bottoms below. The incline careered over the Quality Hill bluffs at an 18.5 percent grade, one so steep that visitor Emma Gage compared it with "coming down Pikes Peak."[54]

— Another New Diocese —

The Roman Catholic Church took note as Kansas City—and its Irish population—swelled in the years after the Civil War. By 1870, almost 9 percent of Kansas City's population—2,869 people—was Irish born, composing the city's largest ethnic group, followed by Germans (1,884) and English (709).[55] By 1880—only a dozen years after the creation of the Diocese of St. Joseph—Kansas City's Irish-born population had grown to about 3,900 with far more first-generation Irish. The city, now with a population of 55,735, had so outpaced St. Joseph that on September 10, 1880, Rome created yet another new diocese in Missouri—the Diocese of Kansas City.

Bishop Hogan was ordered to move again, this time from St. Joseph to the new see in Kansas City, where he set to work planning the copper-domed Cathedral of the Immaculate Conception at 11th and Broadway—a testament to Kansas City's new status as a diocesan city. Though Kansas City still was predominantly Protestant, Bishop Hogan counted 12,000 Catholics within the 23,539-square-mile diocese, which included all of

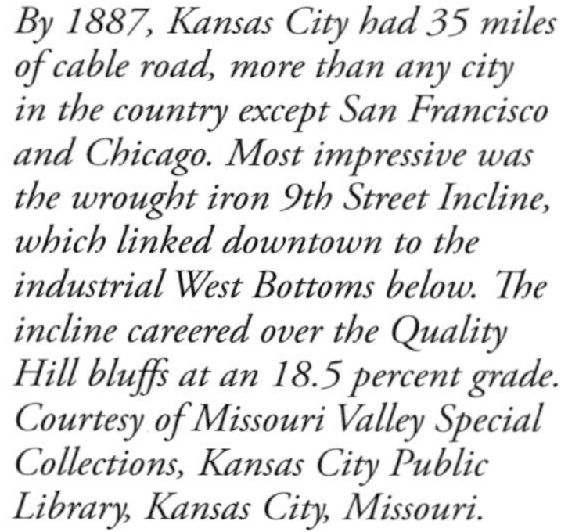

By 1887, Kansas City had 35 miles of cable road, more than any city in the country except San Francisco and Chicago. Most impressive was the wrought iron 9th Street Incline, which linked downtown to the industrial West Bottoms below. The incline careered over the Quality Hill bluffs at an 18.5 percent grade. Courtesy of Missouri Valley Special Collections, Kansas City Public Library, Kansas City, Missouri.

Father Bernard Donnelly took up residence at the old log church at 11th Street and Broadway in November 1845 and ministered uninterruptedly for 34 years, forming the link between pioneer and modern eras of Catholic development in Kansas City. In 1856, he built the brick church pictured here, Immaculate Conception, which was used until a new cathedral was completed in 1883. Courtesy of Diocese of Kansas City-St. Joseph.

Missouri south of the Missouri River and east to the border of Moniteau, Miller, Camden, Laclede, Wright, Douglas, and Ozark counties.

At 8th and Cherry streets, the Irish St. Patrick Church had grown to nearly 400 families, and plans were in the works for a 3-story school building. Among congregants was the elderly Berenice Chouteau, who attended regularly, sitting in the twentieth row from the altar, a woman now almost 80 years old and still active in her parish, though she represented a bygone era.[56] Her husband, Francois, had died years ago, and Father Bernard Donnelly, who had recruited his Irish countrymen to Kansas City to cut bricks and build up the Catholic Church, now lay buried in Mount Saint Mary Cemetery way out in the farmlands beyond Woodland Avenue and beyond the city limits.

Chapter Two

A Jesuit Parish

As the cornerstone was laid for the grand new Cathedral at 11th and Broadway on May 14, 1882, Bishop Hogan found himself doing double duty, serving as administrator of the Diocese of St. Joseph, north of the Missouri River, and as bishop of the Diocese of Kansas City, south of the river. Wright's 1880 map of Kansas City distinctly marks off the "Catholic Church Property" where Hogan now made his home. It stretched from Jefferson Street on the west to Broadway on the east, with St. Teresa's Academy in the middle. Unlike the overgrown hilltop where the Kawsmouth Creoles had built their log church so long ago, the countryside now was laid out in a grid of streets and new additions to the city: Lykin's Place, Aldine Place, and the Broadway Addition across 11th Street to the south. Wright's map drew Coates Addition to the north of the Catholic property, Ashburne's Addition to the east, and to the west, down over the bluff, were heavy black lines representing the tracks of the various railroads now passing through Kansas City: the St. Joseph and Hannibal Railroad; the Chicago & Alton; the Kansas City, Fort Scott and Gulf; the Atchison, Topeka & Santa Fe; the Missouri Pacific; and the Kansas Pacific. Clearly marked along St. Louis Avenue was the big Union Depot and, on either side of Genessee Street, taking up block after block amid the maze of railroad tracks, was the Kansas City Stockyards.

Father Bernard Donnelly's 1856 brick church, Immaculate Conception, was used until after his death in 1880, then replaced by this imposing Cathedral, completed in 1883. Courtesy of Diocese of Kansas City-St. Joseph.

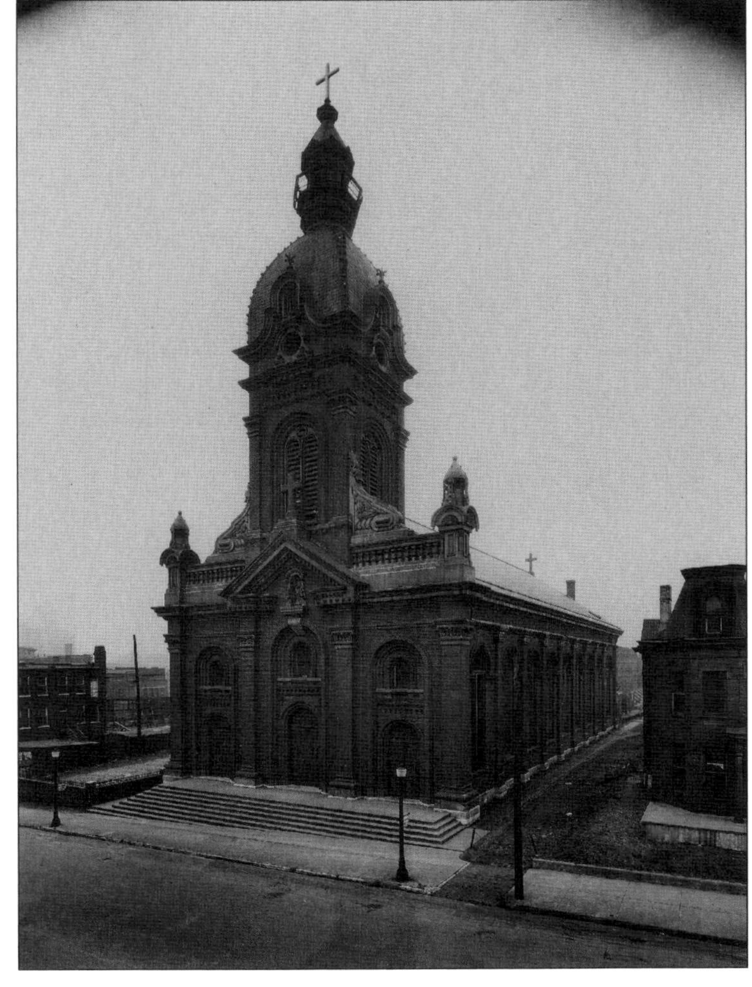

It was here that Father Dalton ministered to the Irish working class at Annunciation Parish. By the 1880s, however, as packinghouses and industry crowded into the bottoms, more and more working people moved to higher ground nearby. By 1887, so many Irish Catholics lived on "Irish Hill," in the vicinity of 25th and Madison streets, that Bishop Hogan established Sacred Heart Parish with boundaries that encompassed the West Side from 20th Street, on south past 29th Street, and east to Broadway. A school and rectory soon went up at 26th and Belleview, and Sisters of Providence arrived from Indiana in 1889 to teach. As school bells rang in the fall of 1892, 11 Sisters of Loretto had taken over the school. They counted 280 families in the parish and 280 children in their "academy."[1]

As Kansas City grew and the city limits pushed farther east and south, Bishop Hogan established more parishes. He often turned to religious orders to supply priests for these parishes. In 1878, the Redemptorist fathers laid the cornerstone for this 3-story monastery and church just to the east of what is now Broadway and Linwood. The Redemptorists were the first religious order to minister in Kansas City since the Jesuit Nicholas Point left Kawsmouth for the Rocky Mountains. Courtesy of Diocese of Kansas City-St. Joseph.

This was the pattern that would be followed again and again as Bishop Hogan oversaw the Kansas City of the 1880s and 1890s, when the population mushroomed and the city limits pushed farther and farther east and farther and farther south—more immigrants, more parishes, more churches, more schools. Two new parishes were established in 1882 alone: St. Joseph at 19th and Troost and St. John the Baptist in the East Bottoms at Highland and Independence Avenue; St. Aloysius at 11th and Prospect in 1885; St. Vincent's at 17th and Oak in 1887; Our Lady of Perpetual Help on Broadway; St. Stephen's, way out east in Sheffield, in 1888; and, in 1889, Holy Trinity on the high bluffs north of Independence Avenue. If Bishop Hogan was feeling overwhelmed, it was easy to understand. His new diocese had 9,000 Catholics in Kansas City alone, and, all told, 42 churches, but only 30 priests. So it was that Hogan turned to religious orders to help him out.[2]

The Redemptorist fathers were already in Kansas City, living in a house on the road to Westport. In 1878 they had laid the cornerstone for a 3-story monastery and church just to the east of what is now Broadway and Linwood. The Catholics of Kansas City were so happy to have them that the *Kansas City Journal of Commerce*, on May 28, 1878, reported that 2,000 people came out from the city "in carriages, buses, horse cars and on foot, and filled every available spot about the building." The next year, the Redemptorist order relocated its preparatory college and novitiate from Chatawa, Mississippi, to Kansas City. Young men came from all over the United States to attend, making the Redemptorists a boon for Kansas City merchants.[3] The Redemptorists were the first religious order to minister in Kansas City since the Jesuit Nicholas Point left Kawsmouth for the Rocky Mountains and the other long ago members of the Society of Jesus had visited Kawsmouth from the Indian missions over the Kansas border. But now the religious orders came in waves: the Dominicans, the Lazarists, the

Jesuits, and Christian Brothers in 1887, the Franciscans in 1890, and the Scalabrini fathers in 1891.

The Dominicans arrived in 1886, just a year after the burgeoning Kansas City extended its boundary another 1-1/2 miles east—to Cleveland Avenue—and another 1-1/4 miles south—to 31st Street. This was new territory in need of new parishes and new priests. The Dominican provincial entered into negotiations with Bishop Hogan, and on January 1, 1886, Holy Name Parish was established. It covered a huge swath in the expanded eastern boundary of town—from Brooklyn Avenue on the west to the new city limit at Cleveland Avenue on the east, and from 18th Street to 27th Street. The Dominicans set to work building a rectory and a church at the corner of 23rd and Walrond streets (called Monroe then). And just as the Sisters of Loretto would do on Irish Hill on the West Side, the Dominicans did on the East Side—they established a school next door to the church and invited the Dominican Sisters to come from Sinsinawa, Wisconsin, to staff it. The school opened with 67 pupils in September 1890.[4]

The story was repeated again and again. The Lazarists, or Vincentians as they also were known, arrived in 1887, built a church at 1715 Oak Street, and ministered to working-class people, many of whom lived in McClure Flats, an Irish slum between Main and McGee streets. The parish found itself so engulfed by the city's growing commercial district that, in 1894, the Vincentians would relocate to 31st Street and Flora Avenue, where they built another church, St. Vincent's, and a parish school, overseen by Sisters

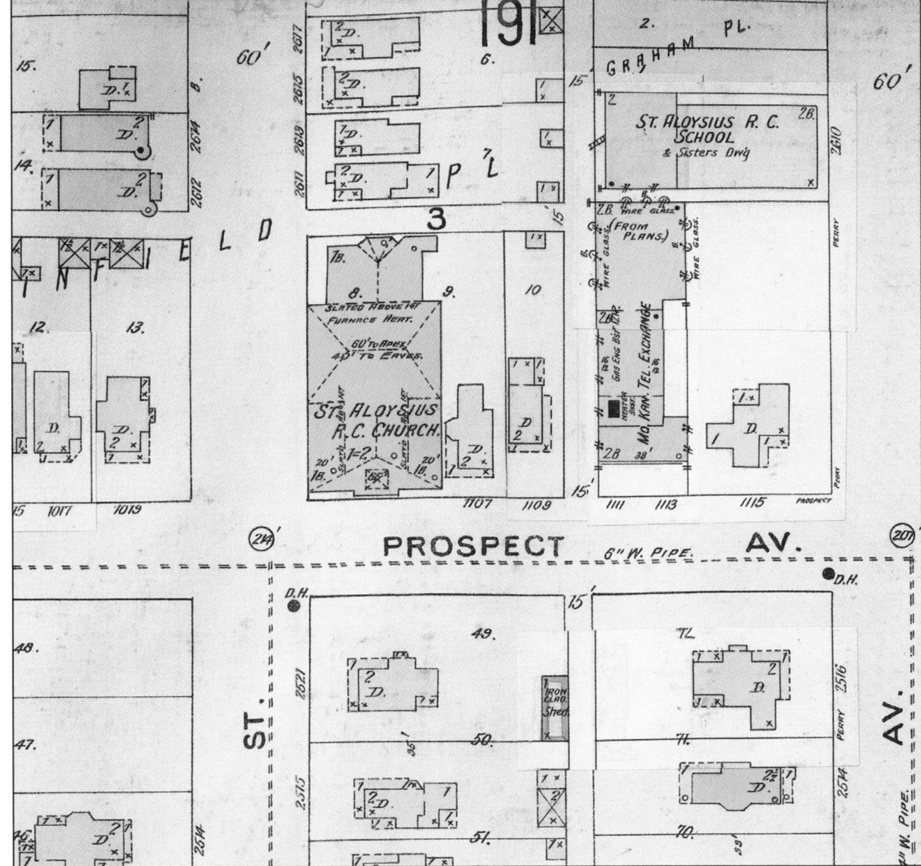

In a letter dated August 31, 1885, Bishop Hogan responded enthusiastically to the Jesuits' desire to return to Kansas City and establish a church and college. Hogan directed the Jesuits to locate in a district bordered by Woodland Avenue on the west and Benton Boulevard on the east, with the northern border set at Independence Avenue and the southern boundary at 18th Street. The parish, established on January 1, 1886, was to be called St. Aloysius. Sanborn Map, Kansas City, Vol. 2, 1896-1907, page 173. Courtesy of Missouri Valley Special Collections, Kansas City Public Library, Kansas City, Missouri.

of Charity of the Blessed Virgin Mary. In September 1908, a parish high school, called St.Vincent's Academy, opened and attracted students from all over the city.[5]

— St. Aloysius Parish —

And just like the Vincentians and the Dominicans before them, the Jesuits entered into an agreement with Bishop Hogan, authorizing the Society of Jesus to erect a church and ecclesiastical residence in Kansas City. The provincial of the society's Missouri Province, Father Leopold Bushart, S.J., had contacted Hogan some months before, informing him that he had received permission from the society's Father General to purchase ground in Kansas City. The news seemed to please Bishop Hogan, who responded in a letter of his own on August 31, 1885: "In reply to your letter informing me that the Very Rev. Father General of the Society has given permission to secure a site here for a church and college to be built in this city soon or in the future, I assure you such pious enterprise and project has my entire approval and most fervent prayers for success...."[6]

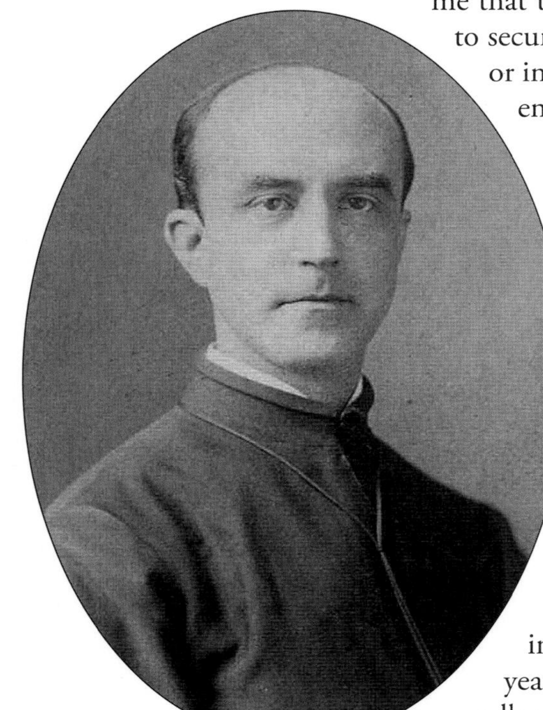

Father Henry A. Schaapman, S.J., first pastor of St. Aloysius Church. Fr. Schaapman said his first Mass on Sunday, January 17, 1886 at a house he purchased on the southeast corner of 11th and Prospect. Courtesy of Midwest Jesuit Archives.

A college? A college to be built in Kansas City? This was among the first indications that the Jesuits were planning to extend their collegiate efforts to Kansas City. By 1885 the Society of Jesus had built 22 colleges in the United States, including the 7-year-old Creighton College, established in Omaha in 1878, and Detroit College, established the year before in Michigan. Jesuit colleges had multiplied after the Civil War—St. Ignatius (the predecessor of Loyola) in Chicago in 1870; Canisius in Buffalo, in 1870; Saint Peter's in Jersey City, in 1872; and St. Mary's College in St. Marys, Kansas, in 1869.[7]

St. Mary's, just 90 miles west of Kansas City, had been an Indian mission and school until the Potawatomi people it served moved to a new reservation in Oklahoma. After that, the Jesuit-run St. Mary's grew into a thriving college—the first in Kansas, where many a Kansas City boy would attend over the years and where many a Jesuit would come for a peaceful retreat. The college stood on the outskirts of the little town of St. Marys, its brick buildings climbing a hill just beyond. At the foot of the hill, and practically at the St. Mary's College gate, ran the tracks of the Union Pacific Railroad, making the college easily accessible.

In a few years, St. Mary's College would figure prominently in the Rockhurst story, but in 1885, St. Mary's seemed far away as Bishop Hogan laid out a course for the Jesuits in Kansas City. As he had done with the Dominicans, Hogan directed the Jesuits to locate in the recently incorporated eastern part of the city, beyond Woodland Avenue, where the district was sparsely settled and the city so new that the streets had yet to be paved. A committee of Jesuits followed Hogan's orders nonetheless and spent that December scouting a place to locate a church within the boundaries the bishop had laid out for a new Jesuit parish—to be called St. Aloysius.

Hogan drew the western border at Woodland Avenue and the eastern border at Benton Boulevard, which was so far east in 1885 that entire quarter sections just beyond still lay in farmland. The northern border was set at busy Independence Avenue, a main artery served by the cable line railroad, and the southern border ran to 18th Street, where it abutted the Dominicans' Holy Name Parish, established the very same day, January 1, 1886.

It was within these boundaries that Bishop Hogan gave the Society of Jesus permission to erect "a school or schools for the instruction of children of both sexes." When it came to a college, however, the bishop was more expansive, instructing the Jesuits to locate "a college for the education of boys and youths" in "such part of the diocese...as may be thought suitable by the said Right Reverend John Joseph Hogan, or his successors, and by the said Society of Jesus...."[8] The college would have to wait, however, as the committee of Jesuits settled first on a site for a church. They found it in a city addition called South Winfield Place, between the Independence Avenue and 9th Street cable car lines. On December 4, 1885, Jesuit Provincial Rudolph Meyer took title to Lot 8 in Block 3 of South Winfield Place, at the southeast corner of 11th Street and Prospect Avenue. Then, on December 10, he added Lot 9.[9]

St. Aloysius' first pastor, Father Henry A. Schaapman, S.J., arrived in Kansas City on December 31, 1885, and got right to work. Within a week, he finalized the purchase of a house on the southeast corner of 11th and Prospect and said his first Mass there on Sunday, January 17. He celebrated a second Mass that Sunday and, all told, 68 persons attended. By Thursday, January 21, Brother Murtagh arrived to take charge of the household, and the Sisters of St. Joseph kindly donated articles for the bedrooms, dining room, and kitchen. On only the second Sunday in the new parish, January 24, 1886, the Jesuits held their first Catechism class, attended by 21 pupils. By February 6, the parish had an Altar Society. By the fourteenth it had collected $67 to rent seats for 6 months, and on February 21, it held its first baptism, for Mary Steward, daughter of Mr. and Mrs. Henry A. Steward. By April 11, St. Aloysius had a Young Ladies Sodality and, by April 12, a Building Committee with a subscription list of $400. Provincial Rudolph Meyer paid his first visit to the new parish on Wednesday, May 19, and gave his permission to begin building a church basement, where exactly a year to the date of its founding, St. Aloysius opened its first chapel.

— Catholics Face Prejudice —

It was clear by then, January 1, 1887, that the Society of Jesus, after an absence of 40 years, had returned to Kansas City with all its historic devotion. For all that, it would be another quarter of a century before "a college for the education of boys and youth" took root. That ambitious project was put on hold as the Jesuits turned their attention to the founding of a parochial school. Their plans were set in motion that July when Father James A. Dowling, S.J., arrived to replace Father Schaapman. James Dowling, who was the older brother of Rockhurst founder Michael Dowling, had a genial disposition and a fun-loving personality that suited him well in building up the parish and school. At home in almost any gathering, Father Dowling had a talent for directing sodalities and even wrote a booklet called *Practical Questions on the Sodality*, which was widely circulated and

— ANTI-CATHOLICISM IN KANSAS CITY —

Kansas City was not immune to anti-Catholic outbursts. On Tuesday night, January 16, 1894, a riot erupted outside Turner Hall at 12th and Oak streets during what *The Star* described as an "abusive lecture" by one J.V. McNamara, who claimed to be an ex-priest. McNamara appeared on stage with his wife, who had held a revolver in her lap while selling tickets "to men only," at 35 cents for the main floor, 25 cents for the gallery. By 8:10 p.m., the hall was packed with what *The Star* described as "large delegations of members of the A.P.A." who had come from Kansas City, Kansas, Argentine, and other suburbs to hear McNamara's anti-Catholic spiel. Turner Hall still sported the gaudy decorations of a recent German dance when McNamara appeared on stage shortly after 8. He stood beside a dry goods box serving as a speaker's table. It was covered with American flags and piled high with copies of the book, *Confessions of a Nun*, which McNamara was offering for sale.

Though *The Star* did not say, the book probably was written in the style of Rebecca Reed's *Six Months in a Convent* (1835), which sold 200,000 copies. Reed claimed she had been a nun, held captive in an Ursuline convent near Boston. Though the Mother Superior of the convent denied Reed had been a nun there, an angry mob burned the convent anyway. Reed's story led to other anti-Catholic publishing tales, including Maria Monk's best-seller, *Awful Disclosures of the Hotel Dieu Nunnery of Montreal* (1836), which titillated readers by claiming that nuns served as a harem for priests.

AWFUL DISCLOSURES,
BY
MARIA MONK,
OF THE
HOTEL DIEU NUNNERY OF MONTREAL,
REVISED, WITH AN
APPENDIX,
CONTAINING,
PART I. RECEPTION OF THE FIRST EDITIONS.
PART II. SEQUEL OF HER NARRATIVE.
PART III. REVIEW OF THE CASE.
ALSO, A SUPPLEMENT,
GIVING MORE PARTICULARS OF THE NUNNERY AND GROUNDS.

ILLUSTRATED BY A PLAN OF THE NUNNERY, &c.

NEW-YORK:
PUBLISHED BY MARIA MONK,
AND SOLD BY BOOKSELLERS GENERALLY.
1836.

Though less famous than Maria Monk's disclosures, *Confessions of a Nun* apparently had the ability to stir similar ugly passions. A squadron of policemen was on hand in the hall, though not a single woman as J.V. McNamara took the stage. He carried a Winchester repeating rifle in one hand and a pistol, *The Star* wrote, "which he placed with much ostentation" on the table before him, its barrel gleaming under the stage lights. He had donned a priest's long, black, frock coat and white collar, and started in on the Catholic confessional.

Trouble began when a man in the crowd stood and called McNamara a liar. Two policemen seized him and took him outside, where a gathering of Catholics was trying to gain admittance to the hall. Police turned them back, and before long stones and other missiles crashed through the glass windows of the hall. An iron bolt struck John Waldron, a motorman who lived at 2531 Woodland Avenue, and he was led from the hall, bleeding profusely from a deep scalp wound.

"Keep your seats," McNamara shouted. "This is a bad night for Rome. Let the hoodlums do

Continued

their worst." But as the bombardment increased, McNamara seemed rattled and spoke so fast it was hard to understand his words. Then he closed his lecture and called on all who were his friends to rise. "Be brave," he said to the 500 standing and exhorted them to protect him and his wife by gathering around them as they left the hall. "Keep cool. Be brave," he said. "We stand under the protection of the A.P.A."

The next day, *The Star* ran a sketch of the "sorry" looking hack that had carried McNamara and his wife from the scene. They had run "a gauntlet of stones," the newspaper said, and the hack, owned by the Kansas City Omnibus and Carriage Company, had come away with a broken window and many scratches and dents. "HE BARELY ESCAPED ALIVE" the headline read the next morning.

much in vogue at the turn of the century. Father Dowling also believed in the healing power of the Holy Water of St. Ignatius and was described as a "veritable apostle" in spreading the use of the holy water for cures.[10]

It was James Dowling who extended an invitation to the Sisters of Charity to take charge of the school, and when they agreed to send a few sisters from Dubuque, Iowa, Father Dowling entered negotiations to buy property south of the parochial residence. As he did so, he ran into a prejudice that would plague Catholic people in Kansas City in the years to come. Not only was the land he sought being offered at the "exorbitant price of $5,000," but also, as a church historian recalled, "some of the neighbors were bitterly opposed to a Catholic school in the vicinity."[11]

Although the historian did not list their reasons, opposition to parochial schools was long-standing in the United States. Catholic schools stood apart from the public—and ideologically Protestant—school system that developed in America in the reform-minded days of the pre-Civil War. By the late nineteenth century, the state-supported public school was so revered that it had acquired what historian Jay P. Dolan describes as "a sacred aura." Driving the public school movement, Dolan writes, was an ideology centered on "Republicanism, Protestantism, and Capitalism," a belief system rooted in Puritan John Winthrop's vision of America as a "city on a hill."[12]

With its Protestant hymns, prayers, and Bible reading, the system was not very tolerant of people of other religious heritages. So it was that Catholics determined to have their own schools, where their faith and morals would be secure, and where their children would not be denied the sacraments. Because Catholics challenged the public school system, they were labeled as un-American and enemies of the republic. "Catholics," Dolan writes, "were perceived as assaulting the basic Protestant ideology that inspired not only school, but also the nation. Thus, to attack the school was to attack God, nation, and government as well."[13]

Anti-Catholicism grew with the influx of Catholic immigrants from southern Europe in the late nineteenth and early twentieth centuries. The prejudice against immigrants was nothing new, particularly against the early-arriving Irish, who were poor, tended to affiliate with big-city political machines, and were vilified for their drinking habits.[14] Protestant Americans also feared that Catholics were more loyal to the pope in Rome than the president in Washington. Nativist movements sprang up periodically in the United States and, famously, led to riots in Philadelphia in 1844 and the creation, in the 1850s, of a new political party, the Know-Nothings. Anti-Catholicism flared again in the 1876 and 1884 presidential elections, when a Protestant minister warned against "rum, Romanism, and rebellion."[15]

Despite the absence of large numbers of Catholics in Kansas City, the town was not immune from anti-Catholic outbursts. By 1893, the American Protective Association, a nativist group founded 6 years before in Clinton, Iowa, had set up shop in Kansas City, and by 1894 was deep into city politics. As Kansas City suffered in the throes of a nationwide depression, the A.P.A. called for immigration restrictions, more stringent naturalization requirements, hiring bars against non-naturalized residents and Catholics, and the teaching of the "American" language in schools.[16]

During April 1894, an election riot led to bloodshed when "Fighting Jim" Pryor, boss of the Fifth Ward, commissioned about 50 men as deputy constables to oversee the ward elections. On Election Day, April 4, the Pryor gang, as *The Kansas City Star* referred to the deputies, was out

— THE AMERICAN PROTECTIVE ASSOCIATION —

The American Protective Association, a nativist group founded in 1887 in Clinton, Iowa, did great harm in America during the 1890s, including Kansas City, where they set up shop in 1893. The A.P.A. called for immigration restrictions, more stringent naturalization requirements, hiring bars against non-naturalized residents and Catholics, and the teaching of the "American" language in schools. In 1893 a Detroit paper published an item that purported to be an encyclical of Pope Leo XIII instructing American Catholics to massacre all heretics on the feast of St. Ignatius Loyola, July 31, 1893. The lie was exposed, along with a secret oath that came to light. Included in the oath was the following:

I do most solemnly promise and swear that I will always, to the utmost of my ability, labor, plead and wage a continuous warfare against ignorance and fanaticism; that I will use my utmost power to strike the shackles and chains of blind obedience to the Roman Catholic church from the hampered and bound consciences of a priest-ridden and church-oppressed people; that I will never allow any one, a member of the Roman Catholic church, to become a member of this order, I knowing him to be such; that I will use my influence to promote the interest of all Protestants everywhere in the world that I may be; that I will not employ a Roman Catholic in any capacity if I can procure the services of a Protestant.

The A.P.A. would linger on until 1911.

Source: Michael Williams, *The Shadow of the Pope* (New York: McGraw-Hill Book Co., Inc., 1932), p. 103-04.

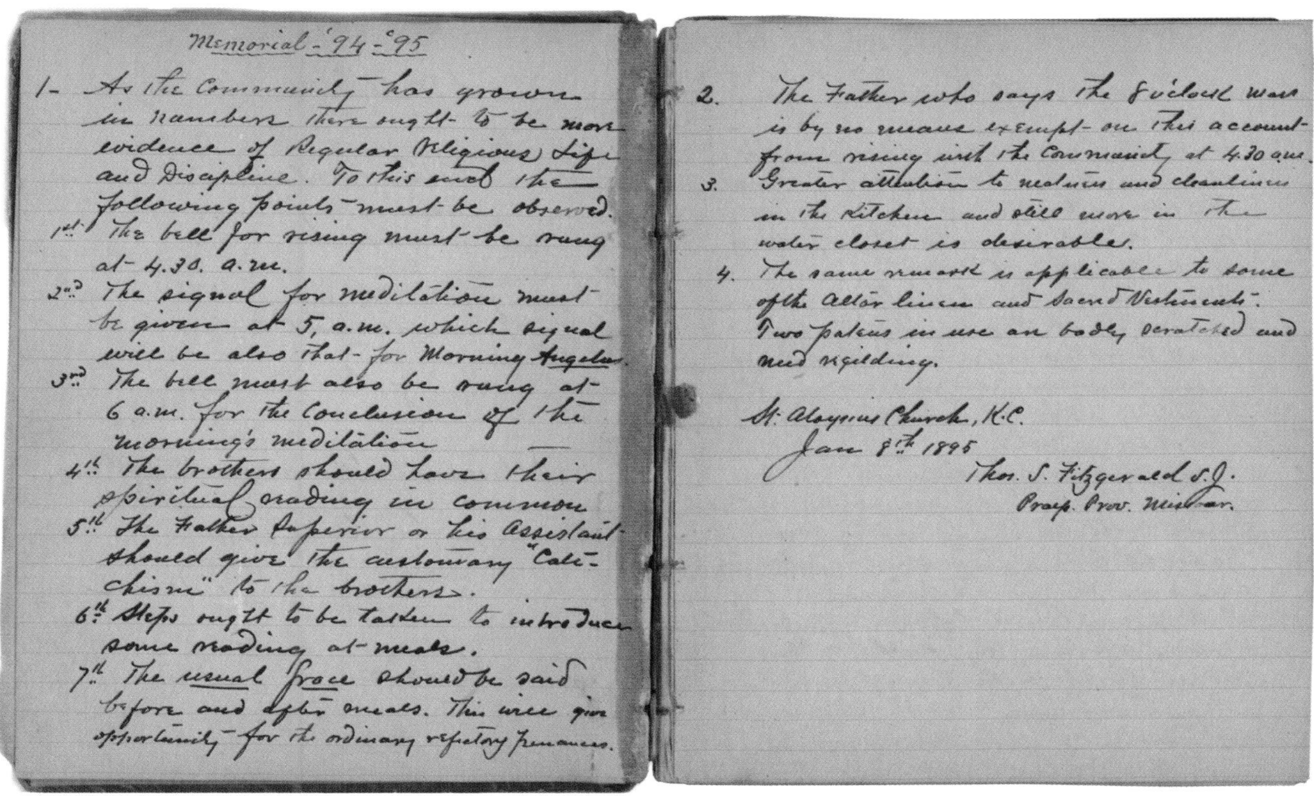

Memorial - 94 - 95

1- As the Community has grown in numbers there ought to be more evidence of Regular Religious Life and Discipline. To this end the following points must be observed.

1st The bell for rising must be rung at 4.30. a.m.

2nd The signal for meditation must be given at 5, a.m. which signal will be also that for Morning Angelus.

3rd The bell must also be rung at 6 a.m. for the Conclusion of the morning's meditation.

4th The brothers should have their spiritual reading in common.

5th The Father Superior or his Assistant should give the customary "Catechism" to the brothers.

6th Steps ought to be taken to introduce some reading at meals.

7th The usual grace should be said before and after meals. This will give opportunity for the ordinary refectory penances.

2. The Father who says the 8 o'clock Mass is by no means exempt on this account from rising with the Community at 4.30 a.m.

3. Greater attention to neatness and cleanliness in the kitchen and still more in the water closet is desirable.

4. The same remark is applicable to some of the Altar linen and Sacred Vestments. Two patens in use are badly scratched and need regilding.

St. Aloysius Church, K.C.
Jan 8th 1895
Thos. S. Fitzgerald S.J.
Praep. Prov. Missouri.

Missouri Provincial Thomas S. Fitzgerald, S.J., paid periodic visits to the community of Jesuits at St. Aloysius and recorded his findings in the book of Memorials. *Based on a visit in the winter of 1894-95, Fr. Fitzgerald admonished the Jesuits to give greater attention to neatness and cleanliness and to keep parish debt to a minimum. Courtesy of Rockhurst University Archives.*

early and in force for Frank Johnson, the Republican candidate for mayor. Their tactics of abusing or assaulting "every voter who was known to favor either Davis or Cooper" got ink in *The Star* after a fight erupted about 2 o'clock that afternoon near the No. 9 engine house, between Summit Street, Southwest Boulevard, and the long viaduct over the nearby railroad tracks.

"BLOODSHED! MANY MEN WOUNDED; MIKE CALLAHAN KILLED" the headline screamed that afternoon.[17] Callahan, a city sidewalk inspector, had been shot through the right side by deputy constable Jerry Pace, who lay near death himself from a shot to the face. Also suffering grievous wounds were Perry Fowler, a West Side laborer, shot through the back, and Con Brosnahan, a West Side contractor, shot in the kidneys. *The Star* pointed a finger at members of the A.P.A. who, it reported, went to the defense of Constable Pace, causing a riot.

Even as such chaos occurred in the Fifth Ward, the Jesuit love of order, ritual, and punctuality reigned inside the rectory at St. Aloysius Parish. A glimpse into the private lives lived there is revealed through the words of Missouri Provincial Thomas S. Fitzgerald, who paid periodic visits to the community in Kansas City and recorded his findings in his book of *Memorials*, preserved in the Rockhurst University Archives.

"The bell for rising must be rung at 4:30 a.m.," the provincial demanded after a visit in the winter of 1894-1895. "The signal for meditation must be given at 5 a.m.," he continued, and "steps ought to be taken to introduce some reading at meals." He was not pleased with the disorder he found in the kitchen and bathroom and admonished the Jesuits: "Greater attention to neatness and cleanliness in the kitchen and still more in the water closet is desirable."[18]

His admonition for more cleanliness was repeated the next winter, and the next, and the next. There were unsightly cobwebs on the library ceiling, rubbish in the cellar, and a mess in the hallway and basement playroom at the school. He found a soiled and partly torn altar cloth in the church, and, then, there were manners to be followed. When the fathers smoked cigars, cigars should be offered to the brothers, as well, and anything that resembled criticism or faultfinding at table, or meals, Fitzgerald wrote, "must be studiously avoided by all."[19]

And, of course, the provincial said, the fathers needed to make every effort to keep the parish debt within limits and to diminish it if they could. The biggest expenses had come in the preceding years when the Jesuits of St. Aloysius secured property and built a wood frame school on the north side of Peery Avenue, east of Prospect. When the school opened on September 26, 1887, 34 pupils were present.[20]

Two years later, in the fall of 1889, St. Aloysius School counted 170 pupils and boasted a new, 3-story building with a parish hall. The next year, ground was broken for a church, its cornerstone laid in the summer of 1890 with the pomp and dignity befitting the occasion. Bishop John Joseph Hogan rode in a carriage from his residence at the Cathedral, escorted by Provincial Rudolph Meyer, S.J., who had made the trip from St. Louis. As the carriage crossed Woodland Avenue and wended over the border of the young St. Aloysius Parish, all the parish societies waited in greeting and the Dominican Band, which had kindly come over from nearby Holy Name Parish, supplied the music. In an act no doubt signifying parish ambitions to yet build that "college for the education of boys and youths," a catalog of Saint Louis University—and another of St. Mary's College—was deposited for all time behind the cornerstone.

Over the next several months, the sanctuary was frescoed, the pews and carpet put in, and the altar and furnishings moved up from the basement—which had been serving as the church. On April 5, 1891, the new church, built of stone and pressed brick in an English Gothic design, was dedicated at the southeast corner of 11th Street and Prospect Avenue in another ceremony befitting the occasion. Bishop Hogan came again from the Cathedral, and Father Provincial Meyer from St. Louis. And perhaps in another omen of things to come, Father Michael Dowling, S.J., the future founder of Rockhurst University, came all the way from Michigan, where he was president of Detroit College, to say Mass and lecture in the evening. That same year of 1891, a convent was erected in front of the school on Peery Avenue for the Sisters of Charity of the Blessed Virgin Mary, who had come from Dubuque to teach, just as they had promised.[21]

In time, 3 bells were christened and placed in the tower, and at 6 o'clock on the evening of September 14, 1893, they rang out the *Angelus* for the first time. It was with hopes bright for the future that the Society of Jesus also purchased Lots 47 and 48 in the Clouser & Cole Addition directly across from the church, on the northwest corner of 11th and Prospect. Here, they hoped to build their college.[22]

— A HOST OF RELIGIOUS ORDERS —

As the years went by, the parish grew. By 1900, it listed 303 households who were contributing some $6,000 a year in support, nearly half of which came from pew rent and seat money. St. Aloysius was a thriving parish. On Sundays, early Mass was at 6 a.m., followed by another at 8 and 10:30, at which the rented pews were held in reserve for those who had paid. But if they failed to show by the time the service began, others could be seated there. Sunday school was at 2:30 p.m., baptisms at 4, and vespers and benediction at 8, with a lecture and Rosary. Confessions were held from 3 to 6 p.m. and again from 7 to 10 p.m. every Thursday and Saturday, as well as before and during the daily Mass. To see a confessor, all one had to do was ring the electric bell on the confessional.[23]

As the Jesuits ministered to the faithful at St. Aloysius, other religious orders were doing the same in other parts of the city. Franciscan priests came from Kansas City, Kansas, to preach to the German Catholics at Our Lady of Sorrows Parish, established in 1890 on the site of the future Union Station, and the Scalabrini fathers were working among the newly arrived Italian immigrants in Holy Rosary Parish, established in 1891. Like the Irish on the West Side and the Croatians across the Kaw on Strawberry Hill, the great majority of Italian immigrants were Catholic. They arrived in America years after the Irish and Germans, who were well-established by the time railroad agent Anthony Basile, an Italian immigrant himself, began recruiting his countrymen to come to the Midwest to work on the railroads. Many Italians arrived from Basilicata and Calabria, then from Sicily. But even as late as 1890, when the Scalabrini priest Ferdinando Santipolo arrived from Italy, he found fewer than 800 Italians in Kansas City. Numbers would swell, however, to 1,712 by 1900 and 7,804 by 1920.[24]

St. Aloysius Church (above). The cornerstone for this building was laid in the summer of 1890. In an act signifying parish ambitions to build a college in the future, catalogs of Saint Louis University and St. Mary's College were deposited behind the cornerstone. The church was dedicated on April 5, 1891. Father Michael Dowling, S.J., the future founder of Rockhurst, came from Michigan, where he was president of Detroit College, to say Mass and lecture in the evening. In time, 3 bells were christened and placed in the tower. When this building was demolished in 1969, the bells were reinstalled at the Benedictine Monastery in Pevely, Missouri, now dissolved. They were moved a second time, to the Pius X Benedictine monastery in Columbia, Missouri, where they were kept until 1999 when the bells were installed in the steeple of the new church building at Our Lady of Lourdes in Columbia (left). Courtesy of Diocese of Kansas City-St. Joseph and Fa'tima Miller.

Mostly poor, illiterate, and speaking no English, Italians tended to isolate themselves, settling on the northern fringe of downtown—the north side of the old Fifth Ward, which became Kansas City's "Little Italy." Like the Irish Catholics of Annunciation Parish, who held their first Mass in a storefront in the West Bottoms 2 decades before, the Italian Catholics did likewise, though on the other side of town, in a storefront at 5th Street and Forest Avenue. It took them 4 years to build a church—the first Holy Rosary Church—a modest wooden building that went up in 1895 on the southeast corner of Missouri Avenue and Campbell Street.[25]

Holy Rosary Parish. As St. Aloysius grew, other religious orders were doing the same in other parts of the city. The Scalabrini fathers established Holy Rosary Parish in 1891 to minister to the newly arrived Italian immigrants. Mostly poor, illiterate, and speaking no English, Italians tended to isolate themselves, settling on the northern fringe of downtown—the north side of the old Fifth Ward, which became Kansas City's "Little Italy." Their first church, a wooden building, burned down. The present brick building was constructed in 1903. Courtesy of Diocese of Kansas City-St. Joseph.

As immigration swelled Kansas City's Catholic population, the Christian Brothers arrived, as well. Unlike the Jesuits, the Christian Brothers were not a brotherhood of priests, but a teaching order, founded 200 years before in Europe by John Baptist de la Salle, who forbade the brothers to become priests, lest they neglect their fundamental calling—Christian education. The Christian Brothers arrived in America in 1846 and by 1849 had opened a parochial school for boys in the St. Louis Cathedral. Three years later, they established their first college, in St. Louis' Rider Mansion, at the corner of 8th and Cerre streets, and in 1855 the Academy of the Christian Brothers was chartered by the Missouri General Assembly. By 1870, 57 brothers were teaching hundreds of boys in 8 St. Louis parish schools, as well as hundreds more in the college and Cathedral academy.[26]

The Jesuits of St. Aloysius Parish hardly had their grade school off the ground when the Christian Brothers arrived in Kansas City in 1887 and started offering classes in September 1888 in 2 rooms of the parish school at St. Patrick Church at 8th and Cherry streets. By June 1889, the brothers' school had so outgrown its quarters that Father John J. Glennon of the Cathedral of the Immaculate Conception invited them to come to the Cathedral and teach in the Cathedral school, a 3-story building facing 12th Street. Because the brothers taught business courses, including typing and shorthand, their school often was called The Cathedral Commercial School.[27]

— Perfect Man for the Job —

The Christian Brothers' 3-year business course was a huge success and was going strong in 1908, when Father Michael Dowling arrived in Kansas City from Omaha to be the new pastor at St. Aloysius Church. He came with the announced purpose of finally, at last, after nearly a quarter of a century, following through on the Society of Jesus' longtime intentions of starting a "college for the education of boys and youths" in Kansas City.

Father Dowling seemed the perfect man to do the job. At 56 years old, he came to Kansas City with an impressive record of success behind him. Born in Cincinnati on June 14, 1851, he had attended St. Xavier's Parish school and moved on to St. Xavier's College. Following the example of his older brother, James, he entered the Missouri novitiate of the Society of Jesus at Florissant shortly after his eighteenth birthday, on July 10, 1869. After his noviceship and one year of juniorate, he completed his philosophy course at Woodstock College in Maryland and returned to the Midwest in 1875, where he taught classes in poetry and rhetoric at St. Xavier, Detroit,

PRESIDENTIAL PROFILE

— MICHAEL PATRICK DOWLING, S.J. —

Father Michael Dowling, founder and first president of Rockhurst, was born in Cincinnati on June 14, 1851. Shortly after his eighteenth birthday, he entered the Missouri novitiate of the Society of Jesus at Florissant on July 10, 1869. He was ordained on December 21, 1881 in the Cincinnati Cathedral. Dowling studied at Xavier and Woodstock College, taught poetry and rhetoric at Xavier, Detroit, and Saint Louis University, and served Holy Family Church in Chicago and Church of the Gesu in Milwaukee.

In 1885 Michael Dowling was appointed vice rector of Omaha's Creighton College. He oversaw construction of an addition to the original college building, as well as a university chapel. That success led to his appointment, on March 17, 1889, as president of Detroit College, where he again tackled new construction. Dowling returned to Creighton in 1898 and added schools of law, pharmacy, and dentistry, as well as a number of new departments. He constructed new buildings, advanced the library, and improved the science laboratories.

In spring 1908, Fr. Dowling came to Kansas City to become pastor of St. Aloysius and to establish the long-awaited "college for the education of boys and youths" that Bishop Hogan had so enthusiastically embraced. Dowling could scarcely have imagined the problems that lay ahead in securing a new Jesuit parish, raising money, and constructing a building that was not only practical but also visionary. Fr. Dowling would live to see the fruit of his labor when Rockhurst opened its doors on that stormy morning of September 15, 1914. Michael Dowling died on February 13, 1915, after a 2-year struggle with cancer. His older brother James Dowling, who had entered the Jesuit order at the same time as Michael and was himself a former pastor at St. Aloysius, died a week earlier. Father Michael was 64. He is buried at Holy Sepulchre Cemetery in Omaha.

Father Michael Dowling and John A. Creighton, October 15, 1906, on the occasion of Creighton's 75th birthday. Creighton, adorned with a flowered Rosary around his neck, had been made a Count of the Holy Roman Empire by Pope Leo XIII in 1895. The honor was bestowed in recognition of his many charitable contributions in support of the Church and its ministries. During his first years in Omaha, Fr. Dowling forged a close friendship with John Creighton, the younger of the two Creighton brothers that are credited with providing the money to found Creighton College. When John Creighton died in February 1907, Fr. Dowling preached his funeral sermon. In attendance was another of John Creighton's close friends, William Jennings Bryan, who was an honorary pallbearer. The great orator himself called Fr. Dowling's sermon "a very remarkable and masterly discourse." Courtesy of Creighton University.

and Saint Louis University. He was ordained on December 21, 1881, in the Cincinnati Cathedral.

Michael Dowling's life took a new turn in 1885 when he was appointed as vice rector of Omaha's nascent Creighton College, founded only 7 years before and described by one biographer as "rather backward." Father Dowling, displaying what one colleague described as "unflagging zeal and uncommon business ability," oversaw construction of an addition to the original college building, as well as a university chapel.[28] That success led to his appointment, on March 17, 1889, as president of Detroit College, where he again tackled new construction. Despite a carpenters' strike, he oversaw the demolition of the old houses that had served as college buildings and laid the foundation for a new college building.

By the time Father Dowling came to Kansas City, he also had served as prefect of Holy Family Church in Chicago, which adjoined St. Ignatius College. The parish had an immense congregation of more than 20,000 souls, and Father Dowling was one of 12 priests. From Chicago, he went to the Church of the Gesu in Milwaukee, where he erected a building for the parish school and was said to have "worked wonders."[29]

But it was at Creighton that Father Dowling left his biggest mark. All told, he would spend 14 years there, first arriving when the college "was little more than a struggling academy, with perhaps 150 pupils," a friend of the college recalled. Over the next 4 years, Father Dowling established Creighton's college course, a labor he was said to have approached "with unflagging zeal and in the face of vexatious obstacles." He had increased the number of faculty and had overseen construction of a spacious residence for them, as well as obtaining the money to build St. John's Church.

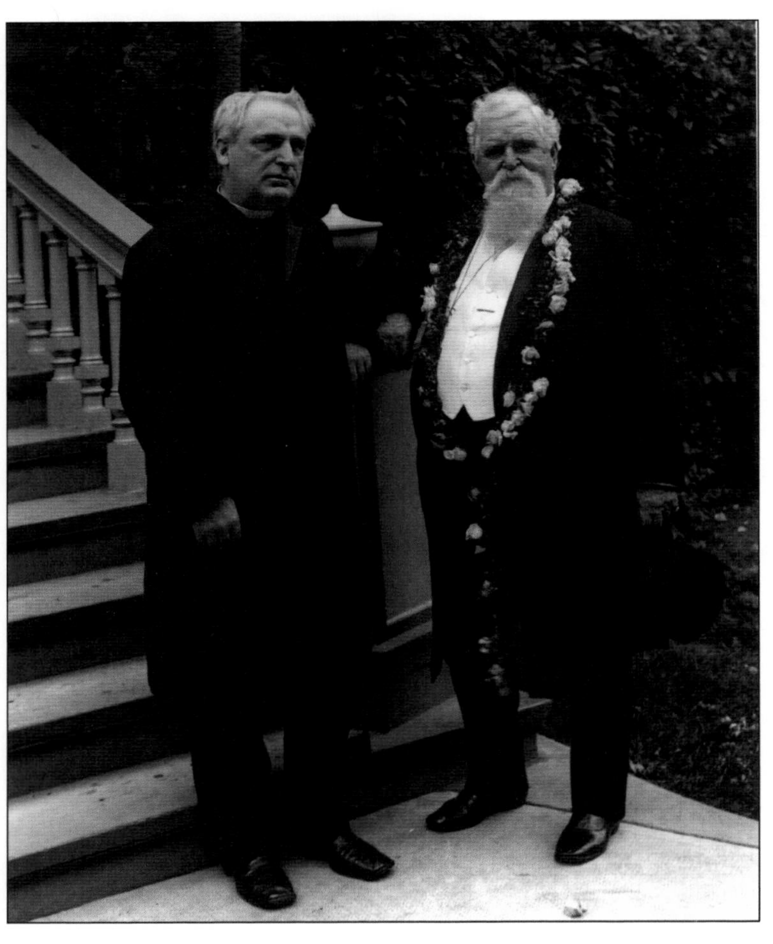

It was during his first years in Omaha that Father Dowling established a close friendship with John A. Creighton, the younger of the two Creighton brothers that are credited with providing the money to found Creighton College. John and his brother, Edward, were Ohio boys who went to Omaha in the 1850s and got their start in life by constructing roads and telegraph lines. Edward was primarily responsible for the laying of the transcontinental telegraph lines from Omaha to the West Coast, and John was actively engaged in mining, stock-raising, and investments in land. When Edward died in 1874, his widow, Mary Lucretia Creighton, inherited his fortune and left $100,000 in her own will to establish the college in her husband's memory. John Creighton, who would live into the twentieth century and had married Mary Lucretia's sister, Sarah Emily Wareham, would leave huge bequests to the university, totaling more than $1.5 million.[30]

The friendship that grew between John Creighton and Michael Dowling "was genuine, deep-seated, inspiring, the spontaneous outburst of kindred natures which naturally attracted each other," a writer for the *Creighton Chronicle* once said. "Both were singularly generous, both animated by high ideals; the one gave lavishly of his ample fortune that with it the other might develop a university where a thorough education could be had by all for the asking."[31]

On November 12, 1898, after an absence of nearly a decade, Dowling was recalled as rector to Creighton when the college was in such financial straits that there was talk of closing the school or petitioning the courts to allow the college to charge tuition, which was in direct opposition to the requirements of the original charter and purpose of the founders. Creighton's financial crisis dated to the Depression of 1893, which had been disastrous in Nebraska, where several years of drought had added to troubles, causing blight and a failure of crops that brought poverty and suffering over the entire region from eastern Iowa to the Dakotas—the very region that Creighton depended on for students.

In Dowling's absence the college had added a medical school and become a university. Dowling threw himself heart and soul into Creighton, assessing the situation and once again enlisting the support of John Creighton. Over the next 10 years, Father Dowling not only solved Creighton's financial embarrassment, but also added schools of law, pharmacy, and dentistry, as well as a number of new departments. He constructed new buildings, advanced the library, and improved the science laboratories.

"For this kind of work," the *Creighton Chronicle* wrote in a eulogy, "he was specially gifted. He was a skillful organizer, a tireless worker, with a clear and logical mind, prudent and farsighted, giving close personal attention to details while leaving much freedom of initiative and action to subordinates and heads of departments. By nature strong and forceful, he was always patient and cordial, readily listening to suggestion, and invariably genial and cheerful in intercourse with others."[32]

But it was Father Dowling's relations with John Creighton that undoubtedly helped secure the university's future. When John Creighton died in February 1907 and his will was opened, it was found that, without any immediate heirs, he had bequeathed the principal part of his estate to Creighton University. It was Father Dowling who preached the funeral sermon in St. John's Church. In attendance was another of John Creighton's close friends, William Jennings Bryan, who was an honorary pallbearer. The great orator himself apparently was so impressed by Father Dowling's sermon that he was moved to comment, calling it "a very remarkable and masterly discourse."[33]

For all the success and intimate times at Creighton, Dowling's work there ended on a sour note when John Creighton's will was contested, a matter of business that consumed Dowling's energy and placed him under such a strain that he was said to have aged visibly. Thus, when he was asked to transfer to a new scene of labor in Kansas City, Father Dowling gladly accepted.

On the eve of his departure from Omaha, students thronged the auditorium at Creighton University's College of Arts to bid him farewell. With the proper dignity befitting his position, he gave credit for his success to the loyal support he received from members of the faculty who, he said, had spent their lives in unselfish devotion to the welfare of their pupils, hoping to promote in the world the higher interests of religion and morality.

"As for myself," Dowling said, "I have given to the university my best years. I have devoted to it the best that was in me, and now after fourteen years, out of 'the Creighton millions' to which someone alluded a moment ago, I take with me six dollars—just enough to pay my fare to Kansas City."[34]

— NO BUILDING, NO MONEY —

On March 4, 1908, Father Michael Patrick Dowling arrived in Kansas City and took up residence in the rectory next to St. Aloysius Church. In what turned out to be a sad irony, Father Dowling's reassignment to Kansas City was intended "to give him rest after his long years of labor." As he arrived in Kansas City that spring of 1908, wrote the Rev. Patrick Harvey, Rockhurst's first historian, Father Dowling "could scarcely have envisioned the poverty, discouragement, and opposition that had to be overcome before the new work was finished...."[35]

He counted 496 families in the parish and described St. Aloysius "as a model Catholic parish" whose members were "loyal, faithful, responsive to every effort undertaken for their spiritual advancement."[36]

The altar of St. Aloysius Church. When Fr. Michael Dowling arrived in the spring of 1908, he described St. Aloysius "as a model Catholic parish" whose members were "loyal, faithful, responsive to every effort undertaken for their spiritual advancement." Courtesy of Rockhurst University Archives.

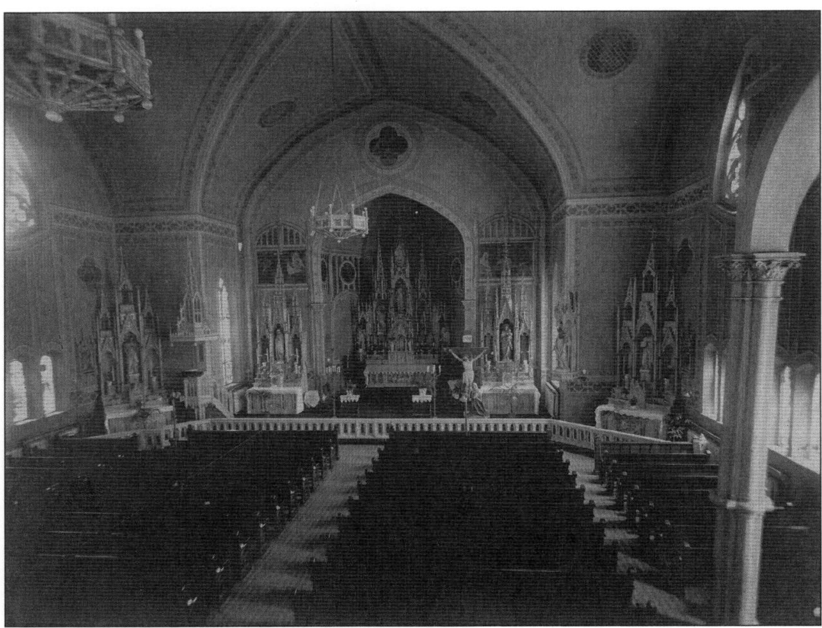

Prospects for a college were another matter. Father Dowling had no building and no money—though a forward-looking Society of Jesus had purchased, in 1904, 2 lots across from St. Aloysius Church for the future college. But, of course, plans have a way of going awry. At St. Aloysius, the once quiet neighborhood began to change. When word came that the city was planning to turn the old Exposition grounds between Montgall and Agnes avenues—just a few blocks from the church—into a factory district, St. Aloysius Pastor John C. Kelly, S.J., was so upset that, in 1907, he led a fight to stop the plan. No longer was Prospect Avenue a dirt street on the edge of the city limits. By the time Father Dowling arrived, the racket of the Prospect Avenue car line had grown so loud that it disturbed Mass. Parishioners took the matter, to no avail, to the City Council.[37]

Surely, Father Dowling noted the poor immigrants in the North End and the obligations his parishioners felt toward the many Catholic charities: the St. Joseph Orphan Girls' Home and the Kansas City Orphan

Boys' Home; the Little Sisters of the Poor and their home for the aged and impoverished; the House of the Good Shepherd for wayward girls; and that wasn't to mention the Catholic hospitals—St. Joseph's, St. Vincent's, and St. Mary's. After only a year in Kansas City, Dowling wrote bluntly to the Father Provincial that it was "an arduous task to establish a college under existing circumstances in Kansas City."[38]

The presence of the Christian Brothers didn't help. They had just been promised $70,000 from the estate of the late Joseph Benoist and were making plans to move to a brand new academy on The Paseo at 16th Street. It was along the beautifully landscaped The Paseo and just across from The Parade, the city's first playground, that the Christian Brothers opened De La Salle Academy on September 12, 1910, months before Rockhurst had been platted or even given a thought to college design. In 1911, De La Salle would incorporate and in 1912 graduate its first class of boys.[39]

Bishop Hogan made it clear that he did not want a Jesuit college locating near De La Salle, a declaration that complicated everything for the Jesuits because the boundary of St. Aloysius Parish began just 3 blocks west of The Paseo, and the ground set aside for the college across the street from St. Aloysius Church was a mere mile from the new De La Salle Academy. On top of that, Father Dowling seemed to be struggling in his efforts to enlist the support—and money—of Kansas City businessmen. As the months passed and still there was no Jesuit college for the education of boys and youths, Father Dowling began to sound discouraged. "This is the poorest place I have ever been," he wrote to the Father Provincial, "for rousing enthusiasm for Higher Catholic Education."[40]

Where, he must have prayed, was Kansas City's John Creighton?

ST. ALOYSIUS CHURCH
KANSAS CITY, MISSOURI
Financial Report of the Pastor, for the Year 1908

RECEIPTS

From the Church

Pew Rent		$ 2,527.50	
Seat Money		1,147.54	
Sunday Collection		1,899.62	
Coal and Boiler Renewal-Special Collection		688.25	
Mission-Goods Sold	$214.55	631.27	
" Collections	416.72		
Cathedraticum, Special Collection		132.85	

Diocesan Collections

Indians and Negroes	$ 34.00	309.80	
Seminary	200.00		
Holy Land	8.30		
Peter's Pence	43.00		
Catholic University	24.50		
Special Services		337.22	
Votive Offerings		400.00	
Lawn Socials		958.64	
School Additons, Subscriptions		245.00	
Bequest, Mary F. Lang		100.00	
Funeral Offerings		120.00	
Raised by Pastors, to Reduce Church Debt		566.72	
			$10,059.41

From the School

Tuition, from Pupils	$ 2,139.75	
Entertainment, Net Proceeds	288.74	
Minstrel Show, Net Proceeds	199.00	
Use of Hall	25.00	
		$ 2,602.49
Total from Church and School		12,661.90
Cash Balance, Jan. 1, 1908		127.78

GRAN[illegible]
P. H. Madde[illegible]
E. J. Reardo[illegible]
Geo. H. Kah[illegible]
P. H. Slatte[illegible]
J. A. McLi[illegible]
H. P. Stew[illegible]

EXPENDITURES

For the Church

Interest Paid on Debt		$ 1,775.00	
Loans Paid From Church Funds	$1,933.28	2,500.00	
Funds Raised by Pastors	566.72		
Salary of Pastors		1,400.00	
Salary of Brother Sacristan		300.00	
Organist, Music, Choir, Organ Respaire		886.07	
Janitor and Extra Help		150.00	
Insurance		55.00	
Special Taxes		77.59	
Heat, Light and Water		365.97	
Church Laundry and Altar Supplies		225.07	
Repairs and Furniture in Church and Residence		1,391.60	
Cathedraticum, Paid to Rt. Rev. Bishop		279.02	
Diocesan Collections Paid		309.80	
Mission Expenses		400.00	
Church Supplies, Incidentals, Sundries		224.59	
Priests Assisting During Year		40.00	
			$ 9,879.71

For the School

Salaries of Teachers	$ 1,750.00	
Janitor and Occasional Help	150.00	
Premiums, Incidentals and Supplies	328.90	
Piano and Wiring for the Hall	310.00	
Repairs and Furniture	50.00	
Heat, Light and Water	321.02	
		$ 2,909.92
Total Expenditures for Church and School		12,789.63
No Cash Balance on Hand		.00
		$12,789.63

But all Current Expenses, Bills and Interest due have been paid in full, and the Church Debt has been reduced $2,500.00 as follows:

Church Debt

Loans at 5 per cent, Jan. 1, 1908	$35,500.00
Paid on Debt, During 1908	2,500 00
Debt Remaining Jan. 1, 1909	$33,000.00

JAN. 7, 1909.

M. P. DOWLING, S. J.
PASTOR.

Financial report for St. Aloysius Church, 1908. Almost from the beginning of his ministry in Kansas City, Fr. Dowling struggled with finances. When Dowling purchased the land for the future Rockhurst College in 1909, he requested from Bishop Hogan a new Jesuit parish for the college. In order to get a new parish, Bishop Hogan insisted that the Jesuits would have to give up St. Aloysius, debt free. The financial report of 1908 shows payments of only $2,500 on church debt during 1908, leaving a remaining debt of $33,000. Courtesy of Rockhurst University Archives.

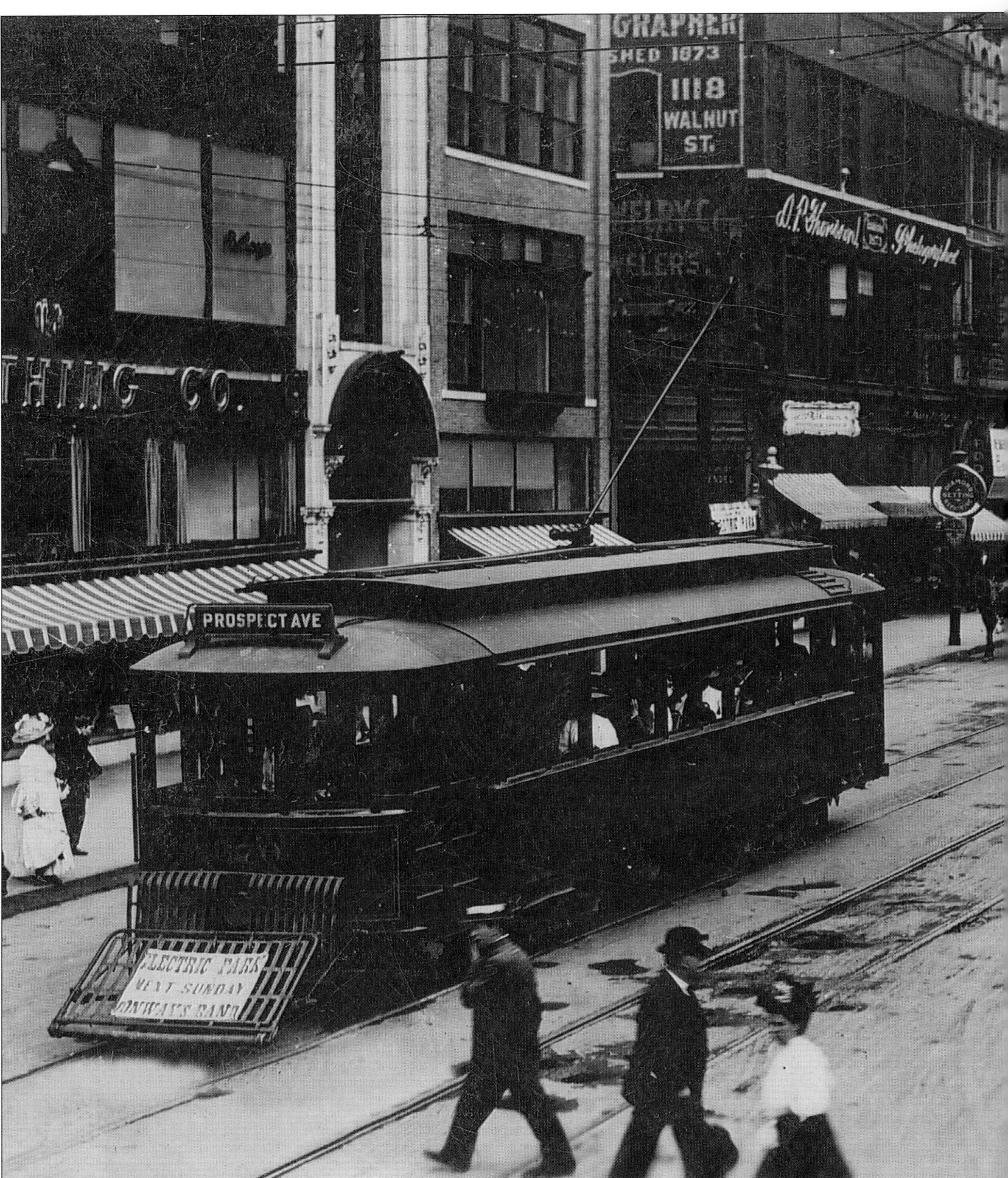
GRAPHER
SHED 1873
1118
WALNUT
ST.
THING CO.
PROSPECT AVE
ELECTRIC PARK
NEXT SUNDAY
ONWAY'S BAND

Chapter Three

A Well-Chosen Name

When Father Michael Dowling arrived in Kansas City in the spring of 1908, he would have noticed a city on the move. Downtown boasted 3 new skyscrapers that year and so many other buildings recently completed or under construction that the list ran for 2 pages in the annual report of the Business Men's League.[1] The R.A. Long Building at 10th and Grand was the city's first steel-structure skyscraper, and the nearby Scarritt Building and Arcade was considered an architectural gem with its Sullivanesque terra cotta façade. Of the new "Big 3," the 16-story Commerce Bank building at 10th and Walnut was the biggest of all. Just 2 blocks over on Baltimore, the New England Bank Building and the First National Bank were under construction. The Montgomery Ward Co. was building at 19th and Campbell streets and the Jones Brothers Dry Goods Co. at 13th and Main. Near the Missouri River, halfway to Independence, the Standard Oil Company had erected a huge refinery, and North Kansas City was being promoted—with the soon-to-be-completed Armour-Swift-Burlington Bridge—as a great location for industry and commerce.[2]

Kansas City's Catholic population was on the rise, as well, as a wave of new immigrants from southern and eastern Europe arrived in the years around the turn of the century and went to work in the city's meatpacking

View of downtown Kansas City at about the time Fr. Michael Dowling arrived in the city. This postcard looks west from the roof of the YMCA Building at 10th and Oak streets. The YMCA was built in 1909 and opened in January 1910. The tall building flying the flag at left is the R.A. Long Building. At right center is the Scarritt Building. Both buildings were erected in 1907 and were two of the first three skyscrapers to be built in Kansas City, the third being the Commerce Trust (not shown). The dome of the old Post Office at 8th and Grand is seen at far right. In the foreground are old homes of an earlier day, which soon were crowded out to make way for business buildings in the fast-growing city. Courtesy of Missouri Valley Special Collections, Kansas City Public Library, Kansas City, Missouri.

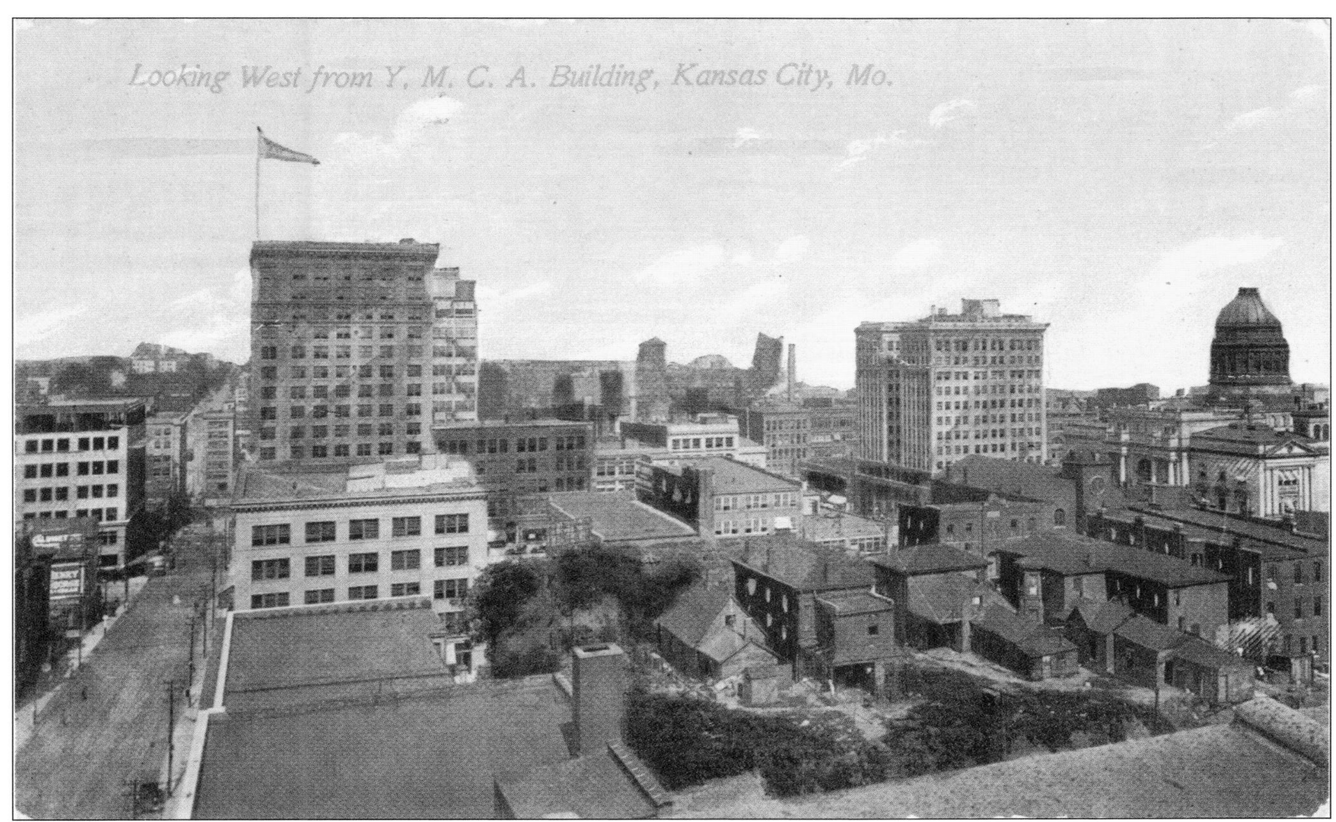

Looking West from Y. M. C. A. Building, Kansas City, Mo.

A 1910 postcard of the pergola at 10th Street and The Paseo. A high-seated motor car and a horse and buggy are the only traffic on the fashionable boulevard. Kansas City's pride and joy were its parks and boulevards system, which extended from the limestone outcroppings along Cliff Drive, south to 47th Street. In 1910, plans were being made to extend the boulevard system farther south to the brand new, exclusive Country Club District. Courtesy of Missouri Valley Special Collections, Kansas City Public Library, Kansas City, Missouri.

plants, flour mills, and garment factories. Kansas City had mushroomed from a population of 55,000 in 1880—5 years before the founding of St. Aloysius Parish—to 163,000 by 1900. In the next 10 years, the population would almost double—to 248,281. The city's Catholic population had always been relatively small—and mostly poor—but by 1905, it had increased substantially enough that Bishop John J. Hogan of the Kansas City Diocese and Bishop Thomas Lillis of the Leavenworth Diocese had announced plans for a new seminary, St. John's, as a way to attract priests to the area.[3]

Away from downtown, the city was growing as well. Handsome new apartment buildings and private residences were evident everywhere, and at least 4 new churches were under construction, including the Redemptorists' imposing Catholic church at Broadway and Linwood Boulevard.[4]

The city's pride and joy were its parks and boulevards system, which now extended from the limestone outcroppings along Cliff Drive, south to 47th Street, where the magnificent home of *The Kansas City Star* Editor William Rockhill Nelson stood as a showplace along Rockhill Road, which wound down the hill to Brush Creek and crossed a picturesque stone bridge. Although the boulevard system stopped at 47th Street, plans were being made to extend it farther south to the brand new, exclusive Country Club District.[5] By 1905, the Metropolitan Street Railway Company was running 500 electric streetcars over 216 miles of track crisscrossing the city. Thanks to universal transfers, a person with a nickel could ride for 15 miles.[6]

Father Michael Dowling would have taken all this in as he arrived in Kansas City from Omaha via rail. The city had so many rail lines and so many passengers passing through that, in fact, plans were being laid for a new Union Station to replace the old Union Depot in the West Bottoms. The new station was still just talk as Father Dowling arrived in 1908, but railroad men such as George Sedgwick, who had been around for years, owed their livelihood to the tracks.

— The Sedgwicks —

George Sedgwick was a New Englander by birth who had made his way west to Pennsylvania, where he married and had 3 children, Georgia, Frank, and the youngest, Lee. George Sedgwick brought his young family to Kansas City shortly before the Civil War. He came as purchasing agent for the Missouri Pacific railway, which slowly was snaking its way across Missouri, from St. Louis to Cheltenham, Hermann, Jefferson City, and Tipton. Progress was torturously slow, reflecting the troubles the road was having selling its stock to people along the route or making a profit from the sale of its land grant acres. By 1859, the tracks still had not reached Sedalia.[7]

Perhaps it was the railroad's ongoing struggles, or Sedgwick's New England roots—after all, he had named his youngest son Lee Massachusetts John Sedgwick—that led him to a new career in the years after the Civil War. He left the Missouri Pacific and partnered with Kansas City businessman E.A. Phillips, an outspoken Union man who was in the railroad construction business. In 1879, Phillips was named superintendent of the Osage Valley Construction Company, which built the entire Sedalia, Warsaw and Southern Railroad. By the fall of 1880, he had formed a partnership with George Sedgwick in the railroad supply business. They called themselves Sedgwick & Phillips, tie contractors, with offices on 6th Street, at the southwest corner of May Street.[8] "The two did an extensive business, employing at one time several large steamers in transporting cross-ties up the Missouri River for the use of the Union Pacific Railroad," Theodore Case wrote in one of Kansas City's earliest histories. George Sedgwick, whom Case described as "one of the most reliable citizens of Kansas City," became wealthy. He brought his son Lee into business with him and formed G.W. Sedgwick & Co., seller of railroad ties, with offices at 903 Broadway.[9]

Men laying the rails of the Union Pacific Railroad at the rate of two miles a day. Shortly before the Civil War, George Sedgwick brought his family to Kansas City from Pennsylvania and partnered with another Kansas City businessman in the railroad supply business. At one time, they employed several steam boats to transport cross-ties up the Missouri River for the building of the Union Pacific Railroad. George Sedgwick's youngest son, Lee, took over the business in 1899. In time, Lee Sedgwick would become Rockhurst's first great benefactor. Courtesy of Kansas Historical Society.

George Sedgwick, like other wealthy Kansas City men, followed the boulevards and the city south. He moved to a home on the southeast corner of Troost Park, at Virginia and 31st Street, while his son Lee, a lifelong bachelor, took to living in well-appointed hotels. When his father died suddenly in 1899, Lee took over the business and, in his spare time, became a student of religion and philosophy. Although the Sedgwicks were Presbyterian,[10] Lee was interested in Catholicism, an interest that undoubtedly dated to his days as a student at St. Mary's Academy, the Jesuit college for boys just 90 miles west of Kansas City. According to the college register, Lee first attended St. Mary's Academy in September 1875, when he was 14 years old. He attended the next year, as well.

It was at St. Mary's, though a Protestant, that he probably received his first introduction to Catholicism. If his life there was anything like that of

St. Mary's Academy, the Jesuit college for boys, was located 90 miles west of Kansas City. Lee Sedgwick attended St. Mary's for two years in the mid-1870s. Though a Protestant, Sedgwick received his first introduction to Catholicism at St. Mary's. The two wings of the building depicted in this artist's rendering were never completed. The building was destroyed by fire in 1879. Courtesy of Midwest Jesuit Archives.

fellow student Michael Boyle, who kept a diary,[11] Lee Sedgwick would have enjoyed his time at St. Mary's Academy. Boyle wrote of long walks along the Kansas River to pick strawberries and of shooting jaunts after quail and prairie chickens. He swam in the summer and skated in the winter, culled grapes in the vineyard, and played ball on the hill (with 500 marbles at stake). Michael Boyle's diary told how he joined the brass band, went to Mass every morning and to classes in the forenoon. There were competitions in Latin, history, geography, and Christian doctrine, and then there were debates on the questions of the day: "Are railroads or steamboats doing more good for this country?" On the feast of St. Aloysius, there was lemonade and ice cream, and, on St. Patrick's Day, the band went downtown to accompany a procession that marched through the streets to the Catholic church.

In April, there was an all-day retreat, where students prayed, meditated, and received Christian instruction. In May was the annual pilgrimage in honor of the Blessed Virgin. Every night after supper, students formed ranks in the yard and marched to the little chapel on the hill, reciting the beads as they went. In such a setting, Lee Sedgwick undoubtedly became immersed in Catholic ways. Students attended Mass, received Communion, sang vespers—and, importantly for the future of Rockhurst University, heard sermons on the necessity of a Catholic education. Years later, Lee Sedgwick told how his "intimate chum" at St. Mary's "was a red-headed Irish lad from the far West."

"He was as wild as a March hare and was a problem child to all the prefects and teachers of the school; at the same time the boy had strong faith and was fundamentally very good," Lee Sedgwick wrote. "At the end of our last year at St. Mary's when we were saying good-bye, (the boy) in his usual light-hearted manner handed me a rosary and said to me, 'Lee, you are an old heretic and you don't know any prayers except those you learned at St. Mary's. Now if ever you feel the need of prayer, say the rosary—that one thing you learned to do at St. Mary's.'

"I thanked him for the gift and the advice," Lee wrote. "We parted sorrowfully and I never met him afterwards."

Lee Sedgwick left St. Mary's Academy and went on to a successful life as a Kansas City businessman. He would emerge years later just when Rockhurst needed him the most.

— LAND IN THE COUNTRY —

Although the founding of a college in Kansas City would tax his talents to the utmost, Father Dowling would remain ever optimistic in his public statements and pronouncements. In an undated report to his superiors in St. Louis, titled *On the advisability of locating a high school and college at Kansas City, Mo.*, Dowling showed himself to be forward-thinking and knowledgeable of the city as he scouted every section for a site to locate a new Jesuit college.

He looked north and ruled out that direction because growth stopped at the Missouri River. He looked east and noted that the city's transportation and railroad growth was in that direction—beyond St. Aloysius Parish and over to the Big Blue River. Close-in real estate prices, however, made an eastern campus out of the question. Still farther to the east was no better because the Big Blue district was industrializing and filling up with the humble residences of factory workers—not those of the more affluent Catholics who would have the financial means to help the Jesuit cause.

Father Dowling looked west and liked what he saw between Broadway and Oak streets, south of Brush Creek, but developer J.C. Nichols, by April 1908, already had gained control of more than 1,000 acres in the area. He had staked out his Country Club District and was beginning to impose restrictive covenants on what types of buildings could be constructed and to whom they could be sold. Notably, black people were not allowed. Nichols insisted, as well, that no flats or apartment buildings be built, only single-family homes with a minimum cost of $5,000, a considerable sum in those days. By early 1909, the initial plat for Nichols' first truly elite subdivision, Sunset Hill, was filed, with minimum home prices placed at $10,000 in certain blocks.[12]

"That was no place for us to go" anyway, Dowling wrote, noting that "there would not be many Catholics in so exclusive a district." Locating nearby, however, would be a good thing, he thought, because "it is of advantage to be in touch with a district where people of wealth, prominence and influence live, on account of the improvements they will bring."

Dowling's search also was dictated by Bishop Hogan, who had told the Jesuits they must not locate near De La Salle Academy at 15th and The Paseo or infringe on the territory of St. James Parish, founded just a few years before. It was in the summer of 1906 that St. James Parish held its first church services in old Wallsman Hall at 38th and Woodland Avenue. The pastor, Father Keyes, lived across the street in rented rooms above Brinkleh's drug store. On Christmas Eve 1906, the congregation moved into a frame church at the northeast corner of 40th Street and Tracy Avenue, a location that undoubtedly had sent Father Dowling looking for land farther south, south of Brush Creek and beyond 48th Street. By degrees, Kansas City had been marching steadily south. It had annexed Westport and pushed to Brush Creek in 1897, and in January 1909 would push its boundary all the way south to 79th Street. Father Dowling took all this into account, noting of his search for land: "Naturally we did not want to get too far south of the present city limits."

Sanborn Company insurance maps for 1909 show 48th Street, west of Harrison Street, to be a sparsely developed area, although the Troost Avenue Division of the Metropolitan Street Railway Company filled entire blocks between Harrison and Troost with its car yard, car barn, offices, and employee locker room.[13] The area east of Troost and 48th Street was more bare still, the Sanborn map showing only J.W. Gunn's planing mill with its dry kiln furnace, lumber shed, and work benches. Farther south,

Electric Park at night, 1910. Electric Park was opened May 19, 1907, to a crowd of 53,000. Its owners, J.J., Mike and Ferdinand Heim, also owned the Heim Brewery. The park extended from 46th and The Paseo to Woodland and was built at the close of an era of kerosene and gas lights. The park boasted 100,000 light bulbs outlining buildings, towers, and high rail rides. By degrees, Kansas City had been marching steadily south. Although Fr. Dowling was criticized for picking a location for the college too far out in the country, he decided the future of the city was to the south, far from the city center. Courtesy of Missouri Valley Special Collections, Kansas City Public Library, Kansas City, Missouri.

at Lydia Avenue beyond 59th Street, was the Elm Ridge Racetrack, and just north of Brush Creek, at 46th Street and Woodland Avenue, was the newly opened Electric Park, billed as "Kansas City's Coney Island" with its electric illuminated fountain, moving pictures, indoor pool, and Loop-the-Loop. The park was said to attract 1,000,000 people a year, or more than 8,000 a day.

Just a few blocks west of Electric Park was Troost Avenue, running parallel—and midway—between J.C. Nichols' coveted Country Club District and the emergent The Paseo, the jewel of Kansas City's new boulevard system. Although far from the city center, Troost Avenue at 52nd Street was a central spot—a seemingly ideal location for a college as it skirted up the hill south of Brush Creek, affording a view of what in 1908 was little more than farmland. Though he would be criticized for picking a location too far out in the country, Father Dowling decided this was the spot for his college.

The property, originally purchased by the Mormon Edward Partridge and sold at sheriff's sale to the Jackson County pioneer Jesse Thomas in 1845, had passed down to Thomas' daughter, Lurinda Thomas Peers, who died intestate on May 6, 1904. So extensive were the probate dealings that followed Lurinda Peers' death that the Abstract of Title to the land ran for 50 pages before the old Peers' estate, as it was known, finally was purchased on December 31, 1908, for $50,000. The purchaser was Robert W. Cary and his wife.

When and where Robert Cary and Michael Dowling met are not known, and the details of what exactly passed between them are sketchy, although letters that flew fast and furious in those first few months of 1909 between Dowling and the Missouri provincial in St. Louis, Rudolph Meyer, indicate that Dowling had put down $1,000 on a contract with Cary, who would hold the property in trust for the Jesuits and deliver it "as soon as we find the title and abstract satisfactory," an abstract that all agreed was "quite voluminous."[14]

While waiting on the abstract—and approval from Rome—Father Dowling went out to 52nd Street and Troost Avenue one more time to examine the property. "I am better pleased with it even more than I was at first," he wrote to Meyer on January 8, 1909. The site, Dowling said, "seems to comprise all the advantages sought for in a college mapped out for the future rather than the present." The ground was high and sightly, it was within easy reach of the city's boulevard system, and, perhaps most importantly, it bordered J.C. Nichol's exclusive residential district, which surely meant, Dowling wrote, that the site would "secure ample transportation facilities and other civic advantages" and that it would "enable us to draw around us the class of people that we wish; it will never be invaded by railways and factories."[15]

Although Dowling could envision a future college there, at the moment the property was no more than a rough farmland dotted with a few stands of trees and the Peers' old frame house, which faced Troost Avenue. Behind the house was a large barn, still used by dairymen. On January 29,

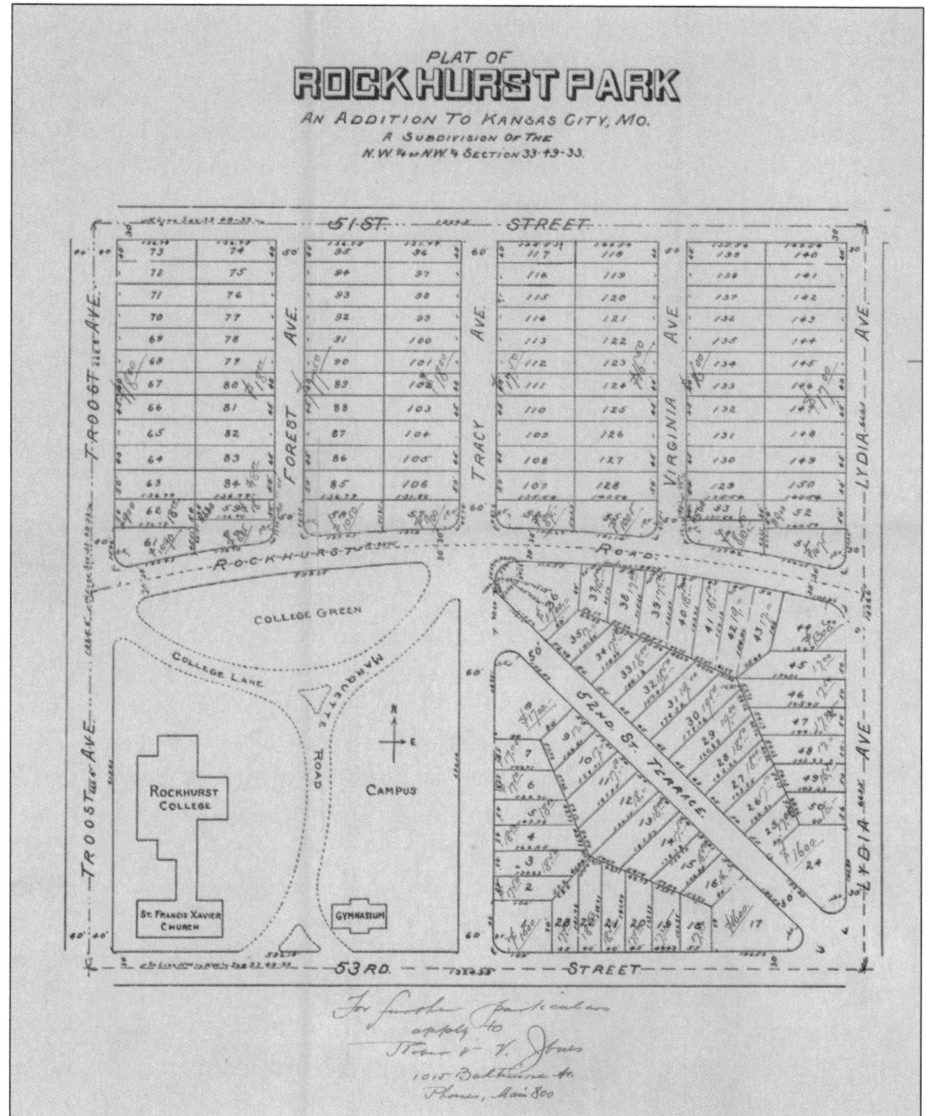

The property that was originally purchased by the Mormon Edward Partridge and sold at sheriff's sale to the Jackson County pioneer Jesse Thomas in 1845 had passed down to Thomas' daughter, Lurinda Thomas Peers. The old Peers' estate, as it was known, was purchased in 1908 by Robert W. Cary and his wife. In 1909, Fr. Dowling put down $1,000 on a contract with Cary. In 1910, Cary filed a plat called "Rockhurst Park" at the Jackson County Courthouse. He had subdivided the land east of Tracy Avenue into 62 lots for homes. The land west of Tracy and running to Troost and south to 53rd Street—about 12 acres—was set aside as "Outlot No. 1," to be used as the campus of the new Rockhurst College. It was Dowling's plan, in time, to sell lots 1 to 62 at a profit to pay off the debt. Courtesy of Rockhurst University Archives.

Looking east along 53rd Street from the future site of Rockhurst. In 1909, the 25-acre tract purchased by Fr. Dowling was rough farmland dotted with a few stands of trees and the occasional farmhouse. "We wanted high ground," Dowling wrote the provincial, so "we selected the first plateau beyond Brush Creek, and that was 52nd Street. This location is pretty far out now; yet if the city continues its present rate of growth, a very few years will make it a desirable and attractive situation. The ground lies well." Courtesy of Rockhurst University Archives.

1909, less than a year after arriving in Kansas City, Father Dowling purchased the 25-acre tract where Rockhurst now stands, intending to keep part of it for the campus and selling the rest to pay for the purchase. "We wanted high ground," he explained, so "we selected the first plateau beyond Brush Creek, and that was 52nd Street."[16]

Nearly a year later, on December 13, 1910, Robert Cary filed a plat, called "Rockhurst Park," at the Jackson County Courthouse. He had subdivided the land east of Tracy Avenue into 62 lots for homes. The land west of Tracy and running to Troost and south to 53rd Street—about 12 acres—was set aside as "Outlot No. 1," ostensibly to be used as the campus of the new Rockhurst College. It was Dowling's plan, in time, to sell lots 1 to 62 at a profit to pay off the debt.[17]

— A SECULAR NAME —

Rockhurst was an unusual name, and, over the years, visitors often would ask how it was decided upon.[18] The name had everything to do with the Kansas City of 1910 and the anti-Catholicism that Father Dowling found there. "I would suggest that you call it by some secular name," he wrote to the provincial. "It will give the bigots less opportunity to discriminate against us secretly, because they will not know from the name that it is a Catholic Institution. Also for some years it will be needful to conciliate public opinion till we get well started. This is very much of a non-Catholic city." With a name in hand, Father Dowling also would be able to go to the press and "take advantage of any publicity to get our title known as well as our location."[19]

But what name could it be? Dowling knew he wanted a secular name, because, as he noted once again, "It is not pleasant to have every little bigot secretly injuring us on account of a distinctively Catholic name."[20] He walked the site with H.P. Stewart, vice chairman of the Stewart-Peck Sand Company, and Father Michael J. Ryan, who had recently been reassigned from Kansas' St. Mary's College to help with the new college. The trio looked out at the stony landscape and nearby grove of woods, and someone apparently said it made him think of the Jesuits' Stonyhurst College, a stately institution noted for its architecture and setting in the breathtaking countryside of Clitheroe, Lancashire, England.[21]

The men noted the hilly bluff above Brush Creek and commented that "Rockhill" was a perfect name, especially because city fathers already were calling the area around 47th and Oak streets by that name. "We would have liked to name the college Rockhill, after a restricted district in the immediate vicinity," Dowling said, but he explained that the Christian Brothers already had a college by that name: Rock Hill, in Ellicott City, Maryland, so the name was out of the question.[22]

So it was that Father Dowling improvised and cut and pasted a name: "Rock" from Rockhill and "Hurst" from Stonyhurst. "We finally determined ROCKHURST COLLEGE as the name," he said. "We expect the district around to take the name of Rockhurst. On a visit here the Very Rev. Father Provincial noticed that the people hereabouts are fond of English names, which are given to additions, hotels, parks and private grounds." It must have been shortly after that the father provincial gave his nod of approval, calling Rockhurst a "well-chosen name."[23] Purchase of the land was consummated, although the Kansas City Title & Trust Company continued to hold the title. With the name and purchase in hand, Dowling went to the press, where *The Kansas City Star* Editor William Rockhill Nelson considered the announcement so important that he put it on Page One of the Saturday paper of February 6, 1909.

"A SITE FOR A COLLEGE," the headline read.

"The twenty-five acres selected will afford accommodation for all the buildings that may be needed, for athletic field, playground and observatory." The east end of the site, the paper noted, "was within a block of the Marlborough trolleyline, and the west end will have the advantage of the Troost avenue line when extended." Father Dowling told *The Star* that

— THE UNIVERSITY SEAL —

The official seal of Rockhurst University was inspired by the history of Rockhurst. It was officially adopted on May 1, 1945 and modified on July 1, 1999.

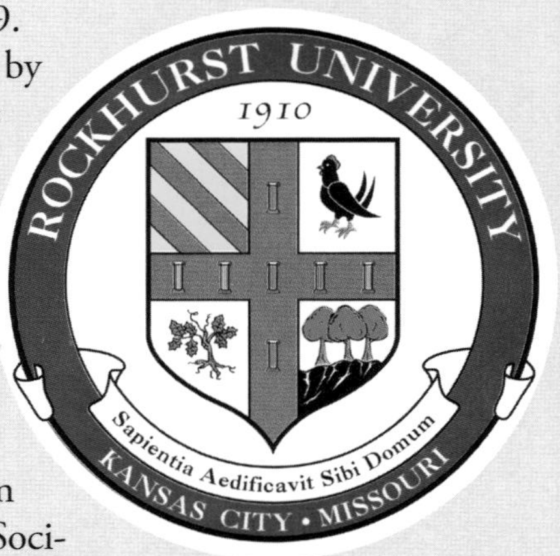

The shield in the center comprises four quarters separated by a cross with seven pillars. The pillars symbolize the seven pillars of wisdom and the seven liberal arts.

Reading clockwise from the upper right quadrant, the moorcock (a mythical bird) is from the family shield of Saint Thomas More, patron saint of Rockhurst. The stony, wooded hill represents the ground on which Rockhurst was built and for which it is named. The holly sprig is from the coat of arms of the Dowling family, in honor of Fr. Michael Dowling, the University's founder. The quarter-bars are from the family shield of St. Ignatius of Loyola, founder of the Society of Jesus. The Latin words at the bottom are the university's motto, "Wisdom has built herself a home."

Rockhurst "would be non-sectarian" and added that a construction date could not be given because more funds needed to be raised first. Over the next several weeks, Father Dowling was so busy that at one point he received a letter from his friend Mother Rock in Omaha asking half in jest "whether he were still alive."[24] Father Dowling was indeed alive and was making time to meet with influential men in the city, including bankers William Kemper and E.F. Swinney, prominent lawyer J.V.C. Karnes, and businessman and philanthropist William Volker. What exactly he said to these men is not known, but his words must have been persuasive because following his visits they and 33 other leading residents wrote an open letter to "the Citizens of Kansas City," which was published in *The Kansas City Star* on March 22, 1909.

The letter did not mention the Society of Jesus, saying only that "some of our Catholic fellow citizens have invited a competent teaching order of their denomination to establish in our midst a high grade college, which they hope, in the near future, to see grow into a university." In an apparent attempt to downplay its Catholic connections, the letter emphasized that Rockhurst would appeal to "all classes" and that "every shade of religious belief" would be received "on equal terms."

The letter writers envisioned Rockhurst to be a center of "conservative teaching," an important point that probably went a long way in explaining their endorsement. Rockhurst, they wrote, would spread "the benign influence of education, religion and morality" in a turn-of-the-century Kansas City where "social discontent is so widespread" and "the movements of anarchy are so threatening."

— MODERN WAYS —

If Kansas City's elite businessmen sounded concerned, it was understandable. The early years of the twentieth century were ones of great change in America as the country entered the modern age. The decade of the 1910s would set, as scholar Vincent Tompkins writes, "the broad patterns" of twentieth-century America. The decade would bring the first U.S. income tax, the first assembly-line automobiles, and, of course, the first world war. It was a chaotic time born of the Industrial Revolution, when the country saw more and more immigrants and more and more people moving to cities to find work and, in the process, turning old lifeways upside down.

The word "modernism" entered the lexicon as the new secular culture transformed society and as new scientific theories like Charles Darwin's *Origin of the Species* brought into question fundamental religious dogmas. Pope Pius X (1903-1913) defended the Catholic faith against popular views such as relativism and promoted Thomas Aquinas and Thomism as the only theology to be taught at Catholic institutions. He denounced the modernist views of those who wanted the Catholic Church itself to be modernized and blended with the new philosophical trends. Modernists, on the other hand, justified their stance, saying that beliefs of the Church had evolved throughout its history and continued to evolve. Anti-modernists viewed those notions as contrary to the dogmas and traditions of the Catholic Church.

The turn of the century also was a time of questioning and change for American higher education. Beginning in the 1890s, academic modernization led to the emergence of the free public high school as the standard agency of secondary education in America. Reforms included the introduction of an elective system that broke down the classical curriculum in favor of new fields of study that included "new" subjects such as English, modern languages, and history. The research university and the professionalization of learning led to many new jobs in education. Regional accrediting agencies, such as the North Central Association of Colleges and Secondary Schools, came into existence, as well as the College Entrance Examination Board, and associations like the Catholic Education Association, created in

St. Ignatius of Loyola is depicted with students from diverse cultures, including contemporary students, a representation of the continuation of the Jesuit mission in education today. The beginning of the 20th century was a time of change for American higher education. Innovations included the introduction of new fields of study and the rise of research universities and accrediting agencies. The trends toward standardization, centralization, and specialization proved to be challenging for the Jesuit system of education, which was based on the 300-year-old Ratio Studiorum. *Painting by Dora Nikolova Bittau, acrylic on wood panel with gold leaf. Courtesy of Chapel of St. Ignatius, Seattle University.*

1904, all of which reflected the standardization that was so characteristic of the twentieth century. The trend toward centralization and specialization created a bureaucracy of school boards, superintendents, examiners, truant officers, compulsory attendance and certification of teachers. From now on, as historian Philip Gleason writes, students would measure progress by "units" or "credit-hours" of work. The changes, Gleason writes, "constituted a veritable revolution which reshaped American higher education."[25]

Traditionally, the Catholic system of higher education centered on private academies, which principally were college preparatory schools for men and finishing schools for women. While many of the private academies called themselves colleges, they actually offered both high school and college education, with the high school classes enrolling the largest number of students. Rather than the prevailing system in the United States of the 4-year high school and 4-year college, the Catholic college was a 7-year institution combining both secondary and collegiate instruction. Not only did the system invite ridicule of colleges attended by "little boys in knickers," but it also baffled non-Catholic educators who considered the system out-of-date.[26]

The emergence of a Catholic school system separate from American public schools dated to reform movements of the 1830s and 1840s that were rooted in the nation's Protestant culture. As historian Jay Dolan explains, Catholics found it necessary to form their own common schools because the nation's public schools were rooted in a Protestant ideology that did not tolerate those outside the cultural matrix. Determined to safeguard their own culture, Catholic bishops at the important Third Plenary Council of Baltimore in 1884, called for the building of a parochial school "near each church where it does not exist" and demanded that all Catholic parents "send their children to the parochial schools." The parochial school, rather than the men's college, became the most important educational institution for Catholics, even though many Catholics did not have the financial means to send their children there. By 1900, reflecting the impoverishment of the nation's many Catholic immigrants, no more than 37 percent of the nation's parishes were able to support schools, and then, most parochial schools had only 4 or 5 grades, suffered from overcrowding, and drew complaints that Catholic schools were inferior.[27]

Difficulties with the organizational structure of Catholic education started in these elementary years. While Catholic schools were under the supervision of the local bishop, priests were responsible for individual parishes and for financing the parochial schools themselves, which usually were taught by nuns of various religious orders. Religious communities, with Jesuits at the forefront, also oversaw Catholic colleges. Because the communities were responsible for financing their own colleges, it was necessary to enroll preparatory boys as well as college men if enough tuition was to be had to run the college.

Because Catholic colleges and Catholic parochial schools operated on different systems, there was no "natural step" on the "education ladder," as Gleason writes, for students to move up from the parochial school. They had either to go to a public high school or shift to the Catholic "college"

— Catholic Higher Education —

Even though the Jesuits moved toward modernization in higher education by adopting a new "Course of Studies" in 1915, and then another in 1920, the first catalog for Rockhurst College describes its aim in a much more traditional way.

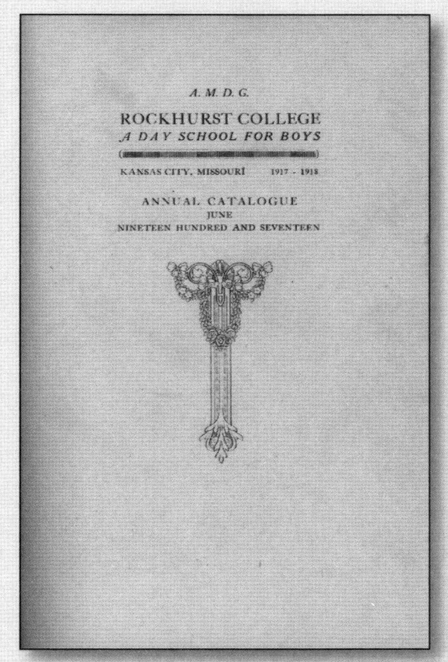

A. M. D. G.

ROCKHURST COLLEGE

A DAY SCHOOL FOR BOYS

KANSAS CITY, MISSOURI 1917 - 1918

ANNUAL CATALOGUE

JUNE

NINETEEN HUNDRED AND SEVENTEEN

"The training in the new Rockhurst College is of the sort which three hundred years of Jesuit educational work has made known throughout the world. The aim of this institution is to turn out young men whose mental faculties have been so developed and formed that they may successfully enter upon the immediate preparation for any career.

"Long experience has proven, to the satisfaction of the best educators the world over, that a young man well trained in general and classical studies succeeds better afterwards in professional preparation than one whose early training was distracted by an assorted smattering of quasi-professional studies. In other words, it is almost universally admitted that a well developed and properly formed mind is a more valuable asset in any career or profession than a heterogeneous and half-assimilated mass of information. The vast number of men, products of the classical course, who have been eminently successful both in PROFESSIONAL and BUSINESS life, proves beyond a doubt the value of such a course of study."

track, which meant more expenses and implied a higher education goal—"college" not "high school."[28]

Catholic colleges also gained a reputation for backwardness because they spurned the modern call for elective courses. This was particularly troublesome for the Jesuit system because it had always keyed on the *Ratio Studiorum*, with its classical-rhetorical emphasis and mastery of Latin, even though Latin had long ago lost its practical value for lay students. The classical versus elective debate raised questions that went to the very heart of the meaning of Jesuit higher education: was it to instill mental discipline in students or prepare them for a career?[29] By 1904, with modernization in full swing, a movement was afoot among Catholic educators to create centralized Catholic high schools rather than single-parish schools, and the more progressive Catholic colleges, such as Holy Cross in Massachusetts, eliminated their prep students. But other Catholic educators shunned the high school movement, especially if they thought their colleges couldn't survive financially without high school students.[30]

By 1913, when the North Central Association's first list of approved colleges came out, only one Catholic college, Notre Dame, was on the list. Against this ominous background, Gleason writes, the Catholic Education Association, in 1915, adopted standardization, agreeing on 128 semester hours as a minimum for graduation from college, and that to be regarded as a college, an institution must have at least 7 departments, each with a full-time professor holding a college degree or its equivalent. Other provisions dealt with things from library holdings to laboratory equipment to teaching loads.[31]

The call for separation of prep school and college was not so easily addressed. The issue was particularly hard for the Jesuits, Gleason explains, because they were unshakably attached to the 300-year-old *Ratio Studiorum*, which treated high school and college as an integrated unit and called for a narrowly classical course of study—rhetoric, poetry, and grammar. Characteristic of Jesuit discipline and order, the *Ratio* demanded that certain subjects be taken in a hierarchical, sequential order. The *Ratio* emphasized the mastery of Latin and ruled out the elective "new subjects" that were so important to the modernist movement.[32]

Amid the debates, Catholic educators found it troubling that more and more Catholics were choosing to attend secular colleges, a trend that was testament, Gleason explains, to the burgeoning professionalization of the twentieth century and the upward mobility aspirations of second- and third-generation Catholics. Although Italian and Slavic "new immigrants" had only recently arrived in America, the children of Irish and German "old immigrants" had been in the United States all their lives and were assimilating into the middle class as they attained a socioeconomic status that allowed for college attendance. The trend was so alarming that many Catholic educators feared that Catholic colleges would fade away altogether. So concerned, in fact, was Missouri's conservative Jesuit provincial, Rudolph Meyer, that he advocated prohibiting Catholics from attending secular undergraduate colleges. [33]

The movement toward secular colleges and universities diverged from early traditions when religious groups often founded America's earliest colleges. In Kansas City, for instance, the area's first college was the Baptist-affiliated William Jewell College, founded in 1849, followed by Park College, established by the Presbyterian John A. McAfee in 1874.[34] By 1908, vocational colleges had opened, including the new Spalding's Commercial College at 10th and Oak streets and another—the Christian Brothers' De La Salle—soon to open on The Paseo between 15th and 16th streets. Although the Christian Brothers promoted De La Salle as a Catholic "college," it actually was the city's first Catholic high school for boys, and a commercial school, offering a practical curriculum of bookkeeping, typing, and shorthand. It would lack the rigor and emphasis on classical education that the Jesuit Michael Dowling brought with him from Creighton.[35]

The debate between a classical curriculum and one more in tune to academic trends raged as Father Dowling corresponded with his conservative provincial and set about trying to found Rockhurst College. Judging from a paper Dowling presented at the second annual Conference of Catholic Colleges, held in Chicago in April 1900, Father Dowling was much more progressive than his superior. In his paper, titled *Development of Character in College Students*, Dowling addressed college discipline and the dormitory versus room system. A summary of the paper, published that year in

53rd and Troost, looking northeast, with Father Michael J. Ryan, S.J., standing in the foreground. Fr. Ryan, who had been reassigned from St. Mary's College to help with the new college, was described by Fr. Michael Dowling as a "busy toiler," a man full of "wonderful endurance and vitality." Ryan oversaw the opening of the rock quarry, supervised the laborers that worked on Sedgwick Hall, and helped found the Jesuit parish at Rockhurst. When the college was incorporated in 1910, Ryan was designated as treasurer of the corporation. Courtesy of Rockhurst University Archives.

the *Woodstock Letters*, noted that Dowling's paper "was a strong appeal for the development of manliness and honor in the building up of true character, and asserted that no small element in character building was to be found in athletics, since character is developed on campus as well as in the classroom."[36]

It would not be until 1913, when Rudolph Meyer was replaced by a moderate provincial, Alexander J. Burrowes, that the Missouri Province moved toward modernization in higher education. A new "Course of Studies" was adopted in 1915, and then another in 1920, which was considered so important that historian Philip Gleason says it amounted "to a radical break with the Jesuit past." The 61-page report, in the vein of academic modernism, adopted the semester-hour system, provided for elective courses, and created 3 degree programs (A.B., B.S., and Ph.B.). Almost half of the document, Gleason writes, was devoted to an alphabetical listing of 21 departments from "Astronomy" to "Spanish," with 200 numbered courses assigned a value in credit hours.[37] No longer would the Jesuit system demand particular subjects be taken in a particular sequential order.

It would be years, however, before Rockhurst could afford to follow academic trends by separating its high school and college.

— An Unexpected Problem —

With land purchased and a name selected, hopes were so high for the beginnings of Rockhurst College that in March of 1909 Father Dowling told how Rockhurst eventually would offer not only undergraduate courses, but also postgraduate studies, including medicine, dentistry, and "advanced science." Dowling told how his life that March was "in a continual whirl" as he went about setting up a board of trustees, meeting with Jackson County officials, and moving the house and barn off the old Peers estate so the county could grade 53rd Street and put in a storm culvert. He opened the limestone quarry on the far side of the property and held high hopes of getting stone there for the college's first building.[38]

In addition to his Rockhurst duties, Father Dowling was busy at St. Aloysius Parish. "Confessions and communions are abundant; and just now sick-calls are more numerous than usual," he wrote to the provincial that March of 1909. "We have had some flattering invitations to preach, which we would be glad to accept, for the sake of the good will so desirable everywhere; yet we absolutely cannot, for we are worked to death as it is." There were 2 Masses on Sunday, baptisms, confessions, night sermons and vespers, sodalities, visits, and pew rents to attend to. On top of that it was the Lenten season, and the church was so packed for the weekly sermons on Wednesday and Sunday nights that people were standing in the back of the church and in the galleries.[39]

In the midst of all this—and just as everything seemed to be getting under way at Rockhurst—Bishop John J. Hogan sent for Dowling and applied the brakes. It wasn't the college that was the problem, the bishop said, but rather the assignment of a new parish to a religious order such as the Jesuits. Father Dowling had made it clear that he wanted to connect Rockhurst to a parish with a church, something he felt was a necessity if the college were to succeed. So adamant was he about the new parish that he told the bishop the Society of Jesus would not begin a college without one. Considering that the Society already had a parish in Kansas City—St. Aloysius—this demand created a touchy situation for Hogan, who told Dowling he had found out—how, he did not say—that he was not allowed, under Canon Law, to give a new parish to the Jesuits without talking to his diocesan consultors first and then referring the matter to Rome.[40] Hogan did as he said he must and met with his consultors. When he reported back to Dowling, the news was not good.

"They want our present parish (St. Aloysius), if we are to get another; and they want it free of debt," Dowling explained to the provincial on April 10, 1909. Apparently, Kansas City's other Catholic clergy were wary of religious orders such as the Jesuits, fearing that if they established another parish, "all the rich people would follow them."

Dowling took a breath and considered. Turning over St. Aloysius Parish certainly was possible, but turning it over debt-free? That simply could not be done immediately. The parish, now 25 years old, was thriving in the spring of 1909, but its $35,000 debt was far from paid off. The debt, understandably, had been incurred over the years to build and furnish the church with its commodious basement, to erect the parish hall, the school, the pastoral residence, and sisters' house. St. Aloysius' 496 families were "loyal and responsive" and were reducing the debt year by year, Dowling said, but they could not be expected to pay it off all at once.[41]

Looking for more information on exactly what was going on, Dowling went to see one of the consultors, Father Ernest Zechenter of St. Peter and St. Paul Church, known as the German church, at 9th and McGee streets. "I could not get him to talk," Dowling told the provincial. "All he would say was they had talked the matter over and came to the conclusion that

that was the right thing to do. Evidently it is to be a conspiracy of silence as well as injustice."

Dowling reasoned and pleaded. "I asked him if he thought it right to encourage and urge us to so great an undertaking (as a college) and financial loss and disregard the fact that it was with the full consult of the Bishop that we went as far as we did; his promise ought to count for something." Zechenter reminded Dowling that the Jesuits of 25 years ago had agreed to establish their college at 11th Street and Prospect Avenue, so why not, he asked, build it there, as promised?

Dowling sparred. "I reminded him that the location was not the right one and it was useless to spend money on the wrong site; moreover the Bishop did not want us to have a college there, because he did not want any rivalry between us and the Christian Brothers." The Christian Brothers, of course, had just established De La Salle Academy on The Paseo, only a mile from St. Aloysius Church. But it was no use talking to Zechenter, so Dowling went to see the Very Rev. Thomas E. Lillis, bishop of the Diocese of Leavenworth, who, in just a few months, would be named coadjutor, with the right of succession, for the aging Bishop Hogan. Lillis urged Dowling to be patient and wait for developments to unfold. The topic was touchy enough that Lillis asked Dowling not to let on that the two had talked.[42]

Rumors were flying. "I hear that the secular clergy believe that we have enriched ourselves at St. Aloysius, meanwhile allowing a large debt to accumulate on the church," Dowling told the provincial in St. Louis. "Also that they doubt whether we really intend to build a college, but may be seeking to secure another good parish, as we did at St. Aloysius. That view does not argue great confidence in our integrity; but it is sometimes good to see ourselves as others see us."[43]

Father Dowling was realistic. When a layman supportive of Rockhurst had wanted to "get up an agitation among the laity," Dowling discouraged him. "It is easier to raise a storm of the kind than to quell it," he reasoned. "Besides if we had to start here in face of relentless opposition, what could we hope to accomplish, with all the clergy solidly against us as interlopers? If we can't convert them to more rational views, our college work would be uphill from the very beginning. It is quite clear that now at least they do not want us and look on our establishment of a college as a menace to their prosperity. They want that part of the city (south of Brush Creek) for themselves, without any Religious to interfere with them."[44]

There seemed nowhere to turn but to providence. "You would do well," Dowling urged the provincial, "to get some of the brethren to help us with their prayers in this emergency; that we may act wisely and with an upright intention, free from human bias."

Kansas City, May 4, 1909
Rev M P Dowling S J
Rector St Aloysius' Church
Kansas City,
Rev Dear Sir
The Diocesan Consulters voted unani= mously today that the Jesuit Fathers be given charge of a new parish at Rockhurst in this city when they will have surrendered St Aloy= sius' parish to the Bishop free from debt.
I remain Rev Dear Sir
Yours faithfully in Christ
+ John J Hogan,
Bp of Kansas City

Over a period of a couple of months in spring 1909, Fr. Dowling and Bishop John Hogan met in person and exchanged letters about the assignment of a new parish to the Jesuits at Rockhurst. Fr. Dowling was convinced that Rockhurst had to be connected to a church if the college were to succeed. Bishop Hogan, following the advice of his consultors, would agree to give the Jesuits a new parish only if they surrendered St. Aloysius to the diocese, debt-free. Though St. Aloysisus was thriving, Dowling knew that it would be many years before the parish would be debt-free. The letter above from Bishop Hogan to Fr. Dowling on May 4 reflects the position of the diocese. In June, however, Dowling drafted a compromise that was agreed upon by both parties: the Society of Jesus would turn the deed over to the diocese, while continuing to pay off the debt. That way, there could be no doubt of the Jesuits' intentions. Courtesy of Rockhurst University Archives.

Father Michael Dowling's cross, which he carried on his watch chain. Photo by David Spaw. Courtesy of Rockhurst University Archives.

That March, Father Dowling had been discouraged enough that he offered to give up the Rockhurst project altogether if Bishop Hogan saw fit. "I told him we were prepared to acquiesce in any judgment he and his consultors would reach; that it was an arduous task to establish a college under existing circumstances in Kansas City, and that we felt we were doing a favor to the diocese in attempting it; that if they were not anxious for it, we could give up the enterprise without any regret...."[45]

But then Dowling drafted a compromise, agreeing to turn St. Aloysius Parish over debt-free—but not right away. It would take "about fifteen years," he said.[46] The intervening years not only would allow time to pay off the debt, but also would give the new Rockhurst parish time "to reach some considerable growth." Dowling was open to compromise, but on the subject of a new parish, he would not budge. Just look, he argued, the location selected for Rockhurst was still so remote that a new parish there surely could not be a threat.

"There is at present no church, no parish, no congregation, perhaps few Catholics, in the vicinity of the location we have recently purchased at 53rd and Troost; and it is not likely that for many years, if ever, there will be a parish as large and flourishing as St. Aloysius is," he wrote to Bishop Hogan on April 26, 1909. "<u>It is not even reasonable to suppose that inside of fifteen (15) years that district will grow into a parish of respectable size</u>." He emphasized his words by underlining them, then continued: "For that reason we could not be expected to give up at once the present parish, taking instead a new parish, with all the pioneer work to be done over again, without any resources for either church or college."

Reasonable as his plea was, Dowling received a succinct note from Bishop Hogan the next week informing him that the diocesan consultors had voted unanimously that the Jesuits must surrender St. Aloysius free of debt before they could have a new parish at Rockhurst.[47] Perhaps it was that note, or the rumors, or the lack of trust in his motivations that, by May, had started to harden Father Dowling's heart, as well. "It is a pretty hard thing to deal dispassionately with such a crisis," he wrote. "We feel like wanting to get even with them somehow." Dowling considered issuing an ultimatum that if the bishop and consultors persisted in their course, he would tell them: "either a college with parish at Rockhurst, or we go."[48]

Things came to head on June 1 when Dowling paid a visit to Hogan and told him the Jesuits were quite willing to drop the project if he and the clergy of the city didn't want it. "We do not want to force it on you," Dowling told him. "It means only labor, expense and responsibility for us."[49] He minced no words: "You say that all of you are in favor of it, anxious for it; but if that were so, you would not impose impossible conditions. To say that we must first give up St. Aloysius parish, free of debt, before we can have any district assigned to us elsewhere, is equivalent to stopping the enterprise. It will take years to pay that debt, and meanwhile you do not engage to hold the other parish for us. Our superiors will never consent to build at Rockhurst, without an understanding that we are to have a parochial district there. To do otherwise would breed dissention and trouble."

Father Dowling did not let up: "We have no fund to draw upon for paying off that debt at once; and even if we had, it would be equal to saying that we pay to the parish or diocese $30,000 for the privilege of surrendering a well established parish, and starting a new one, as well as a college, in a sparsely settled district, without any resources whatever." And then he put the entire future of Rockhurst College on the line: "If some different determination is not reached soon," he told the bishop, "there will be nothing left but for us to sell the property we purchased and abandon the project. It costs three thousand dollars a year to hold that property; and that we cannot do, unless we know clearly in the near future that there is some likelihood of our being able to use the ground."

Do the math, he might as well have said. "We have spent $50,000 for land and will be obliged to spend at least an equal amount on building at the very beginning. An outlay of $100,000 means that we would have to get one hundred paying students, at fifty dollars a year, merely to meet the interest on the debt; without counting the support of the school and Faculty."[50]

Dowling pressed and pressed, but Bishop Hogan seemed unmoved—especially on the point that the debt must be paid on St. Aloysius Parish before the Jesuits would be given a new Rockhurst parish. Hogan insisted that he could not go against the unanimous opinion of his consultors.

But still, in yet another meeting with Bishop Hogan, Dowling persisted: "I showed him that as that debt could not be paid for a number of years, his answer was equivalent to saying that we could not begin a college for an indefinite period. If he had told us that in the beginning, it would have been easy enough for us to have done nothing, but now we were in a different position, because we had assumed a large debt, incurred large expense and committed ourselves to the public, on the strength of his word."

Hogan felt that he, too, was in a difficult position, and his worries spilled out: It was difficult, he told Dowling, to procure places for his own diocesan priests. Just look around. The Redemptorists were building Our Lady of Perpetual Help Church at Broadway and Linwood, with its planned 225-foot spire, and the Dominicans of Holy Name Church also were talking about a new, cathedral-size church to seat 1,000 worshippers at Benton Boulevard at 22nd Street.[51] And now another community of Religious—Dowling's Jesuits—wanted 2 parishes in Kansas City. "The Religious," Hogan told Dowling, "were draining the city," and his own clergy "were being relegated to little country parishes where they could hardly live...." If the Jesuits had 2 parishes, Hogan exclaimed, they "would own the city."[52]

The meeting ended on a softer note: "You must have patience; do not get discouraged; these things will all come out right in course of time," Hogan told Dowling, who embraced the bishop's words but added in his letter to the provincial: "But he did not indicate what would cause a change of conditions." It occurred to Dowling that Bishop Hogan, who was 80 years old, was hoping to hedge the issue. "It looks to me as if he intended to temporize till he dies, which he thinks will come soon; after which it will be up to somebody else to solve the difficulty."

— THE JESUITS GET A NEW PARISH —

By July 1, 1909, the Jesuit provincial had drawn up a "memorandum of agreement" for Bishop Hogan to sign. It outlined all that had been agreed to, giving the Society of Jesus a parish within the boundaries of where the new college would be located. The terms of the agreement were these:

- The Very Rev. R.J. Meyer, S.J., transfers to Rt. Rev. John J. Hogan, D.D., St. Aloysius church, school, parochial residence, sisters house and all parochial appurtenances; and he will at once have the necessary deeds executed.
- The Fathers of the Society of Jesus shall continue to administer St. Aloysius Parish for ten years; and at the end of that time, or sooner if possible, shall hand it over to the Diocese, free of debt....
- Rt. Rev. John J. Hogan, D.D., hereby assigns to the Fathers of the Society of Jesus a parochial district, whose limits are Forty-ninth and Fifty-seventh streets, McGee Street and Woodland Avenue.

"Since at present no parishes adjoin this parochial district either on the east, west, or south sides, the Fathers of the Society of Jesus may attend and administer the sacraments to the faithful half way to the boundaries of the nearest parishes on these three sides. As there is a neutral zone lying between their parochial district above defined, and St. James' parish north of them, as also Our Lady of Good Counsel parish northwest of them, they may divide the intervening territory, by amicable arrangement with the pastors of these aforesaid parishes or otherwise as the Bishop of Kansas City may decide. If in the course of time the Catholics of this neutral zone may call for parish autonomy, the new parish will be so aligned as not to trespass upon any of the above named parishes whose limits are given as one square mile to each parish."

"Memorandum of Agreement," Rockhurst University Archives.

— A SOLUTION —

Dowling pressed the matter again in a letter to Hogan on June 18, 1909, restating his conditions but adding something new to address the consultors' distrust: would the consultors and the bishop reconsider if the Society of Jesus turned the deed to St. Aloysius Church, school, residence, sisters' house, and parish appurtenances over to him? That way, there could be no doubt of the Jesuits' intentions.

Perhaps it was that offer—his turning over of the St. Aloysius deed—that erased any suspicions the consultors had. No sooner, in fact, did Dowling make this offer than he saw a marked change in attitude. Within a week, he had the agreement he sought. "At last everything is satisfactorily arranged," he wrote to the provincial on June 25, 1909. "All that remains is for you to send the Bishop a deed to the St. Aloysius Property. He has given us the new parish, assigned us limits and authorized us to go ahead as soon as we want. I think it was the idea of giving the bishop the deed that caught the consultors."

Father Dowling got down to business. He sent the necessary papers to St. Louis, telling Provincial Rudolph Meyer that it would "be advisable to keep all those memorandums, at least for the present." Here, he told Meyer, was the bishop's letter of consent, and here was the assignment of parish limits, "in the bishop's own handwriting."[53] The parish limits, at one square mile, were "altogether satisfactory," he wrote. "Till other parishes are established in the immediate vicinity, we can take in everything in the neighborhood, south, east, and west." The northern neighborhood would be shared with Father Keyes' one-square-mile St. James Parish. A neutral district would lie between.

Father Dowling already was thinking of the future. That same day he wrote another note to the provincial asking him to assign Father Michael Ryan to Rockhurst for the time being, since "we will need one of Ours out at Rockhurst during the day, to see about the opening of a quarry there, till we know what stone we have there and can make a contract for the working." Ryan also could use any spare time to walk the neighborhood "and drum up the Catholic families and find out how many there are."[54] If enough Catholics were found, Dowling envisioned saying Mass "in the house that is on the ground, till a chapel has been built."

His mood was decidedly upbeat as all thoughts turned now to the future. "A whole lot must be done," he wrote, "putting in sewer, cutting down trees, grading, removing fences, gathering up the loose stones in the field for crushing for concrete." A "capable man" like Father Ryan could hurry things along. Father Ryan, 45 years old, was lauded as a "busy toiler," a man full of "wonderful endurance and vitality," despite a hacking cough that had accompanied him throughout life. Father Ryan insisted it was nothing, though at times the cough so worried his superiors that they urged him to move to Arizona.[55] Instead, Ryan kept on working. He would spend a year helping to found Rockhurst parish.

By July 1, 1909, the provincial had drawn up a "memorandum of agreement" for Bishop Hogan to sign, outlining all that had been agreed to. By the end of July 1909, Father Dowling was moving ahead again with the material work of Rockhurst College; 900 feet of sewers to drain the property were laid, and fences were put up. In order to grade the Troost Avenue frontage, the old farmhouse was moved from Troost to the back of the property, near Forest Avenue, facing 53rd Street, which now boasted temporary sidewalks. Stones were laid the rest of the way to the Marlborough streetcar line.[56] The stones and sidewalks undoubtedly helped parishioners navigate the mud as the first Mass was said in the old farmhouse on August 1, 1909. That August, the new parish, named St. Francis Xavier after the wishes of Bishop Hogan, also saw its first baptism, that of W.J. Sharon.[57]

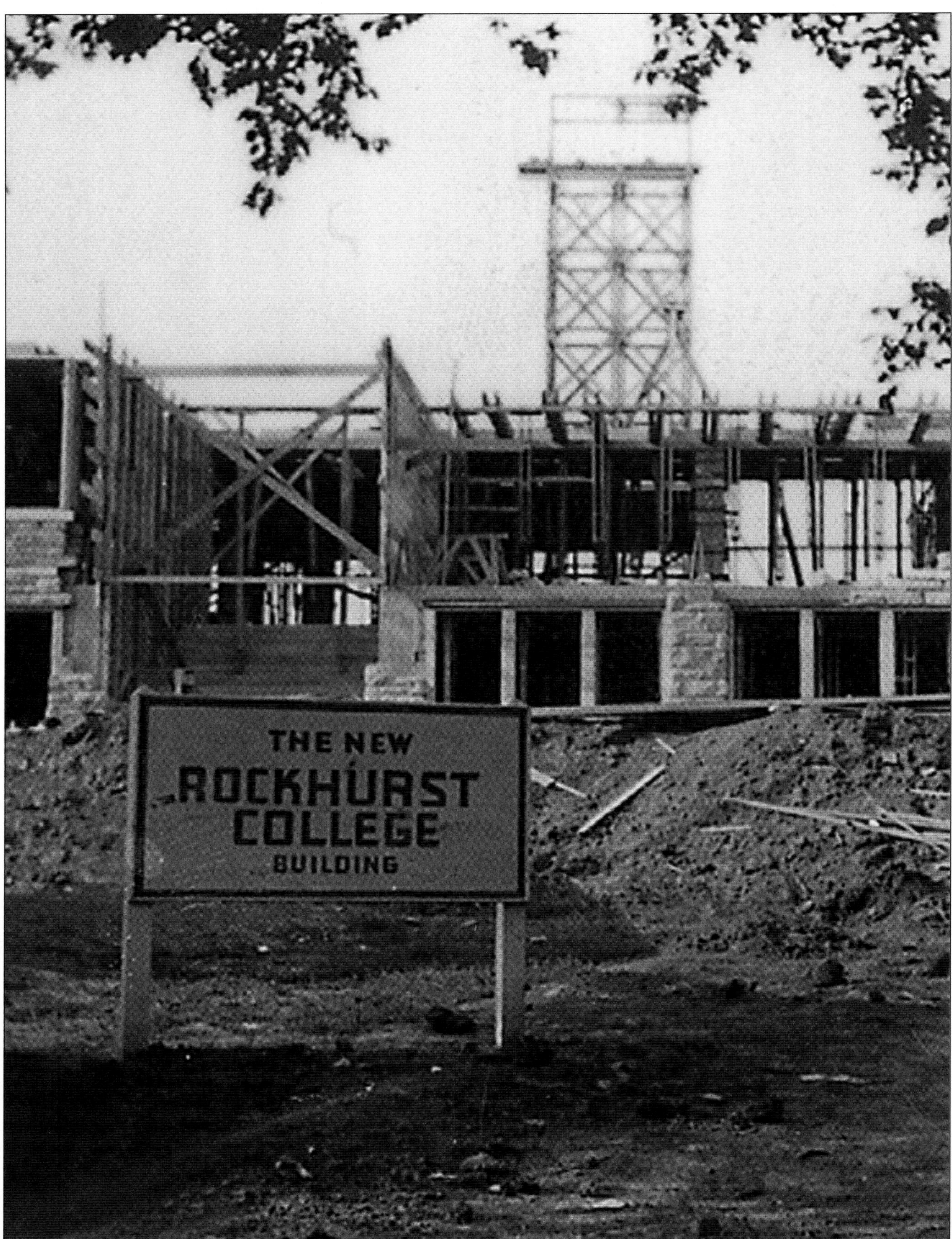
THE NEW
ROCKHURST
COLLEGE
BUILDING

Chapter Four

A College Building 1909–1914

Father Dowling's mind was filled now with the details of construction and the costs that went with it. He not only knew that 900 feet of sewer had been laid to drain his property, but also that it was an 18-inch sewer that could handle water from the watershed that ran diagonally from 55th Street and Troost Avenue to 52nd and Lydia. He grew familiar with cement prices and stone crushers and kept an eye on the digging of prospect holes at the quarry at 53rd Street and Virginia Avenue. He felt optimistic that Rockhurst could get good building stone there for the college's first structure. It was probable, he said, that the site held plenty of blue stone as well as ordinary rubble.[1]

He took advantage of a price war among cement makers, which dropped the price of Iola Portland Cement to 85 cents a barrel, down from $1.50 a barrel. He had 1,300 barrels of the cement delivered that September of 1909 on a siding at 46th and Main streets and hauled it to Troost with Rockhurst's own horse team. Then, Father Dowling went to town buying 300 tons of plaster, which also had plunged in price, from $9 a ton to $5.35. "It will be delivered to us as we need, by the car load, any time within a reasonable period. Mr. Geo. H. Kuhmann of St. Aloysius Parish, a bridge builder, says he will take off our hands any we do not want."[2]

He got permission from surrounding property owners to curb, gutter, and pave 53rd Street by private contractor. Ever mindful of costs, Dowling looked to trim expenses by furnishing the stone right off the Rockhurst property. The work went on and on. A grade had been established for Lydia Avenue, but the work remained for 52nd Street, which Dowling planned to have graded, guttered, and paved. The lots north of the street would be platted and sold as a new addition to the city.

He intended to hire a contractor to build the church and school and was thinking of insurance and finding carpenters to make signs for the college and the chapel. Someone would have to build a roadway in from Troost, paint the old farmhouse, and oil the machinery. They were little things, but they needed to be done.[3]

Exhausted as he was, his spirits were high that September as so much progress was being made. A chapel with schoolroom attached had been erected facing 53rd Street, and weekly

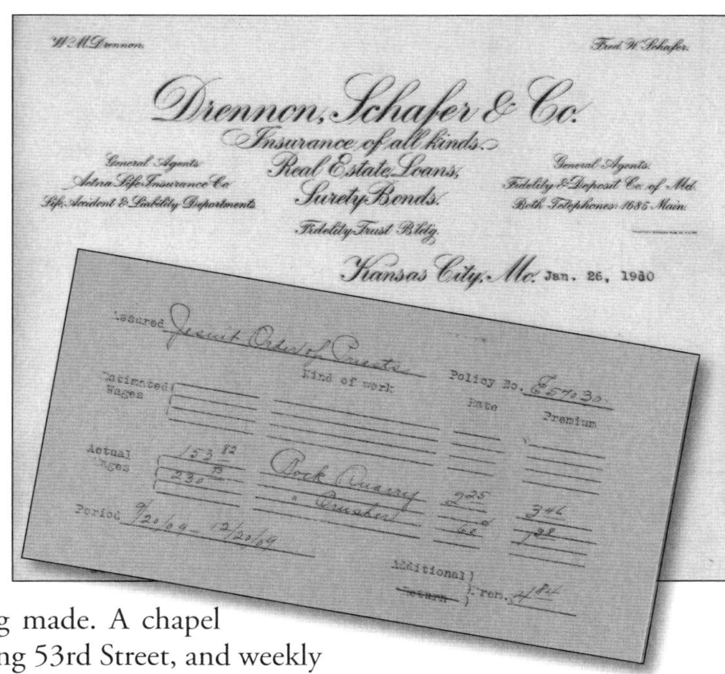
W. M. Drennon. Fred. W. Schafer.

Drennon, Schafer & Co.

Insurance of all kinds.

General Agents Aetna Life Insurance Co. Life, Accident & Liability Departments

Real Estate Loans, Surety Bonds.

General Agents: Fidelity & Deposit Co. of Md. Both Telephones 1685 Main.

Fidelity Trust Bldg.

Kansas City, Mo. Jan. 26, 1910

Assured Jesuit Order of Priests

Estimated Wages

Kind of work

Policy No. E 5703

Rate

Premium

Actual Wages 153.82 / 230.73

Rock Quarry / " Crusher

Period 9/20/09 – 12/20/09

Additional Prem.

Insurance receipt, 1909. The stone used for the building of Sedgwick Hall was quarried from Rockhurst acreage at 53rd and Virginia. Father Dowling took out an insurance policy with the Aetna Life Insurance Company against injuries that might be incurred during the work in the rock quarry. In 1910, a worker brought suit against the college for injuries sustained when the fly wheel of a rock crusher malfunctioned. The suit was settled out of court. Courtesy of Rockhurst University Archives.

St. Francis Xavier Church and the Peers farmhouse. The first Mass was said in the old farmhouse on August 1, 1909. The farmhouse originally faced Troost but was moved to 53rd Street near Forest Avenue to make room for construction of Sedgwick Hall. The chapel, with a schoolroom attached, was erected in the fall of 1909. The new parish drew a weekly attendance of 60 to 70 people. The parochial school opened in September 1910. Courtesy of Rockhurst University Archives.

attendance seldom varied from between 60 and 70 people. Two nuns who resided in the St. Aloysius convent, Sister Mary Sylvester and Sister Mary Catherine, came every Sunday to run the Sunday school, and two Sisters of Charity, B.V.M., Sister Mary Evangelista and Sister Mary Hildegarde, came on Sundays to teach Catechism.[4]

By January of the new year of 1910, architects had returned their conceptions for Rockhurst's first building, and Dowling's spirits were still so high that he was able to joke even when he received a note from St. Louis reprimanding him for not sending along copies of the architectural plans in time for the next consultorial meeting. "When I received your explanatory letter it was too late to get the plans to you in time…either by express or mail," he wrote to the father provincial on January 20, 1910. "The only possible means might be aviation, but Father Kieffer has not got his aeroplane sufficiently advanced to permit of immediate use."

Perhaps a little humor, tinged as it was with sarcasm, would not hurt, he must have thought, in what most likely was an effort to keep too many hands out of the planning process. There were, after all, 4 separate architectural plans for the college. Dowling had sought competitive bids for the first college building months ago and offered a $200 prize to the architect who emerged victorious, $150 to the second-place finisher, and $100 to the third. He had told the architects he wanted their plans by January 1, 1910, would make the awards by May 1, and begin building that spring.[5] He already could envision Rockhurst's first building; it was to be a 2-story, 124-foot by 95-foot structure with a basement—a "substantial building with good architectural lines," but in "an economical style."

There were so many matters to attend to.

He needed to get authorization from his Jesuit superiors to go an additional $50,000 in debt to begin building, promising that "we shall do no more building than we can do with that amount, plus any additional money that we may be able to raise from donations."[6] The debt ultimately would be paid off, he said, from the sale of Rockhurst's unneeded 13 acres between Tracy and Lydia avenues. That, after all, is why he purchased all of those original 25 acres from Robert Cary. Dowling was counting on the land to increase in value once people saw the college going up. All, he emphasized, hinged "on our ability to begin," especially the raising of donations, an effort that, to say the least, had been disappointing so far.

An early publicity drive, in May 1909, had netted only $7,000, but Father Dowling is said to have shrugged off his disappointment: "Let us thank the Lord for that much and begin," he said, words that would become Rockhurst's slogan through the years.[7] Despite his inspiring words,

Father Dowling must have realized that "beginning" was not going to come easily, especially with lack of funds. Already, he faced an $8,500 debt on the chapel and schoolroom, and the debt on St. Aloysius Parish, while being trimmed by $2,500 during 1908 and another $3,300 during 1909, still stood at $29,700.

In addition to the college's financial troubles, there were personnel problems. Dowling wasn't getting the help he felt he needed and begged the provincial to "figure on a new alignment of our Kansas City forces." Aloysius Breen, president of St. Mary's College, was lending men from the college, but what use were they, Dowling complained, when they arrived at the St. Aloysius residence at 8:30 on a Saturday night and left at 5 the next evening? Father Dowling knew he sounded "a little more testy than usual" and said it might be because he was "wrestling with the grip." He'd been trying his best "to do what I ought," he told the provincial, but half the time he felt "as cross as a bag of cats."[8]

He needed help and asked specifically for Father Ryan, who had returned to St. Mary's College, to be sent back to Kansas City. "Father Ryan is the only one that has been a real help to us, because he is ready and willing." It took a man with special qualities to establish a college, Dowling told the provincial.[9] He needed a good memory for names and faces and the disposition of a diplomat or "jollier." Initiative was imperative, as was the ability to meet unexpected conditions. And a man needed a prescience for places, knowing where streets were and where parish lines ran.

Before all was said and done, Father Dowling and his Jesuit assistants would have some harrowing experiences with their hired help. Father Patrick Harvey, in his early history of Rockhurst, tells how one workman had "every promise of great efficiency" but lasted only 12 days before deserting. Another workman, Harvey writes, "was nearly the cause of the death of the sisters on Troost Ave. hill." The workman, John Miller, apparently knew little or nothing about hitching horses to a wagon. "It was his duty to drive the sisters from the car-line at 48th and Troost to the college each morning," Harvey writes. "The harness slipped from the back of the horses and the buggy ran down the hill and into the ditch, and the sisters had a very narrow escape from being seriously injured."[10]

Early June 1910 came, but still nothing had been started on the college building. Father Ryan, at least, was back on hand, sent from St. Mary's to take the place of 2 other priests who did not work out. That summer—with no building, no students, and short of money—Father Ryan and Father Dowling sat down on

In the summer of 1910, with no building, no students, and short of money, Father Michael Dowling and Father Michael Ryan made application for a state charter. They did so after organizing a prospective corporation with Dowling as president, Ryan as treasurer, and John F. Weir, S.J., who was serving in St. Aloysius Parish, as secretary. The 3, along with Adolph J. Kuhlman and Edward Cody, were designated to be the college directors. On August 30, 1910, Rockhurst College was legally founded and chartered by the state of Missouri to grant degrees. Courtesy of Rockhurst University Archives.

In the Matter of the Application
of Michael P.Dowling and others
for the Incorporation of Rockhurst
College

Pro Ferma Decree
Dated Aug,30,1910
Filed Sept,3,1910
Book B-1274,page 115
#776513
Circuit Court,Jackson Co.Mo.
at Kansas City,April Term -
August 30,1910 #52995

Now on this 30th,day of August,1910,come Michael P.Dowling,John F.Weir and Michael J.Ryan,respectively President,Secretary and Treasurer of Rockhourst College,and it appearing to the Court that the petition and articles of agreement of said Rockhurst College were presented to the Court on the 23d,day of August,1910,and have remained on file in the office of the Clerk thereof at least 3 days since such presentation, and John M.Cleary,a member of the bar of thisCourt who was on said 23d day of August,1910,appointed by the Court to examine into the merits of said application,now files his report and the Court having carefully examined said petition and Articles of Agreement,and also the report of said John M.Cleary this day made and being fully advised in the premises entertains no doubt of the lawfulness and public usefulness of said proposed corporation,and being of the opinion that such Articles of Agreement and the purposes of the corporation come properly within the provisions of Article XI,of Chapter 12 of the Revised Statutes of 1899 and are not inconsistent with the constitution and laws of the United States or of the State of Missouri,so finds,and it is,

Ordered,Adjudged and Decreed that said petitioners and their associates named in said Articles of Agreement be,and they are hereby declared a body corporate and politic by and under the name of Rockhurst College.

State of Missouri
County of Jackson - ss

I,Oscar Hochland,Clerk of the Circuit Court within and for the County and State aforesaid,do hereby certufy the above to be a true copy of the order of Court made in the matter aforesaid,as fully as the same remains of record in my office. and that the original articles of agreement are attached hereto.

47

August 17 and made application for a state charter. They did so after organizing a prospective corporation with Dowling as president; John F. Weir, S.J., who was serving in St. Aloysius Parish, as secretary; and Michael J. Ryan, S.J., as treasurer. The 3, along with Adolph J. Kuhlman and Edward Cody, were designated to be the college directors. Just a few days later, on August 30, 1910, Rockhurst College was legally founded and chartered by the state of Missouri to grant degrees. The college was incorporated under Article 11, Section 10264 to 10289 of the Missouri Revised Statutes.[11] But even now, with charter in hand, an actual college was years away.

— AMBITIOUS PLANS —

With construction starting on a college building, an optimistic Father Dowling placed another notice in *The Kansas City Star*. "ROCKHURST COLLEGE BY '11," the headline read that summer of 1910. "By the middle of September 1911, Rockhurst College, for purposes of general collegiate education, will be ready for the entering classes," the newspaper reported. At the top of an inside page, *The Star* ran an artist's rendering of what the new, 3-story administration building would look like when finished. Just below was a campus map illustrating Father Dowling's fondest hopes for the future college, which, he told *The Star*, eventually would "become a university." Dowling's ambitious plans called for schools of dentistry, medicine, science, and law. There the future buildings were, all lined up on a map of the campus with its quadrant at the center. The administration building would have a gymnasium at its center. There would be a library, auditorium, and chapel, and, at the southern end of the campus, would stand a new church with pastor's residence and infirmary.[12]

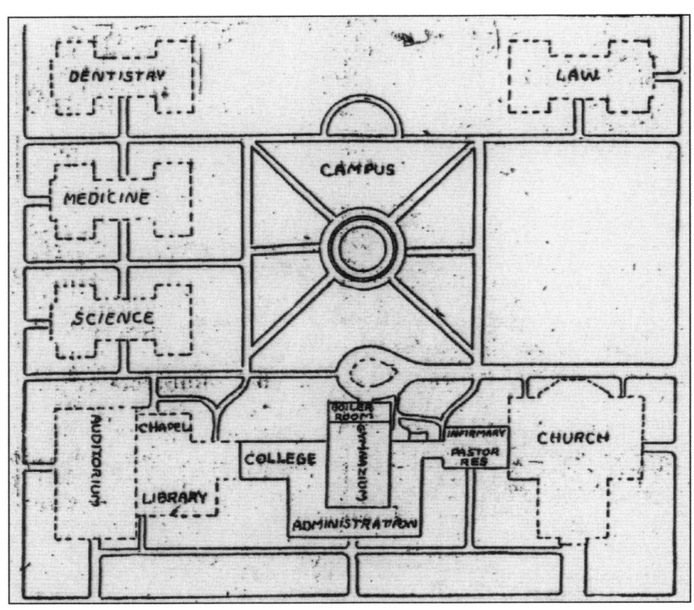

In 1910 an artist's rendering of the future campus appeared in The Kansas City Star. *It illustrated Father Dowling's ambitious plans for future schools of dentistry, medicine, science, and law. The administration building would have a gymnasium at its center. There would be a library, auditorium, and chapel, and, at the southern end of the campus, would stand a new church with pastor's residence and infirmary.*

Dowling's ambitions for Rockhurst were in keeping with the times. The first quarter of the twentieth century were years of great expansion in education. Historian Philip Gleason writes that, in 1900, only a handful of professional programs existed in Catholic institutions, but they "sprang up like mushrooms" over the next 25 years. The Jesuits, in fact, monopolized the field of health care. Father Dowling's beloved Creighton already had a medical school, and many other Jesuit colleges, including Saint Louis University, would add one before World War I. Law schools blossomed, as well as schools of commerce, finance, and business administration.[13]

As president of Creighton for nearly 10 years, Father Dowling, Gleason writes, had been one of the "most energetic promoters" of the blossoming university movement. He had worked tirelessly to open Creighton's departments of law, dentistry, and pharmacy, and to equip the existing medical department.[14] Dowling's enthusiasm was palpable in a letter he wrote to the Catholic Education Association in 1906. He told how Creighton's course of study had won such high approval from the public school system that students could earn "a first class teacher's certificate, without any examination." The certificate allowed Creighton graduates to teach "in any university, college or school in the state, and to have it made a life certificate, also without examination, after three years of teaching." A certificate wasn't needed to teach in a Catholic school, Dowling noted, but "it often adds prestige." It was the "exuberance" in Dowling's letter and the feeling of "cascading change" that was especially telling, Gleason writes, and "helps us recapture the vision of new possibilities that opened before the bolder Catholic educators in the first two decades of the twentieth century."[15]

Coming off such great success in Omaha, Father Dowling undoubtedly brought the same enthusiasm and futuristic outlook to Kansas City. "While the idea of the founders is to make the college a day school at first," he said of Rockhurst, "we hope in time to build dormitories for out-of-town students."

Progress did seem at hand. The parochial school was set to open that September of 1910, and the foundation for the college building had been laid. Dowling had hired a maintenance man to care for the church and schoolroom, barn and horses, and another to take care of the quarry and its apparatus. He hired a carpenter to build window frames and a contractor to cut stone, but as the winter of 1910-11 set in, he advised both to let up on their work, probably hoping to have more money to pay them come spring.[16]

Administratively, Dowling selected a Board of Trustees, composed of prominent men of the city who met twice a month at a downtown hotel. "A thorough canvass of the city," as Dowling phrased it, was under way to gauge the best sources of raising funds and to enlist pledges. The administration building alone was expected to cost $90,000.[17]

— "Promises Will Not Pay Bills" —

By the spring of 1911, the canvass of the city was complete, but the results were not good. An alarmed Dowling wrote to the provincial in St. Louis: "The result is neither encouraging nor satisfactory. It is true we have a number of promises, but not for large sums; and anyhow promises will not pay bills." Part of the problem lay in Kansas City's growth and progressive spirit. "Non-Catholic citizens, and even Catholics, complain that they have been taxed to the limit for various civic enterprises," Dowling said, leaving little surplus to help the Rockhurst cause.[18] Dowling specifically mentioned the Boys Hotel for homeless and troubled boys and the Girls Hotel, a "haven" to keep young women from "temptation." Both were founded in 1908 during the zealous Progressive Era and by 1911 were expanding into newly built quarters.[19] City residents also footed bills for Mercy Hospital, the new Y.M.C.A. and Y.W.C.A., and improvements to river navigation as Kansas City tried to encourage factories to locate in the city.

Besides these civic projects, Catholics were compelled to support their own parish schools and building projects. A new church for Kansas City's African-American residents was under con-

With many charitable enterprises asking for support from Kansas Citians, Fr. Dowling found fund-raising for the new college to be a formidable task. He wrote to the provincial about the various civic projects competing for local money, including the Boys Hotel for homeless and troubled boys. Founded in 1908, the Boys Hotel quickly outgrew its facilities and by 1911 was soliciting money from major Kansas City donors for a new building. The token shown in the picture was uncovered in 2009 from a time box encased in the cornerstone of a later Boys Hotel building constructed in 1921. Photo courtesy of Brad Finch.

struction, the Cathedral of the Immaculate Conception was being renovated at a cost of $25,000, and, in the Redemptorist parish, the new cathedral-like parish church at Broadway and Linwood Boulevard was costing so much to build, Dowling said, that the C.S.S.R. fathers themselves admitted it was a mistake.

"For these reasons we cannot rely upon getting any considerable donations, at least for the present," Dowling told the provincial.[20] As if all the difficulties of securing permission to build the college were not enough, Father Dowling now was confronted with a whole new set of problems—where was he going to get enough money to construct a college building and to pay off the hefty debts not only of St. Aloysius Parish, but also for the 25 acres he had purchased from the Carys?

Madonna, ca. 1490-1500. A very rare Netherlandish Madonna by the Master of Elsloo. This wooden Gothic piece is 53 inches high. Courtesy of Greenlease Gallery.

So dire was the financial picture in Kansas City that spring of 1911, and so tired of the situation was Father Dowling, that he pleaded in desperation for help from the Society of Jesus' provincial headquarters in St. Louis. "It is an awful worry to be kept in hot water every time you need money to meet the pressing demands of contractors," he wrote. "I cannot stand it any longer; and I must ask you to relieve the tension and say what assistance we may rely upon. We are at the end of our resources. Under these circumstances, the question is whether and how we are to continue building. There is no way of doing it except to have the Province finance the undertaking."[21] His thoughts were racing. "We cannot borrow money without giving security; and there is nothing to furnish it but College ground," he wrote. "It would be foolish to mortgage the property we want to sell; and it would be rash to mortgage the ground on which we are building, where there will be no money in sight to pay interest, till some lots have been sold or donations received, instead of promises."

He needed the Missouri Province to lend Rockhurst more money and, as he put it, to "carry us" until the school was able to pay back both the original and new loan. He had gone to St. Louis to press the matter in person with the procurator, who had agreed to take out a loan of $10,000 and give it to Rockhurst. Dowling spent that money on concrete and stonework for the college building and soon recognized that he would have to call on the procurator again, this time to ask for $35,000 more if work on the college was to progress.

"I cannot but see trouble again," he wrote that May of 1911. "The money must come from the Province and the Province must back the undertaking, if a college is wanted here. It would be a brain-racking and insanity-breeding proposition to make ourselves responsible for either principal or interest, without knowing where the means are to come from."

He outlined the options and his growing headaches over Rockhurst:

1. Continue with the work if the province would furnish about $6,000 a month—up to the borrowing limit of $35,000.

2. Discontinue the work altogether, though Rockhurst likely would be liable for $4,000 or $5,000 to contractors who already had put in concrete and stonework.
3. Let the contractors "putter along slowly and quietly, if they can be induced to do so, working merely enough to keep things moving, with a small force of men." That would cost about $4,000 a month through late fall, when work could be shut down for the winter.

Dowling's words must have impressed upon Meyer the dire situation because in just a matter of days, Meyer replied that it had become apparent "that we cannot prudently go on building as we have been doing, the province furnishing you $6,000 monthly."[22] Although he said the province wanted to do all it could for Rockhurst, Meyer told Dowling that he simply was expecting too much if he wanted the province to finance the building of Rockhurst College. "We have no mine from which we can extract gold or silver on short notice," he wrote. Sometimes the province had extra money not invested and "this we shall cheerfully loan to you, in preference to any one else," Meyer wrote. "But we cannot sell our stocks and bonds, sacrifice our interest on them or cripple our own resources for the sake of the particular college."

Meyer, too, was beginning to see that building a college in Kansas City was not going to come easily. "The very fact that you find it hard to get the help you expected in Kansas City, and the dullness of the Real Estate market there, warn us to be prudent, and not to 'bite off more than we can swallow.'"[23] Even though prospects looked bleak, Meyer did not blame Father Dowling and must have sensed the great discouragement in his words because he added: "… do not overtax your physical strength. The Province needs your services." More than "needing" Father Dowling's services, Meyer acted as if no one else could do the job. "I am overworked (too)," he told Dowling, "but if I break down, some one else will be found to succeed me."

He went on: "At any rate, you have more than redeemed your promises to the people of Kansas City. They cannot say that we do not mean business. It is time they should redeem their promises 'given or implied,' as we have redeemed ours. There is no particular reason, on our part, to rush the building of a college. Even when it will have been built, we shall find it difficult to man it, as we would like."[24] Meyer looked over the 3 options Dowling had listed and selected No. 3, explaining that puttering along would at least "look better to the public at large, I suppose; it would save appearances."

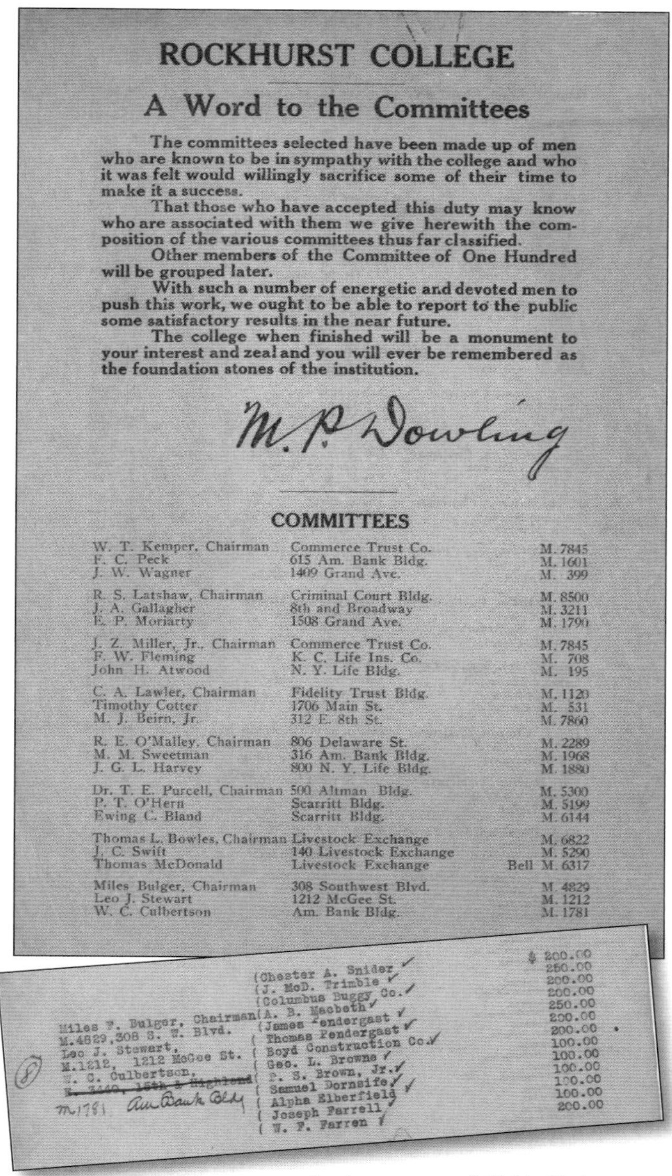

ROCKHURST COLLEGE

A Word to the Committees

The committees selected have been made up of men who are known to be in sympathy with the college and who it was felt would willingly sacrifice some of their time to make it a success.

That those who have accepted this duty may know who are associated with them we give herewith the composition of the various committees thus far classified.

Other members of the Committee of One Hundred will be grouped later.

With such a number of energetic and devoted men to push this work, we ought to be able to report to the public some satisfactory results in the near future.

The college when finished will be a monument to your interest and zeal and you will ever be remembered as the foundation stones of the institution.

M. P. Dowling

COMMITTEES

W. T. Kemper, Chairman	Commerce Trust Co.	M. 7845
F. C. Peck	615 Am. Bank Bldg.	M. 1601
J. W. Wagner	1409 Grand Ave.	M. 399
R. S. Latshaw, Chairman	Criminal Court Bldg.	M. 8500
J. A. Gallagher	8th and Broadway	M. 3211
E. P. Moriarty	1508 Grand Ave.	M. 1790
J. Z. Miller, Jr., Chairman	Commerce Trust Co.	M. 7845
F. W. Fleming	K. C. Life Ins. Co.	M. 708
John H. Atwood	N. Y. Life Bldg.	M. 195
C. A. Lawler, Chairman	Fidelity Trust Bldg.	M. 1120
Timothy Cotter	1706 Main St.	M. 531
M. J. Beirn, Jr.	312 E. 8th St.	M. 7860
R. E. O'Malley, Chairman	806 Delaware St.	M. 2289
M. M. Sweetman	316 Am. Bank Bldg.	M. 1968
J. G. L. Harvey	800 N. Y. Life Bldg.	M. 1880
Dr. T. E. Purcell, Chairman	500 Altman Bldg.	M. 5300
P. T. O'Hern	Scarritt Bldg.	M. 5199
Ewing C. Bland	Scarritt Bldg.	M. 6144
Thomas L. Bowles, Chairman	Livestock Exchange	M. 6822
J. C. Swift	140 Livestock Exchange	M. 5290
Thomas McDonald	Livestock Exchange	Bell M. 6317
Miles Bulger, Chairman	308 Southwest Blvd.	M. 4829
Leo J. Stewart	1212 McGee St.	M. 1212
W. C. Culbertson	Am. Bank Bldg.	M. 1781

(8)

Miles F. Bulger, Chairman
M.4829, 308 S. W. Blvd.
Leo J. Stewart,
M.1212, 1212 McGee St.
W. C. Culbertson,
~~M. 3440, 15th & Highland~~
m1781 Am Bank Bldg

(Chester A. Snider
(J. McD. Trimble
(Columbus Buggy Co.
(A. B. Macbeth
(James Pendergast
(Thomas Pendergast
(Boyd Construction Co.
(Geo. L. Browne
(P. S. Brown, Jr.
(Samuel Dornsife
(Alpha Elberfield
(Joseph Farrell
(W. F. Farren

$ 200.00
250.00
200.00
200.00
250.00
200.00
200.00
100.00
100.00
100.00
100.00
100.00
200.00

In the summer of 1911, Father Dowling initiated a fund-raising campaign called The Committee of 100. The group was an impressive list of influential businessmen, including, among others, banker William T. Kemper, lumberman R.A. Long, brewing magnate George E. Muehlebach, and meatpacker Charles W. Armour. Each committee member was given a list of about a dozen names with an amount of money to be solicited. For example, the subcommittee headed by Miles F. Bulger was asked to contact the Pendergast brothers, James and Thomas, and secure a pledge of $250 from James and $200 from Thomas. Courtesy of Rockhurst University Archives.

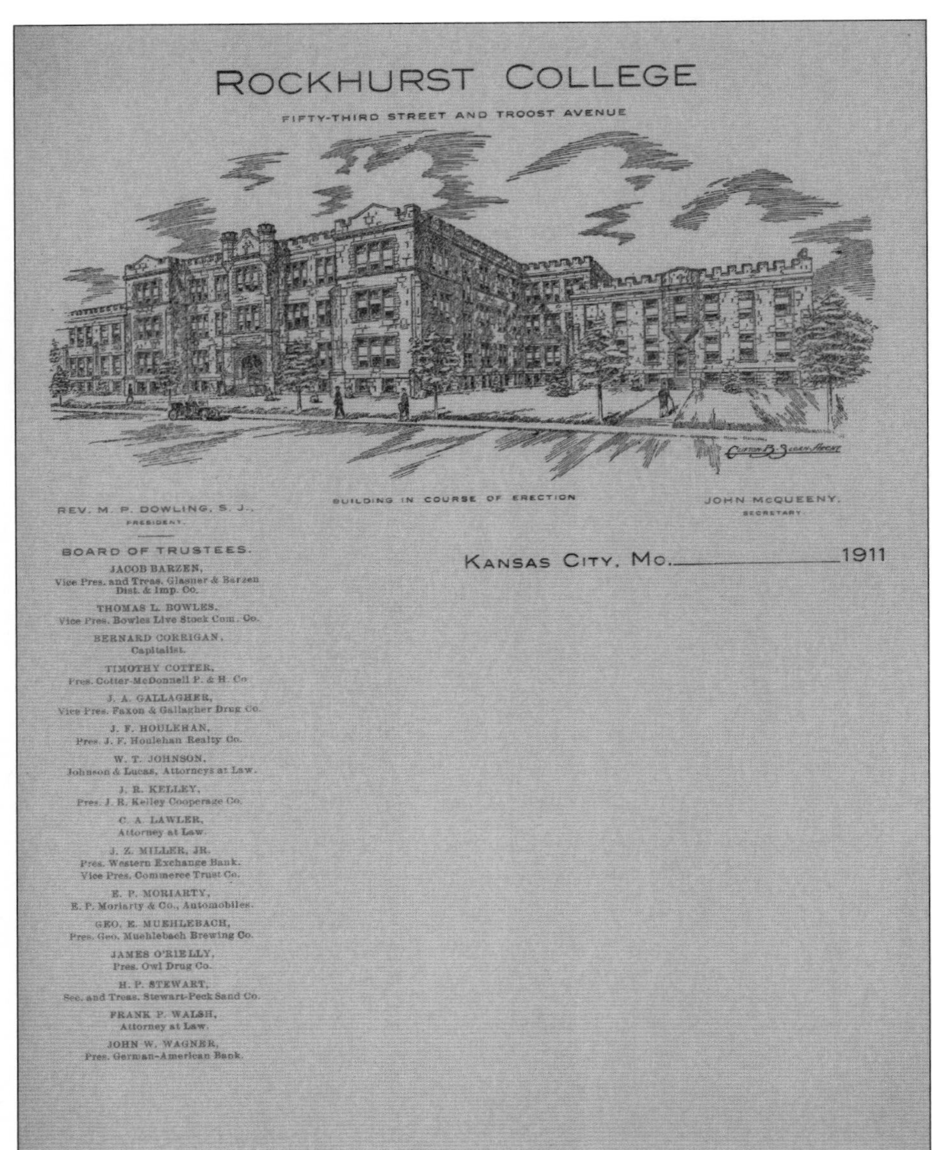
ROCKHURST COLLEGE

FIFTY-THIRD STREET AND TROOST AVENUE

BUILDING IN COURSE OF ERECTION

REV. M. P. DOWLING, S. J.,
PRESIDENT.

JOHN McQUEENY,
SECRETARY.

KANSAS CITY, MO.______________1911

The members of The Committee of 100 used this letterhead to solicit funds for the college. Form letters were drafted, such as this one addressed to the president of the National Biscuit Company in New York City.

"Dear Sir,

"Rockhurst College, an institution for the education of young men without regard to their religious affiliations, is now in the course of construction, but for its completion it needs the active support of the citizens of Kansas City irrespective of creed.

"The Board of Trustees whose names are found on this letter head recognizing your influence and past efficient services in behalf of our civic enterprises desire to enlist your help for this worthy object.

"We feel that you cannot afford to stand aloof from an undertaking that means so much to Kansas City and which will attract many to live here for the advantages to be derived from the existence of such an institution.

"You do not need to be told what this college will mean to the youth of Kansas City who have no opportunity for a higher education unless it be furnished at home; and what an important want it will fill in our midst."

Courtesy of Rockhurst University Archives.

— THE COMMITTEE OF 100 —

While the workmen puttered, Dowling initiated a fund-raising campaign for the summer of 1911. Again he turned to Kansas City's influential businessmen, hoping to enlist their help to get the college off the ground. He formed what he called The Committee of 100—an impressive list of men that now included not only banker William T. Kemper, but also lumberman R.A. Long, and meatpacker Charles W. Armour. Representatives were listed from the Cudahy Packing House, the Loose-Wiles Biscuit Co., Peck's Dry Goods Co., the Abernathy Furniture Co., and the Jenkins Music Co. Brewing magnate George E. Muehlebach, livestock man Thomas L. Bowles, and lawyer Frank P. Walsh were among The Committee of 100 who "willingly sacrifice some of their time to make the college a success."[25] John McQueeny was named Rockhurst College secretary and placed in charge of the fund-raising campaign. He set up his office in the Lillis Building downtown, Room 504, and gave each of the subcommittees a list of about a dozen names, charging committee members to contact all the names on the list and solicit funds.

The subcommittee headed by Miles F. Bulger, for example, was asked to contact the Pendergast brothers, James and Thomas, and secure a pledge of $250 from James and $200 from Thomas. William Kemper's subcommittee would contact E.F. Swinney, president of the First National Bank, and request $500. The Cudahy Packing Co. was asked to pledge $1,000, the Ash Grove Lime & Cement Co. $500, and the Baltimore Hotel, where the Board of Trustees held its meetings, $250. The least amount—$50—would be sought from the Liebstader Millinery Co.[26]

Dowling set up an installment plan for those least able to pay, offering to accept $10 at a time until the pledge was met. If all the pledges came in, they would top $75,000. Form letters were drafted for the committees to send to Kansas City residents and landholders living elsewhere. When Dr. Owen Krueger, a surgeon, was asked to be chairman of one of the subcommittees, he responded with zeal: "Dear Sir," Krueger wrote to McQueeny: "Your letter received and it will give me great pleasure to be present at the meeting tomorrow evening at eight o'clock, provided business does not interfere. You may be sure I am interested in this institution and wish it Godspeed. I will be glad to do anything I can at anytime to further its interests."[27] His enthusiasm soon waned, however, after he called his subcommittee to a meeting and no one attended, though he waited for 2 hours. "I wish you would rearrange this committee," he wrote now to McQueeny, "make someone else chairman and I will work in conjunction and do all I can, but prefer not to be chairman."[28]

Although several prominent businessmen declined to contribute for various reasons, including their commitments to other worthy causes in the region, some did make a subscription. If a committee member agreed to help but then slacked off, Father Dowling and Secretary McQueeny kept after him, as evidenced by this form letter:

"Dear Mr. ______: We would regret to find it necessary to place some one in your place on the Rockhurst College Soliciting Committee....

"It is quite essential to the success of this movement that those who are in sympathy with it give it their active support. You are regarded as one of the friends of the institution and we trust that you will see fit to give a little of your time to its establishment.

"The work assigned to your committee is not great and no doubt can be completed in one day.

"Please think it over again Mr. ______ and let us hear that you have concluded to accept this task and give this great enterprise the benefit of your efforts....

"I hope to be advised within the next few days that you have met with your committee and that arrangements have been made to begin at once the work assigned to you."[29]

When someone failed to submit their pledge on time, the college wrote:

"Dear Mr. ______: A remittance for $______, the payment upon your subscription to Rockhurst College would be gratefully received.

"Hope you will find it convenient to mail same within a short time."

When Judge R.S. Latshaw gave an "eloquent and impressive discourse on the subject of Rockhurst college," McQueeny didn't miss a beat. He fired off a letter to the judge, suggesting that "it would be very beneficial if your words could be placed before the people in some manner." His words, McQueeny wrote, "would have a great effect towards enlightening the people and awakening them to the importance of establishing this school in this city." As always, there was work involved. Could you please, McQueeny wrote, "reduce your words to writing and furnish (us) with a copy."[30]

McQueeny was not shy about asking for help. One day he called on committee leader H.P. Stewart to add beer barons M.G. Heim and George Muehlebach to his committee list: "Each of these gentlemen has contributed $500.00," he wrote, "but it is hoped they may be prevailed upon to increase their subscriptions to $1000.00."[31] Rockhurst looked to wealthy women, as well, including the widow of George Dugan:

"Dear Mrs. Dugan: I regret very much that I was unable to see you twice that I called recently in the interest of Rockhurst College.

"Knowing your good will for the cause, I have based great hopes on your help.

"The well-known liberality of your husband, which would no doubt have secured us a substantial donation had he lived, may be an additional reason for your greater personal interest. We already have a number of ladies of position and influence in this community who have guaranteed their support and this gives us reason to believe that we can rely upon yours also.

"Will you authorize us to put down your name for a subscription of $250.00 to be paid at your convenience?"

A similar letter went out to the widow of James B. McGowan, noting that her husband had "promised a contribution which his early demise prevented him from giving." Would she kindly authorize Rockhurst to put down her name for a subscription of $200? A little friendly persuasion could go a long way:

"Dear Mrs. Foran," another letter began. *"The Bishop and your brother Jere have each contributed $200.00 and Miss Bessie $100.00. It would not do for you and Mr. Foran to be left out of the list of contributors for as good a cause and I therefore, ask you to subscribe such an amount as you consider proper...."*[32]

— THE "JESUITS' FOLLY" —

Progress on the first college building was visible enough that on August 3, 1911, Father Dowling invited members of the Board of Trustees and The Committee of 100 to attend a summer outing, where light refreshments would be served on the college grounds "to see how far the building has progressed and to learn more fully the scope of the college."[33] He instructed the men to meet at the Kupper Hotel, on the corner of 11th and McGee streets, and arranged for automobiles to carry them to the college site. After the men arrived and Father Dowling gave what Rockhurst historian Patrick Harvey described as an "eloquent speech on the benefits of the educational institutions to the town and to the individual," the committee "redoubled its efforts at raising money." How sobering it must have been when the total contributions garnered by the campaign amounted not to the hoped for $75,000, but only $15,000.[34]

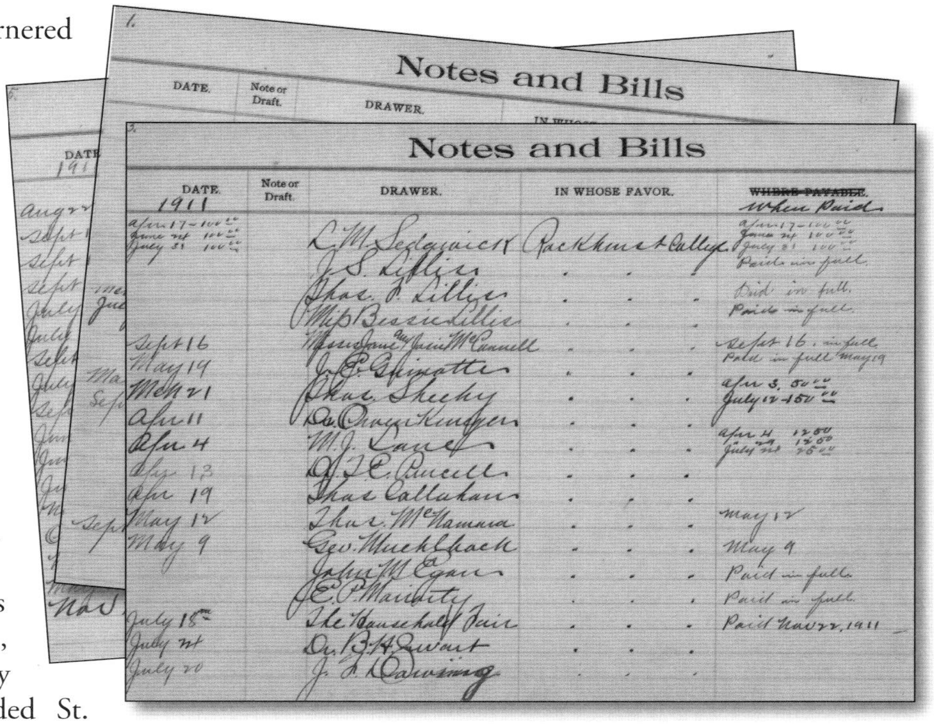

As Dowling and Secretary McQueeny counted contributions, they would have noticed that Board of Trustees Chairman J.Z. Miller, Jr. had done his part—sending along $100 in April and another $250 in November. H.T. Abernathy had sent $200 on behalf of the First National Bank, and Hugh J. McGowan of Indianapolis had promised $500.[35]

Among other subscriptions was one dated June 24, 1911, from L.M. Sedgwick, the wealthy railroad man who had attended St. Mary's College as a boy. "Dear Sir," Sedgwick wrote: "Enclosed please find check for One Hundred Dollars as a subscription toward the building of an adequate University in KCMO, both grounds and bldgs." He added: "Don't build small" and emphasized his words by underlining them. *Don't build small?* We'll be lucky, Father Dowling must have thought, if we can finish building at all.

This 1911 ledger records progress on fund-raising. The name of Lee Sedgwick, soon to be Rockhurst's first major benefactor, appears at the top with 3 donations of $100 each from April to July 1911. In his June contribution, Sedgwick included a note of encouragement saying, "Don't build small." But the campaign produced only $15,000 of the needed $75,000. By September 1911, work on the college building stopped altogether, with only the unroofed, first story completed. Courtesy of Rockhurst University Archives.

It was just a few months later, in fact, in September 1911, that work on the college building stopped altogether, with only the unroofed, first story completed.[36] Nonetheless, Father Dowling put on a confident face for a newspaperman who interviewed him on September 20, 1911. "We have passed the doubtful stage if there ever were any," he told the reporter, "and we shall be ready for students Sept. 20, 1912."[37] But Dowling's prediction would not come true. A year passed, September 1912 came and went, and still Rockhurst had no students and the college building stood unfinished—just one, unroofed story high—still a work in progress along the east side of Troost. And still, no carline ran up the Troost Avenue hill to the college site. Recognizing that easy accessibility was a key ingredient if the college were to succeed, Dowling had gone back to *The Kansas City Star* in January 1912 and pleaded through the pages of the newspaper for the city to build a bridge across Brush Creek at Troost Avenue and to pave Troost at least to 53rd Street.[38]

When nothing came of his plea, Dowling sounded more and more forceful as he spoke again to the press, this time to the *Kansas City Times*. In an article published on February 16, 1912, he pleaded with the people of Kansas City to come to the aid of the college. "Work on the building is going forward as fast as available funds will permit, but the funds we have on hand are not sufficient," he said. He told the public that "it was understood from the beginning that we would not be able to complete it without

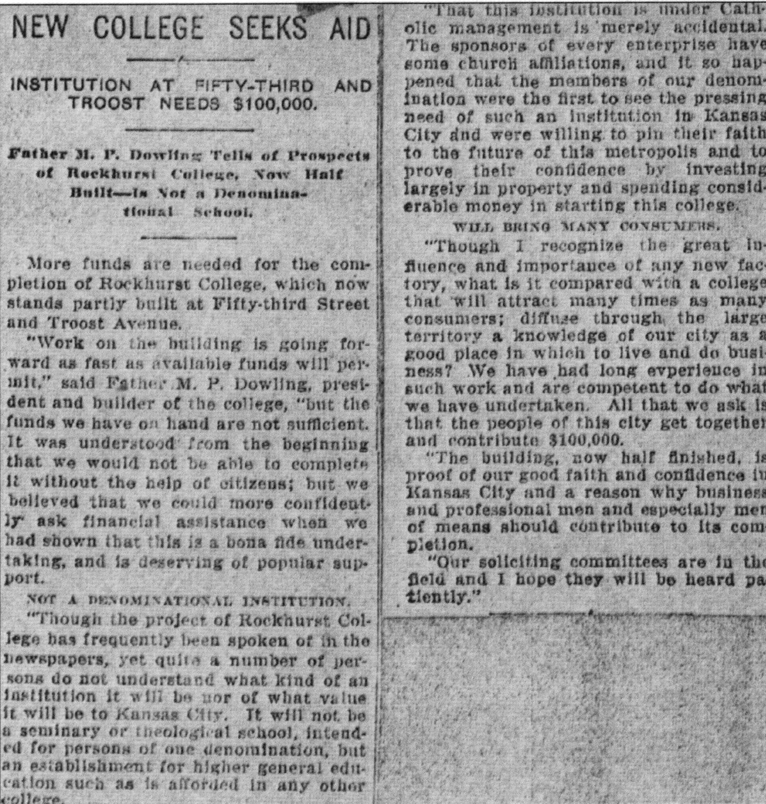

NEW COLLEGE SEEKS AID

INSTITUTION AT FIFTY-THIRD AND TROOST NEEDS $100,000.

Father M. P. Dowling Tells of Prospects of Rockhurst College, Now Half Built—Is Not a Denominational School.

More funds are needed for the completion of Rockhurst College, which now stands partly built at Fifty-third Street and Troost Avenue.

"Work on the building is going forward as fast as available funds will permit," said Father M. P. Dowling, president and builder of the college, "but the funds we have on hand are not sufficient. It was understood from the beginning that we would not be able to complete it without the help of citizens; but we believed that we could more confidently ask financial assistance when we had shown that this is a bona fide undertaking, and is deserving of popular support.

NOT A DENOMINATIONAL INSTITUTION.

"Though the project of Rockhurst College has frequently been spoken of in the newspapers, yet quite a number of persons do not understand what kind of an institution it will be nor of what value it will be to Kansas City. It will not be a seminary or theological school, intended for persons of one denomination, but an establishment for higher general education such as is afforded in any other college.

"That this institution is under Catholic management is merely accidental. The sponsors of every enterprise have some church affiliations, and it so happened that the members of our denomination were the first to see the pressing need of such an institution in Kansas City and were willing to pin their faith to the future of this metropolis and to prove their confidence by investing largely in property and spending considerable money in starting this college.

WILL BRING MANY CONSUMERS.

"Though I recognize the great influence and importance of any new factory, what is it compared with a college that will attract many times as many consumers; diffuse through the large territory a knowledge of our city as a good place in which to live and do business? We have had long evperience in such work and are competent to do what we have undertaken. All that we ask is that the people of this city get together and contribute $100,000.

"The building, now half finished, is proof of our good faith and confidence in Kansas City and a reason why business and professional men and especially men of means should contribute to its completion.

"Our soliciting committees are in the field and I hope they will be heard patiently."

In this February 16, 1912 article in the Kansas City Times, *Father Dowling pleaded for the people of Kansas City to come to the aid of the college. "Work on the building is going forward as fast as available funds will permit, but the funds we have on hand are not sufficient. All that we ask," he said, "is that the people of this city get together and contribute $100,000." He hoped that people would hear Rockhurst's "soliciting committees" patiently, especially business and professional men "of means."*

the help of citizens; but we believed that we could more confidently ask financial assistance when we had shown that this is a bona fide undertaking, and is deserving of popular support."

That Kansas City was not a Catholic town was turning out to be a sticking point. It seemed that many Kansas Citians balked at supporting Rockhurst because they were under the impression that it was to be a seminary or theological school for Catholics. Not so, Dowling reiterated in the *Times* that February. It would be "an establishment," he had explained over and over again, "for higher general education such as is afforded in any other college." That the college was under "Catholic management," he said, "is merely accidental. The sponsors of every enterprise have some church affiliations, and it so happened that the members of our denomination were the first to see the pressing need of such an institution in Kansas City and were willing to pin their faith to the future of this metropolis and to prove their confidence by investing largely in property and spending considerable money in starting this college."

Dowling went on trying to persuade: "Though I recognize the great influence and importance of any new factory, what is it compared with a college that will attract many times as many consumers; diffuse through the large territory a knowledge of our city as a good place in which to live and do business? We have had long experience in such work and are competent to do what we have undertaken. All that we ask is that the people of this city get together and contribute $100,000."

Although privately he told the provincial that the half-finished and unroofed building on Troost "acted as a deterrent" to any prospective sales of Rockhurst's extra lots, he told a different story to the newspapermen, pointing to the half-finished building as proof "of our good faith and confidence in Kansas City." He drove home the point that Rockhurst College was intended especially to serve students who could not afford to attend college in a city away from home. Rockhurst's "soliciting committees" were still in the field, he said, and he hoped that people would hear them "patiently," especially business and professional men "of means."[39]

All the while, Father Michael Ryan, who was more used to the quiet academic life at St. Mary's College than the noisy world of rock quarries and cement, was stationed at the half-finished building on Troost, where he lived alone in the old farmhouse, doing his own housework—a situation that said much about the poverty of the new parish.[40] A newsman from *The Kansas City Star* found him there one afternoon in March 1913, a ruler and pencil in his hands, a map spread out before him. "The life of a university is long," he told the reporter when quizzed about the building delay. The work had progressed slowly, the reporter wrote, as workmen had cut huge stone blocks from the quarry on the property, crushed rock, and built the walls "stone upon stone" until the first floor was complete. Yes, the building stood unfinished, Ryan told the reporter, but as soon as enough funds came in, other stories and a roof would be added.[41]

Like Dowling, Father Ryan put on a confident face. Once opened, Rockhurst College would grow, he said. The first class would be freshmen of high school rank, but year by year, as that class advanced and new classes entered, the school would advance until it grew into a real college with its first preparatory class, and then would add post-graduate and professional schools — medicine, dentistry, law, and science. The boys would play football and baseball, too.

"The boys of the football squad. Honestly, can't you see them in this room?" he said with a twinkle in his eye to the reporter. "No? Then look closely at this map and perhaps you can picture them in a like room a few years from now." Ryan was making plans in his head for a future football field and a free-standing gymnasium, not the simple room for a gym that the architect had included in his drawings for the main college building. *The Star* ran a photograph of Father Ryan standing in his robes before the unroofed college building. "Father M.J. Ryan, workman-priest," the caption read, "who is building Rockhurst College, a great university of tomorrow."[42]

Another year would pass before news of Rockhurst College would again make the pages of *The Star*. The "great university of tomorrow" was slow to progress, with work resuming on the main building only in spurts, then stopping again. In the meantime, Missouri Provincial Rudolph Meyer, S.J., died on December 1, 1912, and the new provincial, A.J. Burrowes, demanded a financial report on the college. Once again, Father Dowling had to plead not to abandon the project and lose all of the effort expended so far.

In September of 1913, with the college building still not finished, Father Ryan was transferred to Cincinnati and Father W.F. Hoffend, S.J., came from Detroit to oversee construction and the little parish at Rockhurst. He struggled with workmen who quit soon after beginning and complained of being lonely. "Nothing worth recording has happened these last few months," he wrote in January 1914. "Loneliness and lack of the ordinary comforts of life are the usual characteristics of this place."[43]

This Blickensderfer typewriter, vintage 1900-1915, was probably used by Father Dowling. It was recovered from St. Aloysius residence when the Jesuits vacated it in 1942. Photo by David Spaw. Courtesy of Rockhurst University Archives.

And so another dark winter passed. So utterly hopeless did prospects for the college seem that Rockhurst historian Hugh Owens described the skeleton of the college building as it stood that winter along Troost Avenue as "the 'Jesuits' folly' of the southern skyline." Privately, Father Dowling said it looked "like a ruin" to passersby.[44] "How much would it cost to finish the building?" the new provincial asked Dowling. The answer was sobering—$59,500 ($25,000 would put it under roof, but it still would not be livable). That $59,500 did not include the present debt for the land and construction so far—$64,238. Of the total, $43,988 was owed to the Missouri Province; $10,500 to Creighton University; $3,000 to M. Dulse; $6,000 to the Sisters of Poor Clares; and $750 to Father Kieffer.[45]

Things just hadn't worked out as planned. The extra land that Dowling hoped to sell was not selling. The lots, conservatively, should fetch $50,000, he told Provincial Burrows, "but there is no market for real estate just now." Pending an economic boom, "there is little prospect of additional donations," he said. "We have received all the money there is in sight from prospective givers." What was in sight was only more expenses—$7,000 for sewers, construction on The Paseo, and taxes.

It was a bleak report indeed that Dowling sent to the new provincial. "This is the poorest place I have ever been for rousing enthusiasm for Higher Catholic Education," Dowling wrote to Burrowes in the dark winter of 1913–14.[46] As if things could not possibly get worse, Dowling's health deteriorated along with his efforts on behalf of Rockhurst. That past August of 1913, he had undergone surgery for what he described as tubercular ulceration of the peritoneum, a transparent membrane lining the abdominal cavity. Simply, Father Dowling had cancer. "The Doctors cut me open, but they found conditions inside so hopeless, that they could not do anything without fatal results," he told the provincial. "So they sewed me up again, without doing anything; and left me to my fate. They said I would continue to suffer intensely, but it would not be of long duration; a few days would finish me."

But a few days did not finish him. Friends offered prayers, his suffering ceased, and Father Dowling got back to work, although he told the provincial it was doubtful he would be able "to do the strenuous work needful for Rockhurst; but as long as I last, I will give all the help I can to any one else on whom Father Provincial may impose the burden."[47]

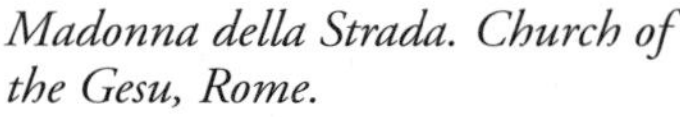

Madonna della Strada. Church of the Gesu, Rome.

— A SECRET DONOR —

If Father Dowling's fragile health played a role in what happened next, there can be no way to know, but sometime during those months of struggle in late 1913 and early 1914, the wealthy railroad man Lee M. Sedgwick took a personal interest in Rockhurst that renewed Dowling's hopes that the college could succeed.

Although he was a middle-aged man now, Lee Sedgwick had never forgotten his boyhood years at St. Mary's College. In fact, he had returned just recently to attend a popular series of Jesuit retreats offered there for laymen, be they lawyers, doctors, businessmen, merchants, or retired farmers. The college was a perfect setting for retreats, situated as it was in a charming spot overlooking the Kaw River Valley and with its Loyola Hall able to accommodate 100 men. Retreats began in the summer of 1909 and would continue for several years. A photograph

Layman's retreat, St. Mary's College, 1909. Wealthy railroad man Lee M. Sedgwick was baptized into the Catholic Church at St. Mary's College on August 14, 1908. In 1909 St. Mary's began offering retreats for laymen, a practice that continued for several years. This photograph of attendees taken that first year shows a tall, bearded Lee Sedgwick (circled). Courtesy of Midwest Jesuit Archives.

of attendees, taken that first year of 1909, shows a tall, bearded Lee Sedgwick, standing amidst the attendees.

Lee Sedgwick, in many ways, was a peculiar man who kept mostly to himself. One of Rockhurst's early Jesuits, Father Joseph Matoushek, S.J., went so far as to call Sedgwick a "hermit" who refused to sit in a comfortable chair because he practiced mortification. The Rev. Daniel Conway, S.J., who would say Mass at Sedgwick's funeral in 1935, described Sedgwick as a "very pious man who made a half hour mental prayer every morning." Even in his coffin, Conway said, Sedgwick "looked the part of a noble-minded-ascetical man."[48] Early Rockhurst President Aloysius Breen told how Sedgwick kept a large collection of books on the Roman Catholic Church, but for years did not join the church, turning for instruction instead from a pastor at Kansas City's Cathedral of the Immaculate Conception.

That he was an opinionated, moralistic man is suggested by his disdain for England, even though "he was thoroughly English in his make-up." According to Breen, Sedgwick "had no use for England because he thought she was exploiting this country for her own selfish ends." Whether he meant in America's colonial days or in the present, Breen did not say. But so angry at England was Sedgwick that "he was dead set against our going to England's aid in the First World War and didn't hesitate to say so in strong terms even after the United States had gone into the conflict."[49]

His moralism came through, as well, in his reasons for not joining the church. "Often I made up my mind to become a Catholic," he told Breen, "but was kept back by the scandalous lives of some Catholic business men with whom I had come in contact. Then, too, I was shocked at some of the means which certain parishes made use of to get money. This latter objection may seem foolish, but even now I hate to see in the back of the church an ugly sign, SEATS 10¢."

He seemed an exacting man, extremely successful in business. Though a near millionaire who had taken many trips around the world, Lee Sedgwick, according to Breen, never spoke of business matters and insisted on secrecy to the point that even his banker did not know much about his business connections.[50]

In what turned out to be an uncanny coming together of events, Lee Sedgwick was baptized into the Catholic Church at St. Mary's on August 14, 1908, just months after Michael Dowling arrived in Kansas City with the express intent of founding a Catholic college.[51] Lee Sedgwick apparently had been watching from afar during all the bleak months that Rockhurst struggled to complete its first college building. On occasion, he had sent a few hundred dollars to Dowling, including the $100 he contributed during the campaign of 1911, when he had seemed so enthused about the college project that he had told the Jesuits "to build big."

Another $100 contribution came from Sedgwick on July 31, 1911, this time with an admonition: "I do not wish to be a member of any committee without first having my assent," he scribbled in the margin of a letter he had received from Rockhurst Secretary John McQueeny, inviting him to Father Dowling's campus picnic in the summer of 1911. McQueeny mistakenly had sent to Sedgwick a form letter intended only for members of The Committee of 100, of which Sedgwick was not a member. McQueeny quickly wrote back, apologizing for the error and explaining that "Father Dowling desired to have a few of the good friends of the institution attend the outing.... and knowing your interest in the college, requested me to extend an invitation to you." He included a list of members of The Committee of 100 and told Sedgwick: "you will observe that the list does not include your name."[52]

All apparently was forgiven because another $50 soon came from Sedgwick, who took to enclosing notes to Dowling, who dutifully answered them. "I cannot tell you what a source of encouragement your several brief but effective notes have been to me," Dowling wrote back to Sedgwick on December 2, 1911. "Your last contribution of $50.00 should have been acknowledged before this, only that I wanted to write the acknowledgement myself instead of having it done. Shall I not have the pleasure of meeting you some time and learning to know a friend whose acts I value so highly?" The two were introduced, probably in 1912, by their mutual friend, Father Aloysius Breen of St. Mary's College.[53]

ST. MARY'S COLLEGE
ST. MARYS, KANSAS

Transscript of Register of B aptism of Mr. Lee
Massachusetts John Sedgwick at St. Mary's College
St. MarysKansas.-- Ag. 14, 1908.

"Hodie solemniter baptizavi sub conditione Lee Massachusetts
Joannem Sedgwick, ex secta Presbyterianorum conversum. Natus
est die 9a Aprilis 1860 in oppido Indiana, Indiana Co., Pennsylvania, ex Georgio W. Sedgwick et Margarita Phoebe Bell, ejus
uxore. Has nostras scholas frequentavit per duos annos 1876
et 1877.- Sponsor fuit Ioannes Shyne ex oppido nostro.
Die 14a Aug. 1908.
Georgius H. Worpenberg, S.J."

Transcript of Register of Baptism of Lee Sedgwick, August 14, 1908, St. Mary's College. Though Sedgwick had been reared in a Presbyterian family, he had attended St. Mary's for 2 years, read from his large collection of books on the Roman Catholic Church, and also received instruction from a pastor at Kansas City's Cathedral of the Immaculate Conception. Dowling and Sedgwick were probably introduced in 1912 by their mutual friend, Father Aloysius Breen of St. Mary's College, who was an important influence in Sedgwick's life, and who later became Rockhurst's second president at Dowling's death in 1915. Courtesy of Rockhurst University Archives.

When the eccentric Sedgwick met with Father Dowling, he did not arrive with a simple handshake; he came, instead, with a plan of his own for the future college. He told Dowling he would set up a trust fund of $10,000 for Rockhurst, invest the money in the "best securities that can be found," and use the interest paid every 6 months to enable the college to finance a course of lectures to be delivered in Kansas City "upon Christian philosophy, and subjects germane thereto." He wanted the lectures to be published in pamphlet or book form and distributed to anyone who came to hear them. The subjects of the lectures, to be delivered "from time to time by the Faculty of said Rockhurst College," would be left up to faculty members.[54] Sedgwick was so serious about his proposal for a lecture series that he had drawn up a formal document, needing only a few signatures, to institute it.

"My Dear Sir," he had written to Dowling on February 16, 1913. "Will you kindly give your full and mature deliberation to the following outline of a plan which has obsessed me for some time and then give me your honest and candid opinion of its practicability and if it meets your approval, the manner in which in your judgement it should be handled."

The Prayer of a Soldier of Christ by St. Ignatius of Loyola.

He wanted Dowling to appoint a "Chair of Christian Philosophy," or, if Dowling preferred, a "Chair of Moral Sciences" who would oversee the course of lectures, which he insisted be delivered "by a good orator" who was "pleasing yet forcible." The subjects should be "generally along the line that Religion is teaching what God has revealed," and what He has revealed, Sedgwick believed, was that "Truth" was "a moral Science," as rigid in its enforcement as "physical Science."

His instructions for the lecture series went on for 7 pages, in which the man who would become Rockhurst's secret benefactor revealed much about himself. His motive for the lectures, it seemed, was to reach non-Catholics, as he himself once was, with the moral teachings of Christ. He seemed to think that "the conduct of too many of the Catholic people" hindered this. "We are not needing more revelations from God to give us an adequate conception of Christ's teaching but we are badly needing Men, men with brains and hearts too big to use the 3rd Commandment of God as a means of getting money under pain of mortal sin and Hell fire." He wanted God's truth to be presented to non-Catholics "as it is, and not as many Catholic people purport it to be by their actions."[55]

If Father Dowling would agree to his plan, Sedgwick would continue to help the college financially. His only stipulation was that his name remain anonymous. "I hope you catch the thought I have in mind and that you can carry it out and allow me to participate that much in your labors & in your eternal reward and yet I wish to remain entirely unknown—you can handle it without my being known. Respectfully, L.M. Sedgwick."[56]

The realistic Dowling—struggling as he was simply to finish a *building* for the college—must have read that letter and shaken his head. "It seems a great deal like building from the top down, seeing that we have as yet no college and no place to house one," he wrote to Provincial Burrowes. But the man, Lee Sedgwick, was another matter. "He is a well meaning man," Dowling wrote, "who even last week gave me another hundred dollars for the building. I deem it advisable to humor him in this idea, which he has much at heart; and I have no doubt it will result very favorably in other directions, when he has provided for his pet plan."[57]

Dowling found Sedgwick, "something of a crank," but "quite amenable to direction and advice, provided you do not try to force him into something." They were talking money—$5,000, $10,000, or even more. Sedgwick "suggested that we could use the principal for building, till such time as we would be in a condition to start the lecture course." Dowling was upfront, telling Sedgwick he could not "devote any sum for a specific purpose...even temporarily" and that the spending of any money Sedgwick gave, as well as the subjects and methods of a lecture course, would have to be left to the college authorities to decide. Sedgwick "readily agreed" with that, and Dowling and the provincial, perhaps to humor Sedgwick but also thinking that the lecture series he envisioned could be shaped into "practically whatever we want," decided to accept his money and set up a foundation. They could, for instance, have public lectures on topics of current interest such as race, suicide, eugenics, socialism, and comparative religion.[58]

Michael Dowling and Lee Sedgwick must have had further meetings that spring and summer of 1913, and it probably was Dowling's gentle but persistent persuasion that convinced Sedgwick that his money could be put to better use than funding a lecture course at a college that did not, for all practical purposes, exist. John Creighton's name undoubtedly came up as Dowling explained to Sedgwick how his old friend in Omaha had been the lifeblood behind the establishment of Creighton University. John Creighton, Dowling explained, had given the Jesuits a deed to his property outright, and the Jesuits had given Creighton a contract authorizing him to administer the property, pay all expenses, and use all the revenues during his lifetime. That way, Mr. Creighton had had plenty of his money to live on, but when he died his property already was in the Jesuits' hands with no inheritance tax to pay.[59]

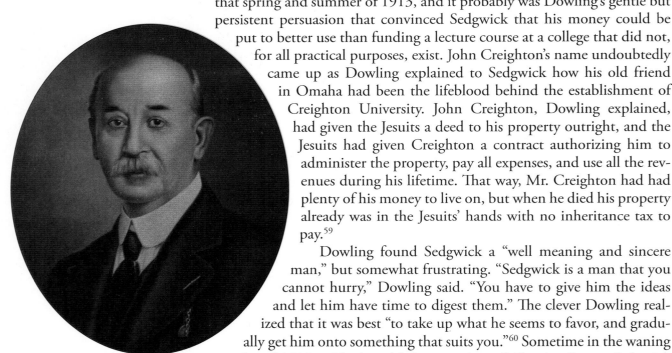

Lee M. Sedgwick, Rockhurst's first major benefactor. Sedgwick's pledge to contribute $500 a month for 5 years—or $30,000, was the boost that Rockhurst needed to put the building under roof and prepare to receive students in September 1914. Sedgwick's contributions, according to his own wishes, would remain a secret for many years to come. He died in 1935, and in 1942 Rockhurst named its original building in his honor, Sedgwick Hall. Courtesy of Rockhurst University Archives.

Dowling found Sedgwick a "well meaning and sincere man," but somewhat frustrating. "Sedgwick is a man that you cannot hurry," Dowling said. "You have to give him the ideas and let him have time to digest them." The clever Dowling realized that it was best "to take up what he seems to favor, and gradually get him onto something that suits you."[60] Sometime in the waning weeks of 1913, with the added persuasion of Aloysius Breen, Sedgwick had a change of heart about his pet lecture course project. No moment would be more important for the future of Rockhurst College.

"Mr. Sedgwick has given up the idea of establishing a lecture course... and he has now come to the determination to do what I wanted him to do from the beginning, and that is provide for advancing the building project," Dowling wrote to the provincial on December 16, 1913. Sedgwick had agreed to contribute $500 a month for 5 years—or $30,000, "provided we get to work now and finish that building." Dowling did not mince words with Sedgwick. "I told him that he would have to provide so that the money would be forthcoming whether he lived or died. This he found reasonable and agreed to." Sedgwick simply insisted that his money "be employed in something that can be seen, that is the building."

It must have been quite a meeting where the deal was struck because the 2 men "threshed over the whole matter for two hours." Sedgwick was planning to leave town shortly for a 6-month excursion so brought along his secretary, Frank Webber. "He wanted him to know all about the affair and his engagement, so that the secretary will send the check for $500 every month faithfully, beginning next month, January, 1914," Dowling told the provincial.[61]

The deal seemed to renew Dowling's enthusiasm as his hopes soared again for the "Jesuits' folly" on Troost Avenue. He just needed approval to go ahead from the father provincial, who remained skeptical, writing from St. Louis to ask whether $30,000 was enough to complete the building without incurring further debt. Well, probably not, Dowling responded, but $30,000 was enough to put the building under roof, pay some interest, and go from there. "We must have some confidence in the future and in the divine providence," he wrote. "It will be a considerable step to have the building under roof."[62]

There was no time to waste. Sedgwick "is waiting to hear from us, in order that he may go on his prospective trip," Dowling told the provincial on January 2, 1914. "He has already made out the checks for the present year and they will come regularly." Just days later Dowling received the approval he needed from St. Louis, and, with Sedgwick's money in hand, Dowling dickered again with contractors, who resumed work on the college building that March with a promise to have it under roof by June 1914.

By the end of April, Rockhurst was back in the pages of *The Kansas City Star*, a sketch of what was now a proposed 3-story college building atop the page. "Active construction work is now in progress on Rockhurst College," the newspaper reported. The Martin Carroll Company was doing the stonework according to the original plans drawn by architect Clifton B. Sloan. Contracts hadn't been let for interior work, but still, the paper said, "the Jesuit fathers hope to have their first classes in the building in September."[63]

All the months and years of waiting finally came together that spring and summer of 1914. In March, work again was begun on the college building, and in May, Bishop Thomas Lillis came to Rockhurst and administered the parish's first confirmation. Fifty people were confirmed and 120 received communion. That June, as Dowling's health continued to fail, Aloysius Breen came to Rockhurst to take charge of the parish and oversee construction. That July, the first member of Rockhurst's faculty, Patrick F. Harvey, S.J., arrived from St. Louis, and that August, he set to work canvassing the city for prospective students.[64]

More than 6 years had passed since that day in March 1908 when Michael Dowling arrived in Kansas City, fresh from his victorious days in establishing Creighton University in Omaha. At last, after all the struggles and frustration, providence had indeed produced Kansas City's John Creighton. He was the eccentric but well-meaning Lee M. Sedgwick, Rockhurst's first great benefactor, whose name, according to his own wishes, would remain a secret for many years to come.

Chapter Five

First Years at Rockhurst 1914–17

Rockhurst's first teacher was also its first historian—the Rev. Patrick F. Harvey, S.J., whose 39-page *History of Rockhurst College* offers an eyewitness account of the first months and years of the new college. Harvey arrived at Rockhurst from St. Louis on July 27, 1914, just 7 weeks before the Society of Jesus hoped to open the college that coming fall. At 35 years old, Father Harvey had 7 years of teaching experience under his belt, including time spent at St. Xavier Academy in Cincinnati and Gonzaga Hall in St. Louis. He was a youthful man in looks—and likewise in spirit, friendly and always willing to help others. Although no one said, perhaps it was Father Harvey's familiarity with Kansas City that led to his appointment as Rockhurst's first teacher. He was born in Locust Gap, Pennsylvania, but had moved with his family to Kansas City when he was only 8 years old. He was a graduate of St. Benedict's high school and college in Atchison, Kansas, and attended Kenrick Seminary in St. Louis, where he was ordained on June 14, 1902.[1]

Fathers L. Lyons and M.J. Ryan sitting on the porch of the Peers farmhouse at 53rd and Troost. This house was later moved to the back of the property near Forest Avenue, facing 53rd Street, to make room for the construction of Sedgwick Hall. Some of the first Rockhurst Jesuits lived in this house. Courtesy of Rockhurst University Archives.

The names and locations of Kansas City's streets probably came easily to him as he set out that first summer to canvass the city for prospective students. He had been in Kansas City only a few days before setting out, he said, "in the quest for boys." Every day, "starting out after breakfast and returning to the residence at sundown," Harvey said, he visited Catholic family after Catholic family, until, by August's end, he had visited 78 families.[2]

When he arrived in Kansas City that summer of 1914, he had found builders working feverishly to complete the college building—eventually to be named Sedgwick Hall—in time for a September opening. With the help of another $15,000 loan from the provincial office, the exterior structure was completed, but inside, the building's upper 2 floors were left unfinished. Plans called for the Jesuit faculty to live in the new building, but with the upper floors unfinished and nowhere else to go, the little faculty of 3—Harvey, Aloysius Breen, S.J., and Walter A. Roemer, S.J.—huddled in the Peers' old frame house, which still stood on the property. It would be mid-October before they were able to take up residence in Sedgwick Hall, which for years, as the school's only structure, would serve as administration building, classroom, and living space for the Jesuit faculty. A gymnasium, open to the sky and useless in inclement weather, stood in a center space of Sedgwick Hall, and a lunchroom, with benches for the boys, was excavated out of a northeast section of the cellar. So sparse were furnishings in the Jesuit living quarters that when the Rev. John Sullivan, S.J., came to visit from St. Aloysius Parish he was shocked to find that soap boxes were being used as wash stands and that his Jesuit comrades were sleeping on old cots found on the premises.[3]

"The life at Rockhurst at this time was not of a luxurious nature," Harvey understated. He paid his own expenses of about $10 a week and poked fun at the food being served by Brother Patrick Kehoe, who had served at St. Mary's Academy when it was still an Indian mission. "From his little descriptions of the privations endured there, the members of the Faculty of the new college considered themselves not so badly off after all," Harvey wrote, "although Brother Patrick repeatedly assured them their table was as poor as the poorest he had seen amongst the pioneers."[4]

It was Father Harvey who would sit in a first-floor office of Sedgwick Hall on that first class day at Rockhurst, taking down the names of new students as they arrived. That morning was so stormy that Harvey had stood anxiously with Father Dowling at the back door of Sedgwick Hall, wondering silently whether anyone would show up. But still, he said, they kept "looking hopefully towards the Marlborough (streetcar) line," which ran along The Paseo just east of campus. Surely, it was a jubilant moment when a streetcar stopped at 53rd Street shortly after 9 that morning and nearly every passenger who got off looked to be a young fellow. They "formed a procession bound for Rockhurst," Harvey said, "and they marched up 53rd Street—the first students of Rockhurst."

Rev. Patrick F. Harvey, S.J. Fr. Harvey's 39-page History of Rockhurst College *is an eyewitness account of the earliest years of Rockhurst. Just weeks before the opening of the school, Fr. Harvey canvassed the neighborhood for prospective students. On the first day of classes, it was Harvey who took down the names of the 42 boys who began their studies at Rockhurst. Courtesy of Rockhurst University Archives.*

— THE ROCKHURST BOYS —

By the time the first bell rang, at about 9:30 on the morning of Tuesday, September 15, 1914, Father Harvey was sitting in the Prefect of Studies Office, where he took down the names of 42 boys who registered that day. Their Irish names, their Irish backgrounds, and the ways in which their Irish families embraced the American dream are instructive.

As historian James Hennesey, S.J., explains, the first Irish to attend college in the United States usually were the first- and second-generation children of Irish immigrant families. It took time for Irish immigrants, most of whom were Catholic, to become settled and move far enough up the economic ladder that they could afford to send their children to college. By 1910, the overall Catholic population in the United States had grown to 16.4 million and by 1920 to 19.8 million. By then, the earliest generations of Catholic immigrants, Hennesey writes, "were making their way in business, and especially in politics."[5] In 1906 a Catholic was named U.S. attorney general (Charles Bonaparte), and in 1910 a Catholic was appointed chief justice of the United States (Edward Douglass White). On the municipal level, Irish-Catholics were heavily involved in ward politics

First students at Rockhurst. Forty-two boys registered on the first day of class on September 15, 1914. The Jesuits from left to right are Brother Patrick Kehoe, Fr. William F. Hoffend, Fr. Aloysius A. Breen, Fr. Robert Henneman, and Fr. Patrick F. Harvey. Fr. Dowling, although president of Rockhurst, did not live on campus. Fr. Breen became the second president of Rockhurst in 1915 at Dowling's death. Courtesy of Rockhurst University Archives.

as members of the Democratic Party. Tammany Hall, for example, dominated New York City politics from 1902 to 1924, and, in Boston, John F. Fitzgerald, grandfather of the country's first Catholic president, was elected mayor. In Kansas City, politics was an Irish-Catholic stronghold, as well, ruled by the Pendergast machine, which famously parceled out city jobs to fellow Irishmen. By 1914, Roman Catholicism was firmly established in the United States, but Catholics—some 85 percent of whom were descended from immigrants—still were perceived as somehow more "foreign" than other Americans,[6] a perception that Catholics would work hard to dispel in the first decade of Rockhurst's existence.

Many of Rockhurst's first students were second-generation Irish whose families had arrived in Kansas City after the Civil War. Men who worked on the railroad or in the packinghouses tended to settle their families in the West Bottoms, where as many as 500 Irish lived by 1880. They also settled in Old Town, along the river between Cherry and Charlotte streets, where another 400 Irish families lived after the Civil War. As the West Bottoms industrialized and Old Town commercialized, the more prosperous Irish moved "up the hill," to the area around 9th and Pennsylvania streets and then followed the city south in later years. The less prosperous moved east, to the area around Brooklyn Street, not far from St. Aloysius Church. As Rockhurst was founded, it was the Irish who dominated the city's Roman Catholic Church.[7]

— THE SONS OF WORKING-CLASS IRISH FATHERS —

It is not surprising that many boys in that first Rockhurst class were the sons of working-class Irish fathers. The father of brothers James and John Glynn, for example, worked for the railroad, as did Thomas Hogan's father, who was a yardmaster for the Frisco lines. Bernard McKenna's father drove a laundry truck, Martin Mangan's father was a coal merchant, and Michael Ahern's father was a brick contractor.

John Flynn's father, like so many Irishmen during the Pendergast era, landed a job with the city; he was a fireman. Earl Boughan's father worked for the police department, and Vincent O'Flaherty's father was a deputy sheriff, at least when Vincent was a toddler. By 1914, when Vincent enrolled at Rockhurst, the family had moved up in the world. His father now was a lawyer, employed on the third floor of the county courthouse.

Patrick Mason and Edward McCarren were first-generation Irish-Americans, the sons of immigrant fathers who were working hard to move up the economic ladder. In 1900, Patrick's father was a lowly day laborer, but by 1910, he was employed in the saloon business and renting a house at 2314 E. 12th Street in the West Bottoms. Just 4 years later, in 1914, he was listed in the city directory as a conductor for the Pullman Company and had moved his family out of the Bottoms to 2107 E. 36th Street. How far the Masons had come in just a dozen years.

Not all Rockhurst boys were Irish. Arthur Forster and Leo Heinz were children of German immigrants. Arthur's father was a cabinetmaker, and Leo's father, a tailor, who worked out of the family home at 1712 Pennsylvania Avenue and had been in America for more than 30 years. Duff Vilm's father was a Frenchman who had immigrated to America in 1891 and worked as superintendent of a milling company. Jasper Messina, one of 7 children, was the son of Italian immigrants so poor that Jasper would be forced to leave Rockhurst for a time because he was needed at home. His father, who still spoke Italian, was a laborer on the railroad.

A few boys at Rockhurst hailed from families that were much more well-to-do than the large Messina family. Sanford Zwart was the son of a physician who employed 2 servants to help his wife with the family's 5 children. The Zwarts were immigrants from Holland who lived at 1019 Prospect Avenue, near St. Aloysius Church. John Walsh was the son of a nationally renowned lawyer, Frank P. Walsh, who was a great advocate of Irish freedom and a partner in the Kansas City law firm of Walsh, Aylward & Lee at 1112-1116 Grand Avenue. During World War I, Frank Walsh would serve as chairman of the War Labor Board, and after the war would represent the Irish Republic in negotiations with the British that led to the establishment of the Irish Free State. Although Frank Walsh and his wife, Katie, were the children of Irish immigrants, they lived with their 8 children at 2506 Independence Avenue, an exclusive address in 1914 Kansas City. Katie's 77-year-old mother and her 60-year-old brother-in-law also lived with the family, as did a live-in nurse.

Of all the Rockhurst boys, William McHattie may have had the deepest roots in America, although that did not necessarily make the family better off financially. William lived at 3007 E. 7th Street with his paternal grandmother, who was a native of Ohio, as were her parents, which would place the McHattie family in Ohio as early as 1820. William's father, also an Ohio native, was a working-class man who held down a job as a pipefitter for the Missouri Pacific Railroad. William worked, too, as a telephone boy for the George B. Peck Dry Goods Company.

Foreman Thomas J. Burke oversees workers for the Kansas City Street Department. Many of the first students at Rockhurst were sons of Irish immigrants, whose fathers were employed by city boss Tom Pendergast. Courtesy of Kittie D. Adee.

A number of Rockhurst boys who attended in those early years had to work to help pay for their education. Edward Kavanaugh and his brother Robert earned part of their board and tuition by helping out around campus. They fired the boilers, swept the church and classrooms, served the noontime lunch, and then helped wash the dishes.[8] Two other boys were ushers at Union Station, another was a night watchman at an undertaker's establishment, and a dozen delivered newspapers. Others worked in stores on Saturdays. One boy made it through Rockhurst thanks to his cow. In those days, most of the campus was still farmland, so the boy, who was not identified, brought his cow to school and put her in the pasture until evening, when he milked her.[9]

The Dr. Joseph Horigan home at 1107 East 53rd Street. The photo was taken in 1912. Joseph Horigan was the first boy to enroll at Rockhurst, probably because he lived across the street. Joseph "handed in his name" on August 16, 1914, and then "came with the boys" and registered again on September 15. Horigan was the son of a physician, Dr. Joseph A. Horigan, who is listed in the 1915 catalog as the "attending physician" for Rockhurst. The doctor, who was a native of the District of Columbia, was wealthy enough to employ a cook and janitor to help his wife, Katherine, with their 5 children, of whom 16-year-old Joseph was the youngest. Courtesy of Rockhurst University Public Relations and Marketing.

It would not be until the 1930s that Rockhurst started to attract a few out-of-state students. One out-of-state student, from Woodward, Oklahoma, hitchhiked to Kansas City with only 50 cents in his pocket. Another boy drove his old car up from Arkansas and lived in it all one winter. Another boy contracted with Rockhurst's biology teacher to supply the bugs used in class. "He went through college, graduating with honors, on the bugs, frogs, mice, squirrels, and other like laboratory material" he found in the fields around Kansas City, as the then-college president, Daniel Conway, told the story.[10]

— The Rockhurst Faculty —

By Thanksgiving of that first academic year, life was more settled for Rockhurst's tiny faculty. Now grown to 4 members with the addition of William Hoffend, S.J., they had moved into new living quarters in Sedgwick Hall, and, thanks to the generosity of Father Sullivan of St. Aloysius Parish, each of their rooms had acquired new furniture, though their living quarters were simple and frugal. No carpet hugged the corridor, and no rug brightened the Jesuits' bedrooms. Each room had a narrow bed, a desk, a bookcase, and a bench for the resident to kneel at prayer. And, of course, a crucifix hung on the wall above.[11]

But life was not without its pleasures. Father Harvey's mother had donated a Victor Graphaphone with 100 records, and someone else had donated a 5-passenger Ford touring car. The camaraderie of Rockhurst's first faculty came through in Father Harvey's history, as he joked about Father Breen's poor driving and poked fun at Walter Roemer and Patrick Kehoe who got off the streetcar at Troost Avenue near Gillham Road in a blinding snowstorm and started walking in the wrong direction. Instead of walking south across the Brush Creek bridge to Rockhurst, they turned north and kept walking and walking, convinced that something had happened to the bridge. No one escaped Father Harvey's lighthearted ribbing. He must have chuckled as he wrote about Brother Kehoe's assistant, John Miller, who did the cooking, and who, Harvey said, used the same old excuse every time he wanted a day off. Like many Catholics who emigrated to Kansas City at the turn of the century, John Miller was a Croatian who undoubtedly knew many people in the Croatian community across the river in Kansas City, Kansas. "Whenever John wanted a day or two off, there was always a christening in Kansas City, Kansas," Harvey wrote. "And those christenings came so often according to the excuses John gave, that that colony must be over-crowded with children by this time."[12]

On a visit to Rockhurst, Provincial A.J. Burrowes commented on the "fine spirit of charity and religious discipline in the community," though he chastised the fathers for leaving dishes on the table and allowing workmen to dine in the kitchen. He also noted the faculty's need for a new icebox and coffee urn.[13] Father Dowling, although president of Rockhurst Col-

The Rockhurst Jesuit community, 1916-17. Top Row, Left to Right: Bro. Francis X. Polanowski; Bro. Martin Hagerty; Bro. Patrick Kehoe; Mr. Wm. P. Manion; Mr. Robert U. Bakewell; Mr. Adam Ellis. Bottom Row, Left to Right: Fr. Henry R. Ehrhard; Fr. Patrick F. Harvey; Fr. Aloysius A. Breen; Fr. Wm. F. Hoffend; Fr. Alphonse M. Schwitalla.

At the death of Fr. Dowling in 1915, Fr. Breen became president of Rockhurst and served until 1918. "Mr." Wm. P. Manion later became "Father" Manion and served as Rockhurst's fifth president from 1928-33. Courtesy of Rockhurst University Archives.

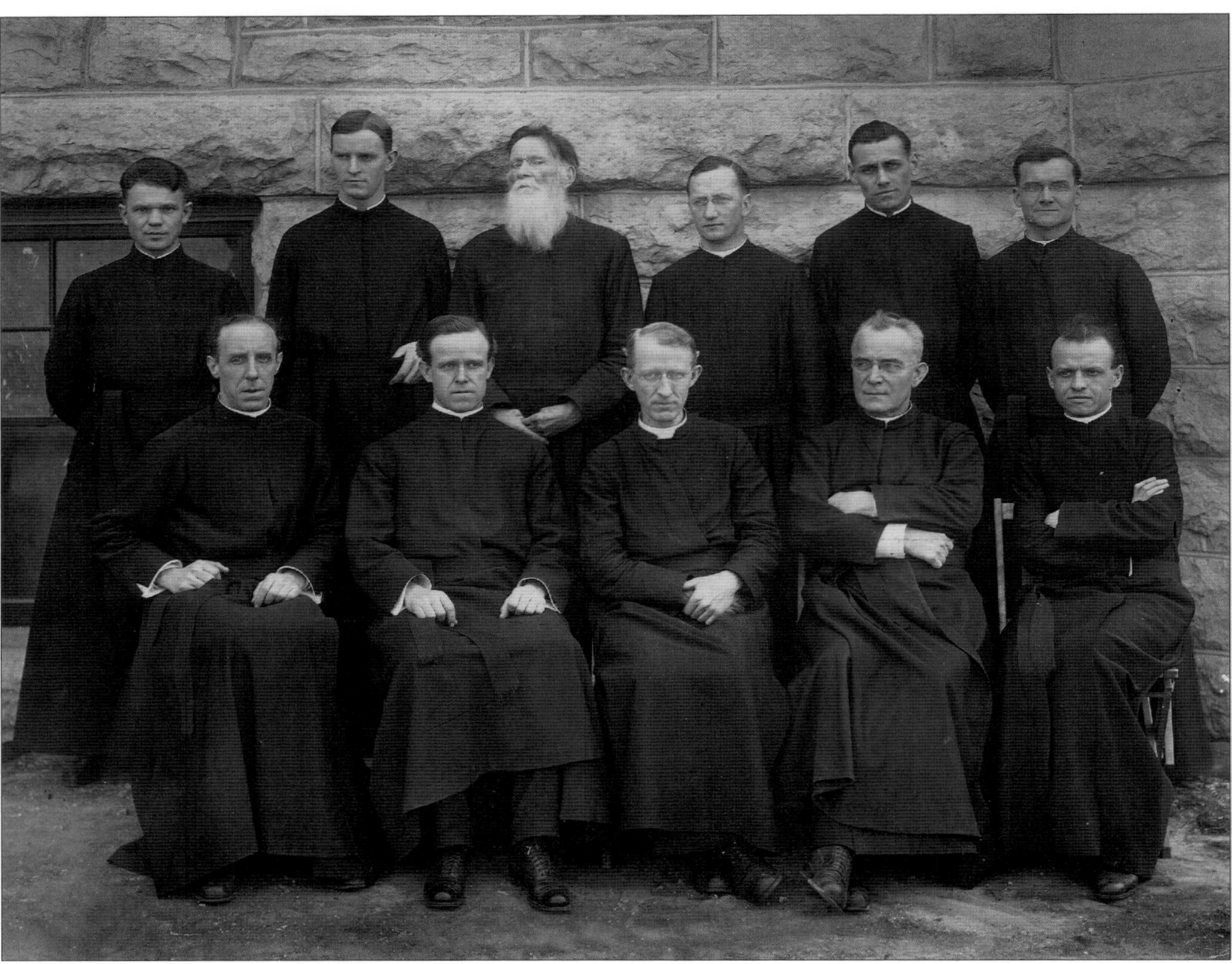

lege, did not live on campus. In failing health, he resided in the Jesuit residence at 11th and Prospect streets, next to St. Aloysius Church. Whether Dowling stayed around on that first opening day to partake in the Jesuits' evening meal, Harvey did not say, though it is likely that he did. After all, Bishop Thomas Lillis came out that evening of September 15, 1914, to, as Harvey put it, "take supper" with the faculty. Perhaps it was fitting after all the difficulties in establishing Rockhurst College that even taking supper did not prove to be an easy matter. The torrential morning storm had played havoc with the electric light system, Harvey wrote, "and when supper time came, it was found that the only light that could be found to illumine the 'banquet table' of the Bishop was a solitary candle." The Jesuits placed the candle on top of a glass in the middle of the table and all began to eat. "His Lordship seemed to enjoy the meal," Harvey wrote, "and said that an institution that had such a hard beginning would surely prove a great success."[14]

Brother Martin J. Hagerty, S.J., known as Brother Pat to thousands of students during his 50 years at Rockhurst, came to take charge of food services and purchase in November 1915. Born in Ireland, Hagerty came to the United States in 1906 at age 16, entered the Jesuit novitiate at Florissant in 1910, and after a brief assignment in British Honduras, arrived at Rockhurst in 1915 where he remained until shortly before his death in 1965. In 1955, the celebration of Bro. Pat's fortieth year at Rockhurst drew alumni from all parts of the nation.

As the college opened, Rockhurst's was an all-Jesuit faculty, from the 70-year-old Brother Kehoe, an Irishman who entered the Jesuit novitiate at Florissant during the Civil War (1864), to the 24-year-old Walter Roemer, who had only entered the Society of Jesus 4 years earlier. Roemer had been studying philosophy at Saint Louis University before he came to Rockhurst to serve his regency.[15] The regency—or 3 years of teaching—was part of the long process that a young man took to become a Jesuit. He had to spend 2 years as a novice in a seminary such as Florissant, where he trained and made sure he could hack the rigorous life that demanded vows of poverty, chastity, and obedience. He then would have to study the classics for 2 years, philosophy for 3, teach for 3 years, and then spend 4 more years in the study of theology, and another year in the study of aesthetic theology.[16]

"Brother Pat Night," September 12, 1955. Left to right: Vincent J. O'Flaherty, Jr., H. Duff Vilm, Brother Martin J. Hagerty, S.J., John B. Spence, Bernard J. Glynn. O'Flaherty was in the first graduating class from the college (1921), Glynn in the second (1922). Courtesy of Rockhurst University Archives.

The life of a Jesuit at Rockhurst was one ordered by routine and a discipline that went beyond the teaching of classes. As Rockhurst historian Hugh M. Owens writes, the fathers prepared their own meals, did their own dishes, swept the rooms, and cleaned the laboratories after classes.[17] In the 1930s, Rockhurst President Daniel Conway told how the fathers rose at 5 a.m., visited the chapel, and offered up the day to God's service. At 7:15 they gathered for breakfast, eaten in absolute silence. Then, before embarking on the day's duties, each man went to his room and examined his conscience to see whether he had had a wrong thought or had been unkind. Lunch was at noon, when the priests said grace in unison, in Latin, of course. Each returned to his duties until 6 p.m., when supper was served, followed by an hour of recreation in the common room. After that, it was back to their private rooms to study lessons for the next day, prepare lectures, or read until 9 p.m., when everyone gathered again in the chapel for 20 minutes of prayer and 15 minutes more of self-reflection. "All are equally poor," said Conway, who, even as the college president, lived exactly as the other Jesuits.[18]

— A College in Name Only —

Although Rockhurst called itself a "college" from the outset, it actually was a high school, a status that would not change until 1917. Most of the students who registered that first day were in their early teenage years. Judging from available records in the censuses of 1900 through 1930, most of the Rockhurst boys were born between 1899 and 1901, making them from 13 to 15 years old when they trekked up the muddy hill to Rockhurst on opening day.

They registered as first-, second-, and third-year high school students, although Rockhurst, after only a week, had to eliminate third-year classes because the school was unable to secure another teacher from St. Louis.[19] Harvey writes that despite the elimination of the third-year class, most of the third-year boys "refused to leave and finished the year in second high." By the end of the first term, a total of 47 boys had enrolled at Rockhurst. The spirit of the first students of Rockhurst "was one never to be forgotten," Harvey wrote. "No one could persuade any of those students to utter a complaint…their motto. 'If you can't say anything good…don't say anything….'" When Rockhurst's first school year ended, on June 21, 1915, each boy, Harvey said, resolved to bring another boy with him the next year.[20]

This sculpture of St. Ignatius of Loyola is by artist Abraham Mathew and was commissioned for the 100th anniversary of Rockhurst University. St. Ignatius is depicted sitting at the River Cardoner in Spain, where he spent 9 months in reflection and prayer, leading to the creation of the Spiritual Exercises. *Courtesy of Rockhurst University Public Relations and Marketing.*

From this inauspicious start, Rockhurst would grow. When school opened for its second year, on September 7, 1915, Rockhurst counted 72 boys in attendance, and in its third year, 125 boys registered on September 5, 1916.[21] It was in that third academic year, on June 21, 1917, that Rockhurst graduated its first class. They were, of course, high school boys all—Luke Byrne, Francis Carroll, Thomas Divine, Bernard J. Hale, Joseph D. Horigan, Leo J. Hulseman, Clem McCormack, Patrick W. Mason, Norbert Mudd, Clarence Mullen, and Clarence Reardon.[22]

With its first high school graduation complete—and no college curriculum for the new graduates to advance to in the fall—Rockhurst faced the fact that it was about to lose the very young men most likely to enroll in Rockhurst College, had there actually been one. With that in mind, high school teacher Alphonse M. Schwitalla, S.J., who had been teaching at Rockhurst since the fall of 1916, contacted the provincial in St. Louis. He stated the situation and asked for permission to offer college classes beginning in the fall of 1917.

"His request was granted," Rockhurst historian Huge M. Owens writes, but "only because Father (Schwitalla) was able to teach all the college classes offered that first year, namely, the Classics, Religion, English, and Chemistry."[23] In addition, the provincial laid down two other conditions: Schwitalla must enroll at least 15 students for the college and he must raise $5,000, most likely to improve the science lab.

Father Schwitalla faced the difficult task of teaching not only the classics, religion, and English, but also the science of chemistry, which spoke to Rockhurst's recognition that education had moved into the twentieth century. The age-old Jesuit curriculum would need upgrading. Rockhurst, as did all Jesuit colleges, based its guidelines for preparing young men for adulthood on the *Ratio Studiorum* (Rule of Studies), which was nearly as old as the Society of Jesus itself, founded between 1553 and 1554 by St. Ignatius of Loyola. Ignatius, as Rockhurst graduate Sean Brennan explains, believed that the development of the intellect went hand in hand with the development of faith. Although Jesuit education would revise and modify over the years, this idea always was at its core.[24]

The *Ratio Studiorum* instructed Jesuit schools to equip their students with a mastery of the written and spoken word, the habit of logical thinking, knowledge of the past and present through literature and history, a clear sense of direction through philosophy and religion, and strength of character through intelligent discipline.[25]

A subject such as chemistry was something new—born of the modern era, when new ideas such as Albert Einstein's theory of relativity were altering views of the universe and leading people to deny that absolute values existed, even in society. As new colleges and universities sprang up all across the country in the first years of the century, the philosopher John Dewey applied scientific methods to education and social problems, arguing that intelligent applications could build a just and harmonious society. A mood of "civic idealism" spread across college campuses, explain historians George Brown Tindall and David E. Shi. "No longer could the university be a 'home of useless and harmless recluses'...but it must dedicate itself to the public good."[26]

Hotly debated reforms between old and new educational structures were important for Catholic higher education, as well. After World War I, historian Philip Gleason writes, the push in Catholic higher education would be for academic excellence, for research, and for developing a faculty dedicated to scholarship. By 1920, a paper presented at the convention of the Catholic Education Association was arguing for these reforms, marking the first time in the history of the CEA, Gleason writes, that the ideal of scholarly research had been set forth. Now that Catholic colleges had been brought into the national standard, it was time, the speaker said, "to breathe into them this breath of the higher academic life which is necessary to give them name and place as essential units in the new intellectual order within the nation."[27]

Thus, at Rockhurst, Jesuits not only would offer their traditional emphasis on the classics—logic, philosophy, ethics, and Latin—but also the modern subjects of science and mathematics, English literature, and his-

The annual catalog for 1918 outlines the courses required in Greek and Latin. In order to be admitted to the A.B. degree program, students must have completed 4 years of high school Latin and 3 years of Greek. Applicants could be admitted "with conditions" in Greek, but these had to be "removed within one year from the time of entrance."

The heavy emphasis on the classics was rooted in the Jesuit educational tradition. The intent of the college course, as stated in the 1918 catalog, was to give "the student a complete liberal education, which will train and develop all powers of the mind, and will cultivate no one faculty to an exaggerated degree at the expense of the others. The college ideal is not to foster specialization, but to cultivate the mind, to build up and strengthen true character, and to impart accuracy of thought and reasoning and that breadth of view which must ever be the foundation as well of more advanced scholarship as of eminence in the professions or others stations in life." Courtesy of Rockhurst University Archives.

OUTLINE OF COLLEGE COURSES.

LATIN.

NOTE—The courses in Latin, Greek and English are, for greater educative effect, made parallel as much as possible. The theory of the different forms of literature is presented in the English courses, and the classic masterpieces studied in the Latin and Greek course furnish illustrative material to enforce the precepts and for comparative work. Poetry, with its various forms, is the subject of Freshman year; Oratory, of Sophomore.

COURSE I.
Precepts: A thorough review of Latin Prosody and versification.
Authors: Horace, "Ars Poetica"; Virgil, "Aeneid," Books III, V and VI.
Four hours a week. One semester.

COURSE II. Livy, Book XXI. (2300 lines).
Sight-Reading: Selections from Christian Hymnology; Livy.
Four hours a week. One semester.
Practice: (Both Semesters.) Practical Course in Latin Composition. Two themes a week. A theme in imitation of the prose authors studied, about every fortnight.
Memory: From the authors read in class.

COURSE III.
Authors: Cicero, Pro Milone; Horace, Select Odes.
Four hours a week. One semester.

COURSE IV. Horace, Epodes, Epistles and Satires; Tacitus, Agricola.
Sight-Reading: Selections from the authors assigned above. Tacitus, Germania or Annals. Selections from the Latin Fathers.
Four hours a week. One semester.
Practice: (Both semesters.) Bradley's Aids, selections from Part II, from Exercise 50 to end of book. Two themes a week. One composition every fortnight in imitation of the author studied. Off-hand translation from English into Latin.
Memory: Select passages from the authors read.

GREEK.

COURSE I.
Precepts: The Syntax of the verb repeated; general rules of quantity; the Homeric Dialect; a brief sketch of Greek Epic and Lyric Poetry.
Authors: Homer, Iliad, Books II-VI.
Four hours a week. One semester.

COURSE II. Plato, Apology and Crito.
Sight-Reading: The New Testament or selections from the authors read in class.
Four hours a week. One semester.
Practice: (Both semesters.) A written theme once a week, based on the authors studied and illustrating the syntax of Attic Greek. Frequent written reviews done in class.

COURSE III.
Authors: Demosthenes, Philippic I or III; anaylsis of Philippic I or III; selections from "On the Crown."
Four hours a week. One semester.

COURSE IV.
Selections from Demosthenes On the Crown, with detailed analysis. Sophocles, Antigones, Oedipus Tyrannus or Oedipus Coloneus.
Sight-Reading: The New Testament or St. Chrysostom, Eutropius, or St. Basil.
Four hours a week. One semester.

tory. Furthermore, Rockhurst's would be a modern, 4-year college curriculum, thus setting aside the traditional 7-year Catholic method in favor of the standard 4 years being offered at secular American and British universities. By fusing the classical with the vocational and by offering the modern 4-year curriculum, Rockhurst was able, as Brennan writes, "to maintain its Jesuit commitments while offerings in English and chemistry appealed to a broader range of students." Importantly, as Brennan argues, this fusion of the classical and modern spoke to the innovative spirit and adaptability of Rockhurst's founders—an adaptability that "became one of the crucial elements in Rockhurst's later successes."[28]

In future years, Rockhurst would become the first college in the Kansas City area to offer evening classes, which, for a time, even admitted women. It also would be among the first to open a School of Management and would stand out nationally in the 1940s and 1950s for its unique Institute of Social Order.

But never would Rockhurst forget the Jesuit traditions of the *Ratio Studiorum*. As stated in its first prospectus that fall of 1917, Rockhurst College aimed "to perfect" a boy's development "during the most plastic years of young manhood." The prospectus went on: "It is the conviction of the Society of Jesus that the final result of a good education is neither distinctively intellectual nor distinctively moral, but rather that combination of capable intelligence and sterling manly virtue which makes up a good character: that it is men who are to be trained in schools, not mere minds."[29]

In other words, Rockhurst was interested in developing the whole man. This aim—to lay "strong intellectual and moral foundations," ensuring "complete development" for a student's "future utility to himself and to the community"—would not change, be it explained in the 1918 or 1932 catalog, or in later years when the college issued statements from its public relations department.[30]

Despite the inclusion of science and mathematics, Rockhurst's emphasis on a humanistic and liberal education was quite an innovation in Kansas City, which, Schwitalla said, always "had been accustomed to education of a more pragmatic character." Kansas City, he said, "had to be converted to Jesuit education, but once converted, it showed all the enthusiasm of the new convert for the classical and philosophical courses."[31]

Rockhurst's new, 4-year curriculum led to one of 3 degrees: a Bachelor of Arts (A.B.), Bachelor of Science (B.S.), or Bachelor of Philosophy (Ph.B.). A list of specific courses that first year has not been located, the prospectus saying only that "in each of these courses a certain number of studies are prescribed, Logic, Psychology, Ethics, together with one or more of the sciences, a branch of mathematics and English Literature."[32]

By 1920 the annual catalog listed requirements for an A.B. degree as follows: 16 credit hours each in Latin, Modern Language, and Philosophy; 12 credit hours in English; 8 credit hours each in Science and Religion; and 6 hours each in Mathematics and History. A credit hour was defined as one lecture, recitation, or class exercise, one hour in length per week, for one semester. The B.S. degree was conferred on the student who concentrated his studies, particularly during the last 2 years, on science or math. The Ph.B. degree demanded concentration in one of the following departments: philosophy, history, English, literature, economics, political science, education, or sociology.[33]

Alphonse M. Schwitalla, S.J., Rockhurst College's first professor. Fr. Schwitalla earned a Ph.D. in zoology from Johns Hopkins University in 1921, becoming one of the first American Jesuits to graduate with a doctorate from a secular university. A man of multiple talents and unbounded enthusiasm, Schwitalla, who had been teaching in the high school since 1916, received permission from the provincial to offer college classes beginning in the fall of 1917. Schwitalla taught the entire first-year curriculum—classics, religion, English, and chemistry. Fr. Schwitalla would later go on to a distinguished career in education and science. He served as president of the North Central Association of Colleges and Secondary Schools, Dean of the School of Medicine at Saint Louis University for 21 years, and in 1960, became the first non-physician to receive the American Medical Association's Certificate of Merit. A Phi Beta Kappa, Fr. Schwitalla held honorary degrees from numerous universities. Courtesy of Rockhurst University Archives.

— A Single Teacher —

Father Schwitalla was the logical choice for Rockhurst's first college professor because he was a man as modern as Rockhurst's curriculum. A German Pole who emigrated with his family to the United States when he was only 3 years old, Schwitalla had attended parochial schools in St. Louis, went on to Saint Louis Academy, and, notably, later would earn his doctorate in zoology from Johns Hopkins University—a secular university. Schwitalla, who distinguished himself at Johns Hopkins with a Phi Beta Kappa key, would go on to a long and distinguished career in education, but when he arrived at Rockhurst in the summer of 1916, he was still a young priest.[34] It was in the dog days of summer, on August 17, when he hopped off the streetcar at 47th and Harrison streets and began the trek up the Troost Avenue hill. He walked because the city had not yet extended the streetcar line—nor paved the avenue. So it was that Rockhurst's first college teacher walked in the dust and heat and was "a sight," Harvey writes, by the time he reached his new home.[35]

Though young, Schwitalla already had taught chemistry at St. Xavier College in Cincinnati (1907–10) and biology and physiology at Saint Louis University (1910–12), which must have strengthened his confidence as he took on the entire college curricu-

Memorial of 1918

1) The spirit of charity is commendable & also the earnestness with which all devote themselves to their work.

2) Care should be taken not to allow students to ascend to higher classes whose examination papers show they are wholly unfit: such laxity is sure to lower the standard & while it may save a few boys will eventually send away many more by destroying the reputation of the college

3) Open disobedience on the part of students must be stopped by very severe measures, else the discipline of the college will suffer great harm

4) Attention is called to no. 4 of the preceding memorial. This past winter has demonstrated again the truth contained there. Doubtless much of the illness of the past winter was due to lack of sufficient heat. If the money can be spared at all, it would prove a good investment.

5) The birretta should be worn at table & also by the fathers when going to & returning from the altar. The latter is a regulation of the church.

6) Scholastics ought not to approach Holy Communion before the half past five Mass. It is usually done without any previous preparation & means no thanksgiving after Mass. This is not a good training in spiritual life

A J Burrowes, S.J.
April 25/18

In his 1918 "Memorial" to the Rockhurst Jesuits, Provincial A.J. Burrowes, S.J., warns against laxity in academic standards and student discipline. "Open disobedience on the part of students," he writes, "must be stopped by very severe measures, else the discipline of the college will suffer great harm." He also instructs the Jesuits that the biretta "should be worn at table and also by the fathers when going to and returning from the altar. The collar is a regulation of the church." Courtesy of Rockhurst University Archives.

lum. That he later would seek a degree from a secular university such as Johns Hopkins—one of the first Jesuits from the Missouri Province to do so—said worlds about his modern ideas on education. He was described as a man "full of youthful zeal," with "unbounded enthusiasm," and a "scintillating intellect." So full of energy was Father Schwitalla that even when he suffered an attack of rheumatism and was confined to his room, he continued to teach his chemistry classes.

He would do his best, though a lack of laboratory equipment had long hindered the science program in the high school. Upon his arrival, Schwitalla ordered 2 lab tables from Schwegers of Kansas City and bought an acetylene tank to fuel the burners for chemistry experiments, an adaptation that probably melted many a test tube. With no city gas yet supplied to the campus, it was the best he could do.

A Dr. Foehling donated a microscope in the Christmas season of 1916, and a Mr. Gallagher of the Faxon and Gallagher Drug Company donated a supply of chemicals, but that was about the extent of the high school's third-floor science laboratory. College instruction would demand better, so in the summer of 1917, before college classes opened that fall, Rockhurst held a drive to raise $2,500 to outfit the chemistry department. Two citizens, Vincent O'Flaherty and Dr. Thomas E. Purcell, went about the city soliciting funds. "They got promissory notes for the amounts promised," Harvey writes, "and as a result, we gathered together $3,600, or $1,100 more than what we had aimed at collecting."[36]

In its first years, the college would accept many needed donations. Books, especially, came from many people—Latin, Greek, English, and French dictionaries from St. Aloysius' John Sullivan; books on history and travel from a Dr. Kruger; 100 novels and 300 nonfiction works of reference, history, and poetry from an anonymous donor; and another 200 to 300 books from Kansas City priest Curtis Tiernan. Mrs. J.Z. Miller donated $25 specifically for the library to buy books, and students in some classes started turning over their used books, setting a good example, the student newspaper reported, for other classes to follow.[37] But still, the col-

Gymnasium and auditorium, Sedgwick Hall. The interior of Sedgwick Hall originally was constructed as an open space, extending upward from the basement to the second floor.

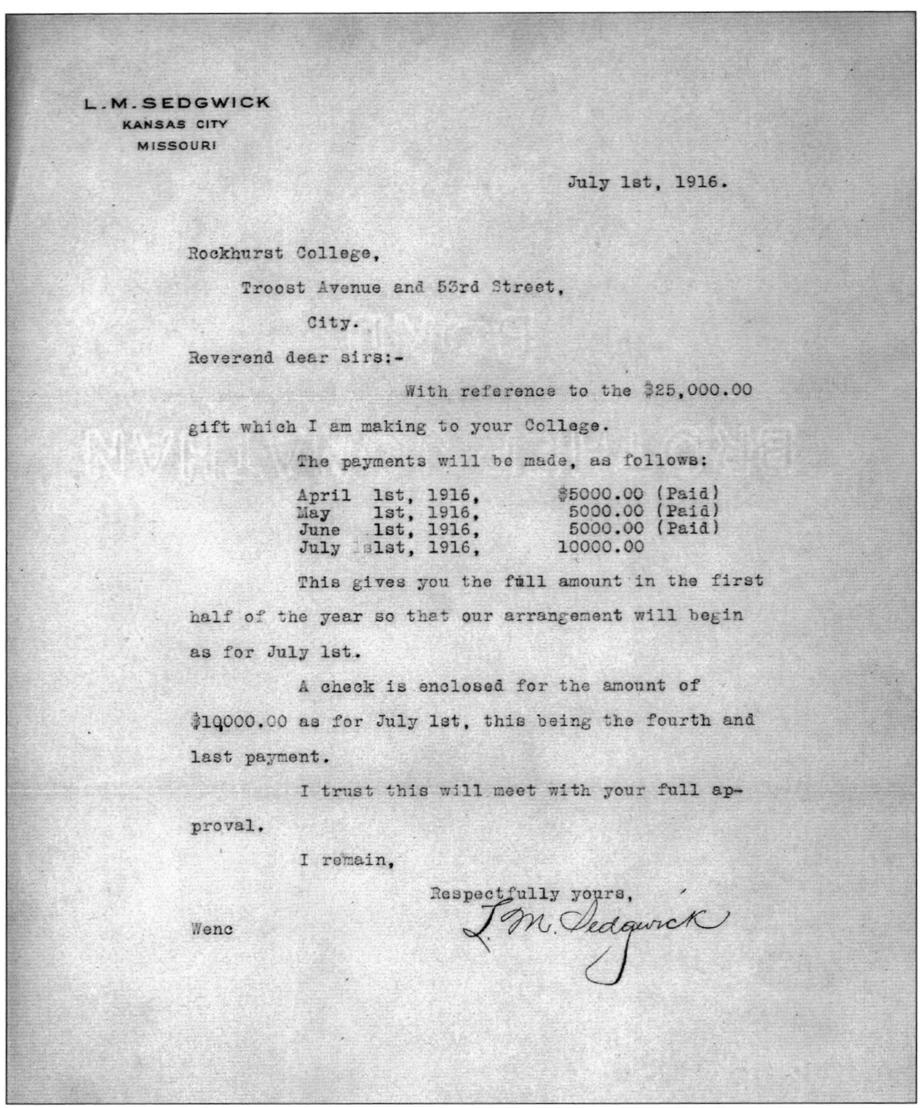

L.M.SEDGWICK
KANSAS CITY
MISSOURI

July 1st, 1916.

Rockhurst College,
Troost Avenue and 53rd Street,
City.

Reverend dear sirs:-

With reference to the $25,000.00 gift which I am making to your College.

The payments will be made, as follows:

April 1st, 1916,	$5000.00	(Paid)
May 1st, 1916,	5000.00	(Paid)
June 1st, 1916,	5000.00	(Paid)
July 1st, 1916,	10000.00	

This gives you the full amount in the first half of the year so that our arrangement will begin as for July 1st.

A check is enclosed for the amount of $10000.00 as for July 1st, this being the fourth and last payment.

I trust this will meet with your full approval.

I remain,

Respectfully yours,
L.M. Sedgwick

Wenc

In 1916, Lee Sedgwick gave Rockhurst $25,000 to complete construction on the second and third floors of the college building. The stipulations of the loan were these: "This day, 31 March 1916, Sedgwick gives Rockhurst $25,000, to be paid in four installments of $5,000 on April 1st; on May 1st; June 1st; and $10,000 on July 1st, in order to help us finish the building now, rather than to wait until his death, at which time he states he would have given us this amount under his will. Rockhurst College promises to pay 5% a year, payable semi-annually on Jan. 1st and July 1st of each and every year during Sedgwick's life and at his death the interest payments to cease and determine." Just 3 months after the final payment of $10,000, Sedgwick forgave the interest completely. Courtesy of Rockhurst University Archives.

lege library was so inadequate, historian Hugh Owens writes, that the few worthwhile books were designated as reference and were not allowed to be checked out. Students were forced to borrow from the public library.[38]

Despite the inauspicious start, there was, Schwitalla said, a spirit of generosity and self-sacrifice in those first years. "We were all of one heart and soul to make something of the underdog of the Province."[39] Donations were always welcome—the graphaphone from Father Harvey's mother; an Edison kinetoscope from Lee Sedgwick; a dining room set from Mrs. Robert Keith; a parlor rug from a Mrs. Doeer; and a large bell, a gift from Dr. Horigan, which was installed at the northwest corner of Sedgwick Hall.[40] It must have clanged often and loud because an early edition of the school newspaper included an essay titled "The College Bell."

"It is," the essay said, "a general messenger. It sends out its little emissaries, the small vibrations, at appointed times, that go everywhere, even to the very crags of the building.…No one cares for the bell. It is exposed to all weather, rain or snowy, warm or cold. Now and then its surface becomes glassy with ice. The clear clang then turns into a dull crank."[41]

Many donations had come in for the college chapel in Sedgwick Hall—a stained glass window from Martin Carroll, the contractor; an organ from Mrs. William Harvey; vestments from Miss Sara Curry; a chalice from Mrs. J. Altman; a ciborium from Miss Genevieve Reardon; and an altar crucifix from Mrs. Robert Ehrhard. The altar itself was a joint purchase by John M. Cleary, Bernard Muller-Thym, V.J. O'Flaherty, and Dr. T.E. Purcell.[42] Other donations to the chapel came in the following year, 1917. They included a statue of St. Joseph from W.P. Reardon; a statue of the Blessed Virgin from Edward Reardon, Jr.; a statue of the Sacred Heart from Jo Zach Miller, III; and a statue of St. Ignatius from Mrs. John Cannon. S. Spence donated the communion rail, and Mrs. John E. Rourke the Way of the Cross. There was another chalice form Clarence Reardon and a sanctuary lamp donated jointly by Mrs. Frank P. Walsh and Mrs. Edward J. Reardon.

— BROTHER DAVID E. SHAUGHNESSY, S.J. —

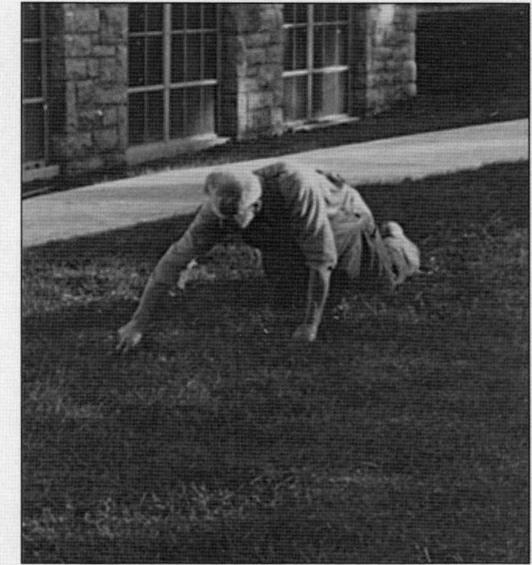

In the summer of 1916 while construction continued on Sedgwick Hall, trees were planted along Troost Avenue and 53rd Street, vines and shrubbery added as an accent for the new, semicircular drive in front of Sedgwick Hall, and the uneven grounds from 53rd to Rockhurst Road leveled and graded. These painstaking jobs were undertaken by the hardworking Brother David Shaughnessy, S.J., who, according to historian Patrick Harvey, S.J., completed the work by himself and without the help of instruments. Though occasionally the school would contract with outside firms for grading, much of the leveling of the hilly campus was the work of Bro. David. Historian Hugh Owens notes that early photos show Bourke Field as little more than a flooded, abandoned rock quarry, overgrown with weeds. "Patiently, methodically, on his hands and knees, and without precision instruments of any kind," Bro. Shaughnessy labored tirelessly to beautify the campus. Amazingly, Bro. David, who was born in 1858, carried out all of this manual labor after the age of 50. When Bourke Field was ready for play in 1927, it was Bro. Shaughnessy who cut the blue and white ribbon that stretched across the field on homecoming day, a tribute to his labors of love. He died in 1939 and is buried in Mount Saint Mary Cemetery, Kansas City.

Cash donations also trickled in. One hundred dollars came from brewer George Muehlebach, $200 from city boss T.J. Pendergast, and $500 from "the Misses Corrigan." Jo Zach Miller, Jr. was a large donor, giving 2 donations of $5,000 each for the science department, and J.Z. Miller, III got creative, donating 5 shares in the Lucky Tiger Gold Mining Company to found the Mass for the Sodality.[43]

Lee Sedgwick also weighed in occasionally with more money for Rockhurst. There would be $50 on August 16, 1920, and $100 on January 31, 1922.[44] Most importantly, he forgave the interest on a $25,000 loan he had given to the college on March 31, 1916, so Rockhurst could complete construction on the second and third floors of the college building. Sedgwick's continued generosity caught Aloysius Breen, Rockhurst president at the time, off guard.

"Here is a bit of news which I am sure you will be glad to get," Breen wrote to the provincial in St. Louis on October 31, 1916. "Yesterday I was down to the hotel visiting our friend Mr. Sedgwick, and after some communication, he handed me the inclosed 'agreement' about the interest on the $25,000, and said I could tear up the document and forget all about it.

"Well, thank the Lord," Breen continued, "this is certainly a great relief; and if you are not too busy I wish you would write a line to Sedgwick—for I am sure he would appreciate your noting his generosity."[45]

— THE NEIGHBORHOOD EXPANDS —

It was Sedgwick's $25,000 loan—made in addition to the $25,000 gift he had given earlier to Father Dowling—that allowed for the completion of Rockhurst's first—and, at the time, only building—which eventually would be named, appropriately, Sedgwick Hall. Completion of the second and third floors came none too soon because the school's enrollment was burgeoning—at least in the high school. The college enrollment never would surpass a dozen before 1920, but the high school grew quickly—from those first 42 boys in September 1914, to 72 boys in 1915, 125 in 1916, 150 in 1917, and 192 in 1918. By October 1920, when still only 10 boys were enrolled in the college department, the high school would boast an enrollment of 241.[46] As early as February 1916, the faculty had met at St. Aloysius Church to discuss the need to complete the second and third stories of Sedgwick Hall. "Plans were made to push this work as soon as possible," Harvey writes, "for it was realized that if the student body would increase the following year, there would not be room for the students in the part of the building that was finished."

An early Rockhurst baseball game, date unknown. The view looks east toward The Paseo, with 53rd street and Virginia at the right of the photo. Courtesy of Ruth Reed and Pat Green.

Just a month later, Lee Sedgwick loaned the $25,000 for the project, and just 2 months after that, on May 20, 1916, a contract was let for finishing the interior of the building, including the unroofed gymnasium. "A Jesuit School Expands," read the headline the next day in *The Kansas*

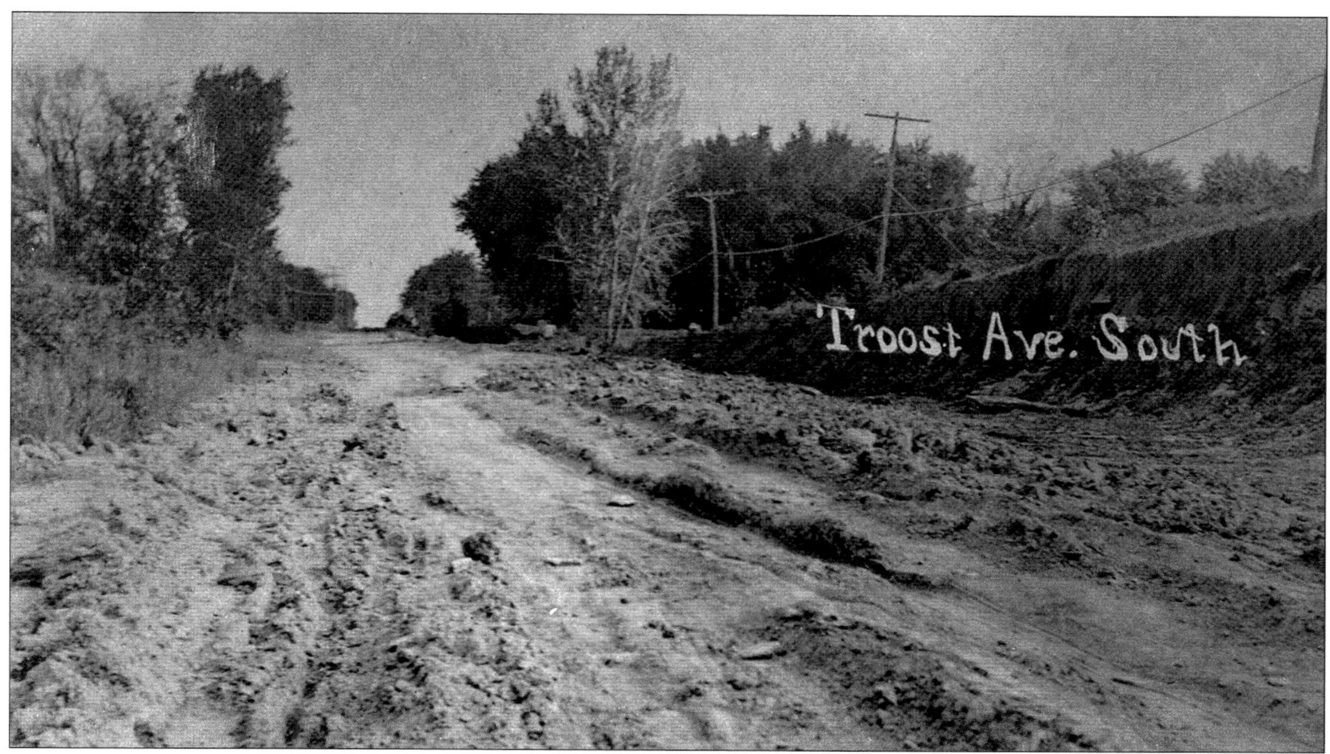

53rd Street and Troost, 1910, prior to grading and paving. Courtesy of Rockhurst University Archives.

City Star. In the fall, the newspaper reported, Rockhurst would open with a "full 4-year high school." And in the months ahead, Rockhurst would build a portable stage for the gymnasium so the gym could be used for lectures, plays, and commencement exercises, as well as basketball games.[47]

All that summer of 1916, despite a citywide workers' strike, construction progressed on Sedgwick Hall. Thanks to police officers detailed to guard duty, work continued even after striking workers stormed the building.[48] Over the next several months, trees were planted along Troost Avenue and 53rd Street, vines and shrubbery added as an accent for the new, semicircular drive behind Sedgwick Hall, and the uneven grounds from 53rd to Rockhurst Road leveled and graded, a painstaking job undertaken by the hardworking Brother David Shaughnessy, S.J., who Harvey said completed the work all by himself and without the help of instruments. In time, the grounds were sodded and 2 new tennis courts put in.[49] In the meantime, the City Council had been persuaded to close the diagonal road that ran across campus from Rockhurst Road to 53rd Street, giving Rockhurst an unbroken campus from Troost to Lydia.

The improvements apparently stoked confidence at the student newspaper, *The Sentinel*, which began voicing high hopes for construction of a second building on campus—a new, 3-story "Science Hall" that would enable Rockhurst to separate its high school and college classes. Even though the completion of Sedgwick Hall greatly improved space for the school's science laboratory, *The Sentinel* correctly recognized that if Rockhurst ever were to gain accreditation for its fledgling college, the college would need its own space. A hopeful staff at *The Sentinel* embarked on a campaign to raise the needed money for a second building: "Wanted: A Rich Man," a headline read in the March 3, 1919 issue. "Nobody has offered yet to build the new science hall; and it is up to somebody to build that hall. Rockhurst can't build it. It is going to take a lot of money to erect this building; and we are looking for a man with lots of money...."

A man with lots of money did not emerge to build a new "Science Hall," but, still, Rockhurst's facilities for science classes in Sedgwick Hall were greatly improved. In the fall of 1919, boxes of new equipment (valued at $1,600) arrived and were carried to the third-floor lab by several students, who then helped chemistry professor Knipscher unpack. By the following school year, the chemistry department was becoming so well equipped that Knipscher declared "that it is threatened with growing pains." By then, the lab had more than doubled its capacity and could accommodate 46 boys, all with individual lockers and their own equipment. The lecture room had been made into an amphitheater that could seat 50 students on comfortable chairs made for notetaking.[50]

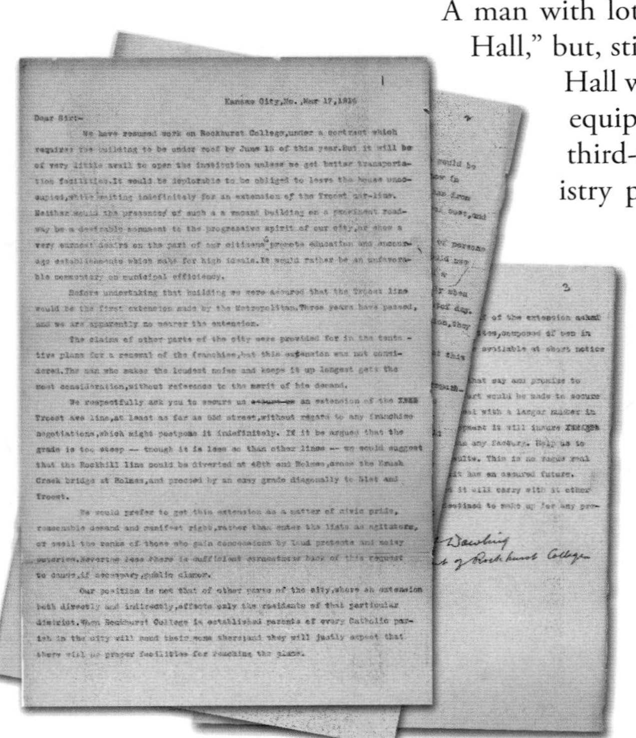

Kansas City,Mo.,Mar 17,1914

Dear Sir:-

We have resumed work on Rockhurst College,under a contract which requires the building to be under roof by June 15 of this year.But it will be of very little avail to open the institution unless we get better transportation facilities.It would be deplorable to be obliged to leave the house unoccupied,while waiting indefinitely for an extension of the Troost car-line. Neither would the presence of such a vacant building on a prominent roadway be a desirable monument to the progressive spirit of our city,or show a very earnest desire on the part of our citizens to promote education and encourage establishments which make for high ideals.It would rather be an unfavorable commentary on municipal efficiency.

Before undertaking that building we were assured that the Troost line would be the first extension made by the Metropolitan.Three years have passed, and we are apparently no nearer the extension.

The claims of other parts of the city were provided for in the tentative plans for a renewal of the franchise,but this extension was not considered.The man who makes the loudest noise and keeps it up longest gets the most consideration,without reference to the merit of his demand.

We respectfully ask you to secure us an extension of the Troost Ave line,at least as far as 53d street,without regard to any franchise negotiations,which might postpone it indefinitely. If it be argued that the grade is too steep -- though it is less so than other lines -- we would suggest that the Rockhill line could be diverted at 48th and Holmes,cross the Brush Creek bridge at Holmes,and proceed by an easy grade diagonally to 51st and Troost.

We would prefer to get this extension as a matter of civic pride, reasonable demand and manifest right,rather than enter the lists as agitators, or swell the ranks of those who gain concessions by loud protests and noisy outcries.Nevertheless there is sufficient earnestness back of this request to court,if necessary,public clamor.

Our position is not that of other parts of the city,where an extension both directly and indirectly,affects only the residents of that particular district.When Rockhurst College is established parents of every Catholic parish in the city will send their sons there;and they will justly expect that there will be proper facilities for reaching the place.

Six months before Rockhurst opened its doors, Fr. Dowling wrote to the Metropolitan Railway Company imploring them to fulfill an earlier promise to extend the Troost Avenue streetcar line at least to 53rd Street. His worst fears would come true on the morning of September 15, 1914, the first day of classes, when a downpour that started in the middle of the night would not let up until about 9 a.m. The steep grade up Troost hill made travel impossible, and had it not been for the Marlborough line running down The Paseo, the 42 boys who braved the storm would never have arrived for that first day of classes. After years of much pleading, finally, in September 1917, the Metropolitan Street Railway Company established service up the Troost Avenue hill, all the way south to 55th Street. Now, streetcars ran directly in front of campus, giving Rockhurst a direct connection to downtown and other parts of the city. Courtesy of Rockhurst University Archives.

As Rockhurst entered the 1920s, the floors in Sedgwick Hall would be oiled, the large entrance parlor painted, a new boiler added, and a portion of the basement excavated for a lunchroom, where business for the "first class" food was brisk, *The Sentinel* reported. New pews had been donated for the chapel, more books for the library, and new electric light fixtures installed in the classrooms and corridors. Even the old Peers' farmhouse and the church building constructed on campus in 1909 had been painted white.[51]

Things were humming in Rockhurst Parish, as well, where talk centered on various sites for a new church and parochial school. The Horigan property at the southeast corner of 53rd and Troost seemed to be the prime candidate, but in April 1918, Bishop Thomas Lillis purchased the northwest corner of Troost and 53rd Street, where St. Francis Xavier Church and School eventually would be built. The parish was growing so rapidly that by September 1923 it would count 350 families within its borders, nearly 100 of whom had arrived in that spring and summer alone.[52]

Father Dowling's keen eye in selecting the campus site so far south of downtown was beginning to bear fruit. It had taken years and much pleading, but finally, in September 1917, the Metropolitan Street Railway Company established service up the Troost Avenue hill, all the way south to 55th Street. Now, streetcars ran directly in front of campus, giving Rockhurst a direct connection to downtown and other parts of the city.[53]

The Sentinel staff as early as 1921 began to reflect on how far the school had come in such a short time. "When Rockhurst first opened, and the first Freshman class came plodding up the hill, the surrounding sight that greeted him is far different from that which passes before our vision today," the paper said. In the old days—before the streetcars ran up the Troost Avenue hill—students left the cars at 48th Street and walked up "a much used dirt road" to Brush Creek, which they crossed on "an old log," the

Sedgwick Hall, 1920. One year before the graduation of the first college class, all floors of the school's only building were in use, trees and shrubs had been planted, and the trolley line had been extended south on Troost Avenue from Brush Creek to 55th Street. Courtesy of Rockhurst University Public Relations and Marketing.

reporter recalled. As a boy climbed the hill, "he saw on both sides of him large fields. In rainy weather it was impossible to make any progress on account of the mud."[54]

How times had changed. Not only did Troost now have streetcar service, but also the avenue was paved and a bridge had been erected over Brush Creek. The neighborhood was growing, too. By 1919, 4 new houses stood north of the school and 4 apartment houses between 50th and 51st streets. By late 1921, houses were springing up so rapidly south of campus that *The Sentinel* had trouble keeping track of them. Forest, Tracy, and Virginia avenues were being paved, and a new grocery store and drug store stood at 51st and Troost.[55]

— Darker Days —

Even as Rockhurst grew, darker days set in—World War I, the influenza pandemic of 1918, and the deaths of a number of Rockhurst pioneers, including Michael Dowling.

Father Dowling's health had begun failing even before Rockhurst opened its doors in 1914. There had been surgery in St. Louis for stomach cancer in December of 1913. The doctors told Dowling there was no hope for recovery, but he pressed on nonetheless.[56] The next spring and summer, as Rockhurst worked feverishly to complete the first floor of Sedgwick Hall so it could start classes in the fall of 1914, Father Dowling was so weak that he had written to the provincial: "I am not physically able to take care of that job." When construction was in its earlier stages, he said, "I used to go out there nearly every day, consuming the best part of half a day in doing so." He hadn't minded then, he said, because if he hadn't met a streetcar on the way from his St. Aloysius quarters at 11th and Prospect, he simply would walk the 4 miles to Rockhurst. "But my days of strenuous life are

PRESIDENTIAL PROFILE

— ALOYSIUS ANTHONY BREEN, S.J. —

Father Aloysius Breen, second president of Rockhurst, was born in Chicago on September 1, 1867. A graduate of St. Ignatius College, he entered the Society of Jesus on August 11, 1890, at Florissant. Breen's two younger brothers, Paul and Frank, followed him into the Society. He studied philosophy and theology at Saint Louis University and was ordained in 1903. After tertianship at Florissant and a year as minister in Detroit, Fr. Breen was appointed as treasurer of St. Mary's College in 1906, then as president in 1907. From St. Mary's he came to Rockhurst to teach theology. At Fr. Michael Dowling's death in 1915, Fr. Breen became president of Rockhurst College. He served as President until 1918 when he left to manage the Jesuit sodality magazine, *The Queen's Work*, in St. Louis. He later became president of Regis College (1926-1931), treasurer of John Carroll (1931-33), and treasurer of Xavier (1933-1953).

In 1957 Fr. Breen was awarded the St. Francis Xavier Medal by Xavier University. The citation noted his "warmth of human understanding and wonderful good humor as priest, educator, administrator, religious superior, and spiritual counselor." Alumnus Luke Byrne, '22, described Breen as "comforting and consoling . . . a nice person all around . . . a person that you would be glad to be considered a friend." Fr. Breen died on January 12, 1960 in Cincinnati at the age of 93.

over," he wrote in March 1914, "and you will have to enlist some young blood in the cause."[57]

Father Dowling had lived to see Rockhurst open that September of 1914, but just a few months later he was admitted to St. Joseph's Hospital, where he died in the wee hours of Saturday, February 13, 1915, after a 2-year struggle with a malady the Woodstock letters described as "a malignant ulceration of the bowels."[58] His death had come quietly, with his 2 sisters at his side, Mrs. Anna New, of Cincinnati, and Mrs. Joseph Hempfling, of Kansas City. Just the week before, their brother James Dowling, who also was a Jesuit, had died in Chicago. Like Michael, James had attended St. Xavier College in Cincinnati, and then entered the novitiate at Florissant. James was 66; Michael was 64.[59]

The Monday following Michael Dowling's death, there had been a eulogy, led by Bishop Thomas Lillis, at St. Aloysius Church, the pews filled to overflowing and people standing in the street. Then a funeral procession had followed Father Dowling's body to Union Station, where it was placed on a train bound for Omaha. Rockhurst's second president, Aloysius Breen, and a delegation of 30 gentlemen from Kansas City boarded the train and accompanied the body to Omaha, where it arrived late in the evening at St. John's Church. There, it lay in state until the following morning, relays of Creighton University alumni acting as a guard of honor until close to midnight.[60]

Michael Dowling was much loved in Omaha, where he had spent 14 years as president of Creighton. "Father Dowling is credited with the principal share in the upbuilding of Creighton university," the *Omaha Sunday Herald* wrote that weekend. "Since he has been in Kansas City, Rockhurst college, a Jesuit institution, has been built there as a result of his efforts." The newspaper recalled how, on the eve of his departure for Kansas City in 1908, "the students of the university thronged the art's auditorium to bid him farewell." When the Creighton Alumni Association and many prominent citizens insisted on hosting a farewell banquet, Father Dowling had protested and begged the group to give the banquet instead as a form of reception to the college's new president, Father Eugene A. Magevney, who had arrived the day before.[61]

As Bishop Lillis had noted in his eulogy, Father Dowling was an unselfish man. He was laid to rest in Omaha's Holy Sepulchre Cemetery on Tuesday morning, February 16, 1915, "near the spot where a tall shaft of stone marks the last resting place of Mr. John A. Creighton, the faithful friend with whom Father Dowling had labored so many years for such noble, fruitful and enduring purposes."[62]

How sad that it would be a few years later in Kansas City when parishioners at St. Francis Xavier, far from recognizing Father Dowling for his work in founding Rockhurst and the parish, were complaining that he had hired his brother-in-law to build the parish church, even though his brother-in-law's bid was $500 higher than that from another contractor. The stink was odorous enough that letters had flown between then-president John A. Weiand and former president Aloysius Breen. "Did you ever hear this report? Is there any truth in it?" Weiand asked Breen, who did not know the answer, so passed the question along to Michael Ryan, who had been transferred from St. Mary's College to Rockhurst in those early years and now was serving in Cincinnati.[63] Yes, Ryan responded, Father Dowling's brother-in-law, a Mr. Hempfling, had built the church. As to whether there were any other bidders, Ryan did not know, and as to listing the costs of various projects before his arrival in Kansas City, he could not. "I was told to keep accounts from the day of my arrival and not to bother about previous transactions. And I did as I was told," he told Weiand. He did remember that the salaries of the 2 sisters teaching in the parish school had not been paid and the burden of finding a way to pay them had fallen on him.

"When I arrived from St. Mary's with 35 cents in my pocket, that represented all the cash to the credit of Rockhurst church," he told Weiand, and then added: "Reports of the great progress you are making at Rockhurst reach us now here. It is consoling to know this—for I assure you that my years there were anything but pleasant."[64]

Breen, too, had been around in those difficult days and shook his head at the lingering rumors over the $500. "Rockhurst owes so much to good

In a letter dated October 31, 1914, benefactor Lee Sedgwick enclosed a check for $500 to establish the Dowling Medal in honor of Father Michael Dowling, S.J., founder of Rockhurst College. Wishing to remain anonymous, the source of the funding is described in the 1915 catalog only as "a friend of Rockhurst College." The medal was to be awarded to the "student of the College who shall deliver the best speech in public debate." Luke J. Byrne was the first recipient of the award. The medal depicted in the photo was won by Caitlin Beller in 2008. Photo by David Spaw.

Father Dowling that it is a great pity his name should be brought into this discussion in such a disagreeable way," he told Weiand, and suggested that the issue be solved by turning $500 in Jesuit funds over to the parish.[65]

Another man who had lived through those difficult times also remembered the "great many years of hard work" that Father Dowling had put in to found Rockhurst College. He was the eccentric Lee Sedgwick, who resolved not to disparage Dowling's name, but to honor it. Just months before Dowling died, Sedgwick wrote a letter, dated October 31, 1914, calling for creation of "The Dowling Medal," to be awarded each year in honor of the Rev. M.P. Dowling, S.J. With his letter, Sedgwick enclosed a check for $500 to help complete the first college building, but added the stipulation that the interest on the money was to be used each year for the medal.[66]

The college honored its pledge to Sedgwick, and soon, as Rockhurst College began establishing its traditions, "The Dowling Medal" would be awarded every year by the school's Debating Society. As the college's first academic year of 1917–18 got under way, Father Schwitalla also honored his pledge to the provincial in St. Louis—that he would teach the entire curriculum. However, the other promise he had made—that Rockhurst's first college class would have at least 15 members—went unfulfilled. It would have only 11,[67] a fact the provincial overlooked, perhaps because of the circumstances in the world at the time.

Chapter Six

The Young School Moves Forward 1917–24

The United States entered World War I on April 6, 1917—just weeks before Rockhurst graduated its first high school class. The stage in the gym had been beautifully decorated for the occasion that June as the first graduates listened to an address from Bishop Thomas Lillis and accepted congratulations from the 22 priests who had gathered from across the city.[1] Within months of that happy day graduates Joseph Horigan, the doctor's son who lived across the street from Rockhurst, and Edward Kavanaugh, the working-class boy who had earned his board by firing the Sedgwick Hall boilers, had enlisted in the armed forces. So, too, had so many other Rockhurst boys, among them Patrick Mason, Edward McCarren, Jasper Messina, Roger Curtin, and John Leonard, all of whom had marched up the muddy hill and enrolled at Rockhurst on that first rainy morning when the school opened in 1914.

Joseph Horigan (right), the first student registered at Rockhurst and a member of the first graduating class of the high school, was one of 54 Rockhurst students who served in the First World War. The photo was taken at Naives, near Bar-le-Duc, France. Courtesy of Rockhurst University Archives.

Anyone passing by now on Troost Avenue could see that Rockhurst had raised a service flag to honor its soldiers. Eleven blue stars—one for each man—stood out on a pure white background, surrounded by a blood red border. By May 1918, the flag had added 4 more stars, including one for Charles B. Allen, Rockhurst's football coach. By October, the student newspaper listed 35 names on Rockhurst's "Roll of Honor," and before the war was over, there would be 54 stars.[2]

Before enlisting, Coach Allen had led weekly military drills on campus, a regimen that Rockhurst, thinking Congress might call for compulsory military training in all the nation's high schools, instituted on its own in January 1918. Allen and his assistant, a Capt. Williams of the Seventh Regiment of the Missouri National Guard—better known as the Kansas City Home Guard—marched the boys in columns and squads. They had no uniforms

In support of the war effort, the April 21, 1919 issue of The Rockhurst Sentinel *advertised the sale of Victory Liberty Loan bonds. The ad was paid for by the Jones Store Company. The sale of bonds was only one of many ways that Rockhurst students and faculty made sacrifices during World War I. Courtesy of Rockhurst University Archives.*

or guns, but the Cadet corps, as it was called, conducted 2-hour weekly drills and were making plans to turn the grounds behind Sedgwick Hall into a honeycomb of trenches—a practice ground for the art of digging.[3]

When the government called for the nation to conserve coal, Rockhurst did its part by postponing classes for 2 days. When the government launched its Thrift Stamp Campaign, asking citizens who could not afford Liberty Loans to buy the 25-cent saving stamps, Rockhurst set its quota at $300 and got behind the campaign, urging students to "Lick a Thrift Stamp and Lick the Kaiser."[4]

The Rockhurst Lecture Club gave a speech about Joan of Arc, illustrated with 121 stereopticon slides, and donated the $205 in proceeds to the Red Cross. The student newspaper, *The Junior Sentinel*, urged students to do their two bits for the war campaign—and thus get people to point to Rockhurst "as an example of patriotism." When the Department of Agriculture said it needed 75 million more bushels of wheat to feed troops in Europe and called for a half million young men to help on farms during the summer, *The Sentinel* urged students to answer the call by volunteering to help on farms during the summer.[5]

For all the patriotic fervor displayed at Rockhurst, World War I would serve as a reminder that the tiny college—with only 12 students[6] enrolled in classes for the fall of 1918—did not yet measure up to the American college standard. The reality had hit home the previous August when the draft age was lowered to 18 (from 21), and the government formally inaugurated the Students' Army Training Corps (SATC), a program combining military and academic training for young men of college age. Trainees on 525 college campuses nationwide would sleep on army cots, eat in mess halls, and be under the command of military officers, all with the intent of finding young men with leadership potential. As historian Philip Gleason explains, those who passed muster would be sent on for further officer training; those who did not would be remanded to a basic-training cantonment.[7]

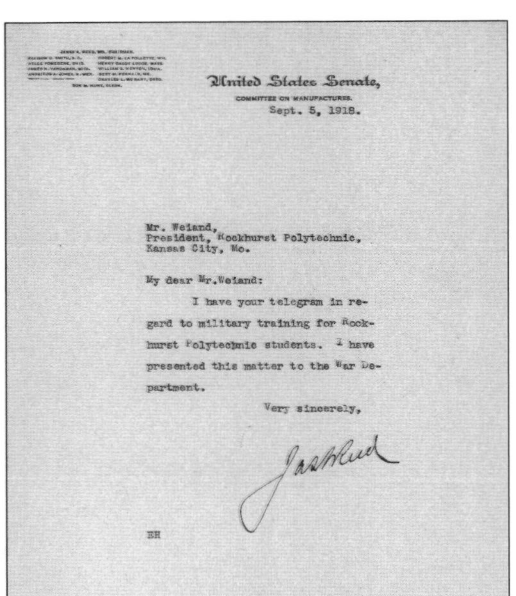

United States Senate,
COMMITTEE ON MANUFACTURES.
Sept. 5, 1918.

Mr. Weiand,
President, Rockhurst Polytechnic,
Kansas City, Mo.

My dear Mr. Weiand:

I have your telegram in regard to military training for Rockhurst Polytechnic students. I have presented this matter to the War Department.

Very sincerely,

Jas A Reed

EH

Because the national Students' Army Training Corps program required a school to have 100 college students for eligibility, President John Weiand wrote to Senator James A. Reed suggesting that Rockhurst combine its enrollment with that of Polytechnic to meet the required number. When his request was denied, Fr. Weiand encouraged students to "transfer to St. Mary's College," which had a SATC program. Eventually, 20 young men did transfer to St. Mary's for the duration of the war. Courtesy of Rockhurst University Archives.

Exactly at noon on October 1, 1918, 140,000 student recruits were sworn in simultaneously across the nation. Rockhurst, however, was not a part of the ceremonies because it lacked the requisite 100 students to establish a SATC unit. Students from other Catholic colleges were well represented, however, including 3,108 from colleges in the Missouri Province.[8] The Students' Army Training Corps exemplified the standardization so characteristic of the modern era. Colleges would

PRESIDENTIAL PROFILE

— JOHN A. WEIAND, S.J. —

The Rev. John Weiand, S.J., became Rockhurst's third president in the summer of 1918, succeeding Fr. Aloysius Breen. Fr. Weiand, born in Milwaukee on May 31, 1871, entered the Society of Jesus on August 5, 1890. He studied at Marquette University and Saint Louis University. He was ordained in 1905. While teaching at Loyola University, Chicago, Weiand was appointed president of St. John's College, Toledo, Ohio in 1911. He remained there for 7 years before coming to Rockhurst in 1918, where he served as president until 1924. After leaving Rockhurst, Fr. Weiand worked in Jesuit high schools in Cincinnati and St. Louis for the next dozen years. In September 1936 he went to the Church of the Gesu in Milwaukee as an assistant pastor.

Father Weiand was described as possessing an "inexhaustible supply of ardor [that] was confined largely to fulfilling duties . . . to which he gave all he had." In his 6 years at Rockhurst, Fr. Weiand oversaw an addition to Sedgwick Hall and the construction of Dowling Hall, the first building exclusively for the college. The first graduates of Rockhurst College received their degrees during Weiand's presidency, as did the first recipient of an honorary degree from Rockhurst, Marshal Ferdinand Foch. Fr. Weiand died on March 25, 1937.

Quote from *The Province News-Letter* (October 1937).

have to meet standards, too, and as Rockhurst's exclusion from the SATC program proved, the little college on the hill did not yet make the grade.

— A NEW PRESIDENT —

In the summer of 1918, a new president arrived—the Rev. John A. Weiand, S.J., who set about improving the Jesuits' residence and beautifying the campus. That summer, the Rev. Aloysius Breen, S.J.—Rockhurst's second president—had moved to the pastorate of St. Aloysius Church downtown, and soon after New Year's Day of 1920 was transferred to St. Louis to be on the staff of the *Queen's Work* magazine.[9]

John Weiand had been president for only 2 months when the national Students' Army Training Corps program was established—and Rockhurst left out because it lacked the necessary 100 college students. Undeterred and probably not wanting Rockhurst to be perceived as a "slacker" school, Weiand wrote to authorities in the nation's capital, asking to establish a SATC unit at Rockhurst. When his request was denied, he called the faculty and the tiny student body together to discuss what Rockhurst should

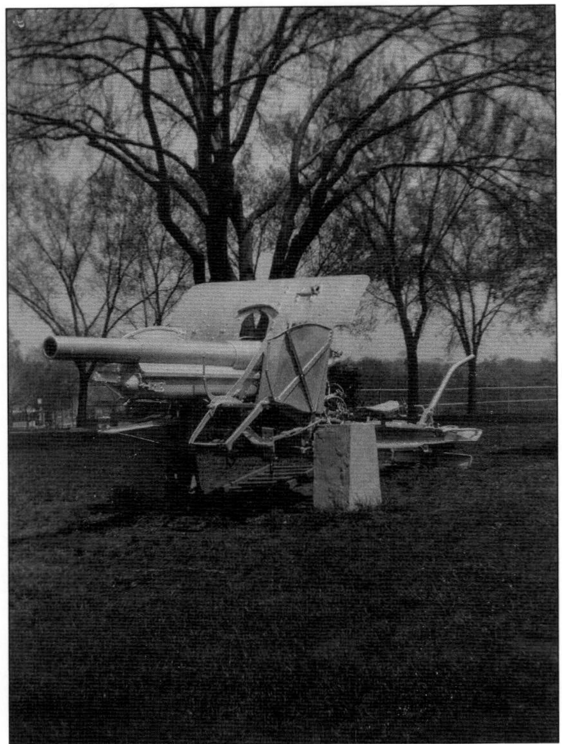

In 1919, this captured German cannon was awarded to the Federal Reserve Bank of Kansas City for its exceptional role in subscriptions to the Victory Liberty Loan bonds. In October 1921, through the leadership of benefactor Jo Zach Miller, Jr., the cannon was loaned to Rockhurst and placed under the flagpole at the northwest corner of Sedgwick Hall. With changing attitudes toward war and symbols of war, Rockhurst sold the cannon in 1972 to a Mr. James C. Smith of Overland Park. The Federal Reserve Bank released its title to the cannon, and Smith had it placed behind the armory in Independence. In 1978 he donated it to the Liberty Memorial Museum where it now remains. Photo by Charles Brenneke. Courtesy of Rockhurst University Archives.

do because a number of students apparently wanted to enter the program.[10]

In what could have proved disastrous for Rockhurst's fledging college program, the boys, at Weiand's suggestion and with his blessing, decided to leave Rockhurst for a SATC program under way at another Jesuit college, St. Mary's College in St. Marys, Kansas. Rockhurst and St. Mary's, of course, had strong ties going back to Rockhurst's earliest days. It was from St. Mary's College that Father Michael Ryan had left his teaching duties to come to Kansas City to help oversee the construction of Sedgwick Hall, and it was from St. Mary's where Aloysius Breen had come when he was tapped to be Rockhurst president. Father Weiand also had served on the faculty there.

Father Weiand, who was intent on building Rockhurst up, organized a college Alumni Association the next day after he arrived. It was during a special meeting of the Alumni Association, called for September 7, 1918, that Weiand explained President Woodrow Wilson's message about the formation of the Students' Army Training Corps and told the group that it was impossible for Rockhurst to meet the requirements. "Hence Fr. Weiand suggested that the boys in a body attend one of our colleges to which the corps had been attached," the note taker at the Alumni Association meeting wrote. "After a discussion it was generally agreed upon to attend (Creighton University in) Omaha."[11] At another special meeting called for September 23, however, Weiand announced that he had received word from St. Mary's College that the government had established a SATC unit there. "Fr. Weiand suggested that the boys, though they were free to choose any school—should choose St. Mary's." He told the boys that their "parents ought to be taken into consideration" and since St. Mary's College was only 90 miles from Kansas City, the parents could visit frequently. A vote was taken, and 17 boys chose St. Mary's. Three chose Creighton, but later changed to St. Mary's, as well. "All agreed," the note taker wrote, "to leave for St. Mary's on Monday."[12]

It was a proud, but sad day indeed, when the Rockhurst boys gathered at Union Station that Monday morning of September 30, 1918, to catch the train to St. Mary's. "Mothers and friends of the brave boys were there and proud of their young soldiers going away," *The Sentinel* reported. When someone in the crowd yelled: "What does the angry mob say?" an answer came immediately back: "Go get 'em."

"Get whom?" the leader shouted back.

"Get the Hun."

"Who said so?"

"Everybody."

"Who's everybody?"

"Rockhurst!!" came back the strong reply.

It was a call-response learned on the Rockhurst football field.[13]

Fewer than 2 months after the boys had departed for St. Mary's, the

First World War ended. "Peace at last!" *The Sentinel* declared.[14] "Whistles screamed their joy, the bells rang out their gladness, and from a thousand, thousand throats came the exultant words: 'Peace at last.'...Parade followed parade through the business section of the city and the vast crowds on the sidewalk, from building to curb, applauded with shout and bell and the firing of guns."

Three years later, in what would become a familiar part of the Rockhurst campus, a 105-mm German cannon captured in the Battle of the Argonne by American soldiers of the 35th Division, American Expeditionary Force, was loaned to Rockhurst by the Federal Reserve Bank of Kansas City, of which longtime Rockhurst benefactor Jo Zach Miller, Jr. was an officer. Rockhurst President Weiand thanked Miller kindly, and the cannon was set up under the high flagpole on the north side of Sedgwick Hall, there to remain for many years.[15] The cannon stood as one more symbol of a college that was beginning to establish its traditions.

— A NEW ATMOSPHERE ON CAMPUS —

Americans entered the postwar era with a new sense of confidence and pride. Caught up in a new mass culture of leisure and consumption, automobiles, movies, radio, advertising, and chain stores were symbols of

— THE MERCILESS FLU —

The great influenza pandemic of 1918 reached Kansas City about the first of October and spread so rapidly that all schools and churches were closed on October 7, 1918, until further notice. At St. Aloysius Church, the priests moved Masses outside to the church yard and took charge of the spiritual welfare of sick and dying soldiers at St. Luke's Hospital. Rockhurst's Father John Knipscher did the same, visiting soldiers and sailors in the 7 local hospitals. On the Rockhurst campus, John Zweisler of *The Sentinel* staff caught the bug the following March and was confined to his home for two weeks. Word came soon after from Chicago that Father Hoffend, a member of Rockhurst's first faculty, had caught the "merciless 'flu'" and died. Hoffend had taught French for 2 years at Rockhurst but now was serving at Chicago's Sacred Heart Church. Those still on the faculty were not immune. Fathers Knipscher, Ehrhard, and Diener, as well as Brother Brzosteck all took sick.

Schools finally were allowed to reopen in mid-November, but then another scare closed them again in early December. Before year's end, Rockhurst student Daniel O'Flaherty would be counted among the number who died during the pandemic. The influenza had played havoc on the Rockhurst High gridiron, as well, where so many boys had become sick that the team was only able to get in 3 games the entire season. A student play scheduled for March 3, 1919, also was canceled and so many classes that the boys were forced to attend on Saturday to make up for all the sick days.

Sources: *The Rockhurst Sentinel*, January 20, 1919, March 3, 31, 1919, May 28, 1919, December 23, 1920; Harvey, *History of Rockhurst College*, p. 34; and Domestic Journal, St. Aloysius folder, Rockhurst University Archives.

the new secular values that defined the United States of the 1920s. This trend greatly disturbed some Americans, and cultural and political conflict would become evident in new laws that restricted immigration and instituted Prohibition.

By 1929, 93 American cities—Kansas City among them—would have a population of more than 100,000. Many Americans, be they old-stock Protestants or more recently arrived immigrant Catholics, worried about a decline of moral values. Religious tensions boiled between modernists who tried to reconcile their beliefs with scientific discoveries such as evolution and traditionalists who favored a literal interpretation of the Bible. Crusaders such as Billy Sunday preached at open-air revivals, and Protestant ministers stood in their pulpits, denouncing the easy morals and patterns of modernity.[16]

The situation for Catholics was different, historian James Hennesey writes. Though by no means all, many Catholics shared in the possibilities of the times. Still somewhat isolated from the American mainstream, Catholics had a new sense of pride, buoyed by their contribution to the war effort, and missed no opportunity to trumpet their patriotism and their religion. Catholic war heroes such as King Albert of Belgium and Cardinal Désiré Mercier, whom the Germans had placed under house arrest for his outspokenness against the Belgian occupation, visited the United States, where they were toasted by Catholic bishops and Catholic universities.

Rockhurst made a coup when it was privileged with a visit from none other than Marshal Ferdinand Foch of France, the war's Allied supreme commander. It was Foch who had turned the tide of the war when he stopped the advance of German forces at the Second Battle of the Marne in July 1918. And it was Foch who had accepted the German surrender.

In November 1921, Marshal Foch was among 5 prominent wartime commanders, as well as then-Vice President Calvin Coolidge, who came to Kansas City for the dedication of the future site of the Liberty Memorial, Kansas City's towering remembrance to those who had died in the war, as well as to the principles of liberty and freedom. The $2 million memorial shaft with its eternal flame was financed through a citywide fund-raising campaign that had climaxed in 1919 with a door-to-door campaign. Then, on Tuesday, November 1, 1921, in an elaborate spectacle that coincided with the national convention of the American Legion being held that year in Kansas City, 100,000 people crammed the street between Union Station and the memorial hillside, adorned with a temporary altar and rostrum. There stood Foch, Coolidge, and a foursome of military brass—the American General John J. Pershing, Italy's General Armando Diaz, Britain's Admiral David Beatty, and Belgium's Lt. General Baron Jacques. They looked out over the crowd, cannons fired, laurel wreaths were laid, and a band played. It was the only

In 1921, 5 prominent wartime commanders came to Kansas City for the dedication of the future site of the Liberty Memorial. In attendance (L to R): Lt. General Baron Jacques (Belgium); General Armando Diaz (Italy); Marshal Ferdinand Foch (France); General John J. Pershing (USA); and Admiral David Beatty (Great Britain). It was the only time that these main Allied leaders ever appeared together in one place. Marshal Foch, who had accepted the German surrender, received the first honorary degree awarded by Rockhurst College. Courtesy of Missouri Valley Special Collections, Kansas City Public Library, Kansas City, Missouri.

On November 2, 1921, Marshal Ferdinand Foch arrived at Rockhurst College for a Requiem Mass, celebrated by Bishop Thomas Lillis, for Foch's son, who had lost his life in the First World War. Foch himself had attended Jesuit schools in Tarbes, France, and his brother was a Jesuit priest in France. Following the private Mass, more than 800 invited guests greeted Foch and saw him receive the Doctor of Law degree, the first honorary degree awarded by Rockhurst. Courtesy of Rockhurst University Archives.

time that these main Allied leaders had appeared together in one place.[17]

The following day, at 5 minutes after 9, a caravan of automobiles filled with military officers and Secret Service men pulled up in front of Rockhurst's Sedgwick Hall. Marshal Ferdinand Foch himself stepped out, and, with military step, walked to the entrance steps, where Rockhurst President John Weiand, S.J., and members of the faculty were standing, waiting to welcome him. They made their way then through crowded halls to the chapel in Sedgwick Hall, where the marshal was seated in a front row pew with one of Rockhurst's priests at his side. Bishop Thomas Lillis emerged and began the Requiem Mass, celebrated for the repose of the soul of Foch's son, who had lost his life in the First World War. "The distinguished visitor had arranged beforehand that this opportunity be afforded," *The Rockhurst Sentinel* reported.[18] Marshal Foch had insisted on a private reception, unattended by the public masses. It was a Catholic affair for a man who apparently had deep faith. Foch had attended Jesuit schools in Tarbes, France, and his brother, Germain Foch, was a Jesuit priest in France.

Following Mass, Foch received visitors in the parlor, shook hands with faculty and clergy, and, immediately afterward, entered the college auditorium to a thunder of applause. The auditorium overflowed with 800 invited guests—friends and patrons of Rockhurst, as well as parents of students—all eager, *The Sentinel* wrote, "to catch a glimpse of the hero of the world." He sat on the stage, flanked by the bishop and Father Weiand, and, behind them, a guard of honor composed of prominent Kansas City Catholics. Here, the honorary degree of Doctor of Law was conferred on Marshal Foch by the college, and the diploma presented by Bishop Lillis. This, *The Sentinel* wrote, was the first public honor given to Foch by any educational institution in the United States.

Before the degree was presented, Rockhurst President Weiand gave a short speech, an interpreter at his side: "This day will ever be memorable in the history of Rockhurst College, for we have with us Marshal Ferdinand

Foch, a man of truly Christian greatness," Weiand said. "In him are conspicuous the simple life, simple ways, dislike for mere display and show. In this age of advertisement he has shunned publicity. He has rarely been interviewed, and his statements to correspondents have been the epitome of briefness....We find him at the zenith of his power, kneeling in humble prayer before the altar of the Lord of Hosts, begging for light and strength to fulfill the task which the world had committed to his charge...."[19]

During the breakfast that followed, Foch mentioned a huge sheath of roses he had noticed on the communion rail in the chapel and requested that they be placed on the Blessed Mother's altar. "The old soldier is still a loyal sodalist and a true knight of Mary," *The Province News-Letter* noted.[20]

— A Religious School —

That Marshal Foch was "a loyal sodalist and a true knight of Mary" spoke to the popularity of devotional Catholicism in the postwar years. It was, historian Jay Dolan writes, a time when the popularity of the novena reached its peak and when Mary enjoyed a resurgence.[21] The Sodality of Mary, established in the sixteenth century by the Jesuits in Rome, experienced a resurgence in the 1920s and 1930s. These religious trends were apparent at Rockhurst, which, in the 1920s and 1930s, still enrolled only a few non-Catholic students.

Rockhurst College graduated its first class on June 16, 1921.Degrees were conferred on Joseph Zachary Miller, III, Master of Arts; Patrick W. Mason, Bachelor of Arts; and Vincent J. O'Flaherty, Jr., Bachelor of Arts. Courtesy of Rockhurst University Public Relations and Marketing.

Rockhurst students went to Mass, searched their souls at yearly retreats, and joined, nearly one and all, the Sodality, where they discussed Catholic teachings and followed up with good works.[22] At one Sodality meeting, *The Sentinel* reported that the entire student body was present and took communion. Faculty members sang the Mass. What a gratifying sight it was, the newspaper reported on another occasion, "to see so many youths go up to the altar and there make their Act of Consecration." On Ash Wednesday, holy ashes were distributed and confessions heard before every First Friday. One Christmas Eve the Sodality sent two boxes of clothing to Holy Rosary Mission and another Christmas sent two truckloads of garments to St. Monica Colored School. The Sodality also raised donations for the missions as twentieth-century American Catholics expanded their horizons beyond the parochialism of the nineteenth century. In February 1920, for instance, Rockhurst students privately collected $20 in "penny collections" and sent the money to 4 missions in British Honduras.

Over the next 2 decades, members of the Rockhurst Sodality would distribute books and Catholic literature around Kansas City, as

The Jesuits of Rockhurst and St. Francis Xavier Church, 1920-21. Back Row, Left to Right: Rudolph Bohn, Bro. David Shaughnessy, Leonard Otting, Raymond Walsh, Henry Sullivan, Bro. Martin Hagerty. Middle Row, Left to Right: Fr. William F. Fitzgerald, Fr. Patrick Harvey, Harry Crimmins, Fr. Henry Ehrhard, Bro. Michael O'Rourke, Fr. John Bankstahl. Front Row, Left to Right: Fr. John Kuhlman, Fr. William Martin, Fr. John Kokenge, Fr. John Weiand, Fr. Thomas Nolan, Fr. John Knipscher. Courtesy of Rockhurst University Archives.

well as setting up 8 catechetical centers, staffed by volunteers. So many college men were volunteering during the 1930s that then-Rockhurst President Daniel Conway praised the students for taking Catholic teachings to "the Negroes, the Mexicans, the Italians, and the orphans of the city."[22]

These were the poorest of Kansas City's people. Italians and other Catholics from southern Europe had emigrated to the United States in great waves at the turn of the twentieth century, just as Irish Catholics had in the nineteenth century. Mexican immigration surged after 1910, when the Mexican Revolution broke out. By the 1920s, nearly 500,000 Mexican people had come to the United States and, of course, most were Catholic. In Kansas City, Our Lady of Guadalupe Parish was started in 1914, the same year that Rockhurst opened. It also was during these years that African-Americans, seeking employment in the new factories of the North, were migrating in huge numbers from the South. Relatively few African-Americans, however, were Catholics. In Kansas City, the number was about 2 percent of the black population—small, but enough to establish a parish—St. Monica Parish, which opened in 1910 with 30 parishioners.[23]

Most established Kansas City Catholics were, like the new Catholic immigrants arriving each day, still members of the working class, but over the generations, many Irish had moved into the American middle class. It was middle-class boys, many with home addresses in the area south and west of the college, who distributed Catholic literature and volunteered to evangelize in the new immigrant parishes.

The movement of Southern black people and the arrival of new immigrants in America gave rise to nativist sentiments and the growth of the Ku Klux Klan. The Klan, as historian Jay Dolan writes, had a long list of enemies, but Catholics were at the top. Hostility evident during the 1928 presidential campaign of the Catholic Alfred E. Smith, who was the grandson of Irish Catholic immigrants, brought reminders of the hateful ways of the Know-Nothings and the American Protective Association of the past.[24] By and large, however, Catholics moved on, viewing themselves, Dolan writes, "as the moral conscience of the nation." Bishops and priests publicly condemned birth control, divorce, and morally suspect movies. To Catholic intellectuals, Catholicism was more than a religion or a creed, it was a culture, and one that educators meant to ensure was presented at the Catholic college, a goodly number of which were run by the Society of Jesus.[25]

— Rules from Rome —

Against this background of moral purpose and sundry attacks on the Catholic Church came the rumblings of authority, emanating all the way from Rome, where Jesuit General Wlodimir Ledóchowski, S.J., was looking closely at the Society's colleges and universities in the United States and finding much that needed correcting. He had distributed a questionnaire to all the American Jesuit institutions, and, when they were returned, he studied the replies long and hard. In a 12-page letter dated June 7, 1928, and sent to every American Jesuit college, including Rockhurst, Ledóchowski spelled out his concerns and his recommended remedies, emphasizing at the start that he was aware of "the great difficulties" faced in "the struggle for Catholic Higher Education" in a Protestant country like the United States.

The issues Ledóchowski addressed—from the lack of a religious spirit on campuses, to the use of non-Catholic textbooks, to the enrollment of women, and what he regarded as the overemphasis on athletics—were topics that would challenge Jesuits at Rockhurst over the next half century. At the top of Ledóchowski's list was the admittance of non-Catholic students. "I do not think that they should be admitted unless with extreme care and discrimination," the Father General wrote. This was especially true, he said, "where there is little or no hope of conversion," which, he added, "is the case in most instances." He chastised American colleges for failing to make a "systematic attempt" to at least bring these students "nearer to the Catholic faith." The crucifix should be placed in every classroom, he admonished, and if any student objected, then his presence was "undesirable" in a Catholic institution.[26]

Non-Catholic professors were an issue, as well. "The large number employed in our schools seems to be unwarranted," Ledóchowski wrote. He directed all superiors "to take steps at once" to secure Catholic teachers in college departments. And, he insisted, they must not be Catholics in name only, but in practice. He begged to differ with college officials who insisted that non-Catholic teachers did no harm. "I have received frequent reports to the contrary," he said, noting comments from American bishops who had visited him in Rome. They had told him of statements made by these non-Catholics that were "either directly contrary to faith or morals, or at least of such an equivocal nature as to be quite out of place in a Catholic institution."[27]

But where, Rockhurst President John Weiand must have thought, was the little school on the hill supposed to find Catholics highly trained enough to teach the modern sciences and new courses emphasizing commerce and finance? While Rockhurst enrolled no more than 4 or 5 non-Catholic students during the 1920s, a glance at the Rockhurst College catalog for 1932–33 is testament to the problem of finding qualified religious to teach the sciences. Rockhurst's biology, chemistry, physics, and mathematics courses all were being taught by non-Jesuits. Even if the men were Catholics, they had been educated at secular schools. August M. Meulemans, assistant professor of biology, had attended the University of Wisconsin and currently was working on his dissertation through the University of Cincinnati. Chemistry professor Vanston H. Ryan was a graduate of the University of Kansas, and physics and mathematics professor Paul V. Ryan was an Iowa State and Chicago University alum.[28]

This diploma was one of 3 awarded at the first graduation ceremony of Rockhurst College in 1921. The recipient was Pat Mason. Courtesy of Virginia Mason Waters.

The Father General recognized the problem of finding qualified science teachers but insisted that something must be done. "I propose," he wrote, "that Rectors immediately begin to establish a fund which can be used to afford graduates of exceptional ability an opportunity for special studies, with a view to developing future professors.…a foundation for such a purpose would be an excellent investment and would in a relatively short time yield returns." If lack of money to pay them a sufficient salary was the chief difficulty, then a similar fund must be established for that purpose, he insisted.

All well and good, Weiand surely thought, but Rockhurst had no endowment fund for its own needs, let alone a foundation to educate and attract teachers. The college's financial strain was great, and its lack of accreditation a constant concern. Rockhurst's financial records for 1923–24, in fact, showed a deficit. Income for both the high school and college was $22,809.50, while expenses were $37,822.19—a deficit of more than $15,000. Besides that, Rockhurst was carrying a debt of $152,191, which demanded an annual interest payment of $8,315.50.[29]

And truth be told, many students were attending Rockhurst at reduced rates or paying nothing at all of the annual tuition bill, recently raised from

1923 Rockhurst College basketball team. Courtesy of Rockhurst University Archives.

$80 to $100. "Such charity, as Religious men, we cannot very well refuse to practice," future Rockhurst President Arthur Spillard, S.J., would say. "A student turned away because he could not afford the required tuition… might mean a loss to the priesthood, or even to the Faith."[30] Even as finances lagged, enrollment soared. On October 17, 1921, *The Sentinel* reported the largest enrollment in Rockhurst's history—319 students. Among them were 45 boys registered in the college department, 32 of whom were freshmen. "This is a record that we can be proud of, considering that Rockhurst is now starting her eighth year," the newspaper wrote. With 32 new college freshmen, *The Sentinel* said, Rockhurst "can now feel confident that her mission in this community is started on the highway to its fulfillment."

According to *The Province News-Letter*, enrollment in Rockhurst's college department increased steadily throughout the 1920s: from 10 in 1920, to 46 by 1923, to 85 by 1926, and 159 by 1929. Even after the stock market crashed and the years of the Great Depression set in, Rockhurst enrollment continued to rise—to 172 in 1931 and 209 in 1932. With the addition by then of night and Saturday classes, the total college enrollment in 1932 stood at 266, though it would take time for the number of actual graduates to catch up.[31] "Each year the enrollment grows and new demands are made on its faculty for increased facilities," *The Jesuit Bulletin* reported.[32]

For Rockhurst's first 8 years, the yet unnamed Sedgwick Hall did double duty, housing both high school and college classes, including the all-important science laboratories, shared by both. Sedgwick also held Rockhurst's administrative offices, its chapel, gymnasium, and lunchroom, not to mention serving as a residence for the Jesuits.

— NEW ADDITIONS —

As early as 1922, Rockhurst dreamed of creating an endowment fund and erecting a substantial building just for the college, but it would be years before such things became possible. But still, with enrollment on the rise, college President John Weiand felt he needed to do something. According to Rockhurst historian Hugh Owens, Weiand was an energetic man, deeply interested in the welfare of the college. He was highly respected in education circles, having served as president of St. John's College in Toledo, Ohio, and had made a host of friends, whom he turned to now.[33]

In the summer of 1923, probably with the help of friends and with money from the sale of 2 Rockhurst lots, he oversaw an addition to Sedgwick Hall. A single-story space that housed the school's kitchen, workrooms, and storerooms, was raised two stories to correspond with the rest of the building. When finished, the Jesuit living quarters had an additional 6 private rooms and a few badly needed guestrooms. A rec room was added, and the school library, now overflowing with books, was relocated to the new wing. "The appearance of the building from the Paseo will also be greatly improved by this addition," *The Province News-Letter* said.[34]

The addition to Sedgwick Hall followed an even larger project the summer before, when Weiand had scraped together enough money to build a small, 2-story brick building facing Troost Avenue. Named Dowling Hall, it stood north of Sedgwick Hall and across Rockhurst Road. Weiand made clear that Dowling Hall, constructed in the summer of 1922 at a cost of $18,000, was intended only as a temporary solution until a new, "college building proper" could be erected.[35] There was talk that summer of building a new Science Hall, too. When that day came, *The Province News-Letter* said, Dowling Hall would be converted into a dormitory, a need that already was apparent. Out-of-town students were few, but with no dormitory, they were living in the private homes of nearby Catholic families.

In the summer of 1922, President Weiand oversaw the construction of Dowling Hall, a 2-story brick building situated at the northeast corner of Troost Avenue and Rockhurst Road. Weiand intended the building to be only a temporary solution to a space problem until a new "college building proper" could be erected. For the first time, Rockhurst's collegians had their own space, separate from the high school boys. Dowling Hall was razed in 1999. Courtesy of Rockhurst University Archives.

Hopeful as the plans sounded, a "college building proper" was years away, and Dowling Hall would end up serving as Rockhurst's main college building for the next 15 years. Science classes continued to be taught in the laboratory on the third floor of Sedgwick Hall, and the library, chapel, and gymnasium continued to do double duty, as well, for high school and college boys alike.[36]

— A SYMBOL OF IMPORTANCE —

Temporary building though it was, the erection of Dowling Hall was a huge symbolic step for the college. Dowling Hall—to be used only by the college—contained 4 classrooms on the first floor and 2 on the second, as well as an assembly hall and biology lab. An office for the dean was situated on the first floor, and in the basement was the heating plant, a cloakroom, lavatory, and, importantly, a clubroom with a pool table for the college men. For the first time, Rockhurst's collegians would have their own space, separate from the younger boys.

The importance of this comes through in an essay written by collegian Frank Meyer, Class of '24, and published in *The Rockhurst Sentinel* of October 30, 1922. The college men were "greatly pleased" with the new building, Meyer wrote, and noted that "a new atmosphere" already was apparent on campus.

"There are certain characteristics...which distinguish a college from a high-school," Meyer explained. "Take for example a boy in his first year away at college. His letters are filled with descriptions of his new life, of the general tone of his new surroundings, and their difference from high-school days. He is made aware of a higher and an entirely different atmosphere. This can hardly be expected to exist unhindered in a building with younger boys."

Frank Meyer went on to describe his view of "a true college." Besides scholastic enthusiasm and religious fervor, it must have, he said, "a certain amount of social activity," and, of course, athletics. To this young man, Dowling Hall offered the promise of all that. "Can we not now see what Rockhurst is endeavoring to accomplish?" he asked. "Is not the design of the new building evident? And, with a faculty of men whose whole life is devoted to such enterprise, the goal cannot be far distant...We hold conclusive proof that there will one day be a great college in Kansas City."

That Rockhurst was looking to a bright future was everywhere apparent. On November 2, 1923, a Boosters Club was organized after a Sodality meeting. "The first requisite to belong to it is DOING for Rockhurst," minutes of its founding say. "Eligibility is universal, open to all students; however, academic standards are maintained....a student is expelled from the club the moment he is found wanting."[37]

"DOING" for Rockhurst was key in these early years when the college was trying to establish itself in Kansas City and gain accreditation. The occasional gift arrived, including a Gardner automobile donated by a downtown businessman and $100 given to Father Gettelman so he could buy wall maps for his history class. Many more books were donated to the library, including a 1,200-volume acquisition from the estate of a Mr. G.O. Huling. The estate included beautiful sets of Dickens and entire issues of the *Spectator*. Another $5,000 for the science department came from Jo Zach Miller, Jr. and $10,000 from Mr. Thomas C. Bourke, given in memory of his brother, Lt. Wilfrid Corrigan Bourke, who had died in an airplane accident. The money soon would be used for an athletic field, which would complement 2 recently built tennis courts and replace a cinder straightaway for the track team.[38]

Father Weiand, interested in beautifying the college grounds, had encouraged the generous and hardworking Jesuit Brother David Shaughnessy in his efforts to level the hilly campus.[39] Surely, a beautified campus would help gain the attention of a Kansas City that had never seemed to pay much heed to the little school that had built way out on the southern edge of town. But now, in the first half of the 1920s, single-family homes were going up at the fastest clip in the city's (and nation's) history. South of Rockhurst, bungalows already stretched to 63rd Street. The Armour Hills subdivision, with its modestly priced homes in the $8,500 range, would open in 1922, and between 1926 and 1930, a string of high-rise apartment buildings went up to the west and south of J.C. Nichols' new Country Club Plaza, a mile or so from the Rockhurst campus. The housing boom peaked in 1925 when Kansas City counted 3,645 single-family housing starts, a local record that would stand until after World War II. In 1924, there were more than 2,600 housing starts, and, in 1926, almost 2,200. The wealthy Sunset Hill and Mission Hills subdivisions had been laid out earlier in the century.[40]

It was during these boom times, in December 1925, that Rockhurst consultors sat down and outlined a "Contemplated Program of Rockhurst College" with the express purpose of establishing a foundation, looking to build, clearing debt—and becoming accredited by the North Central Association of Colleges and Secondary Schools.

— The North Central Association —

The North Central Association (NCA) was formed in 1895, a time when groups from doctors to lawyers to educators were looking to professionalize by setting standards and forming organizations. The NCA was not the first accrediting agency for schools. New England had one as early as 1885 and the Middle Atlantic States by 1892. The Southern Association was set up a few months after the NCA, whose authority centered on schools in the Midwest. All, historian Philip Gleason writes, "concerned themselves with the problem of articulation between secondary and collegiate institutions." The process culminated in 1900 with formation of the College Entrance Examination Board.

The NCA took a quantitative approach to education, evaluating colleges by criteria such as the number of students per teacher, the cubic feet per student in each classroom, the expenditure per student, and the number of hours of subject matter taught. This stress on the quantitative, with its emphasis on electives, units, and credit hours, symbolized, Gleason writes, "the process of bureaucratic rationalization that was reshaping higher education," a process clearly linking modernization and secularization. In 1913, just a year before Rockhurst opened its doors, the NCA issued its first list of approved colleges and universities. To graduate, a student would need 120 semester hours of college credits, and the college, to be accredited, was required to have at least 8 departments in the arts and sciences, each with at least one full-time professor holding a master's degree; an adequate library and laboratory facilities; and a productive endowment of $200,000 if, like Rockhurst, it was a private institution. Tellingly, only one Catholic college, Notre Dame, made the NCA's first list.[41]

Catholics responded to the new challenges of quantitative education by forming, in 1899, the Association of Catholic Colleges in the United States, which defined the purpose of higher education as forming "citizens for the city of God" while fitting "them for the business for life." In 1904, the association became part of the newly created Catholic Education

Association, which joined three separate Catholic groups in the hope of bringing Catholic educators together to exchange information and ideas, and it didn't take long to see the wide division that existed. Most Catholic educators favored a liberal education and scorned the elective system, though others pointed to the unwillingness to change as a sign of Catholic backwardness. It would take until 1915 for the CEA (which became the National Catholic Educational Association in 1927) to get on the modern bandwagon, adopting standards that required 128 semester hours as "a minimum for graduation" from college. In addition, it said the "standard" Catholic college must have at least 7 departments, each with a full-time professor holding a college degree or its equivalent, as well as other requirements regarding library holdings, laboratory equipment, teaching loads, and maximum and minimum credit-hour loads for students.[42]

In 1918, when the CEA published its first list of approved colleges, Rockhurst could not even dream of being on it. The college was still in its infancy and had yet to graduate its first college students, let alone meet all the new requirements. It had been more than 30 years since the Missouri Province of the Society of Jesus, in 1887, had drawn up its "Course of Studies," which set forth the Jesuits' classical course, which alone led to the baccalaureate degree. It demanded studies in philosophy, rhetoric, poetry, and humanities. Readings in Latin, Greek, and English were specified in detail, while history, elocution, physics, and chemistry were simply "accessory branches." As Gleason explains, learning Latin made sense when the *Ratio* originally was drawn up in the 16th century because mastery of Latin was a prerequisite to careers in the church, medicine, law, and government. In the 19th century, when Latin no longer had a utilitarian purpose, Jesuits still argued for its importance, citing its cultural value and mental discipline.[43]

Although Latin would continue to be important at Jesuit schools, big changes came to the Missouri Province when the conservative Provincial Rudolph J. Meyer (1907–12) was replaced by one more progressive (Alexander J. Burrowes, followed by Francis X. McMenamy). In 1920, the Missouri Province accepted standardization, and, as Gleason puts it, with "the zeal of new converts" issued a 61-page *Report* laying out a structure for

Students of the high school and college, 1920-21. Courtesy of Rockhurst University Archives.

education that soon would be reflected at its colleges, including Rockhurst. In the *Report*, Jesuits of the Missouri Province adopted the semester-hour system, with 128 hours as the graduation requirement. There would be 3 degree programs: A.B., B.S., and Ph.B, with 2 years of Latin, but no Greek, required for the A.B. The *Report* also made provision for electives, grouped as "majors" and "minors." As Gleason explains, the *Report* instructed college administrators how to lay out a college catalog, then went on to list a possible 21 departments, from astronomy to Spanish, with some 200 numbered courses assigned a value in credit hours. Unremarkable as the catalog might seem today, it was, in fact, Gleason writes, "a startling innovation that symbolized in its very format effective abandonment of the *Ratio*." Because the educational model was rationalized, departmentalized, and bureaucratic, it amounted to the modernization of Jesuit undergraduate education.[44]

With these new standards in mind, Rockhurst consultors sat down in the academic year 1923–24 to figure out what action Rockhurst must take if it ever were to meet the criteria. Bottom line, it was going to take money. The consultors made a to-do list, topped by the need "to sell the idea of Rockhurst College to wealthy citizens" for miles around. The consultors determined to conduct a letter-survey to determine the "educational forces at work" against the Catholic Church and the Catholic college in the Kansas City area. Once they had a handle on the "false philosophies" being taught elsewhere in Kansas City and environs, they were sure they could offer "an indispensable source of uplift to this whole section of the country." They would ask wealthy Catholics what part they were willing to play in that goal. They stated their intentions to become "a First Class College, to demand attention and to hold prestige," all necessary if Rockhurst were to attain accreditation.[45]

Rockhurst students already had been enlisted in the campaign to help Rockhurst grow. At the final school assembly on May 8, 1924, they were urged to accept a new slogan: "One new boy for every student." The Jesuits said they would help by supplying the names and addresses of good prospects.[46] Many of those "good prospects" undoubtedly lived in the St. Francis Xavier Parish, once considered on the outskirts of town, but now at the center of a Kansas City expanding so rapidly to the south that, by 1932, 4 other parishes existed south of St. Francis Xavier—St. Augustine, St. Catherine's, St. Peter's, and St. Teresa's—all cut out of territory that originally belonged to St. Francis Xavier.

— SAINT FRANCIS XAVIER PARISH —

The need to enlarge the parish church was apparent as early as 1922, when a new pastor, Father Michael Leary, arrived. The original St. Francis Xavier Church, now bursting at the seams, still stood on the Rockhurst campus, where Father Michael Dowling had built it in 1909 when the parish was home to perhaps a dozen families.[47] How times had changed. During Father Leary's first year at St. Francis Xavier, the parish nearly doubled in size—from 135 families in the summer of 1922, to 250 by the summer of 1923. Four Masses were being celebrated, but the need for a fifth was apparent. A new parochial school was added in the fall of 1922 for a neighborhood described as "young and vigorous." The school was built on the west side of Troost Avenue, across the street from Rockhurst, on land purchased by the diocese in 1918. As the number of religious women who taught there grew with the student body, a convent also was built on the grounds, in 1924.[48]

But disaster struck the next fall, on September 19, 1925, when a fire of undetermined origin destroyed the original frame church, which stood on the east side of Troost, at 53rd Street, facing Forest Avenue. The church burned early on a Saturday afternoon, following that morning's 8 a.m. Mass. The old frame structure, fueled by a south wind, had gone quickly, but thankfully, no one was injured seriously, although timber from the steeple had fallen on a fireman.[49]

After the fire, St. Francis Xavier Parish dreamed of building a great new church on the model of St. Ignatius Loyola in Chicago. The diocese offered Rockhurst $12,000 for a 150-foot by 300-foot plot of campus land south of Sedgwick Hall, on the northeast corner of 53rd Street and Troost Avenue. Long discussions followed with the bishop as the Rockhurst Jesuits demurred, insisting they could not accept $12,000 because the land was worth $22,000 and "the college could not afford to make a present of $10,000 to the Parish, especially as the College is not able to pay even the interest on its heavy debt." A compromise finally was reached, and in January 1926 the bishop paid Rockhurst $17,500 for the piece of land.[50]

But after all that, a church never was built on the east side of Troost Avenue. Worried about the financial resources of St. Francis Xavier's Father Leary, the bishop advised putting off plans for the church. Instead, he instructed the parish to settle, for the time being, on building a temporary church—a parish hall—on the west side of Troost, adjacent to the parochial school and convent.[51] A year would pass before construction started on the new stone and brick church, and, until it opened in 1927, services were held in the basement of the parochial school. St. Francis Xavier pastors, who always had lived with the Rockhurst Jesuits in their Sedgwick Hall quarters, continued to do so until 1929, when Father Leary oversaw construction of an addition to the rear of the new St. Francis Xavier

HONOR ROLL
ERECTED BY THE ALUMNI 1917 AND 1918
IN HONOR OF THE ROCKHURST STUDENTS WHO
GAVE THEIR SERVICES IN THE GREAT WORLD WAR 1914-1918.
EARL J. BOUGHAN
EDMUND J. BYRNE
LUKE J. BYRNE
JOSEPH F. BYRNES
FRANCIS X. CARROLL
ARTHUR A. CLIFFORD
JOSEPH V. CRANE
JOHN V. CROWE
ROBERT F. CURTIN
ROGER C. CURTIN
EDWARD W. DOERR
CHARLES H. DUNN
THOMAS R. FINN
ARTHUR A. FORSTER
MARION A. GRIFFIN
WILLIAM J. GROOMS
RICH'D F. HANRAHAN
LEO J. HEINZ
JOSEPH D. HORIGAN
LEO J. HULSEMAN
RAY. F. HULSEMAN
J. EDWARD JOY
EDW. V. KAVANAUGH
GEORGE L. KORTY
JOHN P. LEONARD
LOUIS J. LUCAS
JOHN G. LYNCH
EDW. W. McCARREN
J. CLEM. McCORMICK
FRED. J. McDONALD
THOMAS F. McGRAW
CHARLES A. McKENNA
EDWARD D. McKIM
MARTIN A. MANGAN
PATRICK W. MASON
JASPER MESSINA
EDWARD J. MORRIS
NORBERT F. MUDD
ROBERT M. NEWELL
VIN. J. O'FLAHERTY JR.
STEPHEN J. POWERS
M. AUGUSTINE RYAN
HERBERT A. STEWART
JOHN B. SPENCE
GEORGE W. SUTTER
PATRICK A. TREAR
JOSEPH D. TRIPP
THOMAS X. VAILE
FRANK P. WALSH JR.
JAMES F. WALSH
JOHN F. WALSH
EDWARD J. WELSH
MATT. J. WILLIAMS
SANDFORD M. ZWART

The Rockhurst Alumni Association raised money to purchase a bronze memorial in honor of all Rockhurst men who served in the First World War. The tablet, displayed in the Troost entrance of Sedgwick Hall, was dedicated in a ceremony on March 18, 1920. Courtesy of Rockhurst University Archives.

Church, comprising several offices and 3 private rooms as living quarters. The parish, with many of its families coming from the old St. Aloysius Parish, boasted the largest parochial school in the diocese, and by the early 1930s numbered 650 families.[52]

— PUBLICIZING THE COLLEGE —

Efforts to publicize the tiny college in the midst of this astounding growth included a new Thursday lecture series given by prominent men of the city. On January 17, 1924, Mr. J. O'Sullivan, manager of the United Press syndicate, gave a lecture on the workings of the UP, and another Thursday, E.C.L. Wagner, a consulting engineer and graduate of Yale University, spoke on the requirements of becoming an engineer.[53] The Rockhurst Alumni Association, organized on June 25, 1917, in the high school, grew with Rockhurst and eventually took steps to publicize the college. Its first large endeavor was the casting of a bronze memorial tablet to honor all the Rockhurst men who had served in the First World War. The tablet, at a cost of $232, was cast at The Michaels Art Bronze Company in Cincinnati and shipped to Rockhurst in time for its dedication during a ceremony in the gym on March 18, 1920. To raise the necessary $232, the association planned to assess a $5 fee on all its members except those who had gone overseas in the war. And they planned entertainment. An elaborate dance was held on October 22, 1919, at the Knights of Columbus Hall, 32nd and Main streets, when 200 couples had taken the floor for the grand march.[54]

In a coup for Rockhurst, the famous magician Houdini gave an address in the college gym on October 30, 1923. Houdini denounced spiritualists and demonstrated how they performed their deceptions. He told students that he believed in God but did not believe that spirits perform physical acts.

The alumni hosted dances at the Catholic Woman's Club at 1018 Walnut Street and, in 1920, began holding a reception for graduating seniors. That June, when the high school had 241 students—25 of whom were about to graduate—the Alumni Association decided to entertain them "royally," with the express purpose, of course, to get them to join the association, which was hurting for members.[55]

In a bigger publicity coup for Rockhurst, the famous magician Houdini gave an address in the college gym on October 30, 1923. The "master of mystery" denounced proponents of spiritualism, a belief, he said, that he once held, but now, after an investigation of 25 years, knew was practiced "by miserable crooks." He held out a challenge of $5,000 to any spiritualist who could "do anything I can't explain, duplicate or have duplicated." For Rockhurst students, he displayed picture slides showing noted spiritualists at work and then demonstrated their subterfuges. "They were all tricksters," he said, admitting that he was a trickster, too, though what he did was accomplished by natural means. "I am a great sentimentalist," Houdini said, "but I don't believe spirits do physical acts.... I believe in God and that my sainted mother is waiting in another world."[56]

— PRIVATE WORRIES —

These efforts to publicize Rockhurst, along with the new college building and the added wing on Sedgwick Hall, were steps in the right direction. Excited as the college men were with the new Dowling Hall, college President John Weiand privately feared that it was far from enough. It would be hard, he thought, for Rockhurst to get even its first 2 years accredited by the North Central Association, let alone recognition as a 4-year college. "We are meeting great difficulty in our college because we are not accredited," he wrote to the provincial on July 9, 1924. Too few students was one concern, but the bigger matter, he said, was "our lack of a good college building and Biology Lab facilities."[57]

Father Weiand had tried to set up an endowment for the college, but his efforts had fallen far short. On November 14, 1922, he called a special meeting of the Alumni Association, where he outlined a plan, "which was quite new to most of us," minutes of the association state. The plan, in brief, was that the alumni establish an endowment fund of $200,000, "which was to be accomplished by 200 of its members taking out endowment policies of $100 each, making the college the beneficiaries." The annual premium on each would be $10, which would run for 10 years. "At the end of the ten years the fund would be invested by the college, and the interest thereof be used for purchasing books for the library," the minutes state. "This plan met with the hearty approval of all present."[58]

Dr. Purcell took the lead by appointing 20 team captains to solicit pledges of the Alumni Association, which had 125 active members and another 280 who were eligible. But it was slow going. By the next spring, only $528 had been paid into the endowment fund and promises made for another $460. A disappointed Father Weiand spoke again before the Alumni Association, "suggesting that new life be put into the drive by the captains and that the failure of the drive would be a disgrace to the alumni." Autumn arrived, but with it no improvement.

At another Alumni Association meeting on October 12, 1923, poorly attended as it was, Father Weiand expressed sorrow at the lack of interest and once again urged the association "to interest itself in student affairs and continued work on the endowment fund." When 2 months passed and still nothing changed, association vice president Jim Walsh stood up at a meeting on December 10, 1923, and declared it "a disgrace the way the drive had lapsed" and called on every alum to do his part. The problem apparently hinged on a misunderstanding of the uses of the endowment fund. Many apparently thought the college could use the money in any way it pleased, though, in fact, the fund belonged to the Alumni Association, which had stipulated that the money could be used by the college only to buy books. Despite the many scoldings and pleadings, by February 1924, the fund still amounted to a meager $640 with a first year's interest payment of $34.50.[59]

In the summer of 1924, in his final days as Rockhurst president, Father Weiand turned to Saint Louis University, asking whether it would be possible for Rockhurst to affiliate its college department with SLU. It would only be for a few years, he asserted, until Rockhurst College could enroll 100 students and build its hoped-for Science Hall. Privately, there was urgency in his voice: "Something must be done and soon," he said, knowing that Rockhurst was losing students because of its lack of recognition. As the new academic year started that September of 1924, Dean George Deglman noted in the daybook that nearly 50 percent of the old students had not returned. "Some of the old boys did not return because of lack of means, some have gone to other schools for professional work, some simply quit, one entered the novitiate," he wrote. "The fact that we are not accredited caused some applicants to stay away and also prevented a few old boys from not returning—four I know of." The problem reared its head again in January when 3 more students didn't return, one of whom had chosen to transfer to the Jesuits' St. Mary's College in Kansas.[60]

Father Weiand had done his best, even getting the father provincial to agree to the idea of constructing another, bigger college building. But the agreement had come with stipulations, the provincial saying that before Rockhurst could build, it would have to be certain it could cover the annual interest and raise $4,000 or $5,000 a year to pay off the capital. In a letter dated May 7, 1924, Weiand had sounded confident: "I am gathering friends and so far have been quite successful," he wrote. "I hope to get all I need."[61] He promised to show the provincial a building plan that could be forwarded for approval to Rome.

As his term as Rockhurst president was drawing to a close, however, Weiand's plans were suspended, and the

Registration, September 12-13, 1924. In this page from his diary, Dean George Deglman notes a decrease of nearly 50% in the return of students from the previous year. Too few students was a contributing factor to the lack of accreditation by the North Central Association. Conversely, as Deglman points out, the lack of accreditation caused some students to stay away. Courtesy of Rockhurst University Archives.

YEAR 1924-25
ROCKHURST COLLEGE

Sept. 12-13. Registration. 48 registered
these two days. Sept. 15, the number
was 58; Sept. 17, 61. There is an
increase very noticeable in the
freshman year. Last year the freshman
numbered 19, so far this year, 35.
Sophomore this year, 14, two of them
new ones; last year's sophomores 18,
only seven of whom returned; junior
this year 7, last year, 6, of whom fiv
returned. Senior 5, last year, 2.
New students up to date 38, old studen
23. A decrease of nearly fifty per cen
in the return of the old students.
Some of the old boys did not return
because of lack of means, some have
gone to other schools for professional work, some simply quit, one entered
the novitiate - L. McHattie. The fact
that we are not accredited caused
some applicants to stay away and also
prevented a few old boys from not returning - four I know of. Twenety five
of the new freshman are our high
school graduates; the rest come from
other high schools.

Sept. 15. Full opening of classes. No
recreation allowed in the building
during any of the class hours. Boys
encouraged to study when not in class.
The new students are a fine lot.
Promising football material. Mr. Mason
head coach, Mr. Ryan, assistant coach,
Father Knipscher, faculty director of
athletics. Classes begin at 8 o'clock.
This was due to two things, more
courses and the necessity to give more
subjects to some professors. Some boys

Rockhurst College's first football squad, 1923. The season included only 2 games, one against the alumni and another against the Olathe Mutes. A third scheduled game against The Hill Reserves was cancelled due to snow. It was not until the academic year of 1924-25 that the college played an official football schedule against other college teams. Courtesy of Rockhurst University Archives.

Society, on July 21, 1924, appointed a new president, Arthur D. Spillard, S.J., who seems to have arrived with a new agenda supported by the father provincial in St. Louis: to cut Rockhurst's curriculum to a 2-year program. In a letter Spillard wrote to the provincial soon after his arrival in Kansas City, he said he had decided to wait awhile before putting his plan into effect.

"With reference to the College—as much as I desired, and particularly since I knew I had your backing, to cut the Course to Junior Grade, I felt that it would not be altogether prudent to do so this year," he wrote on September 2, 1924, and then went on to list his reasons. "1. It would brand me an iconoclast in the minds of certain men from whom I expect to get financial aid; 2. It would point a critical finger at Fr. Weiand, who as a shrewd businessman seems to have won the confidence of very many men here; 3. Both Father Weiand and Father Deglman put forth strenuous efforts to get students since the close of college in June—thus appearances should be kept up for a time, and Fr. Deglman should be let down gradually, for the simple reason that his heart and soul have been deeply ambitious of accomplishing what seems to me an impossibility for the time being; 4. The Bishop needs to be prepared for the change—I have already in a mild way started in to convince him that a Four-year College is beyond the present educational development of Kansas City; that the most urgent need now is a flourishing high school, and that only thru such an institution can we hope to build up a supply-source of students for the college. . . ."[62]

Father Spillard had been in office for only a week when he turned to the University of Missouri, hoping the state university would accredit Rockhurst as a junior college. On a Wednesday, October 29, 1924, he and Dean Deglman made a special trip to Columbia, going with hats in hand. They spent 3 days in Columbia, pleading Rockhurst's case before returning to Kansas City that Friday evening. Two weeks later, on November 13, 3 officials from MU, at Spillard's invitation, arrived on campus to inspect Rockhurst College.[63]

"They came at our request to examine our college, with the prospective hope that they might find us worthy of recognition for the first two years," Deglman wrote in the college daybook on November 13, 1924. The committee, comprised of University of Missouri Dean Tisdel and professors Trenholme and Schlundt, stayed from 9 in the morning until noon, going into classes, visiting the science laboratory and library, and then staying for lunch before returning to Columbia. "I can only say that the inspectors from Missouri U. have been here, and departed seemingly satisfied with conditions in the different departments," Spillard wrote to the provincial after the visit. Then, he prayed to the Blessed Lady, St. Joseph, and the Angels. "If we are ever to get out of this mudhole," he said, "it is they who will pull us out."[64]

Months passed, but finally, on April 14, 1925, word came that the University of Missouri had decided to accredit Rockhurst as a junior college. This meant that Rockhurst students who wanted to transfer to MU or the University of Kansas after completing 2 years at Rockhurst could do so without having to take an exam to prove their proficiency. Though only its first 2 years of classes were accredited, students rejoiced, and Rockhurst continued to offer its 4-year course, though the last 2 years were not accredited.[65]

Chapter Seven

Inventing Traditions 1923–29

With the new Dowling Hall, temporary college building though it be, students began to work in earnest, as *The Sentinel* put it, to organize themselves "along lines that will lead to the development of a true 'College Spirit.'" By the fall of 1923, freshmen were wearing blue and white caps to designate their low status. The Jesuit faculty did not allow hazing by upper classmen, but reports of freshmen forced "to run the gauntlet" still made the pages of *The Sentinel*. Rockhurst now had 2 cheerleaders, and rallies were being called to practice "yells" and to "stir up more life." When the city's Loyalty Parade came around on April 30, 1924, Rockhurst's college men, for the first time, marched separately from the high schoolers, carrying "canes and colors." Rockhurst's own Earl A. Hapke was chosen mayor for the day.[1]

Rockhurst traditions were beginning to take root as a new "spirit of enthusiasm" was noticeable on campus. Students "are proud that they go to Rockhurst and are doing much to make it better known among their friends and the public in general," *The Province News-Letter* reported. "This spirit is being fostered not only by the Jesuit members of the faculty but also by our extern professors who are excellent teachers and loyal enthusiast 'boosters' of the school." On November 13, 1923, the faculty, for the first time, held a reception for all parents of students. Traditions such as the annual alumni-college basketball game and the annual Student Council homecoming dance took hold, and the annual retreat, obligatory for all Catholic students, already was a "landmark" of the collegiate year.[2]

ROCKHURST COLLEGE
ANNUAL RETREAT 1926
FRIDAY & SATURDAY, JAN. 29 & 30

8.40 Mass
9.15 Instruction
10.00 Recess in silence
10.15 Spiritual reading
10.45 Instruction
11.30 Lunch, recess
12.30 Instruction
1:00 Way of the Cross
1.15 Recess
1.30 Instruction and Benediction
(Saturday — Instruction and Confessions)

SUNDAY, JANUARY 31.

7.40 Communion Mass
8.30 Breakfast
9.15 Instruction etc. as on Friday
12.30 Instruction and Benediction

REGULATIONS FOR THE RETREAT

The strict observance of silence during the Retreat is an essential requirement for its success. No one is allowed to leave the college premises before the afternoon exercises. Spiritual reading is to be made privately. Suitable books are available in the library. Librarians: A. Harvey & W. Otterman.

Rockhurst traditions began to take root in the 1920s. The annual retreat, obligatory for all Catholic students, was a landmark of the collegiate year. The retreat became voluntary in the late 1960s. Courtesy of Rockhurst University Archives.

In short order, college students established a separate Sodality, a beefed-up debating society looking to compete with other colleges, and a Student Council reorganized with the college man John McManus at the helm. When the Student Council originally was organized in 1919, each high school class had elected 3 representatives while the college had had a total of only 3 representatives—understandable, considering that the entire college at the time had only 12 students. Pat Mason had been the council's first president, Vincent O'Flaherty its secretary, and John Hauber its treasurer. Among representatives from the high school had been one Henry J. Massman, who would figure prominently at Rockhurst during the 1950s.

Not much was heard from that first Student Council, but that all changed in the fall of 1922, when it went to work with enthusiasm and purpose. It appointed a publicity committee to "get Rockhurst in the daily papers," started to give dances, instituted an all-school picnic every spring, and, according to Rockhurst student John Jennings, provided "many humorous and interesting Kangaroo courts."[3]

The first annual picnic had been an all-day affair at Swope Park in June 1920. It had been "some picnic," *The Sentinel* reported, just "ask anyone who was there." Beginning at 9:15 a.m. sharp, cars enlisted to transport students had pulled away from campus. Twenty minutes later, boys set down the baskets of food packed by their mothers and like "speed demons" went as a bunch to participate in interclass competition, which began with a 50-yard dash. Next came a sack race, a three-legged race, and then the 440- and 880-yard dash, run on "the boulevards about the grounds." Classes competed in a tug-of-war and a ball-throwing contest, won by Matt Williams, with Bud Walter runner-up. "The little men in first year also threw the pellet," *The Sentinel* noted, "and Heinz proved to have the best wing." When it was time to eat, the baskets emptied "before a minute had elapsed, and all the fancy sandwiches and cakes and pies were gobbled up before you could say 'Jack Robinson.'"[4]

May 6th Picnic at Walsh's farm, Hickman Mills. Classes 9-11. then started in 10 autos for farm. Chd keg of near beer from Muehlebach's, indoor base-ball on lawn. Mrs. Walsh invited faculty for lunch. A most enjoyable time for all. Gentlemanly conduct on part of students.

In this page from his diary, Dean George Deglman reports on the annual student picnic, held at the James Walsh farm in Hickman Mills, on May 6, 1926. Deglman writes, "Mrs. Walsh invited faculty for lunch. A most enjoyable time for all. Gentlemanly conduct on part of students." Courtesy of Rockhurst University Archives.

The new Student Council continued this tradition, but by 1927 had moved the picnics to the James Walsh farm in Hickman Mills. All through the day different class baseball teams "fielded and drove long flies over the driveway in right field for three bases." The team called Freshman C "survived these grueling elimination contests" to claim the championship. There was an "excellent lunch," provided by the Student Council, "fictitious beer"—and bugs. "Between the time they spent separating bugs from the delicious potato salad, and eating the excellent lunch which the Student Council provided, or resting after the sixth bottle of fictitious beer, most of the picnickers played 'indoor'" for the rest of the day, *The Sentinel* reported.[5]

The Student Council also instituted a scholarship, gave the occasional "smoker," and, in the late 1920s and early 1930s, sponsored a basketball tournament, the teams comprising any students who wished to play.[6]

— DEBATE AND ORATORICAL SOCIETIES —

The college had had its Debating Society since the second semester of its first year, with one medal awarded for the best speech during the annual oratorical contest and another, the Dowling Medal, first donated by Lee Sedgwick, going to the best debater.[7] Debate, in fact, had been perhaps the most prominent activity in Rockhurst's first years. The Debating Society held its first gathering on May 14, 1917, just a month after the United States entered the First World War. Students had debated whether the government "should have and exercise unlimited control of the food prices." Debates often centered on questions of the day: Should Ireland be a free and independent nation? Should the United States join the League of Nations? Should the right of women to vote be established by constitutional amendment?[8]

"There was an intense interest in debating," recalled Thomas Divine, who was among the first 42 boys to enroll at Rockhurst and who would go on to become a Jesuit priest. "How well I remember upholding before the student body in 1917 the negative side of the proposition: "Resolved that the execution of Sir Roger Casement was justified."[9]

Now, with the possibility of competing against other colleges, there was renewed enthusiasm. A new debating society was formed in the fall of 1922 and was beginning "timidly" to try out "the capabilities of its members" when word came that a new Intercollegiate Debating Society of the Missouri Province had just formed and that Rockhurst was scheduled to compete in just a few weeks against Kansas' St. Mary's College and then Denver's Regis College. Rockhurst was told to argue the negative side of the question: "Resolved that it should be the policy of the United States to claim full payment of all debts owed her by the allied nations (in the First World War)." *The Sentinel* reported with a shudder that the Rockhurst team not only was "untried and without any traditions," but also hadn't even decided yet who was good enough to be on the team. Once that was decided, *The Sentinel* assured readers, the team would "settle down to good hard work in preparation for their first encounter with St. Mary's."[10]

PRESIDENTIAL PROFILE

— ARTHUR DANAHY SPILLARD, S.J. —

Father Arthur Spillard was appointed as Rockhurst's fourth president in 1924 and remained in that position until 1928. Born in Aurora, Illinois, on July 7, 1880, Fr. Spillard entered the Jesuit novitiate at Florissant in 1901. He was educated at St. Ignatius College, Chicago, St. Mary's College, and Saint Louis University. He was ordained in 1916. Prior to coming to Rockhurst, Spillard taught English at Saint Louis University High School, was prefect of discipline at St. Mary's College, and principal of the University of Detroit High School. After leaving Rockhurst in 1928, he returned to the University of Detroit High School as rector and as pastor of SS Peter and Paul's Church.

Fr. Spillard died on July 18, 1947, at age 67. The Chicago Province *Chronicle* (November 1950) noted this about him: "Whatever his assignments, he evidently subscribed to the divine wisdom of the saint's motto: Do what you are doing, and do it as if it were the only thing you had to do in life." During Fr. Spillard's time at Rockhurst, he worked tirelessly toward obtaining accreditation for the college. In 1925, the college did attain accreditation from the University of Missouri as a junior college, though Rockhurst continued to offer its 4-year course.

Rockhurst Song

Out where the fading sunset lingers
Low in the amber West,
Memory traces with golden fingers
A name that we all love best.
Round thy dear walls and lofty towers,
Rockhurst, our thoughts are hovering still,
Fresh as the fragrance of springtime flowers,
That bloom on thy verdant hill.

Chorus
Round thy banners proudly ranging,
Rockhurst we thy praises sing,
Loyal sons with love unchanging,
To thy feet our homage bring.
Through the mists of life's gray morning,
Star-like shines the thought of thee!
Thou our fairest hopes adorning,
Alma Mater, old R.C.

How like a castle rich in story,
High on the city's crest
Stands Alma Mater in youthful glory,
The pride of the golden west.
Far from thy portals life's ways may lead us,
Cordon of earth nor terrors of sea
Shall us dissever when thou shalt need us,
We're thine ever, old R.C.

Music by J.A. Kiefer, S.J.
Words by T.F. Divine, S.J.

Such were the humble beginnings of what, in time, would become a nationally recognized debating squad. Eventually renamed the Dowling Literary Society, members met every 2 weeks for debates or discussions, and a credit hour was given to all who attended faithfully. By 1928, Rockhurst had 2 debating societies, the Dowling Literary Society and the Campion Debating Society. The 2 competed in an annual public debate known as the Dr. T.S. Bourke debate; the best speaker chosen by civic judges won the Bourke Debate Medal. These early gatherings laid the groundwork, Rockhurst historian Sandra Scott Wilks writes, for the outstanding debate teams that would receive national attention in years to come. Over a 5-year period ending with the 1938 season, Rockhurst students participated in 143 debates—6 percent of them intercollegiate debates—and won 80 percent of them. In February 1933, for example, Rockhurst was one of 15 college teams competing at St. Benedict's College in Atchison, Kansas. Rockhurst won 5 of its 6 debates that day, including one with the University of Kansas.[11]

By 1934, Rockhurst was debating teams from local colleges, big and small alike—from St. Benedict's, William Jewell, Park, and St. Mary's, to the University of Kansas, Kansas State University, and Kansas City Junior College. Rockhurst debaters also took on prominent national schools, including the University of California, Stanford, Johns Hopkins, and, perhaps most competitively, Saint Louis and Washington universities.[12]

In addition to debate, a separate college elocution contest, known as the Oratorical Contest, was held every spring, in which students competed for the Kealy Medal, and later the Dowling Medal, founded by Lee Sedgwick and later funded by Mrs. Frank P. Walsh. Thomas Divine remembered these annual elocution contests fondly, too, recalling that they usually were won in Rockhurst's pioneer days by fellow student Brooks Hale, who, like Divine, went on to become a priest. The annual contests in the college gym were prominent affairs, often packing the house. The first one, on Friday night, May 17, 1918, was attended by 400 people. "This is the first time that ever such a feat was attempted at Rockhurst," *The Junior Sentinel* reported. Students in the college department had written the essays, and the best essay of the lot chosen for delivery in the contest. Pat Mason had delivered his speech on "The War and Religion"; Vincent O'Flaherty (the winner) on "Democracy, the Word of Life"; Luke Byrne on "The War and Catholicism"; and Louis Lucas on "Patriotism—Then and Now." In May 1920, O'Flaherty won the Dowling Medal, this time for his oration on "Father Damien, the Servant of the Lepers." In 1927, with the Catholic Alfred E. Smith running for president, there must have been hearty applause when Rockhurst student Edward Larkin stood up at the Catholic Community Club that May and delivered his speech, "Alfred E. Smith, Loyal American." Larkin won Dowling gold.[13]

It was during the oratorical contest in 1927 that the Rockhurst College Glee Club sang Rockhurst's first college song. Composed by Thomas Divine and set to original music by Father J.A. Kiefer, it received, according to the *Province News-Letter*, "a cordial reception."[14] The glee club, according to *The Rockhurst Sentinel*,[15] was formed "one morning last week (when) the

Prefect of Studies met several of the 'old boys' leisurely strolling through the first-floor corridor and asked them to step up to *The Sentinel* room to carry something for him. When they found out that they were expected to carry 'notes,' chagrin and despair surged up in their youthful frames.... They admitted, however, that they had been the victims of a good joke and resolved to keep quiet and quietly enjoy the fun. The good work went on and at the end of the second day a hundred and thirty had gone through the trying-out ordeal, sixty of whom were chosen to establish and maintain a name for Rockhurst in musical circles."[16]

It was on the night of another oratorical contest, in May 1920, that Mr. Bohn, the physics teacher, invited some of the boys up to the physics classroom to see an X-ray machine in action. "Nothing for it then, but that everyone there should take a look at his bones under the powerful rays of the X-Ray machine. When everyone was satisfied that his bones were all in place and that there was nothing at all the matter with them, Mr. Bohn got in a few words of explanation on the subject, and had a very attentive audience," *The Sentinel* reported.[17]

— The Student Newspaper —

Early issues of *The Rockhurst Sentinel* are filled with news of the oratorical and debating squads, their topics, and victors. *The Sentinel* first appeared in 1917 as a publication of the junior class in the high school, thus its first name, *The Junior Sentinel.*[18] Its beginnings were humble. The first issue, dated November 27, 1917, was only 4 pages—a plain, mimeographed sheet 8-1/2 by 11 inches. The newspaper was typewritten until March 4, 1918, when it began to appear as a printed edition, usually of 4 pages, though the graduation issue that year was 16 pages. Beginning with the fall term of 1918, the paper changed its name to *The Rockhurst Sentinel,* and later still, in 1946, to *The Hawk*. In 2000, the name was changed back to *The Rockhurst Sentinel.*

The newspaper, preserved in hard copy and on microfilm in Greenlease Library, is a testament to the parochial atmosphere that existed at Rockhurst in the school's earliest days. The first reporters at *The Sentinel* not only listed newsy items such as the 1918 schedule of the Debating Society, but also little repartees on individual students. "What Never Happens," one headline read, then went on in good humor to list them: the vain Hayde "passing an hour without consulting a mirror"; the pugnacious Gaffney "starting a scrap with a man his own size"; the loquacious Crowe "with his mouth closed"; or Mike Ahern "with a shave."[19]

By the early 1920s, issues had become sporadic, and the paper ceased publishing altogether in the fall of 1924 when advertisements and circulation lagged. The paper was revived in December 1926 under George McLiney, who was Rockhurst's correspondent for *The Kansas City Journal-Post.*[20] Thereafter, its fortunes improved.

In 1932 *The Sentinel* entered the College Newspaper Contest for the first time, and 2 staff members placed. The next year, 1933, it was given an all-American ranking from the National Scholastic Press Association for newspapers of its class, scoring 880 of a possible 1,000 points, as well as

The student newspaper was an important part of Rockhurst from its inception. By the late 1920s, the paper was publishing not only stories of local interest to the college, but editorials on national and international issues. The May 16, 1928 issue of The Sentinel *(right) is typical, editorially weighing in on atheism in America, taking up the issue of financial support for women's colleges in America, and praising Kansas City for its efforts to plant trees throughout the city. From the 1930s on into the 1950s, the paper won national awards in competition with other collegiate newspapers. Courtesy of Rockhurst University Archives.*

ROCKHURST SENTINEL

VOLUME TEN — KANSAS CITY, MISSOURI, MAY 16, 1928 — NUMBER SIXTEEN

SEVEN SPEAK FRIDAY FOR DOWLING MEDAL

Winning Orator Will Get Award Given This Year by Mrs. Frank P. Walsh

The annual oratorical contest of the Dowling Literary Society will be held Friday night at 8 o'clock in the college auditorium. There will be seven speakers.

The Dowling medal, donated this year by Mrs. Frank P. Walsh, in memory of the Rev. Michael P. Dowling, S. J., founder of Rockhurst college, will be awarded to the winning orator. Edward P. Larkin, a senior, received the medal last year.

The names of the speakers and their subjects are, Edward P. Larkin, "World Peace;" Lawrence J. Coleman, "An Evil and Its Remedy;" John F. Halpin, "The Dictator of the Mediterranean;" John A. Lally, "Qualities That Make a Leader;" Paul F. Moore, "Louis Pasteur;" Joseph M. Sheehy, "Catholic Higher Education," and William L. Rossner, "The Man of the Hour."

The judges will be Vincent J. O'Flaherty, Jr., Patrick H. Slattery, and Joseph E. Hogan.

LOCAL DEBATE TEAMS MEET HERE MAY 25

Dowling and Campion Clash in Auditorium—Bourke Medal at Stake

After the Dowling medal has been pinned on the bosom of one of the seven speakers in the oratorical contest next Friday night at 8 o'clock in the auditorium, most of the contestants will turn at once to new themes.

On the following Friday, May 25, at the same hour and in the same place, there will be a public debate between members of the Dowling and Campion debating teams.

The subject under discussion will be: "Resolved, That the United States should cease to protect by armed force private capital invested in foreign fields except after a formal declaration of war."

The debaters for the affirmative are, James E. Burke, Edward P. Larkin and Bernard J. Muller-Thym; for the negative, Lawrence J. Coleman, Paul F. Moore and William L. Rossner.

A gold medal for the best speaker in debate is awarded annually by Dr. T. S. Bourke. The winner will be announced immediately after the decision of the judges. The medal will be presented at the commencement exercises.

INDIAN LECTURER TELLS "STORY OF THE ATOM"

"The Story of the Atom" was the subject of a one hour talk by Chandoo N. Shah of Bombay, India, to the college students and the members of the third and fourth years of high school Monday morning.

Mr. Shah, a native-born Indian, is a former student of Chicago university. He held a fellowship there from 1925 to 1927.

In his lecture, which has been given at Northwestern university, Loyola university, St. Louis university and Chicago university, Mr. Shah outlined very briefly the speculations of philosophers, chemists and physicists on the nature of the atom and said that it has now been demonstrated that the atom is made of tiny particles, protons and electrons.

The protons and electrons, which have opposite charges of electricity, exist around a nucleus. The atom is not solid, but hollow, to a great extent, for the protons and electrons are relatively far from the nucleus.

HOLD SCHOLARSHIP EXAMS IN HIGH SCHOOL SATURDAY

The annual examination for the scholarships to Rockhurst academy will be held Saturday, May 19. Boys graduating from the parochial schools of greater Kansas City are eligible to take the examination.

Four scholarships will be awarded, one for four years, one for three years, one for two years, and one for one year.

GOLDREN CAULDRON DINNER POSTPONED

Will be Held a Week From Today At the Newbern Hotel

The time and place of the Golden Cauldron fraternity dinner for the college graduates of this year have been changed. It will be held on May 23 at the Newbern hotel. Previous plans had been for the dinner tonight at the Mission Hills Country club.

Al V. Van Hee, one of the organizers of the fraternity, said the change was made in order that all college alumni might be notified and invited to the dinner.

Frank L. Davis, president of the Kansas City chapter, has announced that there will be no lengthy speeches at the dinner. The few speakers have been warned not to prepare lengthy discourses.

The toastmaster will be James G. Walsh, a graduate of last year.

The membership of the Golden Cauldron is taken from the Arts and Science graduates of all Jesuit colleges throughout the country. At present there are about 185 members.

TWO TROPHY CASES WILL MATCH NOW

College Specifications Changed to Secure Harmony—Ready in Two Weeks

A change has been made in the specifications for the college trophy case. In order to harmonize with the high school trophy case which will stand opposite it in the hall of the main building, the college case will exactly match the one ordered by the high school department.

The cases will be 8 feet high, 3 wide, and 18 inches deep. The wood will be mahogany and the sides will be of plate glass.

A local cabinet maker is at work on both. They will be ready in about two weeks.

ALL LOG SECTIONS AT PRESS TODAY

All sections of the Log, high school annual, are at press today.

The work of lining, printing and binding the book will take a week or more. Then, if all work is completed on time, the Log will be distributed about May 23.

Robert Hogan, in charge of the subscription department, reports that 174 orders have been received. Class IA leads the list of the sales groups with 32 books bought.

A broadside of literature around the campus is being directed at the student body. Drawings by a staff artist and snappy phrases are designed to keep the Log before the readers' attention and to promote sales.

CIRCLE DANCE JUNE 4

The Rockhurst Circle will give a dance, Wednesday, June 4, at the Garret, for the graduates of the College and High school. Bob White's Missourians will furnish the music.

SCHOLARSHIP VOTED BY STUDENT COUNCIL

At Last Meeting of the Year Many Appropriations Were Made

One hundred and twenty-five dollars was appropriated by the Student Council of Rockhurst college at its last meeting of the year on May 10, to establish a one year scholarship to Rockhurst. The college president will employ the fund at his discretion.

Other expenditures voted by the Council were an estimated $100 for the student picnic, an estimated $60 for individual trophies for members of the baseball, tennis and golf teams in the event they win the Missouri State Conference championships, $35 for the missions, $18 to send a delegate to the sodality convention in St. Louis in August, and an unknown amount with which to have a medal struck in honor of Bernard J. Muller-Thym, winner of second place in the intercollegiate Latin contest.

Harry Charles Nelson, sitting as president of the Council for the last time called upon the treasurer for a report. It was revealed that there would be a balance of about $400 in the bank after all dues had been paid. It was explained that much of this sum was profits from the three Council dances.

T. Galvin Scanlon reported that the Student Council dance on April 25, the "Kat and the Fiddle" was a decided success both socially and financially. A surplus of $165 existed after all expenses had been met.

In thanking the members, Scanlon named the other members of the committee, James J. Riley, publicity man; Wayne T. O'Donnell, art advertising; and Robert T. Gibbons, who was general secretary.

William T. Smith, speaking for the special committee which was appointed to purchase a trophy case for college athletic trophies, said that the case had been ordered and would be delivered in two weeks.

J. Ward McQueeny, recently named general chairman of the picnic committee, spoke a few words on the preliminary work of his group. Assisting him on the main committee are John F. Halpin and Theodore Tobin.

Two branch committees are on transportation and program. The members of the former are, John G. O'Flaherty, William T. Smith and James Gleeson, and of the latter, chairman, Jerome T. Donnelly, John A. Lally, and James Lamb.

CONSIDERS RAFFLE OF OLD RECORDS

No more victrola records will be purchased by the house committee of the Student Council.

Frank R. Connaughton, chairman of the committee, was of the opinion that the students would not get seventy-five cents worth of use out of new records before the examinations.

He said also that a lottery was under consideration whereby the records bought during the year would be disposed of to any and all interested in the popular melodies of the past months. These records would be out-of-date next year.

A SODALITY RECEPTION MAY 2

A private reception into the college sodality was held on Thursday, May 2, in the chapel. Nine members were enrolled.

A second reception for a small number of candidates who were unable to attend the services on May 2 will be held today, if possible.

The regular sodality meeting on next Thursday will not be held because of the picnic.

LATIN ESSAYIST

—Haines Studio.

BERNARD J. MULLER-THYM

MULLER-THYM WINS SECOND IN CONTEST

Takes High Honor in Competition With 1000 Students in Middle West

Bernard J. Muller-Thym, a sophomore, is the winner of second place in the intercollegiate Latin contest in which 1000 students in the Missouri province of the Society of Jesus recently took part. The names of the first 10 honor men were received at Rockhurst last week.

The Rev. Joseph A. Kiefer, S. J., is professor of Latin. He has taught Muller-Thym for two years.

St. Xavier's college of Cincinnati is the school which produced the winner of first place.

Last year Muller-Thym was sixth in the standings. It was the first time in the history of the annual contest that Rockhurst had placed a man among the ranking 10.

Rockhurst is honored in the list of winners more especially when it is considered that the college is in competition with large universities such as Creighton, Marquette, and Detroit, each of which has over 1000 students.

WALSH FARM TO BE SCENE OF PICNIC

J. Ward McQueeny, General Chairman of Arrangements, Announces Outing Will Be Held May 24

The fifth annual college picnic will be held May 24, at the Frank P. Walsh country home, announced J. Ward McQueeny, last night. "We wish to acknowledge," said Mr. McQueeny, "the kindness of Mrs. Walsh in allowing us to use the grounds for our picnic. The arrangements are well under way and the success of the affair, if it can be measured by the efforts of my contemporaries, is assured."

The transportation committee, headed by John G. O'Flaherty, has announced that it has secured sufficient cars to convey the collegians to and from the Walsh farm. The program group, Jerome T. Donnelly, chairman, has declared that as far as entertainment is concerned "no stone will be left unturned" and all activities will be so distributed as to spread the entertainment out over the morning and afternoon.

When asked about the food, Mr. McQueeny said, "I don't think that there need be any fears about the food. We will serve a regular outing luncheon, with an abundance of everything."

The picnickers will leave the college building at about ten o'clock, after the first class period.

SODALISTS TO MARCH IN PUBLIC SUNDAY

Students of Twenty-Five Schools Will Participate in a May Celebration

Twenty-five Catholic schools will participate in the public sodality demonstration next Sunday, on the grounds of St. Teresa college and academy, Fifty-sixth and Main streets. About 500 students are expected to be in the procession which will begin at 3 o'clock.

The purpose of the activity is to give a public demonstration of Faith in the form of a special devotion to Mary, the mother of God.

While marching around the grounds the Litany of the Blessed Virgin will be recited. Leaders will be appointed from the various academies to lead the parochial schools in the prayer.

The outstanding event of the day will be the crowning of the statue of the Blessed Virgin by the "May queen," who will be chosen from a list of names submitted by the girls' academies of the city.

A short talk will be given by a priest not yet named.

Men will be on the grounds to direct the different delegations to the places of assembly at 2:30.

The Country Club street car runs one block east of St. Teresa's.

The director of the demonstration, Harry Charles Nelson of the Rockhurst college sodality, has announced that if it is raining between 11 and 12 o'clock Sunday morning, the procession will be called off.

ELOCUTIONISTS JUDGED IN CONTEST THURSDAY

Stephen S. Spengler, Walter J. Ong, Edmund J. Stein, and Charles E. Prather Are the Best

In the annual high school elocution contest last Thursday in the Rockhurst auditorium, Stephen S. Spengler, senior; Walter J. Ong, junior; Edmund J. Stein, sophomore; and Charles E. Prather, freshman, were the victors in their respective divisions. There were 16 speakers in all.

The judges were Charles L. Aylward, William J. Leahy, and Jozach Miller, III.

Gold medals will be awarded to the winners of the contest on commencement day.

"It was a very difficult task to decide the four best speakers," said William J. Leahy, who announced the judges' decisions. "All showed splendid ability in elocution. We congratulate each one individually."

Stephen S. Spengler, the winner in fourth year, delivered "The Bells." Other best speeches were, "The Soul of the Violin," by Walter J. Ong; "Smiting the Rock," by Edmund J. Stein; and "Kentucky Philosophy," by Charles E. Prather.

The Rockhurst orchestra entertained the audience with several selections during the intermissions.

Joseph D. Murphy Wins Scholarship At "Boston Tech"

Joseph D. Murphy, a sophomore at Rockhurst college last year, has won the Fontainbleau scholarship in architecture at the Massachusetts Institute of Technology. This award is the highest which "Tech" can give.

Murphy will go to Paris the latter part of this month to study until October.

Last year the art drawings for the Log, high school annual, were drawn by Murphy.

Phil Koury, '34, editor of The Sentinel, *displays trophies and medals won by the student newspaper in competition with other collegiate newspapers. Courtesy of Rockhurst University Archives.*

being judged the best college paper in Missouri, an honor that would be repeated 3 more times in the 1930s.[21] During the 1934 Missouri Newspaper Association contest, held under the auspices of the School of Journalism of the University of Missouri, *The Sentinel*, though the smallest of the 12 competitors, garnered 5 of 7 first-place awards and 2 third-place awards.[22] Success continued into the 1950s, when *The Hawk* received a first-class rating 7 years in a row during the Associated College Press Contests.

Another early institution at Rockhurst was the Lecture Club. Organized by Father Schwitalla in January 1918, club members gave lectures in the community as a way to advertise Rockhurst, adding interest to their talks by including as many as 50 lantern slides. On St. Patrick's Day 1919, for instance, the club appeared before the nuns and nurses at St. Joseph's Hospital when students Vincent O'Flaherty and Arthur Forster presented "Ireland: An Illustrated Lecture." They gave a similar showing at the Knights of Columbus Hall at 33rd and Main streets, where Father Schwitalla himself, for a time, gave 2 lectures a week on Catholic philosophy.[23]

— A SOCIAL LIFE —

During the 1920s and 1930s, a number of clubs took root and flourished at Rockhurst—the Philosopher's Club, Latin Club, Modern Problems Club, Spanish Club, and Culture Club, as well as social clubs often linked to various city parishes. Rockhurst students joined the Jolly Old Owls, the Majella Club, the St. James Club, and the Antill Club.[24] Not surprisingly, these social clubs held the greatest interest for a Rockhurst student. If he belonged to any one of them, *The Sentinel* wrote, "his social life is maintained and formed through their activities."

The Owls, an invitation-only club, actually was a fraternity with the Greek letters Phi Alpha Nu. Among its 10 members in 1924 were John Stewart, James Lillis, and Chris Jones. The Majella Club, comprising 25 men from Redemptorist Parish, including a number who attended Rockhurst, derived its name from St. Gerard of Majella, a patron saint of youth. It, too, was an invitation-only social club known for its bi-monthly danc-

Sedgwick Hall in winter. Courtesy of Rockhurst University Archives.

es at Garrett Hall. Among Rockhurst members were Raymond Bray, Al Van Hee, Charles Cattanoch, Pierce Shine, Ambrose Duff, and Charles Bombeck.

The St. James Club, as its name suggested, comprised men from St. James Parish, just north of the Rockhurst campus. In 1924, the club had reached its limit of 20 members and maintained a long waiting list to join. The St. James Club held bi-monthly dances, called "Jimmy hops," and also published its own newspaper, the *St. James Comet*, with Rockhurst student Elmer Rehagen as business manager. Other college students in the club were Harry Murphy and Irving Damon.

The Antill Club, named in honor of the late pastor of St. Vincent's Parish, was open to any Catholic man over age 16. It had 52 members and staged a monthly dance. Rockhurst collegians Carl W. Brady and Frank L. Davis were members, as well as 4 high schoolers.

Rockhurst College also was affiliated with the LaCroix Council of the Knights of Columbus through an organization known as the Rockhurst Council. Several current and former Rockhurst students were members and met on the second and fourth Tuesdays of each month at Dowling Hall. "The Rockhurst spirit has joined hands with the K. of C. spirit and the combination foretells a successful and beneficial future," *The Sentinel* reported.[25]

Academic clubs also flourished. The Philosopher's Club, organized by philosophy professor George A. Deglman, S.J., first met in September 1923, when it drew up a constitution stating a fourfold purpose: "to foster a spirit of eager search for truth"; to encourage "a deepening of knowledge" of matters dealt with in classes; to help students "develop a keen and accurate judgment"; and "to intensify the desire to know thoroughly the tenets and doctrines of right philosophy." The Culture Club, founded by English Professor Richard Hickey and reorganized in 1937 as the Beaux Arts Club, made field trips to art centers in Kansas City. The Modern Problems Club explored the underlying causes of modern problems and tried to find solutions, while a club known as the Industrialists wanted to know more about modern industrial methods. Members met bi-weekly and scheduled field trips to industrial plants, banks, and mercantile firms. Members of the Latin Club competed each year for the Intercollegiate Latin Prize. On the day of the contest, they spent the morning translating a Latin theme into English and the afternoon translating an English theme into Latin. Dictionaries were allowed only in the afternoon session. College senior Walter J. Ong and freshman Robert J. Kasper won 2 of the 10 top honors in the 1931 contest, bringing "great honor to the college," because classical students from 12 Jesuit colleges had competed. Ong also served that year as editor of the booklet, *Virgil's Bimillenium* (sic), which commemorated the poet's 2,000th birthday anniversary.[26]

Brooks Hale (left) and Pat Mason, 1916. Courtesy of Rockhurst University Archives.

— Athletics —

What was an all-boys school without athletic competition? Rockhurst High School was playing other high schools in basketball as early as the 1916–17 academic year, when a team comprised of Brooks Hale, Pat Mason, Clarence Reardon, Louis Lucas, George Sutter, and George Korty held the league lead until losing to Independence High School.[27]

According to John Jennings' 1938 senior thesis, Rockhurst's college basketball tradition began in 1919 after Midland College in Atchison, Kansas, proffered an invitation, asking Rockhurst to send a team to Midland for a preseason game. At that time, according to Jennings, the college "had no athletics of any form." Pat Mason, a college freshman who also was serving as coach for the high school, "gathered a group of boys together and they journeyed to Atchison for the game." When the Rockhurst "Blue and White" blew away the strong Midland team, 53-4, it was, Jennings writes, "a great surprise to everyone." Encouraged by their success, the Rockhurst boys scheduled about 6 or 7 more games that season and "finished the season on top."[28] The highlight of that first season came in late March when the Rockhurst team was selected to play Kansas City's high school all-stars, who were bound for Chicago to play for the national championship. To raise money for the trip, a series of games was scheduled against Rockhurst, in the Rockhurst gym. So many people turned out for the games that the Metropolitan Street Railway Company put extra cars on the Marlborough line. Rockhurst lost all 3 games, but split the $500 in gate receipts with the all-star team. "Ever since that time," Rockhurst historian Patrick Harvey writes, "the feeling of the public high schools towards the College has been of a very friendly nature."[29]

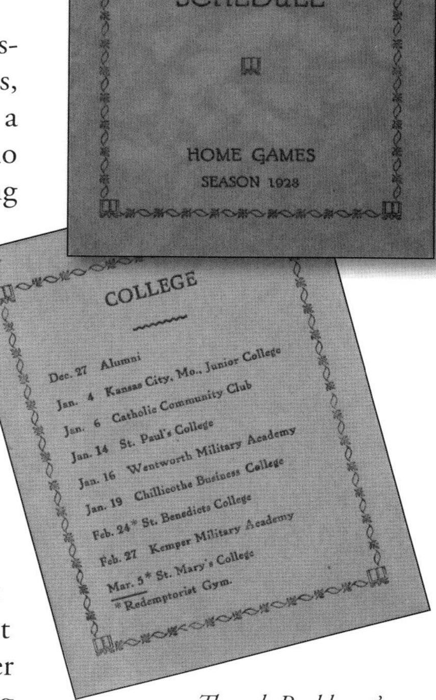

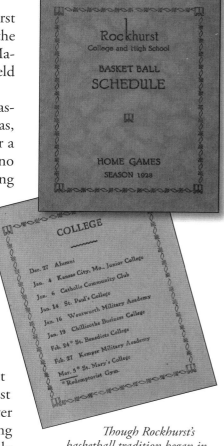

Though Rockhurst's basketball tradition began in 1919, it was not until 1926 that the college joined the Missouri State Conference. Courtesy of Rockhurst University Archives.

A noon-hour basketball league at Rockhurst was an integral part of campus life in the early 1920s. Four games were played each noon, with every student a member of a team. So successful was the program that some gave it credit for the powerful teams that Rockhurst fielded against other schools.[30]

Schedules for the high school and college teams began appearing in *The Sentinel*. The 1919–20 schedule listed only 3 official college games: against Westminster on February 4, Kansas City Junior College on February 21, and the Olathe Mutes on February 28.[31] By playing each team twice, the schedule of games doubled by the next season, 1920–21, including a new addition—what was to become the annual, first game of the season against the alumni. "This first game for the basketeers has always attracted considerable attention," *The Sentinel* said. "It not only offers an opportunity for the 'old grads' to get together again and to defend the integrity of the classes of former years against the 'young generation,' but it also affords an excellent chance to compare the fledglings with the stellar performances of teams of other years, for the rooters to begin their yells and for the enthusiastic supporters to make pre-season predictions."[32]

The basketball team gained national attention in 1921–22 when it entered the National Basketball Tournament held in Kansas City's Convention Hall, but it wasn't until 1926 that the college program joined the

Missouri State Conference, comprising Wentworth and Kemper military academies, St. Paul, Chillicothe Business College, and Rockhurst.[33]

Enthusiasm for Rockhurst athletics was running so high by 1926 that the college not only had a basketball team, but also football, tennis, baseball, and track teams. Since the fall term of 1919, an athletic store had beckoned in a third-floor room of Sedgwick Hall. The room was filled with blue and white caps, pennants, basketball supplies, and other sporting goods. One glass case sported pillows with Rockhurst written in broad letters. Students were encouraged to patronize the Rockhurst store rather than go downtown to sporting good stores such as the popular Lowe & Campbell at 11th and Grand, because all Rockhurst profits would be donated to the student athletic fund.[34]

"There is," *The Sentinel* reported on December 16, 1926, "an athletic spirit existing at Rockhurst." Every student, it seemed, desired "to represent the school at some time or another in the field of sport." During the academic year of 1926–27, Rockhurst won 3 Missouri State Conference championships—one each in basketball, baseball, and tennis. The football team, coached for the first time that year by Pat Mason, tied for second place with a 5-2 record, and the track team placed third.[35] Rockhurst outdid itself the next year, 1927–28, by winning 4 Missouri State Conference championships, in basketball, baseball, tennis—and its first ever in football with a 4-1-1 record.[36] The gridiron team sealed the championship with a 45-6 romp over Kemper Military Academy on Rockhurst's Homecoming Day at the new Bourke Field, dedicated that very day.[37]

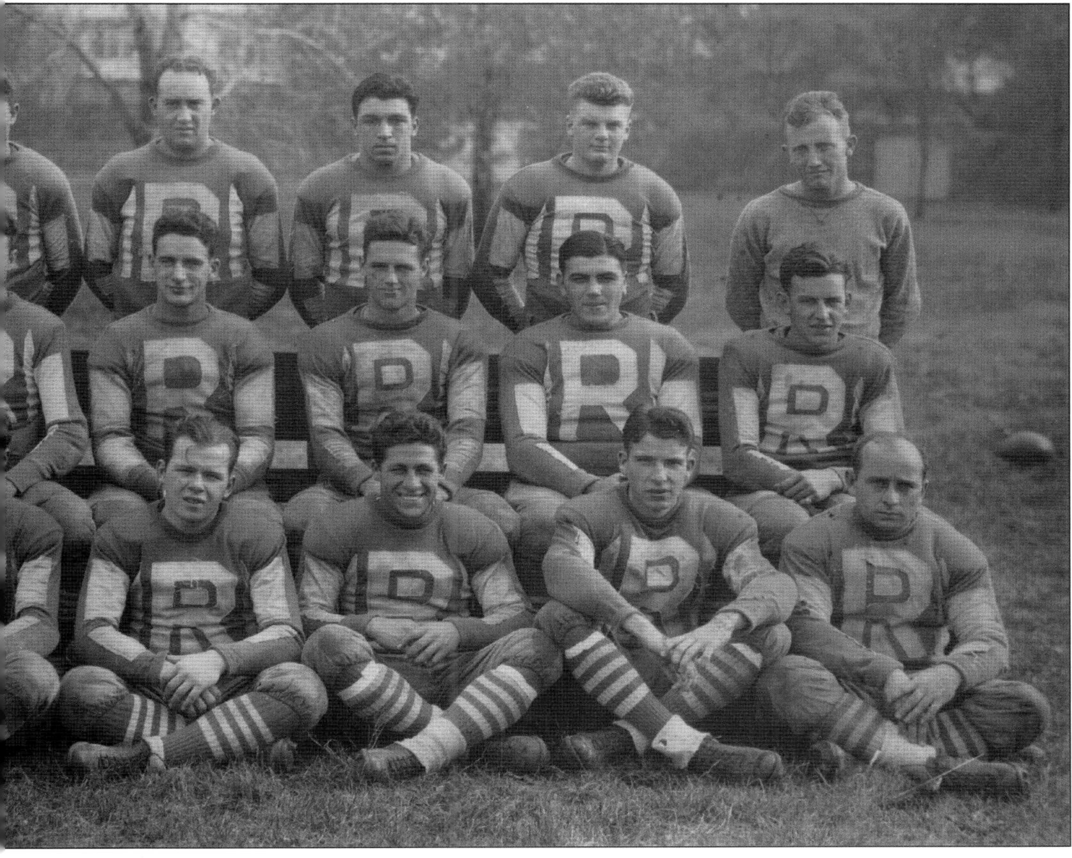

The Rockhurst College football squad, 1929. Rockhurst did not play an official football schedule against other college teams until 1924. That initial effort produced a record of 3 losses, one victory, and one tie. In 1928, the college won the Missouri State Conference football title with a perfect 8-0 record, scoring a total of 260 points to only 24 for its opponents. Courtesy of Rockhurst University Archives.

Alumni and fans had packed the stands that afternoon, November 12, 1927, for the game against Kemper, billed as "the greatest battle in college history."[38] The "zero hour" had arrived as "the 1927 Hawk machine" lined up against the Kemper Yellowjackets, never before beaten in football by Rockhurst. Spirits had been running high all week on campus, the blue and white colors visible everywhere as Rockhurst was set to compete for the conference title. There had been a huge bonfire, cheers, and speeches by alumni. Alum Pat Slattery told of the "old days before the present generation had come into power." He described "the battles of bygone days when the college was still struggling along." Vincent O'Flaherty had stood up, too, and in a voice hoarse with emotion "cried out…for a continuance of the fighting spirit of the days and times Mr. Slattery described." And then, "a mighty shout went up from the crowd" as coach Pat Mason stepped to the platform, followed by his players, one by one. There was team captain Galvin "Duck" Scanlon and George Riordan, "the Rockhurst Rambler," who had "gone off tackle, skirted the ends," and "plunged through the line" of every team Rockhurst had faced. Jack "Piggy" Harrington was short and stocky but had "an uncanny knack of charging through the enemy line to nail plays before they have a chance to get started," and then there was quarterback Ed Henke, "perhaps the greatest passer that ever played on a Hawk team." Over two seasons, Henke had made only 2 bad passes from center.

The dedication of Bourke Field only added to the excitement. Much of the work of leveling the field had gone to Brother David E. Shaughnessy, S.J., and it was he who cut the blue and white ribbon that stretched across the field on homecoming day. A 6-foot-tall wire fence, enclosing the entire lower campus, also had been completed. It ran down 52nd Street, crossed Lydia and went up 53rd Street to the raised upper campus. By hanging a canvas curtain on the fence, Rockhurst's football field was made "spectator proof," an innovation that was expected to greatly increase revenue on game days.[39]

— NEW STADIUM —

By the next fall, of 1928, the first unit of a stadium expected in time to seat 12,000 people had been erected on the west side of Bourke Field. "New stadium to be ready for first home tilt," *The Sentinel* heralded on October 10, 1928. "Along with other signs of the times, comes Rockhurst's new stadium." Three thousand bleacher seats, arranged in 17 tiers, were being constructed on a concrete base on the west bank separating the lower campus from the upper. Rockhurst alum Eddie Doyle, of the Doyle-Moore Lumber Company, had furnished the lumber for the stands, which were to be 300 feet long—exactly the length of the football field and affording an unobstructed view to all. Overseeing the project was the Rev. David A. Shyne, S.J., a member of Rockhurst's athletic board, who would receive much praise for his part in the opening of Bourke Field.[40]

"The project, backed by the Alumni Association, is but the first step forward towards a Rockhurst athletic plant in keeping with those of other colleges in the Middle-West," *The Sentinel* said. It had been only a few short

— THE DEDICATION OF BOURKE FIELD —

Rockhurst received a $10,000 gift in 1922 from Thomas C. Bourke in memory of his brother, Lt. Wilfrid Corrigan Bourke, who was killed in an airplane accident on October 14, 1918, at Fort Sill, Oklahoma. Lt. Bourke was a Kansas City native, 23 years old, when he died. He had graduated from Westport High School in 1912 and from Yale University in 1916, where he was a member of the crew team. When the First World War broke out, Bourke entered the first officers training camp at Fort Riley, Kansas, was commissioned a second lieutenant in August 1918, and served at Camp Funston and then Camp Jackson in South Carolina before entering the School for Aerial Observers at Fort Sill's Post Field. He was within one week of completing the course when he was killed in a crash while flying as an observer with a Lt. Brown of the Air Service.

Lt. Wilfrid Corrigan Bourke

On November 12, 1927, homecoming day, alumni and fans packed the stands to see the dedication of the new Bourke Field and to witness a 45-6 romp over Kemper Military Academy. Much of the work of leveling the field had gone to Brother David E. Shaughnessy, S.J., and it was he who cut the blue and white ribbon that stretched across the field that day.

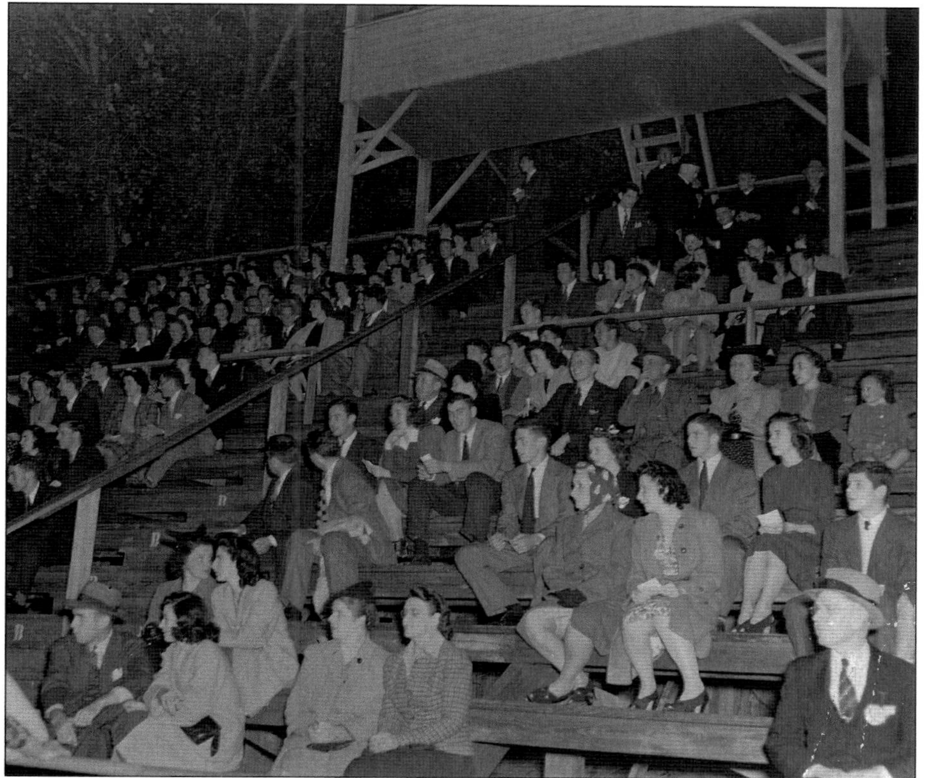

In the fall of 1928, the first unit of a stadium, expected in time to seat 12,000 people, was erected on the west side of Bourke Field. Three thousand bleacher seats, arranged in 17 tiers, were built on a concrete base running 300 feet long—exactly the length of the football field. Courtesy of Rockhurst University Archives.

years ago that the lower campus was "nothing more than an abandoned rock quarry, flooded most of the time with stagnant water and overgrown with weeds." People had referred to the area as "out in back," a place rough with ridges, holes, small hills, and "rocks all over the place."[41]

How far Rockhurst had come in just a few years. Since 1920 Rockhurst had acquired not only the new gridiron stadium, but also 2 tennis courts, situated on a grassy plot just north of the driveway, as well as handball courts and 2 baseball diamonds. There also was talk of building a fieldhouse to seat 5,000 spectators. Construction was expected to begin in the spring or summer of 1929, but the devastating economic collapse that lay just around the corner would interfere, and Rockhurst would not get its fieldhouse for another 10 years.[42]

John S. "Red" Sullivan, '30, a member of the undefeated 1928 Rockhurst College football squad. Sullivan, one of 7 Rockhurst players selected for The Sentinal's *1928 Missouri State Conference All-Star team, was in the first class of inductees to the Rockhurst Athletics Hall of Fame in 1981. Courtesy of Rockhurst University Archives.*

— FOOTBALL —

Rockhurst boys had been playing football since the fall of 1915, when Father Kennedy of Our Lady of Good Counsel Church had offered to come to campus 3 nights a week and teach the boys the game, which they apparently had never played before. Father Kennedy had learned the game while studying at Allegheny College in Pennsylvania.[43]

The next fall, of 1916, Charles Allen arrived from Warrensburg North School to be Rockhurst's athletic coach. "He immediately took charge of the football team and drilled the boys so thoroughly that they had a remarkably successful season," Harvey writes. The city newspapers took note, writing that "Charlie Allen was physical instructor at the school this year and all of the championships were won under his tutelage." The Rockhurst team, still high schoolers all, lost only one game in the 1916 season, 12-0,

Pat Mason, who himself was an outstanding athlete, at one time coached all of the Rockhurst College teams, while serving as athletic director. Mason was a second-year high school boy when Rockhurst opened in 1914. He stayed on for college, graduating in Rockhurst's first college class in 1921. Pictured is the whistle he used in coaching football and basketball. Courtesy of Rockhurst University Archives and Virginia Mason Waters.

against archrival Country Day School, which had shellacked Rockhurst the year before, 66-0. "Our hats off to Rockhurst," *The Kansas City Post* wrote of the 1916 season: "Starting with absolutely nothing and their first year in the football field, they made a wonderful record. Out of a school of 140 students of varying ages, a football squad of 26 was gathered. The majority of the squad had never played a game of football." The greatest credit for Rockhurst's success went to high school senior Pat Mason, captain and quarterback. "His forward passing was nothing short of marvelous," *The Post* wrote. So talented was Pat Mason that Coach Allen had said he "had more control of the ball than any other quarter (back) he had witnessed in action this year."[44]

On December 12, there was a football banquet for the players in the Jesuits' dining hall. Thirty-two people were there, including members of the faculty and then-Rockhurst President Aloysius Breen, who had stood up and given a speech, as had Fathers Harvey and Ellis, and Coach Allen. Team captain Pat Mason had spoken and then turned the floor over to Leo Heinz, selected captain for the next season.[45]

Games in those early years were high school games played against other high schools. The football season of 1916, for instance, opened against the Mohawk Athletic Club, an aggregation of Westport High School players. Rockhurst played schools in what was known as the School and College League of Kansas City. Sponsored by Lowe & Campbell Athletic Company, it comprised Rockhurst; De La Salle; Country Day; Kansas City, Kansas, High School; and Kansas City, Kansas, Catholic High School (later renamed Bishop Ward High School). Without an adequate football field, Rockhurst played its opponents on the Kansas City Athletic Club field at Linwood Boulevard and Gillham Road.[46]

Rockhurst's college men were playing football as early as November 1919, but the team was in no way official, organized as it was by the students themselves. The team's first game was on Friday, November 7, 1919, at the Kansas City Athletic Club field. "This will be the first time that Rockhurst has put a football team on the field," *The Sentinel* reported. The players, on what apparently was a 6-man team, were veterans of former Rockhurst high teams: Pat Mason, Jim Walsh, Herbert Stewart, Matthew Williams, George Korty, and Val Schroeger. Also on the team was Hugh Downey, captain of the De La Salle team the previous year.[47]

It would not be until the academic year of 1924-25 that the college played an official football schedule against other college teams. Rockhurst football historian Philip Dynan credits mathematics teacher Paul V. Ryan with "stirring up enough spirit to make the start possible." Ryan whipped the team into shape to compete with much larger schools, which was, Dynan writes, "no small task."[48] That kickoff year, with a record of 3 losses, one victory, and one tie, was less than impressive, but it bode well for the future. The tie came in the first official football game Rockhurst College ever played—against the Wentworth Military Academy Cadets, who were 1924 league champions. "The Cadets took a taste of the 'fighting Irish' football as time after time they held the ball in the shadow of the Rockhurst goal posts, once having a first down on the six inch line, only to see the stubborn Hawk defense turn them back," Dynan writes. In the last game of the season, against powerhouse St. Benedict's College, considered the best team in the region, the Hawks stunned everyone with a 13-6 victory. It was the first time all season that a team had scored a touchdown, let alone a victory, against the St. Benedict Ravens.

This, Rockhurst historian Hugh Owens writes, "might well mark the beginning of the modern Rockhurst athletic tradition." A more dramatic Philip Dynan writes that the game with St. Benedict's was "the birth" of Rockhurst's fighting spirit. "There were eleven fighting fiends wearing the blue and white jerseys that day," he writes. "It was not the fight they had shown in others games, but a new fight that made every player tackle harder, run faster, and play the game determined to win or to die trying." The biggest star of the day was Jim Walsh, who had entered the game as a substitute in the final quarter with time running short. "On the first play he ripped through the Raven line for twenty yards and another touchdown to give the Hawks their first victory over St. Benedict's. Say what you may," Dynan argues, "that game made Rockhurst tradition."[49]

Charles "Junior" Bombeck was Rockhurst captain and quarterback; Harry Nelson, Charles Heinz, and Jimmie Walsh were the halfbacks; and Mike Spittle played fullback. In the line were Dick Flucke, Jim Lillis, Pierce Shine, Frank Davis, Joe DeMerea, Bud Riley, and George McLiney. Completing this historic Rockhurst team were Mike DeMerea, Ray Natchman, and George Christ at tackle, and Frank Harrington, Charley Gattanack, Dutch Damon, and James Casey playing end.

There would be many bonfires and pep rallies as Rockhurst went on to establish an excellent reputation in sports, including, in 1928, a second straight Missouri State Conference football title, this time with a perfect 8-0 record in what *The Sentinel* called "the most difficult schedule ever arranged" for a Rockhurst team.[50] The biggest upset had come during the Thanksgiving game when Rockhurst shut out its big Catholic rival, the St. Mary's College Knights, 9-0. It was such a big deal, *The Kansas City Journal-Post* explained, because Rockhurst was only 10 years old and St. Mary's, founded in 1869, was the oldest college in Kansas. "It was like a 3-year-old yanking the beard of a grandfather, punctuated with a kick in the pants," *The Journal-Post* wrote.

The record for the 1928 season:

Rockhurst 80	K.C.K. Junior College 0
Rockhurst 59	St. Paul's 6
Rockhurst 28	Wentworth 6
Rockhurst 13	St. Benedict's 6
Rockhurst 9	St. Mary's 0
Rockhurst 26	Kemper 6
Rockhurst 45	Chillicothe 0

Rockhurst had scored a total of 260 points to only 24 for its opponents. Hawk followers were so happy that they "went about for weeks after

By spring 1928, Rockhurst had a total of 13 athletic trophies, many of them won by John C. Egelhoff for tennis. This trophy went to Egelhoff in 1927 for his victory in singles at Chillicothe. Photo by David Spaw. Courtesy of Rockhurst University Athletics Department.

the last game shouting of the undefeated season." Perhaps the team had been spurred on by an exclusive, 40-member college pep club formed that fall; members were required to attend every home game to cheer on the team. Topping off coach Pat Mason's "dream year" was the selection of 7 Rockhurst players to *The Sentinel's* Missouri State Conference All-Star football team—Galvin Scanlon, John Sullivan, Earl Wright, Barnard Cahill, Vic Zahner, Raymond "Red" McKee, and Joseph Halpin. Another star was Jerry Donnelly, whose sweetheart clipped article after article about the team and pasted them in a scrapbook, now in the Rockhurst University archives.[51]

By 1932, Rockhurst athletic teams were so dominant that other members of the Missouri State Conference started to complain, saying that Rockhurst, as a 4-year college, accredited or not, had an unfair advantage. In a gesture of protest, Kemper Military Academy, a junior college, withdrew from the conference, and Rockhurst, undoubtedly in response to the criticism, soon followed suit. "The years have dealt well with the home of the Hawks, and have seen the school grow until it was almost customary for her to dominate in the conference every field of athletic competition which she entered," *The Sentinel* editorialized on March 9, 1932. "An uncanny ability on the gridiron, hardwood floor, and court, coupled with the fact that a four year course was available for her students soon made it evident that Rockhurst had outgrown her boots." Surely, *The Sentinel* wrote, that was a healthy sign of a growing college. Whether Rockhurst had a new conference to join any time soon was immaterial because "the Hawks can at least stretch their wings." By the early 1930s, new teams were appearing on Rockhurst's "free-lance" schedule, among them Kansas Wesleyan, Baker University, the Haskell Reserves, Missouri Valley, Central, Parsons, and William Jewell.[52]

By the football season of 1939–40, Rockhurst embarked on an even tougher football schedule, adding Loras College of Dubuque, Iowa, and Regis College of Denver. The "bolder" schedule, *The Kansas City Star* wrote on October 17, 1939, was "the first step toward a building policy intended eventually to raise the local school to prominence in the national gridiron picture." Rockhurst, *The Star* said, "has no ambition to be another Notre Dame. But she does hope to be known eventually in the very select group of small colleges which annually turn out teams worthy of attention more than merely local....Kansas City is beginning to watch Rockhurst. Something is going on out on the Hawk campus. This year is only a starter."[53]

— TROPHIES AND PEP CLUBS —

Rockhurst always seemed to excel. Despite the admonition from Rome decrying the overemphasis on athletics, Rockhurst encouraged its boys to take part in some athletic activity. By the spring semester of 1928, Rockhurst had a new pep club and a total of 13 athletic trophies, many of them on display in Father Shyne's office, where a *Sentinel* reporter admired them on a winter day in 1928. He counted 3 trophies for baseball, 2 for basketball, one for football, and a loyalty cup awarded for intramural competition. Tennis had the most trophies, 5 in all—3 for doubles and 2 for singles. "The man to whom a great deal of credit belongs for winning these cups is John C. Egelhoff," *The Sentinel* said. In fact, Egelhoff's name was on every one of Rockhurst's tennis trophies; in 1925, teamed with doubles partner Raymond Bray, Egelhoff had won the conference championship at Lexington, Missouri; in 1926, this time with doubles partner Anthony Christ, he had won another trophy at Boonville, Missouri; and, in 1927, with John R. Callan as his partner, had won the doubles trophy at Chillicothe. The college's 2 singles trophies belonged to Egelhoff, as well. He won one at Boonville in 1926; the other at Chillicothe in 1927.[54]

As early as 1920, letter sweaters were being awarded. In 1927, Rockhurst organized a letterman's club, the R Club, to aid "in any way possible the advancement of Rockhurst athletics." Courtesy of Virginia Mason Waters. Photo by David Spaw.

As early as 1920, letter sweaters were being awarded. "They are here and they are very natty," *The Sentinel* reported on March 29, 1920. In 1927, Rockhurst organized a letterman's club, the R Club, to aid "in any way possible the advancement of Rockhurst athletics and to follow a busy outline of activities." It also launched a campaign in *The Sentinel* to select a new name for its college teams, which sportswriters long had referred to as the "Blue and White," the "Southsiders," the "Irish," or, in the school's earliest days, the "Catholics." The 5-week campaign conducted by *The Sentinel* drew 300 suggestions that named "nearly every bird and beast in the animal kingdom."

The winning bird was submitted by John Cauley, a college freshman, and Donald Rossner, a high school student. "The new name, Hawks, is distinctive and indicative of dash and courage," *The Sentinel* wrote. The selection committee comprised the Jesuits David Shyne and Laurence J. Lynch and coaches Pat Mason, Paul Ryan, and Eddie Halpin.[55]

— THE ROCKHURST CIRCLE —

Over time, Rockhurst would have various fund-raising organizations, but perhaps none ever would do as much for Rockhurst finances as the Rockhurst Circle, organized on April 3, 1927, at a meeting in the Rockhurst gym. Eighty mothers, sisters, and aunts of Rockhurst boys, both college and high school, showed up that day and, as they always would, wasted no time in getting to work. "Mothers and Aunts of Students to Unite for Benefit of School," *The Sentinel* announced just 3 days after the initial meeting. Mrs. James H. Hale had been elected president; Mrs. John J. Sullivan, vice president; Mrs. William Moore, secretary; and Mrs. Joseph Halpin, Sr., treasurer.[56] According to the diary of Victor F. Gettleman, S.J., and a short history of the organization written in 1951, these women, as well as Mrs. William Bannon and Mrs. Margaret Mongoven, had discussed organizing a fund-raising group as early as September 10, 1926. They had met with Father Shyne, principal of the high school, and the idea had been broached to Rockhurst President Arthur Spillard, but, preoccupied, Spillard had thought it best to postpone the idea.

It wasn't until the meeting in the gym the next year that the Circle officially got underway. From that day on, news of its doings would appear again and again in the pages of *The Sentinel*. "Rockhurst Circle Will Give

The Rockhurst Circle was officially organized on April 3, 1927, when 80 women—mothers, sisters, and aunts of Rockhurst boys, both college and high school—gathered at Rockhurst to organize a fund-raising group. Through its sponsorship of monthly dinners, card parties, picnics, dances, and fashion shows, over the years the Circle contributed substantial sums to the college. In 1972, the Rockhurst Circle Scholarship was established as a permanent fund to help students achieve their educational goals by providing financial assistance. Courtesy of Rockhurst University Archives.

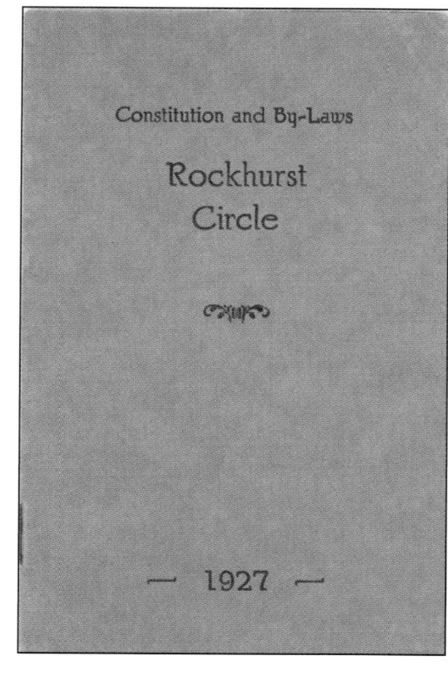

Constitution and By-Laws

Rockhurst Circle

— 1927 —

In 1959, past presidents of the Rockhurst Circle gathered for a luncheon. Courtesy of Rockhurst University Archives.

Banquet," the paper announced just a few weeks after its initial meeting. Invitations had been mailed to 150 Kansas Citians who were not members of the Circle but whom the women knew had "shown themselves, in the past, to be actively interested in the promotion of higher education."

The Circle's first dinner gathering, in honor of President Spillard and the faculty, was held in the Rockhurst gym and given free of charge to attendees. "Members of the Circle have been busy during the past week securing the service of a caterer and in inspecting the cooking facilities offered in the College cafeteria," *The Sentinel* reported on April 29, 1927. According to "Rockhurst Circle, A Short History," however, the women cooked these early dinners in their own homes and carried the food, as well as linen and silver, sugars, creamers, and salt and pepper shakers to campus. They borrowed plates, cups, and saucers from the Knights of Columbus and from Good Counsel parish hall. "Two days before the dinner," the history states, "the ladies would meet to wash the dishes, prepare the vegetables and set the tables. The old gym was used and it was always transformed from the drab gymnasium to a beautiful banquet room." For that first dinner of 1927, Mrs. Hale, Circle president, had enlisted members of the Rockhurst college and high school basketball teams to act as waiters, and members of the Rockhurst orchestra to entertain. That Thursday night, the banquet opened with a shout as the basketball teams led a school cheer and then said the Pledge of Allegiance. President Spillard gave a speech, thanking the women and laying out the challenges that Rockhurst faced.

The biggest challenge was lack of accreditation, Spillard told the women. An inspector from the North Central Association of Colleges and Secondary Schools had been to campus and laid out the conditions that must be met if the college department were to gain the association's stamp of approval. "There was only one way to meet the conditions," Spillard explained, and that was "to erect a new high school building and to transfer the students of the college department to the present building, which was originally intended for them."[57]

"The present building"—meaning the yet unnamed Sedgwick Hall—was being used by the 293 high school boys enrolled that year, while the college students—91 in all—still were taking classes in Dowling Hall, except for science classes. The science lab and lecture rooms in Sedgwick Hall were newly outfitted, but continued to be shared by one and all. This was unacceptable to NCA inspectors, who insisted that Rockhurst must have separate buildings for the high school and college if it hoped to gain accreditation. The high school had been accredited as early as 1918 by the University of Missouri and as a member of the North Central Association, but the college still had not earned the stamp of approval as a 4-year institution. It was regarded as a junior college, a designation awarded by the North Central Accrediting Committee in the spring of 1925.[58]

Despite the addition of Dowling Hall, the shared high school/college science rooms would continue to be a serious sticking point. Besides that, Spillard explained, the student bodies of college and high school departments alike were overcrowded and "taxed to capacity." Rockhurst needed money, he said, if it were to build and meet the conditions to become accredited. Knowledge of Rockhurst's financial situation apparently had spurred formation of the Circle in the first place.

Beginning in October 1927, the Circle started giving monthly dinners—including its annual Thanksgiving turkey dinner—in the Rockhurst gym "in order to bring Kansas City people out to the college and to interest them in the work which Rockhurst is doing." Besides dinners, the Circle orchestrated card parties, picnics, dances, fashion shows, and a play at the Orpheum. Its dinners were an instant hit; so many people wanted to attend that within a year the number had to be limited to 500. In just its first few months, such a substantial sum had been raised from membership dues and donations, *The Sentinel* said, that the Circle "has come to be recognized as one of the big factors in the future growth of the college."[59]

The Circle's own banking records from 1927 to 1929 reveal accounts with receipts and disbursements totaling more than $15,000 at 2 banks. Financial records in the Rockhurst University Archives show the Circle contributing substantial sums to the college over the years, even during years of the Great Depression: $3,000 in 1930; $4,000 in 1932; $800 in 1933; and $900 in 1934. In 1940, records list a contribution of $1,200; in 1941, $2,000; in 1942, $1,800; and in 1943, $1,800. By 1952, on its 25th anniversary, the Circle's contributions to Rockhurst would amount to a total of more than $50,000 in funds and equipment, not to mention, as one historian put it, "several thousand pounds of potatoes peeled for dinners and luncheons, promotion of benefit shows and card parties, operation of refreshment booths at athletic games, assistance in building fund drives, to name but a few."[60]

— College Daze —

As the 1920s drew to a close, Rockhurst students celebrated their new traditions of college life in an all-student musical comedy, titled *College Daze*, which they staged to 2 "capacity crowds" at the Shubert Theater downtown on Friday and Saturday, May 17 and 18, 1929. James McQueeney of *The Sentinel* staff had written the script, James Riley had produced it, and Frank Condon had supplied the original musical score. Members of the cast and chorus—which included "a group of fair maidens" from St. Teresa College—had spent that April and May rehearsing 4 nights a week

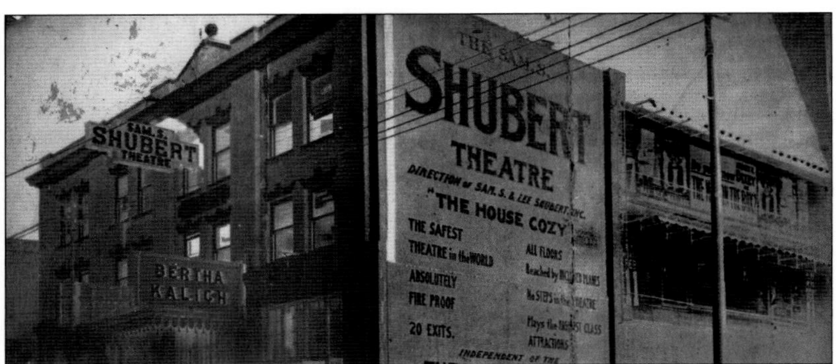

In 1929 and again in 1930, the all-student musical comedy College Daze *was staged to 2 capacity crowds at the Shubert Theater at 10th and Baltimore. Courtesy of Missouri Valley Special Collections, Kansas City Public Library, Kansas City, Missouri.*

in Dowling Hall and at the Dorothy Perkins Dancing Studio.

There had been a free dress rehearsal in the gymnasium-turned-playhouse on Monday night, April 15. The curtain had never gone up "because there was no curtain," but the play had been a smashing success nonetheless. Betty Shirk from St. Teresa did a tap dance routine, and the 3 Soden sisters sang the play's biggest hit, "Lonely," before stepping into what *The Sentinel* described as the "rollicking Rockhurst Stomp," which Miss Shirk "interpreted" on the hardwoods. Other stars included Raymond McKee, who portrayed a witty, sophisticated collegian, while James Bannon was his counterpart, giving a more depressed outlook on college life. Halbert Young played the "hard-boiled" coach, and William Buchholz portrayed the sincere, hard-working college man.[61]

The Sentinel correspondent also attended a rehearsal at the Shubert and found the one-liners so "rib-tickling" and "Rockhurstian" that even Rockhurst's "rigid-visaged ex-president"—meaning the recently departed Jesuit Arthur D. Spillard—"would get a guffaw." The play, with its theme song, "College Days," was, the reporter said, "a delightful exposition of true collegiate life," with all its "witticisms, mannerisms, and idiosyncrasies." You better, he suggested, procure a good seat (for $1.50) and tie yourself to it, "to prevent rolling in the aisles...."[62]

Rockhurst had staged plays since its pioneers days, including its first on February 15-17, 1917, a dramatic performance by the high school titled *For a Greater Crown*, based on the life of Saint Herminigild, who, as the Christian governor of Seville, Spain, had been executed in A.D. 585. It was acted in the Little Theatre at 3214 Troost Avenue and received generous applause from the newspapers. The unsettled conditions caused by World War I had canceled a play planned for 1918, and the influenza pandemic had canceled one for 1919, the proceeds of which were to have been dedicated to the school library. That December, however, practice started for the next year's play, *The Prince and the Pauper*. Rockhurst presented at least one other play downtown, *Let's Go*, at the Grand Theatre on April 6, 1923.[63]

It would be left to *College Daze*, however, to bring down the house. With the modern era in full swing, the play included an extremely popular "radio scene," in which C.T. Falk announced the "big game." The play mimicked life at Rockhurst in 1929, where "motion picture lectures" were being given occasionally in the high school and where students now could listen to speeches over the radio, including one piped in from Saint Louis University on March 30, 1928, and given by Rockhurst alum Thomas Divine.

Radio equipment was installed in the physics lab as early as 1922, but radios still were considered such a luxury that individual Jesuits were not allowed to have one in their living quarters. Someone must have had one, however, because, in the summer of 1932, the community received an unhappy letter from the provincial accusing members of violating "in a very marked degree" the Father General's "prescriptions about the use of the radio." If Rockhurst was using the radio for athletic reports, concerts, or vaudeville, the provincial demanded to know.[64]

Luckily for the success of the school play, no one apparently had told the provincial about the radio scene. As *College Daze* ended its run, Rockhurst was getting ready that May of 1929 to graduate the largest college class in its history—12 students. Few as the graduates were, the future looked promising with a college enrollment that had soared from 63 in the fall of 1924 to 150 just 4 years later. Rockhurst now had Dowling Hall and Bourke Field, with its freshly painted grandstand and its winning teams. The Rockhurst Circle was busily raising money and bringing recognition throughout the city. Yes, even Kansas City was starting to take note of the little school on the hill. On September 15, 1927, the *Kansas City Times* had noted the "substantial increase in enrollment at Catholic schools," and reported that Rockhurst College had hired a new professor, George Donovan, a Harvard graduate who "would take charge of a new sociology course."[65]

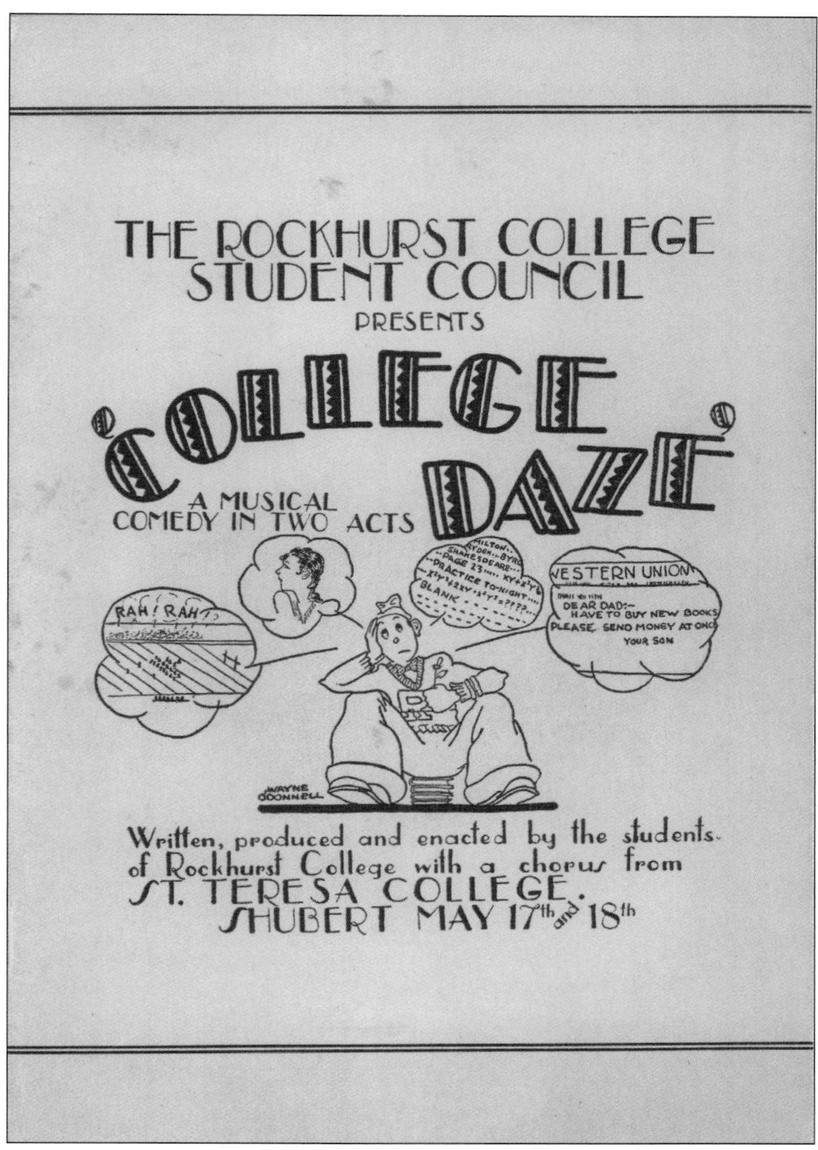

College Daze *was originally produced by Jim Riley, '31, written by Jim McQueeny, '31, with music and lyrics by Frank Condon, '34. Members of the cast and chorus included women from St. Teresa College. The musical was later reprised in 1980 for the 70th anniversary of the college. Courtesy of Rockhurst University Archives.*

No sooner, however, did the hilarious *College Daze* draw to a close than Rockhurst and the nation would find itself struggling to survive the darkest economic depression in the nation's history.

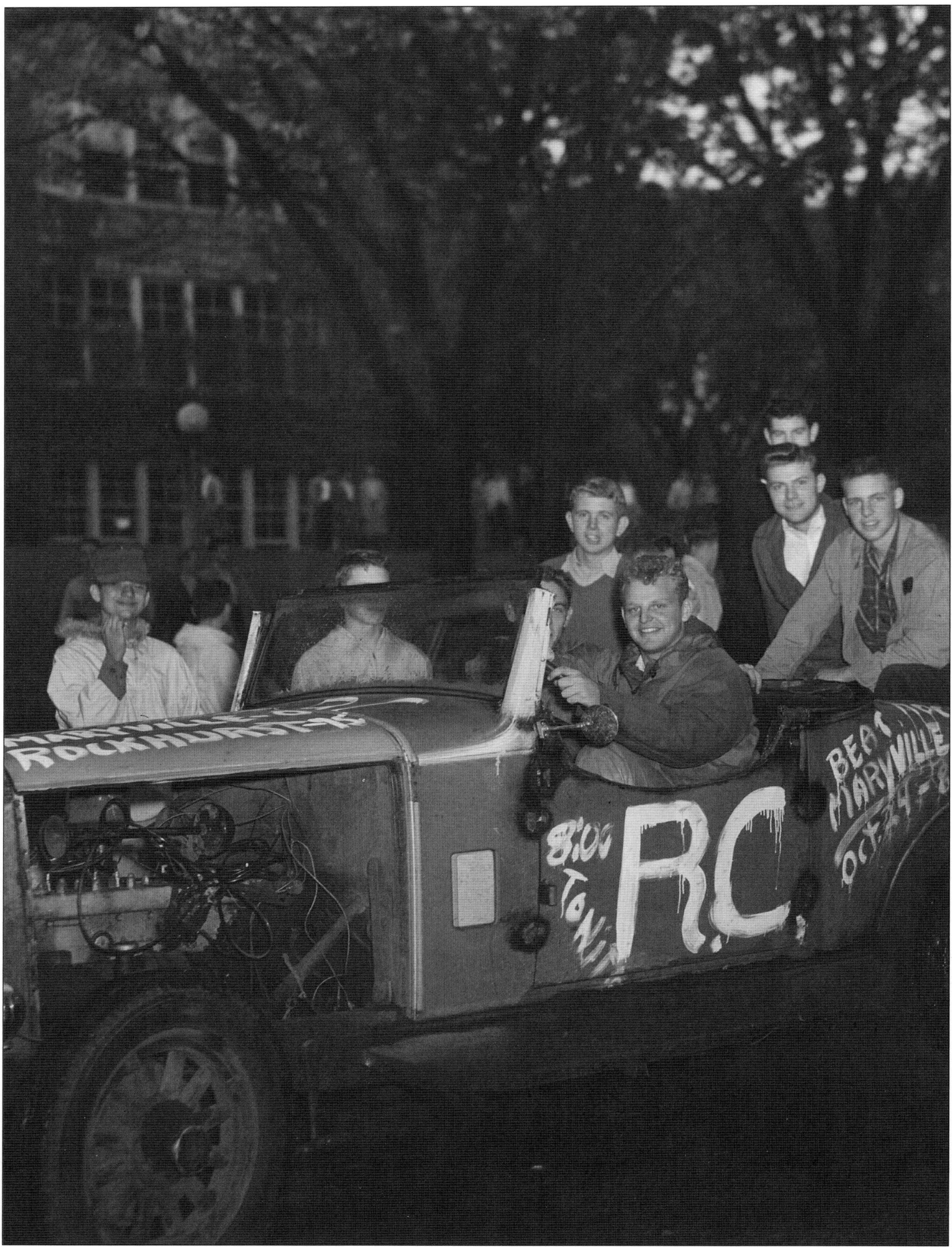

8:00
RC
BEAT
MARYVILLE

Chapter Eight

Struggle for Accreditation 1924–39

In the summer of 1928, the future seemed bright as Rockhurst installed a new president—Father William Manion, S.J., who had been at Rockhurst in its pioneer days, teaching in the high school from the fall of 1916 to the spring of 1919. Father Manion, who took over the presidency in July 1928, on the eve of his 41st birthday, was an enthusiastic man, a St. Louis native and graduate of Saint Louis University, who had been serving as Rockhurst College dean since 1926.[1]

Father Manion picked up where his predecessors, Fathers Weiand (1918–24) and Spillard (1924–28), had left off—looking to build an endowment fund and the new facilities that were key if Rockhurst ever were to gain recognition as a 4-year college. Seemingly unfazed by the discouragement that came to mark Spillard's tenure, Father Manion wasted no time drawing up plans for an addition to Sedgwick Hall and scheduling a visit with Kansas City Bishop Thomas Lillis, hoping to enlist his financial backing for a Rockhurst endowment fund.

Manion apparently broached the subject to the bishop in the summer of 1929, outlining a plan "of getting one thousand men to give $100 each," and voicing hopes for a subscription from the Kansas City Diocese. In a letter written from the episcopal residence at 301 East Armour Blvd., dated July 23, 1929, the bishop praised Manion's plan, but sounded skeptical, wondering whether it were possible for Manion to "find the one thousand men." The bishop held out the promise of a subscription but stipulated that it would come only after Manion had secured his first 99 pledges.

In his letter, Lillis linked his skepticism to an experience just a few years previous when he had given Rockhurst College $5,000, expecting that several more like gifts from the community would follow, which they did not. "We have had a great many promises and quite a few (people) make suggestions what should be done," he wrote. But where were the results? [2]

The bishop probably was referring to the efforts of former Rockhurst President Arthur Spillard, who had tried, but failed, to establish an endowment fund. Father Spillard, in fact, had become so frustrated with Rockhurst that, in 1928, he asked to leave and soon afterwards was appointed superior of the University of Detroit High School.[3] Spillard's letters to the provincial while he was at Rockhurst are revealing, indicating that he never wanted to come to Kansas City in the first place. He apparently had been quite content where he was in Michigan, "until you gave me the call and plunged me headfirst into this mudhole," he wrote just months after his arrival in Kansas City.[4]

He had spent many hours, he said, "racking his brains" and "scheming" for ways to meet and "get in with the 'big Guns' in Kansas City." On a winter day in 1927, he had had some success when he either approached or

PRESIDENTIAL PROFILE

— WILLIAM PATRICK MANION, S.J. —

Father William P. Manion, S.J., took office in July 1928 as Rockhurst's fifth president. A native of St. Louis, Manion was born on August 4, 1887, and entered the Jesuit novitiate in 1909. He earned bachelor's (1915) and master's (1924) degrees from Saint Louis University. From 1916 to 1919, Manion was a scholastic, teaching Latin and Greek at Rockhurst. He was ordained in 1922. Fr. Manion also taught at St. Stanislaus Seminary, Cleveland, Campion High School, Prairie du Chien, and was principal of St. Mary's College High School before returning to Rockhurst in 1926. At Rockhurst, he took on the role of dean of the college until his appointment as president in 1928. He served as president from 1928 to 1933.

Fr. Manion's time at Rockhurst as president was noteworthy for the work he did as an ambassador of good will for the school. At every opportunity, he attended gatherings of Catholic clergy, religious, and lay people throughout western Missouri and Kansas. He formed the Honorary Directors Association, expanded Sedgwick Hall, and oversaw the construction of Bourke Field with its stadium, track, and the first lighted field for night football in the city. After leaving Rockhurst, Fr. Manion was assigned to St. Louis where he engaged in retreat work and student Sodality activities for the next 10 years. He died in St. Louis on June 25, 1943.

had a chance encounter with Charles L. Aylward, vice president of Kansas City's Columbia National Bank. The two had talked about wealthy Catholics in Kansas City, and Spillard had asked Aylward who he thought might contribute to a Rockhurst endowment fund. In a letter to Spillard, dated February 17, 1927, Aylward listed the names of 15 people he thought would, "if solicited, make substantial contributions." On his list were well-known names such as Chamber of Commerce President Conrad Mann, restaurateur Fred Harvey, lawyer Frank Walsh, and political boss T.J. Pendergast. Miss Frances Lillis, sister of the bishop, also might contribute, Aylward said. Spillard's goal was to raise $1.8 million over the next 10 years, $300,000 of it by February 1, 1927.[5]

Despite Aylward's list and many promises from "men downtown" to "organize a committee for raising funds for Rockhurst," Spillard never succeeded in getting an endowment fund far off the ground. There had been promising moments, especially in the summer of 1926, when Spillard wrote to the provincial that "a few women…are organizing a Jesuit Aid Society," undoubtedly referring to the Sanctuary Guild. But in reality, there were few results.

— AN ADDITION TO SEDGWICK HALL —

Father Manion's addition to Sedgwick Hall was ready by September 1929. "Ninety-six tons of steel, draped in concrete, is the new annex to Rockhurst," the *Woodstock Letters* reported that fall. The building's central court, where the original gymnasium, open to the sky, once had been, now was enclosed and resting on its own pillars. The new annex rose the entire height of the building's 3 stories, and its rough-finished walls of white, its oak-colored ceilings, and its noise-absorbent concrete floors made it ideal, the *Woodstock* writer said, "for class purposes."

The entire third floor of the annex was devoted to labs and lecture rooms for physics and chemistry—those all-important sciences needed to win accreditation. Over-crowding also was eased for the biology department as classes moved into the quarters formerly occupied by the old physics lab, facing Troost Avenue. Now, thanks to the work of contractor C.A. Kelly, under the direction of Father Joseph Matoushek, S.J., there would be more room for lectures and experiments. A bright new chapel and study hall filled the annex's second floor, while the entire first floor was devoted to a new gymnasium that would double as an auditorium. The old chapel, where the Requiem Mass had been said for Marshal Foch's son, had been converted into the school's new library, complete with a golden oak circulation desk and 22 sturdy tables with chairs to match. The shiny maple floor contrasted nicely with the olive-green, steel bookstacks and dark green window hangings. The library now had ample space for its 15,000 volumes, and worshippers in the chapel no longer had to contend with the heat and noise of streetcars and automobiles passing by on Troost Avenue. A sacristy also had been added on one side of the sanctuary.

The old gym had been razed, including removal of the balcony seats attached to the walls. In their place were 8 tiers of detachable seats that could hold 800 people. A removable stairway now led from the main entrance hall down to the gym, where assemblies and social functions would be held. More improvements were apparent out back, where a public address system and scoreboard had been installed at Bourke Field, as well as lights, allowing for night games.[6]

Although the improvements forced Father Manion to borrow money, thus creating debt, Hugh Owens writes that he "was eminently justified" in building the additional rooms over the gymnasium, because the North Central Association, especially after the departure of Father Weiand, became more and more critical of what they considered inadequate library and scientific facilities of the college. Father Manion's building

A key to gaining accreditation as a 4-year college was to build an endowment. To that end, Fr. Manion hoped to enlist the financial backing of Kansas City Bishop Thomas Lillis. Though Lillis praised Manion's plan to get "one thousand men to give $100 each," the bishop made it clear that the diocese would promise a subscription only after Manion secured his first 99 pledges. Courtesy of Rockhurst University Archives.

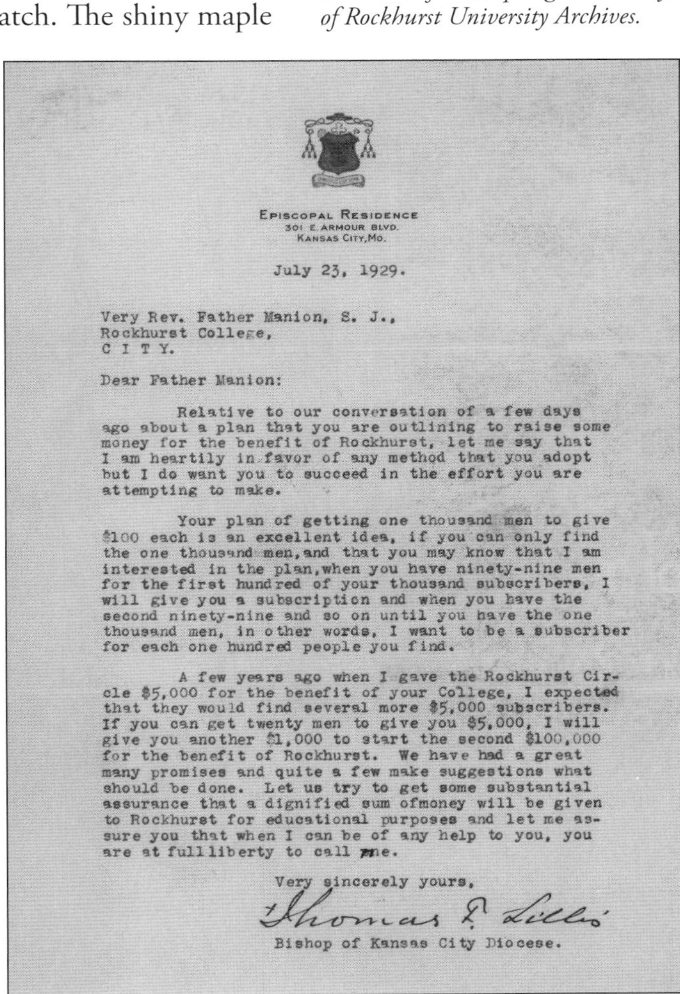

EPISCOPAL RESIDENCE
301 E. ARMOUR BLVD.
KANSAS CITY, MO.

July 23, 1929.

Very Rev. Father Manion, S. J.,
Rockhurst College,
C I T Y.

Dear Father Manion:

Relative to our conversation of a few days ago about a plan that you are outlining to raise some money for the benefit of Rockhurst, let me say that I am heartily in favor of any method that you adopt but I do want you to succeed in the effort you are attempting to make.

Your plan of getting one thousand men to give $100 each is an excellent idea, if you can only find the one thousand men, and that you may know that I am interested in the plan, when you have ninety-nine men for the first hundred of your thousand subscribers, I will give you a subscription and when you have the second ninety-nine and so on until you have the one thousand men, in other words, I want to be a subscriber for each one hundred people you find.

A few years ago when I gave the Rockhurst Circle $5,000 for the benefit of your College, I expected that they would find several more $5,000 subscribers. If you can get twenty men to give you $5,000, I will give you another $1,000 to start the second $100,000 for the benefit of Rockhurst. We have had a great many promises and quite a few make suggestions what should be done. Let us try to get some substantial assurance that a dignified sum ofmoney will be given to Rockhurst for educational purposes and let me assure you that when I can be of any help to you, you are at full liberty to call me.

Very sincerely yours,
Thomas F. Lillis
Bishop of Kansas City Diocese.

program went far, at least for a while, Owens writes, toward placating the accrediting authorities.[7]

Just a few months after Rockhurst moved into its new annex, a welcomed surprise came when it was announced on November 1, 1929, that Mrs. Mary Hanley had willed her house and grounds at 5183 Tracy Avenue to the college. It was a large house, built in 1922 at the northwest corner of Rockhurst Rd. and Tracy and valued at $25,000. With the house so close to St. Francis Xavier Church and right across the street from the Rockhurst campus, Mary Hanley's husband, a prominent Kansas City manufacturer, had become close friends with Pastor Michael Leary and other Jesuits at Rockhurst, which explains why the Hanleys willed their house to the college. Classrooms soon were constructed on the first and second floors of the Hanley house to relieve crowding in Dowling Hall, and the Hanley basement was converted into a locker room for the college football team.[8]

Touting Rockhurst's improvements, Father Manion, just as Father Weiand had done a decade before, approached officials at Saint Louis University, asking again whether SLU would take Rockhurst under its wing until the little college could stand more firmly on its own. "I have been trying for the past fourteen months to have the authorities of our own University, i.e., St. Louis University, include Rockhurst among the 'Corporate Colleges of the St. Louis University,'" Manion wrote on February 7, 1931. His requests had not gone over well, being looked on "askance," he said, by all the men there except the Father Provincial, SLU President Robert A. Johnston, and faculty member Alphonse M. Schwitalla.

Schwitalla, of course, had been Rockhurst's first college teacher, the very man who had taken it upon himself to teach every college class that

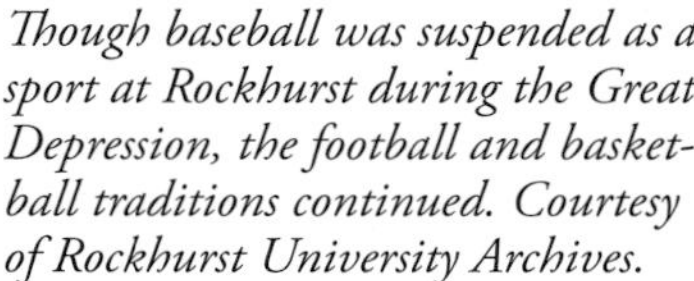

Though baseball was suspended as a sport at Rockhurst during the Great Depression, the football and basketball traditions continued. Courtesy of Rockhurst University Archives.

first year of 1917. It was Father Schwitalla who went the extra mile now, doing his best to persuade Saint Louis University and the Board of Review of the North Central Standardizing Committee to accept Manion's request. The main difficulty, Manion feared, was the distance separating the 2 colleges—256 miles, which created problems in controlling the registrar's office and departmental administrators, as well as maintaining departmental and faculty meetings. He prayed for success, nonetheless, expecting a favorable reply by spring. "It is," he wrote to the provincial on February 7, 1931, "our only hope if we are to continue as a four-year college."

— BAD NEWS IN BUNDLES —

Manion's prayer would have to wait to be answered. On March 31, 1931, his hopes were dashed. "I felt certain that I would be able to communicate some good news in this letter but my hopes have been vain," he wrote. A letter bearing the bad news had come the previous week from Father Schwitalla, informing him that, just as he had feared, Rockhurst simply was too far from St. Louis. "The negative reply has depressed me and all here at our college since we had such high hopes of receiving the necessary recognition," Manion wrote. "This severe blow leaves us almost helpless...."

The news everywhere seemed to be bad as the nation, now in the throes of the Great Depression, slogged along. The flu had wreaked havoc, as well, confining 7 or 8 members of the faculty to bed. Most had returned to the classroom as March drew to a close, but Father John E. Knipscher was still in the hospital, suffering from heart trouble. His condition was so serious that there was no chance he would return to Rockhurst to finish the spring term. The doctor said it was quite possible he wouldn't be able to return in the fall, either. Then, Bishop Lillis continued to be an irritant, demanding that every Rockhurst priest attend a trio of yearly diocesan conferences. Manion and his small faculty had no time for that, so Manion was holding out against the bishop, though he knew that Lillis "may try to force me to comply."

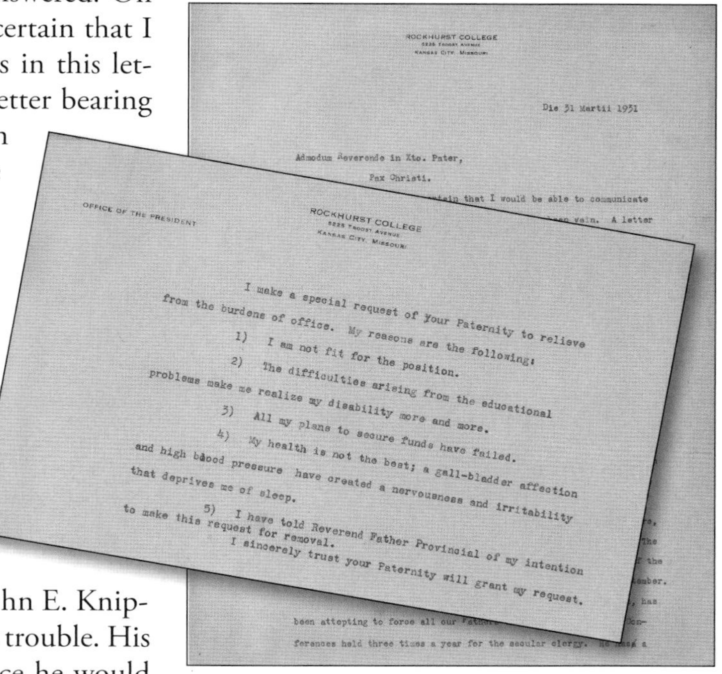
ROCKHURST COLLEGE
5225 TROOST AVENUE
KANSAS CITY, MISSOURI

Die 31 Martii 1931

Admodum Reverende in Xto. Pater,

Pax Christi.

OFFICE OF THE PRESIDENT

ROCKHURST COLLEGE
5225 TROOST AVENUE
KANSAS CITY, MISSOURI

I make a special request of Your Paternity to relieve from the burdens of office. My reasons are the following:

1) I am not fit for the position.

2) The difficulties arising from the educational problems make me realize my disability more and more.

3) All my plans to secure funds have failed.

4) My health is not the best; a gall-bladder affection and high blood pressure have created a nervousness and irritability that deprives me of sleep.

5) I have told Reverend Father Provincial of my intention to make this request for removal.

I sincerely trust your Paternity will grant my request.

Citing problems related to accreditation, finances, and his own health, on March 31, 1931, Father Manion wrote the Superior General of the Society of Jesus, Wlodimir Ledóchowski, S.J., asking that he be relieved of his duties at Rockhurst. The request was denied. A few months later, Provincial Samuel Horine, S.J., wrote to Manion, "Can you live on hope for a couple of years longer?" Fr. Manion would remain as president until 1933. Courtesy of Rockhurst University Archives.

It had been Manion's plan—not to construct a new *college* building—but a new high school building. He then would move the college into the existing high school building—Sedgwick Hall. A wealthy man had promised to donate to the project, but now, with the Depression weighing so heavily on everyone, he was delaying.

All of these troubles weighed on Father Manion as the winter of 1930–31 turned to spring. The letter denying incorporation with SLU apparently had so demoralized Manion that he took the route his predecessor had and asked to be relieved "from the burdens of office." As troubles had compounded, his self-confidence had suffered to the point that he determined he was not "fit for the position." He felt overwhelmed by the "educational

— JIMMY GLEESON, MAJOR-LEAGUE BASEBALL PLAYER —

A 3-letter man starring in football, basketball, and baseball at Rockhurst, Jimmy Gleeson was offered a contract to play baseball with the New York Yankees in his junior year of college. He turned it down to finish his degree at Rockhurst. The day after his graduation in 1933, Gleeson signed a contract with the Cleveland Indians. Later he played for the Chicago Cubs and the Cincinnati Reds, and, after serving in the Navy during the war, he spent the 1948 and 1949 seasons with the Boston Braves' AAA club, retiring after the 1950 season.

On October 24, 1963, Yogi Berra was named manager of the New York Yankees. Two hours after Berra's appointment, Jimmy Gleeson received a phone call from Yogi offering him a job as first-base coach with the Yankees. Gleeson and Berra had become friends during the war when Gleeson was in charge of baseball at a submarine base in New London, Connecticut, and Berra was an apprentice seaman playing outfield on Gleeson's team. Gleeson accepted the job with the Yankees, finally joining the team he had turned down 31 years earlier as a junior at Rockhurst. The 1964 Yankees won the American League pennant.

In 1964 Jimmy Gleeson was inducted into the NAIA Baseball Hall of Fame and in 1981 the Rockhurst Athletics Hall of Fame. Gleeson died in 1996.

Rev. Maurice Van Ackeren, S.J., president of Rockhurst, presents Jimmy Gleeson a plaque at his induction into the NAIA Baseball Hall of Fame.

problems," and, perhaps most discouraging, that "all my plans to secure funds have failed."[9]

The details of what followed after Manion mailed that letter are not known, although his request for removal certainly was denied because he would remain as Rockhurst president for another 2 years. By the fall of 1931, there was a noticeable slowness in his walk, and he seemed to hang his head, as if in deep thought. A sympathetic letter came from the provincial's office. "I hope you are not suffering, either bodily pain or mental worries," Provincial Samuel Horine, S.J., wrote. He told Manion that he had just spoken of Rockhurst that very day, saying that "anyone would find it a care and a burden, especially as the problems there are seemingly at a deadlock and no one able to break that. Some day a good angel will give a very substantial gift to Rockhurst and open up the way out for those then in charge. I really would wish to have this occur while you are still Rector," Horine wrote. "Can you live on hope for a couple of years longer?"[10]

Adding to tensions were the NCA's new financial standards for Catholic schools, requiring all to submit comprehensive data on their finances. If the NCA wasn't satisfied that a college had a sufficient endowment to cover its debts, an on-site survey was conducted. This new approach by the NCA, which de-emphasized discrete quantitative standards in favor of an overall qualitative assessment, sent shivers through Catholic colleges when 5 of their institutions soon were scheduled for an on-site survey and 2, Xavier in Cincinnati and the University of Detroit, lost accreditation.[11]

Rockhurst, with no accreditation to lose, continued its efforts to find favor with SLU and the NCA. With another effort to approach them apparently in the works, another letter came from the provincial's residence in St. Louis, this one dated December 18, 1931, advising Manion on how to deal with the inspectors who surely would come to Kansas City. "You are inclined to give too glowing an account of things in your eagerness to give a good impression," Horine told Manion and advised him to tone it down because the inspectors were men who "strive to be objective in a very disheartening fashion." After reiterating the same old Rockhurst drawbacks—too few teachers with full degrees, the lack of an endowment, the debt, crowded classrooms, and the sharing of a building with the high school—Father Horine suggested that Manion drop a note to Father Deglman, who had been through all this before when he went to Columbia with Father Spillard that Halloween weekend a half-dozen years before.

A year passed and nothing changed, except that the country fell deeper into the darkest days of the Depression. Average earnings in the nation dropped 33 percent, and unemployment, by 1933, stood at 13 million, or one-quarter of the work force. In Kansas City, with a population of nearly 400,000, about one in 10 residents received direct public relief. To avoid layoffs, workers at Hallmark Cards voted twice to take 10 percent paycuts. Housing construction came to a standstill, but public works projects abounded and would leave Kansas City with a new City Hall, Jackson County Courthouse, and Municipal Auditorium. The projects were made possible by voter-approved bonds that launched Kansas City's 10-Year Plan, which aimed at moderating the effects of the Depression through job-creating public works projects. Under the plan, miles of new roads and new sewers were built, and the bed of Brush Creek paved. Despite hard times, the Nelson Gallery of Art and Atkins Museum also went up, built with $14 million from the estates of publisher William Rockhill Nelson and the reclusive Mary McAfee Atkins. More important for Rockhurst, the Depression years also saw the foundation of a new university—the University of Kansas City, founded in 1933. Eventually it would become the University of Missouri-Kansas City.

Students there, as did those at Rockhurst, got assistance during the Depression through the New Deal's National Youth Administration. By working 40 hours a month, often in the school office or library or by assisting in the physical education department, students earned an average of $15—enough to cover the cost of books, college fees, streetcar fare, and lunch. By December 1935, about 230 young men and women in Kansas City's colleges were earning part of their college expenses thanks to the government's NYA. The 2-year-old University of Kansas City reported 73 students receiving aid, while Rockhurst reported 21.[12]

— SPECIAL PRAYERS —

Like most everyone, Rockhurst was taking stock of its situation and trying to figure out ways to cut back on expenses so as to survive. A number of colleges would go under during the Depression, including, in 1931, St. Mary's College in Kansas, which the Society of Jesus had started as an Indian mission in 1848 and where so many of Rockhurst's Jesuits had worked or taken retreats over the years.

On February 9, 1932, Father Manion called a special meeting of the house consultors "to lay before them the financial condition" of the school. Truth be told, Rockhurst had been having difficulties for some time collecting tuition. Following the stock market crash of October 1929, Manion had taken immediate inventory and written to the provincial, bemoaning the school's financial situation. An angry provincial, Matthew Germing, S.J., shot back: "What became of the money you must be taking in for tuition?" That Rockhurst "was not taking it in," was something he had just learned from Father Matoushek. "You will have to stop that at once," he told Manion and went on to explain how the tuition "trouble" was costing Rockhurst a probable $61,000 a year. "People are of course imposing on you," he wrote and instructed Manion "to take away from your Dean and Principal the power to give reductions, if they have it. Better do that at once; just tell them I ordered it." Come mid-year, the provincial said, Manion must "strictly follow the policy" of no examination for anyone who had not paid his bills.

"I tell you, Father, it's absolutely necessary," the provincial wrote. "I am told that now people pay just when they please. No wonder that with 500 boys paying no assessment and hardly any interest to you, you can hardly make ends meet." Of course, the provincial added, "there will always be those who can't pay, but the trouble is there are so many others who try <u>to make our authorities believe</u> that they can't pay. Then when they have finished at our school, or leave us for some reason, they pay $400, even $500 a year, at the other school without saying a word." Manion had tried to explain: because Rockhurst was the only Catholic college in Kansas City, if it didn't keep a boy, the boy would have no other school to attend. The explanation was not good enough for the provincial. "This simply means that you have to look closely into each case but you can not make that a reason for keeping him; if you do your school can not be run at all."

After the stock market crash of October 1929, Rockhurst took inventory of its financial situation. Father Manion wrote Provincial Matthew Germing, S.J., about the worsening financial conditions at Rockhurst. Fr. Germing's response was abrupt. He took the young school to task for not collecting tuition and for giving too many reductions in fees. He ordered Manion not to allow any student to take mid-year exams until his bills were paid and to begin the fund-raising campaign immediately. Courtesy of Rockhurst University Archives.

Provincial's Residence
St. Louis University, St. Louis, Mo.

November 8, 1929.

Dear Father Manion,
P. C.

I was speaking to Father Matoushek a while ago and told him that I didn't understand what became of the money you must be taking in for tuition. He interrupted me at once by saying, we are not taking it in; there's the trouble. Here at the High School they have only about fifty more boys than you have at Rockhurst, but look at the result: they pay at least $20,000 in interest to the U. about $32,000 in teachers salaries about . $9,000 in Province assesment. This makes $61,000. To think that they have an expense of $61,000 which you have not and then come out better than you at the end of the year.

But to come back to not collecting tuition fees, you will have to stop that at once. People are of course imposing on you, as they have imposed on many others of our men. In the first place, take away from your Dean and Principal the power to give reductions, if they have it. Better do that at once; just tell them that I ordered it. Secondly, at mid-year strictly follow the policy, no examination for any one who has not paid his bills. I tell you, Father, it's absolutely necessary. I am told that now people pay just when they please. No wonder that with 500 boys, paying no assessment and ~~no~~ hardly any interest, you can hardly make ends meet. I suppose you have thousands upon thousands of dollars on the books.

No boy respects the college for letting him slip through without paying when he can pay. And they can pay, as is clear from the fact that from Rockhurst they go to other colleges and universities, where they have to pay.

Please start the campaign at once, it has to be done. Excuse my abruptness, but I want to get this off this evening.

Ever yours in Dmno,

M. Germing S.J.

As the Depression worsened, the new provincial, Samuel Horine, S.J., wrote, this time to the Rockhurst procurator, admonishing him that he must learn "to inconvenience himself" to collect tuition because Rockhurst "has so many unpaid tuitions."[13]

At his special meeting of the house consultors, Father Manion also aired concerns that "our loans might be called any moment," and, perhaps following the city's lead, suggested that the college issue mortgage bonds. Added worries came from the provincial's office in St. Louis, which was about to increase by $5 the "man tax" on its colleges, and, as always, pressure came from the North Central Association. The latest blow from the accrediting association was a new deadline for Rockhurst to become accredited as a 4-year college: September 1934. Rockhurst must meet the deadline, the NCA said, or drop its upper level courses. "Our need of a new building and an endowment fund is most urgent," Manion told the Jesuits at Rockhurst, then asked the community "to unite in prayer and sacrifice for help from God." A special Novena was to be held and each evening during benediction "a special prayer" was to be recited to the Sacred Heart.[14]

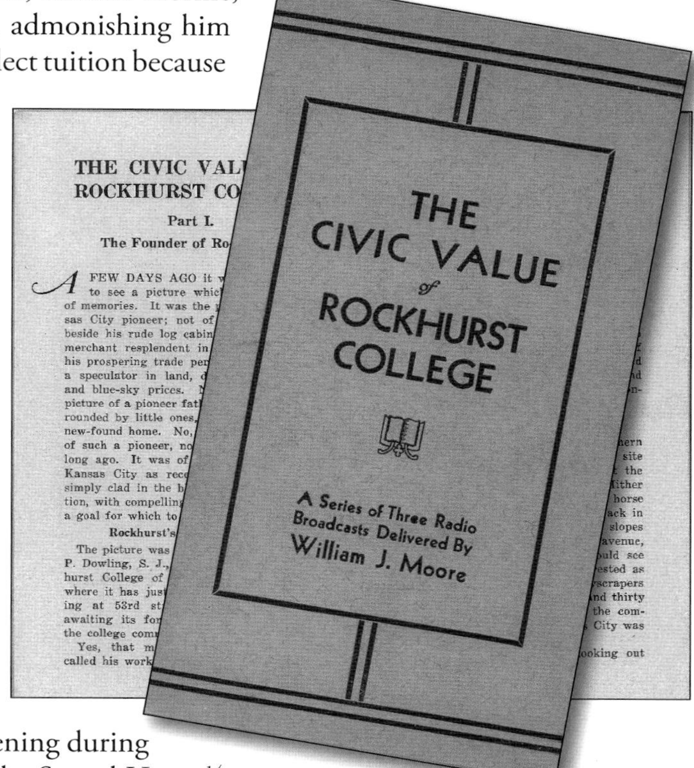

In April and May 1932, Rockhurst graduate William J. Moore, '28, delivered a series of 3 addresses over radio station KWKC. Moore, a former editor of The Sentinel, *explained how all great private colleges depend on the establishment of endowments through the generosity of benefactors. "I ask Kansas City in the name of education to keep alive the light of learning which shines at Rockhurst . . . that it may fulfill its destiny of future greatness." Courtesy of Rockhurst University Archives.*

By April 1932, Rockhurst had taken drastic steps. It gathered all of its lay teachers together and told them, come fall, that their salaries would be reduced by 15 percent. Other employees faced a 20 percent pay cut. Baseball was dropped, and a coach let go for lack of funds to pay him. In the Jesuit dining hall, first-class feasts were limited to one for each season of the year.[15]

Then Rockhurst got proactive. In an editorial published February 10, 1932, the student newspaper wondered aloud why Rockhurst had no publicity department like other colleges and lamented that it was only through the school's successful athletic teams that any notice came. *The Sentinel's* editor urged the Student Council to get busy putting Rockhurst's name before the city's newspapers, who then could write up the school's social, scholastic, and oratorical events, as well as athletics. Someone apparently approached faculty member Thomas F. Divine, S.J., who announced in the article that he intended to form a Rockhurst Press Club.

Then a lecture series was established where prominent men of the city would be invited to speak at Student Council meetings and at evening assemblies open to the public. Credit for the idea, the primary purpose of which was to publicize Rockhurst, went to Council President John W. Dorsey, who explained that "if the Circle and other organizations can accomplish as much as they have for Rockhurst, the students themselves, who are, or should be, much more interested in the Institution, can do as much and more." His statement and a *Sentinel* editorial in support of the lecture series addressed murmurs of discontent heard after it was announced that the entire student body of the college would be required to attend.

The Rockhurst College Student Council sponsored a lecture series to put Rockhurst's name before the public. In addition to religious lectures led by Jesuits, the Student Council invited prominent men of the city to speak at Student Council meetings and at evening assemblies open to the public. Courtesy of Rockhurst University Archives.

The lecture series began the very next week when Thomas Collins, managing editor of *The Kansas City Journal-Post*, showed up at the regular Student Council meeting. After the council conducted its usual business, Collins launched into an impromptu talk about newspaper ethics and how it is not the newspaperman but the public that regulates the moral tone of a newspaper. When Collins finished and students asked questions—including one inquiring why *The Journal-Post* used pink sheets for its final edition—the meeting was declared the most successful of the year.[16]

Then Rockhurst took to the airwaves. In a series of three addresses in April and May 1932, the voice of Rockhurst graduate William J. Moore, Class of '28, went out over radio station KWKC, cajoling, educating, and pleading for Kansas City to come to the aid of Rockhurst College. Moore, a former editor of *The Sentinel*, invoked the image of a pioneer Rockhurst situated in an empty field south of Brush Creek, then argued that the college "was a nucleus" for the recent development south of 48th Street along Troost. Had listeners forgotten that Rockhurst had given a strip of ground on Rockhurst Road that allowed the city to connect Troost Avenue and The Paseo? Had they forgotten what a civic asset the college was?

The great universities of the United States, he explained, depend, not on taxes, but on the generosity of benefactors. Columbia University had an endowment of nearly $70 million, Stanford of $29 million, and Princeton of $18 million. Georgetown University was befriended by James A. Farrell, recently retired president of the United States Steel Company. The University of Detroit had a friend in the Fisher brothers, founders of General Motors' Fisher Body Company, and Marquette University had the Robert A. Johnston family, makers of Johnston Chocolates. Sadly, Rockhurst College had no one, Moore said, though it was looking forward to the day when Kansas City would "recognize its debt to its only college and will come to its aid." What, he asked, would Kansas City be without Rockhurst College? "The Heart of America, but a heart without feeling. A cold heart. Cold to education and learning. A city where intelligence is not prized." If that be so, then Kansas City, he said, should "hang its head in shame."

The radio broadcast appealed to Kansas Citians to send their high school graduates—whatever their religion—to Rockhurst, thus avoiding expenses to live and travel out of town, and simultaneously providing an economic boost for Kansas City as students spent their money with local merchants. "If it's smart to be thrifty, it's smart to attend Rockhurst College," Moore said. If they did so, they could be assured that Rockhurst would ground their sons in "sound principles," lay the foundation "for strong character," and a "love of truth and justice."

William Moore looked downtown at the skeletons of new skyscrapers piercing the sky and at men busily lining the bed of Brush Creek with concrete and declared with alarm, as had newspaper headlines, "the prodigality with which money has been lavished on unproductive monuments to civic vanity." In the past, money had been wasted on education, as well, he conceded, with courses in tap dancing and beauty culture. That wasn't so unbearable "when there was a chicken in every pot," but now, in 1932, schools were being closed for lack of funds.

How, he asked, was Rockhurst going to continue to exist? How, he asked, was it going to receive accreditation, excellent college though it might be, when the standardizing agency kept pressing "the endowment problem." Did Kansas City understand that Rockhurst had no endowment? That it was not supported by taxes? That it had no income from a wealthy estate and no "vault filled with crisp government bonds?" It continues to exist, Moore argued, for one reason only: "the unselfish labor of the Jesuit members of the faculty," who worked without pay.

And then, in the last of his 3 weekly speeches, William Moore got right to the point and asked Kansas Citians to contribute to a needed endowment fund. "I now ask Kansas City to recognize the debt which it owes Rockhurst, the only college of arts and sciences in this city. The debt is a real one. It is an economic debt, a cultural debt, and a debt of gratitude, gratitude for the work, which has been done. I ask Kansas City in the name of education to keep alive the light of learning which shines at Rockhurst. I ask Kansas City in the name of truth to cherish the ministers of truth. I ask Kansas City in the name of justice to be just as a debtor and to generously repay Rockhurst College, that it may fulfill its destiny of future greatness."[17]

— Back to Columbia —

That summer of 1932, Rockhurst approached the University of Missouri again, asking for an extension to give Rockhurst time to work out its accreditation problems. On August 17, 1932, and again on September 7, Rockhurst Dean Daniel H. Conway went to Columbia on a mission of supreme importance. "We have a serious crisis," the minister's diary stated that summer. If MU dropped Rockhurst's junior college accreditation, then "our college is lost," it said, because there would be no chance of securing funds for a separate college or high school building.[18]

In Columbia, Conway was questioned for 2 hours on every phase of the college—"searching, severe and embarrassing—yet eminently fair," he

Rockhurst band members, 1930s. Courtesy of Rockhurst University Archives.

reported. The accreditors brought up the same old difficulty—Rockhurst needed a separate college building with its own library and science hall. Conway pointed out Rockhurst's handicaps, noted the progress made, and came away with the extension he requested for the school year 1932-33. But that was only one year, so the peril was far from over. A letter came from the provincial, stating bluntly that Rockhurst might never rise above junior college status and that President Manion should be prepared to tell the alumni just that.[19]

In November 1932 came more inspections. On November 10, 3 faculty members from the University of Missouri spent the day at Rockhurst, and on November 18, came yet another inspection by representatives of the North Central Association. Rockhurst went all out to put the college in its most favorable light. A competent librarian was hired and a physics teacher with experience replaced one without. Friends of the college formed the all-male Rockhurst Club, charging $100 annual dues and writing a constitution that stated its purpose: "to promote higher education by securing funds to build and equip such buildings at Rockhurst as may be necessary to have Rockhurst College raised to a standard to be affiliated with and recognized as a class A college." But still Rockhurst could not rise above its junior college status.[20]

A few months later, with still no recognition as a 4-year college, Rockhurst changed leadership, installing the current dean, the Rev. Daniel H. Conway, S.J., as its sixth president. Father Manion left for a new assignment in St. Louis, where he joined *The Queen's Work*, the Jesuit Sodality publication. The work suited Father Manion, who was described as a man whose greatest work on behalf of Rockhurst had been "as an ambassador of good will for the school." At every opportunity he had attended gatherings of Catholic clergy, religious, and laypersons throughout Kansas and western Missouri and had taken a special interest in missions to African-Americans in Leavenworth and both Kansas Cities. He was never, *The Catholic Register* said, a man who steered private conversations toward Rockhurst interests, but instead "confined himself almost entirely to making new friendships and cementing old ones."[21] His successor would be much different.

— "THE BUILDER OF ROCKHURST" —

Daniel H. Conway, S.J., was 39 years old, one of 12 children of a railroad worker from Durango, Colorado. He was a towering, lean man, who briefly had played semi-pro baseball and studied at Regis College in Denver and the law school at Creighton University before entering the Society of Jesus as a novice in Florissant when he was 21. He received his bachelor's and master's degrees from Saint Louis University and had taught at John Carroll University in Cleveland and Campion College in Prairie du Chien, Wisconsin, before going to Rockhurst. He arrived in 1930 to teach religion and philosophy. In 1932 he would assume duties as dean of men. Father Manion said of him that he had "a genius for organization" and was "a forceful orator." Others described him as a "hard-headed, practical planner" and noted his "phenomenal memory of people" and his "great sincerity."[22]

PRESIDENTIAL PROFILE

— DANIEL H. CONWAY, S.J. —

A native of Colorado, Fr. Dan Conway graduated from Regis College and entered the Society of Jesus as a novice in Florissant in 1914 at age 21. He held bachelor's (1920) and master's (1921) degrees from Saint Louis University and taught English, Spanish, Latin, Philosophy, and Religion at Campion College, John Carroll University, and Saint Louis University. Ordained in 1927, Conway came to Rockhurst in 1930 as professor of religion and philosophy. In 1932 he became dean of men, and in February 1933 assumed the presidency of Rockhurst. Fr. Conway served as president until April 1940.

After leaving Rockhurst, Conway was appointed president of St. Mary's College, the theological seminary of the Missouri province. In 1947 he was named rector and tertian master at St. Joseph's Hall, Decatur, Illinois. In 1950, he became provincial of the Missouri Province of the Society of Jesus.

Fr. Conway's presidency occurred during an important period of formation and expansion. The building that bears his name, Conway Hall, was built under his leadership, as was Mason-Halpin Fieldhouse. Additionally, during his term of office Rockhurst received full accreditation as a 4-year college from the North Central Association.

Fr. Conway died in 1956.

Those qualities would come in handy as Father Conway set about outlining Rockhurst's needs and embarking on the college's first major expansion since its founding. The past few years of the economic depression had been hard and many colleges, including Rockhurst, had faced financial reversals, the new president said. But Rockhurst "had carried on," even as the demand for more and better education had increased. He pointed out that Rockhurst College had started in 1917 with an enrollment of only 11 students; but now, 170 were enrolled. "These figures," Conway said with emphasis, "leave only one course open to Rockhurst; space and facilities MUST be increased—she must forge ahead—NOW."

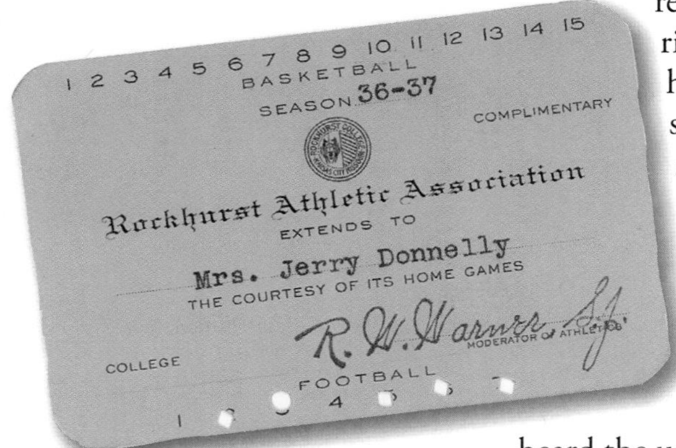

Complimentary pass for 1936-37 Rockhurst football and basketball home games. Courtesy of Rockhurst University Archives.

Rockhurst's Honorary Directors, a newly formed group of businessmen who cared about the college, including Chamber of Commerce President Conrad Mann, heard the urgency in Father Conway's voice and stepped up to help. On a Wednesday night, September 28, 1933, Mann stood up at a dinner given by the Honorary Directors in the main dining room at Union Station and appealed to the people of Kansas City to co-operate with the Jesuit fathers "in the upbuilding of Rockhurst college."[23] The dinner, attended by Catholics and non-Catholics alike, was the kickoff of a drive to enlist an additional 150 Honorary Directors.

"The North Central Association has served notice on Rockhurst that it must have an endowment and a new building if it is to be recognized fully," Mann began. "This condition is not creditable to Kansas City, nor to the Kansas City spirit. Rockhurst has a faculty above the requirements; only the physical requirements are lacking."

Like others before him, he chastised Kansas City for failing to recognize its responsibility "to this college of ours." Mann told how he had devoted much of his time and effort to making Kansas City an industrial center, only to realize that without cultural development the city "would be lopsided and uninviting to prospective residents." So, he said, he had gone on to help organize the Kansas City Art Institute and the Horner conservatory and junior college. Presently, he was involved in plans for what he hoped would become "a great seat of learning"—the future University of Kansas City. "But while we are planning for the future," he said, "let us also remember the college we already have."

Pat Mason and Vincent O'Flaherty, Jr., 2 of Rockhurst's first 3 graduates, Class of '21, also spoke. O'Flaherty, now a realtor, pledged the support of alumni, and Mason, Rockhurst coach since the school first had a team, told of the prospects of the season's football team. In tow were the year's co-captains, Richard Sullivan and Ray Sonnenberg. Dr. John H. Outland, former president of the Kansas City Athletic Club, spoke briefly of football "then and now." Outland was a first-team all-American from the University of Pennsylvania in 1897 and 1898, and later the namesake of the Outland Trophy, given each year to the most outstanding interior lineman. Rockhurst President Conway also was there, admitting the difficulties he faced. Despite the lack of an endowment fund and no considerable reserve of any kind, he felt a "tremendous responsibility," he said, to maintain every standard of educational opportunity.

One of Father Conway's first accomplishments as president was to add a night school, which allowed those who had to work during the day to get an education. Tuition was $5 per semester hour and a special fee of $15 for the third- and fourth-year advanced accounting courses. In keeping with the times, required subjects were of a practical nature: accounting, principles of economics, money and banking, corporation finance, English composition and rhetoric, and public speaking. Among elective courses were auditing, income tax procedure, and principles of investment. The School of Commerce and Finance, as it was called, opened on November 22, 1933, and within 2 years had an enrollment of 156 students. By 1937, it enrolled 219 students, and by 1939, a total of 527. Rockhurst apparently ignored the earlier directive from the Father General forbidding coeducational study because women as well as men enrolled at the night school and, over the course of 6 years, were able to earn a bachelor of science degree in commerce.[24]

In the fall of 1934, pre-business courses were added in the college, but it would not be until the fall of 1937 that a complete course in commerce and finance, leading to a bachelor of science degree, would be available for

— THE ROCKHURST HONORARY DIRECTORS ASSOCIATION —

Perhaps no group has contributed more to helping young people finance their education at Rockhurst than the Honorary Directors. It all began during the depression days of 1931 when 2 members of the Rockhurst football team were short on tuition money. Eight men pledged $25 each, and the Honorary Directors Association was born. By 1932, there were 40 Honorary Directors. In 1933, the Honorary Directors elected their first officers, pictured left to right: Charles G. Haake, president; William J. Teefey, secretary; William Stoneman, Jr., vice president; Louis B. McGee, treasurer.

ROCKHURST COLLEGE MEN'S GROUP ELECTS OFFICERS.

Over the years, thousands of civic, business, and professional leaders have been a part of the Honorary Directors Association. Through their annual dues and in other ways, they have reached out to help deserving students in scholarship aid. Since 1998, the Honorary Directors has presented the Van Ackeren Spirit Award to an individual who has lived and worked to uphold the values of Rockhurst University. The award is named after Rockhurst's ninth president, Rev. Maurice E. Van Ackeren, S.J.

day students. For regular students, college tuition in the 1930s was $72.50 a semester. Prior to 1937, business students could transfer their credits to a 4-year college, which they entered in the junior year. Rockhurst's pre-med, pre-law, pre-dentistry, and pre-engineering students did the same. Although the night school was new, extension courses were not. Since September 1930, Rockhurst had been offering Saturday morning classes for nuns in the Kansas City vicinity.[25]

— AT A CROSSROADS —

By the mid-1930s, with business conditions starting to improve, Rockhurst found itself at a crossroads: either find a way to build or settle for permanent status as a junior college. In April 1934, Father Conway put in a personal appearance at the North Central Association spring meeting in Chicago, which must have paid off because he came home with good news: the NCA had voted to accredit Rockhurst as a junior college—subject to revision in 1936. That meant inspectors again would take up the question of full recognition. In another positive development, the accrediting committee had decided to let Rockhurst, in the meantime, retain its upper division classes. Although the news was far short of Rockhurst's long-sought goal, things were looking up.[26]

Then Father Conway went out on a limb; he decided that the best way to raise money for a new building was to start building, thereby showing the public that Rockhurst meant business. "So many say that they have heard about building at Rockhurst for so long that they are waiting to see the start before they will contribute," he explained.[27] The "great organizer" started making lists and forming a plan. Even a bad cold that had confined him to St. Mary's Hospital was not enough to slow him down. He landed an interview with newspaper reporter A.B. Macdonald, who visited Conway in his hospital room and then wrote a lengthy article about Rockhurst, published in *The Kansas City Star* on December 9, 1934.

Macdonald listened as Conway, sitting in an armchair with pencil in hand and a piece of paper propped up on his knees, drew a rough sketch of the Rockhurst campus for Macdonald's edification. "See those two tiny squares?" he said, directing Macdonald's eye to the map. "Those are the only buildings Rockhurst College has for the education of those many thousands of boys." Macdonald protested, saying that he had just been on campus and knew that only 200 boys attended Rockhurst. Yes, that was true now, Conway agreed, but the future, he said, was another story. He rose from his chair, straight and thin, his eyes glowing. "In my mind's eye I can see boys that are coming from all the country around—Kansas, Oklahoma, Texas, Arkansas, Nebraska—all over the Southwest," he said. "A way must be provided for them." He paused a moment, added that he was sure it would happen, and explained: "'I will provide, saith the Lord,' and His promises are sure."

The Lord seemed to answer in September 1935 when Father Conway gathered his Honorary Directors together and introduced them to John M. Aufiero, president of E.A. Laboratories of Brooklyn, New York, who had pledged $1,000 to Rockhurst. At this dinner gathering, Aufiero increased his pledge to $5,000, spurring others to follow. In short order, Chamber President Conrad Mann, Henry J. Massman, W. List, and Thomas McGee promised $5,000 as well, suddenly giving Rockhurst a $25,000 start on a building fund.[28]

Like Father Conway, these prominent men also felt it was important to move ahead with construction, some even saying they would contribute twice as much when they saw a start made. "The committee and the consultors at the house here are of the opinion that the only way to succeed

Hardships and Heroism Have Gone Into the Making of Rockhurst College

Reprint from The Kansas City Star of December 9, 1934.

Rockhurst College, at Fifty-third Street and Troost Avenue, in this city, with a student body that is increasing in numbers each year, has outgrown its two small buildings. The North Central Association of Colleges, of which it is a member, has decreed that if Rockhurst is to stay in the accredited list of colleges it must put up a new and adequate equipment, the aggregate cost of which would be $200,000.

But where is the necessary $200,000 to come from? That is the problem confronting the Jesuit Fathers of Rockhurst College.

In the following article A. B. Macdonald of The Star's staff tells something of the beginnings and the history of this college of the almost incredible fortitude, courage, and sacrifices of its faculty since it was founded in dire poverty twenty years ago, and of the brave struggles against great odds that many of its students have made and are making to get an education.

By A. B. MACDONALD

IN a room of St. Mary's Hospital, where he had been confined by a bad cold several days, the Rev. Daniel H. Conway sat in an arm chair, a pencil in his hand, and on his propped-up knees a rough drawing of the campus of Rockhurst College. I had called to see him, the president of that college, about the plans for a new main building for it.

[illegible]

ing, too, and a fine knowledge of it.

Bound by Three Vows

A man entering the Jesuit order takes three solemn vows, dedicating his whole future life to "poverty, chastity and obedience" in the service of Jesus. They are "soldiers of Christ," under the command of generals. These generals of the order in this province, which embraced all the country from Kentucky to the Canadian line, and from the eastern line of Ohio to St. Marys, Kansas, had decreed that there must be a college of liberal arts in Kansas City. So, when Father Ryan was ordered to lay aside his text-books in St. Marys college and come here to Kansas City to help Father Dowling, he obeyed, as a good soldier.

It meant the roughest kind of work, with his hands, with the crowbar, and the lifting of heavy stones. When the building had gone up to the first story the money ran out. Work had to stop, and for more than a year the building stood, a jagged line of stones with the unsightly long arms of cranes lifting against the sky. Skeptics said: "It is proof of the impractical thinking of a few priests who are simple-minded enough to try to build a college away out there."

For a long time Father Ryan lived alone in a cheerless room of the unfinished building, where owls and bats hovered at night. And then, just as the project seemed utterly hopeless, as if the good Lord had forgotten His promise, it was fulfilled. A rich man (at his request his name always has been withheld) gave enough to finish the building.

Gloomy Prospect at Opening

In the fall of 1914 a faculty of seven Jesuit teaching priests assembled to open the high school, forerunner of the college. That September morning the rain poured in torrents, and the priests, wondering if even one student would come so far in the rain, stood at the eastern windows of the school watching the Marlborough street cars to see if one would get off. At 9:30 o'clock a car stopped at Fifty-third Street, and a dozen young men got off and trudged up through the mud toward the school. The next car brought a dozen more. In all, forty-two students came that first morning. Rockhurst College was a dream no more. Its birth was in the rain of that September morning.

[illegible]

Rockhurst and coach of its football team, and Vincent J. O'Flaherty.

Money was forever scarce in Rockhurst. Often it ran out, even the last penny, but always the promise, "I will provide," came true. In its firsts four years the classes of Rockhurst College were taught in the high school, because there was no other building on the campus. Then Father Weiand, its president, "scraped together," as he said, a few thousand dollars from a few friends and built Dowling Hall, a small brick building, and in the fall of 1922 Rockhurst College opened there in its own building with twenty-one students.

Eight years later the home of Mr. and Mrs. Edward Hanley, right off the street from the campus, came as a gift to the college. Those are the two buildings used by Rockhurst today. Now the college and high school together have 450 students. They are taught by twenty-nine Jesuit priests and a few lay teachers.

Forsake Everything for Jesus

"Would you like to know how each Jesuit teaching priest is trained for that work?" Father Conway asked me. "Well, first of all, the young man who enters our order must take the vows of poverty, chastity and obedience. He forsakes all — father, mother, relatives, the world—to fol-

[illegible]

ROCKHURST HIGH SCHOOL

HANLEY HALL ROCKHURST COLLEGE.

THE REV. DANIEL H. CONWAY PRESIDENT OF THE COLLEGE

DOWLING HALL, MAIN BUILDING OF ROCKHURST COLLEGE.

our day to His service. Then the priests scatter to say Mass at different places. At 7:15 we gather at breakfast, which is eaten in absolute silence, as are all our meals, except that, as we eat, someone of our number reads to us. Then we go to the duties of the day, which is teaching, until 11:45, when each retires to his room, and, kneeling before the crucifix, examines his conscience, sees if he has had a wrong thought, if by word or act or thought he has been unkind to any fellow man. If we have, we ask to be forgiven and again dedicate our lives to His service.

"Then the noon luncheon, and we all say Grace in common, in Latin. After the meal we return to our duties until 6:00 o'clock when we have supper; followed by an hour of recreation in a common room where we relax and talk together of anything that interests us. At 7:00 we go to our rooms to study the lessons of the next day, or to correct papers, or to prepare lectures, or to read until 9:00, when we all assemble in the chapel and for twenty minutes engage in prayer. Then follows another fifteen minutes of self-examination, each one of us alone in his room, checking up on himself, seeing if every act of the day has been in the service of God. Then we spend fifteen minutes of reading some spiritual book.

"Next 'De Profundis,' a bell rings, and every man of us kneels and offers up that wonderful prayer: 'Out of the depths have I cried unto Thee, O Lord.' Then everyone goes to the chapel again for silent prayer and meditation, each to ask himself, "Master, how have we done today?" Follows, a prayer for grace for the day to come, then to bed."

Share Privations Alike

"As no Jesuit may own anything, so all are equally poor, living actually

[illegible]

also fitting them to go out and be the best of citizens. The value of that to Kansas City cannot be over-estimated."

In Rockhurst are 75 Protestant students. They are not required to take religious teaching. But all Catholic students must take that course.

Strive Heroically for Education

While the majority of the students in Rockhurst are able to pay their way, there are many who have to work their way through and require help. Two of the students are ushers at the union station. One is a night watchman in the establishment of an undertaker. A dozen are newspaper carriers, up and at their work at 5:00 o'clock in the morning. Others work in stores on Saturdays, and do all sorts of odd jobs.

Father Conway knows the name, the history and the home life of every student in the college. He knows and has a deep sympathy for those who have to do their home study work in unhappy surroundings and he makes allowances for that. He knows the struggles that many have to undergo to get an education.

There was the young man whose cow put him through. In the summer he brought the cow with him to the school where she pastured on the grass on the campus until he took her home in the evening, milked her and sold the milk in his neighborhood.

There was the Protestant boy from Woodward, Ok., who hitch-hiked from that place to Kansas City, arriving with only 50 cents. He said to Father Conway:

"I don't know how we'll make it, but I'll work at anything to get through."

"O. K. [illegible] Father Conway told him. "We will go along together," and they did. The priest got the boy a job and he became one of the brightest boys in the college."

Slept in Old Motor Car

There was another boy who drove up from Arkansas in an old car, and, as he had no other place in which to stay, parked his car near the college and slept in it all through the winter. When school was out in the spring, he returned to his farm in Arkansas and put in a crop, which paid for his tuition the next year. So he went through to graduation, and now is teaching a school in Arkansas.

Another boy, without money, observed that the insects and young animals used in the biology classes were bought. He contracted with the teacher in that department to supply them, and he went through college, graduating with honors, on the bugs, frogs, mice, squirrels and other like laboratory material to be found in the fields around Kansas City.

"After a Catholic student is graduated and goes out into the world, we try to follow him all through his life and keep in close touch with him," said Father Conway. "If he outlives those of us who taught him, our successors will be here to keep in touch with him, to welcome him always, to be with him in death if that is possible, and to meet him in heaven, for eternity is the measure of the Jesuits. Time is the mere twinkling of an eye, but eternity never ends."

Assured of Care to the End

"And when you become sick or too old to teach, what then?"

"Saint Ignatius de Loyola, founder of our order, decreed that the sick among us should be well cared for even if the sacred vessels had to be sold in order to do it. One of us, Father Leary, is paralyzed and we have him with us so we can the better care for him. He is the only priest of our twenty-nine who has a radio in his room, a luxury that is justified because it soothes his pain. And here am I, without money, and yet, when an attack of the flu lays me low, I am brought to St. Mary's Hospital and nursed back to health and strength. And, some day, when our work is over, may the end be as happy as that which came to Father Eugene Kieffer one night last February. He was 82 years old and had long been failing. At midnight he came to the room of Father Matoushek and said in all calmness:

"I feel that I am going to die. I would like the last sacrament. Will you prepare it?"

"Father John Driscoll was summoned. They propped Father Kieffer on the bed, with pillows at his back. He crossed himself, bowed, received the last rites—absolution, anointing, communion, last absolution. He grasped the crucifix and his last words were: 'My trust is in the infinite mercy of God.' So his soul drifted out with the tide, to be forever with the Lord."

While confined to St. Mary's Hospital in December 1934, Fr. Dan Conway gave a lengthy interview from his hospital bed to a reporter from The Kansas City Star. *Looking to the future, Conway envisioned a new building exclusively for the college, essential for gaining accreditation as a 4-year college. Courtesy of Rockhurst University Archives.*

is to start with the money we have and we will succeed," he wrote to his friend Zacheus Maher, S.J., apparently seeking advice. He noted that 4 men on his committee were contractors and one, whom he did not name, had agreed to put the building under roof with the money already available. "The men on the committee are absolutely convinced this is the only way to succeed," Conway wrote, and also noted that Rockhurst was facing new competition—the University of Kansas City, "situated," he said, "right at our door." The university was just a few years old, starting in 1933, but already it had built 3 buildings. "It is necessary that we do something or be forgotten," Conway said.[29]

Even through the Depression years, Rockhurst's enrollment held fairly steady and by 1937 was growing. That November, the college counted 170 students (up from 164 in 1936), with another 219 enrolled in the night School of Commerce and Finance (up from 167 in 1936). The high school, with 353 boys in November 1937, also was growing (up from 318 in 1936).[30] Rockhurst was at the point, Conway said, that "we could not accept a single additional high school student right now."[31] The problem centered on the college students, who also used the science rooms in Sedgwick Hall. They "take up three full classrooms with their biology rooms and additional chemistry space," Conway said, as well as sharing the gymnasium, chapel, and library with the high school. For ten years now Rockhurst had been talking of erecting a new college building, but still, most college classes were being held in Dowling Hall, which Conway described in 1937 as "getting quite dilapidated." There was, he said, "absolutely no question about the imperative need" for a new college building. "It is," he said, "simply a necessity."[32]

By 1937, thanks to his Honorary Directors, he had the beginnings of a building fund. A building campaign involving the public, however, did not start until the Honorary Directors pooled $1,500 and published a little booklet outlining Rockhurst's needs. Scribbled notes written in the late fall of 1936 on the stationery of the Rev. D.H. Conway, S.J., and on file in the Rockhurst University Archives, most likely were the beginnings of this booklet, which sketched the history of Rockhurst, including the heroic perseverance of its founders, then outlined the school's needs.

"The Rockhurst of today," the booklet stated, then noted that the campus centered on the "large stone building facing Troost Avenue," that is, the yet unnamed Sedgwick Hall. Under the roof of this one building were 320 high school students; 170 college students; faculty quarters for 19 priests, 6 scholastics, and 3 lay brothers; a chapel to accommodate 200; library; physics laboratory; science quarters; faculty executive offices; refectory; kitchen; reading rooms; and a gymnasium. "All well and good," Conway scribbled on his notepad. Then there was Dowling Hall, a "small, cheaply constructed 2-story building" housing college classes, and the private Hanley residence, which provided space for overflow classrooms. "All well and good," he scribbled again.

"The Rockhurst of Tomorrow" came next. It should have, Conway noted, a college building that would cost approximately $150,000. Preliminary plans, available for inspection in the president's office, called for locating it facing Rockhurst Road at about 52nd Street and Lydia Avenue. A fieldhouse and new gymnasium, costing an estimated $100,000 to $150,000, also were "sadly" needed. As it was, basketball games of any consequence, which drew the largest crowds, were being played on a rented court in another part of the city. A new gym also would provide room for indoor track meets and a clubhouse and training center for the football team. Other buildings were needed, too: a science hall, library, and small dormitory. Twenty acres were available, providing plenty of space to build, and, Conway added, a committee of prominent Kansas Citians had been appointed to make sure the "utmost value" was received "for every dollar spent."[33] Anyone who wished was invited to offer suggestions for "a bigger and better Rockhurst." Just make an appointment by calling Hiland 6800.

According to the senior thesis of Rockhurst student John Jennings, Mr. J.F. Fogarty organized the initial building drive, which kicked off in February 1937. Committeemen held rallies, the Rockhurst Circle held card parties, and the children of St. Francis Xavier Parish, boys and girls, held a basketball tournament and donated the proceeds to Rockhurst. Father Conway organized the "5 Year $500,000 Expansion Plan" with quotas to be

Breaking ground for Conway Hall, April 28, 1937. Pictured (left to right); Fr. Daniel Conway, Rockhurst president; Pat Mason, athletic director of the college; Henry J. Massman, building campaign chairman and contractor; and Vincent J. O'Flaherty, Jr., president of the Rockhurst Honorary Directors. Nearly 500 high school and college students were present for the ceremony and broke into cheers when Fr. Conway announced that classes were cancelled for the remainder of the day. Courtesy of Rockhurst University Archives.

Conway Hall housed the college's library until the opening of the Greenlease Library in 1967 and the college's chapel until the addition to Massman Hall in 1984. Behind the altar of the chapel hung a painting by James Roth of the Jesuit Martyrs of North America, a gift of the L.R. Wood family in memory of Rockhurst student Paul A. Wood, who was killed in a target practice accident. Courtesy of Rockhurst University Archives.

raised by various groups and individuals: $275,000 from the Honorary Directors, $75,000 from the Rockhurst Circle; $50,000 from the Rockhurst Alumni Association; and $10,000 from Rockhurst students. J.M. Aufiero was named national committee chairman with a $100,000 quota.[34] By April 9, $58,000 had been collected in cash and pledges, and, just 2 weeks later, the total was up to $96,000, enough money to get the provincial's go-ahead to build. Another accreditation rejection from the NCA, on March 18, 1937, apparently added to the fund drive momentum.[35]

Like clockwork, Father Conway contacted the newspapers and got an article announcing Rockhurst's building plans published in *The Kansas City Star* of April 18, 1937, just 10 days before ground was to be broken. The new building, he explained, would house the college department, thus fulfilling requirements to become accredited as a 4-year institution. A gymnasium also was included in the building program, and hopes were high for a future campus quadrangle that would include an auditorium, library, and other classroom buildings. The current Dowling Hall, he said, was to be converted into a dormitory for out-of-town boys who currently were living with Catholic families in nearby private homes.

— Breaking Ground —

On Wednesday, April 28, 1937, just as Conway promised, ground was broken for the future Conway Hall at Rockhurst Road and Forest Avenue. Shortly before 11 that morning, nearly 500 students of the high school and college gathered with the black-robed Jesuits at the north end of campus. President Conway thanked a host of people—Mrs. Genevieve Moore, Louis McGee, John F. Fogarty, James Lillis, Mrs. Cora Spence, and Vincent J. O'Flaherty, Jr., among them—then took a spade trimmed in blue and white and inscribed with the letter "R." Urged by the students to "turn it over, Father," Conway dug the spade into the earth and turned up a sizeable clod of dirt. Cheers went up and grew louder, *The Kansas City Star* reported, when Father Conway announced that no classes would be held the remainder of the day.[36]

Exactly 2 months later, on June 28, 1937, Father Conway wrote to the provincial, telling him the building was going up fast, the third floor already under construction. By late August the building was under roof, and on September 12, it was dedicated by Bishop Lillis.[37] Several hundred persons were there and, in a procession, marched to the new building, which was draped with American flags and white and yellow papal colors. Bishop Lillis entered the front door and blessed the building, then went outside again, walked to the northeast corner of the building and placed a copper box of records in the cornerstone. With trowel and cement, he then sealed the stone.[38]

There were speeches, including one by Father Conway, for whom the building eventually would be named. The key to success or failure, he said, was in the training of the will, adding that "an intelligent and good citizenship" was the result of a proper education. "We must illuminate the mind to the knowledge of things in the sciences and arts. But we must not overlook the will," Conway said that day. "Man has duties to his Creator, to his country and to his fellow men. To form Christ in the hearts and minds of men will be the object of our education. To this, we dedicate this building, our lives and our energies."[39]

Thanks to donations of material and labor—architect Chester Dean donated his skills and the Sheffield Steel Company, through its non-Catholic president, Ralph Gray, donated all the steel—the project was going to cost only $125,000 when it should have cost $175,000 to $200,000, Conway said. A special thank you belonged to building campaign chairman Henry Massman and the contractor J.E. Dunn, who had agreed to complete the building for well below the market rate. Mr. Dunn also donated his own services and threw in $8,000 to the building fund.

As the college classroom building took shape, men on the campaign committee pressed Father Conway to start building a fieldhouse, as well, though Conway knew the necessary funds were lacking. Enthusiasm was not lacking, however, and on August 1, 1937, the *Kansas City Times* reported that a new athletic building was to be included in the present building program. According to Rockhurst historian Mary Mattione, it was J.E. Dunn who convinced Father Conway to begin building.[40] Dunn argued that it would be less expensive to start immediately because the construction equipment was already on campus. So it was that the foundation was dug and brought up to ground level before funds ran out. Work would

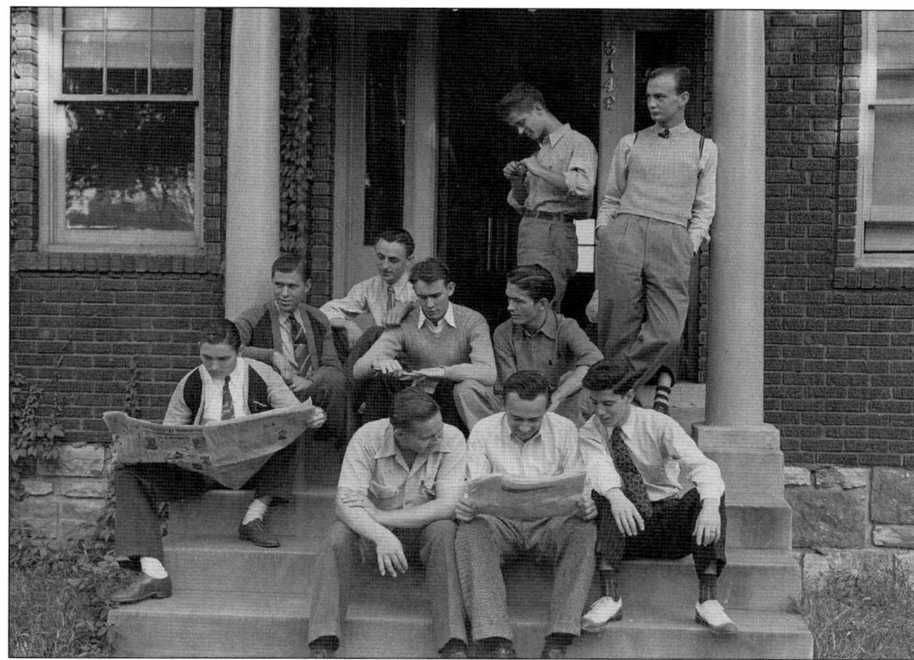

Students relaxing on the steps of Dowling Hall, 1940. After Conway Hall opened in 1938, Dowling Hall was converted into a dormitory. Courtesy of Rockhurst University Archives.

Aerial view of the campus, about 1938. Even while Conway Hall was under construction, members of the building committee pressed Father Conway to start construction on a fieldhouse. The Mason-Halpin Fieldhouse opened in December 1938, less than a year after classes started in Conway Hall. Courtesy of Rockhurst University Archives.

stall until late October, pick up again and stall again, delaying completion of Rockhurst's fieldhouse until the following summer. In the meantime, on September 20, 1937, Bishop Lillis came out to Rockhurst again and blessed what was there.[41]

While the fieldhouse languished, the classroom building was nearing completion. A photograph appeared in the October 31, 1937, *Kansas City Star,* and *The Province News-Letter* reported that work on the new college building was moving so rapidly "that it is now only a matter of days before it will be ready for occupancy." Contractors, in fact, had set Monday, November 15, as the date for completion.[42]

"A Dream Come True," *The Jesuit Bulletin* heralded that December. "From the airy nothingness of a cherished dream a reality has blossomed; the reality of an impressive and beautiful edifice." Rockhurst's new administration and science building, christened Conway Hall, stood as a monument, the *Bulletin* said, "to the generosity of the Catholics of Kansas City." The sturdy, 3-story Norman-Gothic building, with basement, boasted well-lighted classrooms and modern laboratories, as well as administrative offices, a student chapel, assembly hall, library, conference rooms, and student lounge. The building was "a milestone in the growth of the college," a college, the *Bulletin* reported, that "may even be said to have a special mission in a region which has laid so much stress on material progress; she must, as it were, knead the leaven of true progress into the mass of commercial enterprise."[43]

By early February of 1938, college classes were being held in the new hall, and on April 24, 1938, parents and friends of Rockhurst were invited to an open house. It was an informal event attended by more than 1,000 people. Father Conway greeted visitors in the entrance hall but stepped aside for a few moments to deal with a reporter, who later wrote that Conway had given him a complete tour, "even to the showcase of bugs in the biology laboratory and the 11,000 books in the library." On May 11, *The Rockhurst Sentinel* published a special pictorial issue of the ongoing expansion program.[44]

— THE FIELDHOUSE —

Work on the fieldhouse picked up again in the summer of 1938, and by October 6, the finishing touches were being put on the ceiling. In the basement was a heating plant that Rockhurst hoped in time could be enlarged to heat the entire campus. The new fieldhouse, built at the north end of the football field, was designed to take care of all the athletic needs of the college. It had showers and dressing rooms for all sports, quarters for visiting teams, offices for the athletic department and coach, a basketball court and several "cross" courts for the younger students. Around the court were enough seats, counting the balcony, for 2,000 spectators.[45]

How happy coach Pat Mason must have been to see the new facilities for his teams. Mason's life had centered on Rockhurst. He had been a second-year high school boy when he marched up the hill to Rockhurst for the first time—on opening day, September 15, 1914. He had stayed on for college, graduating in Rockhurst's first college class in 1921, then continued to stay on as teacher and coach. Twenty-four years he had been at Rockhurst, earning the admiration and respect of all. He was a Rockhurst legend whose name seemed a part of the school. He had played for the Blue and White in the early days—catching behind the plate for Brooks Hale; scoring a dozen field goals in a single game on the basketball court; and serving as captain and quarterback on the gridiron.

He and Brooks Hale were Rockhurst's first athletic stars. Hale went on to become a Jesuit priest, but Pat Mason stayed on at Rockhurst. Even as a college student working part-time at Loose-Wiles Biscuit Company, he found time to coach Rockhurst's high school teams. From 1917 to 1919 his teams won prep championships twice in baseball, twice in basketball, and once in football.[46] In one game, his basketball team swamped Midland College 53-4, holding them without a field goal. Pat Mason's crowning triumph as a high school coach came in 1925 when his basketball team was named the best coached and his player Jim Hogan was chosen the All-American center at the Catholic basketball tournament in Chicago. After that, Mason focused on Rockhurst College teams,

Pat Mason was a second-year high school boy when Rockhurst opened its doors on September 15, 1914. He would never leave Rockhurst. Mason graduated in Rockhurst's first college class in 1921, then continued on as teacher and coach. He turned down offers to coach at larger universities; his heart was at Rockhurst. Mason suffered from a diabetic condition that took his life in 1938 at the age of 39. At his funeral, Fr. Conway eulogized Mason as a "man whose life was woven into the fabric, ways and traditions of this institution, and who knew no other place." Courtesy of Virginia Mason Waters.

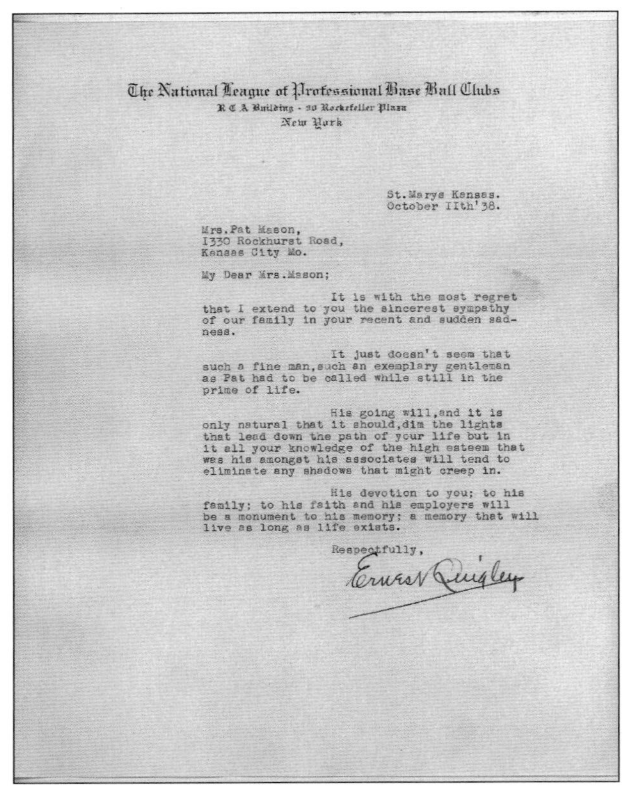

The National League of Professional Base Ball Clubs
R C A Building - 30 Rockefeller Plaza
New York

St.Marys Kansas.
October IIth'38.

Mrs.Pat Mason,
I330 Rockhurst Road,
Kansas City Mo.

My Dear Mrs.Mason;

It is with the most regret that I extend to you the sincerest sympathy of our family in your recent and sudden sadness.

It just doesn't seem that such a fine man,such an exemplary gentleman as Pat had to be called while still in the prime of life.

His going will,and it is only natural that it should,dim the lights that lead down the path of your life but in it all your knowledge of the high esteem that was his amongst his associates will tend to eliminate any shadows that might creep in.

His devotion to you; to his family; to his faith and his employers will be a monument to his memory; a memory that will live as long as life exists.

Respectfully,

Ernest Quigley

At the death of Coach Pat Mason, tributes from the sports world poured in, including this letter to Mason's widow from Ernest Quigley, president of major league baseball's National League. Courtesy of Virginia Mason Waters.

coaching all the teams and serving as athletic director. He turned his high school coaching duties over to his friend Eddie Halpin.

— FAILING HEALTH —

Mason's achievements were many. There was Rockhurst's entry into the Missouri State Conference and the football championships of 1927 and 1928, and in 1936, Mason's Prince Howards captured the pennant in the Ban Johnson baseball league and went on to win the league's Little World Series.

But before the start of the 1937 season, Pat Mason's health started to fail. Suffering from a diabetic condition and a heart ailment, he hung up his baseball spikes with the minor league Omaha club of the Western League, where he had played with various teams on the local circuit. There had been a time when the St. Louis Browns had scouted him, but a leg injury had ended those aspirations, and now his medical troubles finally slowed down what had been a life lived at a dizzy pace. "When he wasn't traveling with his team, he was alone heading for some major athletic event as an official," *The Rockhurst Sentinel* said.[47] "He became well acquainted with every sports writer, coach and official in the Middle West." It was said that Mason had had several offers to coach at larger schools, including at least 2 in the Big Six, but he turned them all down; his heart was with Rockhurst. In the early 1930s, he even moved to a white house at 1330 Rockhurst Road, across from Bourke Field.

On the first Wednesday of October 1938, a critically ill Pat Mason was admitted to St. Mary's Hospital, suffering from the diabetic condition that had plagued him the past few years. As he lay there, his wife, Regina Fetter Mason, at his side, the finishing touches were being put on the ceiling of the new fieldhouse. Mason would not live to see the dedication. He died in the wee hours of Monday, October 10, 1938. He was only 39 years old, the father of 2 children, James, 12, and Virginia, 9. Tributes poured in. "He was one grand guy…a square guy…a guy who wouldn't teach your son any football tricks unworthy of a true sportsman," wrote C.E. McBride, sports editor of *The Kansas City Star*.

"In a small institution where 'material' was scarce and far to seek, he succeeded in a manner almost unbelievable, in building a record of success which has made the Hawks a power in this section of the small college world," wrote another.[48]

"Pat was more than a successful coach, prominent official and a friend—he was an institution," wrote journalist Parke Carroll. "The story of Rockhurst college athletics is the story of Pat Mason," *The Star* said. "Unlike many who rose to the top of their profession, the coach was not a stern disciplinarian. He was enough of a student of human nature to men, their strong points and their shortcomings. Cleverly, tactfully he won the boys over. They loved Pat. They enjoyed his companionship. They went out and made touchdowns for him."[49]

Eddie Halpin began coaching at Rockhurst in 1926, first as an assistant to Pat Mason, then as the high school coach. In the summer of 1936, while visiting 6 Rockhurst boys attending the Jesuits' Camp DeSmet in South Dakota, Halpin was struck by appendicitis. He died 2 days later at the age of 33. Courtesy of Rockhurst University Archives.

And at his funeral, they carried his coffin. Seniors on the 1938-39 football team were the active pallbearers, while all other Rockhurst athletes followed along in an honorary role. Six hundred people filled St. Francis Xavier Church to overflowing that Wednesday morning, October 12, 1938, for an hour-long, Requiem High Mass sung by college students, assisted by the faculty. Outside, almost 400 high school boys had stood as guards of honor, lining Rockhurst Road from the Mason home across from Bourke Field to Troost Avenue, then south on Troost to 53rd Street, as the funeral cortege passed in a drizzling rain to the church.[50]

Father Conway stood up to speak, eulogizing Pat Mason as a "man whose life was woven into the fabric, ways and traditions of this institution, and who knew no other place." He was engaged in a highly competitive field "where the emotional strain was great, where revenge and the meaner side of human nature often gains the upper hand," Conway continued, "but let it be said to his credit and his honor, that he displayed a magnificent self-control, a gentility of nature, a kindly consideration, and humaneness."

On the way to Calvary Cemetery, the procession of cars stretched for more than a mile, so long that by the time those in the rear arrived at the cemetery, the graveside services were over.

News of Mason's death shocked the Rockhurst community, especially coming on the heels, as it did, of the death of beloved Rockhurst High School coach Eddie Halpin, who was only 33 years old. In the summer of 1936, Halpin had taken a weekend trip to visit 6 Rockhurst boys attending the Jesuits' Camp DeSmet, on the Roosevelt Indian Reservation in South Dakota. After a strenuous Saturday of horseback riding and swimming, Halpin had awakened that Sunday with severe stomach pains. He was rushed by airplane to a hospital in Alliance, Nebraska, 150 miles away, where he underwent an operation for appendicitis. He never recovered and died on July 28, 1936, just 2 days after the attack.[51]

"For years no greater shock has come to the athletic-minded citizenry of this community than the news of the death of Eddie Halpin," wrote the sports editor of *The Kansas*

Pat: "Well, Eddie, We'll Still Coach Them from Up Here!"
O'Hern '38

The Rockhurst Sentinel, *October 11, 1938. Cartoon by John B. O'Hern, '38.*

City Star. Halpin was so youthful, so full of zest, that his death was almost unbelievable. Adding pathos was the hurried flight of his young wife, Margaret, to reach his side. Told there was little hope for her husband's recovery, a grief-stricken Mrs. Halpin, accompanied by Mrs. Pat Mason, had hopped a plane piloted by Tex LaGrone and raced from Kansas City to Alliance, Nebraska, arriving at the bedside 3 hours before her husband died.[52]

Unlike Mason, Halpin was not a graduate of Rockhurst, although he had taken a few classes there following his graduation from Kansas City's Central High School. Eddie Halpin was a Jayhawk, earning 3 letters in football and 3 in baseball at the University of Kansas. Halpin was small for a football player but "was a bundle of fight and a blaze of energy." If KU were hard put in a goal line defense, Halpin, *The Star* editor said, "would come dashing in to inspire his mates with the flaming Irish spirit that was his."

He graduated in 1926 and returned to Kansas City as assistant to coach Mason. For the next 10 years he led his Rockhurst squads to all but 2 winning seasons in football and basketball. "The students liked the short, thick-set figure, the ready Irish smile and the ringing laugh," the *Kansas City Times* wrote. He was universally popular, insisting that everyone, even his players, call him Eddie.

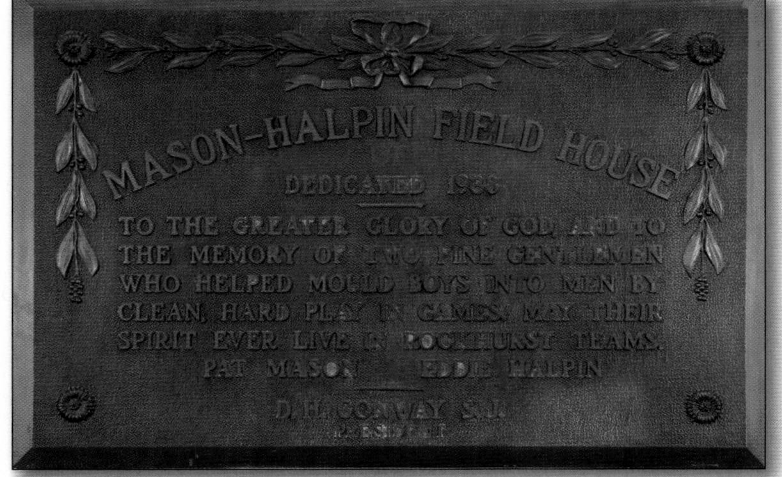

On December 28, 1938, Rockhurst dedicated the new Mason-Halpin Fieldhouse, honoring the memory of its two legendary coaches. Photo by David Spaw.

The pews of St. Francis Xavier Church had overflowed on the Friday of his funeral. Father Conway had gone to Union Station 2 days prior to meet Halpin's widow on her return from Nebraska, and then had stood up at the funeral, saying that Eddie Halpin's greatest achievement was not as a coach, but in his zest of living. "He was not an employee of Rockhurst," Conway said, "he was part of the institution, because he breathed its spirit and lived its ideals."[53]

When it came time to dedicate Rockhurst's new fieldhouse, on December 28, 1938, what more fitting name could there be: the Mason-Halpin Fieldhouse, named in honor of Rockhurst's favorite coaches.[54]

— ACCREDITATION —

With its new college building and fieldhouse, as well as the addition of evening classes, new handball courts, and Brother Shaughnessy's new tree-planting campaign, surely accreditation could not be far behind. Nonetheless, Rockhurst's house consultors decided that fall of 1938 to wait a year before making application because they thought "we will be in much better shape next year." Their thinking hinged on enrollment figures. If the North Central Association did its inspection in the 1938-39 academic year, it would judge Rockhurst on enrollment figures for the previous year of 1937-38, when a total of 389 students, including the night school, were enrolled. By waiting, Rockhurst could present better enrollment figures, currently at 550 for the 1938-39 academic year.[55]

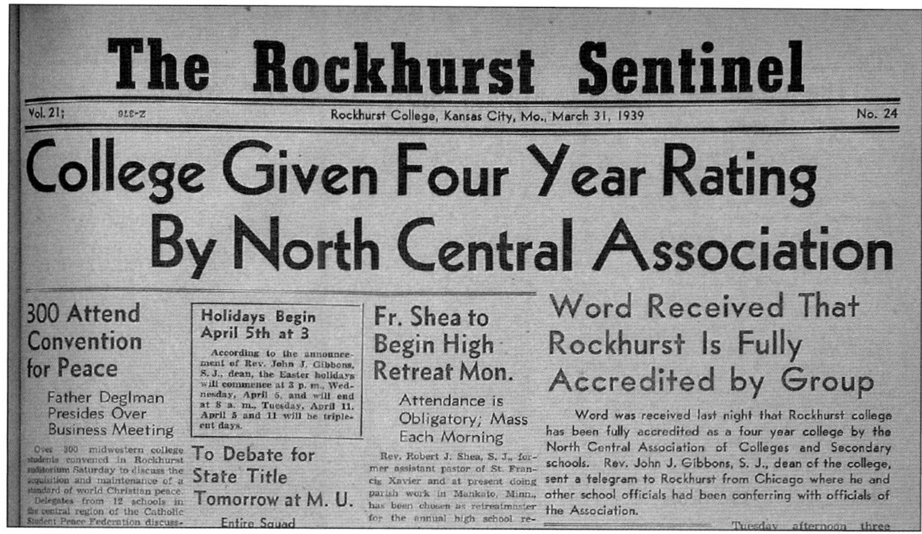

The Rockhurst Sentinel

Vol. 21; Rockhurst College, Kansas City, Mo., March 31, 1939 No. 24

College Given Four Year Rating By North Central Association

300 Attend Convention for Peace

Father Deglman Presides Over Business Meeting

Over 300 midwestern college students convened in Rockhurst auditorium Saturday to discuss the acquisition and maintenance of a standard of world Christian peace.

Delegates from 12 schools in the central region of the Catholic Student Peace Federation discuss-

Holidays Begin April 5th at 3

According to the announcement of Rev. John J. Gibbons, S. J., dean, the Easter holidays will commence at 3 p. m., Wednesday, April 5, and will end at 8 a. m., Tuesday, April 11. April 5 and 11 will be triple-cut days.

To Debate for State Title Tomorrow at M. U.

Entire Squad

Fr. Shea to Begin High Retreat Mon.

Attendance is Obligatory; Mass Each Morning

Rev. Robert J. Shea, S. J., former assistant pastor of St. Francis Xavier and at present doing parish work in Mankato, Minn., has been chosen as retreatmaster for the annual high school re-

Word Received That Rockhurst Is Fully Accredited by Group

Word was received last night that Rockhurst college has been fully accredited as a four year college by the North Central Association of Colleges and Secondary schools. Rev. John J. Gibbons, S. J., dean of the college, sent a telegram to Rockhurst from Chicago where he and other school officials had been conferring with officials of the Association.

Tuesday afternoon three

On March 16, 1939, Rockhurst received the news that the school had been fully accredited as a 4-year college by the North Central Association of Colleges and Secondary Schools. It had taken more than 20 years for Rockhurst to achieve this recognition. Courtesy of Rockhurst University Archives.

For all that, the decision not to fill out an application ended up not mattering. NCA inspectors showed up on campus anyway, on February 22, 1939, and, as usual after their inspection, presented a list of commendations and weaknesses. The inspectors complimented Rockhurst for its "excellent" program of general education, its "well-trained" faculty and "good" instruction, and that the college's business affairs and finances seemed to be in order. Among weaknesses was the college's lack of a dormitory, a problem Rockhurst corrected in 1940 when Dowling Hall was converted into a dorm. Steps also were underway to convert the old Hanley house back into a residence. Since completion of Conway Hall, the house had sat unused, but now, *The Province News-Letter* reported, the new director of student welfare, Father William C. Doyle, had initiated a plan to convert Hanley Hall into a dormitory for 25 students, who would operate it themselves "on a cooperative basis."[56]

Doyle's idea apparently was inspired by a touching incident explained in the *Kansas City Journal* on October 19, 1939. "I'll wager you," the story began, "that a certain Jefferson City boy, when he went to sleep under the grandstand at Rockhurst College on a nippy night last September, had no idea of the activity his bedding down would loose." The story told how the boy was so eager for an education that he enrolled at Rockhurst and started attending classes even though he had nowhere to stay at night. He couldn't afford a room, so decided to sleep under the school's grandstand, where it was sheltered and fairly warm. One night the night watchman found him sleeping there, and the story was out. The alumni heard about it and got busy.

"By cracky!" the *Journal* wrote, "If a boy wanted to go to school badly enough to sleep outdoors for the chance, he deserved better." Members of the Alumni Association went into college and high school classes and launched a program to have students sell scrip tickets for the neighborhood Fox theaters. Each book made a profit, and the proceeds were used to buy furniture for Hanley Hall. "Seven boys already are housed in the hall," the *Journal* wrote, "including the lad from Jefferson City." Rockhurst also took steps to address other problems cited by the NCA, including expanding its student health and placement services.[57]

The momentous news of accreditation came, however, even before these weaknesses were corrected. It came in a letter that arrived in the afternoon mail of March 16, 1939, stating simply that Rockhurst had been approved for full recognition as a 4-year college by the North Central Association of Colleges and Secondary Schools.[58] "Thus we have finally after 20 years of striving and hoping attained the goal," Father Matoushek wrote in the Minister's Diary.

A few months after the good news of accreditation, a less momentous, but more foreboding, announcement of approval came that October: Rockhurst, it said, was the first college in the Kansas City area to be recognized by the Civil Aeronautics Authority to train civil aviators. Just the month before, Adolf Hitler had invaded Poland, setting the stage for World War II. On December 2, 1939, a newspaper clipping included a photograph of Rockhurst's first air student—"the lucky No. 1," Charles Muckenthaler, sitting in the cockpit of "the training ship," instructor Malcolm Canaday standing by his side.[59]

So it was on the eve of World War II that Rockhurst, like the nation itself, embarked on a new era in its history. Soon after the college was accredited, Rockhurst received a visit, in May 1939, from Edward B. Rooney, national secretary of education for the American (Jesuit) Assistancy. He walked the spacious campus with its new college building, its new fieldhouse, and its beautiful landscaping, and noted "the exceptionally fine impression" Rockhurst College made on him. He couldn't, in fact, say enough good things about Rockhurst, which he felt could "become one of our more outstanding liberal arts colleges." He liked the strict entrance requirements and the way Rockhurst administrators did not hesitate to drop students who were deficient in their studies. And he liked the way so many students participated in extracurricular activities. Father Rooney offered his sincere congratulations to Rockhurst for its recent attainment of a 4-year status. "It is a really fine small college," he wrote, "and I hope it will remain such and not go off the deep end of unreasonable liberal arts colleges."[60]

Chapter Nine

The War Years and Afterwards 1940–50

With accreditation, the stage was set for an era of tremendous growth at Rockhurst. "All Kansas City apparently wants to come to Rockhurst," the school's new president, William H. McCabe, S.J., wrote in the summer of 1940. Exaggerated as the statement was, an enrollment of 10 students just 20 years before had mushroomed to nearly 300 by the fall of 1940, including a newly registered 135 freshmen.[1] By decade's end, Rockhurst would have more than 800 students attending day classes, so many that temporary buildings would be brought in to accommodate them.

President McCabe's hyperbole that summer was uncharacteristic of the exacting man that he was. He had taken his doctorate at Cambridge University in England, where he presented his dissertation on the Jesuit theater. His deep interest in history was apparent at Rockhurst, where he would dig into the college archives and strike up a campaign to name the high school building in honor of the school's great benefactor, Lee Sedgwick. It was McCabe, as well, who spearheaded a campaign to name the new college building after his popular predecessor, Daniel Conway, and to find a patron saint for the college, St. Thomas More.

Father McCabe showed up at Rockhurst seemingly out of the blue on a Tuesday afternoon in April 1940. He walked into the college office at 2 p.m., placed his traveling bag on the floor, and by evening was the new president, installed during the Jesuits' evening meal. "This is my first sight of Kansas City and of Rockhurst College," *The* (Catholic) *Register* quoted him as saying. The suddenness in the change of leadership had caught people off-guard, and McCabe quietly had to explain that the Society of Jesus routinely limited a rector's tenure in any one place to 6 years. That the departing Father Conway had served 7 years, McCabe said, "attests to his remarkable record." It was Conway, of course, who had befriended Kansas City's business elite, made them Honorary Directors of the college, and succeeded in getting, at last, an endowment fund off the ground, with the new fieldhouse and college building to his credit. "In his term of office he probably has achieved more for Rockhurst College than in its entire previous history," the *Kansas City Times* wrote, seeming to grieve along with Kansas City's businessmen, who had the deepest respect for Father Conway. It was, the *Times*, said, hard to see him go.[2]

The Kansas City Star was no less chagrined, writing that the abrupt termination "created something akin to consternation among the lay acquaintances of the popular priest." Reporter Henry Van Brunt predicted the shift "might well give rise to misgivings of one sort or another" and revealed his bias by describing McCabe as "a quiet, wrinkled little man with large, expressive brownish-gray eyes and a quick, infectious laugh," which he said

PRESIDENTIAL PROFILE

— WILLIAM HUGH MCCABE, S.J. —

The Rev. William McCabe became president of Rockhurst College on April 2, 1940. Born in 1893, Fr. McCabe was a native of Iowa. He received the A.B. (1918) and the A.M. (1920) degrees from Saint Louis University and a Ph.D. (1929) from the University of Cambridge in England. He entered the Society of Jesus at Florissant in 1911 and was ordained in 1925 in Belgium, where he studied theology 3 years at the French Jesuit house near Brussels. He taught English and classical languages at Xavier High School, Cincinnati and Saint Louis University High School from 1915-1922. From 1930 until his arrival at Rockhurst in 1940, McCabe was an English professor at Saint Louis University.

Father McCabe served Rockhurst during the difficult years of World War II. As enrollment plummeted due to the war, McCabe negotiated an Army contract which, by war's end, had brought an influx of 1,441 cadets to campus for academic and military training. McCabe's interest in the early heritage of Rockhurst led him to name Rockhurst's original building after the school's first great benefactor, Lee Sedgwick. McCabe was also responsible for selecting Thomas More as Rockhurst's patron saint. Additionally, he revised the college seal, which closely resembles the seal of Rockhurst today.

After leaving Rockhurst, Fr. McCabe was appointed president of Creighton University. In 1950 he returned to the classroom as professor of English at Marquette University. He died in Milwaukee in 1962. Father McCabe's doctoral dissertation was published posthumously in 1983 as *An Introduction to the Jesuit Theater: A Posthumous Work*, edited by Rockhurst English professor Louis J. Oldani, S.J.

was McCabe's only resemblance to his "big, physically vigorous predecessor." Van Brunt seemed almost to sneer as he noted that Father McCabe was "half submerged behind the big desk" used by Conway in the college office and that he "almost reaches up to flick the ashes from his cigarette into the ashtray on top of the desk."[3]

There was no doubt that the little man, 47 years old, had big shoes to fill. He would have to guide Rockhurst through the war years, a time when the draft so depleted college ranks that the very existence of some colleges would be threatened. The war in Europe was on everyone's mind as Kansas City officially welcomed William McCabe to town in a ceremony at Mason-Halpin Fieldhouse on April 29, 1940. "We meet in a time of emergency for civilization," speaker Henry Haskell, editor of *The Kansas City Star*, said that day. "H.G. Wells said not long ago that today we see a race between education and destruction....Father McCabe, you accept a rich heritage here, and under your direction I am sure Rockhurst will continue to serve Kansas City and humanity."

That spring, with war clouds darkening in Europe, 10 Rockhurst students already were registered with the government's new Civilian Pilot Training Program, inaugurated in 1939 under the Civil Aeronautics Administration and open to any college student or graduate between the ages of 18 and 26. The government, with the goal of training 15,000 new pilots by September 1, 1940, offered the instruction for free. There would be a 72-hour ground school course, followed by 35 to 50 hours of flight instruction. The program was an instant success, with young men, and at least a few young women, lining up to register even before doors were open. At Kansas City Junior College, 20 young men made application in the first 2 hours. All told, 75 students would apply there, but only 35 would meet the qualifications.[4]

At Rockhurst, 11 students registered for the program and took their physical examinations, but only 10 showed up for training at Ong Flying School, at the old Richards Field in Raytown. There, on December 2, 1939, *The Kansas City Star* snapped a photo of Rockhurst sophomore Charles Muckenthaler, "the lucky No. 1" sitting in the cockpit of a training plane. The boys had drawn straws to see who would take the first lesson. By the following May, Muckenthaler and 2 other Rockhurst students, Tony John Denman, a senior, and freshman Charles Frederick Downey, Jr., were ready to take their final, 1-1/2 hour tests for a private pilot's license. On Friday, May 10, 1940, *The Star* found them doing 6 or 7 take-offs and landings amid the airport's dandelion patches. Fellow Rockhurst trainees stood by, craning their necks upward as the first 3 Rockhurst men to complete the government's training program "did tailspins, vertical banks, normal banks, turns and climbs."

That summer, Rockhurst student pilot William Henderson wasn't so lucky. He was practicing forced landings when his plane struck the treetops and crashed near Liberty, Missouri. Henderson, the 22-year-old son of Mr. and Mrs. Clarence Henderson of 4421 Norledge Ave., suffered head injuries but soon returned home. His 19-year-old instructor, Winthrop C. Cantrell, suffered a broken jaw and was listed in critical condition at St. Luke's Hospital. At news of the accident, several area pilots volunteered to give blood, including John K. (Tex) LaGrone, who had flown Mrs. Eddie Halpin to Nebraska on that sad night a few years before.[5]

From the outset of the Civilian Pilot Training Program until the spring of 1943, Rockhurst would contribute 180 students to the program, almost all of whom went on to enter the Army or Navy air forces.[6]

— THE COUNTRY GOES TO WAR —

Father McCabe's first months at Rockhurst were filled with the everyday. He answered the provincial's inquiries about yearbook photos, installed new bronze lanterns near Sedgwick Hall, and started a newsletter for benefactors, in which he solicited summer jobs for students, appealed for someone to donate redbud and dogwood trees to beautify the campus,

Aerial view of Ong Airport where Rockhurst students trained as pilots in the government's Civilian Pilot Training Program. The airport was located at the southwest corner of Blue Ridge Boulevard and East Gregory Boulevard in Raytown. Originally called Richards Field, this airport served the Kansas City area until 1927 when the Kansas City Municipal Airport opened downtown. Courtesy of History of Aviation Collection, The University of Texas at Dallas.

and campaigned for a name for the new college building.

Privately, he admitted that his staff found him "rigid," but that, perhaps, was just in relation to his predecessor, who apparently had not enforced some basic discipline. Everyone, even students, had been using phones in Sedgwick Hall for long distance; so Father McCabe had the phones removed. He complained that faculty members had been going to the college treasurer for carfare and traveling money without asking permission. He studied budgets and reduced several of them "moderately," finding ways to save money, by handing out, for example, cheaper cigarettes.[7]

It wasn't long, however, before he was deep into the bureaucracy of wartime planning. In his first summer at Rockhurst, Congress began debate on the first peacetime draft registration in the nation's history, spurring a worried letter from Provincial Peter Brooks in St. Louis. The bill had "serious complications for the Society (of Jesus) in America," Brooks said, because it gave "no assurance that our novices and scholastics will be exempted." Brooks politely ordered Father McCabe to write to Missouri's senators, Bennett Champ Clark and Harry S. Truman, urging them to push for an exemption like the one granted in the last world war. Probably thinking of past prejudice against Catholics, the provincial told McCabe to be sure to point out that the request for an exemption "is in no sense due to a lack of willingness on our part to help our country in every way possible."[8]

The efforts were to no avail, and that October the Selective Training and Service Act went into effect, requiring all males between the ages of 21 and 35 to register. A lottery system, first held on October 29, 1940, decided who would be called into service. (The draft later was extended to men aged 18 to 45 and the lottery system dropped in favor of age, the oldest going first.)

Watching all of this closely was the Association of American Colleges, based in New York City. In a mass mailing to member colleges, Rockhurst included, the association noted 2 sections of the draft bill that were of vital importance to colleges:

- Section 5(a) exempted "cadets of the advanced course, senior division, Reserve Officers' Training Corps or Naval Reserve Officers' Training Corps."
- Section 5(f) permitted all students enrolled in arts and sciences to defer response to the draft call until after July 1, 1941.

Section 5(a) "greatly disturbed" many of its member colleges, the association said, because it favored students attending colleges that had R.O.T.C. programs over those without. "If you have the same feeling, it would seem advisable to have immediate request made through trustees, alumni, and other influential friends to Congressmen and Senators to have a bill enacted by the Congress to permit establishment of additional R.O.T.C. units in accredited colleges."[9]

Father McCabe took the suggestion to heart and set to work trying—to no avail—to land a Navy Reserve or Marine Reserve program at Rockhurst. The problem with the Navy, he discovered, was that it required a college to have at least 450 freshmen entering each year before it would start an R.O.T.C. program. The Marines Corps responded to say it had no R.O.T.C. program, although college sophomores could apply for the Corps' Platoon Leaders' Class, held at camps in Quantico, Virginia, and San Diego, California.[10]

McCabe must have shaken his head as he read that letter because he wasn't interested in sending students away from campus. The idea was to use military programs to bring them to Rockhurst, thereby increasing enrollment even as the draft was threatening to deplete it. The timing of the draft was ironic: just as enrollment had caught fire at the newly accredited Rockhurst, world events seemed determined to douse it. That fall of 1940—one year before the Japanese attack on Pearl Harbor—Rockhurst's enrollment of nearly 300 was the largest in its history and included 135 freshmen. The new class of men gathered that September for a 2-day series of tests intended to determine their "mental abilities, college aptitude, knowledge of mathematics, English and reading," after which they were divided into 4 groups and assigned a faculty adviser to help them choose a course of study. With the tests complete, the freshmen gathered in assembly, where Father McCabe, ever mindful of the war raging in Europe, welcomed them and told them the best way to express their patriotism was by applying themselves seriously to their studies. "The liberally educated young

College sophomore Charles Muckenthaler was the first Rockhurst student to fly under the government's Civilian Pilot Training Program. Pictured in December 1939 in the cockpit of a training plane at Ong Field in Raytown, Muckenthaler would see action as a Navy pilot at Pearl Harbor on December 7, 1941, and at the Battle of Midway. Courtesy of Rockhurst University Archives.

man," he said, "who will be of true service to his country both now and when Hitler is dust, is the product of an education inculcating the right view of life and all its relationships, of the individual's rights and duties, of the family, the state and God."[11]

With the influx of freshmen and the new Conway Hall available, Dowling Hall had been remodeled over the summer and converted into Rockhurst's first dormitory, with room for 32 out-of-town students. "The building now has study rooms for small groups, and large unheated sleeping rooms with double-decker beds," *The* (Catholic) *Register* reported on September 8, 1940. "The ground floor, formerly used as a lunchroom, has been converted into a clubroom. Meals will not be served in the building but will be provided by arrangements with the high school cafeteria and nearby restaurants."

Campus life continued apace, up to and immediately after Pearl Harbor. The college seniors that December of 1941 went on to graduate in May, in what up to then was the largest graduating class in Rockhurst's history: 37 students. In honor of 25 years of college classes, the Rev. Bernard Hale, pastor of St. Catherine's Church in Hickman Mills and a 1917 graduate of Rockhurst High School, delivered the baccalaureate sermon at a Sunday morning Mass at St. Francis Xavier Church. Commencement followed that evening in Mason-Halpin Fieldhouse, where Father McCabe made note of the first Rockhurst son to be killed in the war. He was Robert McAnany, a volunteer with Great Britain's Royal Air Force, who had been killed in the line of duty in Scotland on October 1, 1941. "Others are now in the thick of the fight," McCabe continued, adding that he had made count of 201 Rockhurst men serving in the armed forces that May of 1942—76 in the Army, 106 in the Navy, 15 in the Marines, and 4 in the Coast Guard.[12] Of those 37 graduates in the Class of '42, 16 would be joining the armed forces immediately, he said. In fact, 3 already had: Kenneth H. Crone, B.S., had left for Marine officer training 3 weeks before graduation; Richard M. Walker, B.S., was serving in the Army Air Corps; and John J. Hill, A.B., was engaged in meteorological work for the government.

Students Kenneth Crone (left) and Bob Hughes (center) work on radio equipment under the instruction of Father William Doyle (right). Less than 2 weeks after the attack on Pearl Harbor, Rockhurst announced it was beginning classes designed to equip students in subjects vital to national defense. Throughout the Christmas holidays of 1941, courses were offered on meteorology, chemistry, radio operation, and mathematics. Photo by Charles Brenneke. Courtesy of Rockhurst University Archives.

Even as Father McCabe talked up the school's accomplishments that May of 1942—Rockhurst now had conferred a total of 302 bachelor's degrees—the future was far from assured. The previous January, McCabe had traveled to Baltimore to attend the National Conference of College and University Presidents on Higher Education and the War, as well as a meeting of the Association of American Colleges. No sooner had he returned from Baltimore than he announced that Rockhurst, beginning that summer of 1942, would switch to a trimester system instead of the usual 2 semesters. Colleges throughout the nation were adopting this accelerated system, he explained, to permit students to graduate from college in 3 years

— THE ARMY TAKES OVER THE BROOKSIDE HOTEL —

Preparing the Brookside Hotel for the arrival of troops proved to be no easy task. One night in mid-February, just after dinner, each resident was given a terse notice: "Waitresses leaving. Have no help for in the morning. Will be closed. Thanking you for past patronage. Management." Residents, who included 3 or 4 dozen people over 70 years old and some of Kansas City's most upstanding citizens, were outraged.

"Who is 'management'?" fumed Judge Elmer N. Powell. "Try and find 'management' on these premises. That's not legal notice."

"Evasive," sputtered resident Russell F. Greiner, a former police commissioner and now, in the post-Pendergast sweep, a "new broom" city councilman.

Before area attorney Elmo B. Hunter arrived at his office in the New York Life Building the next morning, his home telephone had rung 19 times with complaints. Hunter was annoyed with Mr. Bisno, who had promised when he bought the hotel, not to close the dining room without giving the housing office 3 days advance notice. When Hunter threatened to sue, Bisno arrived in tow with "a new mouthpiece." The lawyer, described as "one of the best the local bar affords," only stirred the brewing pot more by declaring that many of the tenants at the Brookside Hotel, "craving their former luxury and spacious surroundings, don't know a war is on—and don't give a damn so long as they themselves are coddled." Because the Brookside Hotel was so close to Rockhurst and the University of Kansas City, which also had applied for an Army Specialized Training Program, the hotel, the lawyer said, was a natural choice to house cadets.

The Army stepped in to settle the dispute, and a temporary court order required the hotel to keep its dining room running and to give tenants until April 1 to vacate the premises. The few residents who stayed on continued to play bridge in a second-floor room and watch the Brookside transform before their eyes. The built-in bar in the second-floor apartment formerly occupied by Mr. and Mrs. Jay C. Norman was turned into a medical supply room. The deep carpets in the hallways and lounge were pulled up, and the period furniture in the dark-paneled lounge replaced with serviceable desks where the student-cadets could study. Thirty-five double-decker beds were placed in the ballroom and another 8 in the checkroom. The chastely decorated powder room was turned into a shower room, where 3 cadets at a time could wash. When all was done, a bright red, automatic soft drink machine in the lobby was "the nearest thing to a gay note" left in the "fashionable hostelry," *The Kansas City Star* reported.

The hotel guests, some of whom had lived in their suites for 20 years, simply had to adjust. "I don't know where I can find a place to live," one woman complained, but Mr. Greiner acquiesced. "It's all right," he said. "I don't know of anyone I'd rather see move in than the army."

Quotes from The Kansas City Star, *February 17, 23, 24; March 8; and April 5, 1943.*

instead of 4. The fall trimester was to run from September 6 to November 27; the winter trimester from November 29 to February 26; and the spring trimester from March 1 to May 28. Under the system, Rockhurst's current junior class would graduate on March 1, 1943. The purpose of the "victory sessions," as they were called, was to prepare students more quickly for the armed services.[13]

— A LIFELINE —

By the fall of 1942, the war had created severe problems for colleges and universities, which had watched full-time enrollment plummet 14 percent in 2 years. The situation only worsened when the draft age was lowered to 18 that November. By January 1943, just months after Rockhurst had graduated the largest class in its history, it graduated the smallest since its early years—6 students. As enrollments fell nationally, the government came to the rescue of educators, historian Philip Gleason explains, by calling on almost 500 colleges and universities to train specialized military personnel. These programs, which provided an infusion of full-time students, would provide a lifeline, Gleason writes, for 35 Catholic colleges, Rockhurst included. Father McCabe, of course, had inquired about the Navy's series of V programs even before America entered the war. Perhaps he had watched the success of Notre Dame, which had a Navy R.O.T.C. unit as early as September 1941 and in time would be designated as a midshipman's school.[14] By December 1942, the Navy had its V-12 Navy College Training Program, and the Army had its Army Specialized Training Program (ASTP), which would turn college campuses nationwide into miniature military posts, where cadets were housed and trained for the service.

On March 1, 1943, the 73rd College Training Detachment marched from the Brookside Hotel to assemble at Rockhurst. Courtesy of Rockhurst University Archives.

During the war, military troops became a familiar site on campus. Before the program ended in 1944, a total of 1,441 army cadets trained at Rockhurst. Courtesy of Rockhurst University Archives.

Father McCabe wasted no time in filling out the questionnaires that arrived from various government agencies, inquiring about Rockhurst's housing, food service, and classroom space. In time, a telephone call came from the local office of the Civil Aeronautics Administration, requesting a quick tour of the campus. On February 3, 1943, Col. Ferris, commanding officer of the U.S. Air Corps base in Coffeyville, Kansas, and Maj. J.F. Dominic of the same base arrived. As they walked the campus that day, they would have found Rockhurst's administration offices in Sedgwick Hall, and the college library, chapel, classrooms, and science laboratories in the new Conway Hall. The only other buildings on campus were Mason-Halpin Fieldhouse and Dowling Hall, with its 32 beds—far too few to house the 200 cadets the Army was thinking of enrolling at Rockhurst, where they would be trained as pilots, bombardiers, or navigators for the Army Air Forces. The Army's 5-month course, to be taught by the regular college staff, comprised more than 700 hours of academic and military instruction. Subjects ranged from math to history to physical education, as well as instruction in civil air regulations. If Rockhurst was selected for the program, flight training would be given once again at old Richards Field (called at the time Ong Field), in cooperation with the Civil Aeronautics Administration.

That same day, Col. Ferris and Maj. Dominic paid a visit to Mr. Alexander Bisno, a Chicago real estate man who, just a day before, had purchased part interest in the 5-story Brookside Hotel at 54th Street and Brookside Boulevard.[15] Before 2 weeks had passed, arrangements were finalized to use the hotel to house and "mess" the cadets who would come to Rockhurst. The college entered into a contract with Bisno, who then entered into a subcontract with Mr. S.F. Wolfberg of the Brookside Catering Company.

In December 1944, the Aireon Manufacturing Corporation asked for help in completing a rush order for radar parts. Rockhurst dismissed classes for 2 days. Dean John Higgins, S.J., ordered all students to work at the plant, explaining that failure to show up would be treated the same as skipping classes. Courtesy of Rockhurst University Archives.

The Army arrived at Union Station in the wee hours of Sunday, February 28, 1943, its cadets fatigued and sleepy after their train from Missouri's Jefferson Barracks was delayed 3-1/2 hours. The cadets boarded 3 trucks for the ride to the Brookside Hotel, where they fell into their double-decker beds as soon as the order was given.

That Monday morning, March 1, 1943, the entire detachment of 200 student-cadets—known as the 73rd College Training Detachment—rose before dawn to the sound of a sergeant parading the halls and blowing a shrill whistle. By 7 a.m. they had assembled at Rockhurst, where the commanding officer, 1st Lt. R.M. Priesmeyer, called them to order, described the program in more detail, and outlined the daily schedule. Their day would begin with physical training at 7 a.m. and run until after 6 every evening, when, just as they had done in the morning, they would march in formation the 10 blocks back to their hotel. The sight, even after the first few weeks, "continues to give a daily thrill to persons in the neighborhood," *The* (Catholic) *Register* reported.[16]

By April, the first group of 40 cadets began flight instruction and soon found only praise from flight contractor William Ong. "We have had no trouble of any kind disciplinary or otherwise," he would say.[17] By August, the first group of cadets had completed training and was ready for classification tests to determine which branch of the Army Air Forces they were best suited. On Saturday, August 28, 1943, the entire detachment marched in dress parade before a crowd of 1,000 spectators at Bourke Field. The LaCroix Council, Knights of Columbus, presented the colors, followed by a cadet program of drills, calisthenics, and athletic events, including a calisthenics demonstration performed under the direction of Rockhurst coach Lew Lane.

The influx of Army cadets—a total of 1,441 before the program ended—offered the solution to a vexing enrollment problem brought on by the draft. "Thanks to our Army Air Forces contract, Rockhurst College is operating normally, as far as finances are concerned," Father McCabe was able to report. On the eve of signing the Army contract, registration at Rockhurst had plummeted to under 200, and the college was bracing for it to sink as low as 75 from its peacetime average of 300.[18] By the spring semester of 1944, enrollment had, in fact, plummeted to 80 civilian students. The loss in tuition occasioned by this small civilian enrollment was covered by the salaries the Army was paying to the Jesuit faculty, who heretofore had taught, of course, without receiving a salary.

The problem of how to compensate priests and religious, Gleason writes, was a sticking point at all Catholic colleges administering wartime service programs. At first, contracts provided that teachers who belonged to religious orders be paid the same as lay teachers of the same rank. When the question was raised whether this meant Catholic colleges were making a profit off the war, the matter was taken up by the Joint Army-Navy Board for Training Unit Contracts. Quoting a detailed report by Edward B. Rooney, S.J., executive secretary of the Jesuit Educational Association, Gleason writes that the Army-Navy board "ruled in early September 1943 that henceforth teaching salaries for such persons were not to exceed the actual cost incurred by the institution for the 'rooms, meals, clothing, and other benefits furnished the member of the [religious] society or order.'" In other words, no teaching salary.

So against Catholic interests was the ruling that Rooney (and his counterpart in the National Catholic Education Association) took the matter up himself, requested a hearing, and convinced the board to revert to the earlier policy. Getting regular salaries reinstated for religious was, Gleason writes, "Catholic educators' most strikingly successful interaction with national leaders on wartime issues."[19]

The cadet program and the salary questions that came with it created piles of paperwork and much head scratching for the exacting McCabe, who wanted to be fair to everyone involved, government as well as teachers, lay or religious. "Mathematical exactness has been attempted and found impossible," he explained as he laid out the plan for paying Rockhurst's faculty. Before getting to the bottom line that certainly was of most interest to those involved, he explained that "the College is bound by a contract subjecting her to ultimate decisions of the War Department, and cannot bind herself beyond this limit." Come June 13, 1943, and the start of another semester, the ordinary curriculum of the college, he said, would give way to that of the Army, which had required him to hire a few additional faculty members, specifically, to teach mathematics and physics. All regular faculty would be retained, but it was the Army, he explained, who

— CAPTAIN MARTIN M. O'KEEFE, '36 —

Captain Martin M. O'Keefe

Among the 79 Rockhurst College men killed in World War II, the death of Martin O'Keefe was especially poignant. Stationed in Saipan, Japan, O'Keefe was on a homeward-bound plane that crashed. His wife Jean had been widowed in 1937 at the death of her husband, Pat Mason, Rockhurst athletic director and coach. Martin O'Keefe, a 1936 graduate of Rockhurst College, had gone on to succeed Eddie Halpin as Rockhurst High School coach. The O'Keefes were married in 1942.

Jean learned of the death of her husband through a letter sent by Chaplain Arthur M. Tighe, a Kansas City diocesan priest stationed in Saipan. Below are excerpts of the letter.

Saipan
October 5, 1945
My Dear Mrs. O'Keefe:

I have written many letters of condolence since my arrival on Saipan. In my poor way I have tried to ease the pain of loss in letters to people I never knew and never will know. I found the task difficult. But tonight I just don't feel equal to the job. There is so much I want to say to you, so much I want you to know about Marty—yet my own grief only leaves me with a sense of helplessness.

Regina, we picked up this morning a very badly mangled and burned body. It was Marty. One of 14 dead. Six survived the crash; two of these boys will probably die. Yesterday morning Marty drove over for a visit. We chatted and laughed and talked of how surprised you would be to see Marty in a few days. It was another one of those close, intimate visits Marty and I have enjoyed so many times over here.

Marty went to confession (as if Marty ever knowingly offended God) in preparation for his flight. I gave him Holy Communion in my own lovely little chapel. Then last night I was with him at briefing time. That was around eight o'clock. The weather was briefed as suitable for flying, with an unusually strong head wind at take-off. The briefing lasted about a half-hour, then we all piled into trucks to go to the ships and await take-off time at ten p.m. I said good-bye to Marty then, and he put his arm around me affectionately. "Now remember, Father," he said "our home will be on Virginia Street, and you'll have to hurry home for dinner with Jean and me." We set a date for early November.

Father Arthur M. Tighe

At three o'clock I received a call that one of our ships had crash-landed. It was Marty's ship! They had gone out for about two hours toward Kwajelin, lost an engine, and returned to Saipan with one engine. But the poor pilot had to wing in his giant ship under a hurricane cross-wind, with the power of one giant engine gone. The wind turned the ship just as she was putting her wheels down. Marty died instantly.

Continued

Tomorrow I will bury Marty. It won't be easy for me, and it won't be easy to leave Marty behind. Yet, I know this is foolish sentiment on my part, for Marty has gone straight to God! I can never tell you or the world what a wonderful soul Marty had! The men respected him so much! And all through the command tonight, there is many a saddened soldier who grieves over Marty's going.

Will you acquaint the Rockhurst Fathers of the details I have written, and will you be brave—Marty is with God! We can't cry too much over that, can we? I feel wherever I may go now Marty will be there, smiling and encouraging. Quiet, lovable Marty! God bless you.

— Father Tighe

would supervise instructional costs and reimburse Rockhurst for them. Father McCabe went on to outline a policy for paying overtime, noted that the former 10-month school year for each faculty member now would be 12 months, and then released a salary schedule that he hoped the faculty would approve. There was $200 a month for Assistant Dean/teacher J.J. Jolin, S.J., and librarian/teacher H.H. Regnet, S.J.; $220 for history teacher Harry B. Kies; $275 for chemistry teacher Vanston Ryan; and the most of anyone—$300 a month, or $3,600 a year—for noted philosophy teacher George A. Deglman, S.J., who had received the first doctoral degree ever awarded (in 1916) from Marquette University. Football coach Lew Lane, with his added physical training duties for the Army, got a raise of $16.67 a month, to $200, or $2,400 a year.[20]

Wartime demands increased not only coach Lane's duties, but also the teaching load of the Jesuit faculty, which apparently had brought on a few complaints, possibly exacerbated by the denial of vacations during the war. Father McCabe also reported, confidentially, hearing "an occasional whimper about food" and said he didn't like the way in which the heavier teaching load was being used "as an excuse for late rising."[21]

The war colored life at Rockhurst. While the Rockhurst Circle continued to raise money through its monthly card parties and lunches, another women's group, the Rockhurst College Scholarship Club, put on a dozen lectures with titles indicative of the times: "Rationing in War Times" and "Gasses in Warfare and How to Detect Them," a lecture accompanied by a demonstration—which ended up smoking out the room. One day in the auditorium, city fire wardens gave instructions for an upcoming blackout exercise, and, on another day, Rockhurst students were among those who answered an urgent call from the Aireon Manufacturing Corp. for help in completing a rush order for radar parts.[22]

July 4, 1943, came and went with no fireworks, and the Hawk football program was dropped "for the duration" after coach Lane lost his entire first and second squads to the war. The Hawk basketball team continued to play, but it was a team "studded with freshmen." On a more positive note, new half shades were put in the faculty residence windows and a cement sidewalk laid to Conway Hall from the administration building, which finally was given the name Sedgwick Hall.[23]

Father McCabe, meanwhile, had his eye on the old, World War I German cannon that Jo Zach Miller, Jr., had placed on the lawn years before. McCabe thought it a fine idea to melt the thing down and give the proceeds to the Red Cross, an idea he presented to Miller in the spring of 1942. If Miller was insulted by the idea he did not say, but there was no mistaking his fond feelings for the relic. "I do not wish to dispose of the cannon at this time for personal reasons," he wrote back to McCabe, adding that one would be lucky to get $10 a ton for its "junk" value, anyway. To insure its safety, he included a check for $12.50 and told McCabe to just let him know if he ever wanted to move the cannon, and, if so, he would find a place for it.[24]

Harry M. Nearing, Class of '42. Official U.S. Navy photograph. Courtesy of Rockhurst University Archives.

— THE SOLDIERS —

Stories triumphant and tragic filled Kansas City's newspapers during the war years. There was the story, for instance, of Lt. Theodore Marshall, a Navy pilot born and reared in Kansas City and one semester shy of graduation from Rockhurst College when he was presented a Silver Star for his heroics on the day the Japanese attacked Pearl Harbor. In the midst of the attack, Marshall had hurried to Hickham Field in a truck, only to discover upon arrival that his plane had been demolished. He climbed into another fighter plane only to have it riddled by machine gun fire before he could get it into the air. "Undaunted," his citation read, "Lieutenant Marshall rushed to a torpedo bomber, went into the air and pursued enemy aircraft until a depleted fuel supply forced his return to the station." After Pearl Harbor, Marshall went on to serve in the Solomon Islands and New Guinea.[25]

Also in Hawaii at the time was Lt. Charles P. Muckenthaler, the "Lucky No. 1" who had drawn the first straw to begin pilot training when Rockhurst entered the Civilian Pilot Training Program in 1939. After graduation, Muckenthaler had joined the Navy, won his wings at Pensacola, Florida, and, in September 1941, gone to Hawaii, where he was stationed at the naval air base at Kaneoke. How well he remembered December 7, 1941. "The Japs came in about 7:55 o'clock in the morning and strafed our planes," he said. "While we were fighting flames at the hangars, back came the Japs to shower us with bombs. They strafed and bombed at intervals until 10 or 10:30 o'clock that morning. We lost most of our planes, and too many men." Muckenthaler went on to serve in the Battle of Midway and by 1943 was in the Solomon Islands, flying a patrol plane. "In the daytime...we carried depth charges which we dropped on anything that looked like a sub," he said during an interview while home on leave. "We took the offensive at night. Our plane, carrying a crew of ten, made five after-dark contacts with enemy surface vessels. We made some bomb and torpedo hits."[26]

Technical Sgt. Charles J. Doyle, who attended Rockhurst for 2 years before enlisting in August 1942, was awarded a Distinguished Flying Cross for participating in 50 operational flight missions in the Southwest Pacific. Doyle, a flight engineer and the son of Mrs. H.C. Doyle of 5421 Baltimore Ave., served with a troop carrier squadron of the 5th Air Force.[27]

Rockhurst graduate James J. Murphy was a hero of the story "Last Man Off Wake Island," written by Lt. Col. Walter L.J. Bayler and published in *The Saturday Evening Post*. It was Lt. Murphy, the son of Mr. and Mrs. John W. Murphy of 33 W. 57th Street, who landed his Navy patrol plane on Wake Island just days after Pearl Harbor and only a few hours before Japanese forces overwhelmed the American garrison there. "Out of the gray mists came a big navy patrol plane piloted by Ensign Murphy," wrote Bayler, a radio engineer with the U.S. Marines. Murphy landed his plane "as lightly as a gull," wrote Bayler, who was rescued and flown to Midway Island for more radio work. Murphy's parents told a reporter their son had mentioned his Wake Island trip casually as just one of many patrols and trips he had made in the Pacific war zone.[28]

Amid the stories, one exceptional Rockhurst woman stood out. She was Miss Virginia Garst, 23, who was working as secretary to Rockhurst College Treasurer J.F. Hughes when she decided she wanted to become a flying instructor. She quit her job at Rockhurst, earned her commercial and instructor's license and, along with 22 other American women, joined the British Air Transport Auxiliary in England, where they flew fighter planes and bombers as "factory to front" ferry pilots. "We girls fly everything except the 4-motored big ones," Garst said in an interview after she returned to Kansas City in 1943 following an appendicitis operation. "War work isn't so glamorous to the women in England as it is here," she told the reporter. "They wear lipstick all right, and curl their hair, but on sixty coupons a year for clothes rationing, their uniforms usually turn out to be a pair of slacks and a sweater."[29]

By late 1943, the year Miss Garst returned to the States, Rockhurst announced its 15th Gold Star, one each for Rockhurst men killed in the war. The latest belonged to Pvt. William B. Ryan, who died in a collision of 2 training planes north of Spokane, Washington, where he was working as an instructor. Ryan, 32, was a graduate of Rockhurst High School and College, where he had been editor of *The Sentinel*. Former Rockhurst football star Pete Schulte died in a plane crash in San Francisco Bay, and William E. Griffin, flight commander on a B-25 bomber, died in March 1943 when his plane crashed in the jungles of Latin America. "Billy," as he was called by his friends, had written home only days before, telling how he had started out with his crew for a long trip across the Atlantic Ocean to Africa when one of the engines on the B-25 failed "100 miles out." The crew had returned safely to base and planned to begin the trip anew the next day. Lt. Griffin, who was the first Rockhurst student to graduate under the wartime's accelerated 3-year program, was up for promotion when the B-25 crashed somewhere in the jungle before it even reached the ocean. No word had been heard about the 4 other crewmen on the plane. The gunner, at least, had survived because, to reduce the weight of the bomber, he had gone to Africa by boat.[30]

Lt. Ira W. (Bill) Brown, Jr., Class of '39, received the Navy's Distinguished Flying Cross for his bravery in the Battle of the Philippines. Brown was one of many war heroes from Rockhurst. Courtesy of Rockhurst University Archives.

Before the war ended, Rockhurst College would count 79 Gold Stars. Lt. E.L. Mathias, Jr., a Navy fighter pilot, was killed in the line of duty in the South Pacific, and Lt. Charles E. Epp, an aviator in the Marine Corps, was lost when his plane crashed off the coast of California. He was doing maneuvers with 3 other planes from the Marine Air Base at El Toro, California, when his plane fell. He parachuted, but when rescue crews arrived they could find no trace of him. Lt. Epp, the son of Mr. and Mrs. George W. Epp, Sr., of 211 E. 66th Street Terrace, had attended Rockhurst College from 1940 to 1942. Flight officer Martin Coughlin had gone missing when his plane crashed over the Gulf of Mexico in February 1943, only 8 weeks after Coughlin left Kansas City. Coughlin was on submarine duty, escorting a convoy of 26 ships out of the Gulf when his plane went down. Though search planes were out in 5 minutes looking for Coughlin and his pilot, Lt. Paul W. Davis, of St. Louis, there was no sign of them. Coughlin's mother, Mrs. Mary Coughlin, of 2705 E. 35th Street, said her son was 29 years old and had studied law for 2 years before entering the service.[31]

Lt. Albert Monaco, a bombardier on a B-17 Flying Fortress, went missing over Germany in January 1944. Sgt. Roy G. Sanders, Jr., a waist gun-

This plaque hangs in Massman Hall in memory of the 79 Rockhurst men who sacrificed their lives in World War II. Photo by David Spaw.

ner on a B-17, was killed when his plane was hit during a bombing raid over Schweinfurt on April 13, 1944. The pilot and bombardier on the plane, who parachuted, indicated from a prisoner of war camp in Germany that they thought Sanders had left the plane safely with them. But 2 weeks later, word came through the German Red Cross that Sanders was dead. Lt. J.F. Bauman was lost over Tokyo in March 1945. Lt. Frank Hayde was heralded as an ace who shot down 5 Japanese planes in the South Pacific. He had been recommended for the Distinguished Flying Cross when word came in August 1944 that he was missing in action in the Pacific.[32]

Not all of the Rockhurst men who served during the war returned home safely to their families. Sgt. Roy G. Sanders, Jr., was killed in action during a bombing raid over Schweinfurt on April 13, 1944. A graduate of Rockhurst High School, "Bud" Sanders had begun his studies at Rockhurst College when called into military service. In this photo, Sanders is wearing his Rockhurst ring, now the possession of his great-nephew, also a graduate of Rockhurst High School. Courtesy of the family of Mary Jane Sanders Meyer.

Others were wounded or came home with honors: Pvt. James Platt, a radio specialist, was wounded on Saipan; Pvt. Louis Nigro in North Africa; and Pvt. Richard J. Dillon, an infantryman attached to Army intelligence, in France. Pfc. Joseph Phillips earned a Bronze Star and Staff Sgt. Francis J. "Red" Collins, a Silver Star for heroism in Sicily. Collins, a former letterman in football and basketball at Rockhurst, was cited for "gallantry in action" during the capture of enemy territory. His citation explained that "under a hail of bullets, Staff Sgt. Collins went forward to make a reconnaissance and plan his attack, heedless of the fact that the enemy outnumbered his forces five to one."[33]

The Navy awarded a Distinguished Flying Cross to Lt. Ira W. (Bill) Brown, Jr., for his part in the Battle of the Philippines. Brown was an Iowa boy who had lived with his uncle and aunt, Mr. and Mrs. Ralph W. Street, 6444 Summit Street, while attending Rockhurst. Brown's heroics came as he helped to fend off an attack by 6 Japanese planes on a U.S. naval fleet off Jolo Sulu in the Philippine Islands. Earlier, his plane had been shot down, but he swam to an island where friendly natives cared for him and helped him escape to Borneo, where the Dutch aided him in returning to his unit.[34]

— ON CAMPUS —

The war colored everyday doings on campus. "We lost our cafeteria man to the draft," Father McCabe wrote to the provincial on September 12, 1942, adding that it was hard to get any work done because "contractors are not interested in little jobs compared to the govt. jobs." One day, chemistry professor Vanston Ryan spoke to a local group about chemicals and war, and, on another day, Lt. Priesmeyer, now promoted to captain, stood before the entire body of Army cadets—all rigidly at attention—and presented government medals to the widow and mother of a fallen Rockhurst soldier. Another day a statue of St. Thomas More arrived as a gift from the Class of '42 and was placed in a niche in Conway Hall. During a ceremony in the Jesuit dining room, Father McCabe announced that Thomas More had been chosen as Rockhurst's patron saint. "He laboured for wisdom, and wisdom worked together with him," McCabe would say during graduation ceremonies 2 years later. "His life in the sixteenth century encompassed most of the Rockhurst man's twentieth century problems, and that is why you are asked to turn to him for the help you need." Soon, there would be a Rockhurst anthem, "A Song of Wisdom," sung in honor of St. Thomas More. McCabe had spoken that graduation day of June 11, 1944, to a class of only 5 students, one of whom already was in the armed

— SAINT THOMAS MORE, PATRON OF ROCKHURST —

Thomas More was born in England in 1478 and was only 7 at the accession of Henry VII and the establishment of the Tudor dynasty on the throne. He was the son of a barrister, John More, but spent time in the household of Lord Chancellor Cardinal Morton and attended Oxford University and then became a law student at New Inn and Lincoln's Inn. More became a barrister himself in 1497, beginning the practice of law after having seen the inner workings of English politics.

In 1500 he began an intimate friendship with Desiderius Erasmus, the great Christian humanist of the age. After spending two years in a London Carthusian monastery (but without vows), he was elected to Parliament in 1504, and later was made Under-Sheriff of London, part of the King's embassy to Flanders, Under-Treasurer, and finally Lord Chancellor in 1529. After the early death of his first wife, he then married Alice Middleton in 1511.

Attracted to the great movement of Christian Humanism, he wrote the renowned *Utopia* in 1516, placing him in the intellectual forefront of these thinkers. When the Reformation erupted in Europe in 1517, the Christian world was in turmoil. This religious tumult came to England when Henry VIII, concerned about a male heir to succeed him, tried to assume the title of head of the English Church and annul his marriage to Catherine of Aragon, freeing him to marry Anne Boleyn. Thomas More could not in good conscience approve of the king's plan: in 1532 he resigned as Lord Chancellor. Convicted of treason on perjured evidence, though he had always been loyal to the king politically, he was beheaded on July 6, 1535, saying he died the "King's good servant but God's first." Thomas More was canonized in 1935.

Thomas More, as Christian humanist scholar and friend of Erasmus, was a member and supporter of a great Renaissance learning community; as writer of *Utopia* and other works he was a fosterer of the liberal arts; as political office-holder and chancellor he showed his exemplary commitment to serve the world through leadership but only in the light of the Christian principles that informed his whole life. Therefore, it was fitting that in 1942, Father William McCabe named St. Thomas More the patron of Rockhurst. The Class of '42 donated the statue of More, depicted in this picture. Originally located in Conway Hall, the statue is now displayed in the Greenlease Library.

— Charles M. Kovich, Class of '70

services and another who was leaving in a week to sign up. So small was the affair that it was held, not as usual in Mason-Halpin Fieldhouse, but in the Chapel of the North American Martyrs in Conway Hall.[35]

As part of his speech that graduation day, McCabe announced a revision of the college seal, which he said had been authorized by the Board of Directors. The new seal was based on a coat of arms designed by Leonard Wilson of London and San Francisco, "expert in heraldry and genealogy." The shield, McCabe said, would be quartered by a red Christian cross. Three of the quarters would display elements from 3 separate coats of arms: one from that of Jesuit founder Ignatius Loyola, another from patron saint Thomas More, and the third from the family of college founder Michael Dowling. The fourth quarter would display symbols of Rockhurst College—a rock and a hurst, described as a group of trees. Charged on the cross would be 7 gold pillars representing the 7 liberal arts. The motto: "Wisdom hath built herself a house."[36] "This is a monumental landmark in the history of our school," McCabe said of the new seal, "for it denotes our consciousness of tradition and the place in that tradition of wisdom."

Father McCabe's understanding of Rockhurst tradition likely was gleaned as he dug through old files, taking an interest in the school's founding days. He looked hard into Rockhurst's relationship with St. Aloysius Parish, trying to decipher whether he, as college rector, could intervene in parish finances.[37] As early as October 1941 there was renewed talk of turning the church over to the diocese. At pastor John Gerst's request, McCabe paid a visit to the church and premises that autumn and was shocked to find that "everything is dirty" and many of the buildings dilapidated. "Dirt inches thick; window sashes falling out; roofs leaking; walls dirty; etc. A man's job that will cost money." The city sanitary inspectors had come by and demanded repairs and improvements in the grade school building, which was not fireproof. "Toilets positively primitive—only France could duplicate them," McCabe wrote. He also found the bookkeeping primitive and surmised that it would "take good work to put the place into the right shape to save the Society's reputation when it is turned over to the seculars."[38]

He wrote for details to Father Conway and learned that St. Aloysius had been sending money directly to the province in lieu of the tax that Rockhurst, for years, had failed to pay. This, McCabe pointed out, "is rather an argument for the financial identity of the parish house and the college." It would be good to clear up the fuzzy relationship, he said, "since a hazy situation gives rise to bickerings."[39] Declaring himself "but a bird of passage" at Rockhurst, McCabe insisted he was not much concerned about the solution, but suggested that the province should either give the Rockhurst president full control of St. Aloysius, or none at all. What really concerned McCabe was the yearly tax Rockhurst had for so long failed to pay to the province. "One of my chief concerns since coming here has been to pay the Province tax in full as soon as possible; without waiting for an invitation from the Province," he wrote to the provincial. "The income from St. A. would enable me, perhaps, to make a big step in the right direction."

Although Provincial Peter Brooks responded a few days later, instructing McCabe to take control of the finances and books at St. Aloysius, it was only a few months later, apparently at the request of Kansas City Bishop Edwin O'Hara, that the church was turned over to the diocese.[40] "The relinquishment of St. Aloysius took place with proper decorum on June 1," McCabe wrote to Brooks in the summer of 1942. The night before, Sunday, May 31, St. Aloysius parishioners gathered in the school hall to say farewell to the 3 Jesuits stationed there, Fathers Gerst, Grace, and O'Connor, who urged them to give the same loyalty to the new pastors as to the old.[41] The turning over of St. Aloysius Church, symbolizing yet another ending in Rockhurst's early history, came, perhaps fittingly, in the midst of a world changing so quickly that Rockhurst, as did the United States, sat that summer on the cusp of a new age, the atomic age.

As the horrific news of war rolled in month after month, Father John J. Driscoll, S.J., recorded bits of it in Rockhurst's *Historia Domus* (House History). News from Rome, home of Pope Pius XII and the Vatican, as well as the Father General of the Society of Jesus, was of singular concern to Father Driscoll. "Today Rome was bombed by the American planes," he wrote on July 19, 1943, then reassured himself that "the fliers were trained for weeks and given express commands not to bomb any churches or historic monuments." Word came that Nazi soldiers were stationed "with big guns around Vatican City," saying their presence there was to "protect" the Vatican and the Pope. "The Catholics of the world fear this 'protection,'" Driscoll wrote, "and are praying God to protect Christ's Vicar here on earth from those enemies of God & the church." He was appalled at news that Nazi soldiers were "treating the people roughly and stealing treasures of art," as well as gold, from the churches. By the summer of 1944, as the Allies stormed the French beaches at Normandy, Father Driscoll allowed himself the hope that "this terrible war may end sooner than expected. Word comes," he wrote, "that an attempt was made to kill Hitler." The last Nazis had been driven out of Rome, and "His Holiness the Pope," a jubilant Father Driscoll wrote on June 4, 1944, "spoke from the famous balcony thanking God that Rome with its great churches and monuments was not destroyed & the Italian people were freed from the Nazi tyranny."

It was in that hopeful summer of 1944 that the Democratic National Convention nominated Franklin Delano Roosevelt for an unprecedented fourth term as president of the United States. Kansas City buzzed with the news, especially with FDR's choice of a new vice president—Sen. Harry S. Truman of nearby Independence, Missouri. Although both men were Protestants, Father Driscoll found solace that Roosevelt was "a Christian man, fair to all and not afraid to mention God's name when it could be done in a Christian way."[42]

—BUILDING PLANS —

It was during the occupation of Rome that Wlodimir Ledóchowski, the longtime Jesuit Father General, died. His Generalate, from February 11, 1915, to the day of his death in Rome, December 13, 1942, was considered one of the most productive in Jesuit history. During his 27 years of service, the Society of Jesus had increased from 17,000 members to 27,000, passing for the first time the high mark before the Jesuit suppression of 1773. The Polish Ledóchowski, described as wiry and keen-eyed, had started missions among the Eastern Orthodox, fought attacks on Jesuits in Spain, Germany, and Mexico, and, despite threats from Germany and Italy, kept a Jesuit on his staff who regularly disclosed Nazi atrocities in Europe over the Vatican Radio.[43]

Perhaps it wasn't surprising, then, that even at the height of World War II, a letter arrived on the desk of Rockhurst President William McCabe

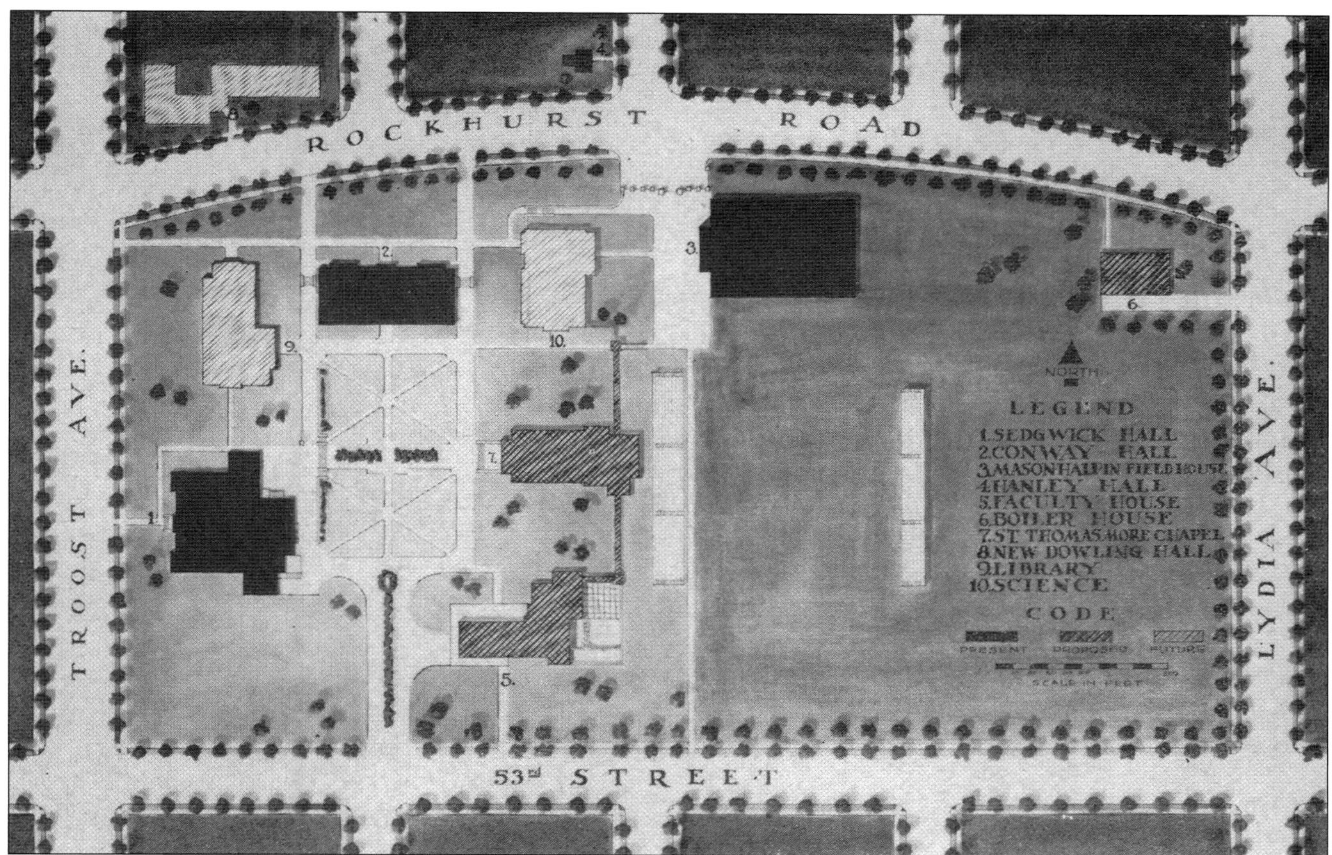

As the war in Europe began to wind down, President William McCabe anticipated a postwar boom in enrollment, requiring expanded campus facilities. In a booklet titled "A Suggestion," McCabe sketched a campus development plan that included a chapel, library, student dormitory, new classroom, and faculty residence for Jesuits. Fr. McCabe's vision would not be realized until many years later, during the presidency of Maurice Van Ackeren, S.J. Courtesy of Rockhurst University Archives.

stating that the Society of Jesus wanted to honor Ledóchowski's memory by raising $500,000 to enlarge the Vatican Radio. "Try to have as many priests as possible raise as much as possible," wrote Zacheus J. Maher, S.J., Ledóchowski's assistant in North America.[44] Maher counted 1,305 priests in the Assistancy able to act as solicitors and figured that if each priest could raise somewhere between $150 and $5,000, the half-million could be had. "Please let me have a list of your solicitors and of the amounts they have pledged to raise as soon as possible," he concluded.

The letter apparently left Father McCabe incredulous because he fired a reply back immediately, noting that Maher's timing was "inopportune." "Some of us are fighting for our existence, both college and high school; any approachable friends whom we may have ought to be asked to save the school," he wrote, and added: "Only a short time ago, we were assessed for a church to be built in Rome as a jubilee gift to the Holy Father. We took this out of our own debt-burdened resources, not asking our friends for it because they have been solicited endlessly for civic and church needs. It seems unwise still to go after them for the present cause. Could it not wait at least until we have some notion whether we shall be bankrupt next year and dependent on our friends?"[45]

The timing was, indeed, inopportune. The situation at Rockhurst was dire enough that McCabe, beginning with the fall term of 1942, had raised tuition from $156 a semester to $200 and then breathed a sigh of relief when "no one kicked."[46] The hike was expected to increase tuition income for the year from $35,000 to $56,000.

Father McCabe's financial pleas surrounding the Vatican Radio proved to no avail, but his prayers to keep Rockhurst financially solvent were answered when the government announcement came in February of 1943 that Rockhurst was among the colleges selected to train a detachment of Army Air Forces cadets. The Army promised to send 200 student trainees and an initial government contract worth $42,000.[47] A relieved and upbeat Father McCabe wrote in his newsletter that February: "Rockhurst is coming through the war. Rockhurst will resume her growth immediately after the war. There will always be a Rockhurst…Rockhurst is twenty-five years young…I can say without boasting that I know of no more promising small college in the land…."

In October 1944, Rockhurst received an award for the college's meritorious service rendered to the Army Air Forces during the war. Bottom row (left to right): Fr. John Higgins, S.J., dean; Fr. William McCabe, S.J., president; Col. George Mundy; Capt. W. Wrape. Middle row: Vanston H. Ryan; Fr. George Hilke, S.J.; Lt. Leonard Lebby; James F. Hughes; Fr. Paul O. Smith, S.J. Top row: Henry J. Massman; Vincent J. O'Flaherty; John F. Fogarty; Harry B. Kies. Courtesy of Rockhurst University Archives.

He went on to predict that Rockhurst enrollment was certain to reach 500 students in the years after the war. Enrollment numbers had been heading in that direction before Pearl Harbor, and the college had realized even then, he said, that "present facilities were fast becoming inadequate" to receive so many students. Rockhurst must, he insisted, get ready for 500 liberal arts students. "We say 500, because that number is all that Rockhurst wants. Her work is best accomplished in the faculty-student intimacy of the small college; and when the number rises beyond half a thousand, that domestic intimacy suffers. That's the way it works. Don't ask me why."

With that, he outlined a building program, specific in its needs:

1. A chapel, and "a beautiful one."

2. A student dormitory to handle 100 out-of-town boys.
3. A library.
4. A faculty residence for the Jesuits.

By May 1943, he was busy drafting the setup of a trust fund, and by July it was officially established as the Rockhurst College Endowment Fund, with the express purpose of raising $250,000 for "the erection or improvements of buildings." McCabe already had a list of contributors, led by Henry J. Massman, Sr., president of the Massman Construction Company, who had pledged $25,000.[48]

"Massman, in a long talk a couple of weeks ago, said the money's in the bank waiting," McCabe wrote to Daniel Conway on May 12, 1943. "In the course of the conversation, he left the gate open for the acceptance of the money in any way I want, even an outright gift with no strings attached." In his "kindly, tentative, undictatorial, miss-nothing-good-for-Rockhurst way," Massman had suggested the name of an attorney to execute the trust document, but, at McCabe's recommendation that the college use its longtime attorney, Hugh Downey, Massman readily acquiesced. McCabe confided that he planned to announce the new trust fund during commencement ceremonies that May, concluding his letter to Conway: "Stand ready."[49]

By the following summer, the trust fund was up to $40,000, and by that fall and winter of 1944–45 the building campaign was going full blast, with Vincent J. O'Flaherty, Jr., Class of '21, serving as chairman of the fund drive. "College to Build," the *Kansas City Times* announced on November 25, 1944, and just a week later, Father McCabe, in a booklet titled "A Suggestion," provided a sketch of the "campus-development plan." The college would be happy, he said, to accept donations in the form of wartime F or G bonds in Rockhurst's name. He reiterated the college's needs as he saw them, "in the following order of urgency": a suitable faculty house, a central heating plant, a student dormitory, a chapel, another classroom building. This, he explained, was a million-dollar, long-range plan. For now, Rockhurst planned to address only one-quarter of it. The faculty house was most urgent, he explained, because it would allow the college to vacate needed space in Sedgwick Hall, where many of the Jesuit faculty lived.[50]

— CADET PROGRAM ENDS —

Only a year after the first cadets arrived at Rockhurst, top brass in the Army Ground Forces, who never favored the aviation-training program, cited an acute shortage of military manpower as it prepared for the long-awaited D-Day invasion. Pressure mounted to terminate the aviation program, and by the summer of 1944, Gleason writes, it had all but disappeared. "This was bad news, not just for the [cadets], most of whom were reassigned to infantry units, but also for the college administrators who had counted on the program's lasting much longer," he writes.[51] The program officially ended on June 30, 1944, but short as its duration was, it had been a godsend for Rockhurst. The Army contract "financially tided over what might have been a calamitous year and a half," McCabe said. Although the

On May 6, 1945, Rockhurst held a Military Mass attended by some 2,000 people. Two days later Germany surrendered, and the war in Europe ended. Victory over Japan came in August, after the dropping of atomic bombs on Hiroshima and Nagasaki. Courtesy of Rockhurst University Archives.

contract was nonprofit, paying only the college's costs, "it paid our way," he said, "during many otherwise very lean months."[52]

An important side benefit stemmed from the religious background of the 1,441 cadets who completed the program at Rockhurst—two-thirds of them were not Catholic. What better publicity agent for a Catholic college could there be than these non-Catholic students? McCabe wondered aloud. "It was a pleasure to watch how…these boys, wary and wondering at first, shortly saw that this is an all-American campus." Plus, he said, they found something new in the Jesuit faculty's spirit of self-sacrifice and devotion to the needs of their students, "especially to those needing extra help."[53] How happy it made him when a cadet, before leaving for military service, would stop by to say how he had grown to like Rockhurst. "A number," McCabe wrote, "have said that, when released finally from military service, they would like to come back to Rockhurst to finish their college education." These cadets were the "finest publicity agency" Rockhurst could hope for. "These men will be telling the whole country that, for excellence of teaching and for fineness of faculty-student relations, Rockhurst College can't be beaten. And that is just what Rockhurst deserves to have said about her. It is much more important that this should be said than that it should be said, *per impossible*, that Rockhurst had beaten Notre Dame."

As the cadet program ended, the Army Air Forces praised Rockhurst for its "high caliber of instruction," and McCabe praised the Army Air Forces for the smooth operation of its program. Even financial negotiations had "been pleasant," he said. He had been impressed by the government's "competence and wish to be fair," and he suspected that Rockhurst's "sincerity in seeking nothing more" than what was its due impressed the government. That October, in a small ceremony in McCabe's office in Sedgwick

Hall, the Army presented a "certificate of service award," to Rockhurst for its "meritorious service" rendered to the Army Air Forces.[54]

As Gleason explains, the wartime programs, as well as service by individual Catholics on various official bodies (Rockhurst's John Friedl, S.J., for instance, had served on the National War Labor Board), "represented a quantum leap in terms of Catholic educator's involvement with secular agencies in general and the federal government in particular." This was true for all institutions of higher education, he explained, but particularly for Catholic schools because "it brought them more actively into the mainstream of public life, thus reinforcing the assimilative tendencies that had long been at work in their adjustment to prevailing norms in educational practice and in other more subtle ways."[55]

At a wartime meeting of the Central Regional Group of the Jesuit Educational Association, for example, education directors and deans discussed the organization of "tomorrow's Jesuit Arts College." Noting that the *Ratio Studiorum*, written nearly 350 years earlier, did not address the objectives of a liberal arts college, they wanted to be clear about their objectives. How, they asked, should science be taught? And what of the study of Latin, which, in 1599, was the core of Jesuit education, seen as it was to effect a humanistic culture? But now, in the 1940s, few students came to college adequately prepared in Latin, which precluded even some of the better students from obtaining the A.B. degree, considered by Jesuits to be the best undergraduate degree. "It is illogical to grant only five A.B. degrees to a graduating class of forty, many of whom are desirous and capable of a more cultural training," stated William J. McGucken, S.J., regional director of education for the Missouri Province. Before the meeting ended, educators recommended making the A.B. curriculum "more flexible," and that the substitution of English for Latin as the core-course of the liberal arts curriculum be considered as a possible solution "for many difficulties."[56]

The war years were the beginning of much change.

By April 1945, as the Allies advanced on Berlin, Rockhurst completed preparations for a Military Mass to be held in Mason-Halpin Fieldhouse. On the morning of May 6, about 2,000 persons, including many servicemen, took their seats and listened to the Rev. Raphael C. McCarthy, head of the department of psychology at Saint Louis University, say that the charity and justice of Christ must come back into the lives of men and nations if the world ever was to enjoy lasting peace. "There can be no lasting peace without religion," Father McCarthy said. "We can have no security without God. The reason for all the slaughter and atrocities is that men, both leaders and people, have forgotten God.....We must bring God back into the planning of our leaders."[57]

He called on those present to show their "reverence, respect, and affection" to the soldiers who had given their lives for their country, as well as to those still serving in the armed forces. To that point in the war, 3,125 former students of Rockhurst High School and Rockhurst College had served in the armed services during World War II. "We should profit by their example—their devotion to an ideal," Father McCarthy said that spring day. "They did not fight a people or a nation but a hideous spirit of evil.

Rockhurst dance, 1946. After the war, the Rockhurst student body sponsored numerous dances, featuring orchestras led by nationally-known band leaders such as Ted Weems, Decca recording artist. Photo by Charles Brenneke. Courtesy of Rockhurst University Archives.

They struggled to defeat a denial of God. This struggle is not between nations but between paganism and Christianity." The Mass concluded with a 3-volley salute outside the fieldhouse by servicemen from Fort Leavenworth. The military guard stood at attention as Capt. Orin Igou, bugler, sounded taps.

Just 2 days later, on May 8, 1945, Germany surrendered on a date that became known as V-E Day (Victory in Europe). Victory over Japan also was in sight, but some of the fiercest fighting of the war was taking place even then in the South Pacific, especially on islands like Iwo Jima, where former Rockhurst College student James E. Platt, Jr., a 19-year-old private, was among the 6,000 Marines killed. Platt was a Kansas City, Kansas, boy who had graduated from Ward High School and worked in the mail and composing rooms of *The Star*.[58]

Victory over Japan would not come until August, after the dropping of atomic bombs on Hiroshima and Nagasaki, but victory in Europe was reason to celebrate. That June, Kansas City put on a grand celebration to honor Gen. Dwight D. Eisenhower, who was reared in nearby Abilene, Kansas, and who had gone on to lead all of America's fighting forces in Europe. "It was a big parade and celebration full of enthusiasm for the great General," Father Driscoll wrote in the *Historia Domus* on June 21, 1945. An estimated 250,000 people had watched the parade or participated in the ceremonies, which ended at Liberty Memorial.

The very next week, President Harry S. Truman, in office fewer than 3 months following the death of Franklin Delano Roosevelt on April 12, arrived by plane at Fairfax Airport. He had been in San Francisco for a meeting of the United Nations Relief Organization. He "rode in a parade of open autos through downtown Kansas City, Mo., and kept on going on 15th Street to his home town of Independence, Mo., where they will have a big reception tonight," Father Driscoll wrote on June 27. The next day, during a luncheon, Truman was granted an honorary degree from the University of Kansas City Law School, which he attended from 1923–25.

That summer of 1945, in its fourth—and last—wartime commencement, Rockhurst graduated only 3 men—John Harvey Affleck, 21; William Henry Breen, 21; and James Edward Burns, 24.[59] They were among the class of 128 freshmen who had entered Rockhurst in 1941, but the war, in one way or the other, had affected the lives of all. More than 80 percent of those 1941 freshmen, *The* (Catholic) *Register* reported, "have had their college course interrupted by service in the armed forces."

Such tiny graduation numbers never would be seen again as the postwar period produced an unprecedented expansion of American higher education, in which Catholics shared. In 1916, historian Jay Dolan writes, the number of students enrolled in Catholic colleges was 8,304. By 1950 the number would reach 112,765 full-time students, two-thirds of whom were male.[60] Significantly, the Jesuit dominance of Catholic higher education would solidify, and by 1950 the Society of Jesus' 25 colleges represented 42 percent of the total number of men's colleges (59) in the United States.

—GI BILL OF RIGHTS —

At Rockhurst, as elsewhere, enrollment mushroomed after the war, with much credit going to the Servicemen's Readjustment Act, also known as the GI Bill of Rights. The bill, signed into law by President Roosevelt on June 22, 1944, and administered by the Veterans Administration, addressed fears that the return of so many veterans would tumble the country into another depression. Among the bill's key provisions were government-financed education for veterans and a loan guaranty for homes. Before the war, college and homeownership were, for the most part, unreachable dreams for most Americans. Under the GI Bill, with the government paying tuition, millions of veterans who would have flooded the job market opted instead for an education. In the peak year of 1947, veterans would account for 49 percent of college admissions. By the time the original GI Bill ended on July 25, 1956, 7.8 million of 16 million World War II veterans would participate in an education or training program.[61]

The influx of veterans at Rockhurst was visible by the fall of 1945, when Father Driscoll counted 21 veterans among Rockhurst's 105-member freshman class.[62] The jump in enrollment seems to have started the previous fall, when a host of boys fresh out of high school—public as well as parochial—joined a returning 30 upperclassmen, pushing enrollment in the fall of 1944 to 151, or half of the prewar total. Notably, the tally included out-of-town students from Pittsburg, Parsons, Paola, and Herington in Kansas, and Liberty and Carrollton in Missouri. One student, Hugh Radigan, had come all the way from Watertown, New York, and another, Harry Halligan, from San Bruno, California. Edward Sanchez had flown in from Cuba, where he had spent several weeks over the summer. His father was the Cuban consul in Kansas City.[63]

Such a rush of enrollment was anticipated for the fall of 1946 that Dean John J. Higgins, S.J., held preliminary registration during the summer and cut off enrollment when the number of registrants reached 750, of whom 70 percent were thought to be veterans. That left another 200 young men on a waiting list. "We have enough instructors to handle 1,200 students," the dean told a reporter, "but the lack of classroom space will make it impossible to take care of more than 750."[64]

Over on Rockhill Road, the University of Kansas City was expecting an enrollment of 3,000 and was screening applicants, giving veterans preference. "Students who were in the lower half of their high school class are being rejected," R.R. Haun, dean of students and registrar, reported. "We make an exception for veterans. They can take a test…and if they pass we will accept them."[65] Housing was in such demand that Haun said the university was only accepting applications from out-of-state students if they already had found a place to live. The story was the same at the University of Kansas and at the University of Missouri, where MU President Frederick A. Middlebush said, "the housing shortage is the factor limiting enrollments."[66]

PRESIDENTIAL PROFILE

— THOMAS MCCARTAN KNAPP, S.J. —

The Rev. Thomas M. Knapp became Rockhurst's eighth president on December 18, 1945, and served until March 1951. A native of St. Louis, Fr. Knapp was born on November 4, 1890. He received his A.B. in 1910 and A.M. in 1917, both from Saint Louis University. He joined the Society of Jesus in 1910 and was ordained in 1924. After teaching at Campion College from 1917 until 1921, Fr. Knapp spent most of the next 25 years at Saint Louis University in various capacities as teacher and administrator.

While at Rockhurst, Father Knapp was noted for the active role he played in community affairs in Kansas City. *The Kansas City Star* spoke of his "humanitarianism and mature judgment" and called him "soft-spoken, realistic and responsive." His most engaging quality, said *The Star,* was his "simple, friendly humanity."

Fr. Knapp arrived at Rockhurst at a strategic moment in the history of the college. The postwar boom in student enrollment produced crowded conditions and the need to enlarge staff and facilities. Knapp tackled these problems in creative ways, most notably bringing onto campus government buildings from military installations for classrooms, housing, and a cafeteria.

After leaving Rockhurst, Fr. Knapp returned to Saint Louis University as regent and director of alumni for the School of Commerce and Finance. He died on October 27, 1965, at age 74.

Quotes from The Kansas City Star, *September 8, 1946 and March 20, 1951.*

There was no letup in the fall of 1947 when Rockhurst's enrollment went over the top with 1,059 registrants—an 18 percent increase over the previous year. According to *America*, the Jesuit weekly of the New York Province, enrollment that fall of 1947 mushroomed at every one of the 60 Catholic colleges it surveyed. Saint Louis University registered an 86 percent increase, to 9,000 students; Regis, in Denver, 117 percent, to 497 students; and Creighton, in Omaha, 94 percent, to 2,948 students.[67]

Enrollment had been heavy even for the second semester the previous spring. When the 3-day, official registration period ended on February 3, 1947, Dean Higgins announced an enrollment of 710 students—of whom 517 were veterans. When late registration was completed, he expected the number to rise to 800. To handle the onslaught of new students, Rockhurst started using a number system at registration. Those with a number from 1 to 160 registered from 9 a.m. to noon on January 30, and those with a number from 161 to 320 from 1 to 4 p.m. that afternoon. Registration spilled into the next day, following a similar pattern. Anyone with a number above 640 was scheduled to register on Saturday, February 1.[68]

The Thomas More Cafeteria (lower photo), situated between Sedgwick and Conway halls. When Father Thomas Knapp became president in December 1945, he wasted no time in planning for the expected boom in postwar enrollment. In a visit to Rosencrans Field in St. Joseph, Missouri, he found a noncommissioned officers' clubhouse and arranged to have it dismantled and shipped to Rockhurst. The new cafeteria opened on December 2, 1946. In all, Rockhurst would set up 8 temporary buildings on campus, including a 2-story structure relocated from Lake City Ordnance in Independence and named Janssens Hall (upper photo). Janssens Hall, situated east of the cafeteria, across from Sedgwick Hall, provided both classroom space and administrative offices. Courtesy of Rockhurst University Archives.

—CHANGING OF THE GUARD—

In the midst of these heady times, William McCabe was ordered to Omaha to become president of Creighton University. "Tonight at dinner there was a big surprise," Father Driscoll wrote in the house diary on December 18, 1945. A letter from the Vicar-General had been read, announcing that Father Thomas M. Knapp, S.J., who had arrived at Rockhurst that very morning, had been appointed president. "After the letter was read Fr. McCabe & Fr. Knapp changed places at table & Fr. Knapp the new Rector gave the Deo Gratias."[69]

Before coming to Rockhurst, Father Knapp had served as Saint Louis University chancellor (1926–37), dean of the College of Arts and Sciences there, and regent of the School of Commerce and Finance, as well as SLU's Senior Corporate Colleges. In 1943 he was named superior of the Missouri Province Jesuit Mission Band, and shortly before coming to Rockhurst

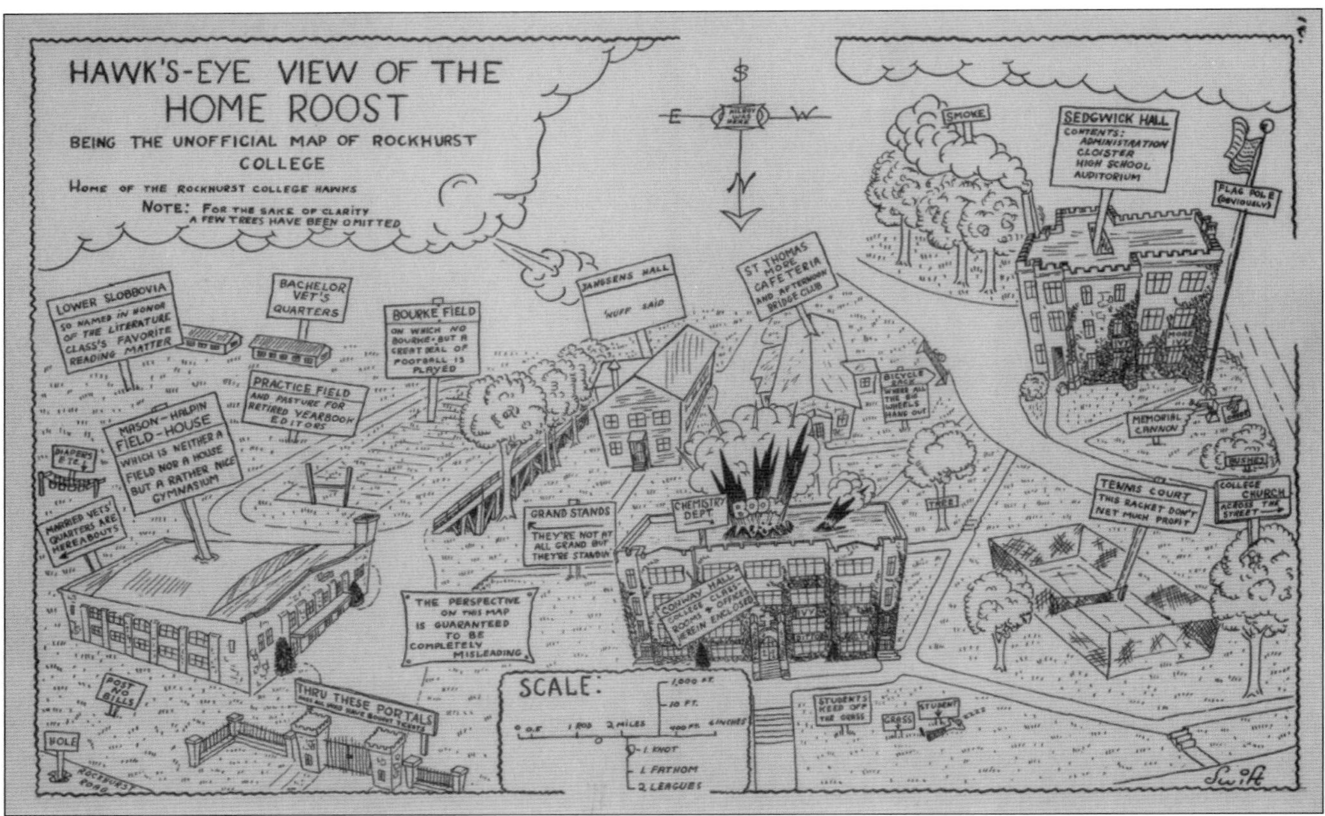

The Rockhurst campus through the eyes of Hawk *cartoonist Mike Swift, '48.*

had requested, but had not received, an assignment in the foreign mission field. Father Knapp was 55 years old, a tall, slender, quick-moving man who, despite his shock of pure white hair, seemed younger than his years. "Father Tom," as his friends called him, was a St. Louis native who traced his lineage to city founder Pierre Laclede Ligueste. His maternal grandfather, John G. Prather, was a powerful man in the Democratic Party, and his paternal grandfather, Col. George Knapp, was editor of the old *Missouri Republican*, the most influential newspaper west of the Mississippi in its day. Neither of his grandfathers was Catholic, but his mother was, and it was from her that he learned the ways of faith, and from the time he was 11, declared that he wanted to become a priest.[70]

In Kansas City, Father Tom wasted no time getting involved in the community. One of his first public appearances was before a meeting of the Knights of Columbus, an organization he joined, along with the Rotary, and South Kansas City Business Men's Club.[71] He inherited a faculty of 16 Jesuits (several of whom were new and had served as army chaplains), 16 full-time lay teachers, 8 part-timers to teach business law and accounting—and a student body so large that his first problem was how, and where, to feed them all.

"So," *The Kansas City Star* told the story, "he started out to find a cafeteria. He went out to the old Pratt-Whitney plant and found cooking equipment big enough to cook an ox, but like Goldilocks with the big bear's bed, it was too big. He visited Commonwealth Aircraft company's wartime plant, but there the cafeteria equipment was too small. Finally he found what he wanted at the Lake City ordnance plant, but the University of Missouri already had put in for it. Father Knapp said the need of M.U. with its big enrollment, was greater than the need of Rockhurst, and withdrew."

When officials at Lake City Ordnance, an Army ammunition plant in east Independence that employed as many as 21,000 people during the war, told Father Knapp of another cafeteria at the plant, he snapped up the equipment, though he had no building to put it in. He solved that problem with a trip to Rosencrans Field in St. Joseph, Missouri, where he found a noncommissioned officers' clubhouse and arranged to have it dismantled and shipped to Rockhurst. When it arrived, it was reassembled between Sedgwick and Conway halls.[72] The new cafeteria, opened on December 2, 1946, and, big enough to serve 300 people at one time, soon became the most popular place on campus. "At any time of the school day several groups of students can be found hurrying to scratch a cup of coffee between classes, playing a round of bridge, or simply sitting around talking," said a release from what apparently was a new publicity office. The Aireon Manufacturing Co. even had installed, on loan, a "colorful juke box."[73]

Cafeteria manager was Mr. William J. Bannon, whose two sons had attended Rockhurst and gone on to noteworthy careers in the movies and the priesthood. His son John Bannon, S.J., was head of the history department at Saint Louis University, and his son Jim Bannon was an actor in radio and Hollywood Westerns, best remembered as the cinema's fourth *Red Ryder* in a series of Westerns released in 1949–50.[74]

Planning and supervising cafeteria meals was Mrs. A.B. Kyle, who estimated that an average of 900 to 1,100 students ate in the cafeteria every day. A typical Monday lunch menu, Mrs. Kyle said, comprised a selection of cube steak, new potatoes, corn, spinach, sliced tomatoes, cottage cheese, fruit salad, sandwiches, cold plate, banana crème pie, cake, ice cream, coffee, and milk. A student, she said, usually selected meat, two vegetables, dessert, and beverage, "and his check is 40 cents." Three meals a day could be had for an average of $1.05 a day. Temporary building though it was, the Thomas More Cafeteria, as it was named, was "a far cry from the cramped, dingy old cafeteria in the basement" of Sedgwick Hall, which since had been converted into 6 small rooms—5 for the high school and one for faculty.[75]

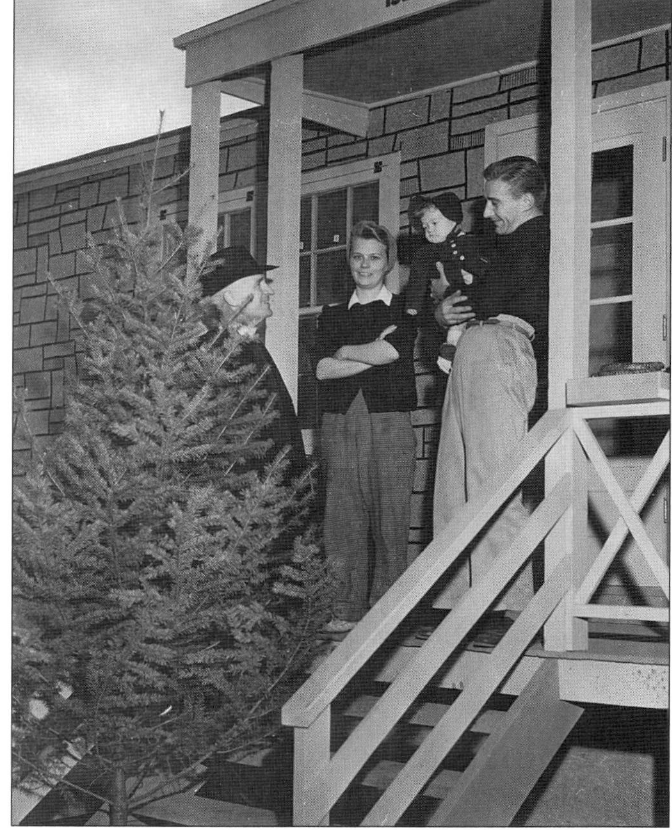

On Christmas Day 1946, Dean John Higgins, S.J., delivered a Christmas tree to the first married veteran to move into the "GI apartments," surplus barracks brought to campus from Rosencrans Field in St. Joseph. Pictured are student Clint Webber, his wife, and 14-month-old daughter. Photo by Roy Johnson. Courtesy of Rockhurst University Archives.

In all, Rockhurst would set up 8 temporary buildings on campus, including a 2-story structure located at Lake City Ordnance and hauled to Rockhurst in the fall of 1946. Named Janssens Hall in honor of newly appointed Jesuit Father General Jean-Baptiste Janssens, it would serve as urgently needed classroom space and to house administrative offices. "It will add tremendously to our facilities here," Dean Higgins said, noting that the additional classrooms would allow Rockhurst to enroll

Robert Dale Seible II was the first baby to be born of parents living on the Rockhurst campus in the converted Army barracks. Fr. Paul O. Smith, S.J., athletic director, presented a cheerleader's sweater to the newborn. Courtesy of Rockhurst University Archives.

250 more college students. And that was not to mention the 340 high schoolers on campus, who must have seemed like little boys to the growing force of veterans.[76]

The Rev. Joseph McCallin, S.J., who taught at Rockhurst from 1946 to 1955, recalled that "the average veteran was 22 years old. The veterans," he said, "were quite serious and excellent students, intent upon making a future for themselves. Many came to college to collect their thoughts." Because classroom space, even with the temporary building, was inadequate, classes were held on Monday, Wednesday, and Friday for one group and Tuesday, Thursday, and Saturday for another. "Trying to teach classes on a Saturday afternoon with a football game going on was a challenge," he said.[77]

All the temporary buildings and equipment, obtained with the financial backing of the Federal Public Housing Administration, would have cost Rockhurst $300,000 if purchased on the open market, Knapp told a meeting of the Alumni Association. The money was part of a $70 million appropriation by the U.S. government for colleges and universities.[78]

Of special interest to the press were the 5 barracks used for housing—3 for single veterans and 2 for married. Father Knapp, just as he had the cafeteria, located the buildings at Rosencrans Field, had them dismantled, hauled to campus, and placed on new foundations near the football practice field—the bachelor quarters on the south side of the field, the married quarters on the north side, facing Rockhurst Road. Having women on campus, except for the occasional secretary, cook, or night student, was a novelty, and the newspapers played it up. On Christmas Day 1946, the *Kansas City Times* ran a large photograph of Dean Higgins delivering a Christmas

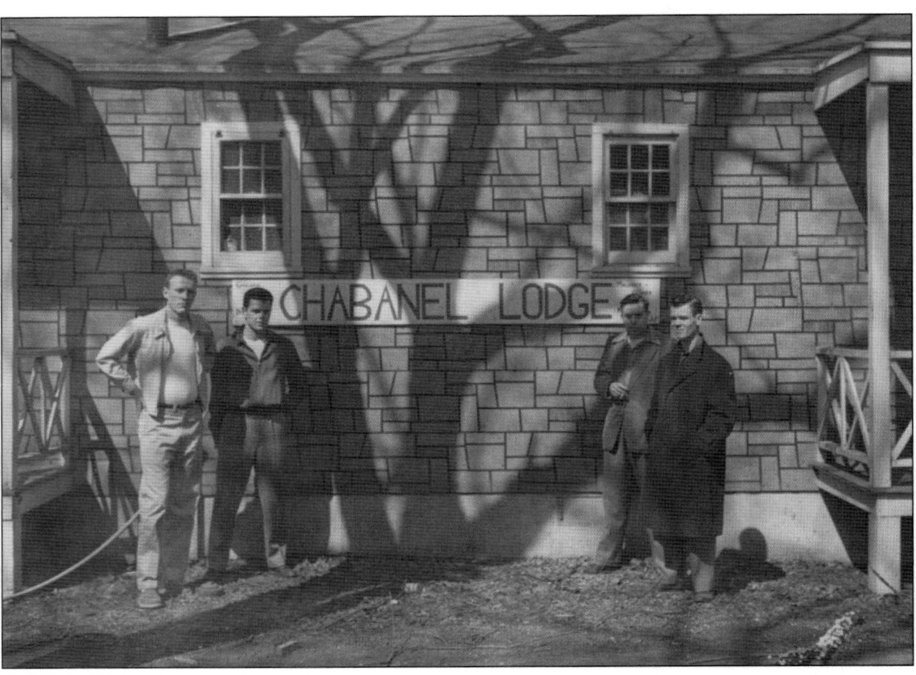

Five wartime military barracks were hauled in for campus housing, all located east of Bourke Field. Three barracks for single men, including Chabanel Lodge, faced 53rd Street, and 2 barracks for married men and their families faced Rockhurst Road. Courtesy of Rockhurst University Archives.

tree to the first married veteran to move into the "GI apartments." There he was, GI Clint Webber, standing with his wife and 14-month-old daughter, Cynthia, on the tiny porch of their home. "We've never had a home of our own where we could use our own furniture," Webber said. He had entered Rockhurst as a freshman in 1942 and earned a varsity letter in basketball before leaving to join the Army Air Forces. Enrolled now as a sophomore, he was playing in the backfield for Rockhurst's gridiron squad.

That Christmas week, 7 more families—including those of 2 faculty members—were scheduled to join the Webbers in the married living quarters. They would find each apartment with a living room, bedroom, kitchen, bathroom, and a small hallway lined with shelves.[79] When the first campus baby was born, it was big news. *The Star* came out to campus and took a photograph of Rockhurst athletic director Paul O. Smith, S.J., presenting a cheerleader's sweater to the newborn, Robert Dale Seible II.[80] It was the perfect gift, considering that the baby and his parents lived in one of the converted Army barracks, which sat within yelling distance of the athletic fields.

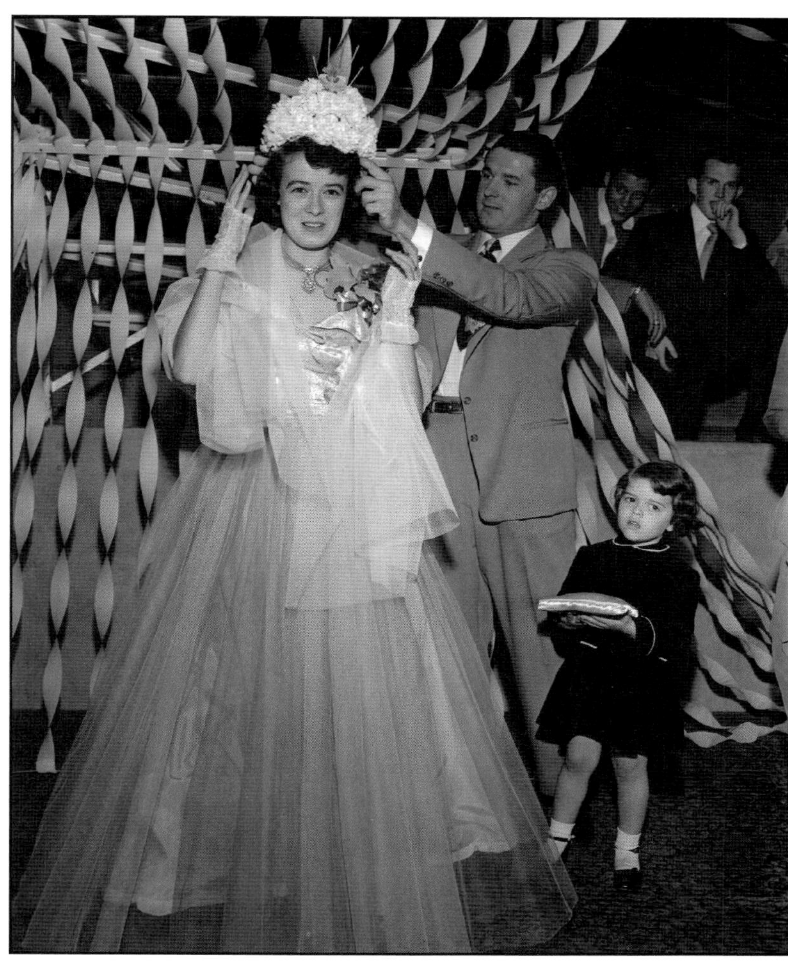

After the war, Rockhurst resumed its tradition of crowning a homecoming queen. Pictured is Audrey Eden being crowned by Mike O'Neil, October 22, 1949. Courtesy of Rockhurst University Archives.

The attention to families and children was characteristic of the postwar period, when America hunkered down to domesticity and longed for security in a world that suddenly seemed more dangerous than ever. American relations with the Soviet Union deteriorated in the late 1940s as the Soviets tested an atomic bomb and expanded into Eastern Europe. The American fear of communism, which dated to the growing power of labor unions and New Deal agencies in the late 1930s, would mark the Cold War era.

For Catholics, the postwar era brought with it assimilationist tendencies, reflected, historian Philip Gleason writes, "in Catholics' new appreciation for liberal democratic values," especially regarding racial equality. The battle against Nazi racism had made it impossible to ignore racial discrimination at home, and the issue, which had been addressed in the 1930s by a cadre of Catholic Actionists, Gleason says, gained visibility during and after the war years. Locally, Bishop Edwin V. O'Hara himself was a noted champion of Catholic Action. On campuses, student movements grew, not only to deal with racial issues, but also to form a national, nonsectarian organization of college and university students.

While Catholic students predictably were anti-communist and would distance themselves from actively pro-communist groups such as American

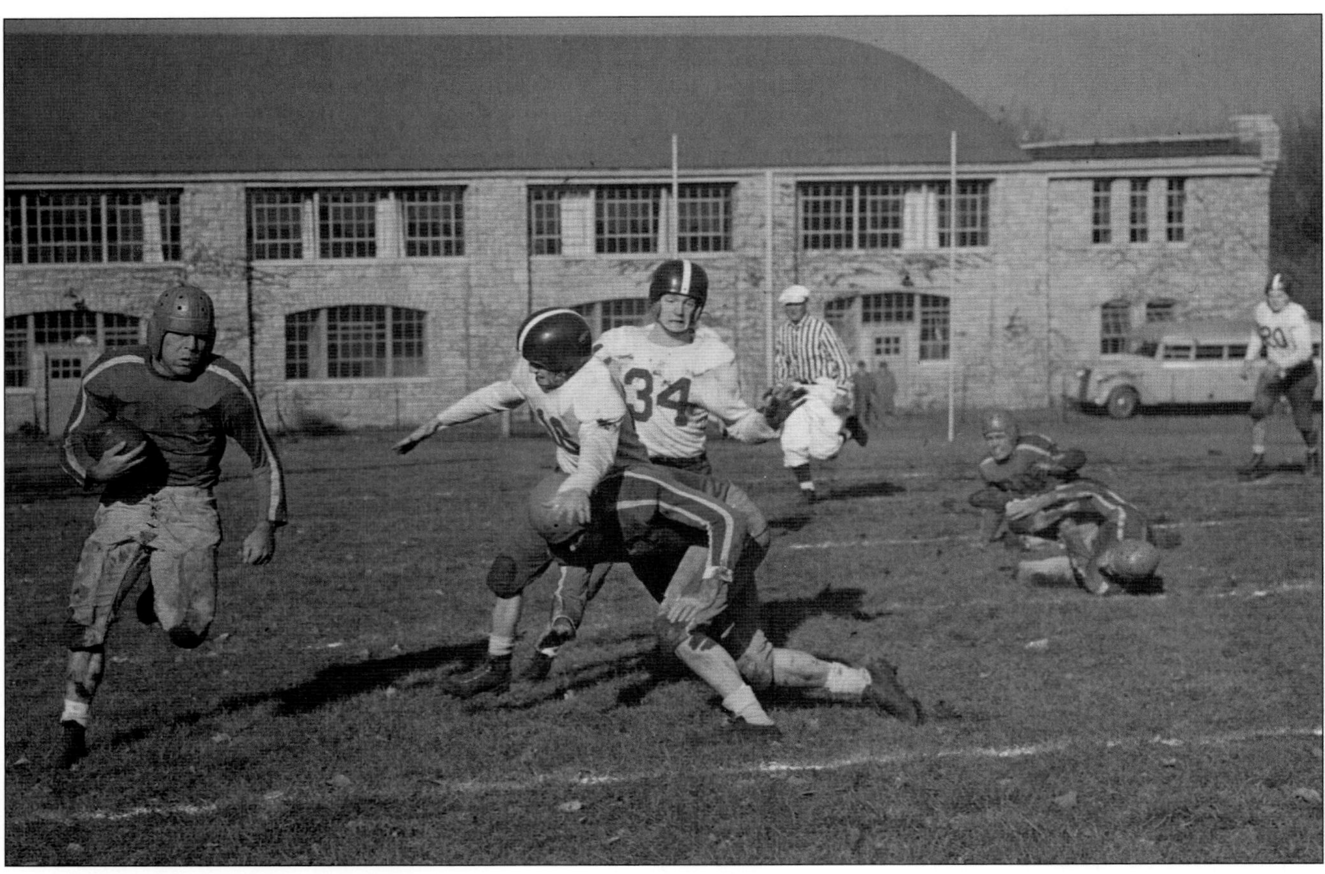

Rockhurst's last football season was 1949. When the Korean War began in the summer of 1950, head football coach Ralph Cormany, a captain in the Marine Corps, was called to active duty. Along with Cormany, the team lost 8 key players to the war. On September 2, 1950, Rockhurst announced it was discontinuing its football program. Photo of shirt by David Spaw. Photo of game courtesy of Rockhurst University Archives.

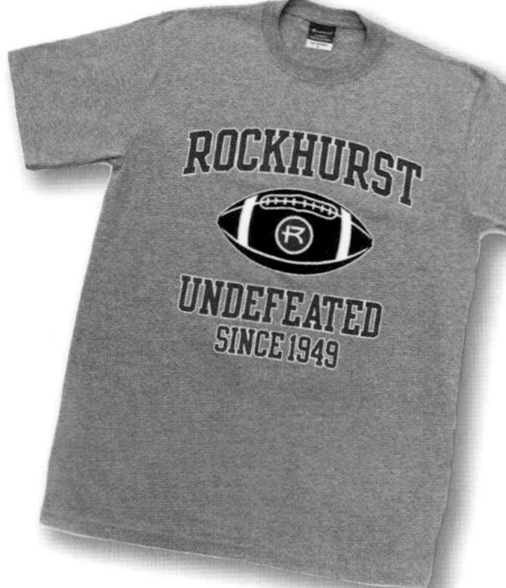

Youth for Democracy, Gleason argues that what was not so predictable was the "quite moderate" stance toward communism adopted by Catholic student leaders and their consistent criticism against red-baiting.[81] To deal with fears of communism, some Catholic leaders took a positive, rather than negative, anti-communist approach by trying to raise "the spiritual tone" of Catholic life. They would emphasize self-criticism and self-improvement, try to find viable solutions to modern problems, and integrate Catholic values into all facets of life. Less progressive Catholics, Gleason writes, dealt with their fear by making a vigorous counterattack, which produced militant anti-communist crusades such as "mass movements to restore decency to the publishing trade."[82]

The postwar emphasis on the family and anti-communism was apparent at Rockhurst, where Father Knapp spoke to the Council of Catholic Women on "Marriage as a Career" and later emphasized the importance of the home during a graduation speech in which he quoted the staunch anti-communist John Foster Dulles. The home, he declared, is "the foundation of a nation and society" and urged graduates to "begin making real homes." That communists were out to destroy the American way of life came as a warning from Judge Kimbrough Stone during Rockhurst commencement ceremonies on June 1, 1947. "No trick is too low, no lie too hard to swallow, in their attempts to gain their final end, revolution," he said, and urged graduates to notify the FBI of any suspicious groups or individuals they encountered. The Rev. A.T. Motherway, a teacher at Rockhurst High School, also spoke that day, warning graduates of the dangers they faced. "Dissatisfaction, unrest, moral laxity—these things are the forerunners of the communists. We must return to a Christian way of life if we are to avoid a clash with the grim ideology of Russia."[83]

The Catholic hierarchy was so concerned about the American family that in 1949 it issued a pastoral letter on family life, which described the family crisis, historian Jay Dolan writes, "as a present danger more fearsome than the atomic bomb." The Catholic position, Dolan explains, was that rapid social change threatened family life. "The procreation and education of children were stressed as the primary goals of marriage."[84]

This theme colored the days and months as the twentieth century neared its midway point. During a student assembly in 1949, it was Emmett A. Scanlon, Jr., a lawyer, who stood before 600 Rockhurst students and urged them "not to fall prey to thinly disguised Communist organizations in this country. I do not expect men trained under the Jesuit systems of logic and philosophy to fall prey easily to Communist propaganda," he said, "but I cannot overemphasize the fact that the propaganda is diabolically clever. Communism pretends to be democratic, and hundreds of American college students are tricked into joining Communist demonstrations and even supporting organizations with seemingly patriotic titles."[85]

—BACK TO NORMAL—

Despite these new concerns, spirits were high at Rockhurst as campus life, except for the crowded conditions, got back to normal. Surely, football coach Lew Lane was smiling as early as the fall of 1944 when 40 freshmen turned out for football practice, just a year after he had been forced to cancel the program for lack of recruits. The Rockhurst Players were back in action, as well, rehearsing for their new dramatic series on the radio. The half-hour Rockhurst program, established in 1939, had become an annual

As postwar Rockhurst got back to normal, sports again captured the attention of the campus. In December 1949, Rockhurst and the University of Kansas made history when they played in the first basketball game ever broadcast on television in Kansas City. Television station WDAF-TV broadcast the game from the Mason-Halpin Fieldhouse before a crowd estimated at 3,400 people. KU won 55 to 34. Courtesy of Rockhurst University Archives.

William Conn (right), assistant professor of mathematics and physics at Rockhurst, explains the principles of the "sun furnace" to Dean John Higgins, S.J. Rockhurst received a Navy contract for research to be conducted on ultra-high temperatures. The "hot spot" of the 120-inch sun furnace, located on the roof of Conway Hall, reached temperatures of about 4,000 degrees centigrade. Life *magazine featured the reflector, calling Conway Hall "the hottest spot on earth." Courtesy of Rockhurst University Archives.*

event, broadcast one evening a week over KCKN radio.[86] Also underway was "freshman court," the "annual student fun feature"—fun, at least, for upperclassmen. Freshmen were required to follow certain rules, with violators "hauled before a mock court, where they are subjected to humorous interrogation by a judge."[87]

In the fall of 1946, the college celebrated its first homecoming festivities since 1942. On a Thursday night in October, 400 students gathered for a pep rally on the lower campus, where a bonfire was lighted in "a flaming, oil-filled, R-shaped ditch." Kansas City Mayor William E. Kemp introduced the homecoming queen, Miss Joan Kelly, a junior at St. Mary College in Xavier (Leavenworth), Kansas, then stood on the back of a truck decorated in blue and white and called for the Hawks to defeat the Warrensburg Mules.[88] In time, the old grandstand on the football field was torn down and a new one, able to seat 3,000 spectators, erected. In the summer of 1949 another grandstand, able to seat an additional 800 spectators, went up, no one apparently realizing that the days of Rockhurst College football were numbered.[89]

In the fall of 1950, after football practice already had begun and a 9-game schedule established, Rockhurst suddenly announced it was dropping its football program. The Korean War had started over the summer, and the new head football coach, Ralph Cormany, a captain in the Marine Corps, had been called to active duty. He had left that very week for Camp Pendleton, California. Not only did the war take the coach, but 8 key players on the team also were lost. Paul O. Smith, S.J., chairman of the faculty athletic board, issued a statement to the press on September 2, 1950: "In view of present war conditions, the loss of coach and players, the Athletic Council of Rockhurst College has voted to announce the immediate discontinuation of its football program." Smith added that Rockhurst, at some point in the future, might reinstate its football program, but that, of course, did not happen. With no football program, Rockhurst decided, as well, to drop out of the Central Intercollegiate Conference, effective June 1, 1951.[90]

Other sports were not affected, and Rockhurst pressed on, boasting a basketball team that made history in December 1949 when it played in the first basketball game ever broadcast on television in Kansas City. The game, against the University of Kansas and broadcast over WDAF-TV, was played in Mason-Halpin Fieldhouse before a crowd estimated at 3,400 people. "We are very glad to have television here, and I want you to know the welcome sign will always be out for WDAF-TV," Rockhurst athletic director Paul Smith said during a half-time interview. The Rockhurst cagers, competing against a Jayhawk team that included star center Clyde Lovellette, lost the match, 55 to 34.[91]

These were years when Rockhurst students still were required to attend Mass, although the student body had grown so large that the chapel in Conway Hall couldn't hold everyone. Overflow students went across the street to St. Francis Xavier Church, where the frame of today's "fish" church was taking shape by the summer of 1949. On June 5 that year, Rockhurst graduated the largest class in its history—153 students.[92]

Progress was, indeed, at hand. In 1947, the college landed a Navy contract to conduct research in ultra-high temperatures. When a 120-inch "sun furnace" was placed on the roof of Conway Hall, *Life* magazine featured Rockhurst, calling the roof of Conway Hall "the hottest spot on earth." That same year, Rockhurst opened a new alumni office and soon would have its first public relations office—as well as a new president who would put the college's long-hoped-for building program into action.

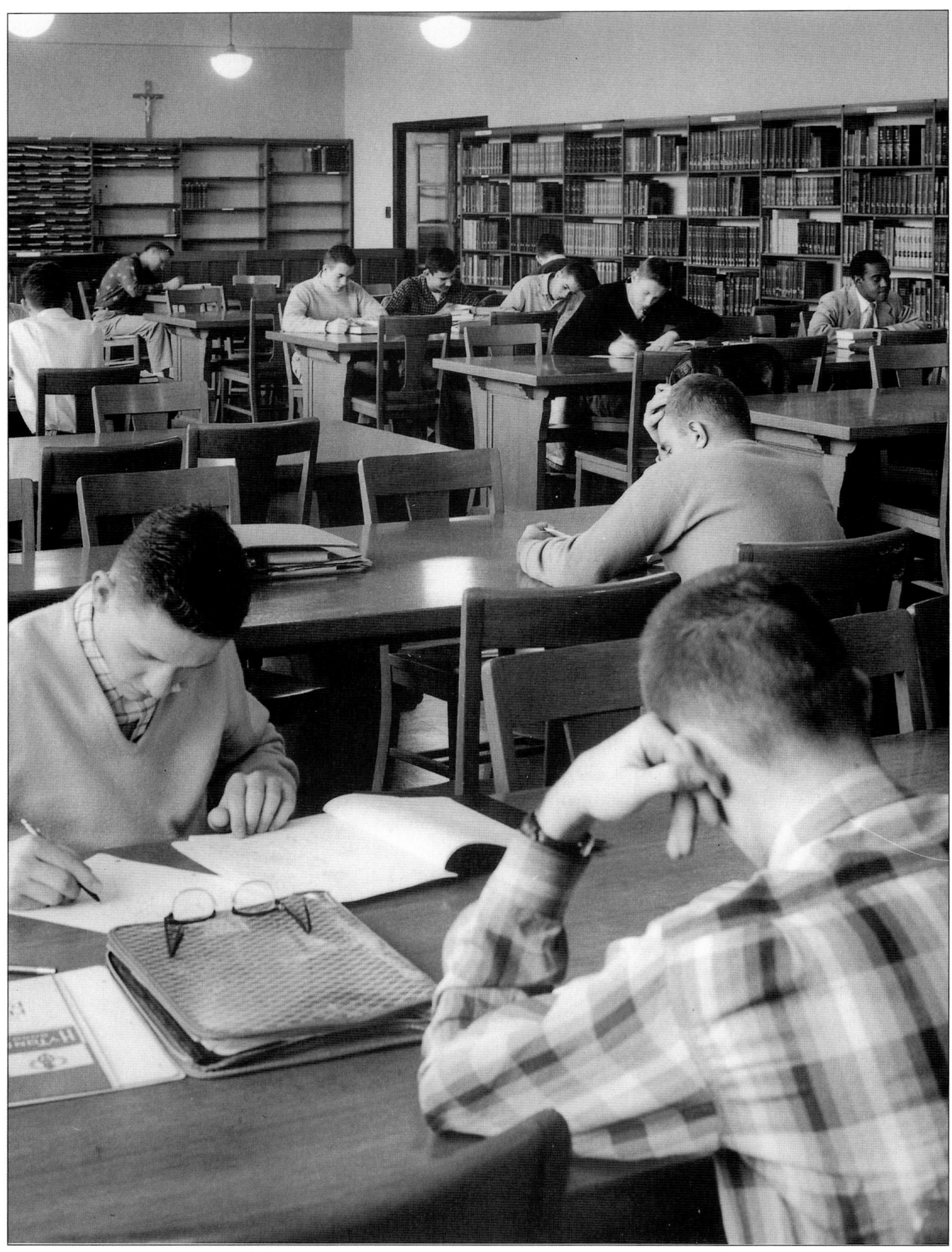

Chapter Ten

Growth and Expansion 1951–63

In the fall of 1951, a small-town Missouri boy named Robert Davis arrived at Rockhurst to begin what he came to call his "lower-middle-class education." The nomenclature fit perfectly the years of the early 1950s when millions of World War II veterans—7.6 million of them by 1952—would take advantage of the free college tuition offered under the GI Bill. The bill was one of the "greatest leveling processes in American history" because it brought a new generation of men to college, men who, like Robert Davis, often were the first in their families to attend college. In years past, a college education hadn't seemed necessary to make a decent living. Davis' father was a workingman who traded cars and cattle. So rare was it for boys from Davis' Boonville Catholic High School to go to college, that one day, he writes, "the nuns brought to assembly a man who was going to night school in Kansas City to show us that it was possible."[1] Robert Davis was not a veteran and, in fact, admitted that he would rather go to college than take a chance on being drafted for the Korean War. He entered Rockhurst College right out of high school (on a partial scholarship), but his lower middle-class background, lacking as it did much family tradition of high culture or higher education, matched that of the typical veteran.[2]

Conway Hall, 1950. Courtesy of Rockhurst University Archives.

The Rockhurst Gun Club was organized in 1947. Its objective was the "promotion of the American ideals of fellowship, sportsmanship and citizenship." The club was affiliated with the National Rifle Association and competed with other shooters in the collegiate division. A range consisting of 5 firing points was located in the basement of Conway Hall. Courtesy of Rockhurst University Archives.

So great was the influx of new students at Rockhurst in the years immediately after World War II that President Thomas Knapp, S.J., (1945–51) had hauled abandoned, wartime military barracks to campus for use as classrooms, administrative offices, a cafeteria, and dormitories. It was to one of these barracks, dubbed Brebeuf Lodge, that Davis was instructed to report on his first day at Rockhurst. Brebeuf Lodge, a one-story building covered with grayish tar paper, squatted on the far southeast side of campus, between 2 other barracks, Daniel Lodge and Chabanel Lodge—all looking so grim, Davis writes, that it reminded him of a German prison camp. The interior of what he came simply to call "the barracks" was war surplus, as well: communal showers and toilets, gas stoves providing the only heat, and alcoves for closets. "We had," he writes, "army surplus bunks, painted brown; desks, painted gray; nondescript chairs. The walls were painted pale, army surplus green."[3]

The "barracks boys," as they called themselves, enrolled in college at a time when not only Rockhurst was burgeoning, but also the population of the Catholic Church itself. From 1940 to 1960, the Catholic population of the United States doubled to 42 million adherents. The number of pupils in Catholic elementary and high schools mushroomed, as well: from 2.6 million pupils in 1949 to 5.6 million in 1959. In the summer of 1956 alone, 408 young men in America entered training to become Jesuits. By 1965, the Society of Jesus would have 8,393 American members, nearly a quarter of its world membership, and a good half of them were involved in education. This plentitude of young men aspiring to the religious life, however, would tumble so dramatically in coming years that by the dawn of the twenty-first century it would become ever harder to a find Jesuits to fill teaching and administrative posts at Rockhurst.

The situation was different in the 1950s, which were, historian James Hennesey, S.J., writes, the "Indian summer" of American religion. During the Eisenhower years, American Catholics got their first significant TV star—Archbishop Fulton J. Sheen, who espoused his religious philosophy in his book, *Peace of the Soul* (1949), and in his 5-volume *Life Is Worth Living* (1953–57). Catholics in record numbers were attending church. A national survey taken in 1957 found 75 percent of Catholic women and 67 percent of Catholic men attending Mass regularly. In contrast to the tidal wave of change that would come in the late 1960s, the *Catholic Digest* in 1953 found that most Catholics were personally devout and accepted church teachings.[4]

Amid these halcyon days came a new drive for "excellence" in Catholic higher education. Questions about the intellectual quality of Catholic colleges dated at least to the 1920s when George Shuster, managing editor of *Commonweal* magazine, sparked lively debate with his essay, *Have We Any Scholars?* University of Chicago President Robert Hutchins, a proponent of the Western intellectual tradition, would lament the absence of Catholic intellectual prestige, and Notre Dame President John J. Cavanaugh would be quoted in *Time* magazine as asking sorrowfully, "Where are the Catholic Salks, Oppenheimers, Einsteins?"[5]

Criticism came to a head on May 14, 1955, when Catholic historian John Tracy Ellis of Catholic University gave a talk in St. Louis to the Catholic Commission on Intellectual and Cultural Affairs. Ellis, searching for answers to Catholic intellectual failures, pointed to many things. Hennesey lists them: the rarity of a cultured or scholarly atmosphere in Catholic homes; the repeated failure of Catholics to fund their colleges and universities; ruinous competition among Catholic colleges; the absence among Catholic professors of the love of scholarship for scholarship's sake; toleration of "intellectual sloth" on supposedly spiritual grounds; and overemphasis in Catholic education on morality, to the disparagement of intellectual developments.[6] Rockhurst's own graduate, the learned Walter J. Ong, S.J., took up the debate with zest, as did others. To stem charges of anti-intellectualism, there were calls for Catholic colleges to employ more lay faculty, to increase the involvement of faculty and students, and to improve the curriculum, especially in the wake of the Soviet launch in 1957 of the space satellite Sputnik.

PRESIDENTIAL PROFILE

— MAURICE E. VAN ACKEREN, S.J. —

Maurice E. Van Ackeren, S.J., became Rockhurst's ninth president on March 18, 1951. He served the longest tenure of any Rockhurst president, 26 years. A native of Nebraska, Van Ackeren graduated from Creighton in 1932 and entered the Jesuit novitiate at Florissant that same year. He studied philosophy at Saint Louis University and theology at St. Mary's College. Ordained in 1943, "Fr. Van" spent one year at Manresa Hall, Port Townsend, Washington, for spiritual preparation and an additional year of graduate study at SLU. From 1946-51, he served as principal of Saint Louis University High School.

Before he left the presidency of Rockhurst, Fr. Van Ackeren would be responsible for campus expansion that included Van Ackeren Hall, the dormitories Xavier-Loyola, Corcoran and McGee, Massman Hall, Greenlease Library, and the Physical Education and Convocation Center addition to the fieldhouse. In 1977, Fr. Van stepped down as president and was appointed chancellor of the college. He died on May 12, 1997. The Rev. Edward Kinerk, S.J., thirteenth president of Rockhurst, said of Fr. Van, "I don't know of any human being who had less ego. He was a man who brought forth generosity, humor, selflessness and determination of purpose in all he met."

Photo courtesy of Missouri Valley Special Collections, Kansas City Public Library, Kansas City, Missouri.

A 1932 graduate of Creighton University, Maurice Van Ackeren played on the university basketball team, serving as captain his senior year. In 1971, Van Ackeren was elected to the Creighton University Athletic Hall of Fame. When Fr. Van Ackeren became president of Rockhurst, the Kansas City Times *(March 18, 1951) called him a "rugged appearing man." Courtesy of Archives, Creighton University.*

— A NEW PRESIDENT —

The man who would lead Rockhurst through these challenging times was Maurice E. Van Ackeren, S.J., who took the reins of the Rockhurst presidency during a simple ceremony conducted at the Jesuit community's evening dinner on Sunday, March 18, 1951. As in the past, the leadership change came unexpectedly, without, the *Kansas City Times* reported, "the slightest hint or suggestion that an important disclosure was to be made." Father Van Ackeren, 39 years old, came to Rockhurst from St. Louis, where he had spent the previous 5 years as principal of Saint Louis University High School. He had spent his young manhood in Omaha, and was a 1932 graduate of Creighton University, where he played on the university basketball team, serving as captain his senior year. A vigorous man with an athletic build, Van Ackeren had followed a typical Jesuit path, entering the Society of Jesus immediately after college. He trained at St. Stanislaus Seminary in Florissant, then went on to study philosophy for 2 years at Saint Louis University and teach for 3 years at Campion High School in Prairie du Chien, Wis. He spent the next 4 years in the study of theology at the Jesuits' St. Mary's College in Kansas, where he was ordained on June 17, 1943.[7]

Maurice Van Ackeren would serve as Rockhurst president for 26 years—longer than any other president in the college's history. In an interview in 1976, as he looked back on his long tenure, he recalled the spirit of the times when he took over the college helm that Sunday evening in 1951. It was still a half-dozen years before Sputnik, but it was Sputnik that came to his mind—one word that summed up the new "drive for excellence" at Catholic colleges. "The idea was that we've got to get a lot more education—we're behind," Van Ackeren said. "So schools got involved and there was a lot of expansion to catch up with other countries. And develop a better quality education."[8]

Although Father Van, as he affectionately came to be known, did not explain what he meant by "a better quality education," the actions he took as president reveal that his ideas encompassed more than better science classes to compete with the Russian space program. In the grand scheme of things, Van Ackeren set out—perhaps without even voicing it aloud—to address the Eisenhower era criticism of Catholic colleges and Catholic anti-intellectualism. He wasted no time in getting to work, be it hiring more lay teachers, involving students and faculty in administrative decisions, or establishing methods to raise money for the necessary physical facilities that would allow the college to grow.

Van Ackeren had been in office less than a month when he instituted a retirement and insurance program for Rockhurst's 60 full-time lay employees, both faculty and administrators—a sure boon to attract talented lay people. "It is increasingly obvious that Catholic higher education, and particularly Jesuit higher education, is a task to be shared jointly by the clergy and the laity," he explained. "Rockhurst College can have no assurance of continued growth in size and excellence unless she conscientiously endeavors to recruit and retain lay faculty."[9] A week later, on April 19, 1951, he announced a tuition hike (an increase of $25 a semester—to $175 for full-time students and an additional $2 per semester hour [to $12] for part-time, day, and evening classes). In May, came word that summer courses were being expanded to accommodate a number of evening classes in the Division of Business Administration.[10] And soon would come notice of a new Visiting Scholar Lecture Series, the name alone a testament to its intent to combat charges of Catholic anti-intellectualism. Over the next decade, the series would bring noted speakers to campus—from Missouri Sen. Stuart Symington to poet Robert Frost to architect/author/philosopher R. Buckminster Fuller.

In September came the college's first public relations office, which Van Ackeren envisioned "as a two-way street" between community and college.[11] Registrar William F. Bartholome was named director and would play a vital role, as Father Van set out next to raise money for the vast physical expansion needed if Rockhurst were to grow. An inventory taken of the college's "physical facilities and human resources" shortly before Van Ackeren arrived, showed the campus to be not much changed—except for its scatter of military barracks and the new St. Francis Xavier Church across the street—from the place that greeted students before World War II.[12]

Indeed, when Robert Davis came up the Troost Avenue hill to campus in the fall of 1951, the building that caught his eye was the stylized

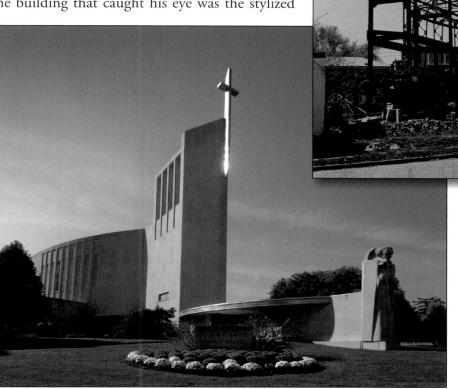

Ground was broken on March 14, 1948 for the new St. Francis Xavier Church. The design of the church was unusual—shaped like a fish, an early Christian symbol. On July 4, 1950, the church was dedicated and the first Mass celebrated. Construction photo, courtesy of Missouri Valley Special Collections, Kansas City Public Library, Kansas City, Missouri. Color photo by David Spaw.

St. Francis Xavier "fish" church, just a year old. Across Troost stood the collegiate looking Sedgwick Hall and beyond Sedgwick, a quite visible Conway Hall—there was not yet a Greenlease Library to block the view. All the buildings that would come to line Troost Avenue in the future simply did not yet exist. The campus, in fact, ended just south of 53rd Street. Only 4 permanent structures stood on campus and even one of those (Dowling Hall) would not survive. At first glance, the view of Rockhurst that fall of 1951 reminded Davis of the "white campus" at the University of Missouri, where the buildings east of the historic quadrangle were not made of red brick, but of white limestone. Many of MU's white stone buildings, just like Rockhurst's Sedgwick Hall, dated to 1913-14.

Rockhurst's beautiful landscaping added to the aura of the campus, but frankly, Davis wrote, "the campus didn't look anything like a movie set."[13] On the quad stood 2 World War II surplus buildings—Janssens Hall and the Thomas More Cafeteria—and just beyond, down the hill on the lower campus, stood Mason-Halpin Fieldhouse. A football field and bleachers ran north to south behind the fieldhouse, and, except for the barracks serving as dormitories, that was it.

The official campus inventory, taken in January 1951, counted a total of 40 classrooms (15 in Conway Hall, 6 in Janssens Hall, and 19 in

— INSTITUTE OF SOCIAL ORDER —

Prompted by the conviction that an educational institution can and should be a guiding force within its own community, the Institute of Social Order was launched in 1939. Founded by the Rev. John C. Friedl, S.J., the institute offered courses in 4 divisions: the Labor School, the Employers' Conferences, the Forum for the Clergy, and the Division of Public Policy and Good Government.

John C. Friedl, S.J.

The Labor School was open to men and women, union and non-union, and awarded a certificate of proficiency for completing the prescribed curriculum. The Employers' Conferences were held weekly to give management and labor an awareness of their mutual rights and responsibilities. The Division of Public Policy and Good Government was conducted as a kind of town hall meeting, bi-weekly, for individuals interested in current topics of government.

In 1942, Fr. Friedl was appointed to the National War Labor Board. In 1946, he organized at Rockhurst the first undergraduate degree program in the United States leading to the B.S. degree in industrial relations. From 1947-49, he collaborated with a group of national industrialists and labor leaders in developing a moral code for labor and management relations, published under the title *Human Relations in Modern Business*. After 17 years of service at Rockhurst, in 1955 Fr. Friedl was assigned to Marquette University. He died in 1956 at age 57 of a heart condition. In John Friedl's time at Rockhurst, the Institute of Social Order served more than 3,000 adults in courses, lectures, and seminars.

Sedgwick Hall) with a capacity for 1,935 students—and that meant high school as well as college. Of the 8 laboratories for biology, chemistry, and physics, 6 were on the third floor of Conway and 2 in Sedgwick. A library/reading room in Conway Hall could hold 238 students, and another in Sedgwick placed capacity at 88, but the Sedgwick library was only available after 3 p.m. Sedgwick also held a theater and auditorium, and Janssens a bookstore. The college chapel was situated on the first floor of Conway Hall, where Robert Davis preferred to attend Sunday Mass rather than the new St. Francis Xavier Church. "It was a positive pleasure to hear (Mass) in the college chapel with a few peers rather than crowd into the parish church across the street," he wrote. For one thing, Mass in the chapel took less time: no sermon or long lines at the communion rail. For another, it seemed less social and more religious.[14]

August M. Meulemans headed up the biology department at Rockhurst for 27 years. Having earned a doctorate in entomology from Iowa State, he joined the Rockhurst faculty in 1931. Meulemans was one of the most popular members of the college faculty. He died in 1958. Courtesy of Rockhurst University Archives.

As Robert Davis entered Rockhurst, the college, just the previous fall, had counted an enrollment of 459 full-time students in its day classes, all undergraduates and all men. Rockhurst's lack of a graduate program—and the research that would have gone with it—stood out against more advanced universities. The credentials of Rockhurst's faculty would not stack up well, either, in today's world: of its 38 full-time faculty, only 4 were full professors, compared with 22 instructors. Another 7 faculty members were only part-time. The evening division counted similar numbers, 449 students, though all were part-time and 43 were women. Davis, who chose English as his major field of study, was in a distinct minority at Rockhurst, where more than one-third of the previous year's graduates (55 of 130) had majored in business and commerce. Only 5 students had majored in English, 4 in history, and 2 in modern language (French or Spanish).[15]

Davis found Rockhurst's curriculum and requirements "almost laughably primitive" by later standards. His "clearest requirement," he said, was 4 years of Latin for a bachelor of arts degree—a requirement so daunting that few students went the B.A. route, opting instead for a bachelor of science degree, which was the primary route taken even by English majors. Every Rockhurst student, Davis writes, was required to take at least 4 religion courses, whose titles spoke to the tenor of the times: Catholic Teaching and Life, Catholic Marriage, Revelation and the Modern Mind, and Bases of Social Reconstruction. Aside from the mandatory requirements of most any college—freshman composition, history survey, math, lab sciences, and a foreign language—Rockhurst demanded courses in philosophy, all taught by Jesuits, as were the religion courses. Much of this would change with the coming social and cultural revolution of the 1960s, but in the 1950s, many students buckled under and endured their religion and philosophy requirements with what Davis describes as "indifference or active resentment." In his 4 years at Rockhurst, Davis estimated that he took courses from 17 teachers, almost 60 percent of whom were Jesuits, all of whom dressed in floor-length cassocks, tied with sashes.[16]

William Louis Blake was awarded a bachelor of science degree in secondary education in 1951, becoming the first African-American graduate of Rockhurst College. While completing his degree at Rockhurst, Blake served as pastor of the First Baptist Church in Liberty, Missouri.

More Jesuits than ever before—an estimated 200 presidents, principals, and deans from the nation's 27 Jesuit colleges, as well as high schools and seminaries, were on campus on April 13-14, 1952, for the annual meeting of the Jesuit Educational Association. Following the J.E.A. meeting was the annual convention of the National Catholic Educational Association, held April 15–18 in Kansas City's Municipal Auditorium. The J.E.A., however, held all its sessions at Rockhurst, including what was being called the "second annual All-Jesuit Alumni Banquet," which drew an estimated 650 alumni and faculty to the event in Mason-Halpin Fieldhouse on Monday, April 14. How Rockhurst managed to house all those Jesuits no one said, but it surely was not on campus, where finding living quarters for Rockhurst's own Jesuits was a challenge. They were scattered across campus—some living in Sedgwick Hall, some in Dowling, some in the Hanley House across Rockhurst Road, and at least one, Father McCallin, in the student barracks. When Maurice Van Ackeren showed up on that Sunday night in 1951 with his appointment as Rockhurst's new president, a total of 44 Jesuits were seated for dinner. They were Rockhurst's Jesuit "community," comprising high school and college faculty and administrators, as well as Jesuits from St. Francis Xavier Church.[17]

—A DEVELOPMENT PLAN—

The need for a faculty residence had long been discussed. President McCabe put it near the top of his wish list during the World War II years. But as McCabe's successor, Thomas Knapp, struggled after the war to house the unprecedented influx of veterans, attention to a new faculty residence fell by the wayside. That changed with the arrival of Van Ackeren, who had been in office less than a year when he called a press conference, on December 13, 1952, to announce what was being called "The 1953 Development Plan."[18] It was the first in a series of campus expansion plans that Van Ackeren would announce during his tenure, marking the 1950s and 1960s as an era of impressive physical expansion at Rockhurst. By the time Father Van stepped down as president, the military barracks—from Robert Davis' Brebeuf Lodge on the far southeastern edge of campus to the 2-story Janssens Hall and the Thomas More Cafeteria in the quad—would be gone, replaced by a string of new buildings: a Faculty Residence (1953), renamed Van Ackeren Hall in 1976; the twin dormitories Xavier and Loyola (1956); the student union/administration building, Massman Hall (1957); the dorms Corcoran (1962) and McGee (1966); Greenlease Library (1967); and the Physical Education and Convocation Center addition to the fieldhouse (1973).

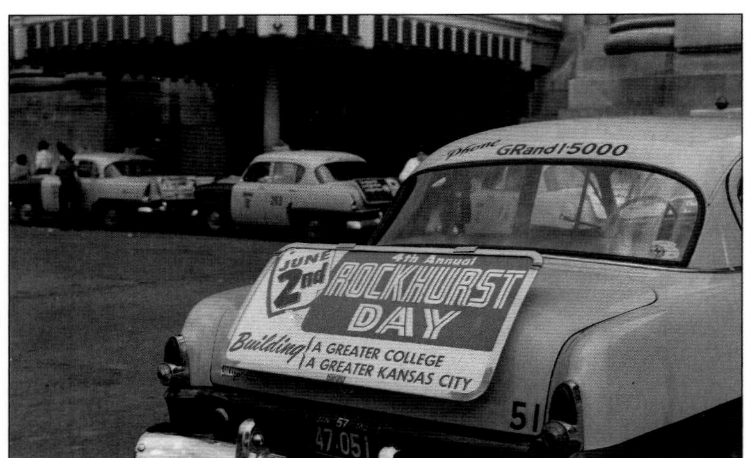

Rockhurst Day became an annual tradition starting in 1953. Courtesy of Rockhurst University Archives.

The first of these many expansion plans carried a price tag of $1,275,000 and called for 2 new structures—a 3-story faculty residence ($675,000) and an administration building/student union ($600,000), which would include a cafeteria and free up space for 8 additional classrooms in Conway Hall and several in Sedgwick. With a nod to history, Father Van scheduled groundbreaking ceremonies for January 28, 1953, almost 44 years to the day that Father Michael Dowling, in 1909, completed purchase

On the first Rockhurst Day, April 20, 1953, Francis Cardinal Spellman, Archbishop of New York, laid the cornerstone of the Faculty Residence, later named Van Ackeren Hall. Cardinal Spellman was presented an honorary doctor of letters degree. Courtesy of Rockhurst University Archives.

of the campus grounds. Father Van stood on a platform at the building site—the northeast corner of 53rd and Troost—and spoke of progress. "Milestones in our school's growth are plainly marked and represent achievement and forward-looking progress," he said to the estimated 800 people gathered round. "Now, in 1953, we begin the first of an extensive building program, a fine new residence hall, which will group all of our priests and Jesuits in one building...." By doing so, he explained, rooms currently being used in Sedgwick Hall and elsewhere to house Jesuits would be freed up for added classrooms. *The Kansas City Star* snapped a photograph of Father Van turning the first shovelful of dirt. Dignitaries of many stripes were on hand, including Kansas City Mayor William E. Kemp and Dr. Clarence R. Decker, president of the nearby University of Kansas City, who expressed his admiration for Rockhurst's growth. Henry J. Massman, Sr., president of Massman Construction Company and general chairman of the 1953 Development Plan, was there; as was J.E. Dunn, contractor; Mrs. John Hodes, Jr., president of the Rockhurst Circle; and future Missouri state senator J. Harry Wiggins, president of the Rockhurst Student Council.[19]

Impressive as the list was, it paled with word that Francis Cardinal Spellman, Archbishop of New York, would be in Kansas City on April 20, 1953, to lay the cornerstone of the Faculty Residence, marking the official opening of the campus development plan. The date, Father Van stated in a letter to friends of the college, "marks the beginning of a new era" at Rockhurst. In keeping with the big day, Father Van instituted a new tradition—the yearly Rockhurst Day.[20]

That first Rockhurst Day, Monday, April 20, 1953, began at 10 a.m. with a Solemn Pontifical Mass in St. Francis Xavier Church, followed by the cornerstone laying at 2 p.m. Invitations for a noon luncheon, to be served by the Rockhurst Circle in St. Francis Hall, 53rd and Harrison streets, had been extended to 250 clergy in the Kansas City area. That night, Cardinal Spellman spoke at a dinner in the grand ballroom of the downtown Muehlebach Hotel, his words reflecting his strong, anti-communist views. "We find ourselves tonight," he told his dinner audience of 550 people, "realizing that we here in America may soon be the last stronghold of our civilization, an isolated and beleaguered citadel of law and of liberty....We must defend that citadel; we must make it the source of the inspiration by which men may be made and kept free; peoples who are subjugated, liberated, and the world we live in purified and made peaceful once more. This is America's destiny, which our college is obliged to fulfill."[21]

A banquet held at the grand ballroom of the Muehlebach Hotel climaxed the first Rockhurst Day. Francis Cardinal Spellman spoke of the university's task to prepare young people to face the enemies of justice and truth, specifically targeting communism. Courtesy of Rockhurst University Archives.

These were the McCarthy years, with the lifelong practicing Catholic Joseph R. McCarthy, a graduate of the Jesuits' Marquette University, at the center of the communist scare. Just a year after Cardinal Spellman's speech, support for McCarthy began to erode following the televised Army-McCarthy hearings, though so staunch was Spellman's anti-communist stance that he continued to support McCarthy. The controversy over McCarthy would become so heated that in the spring of 1954, the Father General in Rome, Jean-Baptiste Janssens, ordered all Jesuits to avoid discussion of such political and secular issues.[22]

But that first Rockhurst Day, as Spellman expressed his convictions, the *Kansas City Times* found the topic of anti-communism so newsworthy that it recorded paragraph after paragraph of his speech. "It is insecurity, doubt and confusion of values which unnerve and unstabilize men," Spellman had said. "Peace of mind comes when a man faces all issues clearly, and without flinching, and decides and resolves them according to the dictates of his conscience and his best mental and physical capabilities. And one of the most important roles of the university in modern times is to fit our youth to face intelligently, purposefully and courageously the varied and mighty problems that confront us as individuals and as a nation." Universities, he said, "have a vital role to play by faithfully fulfilling their mission to be uncompromising opponents of injustice and falsehood."[23]

Following Spellman's address, Rockhurst presented an honorary doctor of letters degree to him, the eighth such doctorate given by Rockhurst in its 40-year history. The tradition would continue through the years, with commencement ceremonies and the annual Rockhurst Day serving as special occasions for announcements and the conferring of honorary degrees.

On May 17, 1954—the second Rockhurst Day—the college conferred its ninth honorary degree, this one on Brig. Gen. Carlos Romulo of the Philippines, who was a war hero and former president of the United Nations General Assembly. But there was bigger news that afternoon as an estimated 1,200 people, including most of the Rockhurst faculty and student body, turned out in the center of campus for the second groundbreaking ceremony in as many years. Again Father Van did the honors, turning the first spade full of dirt for what was to become Massman Hall, where Rockhurst planned to consolidate all of its administrative offices, as well as provide a student union with dining room and cafeteria. The building was to be named after Henry Massman, Sr. Massman, known to his friends as Harry, had served as president of Rockhurst's Honorary Directors since 1934 and as chairman for 3 Rockhurst building programs since 1937, including the present campaign.[24]

The Massman Hall groundbreaking was the second phase of the school's $1,275,000 development plan. The first phase—construction of a new Faculty Residence Hall—had climaxed just a few days before, on May 2, 1954, when the completed building was dedicated by Kansas City Bishop Edwin O'Hara. The new, 3-story residence hall—which in years to come would be renamed Van Ackeren Hall and later converted to classroom and office space—was built of native stone, as well as cuts of expensive Indiana limestone, to blend with Sedgwick and Conway halls. A new, 100-car, asphalt parking lot had been laid just to the east. Inside, the hall provided private study and sleeping rooms for 55 Jesuits.

"This building," Father Van told the press, "provides an inspirational environment in which teachers may carry out holy studies. For the first time in fifteen years the Jesuit faculty will live as a community under one roof. One of the essentials of the true religious spirit is community living. The improvements brought to the lives of the Jesuits by this building will be passed on to the students. It is the good teacher that is the strength of a school."[25]

Construction of the Faculty Residence, later named Van Ackeren Hall. Courtesy of Rockhurst University Archives.

A special, 2-room suite, with bedroom and study, was designated for the Rockhurst president and another for the father minister.[26] A third suite was set aside as a guestroom. The lobby, sporting rift-sawed oak and a floor of red rubber tile, held a reception desk and a buzzer system connecting with individual rooms. Six parlors and a small service pantry filled the west wing, a kitchen and dining facilities the east. More living quarters and a large recreation room stood on one end of the second floor, and on the other, a community chapel. The Kramer Memorial Chapel, with its varicolored, leaded, cathedral glass windows, was donated by the Kramer family in memory of the late Mr. and Mrs. Andrew Kramer. Andrew Kramer, in 1893, had founded the Columbian Steel Tank Company, which now was run by his 3 surviving children at 1509 W. 12th Street. One of Kramer's sons, J.M. Kramer, was president of the firm—and a Rockhurst alumnus.[27]

Other memorial gifts had come in, including a Rockhurst Circle donation that paid for the kitchen and a Sanctuary Guild donation for the chapel sacristy. There was another $5,000 from John M. Aufiero, president of E. A. Laboratories in Brooklyn, N.Y., the longtime Rockhurst supporter who had ignited the 1937 fund drive for Conway Hall. The largest single gift, $50,000, came from Jo Zach Miller, Jr. For those less wealthy, Rockhurst established the Spiritual Stone Society. For any contribution at all, the name of the contributor would be placed on the main altar in the new chapel. All told, Rockhurst's list of benefactors for the year 1953-54 numbered more than 3,000 people.[28]

Fund-raising had gone so well that two-thirds of the needed funds for the Faculty Residence, about $400,000, had been raised within 6 months of the announcement of the 1953 Development Plan. A second $600,000 fund-raising drive kicked off for Massman Hall on June 7, 1954. Fund-raising headquarters were set up in the 916 Walnut Street Building downtown, where Father Van's assistant, Jack F. Fogarty, and public relations director William Bartholome held daily office hours. At the nearby Emery, Bird, Thayer department store, Herbert H. Wilson, president, led a 7-man committee that sent out nearly 4,000 letters, urging business and profes-

— THE SPIRITUAL STONE SOCIETY —

On April 20, 1953, the day on which Francis Cardinal Spellman laid the cornerstone of the Faculty Residence, Fr. Van Ackeren received a letter from an unknown woman who wrote: "Please accept the enclosed donation for your new building at Rockhurst college. I am sorry I cannot give more but, Father, it may be enough to buy a single stone for your building. And could you spiritually inscribe my name on that stone? It would make me very proud knowing that the stone would be there long after I am gone." With that letter, the Spiritual Stone Society was launched.

The anonymous letter was first mentioned by Phil Koury, Class of '38, the evening of the Cardinal Spellman dinner, televised over WDAF-TV. Letters began to pour in with contributions. Father Van Ackeren announced that the name of every person who purchased a stone (there are more than 100,000 stones in the building) would be placed on the altar in the residence's chapel to be remembered at Mass. Less than a month after the formation of the society, it boasted almost 2,000 members.

The fourth annual Rockhurst Day marked another progress point in the development program of the college, as ground was broken for the twin dorms Xavier Hall and Loyola Hall. Left to right: Robert L. Sweet, president of the Kansas City Chamber of Commerce; J. Ernest Dunn, vice chairman of Rockhurst's Board of Regents; Archbishop Edwin V. O'Hara, Diocese of Kansas City; Rev. Maurice Van Ackeren, S.J., Rockhurst president. Courtesy of Rockhurst University Archives.

sional leaders to support the Massman Hall building project. "I don't know of anything in the world that would give me greater satisfaction than to raise a building for Harry Massman," Wilson told the *Kansas City Times*. By mid-July, $33,000 had been raised and the architect's plans, drawn by the firm of Shaughnessy, Bower, and Grimaldi, had come back from Rome with a stamp of approval. Construction officially began in April 1955. The cornerstone was laid a month later, on May 24, the third annual Rockhurst Day.[29]

By October, even as construction workers were pouring the concrete to support Massman's steel pillars, the forward-looking Van Ackeren never let up on his plans for "excellence" at Rockhurst, be it physical or intellectual. That November he announced that Rockhurst had applied for a $750,000 loan from the Federal Housing and Home Finance Agency to build 2 dormitories. Father Van counted 120 out-of-town students living on campus that fall and did not exaggerate when he said the college was full to capacity. The campus boys were scattered in 4 buildings that *The Hawk* euphemistically called "dormitories"—Dowling and Sedgwick halls, the Hanley House, and another house so recently acquired at 5005 Troost Avenue that it didn't have a name.[30]

In May 1956, Van Ackeren announced that Rockhurst had received the federal loan, which was used to build the "twin dorms" of Xavier-Loyola, with their common lobby and entranceway. Each would house 106 students, allowing the 120 out-of-towners living in the Hanley House and Sedgwick and Dowling halls to move into new quarters.[31] Again in keeping with tradition, Rockhurst scheduled groundbreaking ceremonies for the fourth Rockhurst Day—June 2, 1956, one of the most memorable in Rockhurst history. It was on that Saturday that the college conferred 127 degrees on graduating seniors—and an honorary doctor of laws on Sen. John F. Kennedy of Massachusetts, who was in Kansas City to address the annual Rockhurst Day banquet at the Hotel Muehlebach. Even then, 4 years before his election as president, Kennedy was attracting much national attention as rumor circulated that he might be drafted as the running mate for Democrat Adlai Stevenson in the 1956 presidential race. *The Kansas City Star* announced Kennedy's coming arrival by leading Page One of its Sunday features section with a large photograph of the youthful senator and Mrs. Kennedy. "Mid-Westerners," wrote *The Star's* Washington Bureau reporter, "will have an opportunity to see one of the most attractive personalities in public life today." The article recounted the story of "the rising political star"—of his large, political family, his Harvard education, his World War II heroism on the PT 109, his best-selling book, *Profiles in Courage,* and his million-dollar trust fund. Many paragraphs into the story, the newspaper noted that Kennedy's Catholicism might even prove an asset if he ran on a national ticket.[32]

— "DOWN AT LAST!" —

By that summer of 1956, as construction began on Xavier-Loyola, Massman Hall took shape, its 3 stories overshadowing the World War II surplus buildings that stood on the quad. An aerial photograph taken by *The Kansas City Star* and published on July 1, 1956, showed the wooden, 2-story Janssens Hall butting up to the west side of Massman Hall, and the low-slung Thomas More Cafeteria wedged under the trees just east of Sedgwick Hall. By February 1957, as Rockhurst celebrated the formal opening of Massman Hall—with its 400-seat cafeteria, its 4 private dining rooms, and its snack bar—the old surplus buildings were removed. "Down At Last!" *The Hawk* heralded on its front page of January 18, 1957, counting the days until the 2 "time-worn eyesores" would be removed. "Let us bid adieu to the sparrow-laden gutters and the hole in the west wall, as the high school rompsters rejoice that they will have a new building in which they can disturb the serene college luncheon scene."

In June 1956, Rockhurst conferred 127 degrees on graduating seniors—and an honorary doctor of laws on Sen. John F. Kennedy of Massachusetts, pictured with Father Maurice Van Ackeren, S.J. Courtesy of Rockhurst University Archives.

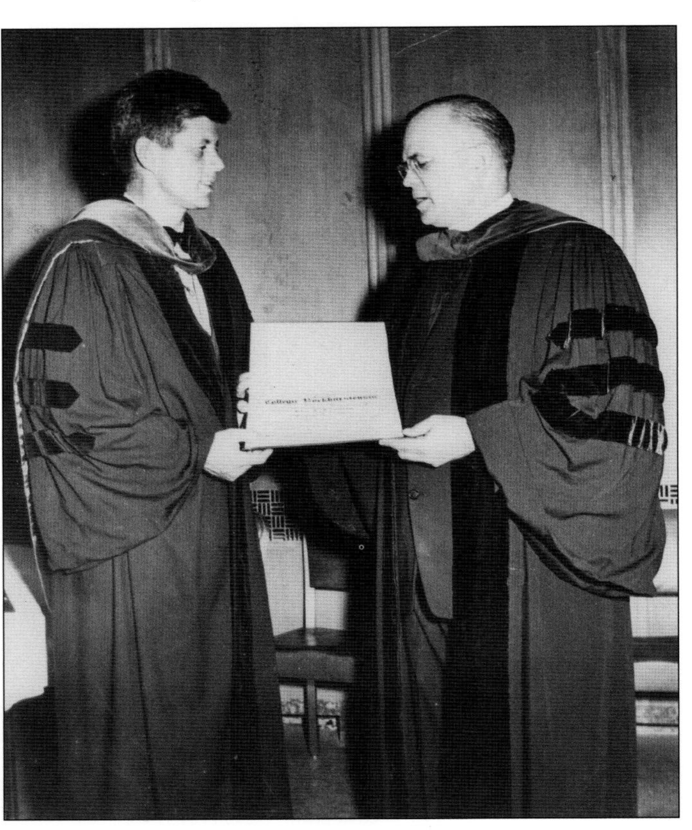

By February, the "beloved but dilapidated hulks," as *The Hawk* now called them, were gone, and on Sunday, the tenth, Rockhurst threw open Massman's doors for public inspection, ending a weeklong celebration to mark the opening of the building that Father Van referred to as the college's "communication center."[33] On Tuesday, February 5, the recently appointed John F. Cody, Kansas City bishop, blessed the building, and on Thursday, the seventh, it was dedicated. Architect Frank Grimaldi said it was unique the way Massman combined, in a single building, faculty and administrative offices, as well as a student union, with its recreation and game rooms, its bookstore, and its offices for the student government and the student newspaper.[34] Four suites of private offices, all air-conditioned, would accommodate 40 fac-

— HENRY JOSEPH MASSMAN, SR. —

When the Rev. Maurice E. Van Ackeren, S.J., announced at the second annual Rockhurst Day in 1954 that the newly proposed building would be named in honor of Henry J. Massman, Sr., Fr. Van was paying tribute to a man who had made extraordinary contributions to Rockhurst and Kansas City. The Massman Construction Company, founded by Massman in 1908, is a bridge, heavy, and marine contracting company with projects all over the United States.

Henry Massman, Sr., not only assisted Fr. Van in fund-raising for the new building, but for 24 years he served as president of the Honorary Directors Association and general chairman for 3 Rockhurst building programs—Conway Hall, Mason-Halpin Fieldhouse, and Massman Hall. In 1943, he initiated a Rockhurst endowment fund with a personal contribution of $25,000. In 1948, Rockhurst conferred an honorary doctor of laws degree on him.

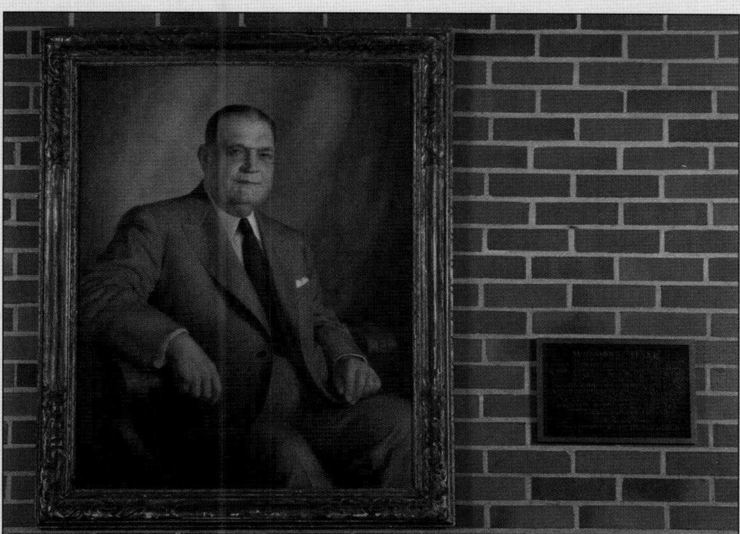

Today, the Henry J. Massman Sr. Scholarship provides tuition assistance for needy students, a cause to which Massman was dedicated. The Massman family has continued to support Rockhurst University through the years, building on the legacy of Henry J. Massman, Sr.

ulty members, and a separate, 5-room suite was set aside for the Institute of Social Order. President Van Ackeren would have his office in Massman, as would the public relations director and other college administrators. With its extensive use of glass and modern materials—including the 2-story terrazzo panel adjoining the main entrance—Massman Hall looked decidedly modern. One stepped inside to find the college seal and coat of arms emblazoned in various-colored terrazzo on the lobby floor. Just off the main lobby was the memorial lounge, dedicated to the 79 Rockhurst alumni who lost their lives in World War II, their names displayed in raised aluminum letters on the north wall.

That May, with the twin dorms nearing completion on what then was the far southeast corner of campus, Rockhurst enlisted Ambassador Ricardo M. Arias, former president of Panama, to speak at the fifth annual Rockhurst Day banquet, which was held, not as usual at the Hotel Muehlebach, but in the new Massman Hall. Earlier that day, Bishop Cody laid the cornerstone on Xavier and Loyola halls. By October, the twin dorms were ready for occupants. Xavier Hall, on the west, would take freshmen; Loyola

As a result of the generosity of Robert and Virginia Greenlease, in 1955 Rockhurst acquired land for a future high school. During the college's Jubilee celebration in 1960, Father Van posed for a photograph in a field at 93rd Street and State Line Road (lower photo), future site of Rockhurst High School. The photograph mimicked the one taken in 1909 of Michael Ryan, S.J., standing in a muddy field atop the Troost Avenue hill (upper photo), future site of Rockhurst College. Courtesy of Rockhurst University Archives.

Hall, on the east, would house sophomores on the third floor and juniors and seniors on the first and second floors.[35] Six Jesuits, with Aloysius M. Rieckus, S.J., as prefect, were tapped to reside in the dorms, as well.

— A NEW HIGH SCHOOL —

The physical changes would continue during Van Ackeren's tenure, but no building project would prove more important than the one that began quietly in the summer of 1955 when Rockhurst acquired land on State Line Road, at 93rd Street, for a future high school.[36] The separation of high school and college had been a central issue since the 1920s, when the college had struggled so mightily and for so long, but to no avail, to gain accreditation. It wasn't until 1939, when the college was able to move its classes into the new Conway Hall, that accreditation finally was attained. But the presence on campus of what *The Hawk* referred to as those "high school rompsters" continued to be an issue.

It was during the college's Jubilee celebration in 1960 that Father Van, in another clever nod to history, posed for a photograph in a scrubby field at 93rd Street and State Line Road, future site of Rockhurst High School.

The photograph mimicked the one taken in 1909 of Michael Ryan, S.J., standing in a muddy field atop the Troost Avenue hill, future site of Rockhurst College. Just as Fathers Ryan and Dowling had looked to the future lo those many years ago, so, too, did Father Van Ackeren. The children of the "baby boom" generation (those born between 1946 and 1964) were growing up and were certain to swell college enrollments by 1965. Even more pressing were statistics indicating that 1961 would be the year of the greatest influx of high school students. To preserve Rockhurst's Troost Avenue campus for future college growth, Rockhurst must, *The Rockhurst Magazine* of March 1960 explained, build a new, separate high school.

Providing the money to buy the land were Robert and Virginia Greenlease, longtime Rockhurst supporters who had made headlines in 1953 when their 6-year-old son, Bobby, was kidnapped and slain. Robert Greenlease was a prominent Kansas City Cadillac dealer, a longtime member of Rockhurst's Honorary Directors, and a charter member of the Board of Regents.[37] Excavation began in the spring of 1961, and a year and a half later, the $2.25 million high school was completed. At an open house on September 30, 1962, Van Ackeren praised Mr. and Mrs. Greenlease for their generosity, and Kansas City Mayor H. Roe Bartle praised Van Ackeren, calling him a " dreamer," but one who had made his dreams come true. Administrative duties for the high school passed from Father Van Ackeren to Louis Mattione, S.J.[38]

Just days after the high school was dedicated, *The Hawk* turned its attention to construction on the college campus, where the yet unnamed Corcoran Hall had been under construction along Rockhurst Road since the previous May. Completion had been scheduled for the opening of the fall semester in September 1962, but students had arrived on campus that fall to find the dorm not ready to be occupied. Rockhurst made do by put-

Artist's drawing of the "Blueprint for 1970," a $6 million plan announced by Father Van Ackeren in December 1958. In addition to increased faculty pay and student aid, the plan called for the addition of several new buildings. Courtesy of Rockhurst University Archives.

ting them up in impromptu quarters in Sedgwick Hall, where classrooms were converted to living quarters, and 2 or 3 showers had to suffice for 100 men. The inconvenience was stressful enough that several men chose to move into the new dormitory even though doors for their rooms, just arrived from Mississippi, weren't up yet. Administrators allowed the move, but stipulated that the college would not accept responsibility for any stolen property. By December, the rest of the Sedgwick men had moved in, floor by floor, and voiced satisfaction with the accommodations. They found adequate closet space, built-in wooden bookshelves, air-conditioning, and a basement lounge and study area.[39]

The dorm, dedicated in December 1962 during the third annual Father-Son Weekend, took the name Corcoran Hall, commemorating the 2 Corcoran sisters, Grace and Ella, who had been longtime Rockhurst benefactors and regular attendees at Rockhurst Circle luncheons. Grace Corcoran, who had served as secretary to 4 presidents of *The Kansas City Star*, including newspaper founder William Rockhill Nelson, died in February 1961, leaving an estate in excess of $300,000, which she bequeathed to Rockhurst. At the time, it was the largest bequest in the school's history. Ella Corcoran had served at *The Star*, as well, working for 38 years as a switchboard supervisor. She died in 1947.[40]

In the fall of 1933, Rockhurst opened college-level evening classes in accounting and business administration. The classes offered an opportunity for study to persons who were employed during the day and could not attend college fulltime. Over time, the program expanded so that students could earn either an associate or a bachelor's degree. Courtesy of Rockhurst University Archives.

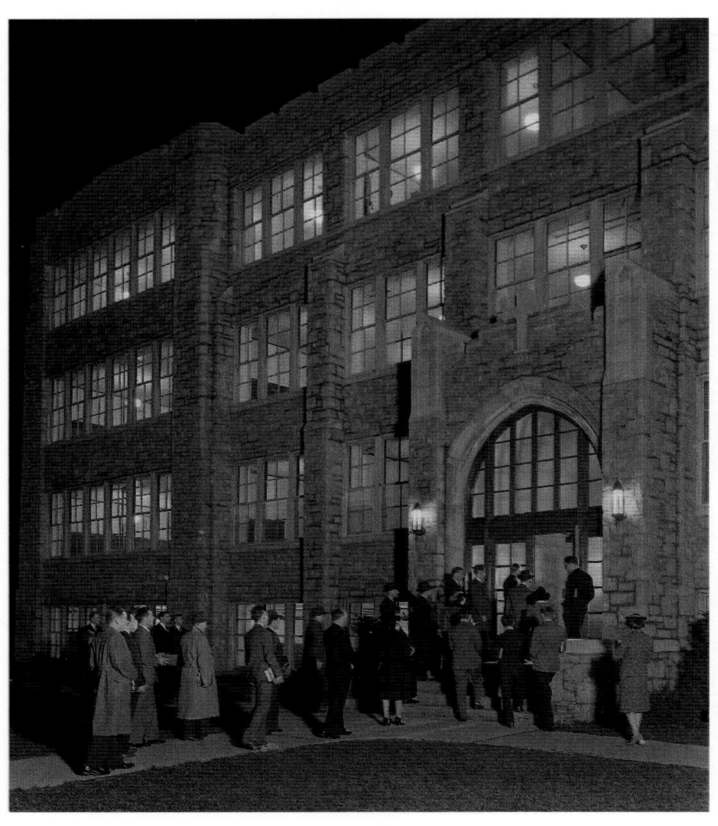

— AMBITIOUS GOAL —

To survive and prosper, Catholic colleges depended on bequests like that from the Corcoran sisters. Also necessary was a healthy endowment, the lack of which had plagued Rockhurst's early presidents. By the college's Jubilee year of 1959-60, however, the college endowment stood at a comfortable $532,456. With the high schoolers now gone and its new dormitories and student union up and running, Rockhurst was prospering. Physical needs—especially a new library—still were apparent, but as Rockhurst prepared to celebrate its 50th anniversary, Father Van shared his larger dreams for the college. "Our common objective is to make Rockhurst one of the top 10 colleges for men in the United States," he told *The Kansas City Star*. "That's an extremely ambitious goal. We have no timetable set for reaching it, but would certainly expect that by 1970 we will have made substantial progress as a result of co-operative efforts of friends, alumni, parents, students, faculty and regents."[41]

Father Van's roadmap for getting there was what he called "The Rockhurst Mid-Century Program," or for short, the "Blueprint for 1970." He announced the program in December 1958, calling it "the biggest single step ever taken by the college."[42] The 12-year development program, *The Hawk* announced, would cost $6 million and provide several new buildings, higher pay for teachers, and increased student aid. The Blueprint was formulated, Van Ackeren explained, "in accordance with Rockhurst's goal—to achieve and maintain 'quality in education' as a liberal arts college." The Blueprint would be tackled in stages, the first in conjunction with the Jubilee year and the second to address college needs from 1961 through 1970.

In 1958, Rockhurst hosted a national symposium titled "Progress or Annihilation." Participants included: (left to right) Gen. Jimmy Doolittle, Col. Thomas Lanphier, Dr. Edward Teller, Fr. Maurice Van Ackeren, Sen. Stuart Symington. Courtesy of Rockhurst University Archives.

Van Ackeren's announcement came, not coincidentally, a year after the Soviet launch of Sputnik, which had sent Americans into fits of anxiety over their lack of preparedness, especially in areas of science, to keep up with the Russians. Rockhurst addressed these concerns in a nationally headlined seminar titled "Progress or Annihilation," which convened on January 24, 1958. Among speakers were national authorities on science and the military—Edward Teller, father of the H-bomb; the famous World War II general, Jimmy Doolittle, now chairman of the National Advisory Committee for Aeronautics; and Thomas Lanphier, Jr., vice president of Conair Division of General Dynamics Corp. The ever-increasing emphasis on research and science was reflected on the roof of Conway Hall, where a solar furnace, installed in 1947, was now being used by the Consolidated Vultee Aircraft Corporation of San Diego.

While acknowledging science, Rockhurst President Van Ackeren would not stray from the importance of the liberal arts, declaring them "the traditional training ground of our nation's leadership." There would be, he said, no expansion into a graduate or professional curriculum at Rockhurst. He would strive, instead, for strengthening the school's current programs with an eye toward quality—quality of instruction, as well as facilities. He wanted, he said, "to build a strong college into a great college."[43] Thus, when he listed his immediate goals that December of 1958, "faculty development" was as important as adding a fourth floor to Conway Hall to expand Rockhurst's science laboratories. "The heart of education is to be found in great teaching," the Blueprint declared.

With 1957-58 enrollment at 2,089 (718 in the day college) and expected to soar to 3,000 by 1970, the need to hire more lay teachers was ever apparent. The college already counted 66 lay professors on its staff. To keep quality teachers and attract new ones, Rockhurst must, the Blueprint said, improve lay salaries. Van Ackeren voiced hopes for a $200,000 bequest to establish an Endowed Chair and then set a goal of $2.5 million for an expanded college endowment fund. The money would be used, not only to improve the faculty, but also for student scholarships, library books, educational equipment, and to support the Visiting Scholar program.

Although it had no graduate programs of its own, in September 1954, Rockhurst began offering a 5-year, cooperative engineering program in conjunction with Saint Louis and Marquette universities. Under the program, students would spend 3 years at Rockhurst and 2 at either of the other universities, graduating with an arts degree from Rockhurst and an engineering degree from the professional school.[44] Ten years later, in 1964, Rockhurst inaugurated a 4-year degree program in engineering science. In the summer after the junior year, the engineering student was given the opportunity either to work with a Kansas City engineering firm or participate in a research project at Rockhurst.[45] A year later, the idea of having students alternate terms of class attendance with full-time employment in their field of study took root as the Cooperative Education Program.[46]

The night school marked its 21st year in 1953, with an enrollment of about 600 students. Some 56 courses were offered, from accounting, business administration, economics, and industrial relations to speech, leading to an associate or bachelor of science degree in business administration. Business courses had always been popular at Rockhurst. In 1946, with the assistance of a $25,000 grant from the William Volker Fund, Rockhurst had added a Division of Business Administration, which enrolled about 150 day students by the early 1950s.[47] The Division of Business Administration was a noted departure from Rockhurst's traditional liberal arts curriculum and made Rockhurst the only college in the Kansas City area to offer a full 4-year business curriculum.

— PROGRESS —

By early 1963, with nearly 4,300 contributions having been made to the Mid-Century Program, Rockhurst had made tremendous progress since Father Van's arrival in 1951: the Jesuit Residence, Massman Hall, the new Rockhurst High School, the fourth-story addition to Conway Hall (added in 1959), and Xavier-Loyola and Corcoran dormitories. As Van Ackeren compiled his annual report to shareholders that March of 1963, he undoubtedly heard the sound of hammers and saws coming across the quad, where workers were renovating Sedgwick Hall to accommodate another 500 students, add air-conditioning, and install an elevator near what was to be become the primary entrance to the stately old building on its east side. The west doors on Troost Avenue, so familiar to passersby, would remain open but were to become an auxiliary entrance.[48]

Thomas S. Bowdern, S.J., who taught in the Department of Education at Rockhurst from 1958-83, displays his extensive collection of Rosaries, showcased in Greenlease Library. Courtesy of Rockhurst University Archives.

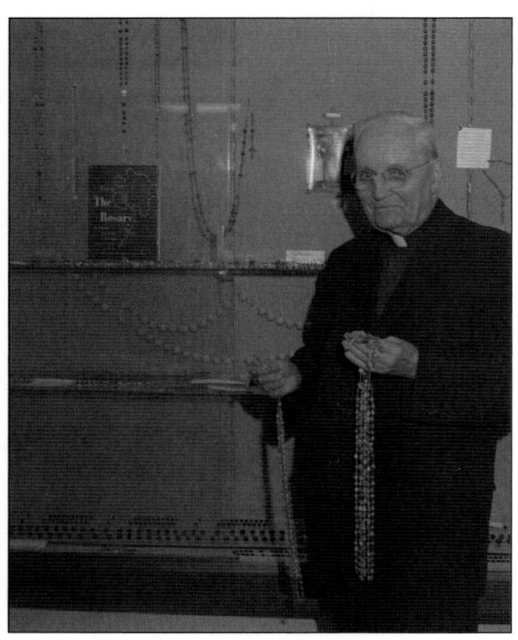

The space would be needed as Rockhurst prepared for the tidal wave of "baby boomers" expected in the next few years. "The wave is now less than two years away," Van Ackeren wrote that March of 1963. It had started with the end of World War II, when nearly 3.4 million babies were born in 1946 alone. The "baby boom" continued into the next decade, when annual birth rates climbed above 4 million by the middle 1950s. Coupled with the increasing number of high school graduates who entered college (58 percent in 1962), the future, from Father Van's desk, must have looked somewhat daunting. Even national predictions of a 100 percent enrollment increase in the 1960s, he wrote, "seem exceedingly conservative."[49]

The festivities surrounding Rockhurst's Golden Jubilee began on Sunday, October 4, 1959, with a solemn Pontifical Mass at St. Francis Xavier Church, celebrated by Bishop John P. Cody. Courtesy of Rockhurst University Archives.

That spring, as Van Ackeren compiled his annual report, he focused on the caliber of Rockhurst's faculty, students, and curriculum, because those elements, he said, were the true measure of a college. By 1970, he wanted 50 percent of the faculty to hold a doctorate (compared with the current 37 percent). He wanted Rockhurst to raise the student entrance bar so that 25 percent of the 1970 freshman class would come from the upper 10 percent of their high school class (compared with 18 percent in 1961). That spring he noted progress on a number of fronts: faculty had better compensation, a new rank and tenure policy, a retirement and insurance program, individual offices, and inducements to study abroad. Three members of the science faculty had received grants, and other faculty members had been published in scholarly journals or had presented papers at academic meetings. The college had hired a full-time director of admissions, a job formerly done by the dean, and, in 1960, established a placement bureau, which expanded its service to include evening students and alumni. The Honors Program was set up in 1962, and, in 1965, the Thomas More Centre would be established to encourage and promote participation in the fine arts by conducting a wide range of cultural programs on campus. In 1966-67, 5 students would go to Italy to study under Rockhurst's first Junior Year Abroad program.[50]

The Visiting Scholar program continued to bring noted scholars to campus for an evening lecture and informal discussions with students the following day. The program was the most visible of a number of new traditions started at Rockhurst during the Van Ackeren era. The annual Rockhurst Day began in 1953, the fall Convocation Day in 1955, and the annual Chancellor's Award in 1959-60. Efforts to involve alumni and the public in Rockhurst's fortunes became much more evident, starting in the fall of 1955, with the establishment of a 26-man Board of Regents, composed of leading business and professional men from the Kansas City area. Henry Massman, Sr., though already serving as president of the Honorary Directors, was appointed chairman, with J. Ernest Dunn, the contractor responsible for a number of buildings on campus, as vice chairman.

While Rockhurst's Board of Regents was largely an advisory and fundraising body, many religious-affiliated colleges of the era were turning over governing authority to a lay-dominated board, a decision made in response to financial pressures to raise more money, to qualify for government loans, and to free college presidents from what historians Susan L. Poulson and Loretta P. Higgins call, "the cumbersome control that inhibited quick decisions." These new governing boards and separate incorporation would play an important role in the decade to come, historian David J. O'Brien writes, as an increasingly lay faculty and involvement with the federal government broke the link of juridical accountability to the church hierarchy in Rome.[51] It also would figure in years to come in the "identity crisis" that came to trouble Catholic colleges as they found it more difficult to develop an integrally Catholic mission statement. While it would be another 20 years before Rockhurst's all-Jesuit Board of Directors transferred its governing authority to a lay Board of Trustees, Father Van Ackeren's 1955 appointment of the new, lay Board of Regents not only was a wise move to involve influential Kansas Citians in the college's future, but also undoubtedly was viewed as a step toward professionalization, which required the adoption of prevailing American standards and academic government.

Important as the formation of the Board of Regents was, the announcement by Van Ackeren that October received surprisingly little notice in *The Hawk*. The paper gave the story 2 columns on the front page, but devoted only 2 paragraphs to the recently appointed board, explaining that its purpose was "to assist in formulating policies concerning Rockhurst's management and growth."[52] At the board's first meeting, at the Hotel Phillips on November 11, 1955, Father Van talked about the school's increasing enrollment (up 23 percent that fall) and the wave of new students (an expected 2,500) certain to hit by 1965 as the "baby boom" generation matured. "The Board of Regents must serve those young men and their community by helping us to be certain that Rockhurst is ready for them," Van Ackeren said that day. He appointed committees, whose titles spoke to their purpose: a development committee, a financial consultant committee, and a community relations committee, whose purpose it was "to help increase the community's awareness of Rockhurst's services and its potential, and to alert Rockhurst to new areas in which we can contribute to Kansas City's growth and development."[53] In Father Van's view, running the college would be a 2-way street.

On the heels of the new Board of Regents came a Gift and Bequest Council, organized in 1956, comprising attorneys, trust officers, life underwriters, and investment specialists who would be on hand to help Rockhurst with financial matters. As part of the Blueprint for 1970, a group

Rockhurst's Golden Jubilee featured a number of prominent guests, including poet Robert Frost in November 1959. Courtesy of Rockhurst University Archives.

known as Ambassadors of Rockhurst College was organized in 1961 to help raise money and support the long-term development plan. Along with the long-established Rockhurst Circle, Alumni Association, and Sanctuary Guild, a new Rockhurst Parents Association was founded in 1957 to get present and past parents of students on board with college development. The important Honorary Directors, founded in 1932, continued to meet and expand, to a membership in the mid-1950s of 1,600 business and professional men, who paid dues of $25 a year. Membership had quadrupled just since 1951—a testament to the wise and hard-working Father Van. Among the influential men who were long-serving directors were City Alderman Jim Pendergast, *The Kansas City Star* Editor Roy Roberts, and banker William Kemper.[54]

— GOLDEN JUBILEE —

Events surrounding Rockhurst's Golden Jubilee marked a shining moment as the 1950s drew to a close. The event kicked off on Sunday, October 4, 1959, with a solemn Pontifical Mass at St. Francis Xavier Church. That afternoon, a procession of Kansas City clergy and faculty from the high school and college formed at Massman Hall for the short walk to the church. Bishop John P. Cody was there and presented a new award that would become a Rockhurst tradition—the Chancellor's Award, a bronze Pattee cross, given for outstanding contributions to the community. The first went to Vanston H. Ryan, professor of chemistry, and Harry B. Kies, professor of history. A buffet dinner for the clergy followed in Massman Hall. Another new award, the Pro Meritis, which expressed the college's appreciation for outstanding individual contributions to the common welfare in Kansas City, was presented to Elmer Ellis, president of the University of Missouri; James A. Hazlett, Kansas City superintendent of schools; and Sister Rose Carmel, S.C.L., formerly of Hogan High School.[55]

The following day, Frank J. Dugan, dean of the Graduate School of Law at Georgetown University, and a 1935 graduate of Rockhurst Col-

— THE FIRST CHANCELLOR'S AWARD —

Vanston H. Ryan and Harry B. Kies

At the opening of the Rockhurst Jubilee celebration in October 1959, longtime professors Vanston H. Ryan and Harry B. Kies received the first Chancellor's Award, named in honor of Rockhurst's patron St. Thomas More, who was Lord Chancellor of England.

When Vanston Ryan arrived at Rockhurst to teach chemistry in 1926 at the age of 22, the first Jesuit he contacted mistook him for one of the students. Over the next 34 years, Ryan provided leadership at Rockhurst in a wide-range of areas including academics, admissions, and athletics. During the Second World War, he was head of the chemical warfare division of the civil defense in Kansas City. When Ryan died in May 1960 at age 55, he was the senior member of the Rockhurst faculty in length of service.

Vanston H. Ryan

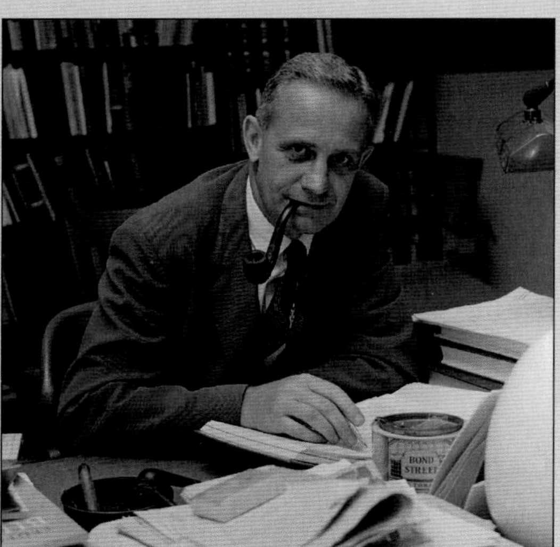

Harry B. Kies

Harry Kies arrived at Rockhurst in 1937 to teach history. He, with Father John C. Friedl, S.J., was instrumental in founding the Institute of Social Order and served as its assistant director for years. Active in politics and community affairs, Kies was a strong advocate for dialogue between labor and management based on shared social principles. In 1962, Rockhurst honored Kies for his distinguished service to the college, and in 1985, the Harry B. Kies Award for Distinguished Service was established to honor exemplary members of the college community.

lege, addressed a convocation in Mason-Halpin Fieldhouse, extolling the contributions of a liberal arts education, which lie, he said, "in the ability of the finished student to think and communicate his thoughts, to analyze, to criticize, to judge, to decide, and to be familiar with basic facts and great ideas." His remarks coincided with an interview President Van Ackeren gave that same week to WDAF-TV. Father Van had shown the TV audience a series of slides marking Rockhurst's progress—from a 1915 photograph of Rockhurst's first class of boys to photos of the ongoing construction on campus. *The Kansas City Star* quoted him as saying that Rockhurst had "decided to remain a liberal arts college." In that way, the college could "devote full time to quality." Never mentioning a 1951 charter change that already had designated Rockhurst a "university," the interview went on to quote Van Ackeren as saying that "expanding to university or professional status would hinder Rockhurst's goal of liberal education."[56]

Talk of launching professional schools and making Rockhurst a university had been heard since 1946. As enrollment grew after World War II and the new Division of Business Administration and Industrial Relations was added, there was talk of next launching a school of law and changing the college charter to designate Rockhurst as a university, plans that had met with vehement opposition from Wilfred M. Mallon, regional director of the Jesuit Educational Association. In a letter dated January 18, 1946, Mallon told Missouri Provincial Joseph Zuercher that he was "convinced that the College should not be permitted to use this title or give itself or the public hope of its becoming a University." The Kansas City "field," he said, simply did not "have a place for a Catholic university." And where, he asked, would the province find enough men, quality men, to teach in another university? Just look at the degree to which the province already was depending on laymen, thereby "not only removing Jesuit influence but also increasing costs beyond our ability to bear them." The financial implications of opening a new professional school were staggering. In addition, any expansion at Rockhurst would require a report to the North Central Association, which might result in a "complete reopening of its accrediting." Did Rockhurst dare go there again?[57]

Mallon also had put the kibosh on a Rockhurst school of law, telling the provincial he regretted that Rockhurst had gone so far as to write to the Missouri Board of Law Examiners, saying it planned to open a law school that September of 1946. A school of business administration was one thing, but a law school could not succeed at Rockhurst, Mallon said, because Kansas City's Catholic population was too small. Any out-of-town Catholic already had the law schools at Creighton and Saint Louis to choose from. And non-Catholics, he said, would not choose Rockhurst over the already strong law schools at the universities of Kansas and Missouri.[58]

Mallon's comments undoubtedly figured in Zuercher's decision in 1947 that Rockhurst *not* open a law school and *not* become a university. Echoing Mallon, Zuercher wrote on February 4, 1947, that the "chief and most cogent reason for this decision is the fact that the Province cannot possibly hope to supply the number of men nor the quality of men necessary to administer and teach in another university in the Province." In his decision against the law school, he cited prohibitive costs, too few prospective students, and the probability that a law school at Rockhurst would, before long, create an annual deficit. "There is to be no use whatever of the term 'Rockhurst University.' Rockhurst is to remain a college, and

The Rev. Aloysius Breen, second president of Rockhurst, reminisced with a group of pioneer students from the early days of Rockhurst. Father Breen, 92, was honored at a reception on October 3, 1959 as part of the Golden Jubilee of the college. Pictured are (top row, left to right) Vincent J. O'Flaherty; Rev. Thomas F. Divine, S.J.; Martin A. Mangan; (bottow row, left to right) Bernard J. Glynn; Fr. Breen; Thomas R. Finn. O'Flaherty was a member of the first college graduating class in 1921. Father Divine was the first alumnus to become a Jesuit. Courtesy of Rockhurst University Archives.

be known exclusively as Rockhurst College," he wrote, underlining the word for emphasis.

Rockhurst's longtime attorney, Hugh B. Downey of the law firm Downey, Morris & Abrams, could not have disagreed more. Archival materials do not shed light on the sequence of events that transpired, but by April 1949, plans were under way to amend Rockhurst's charter, with Downey urging that the name of the college be changed to Rockhurst University. The idea was strictly his own. He had suggested it to then-Rockhurst President Knapp, who directed him to his superior, Father Zuercher, the provincial in St. Louis. So it was that Downey, on April 12, 1949, sat down and composed a letter to Zuercher, listing the "several reasons" that he was proposing amendments to turn Rockhurst into a university.

Chief among them was competition from the nearby University of Kansas City. "Unreasonable as it may be," he wrote, "the people of this section seem to feel that advanced education in a 'university' is of a much higher caliber than in a 'college', and we are losing more and more prospective students to our neighbor, University of Kansas City, merely because it has the name 'university'. Several young men with whom I have spoken have told me that this is the very reason they preferred the University. I agree that their logic is poor, but right or wrong the point is many of our young people are being lost to us in higher learning merely because they look down on the college as not having a 'university' status."

He went on to suggest that some Kansas Citians with substantial means were interested in the development of Rockhurst but were not donating because a general opinion had arisen "that it is futile to donate large sums to a small college." By incorporating the legal word *university* into the Rockhurst name, it "would indicate to the lay mind," Downey argued, "that the school would expand if afforded the opportunity." That "would tend to dispel the present erroneous conception of Rockhurst."

Language faculty test new lab equipment. Left to right: Judson R. McElwee (French); William G. Brown (Spanish); Joseph S. Rydzel (German).

He told Zuercher he wasn't urging "any great expansion program" and never had done so, but "since the sandy foundations upon which [Rockhurst's] start was made have been replaced with footings capable of carrying a great load, I can see no reason for not encouraging a growth in the future." He went on to list one more reason for the name change: it was probable that unforeseen, future requirements would make the change more difficult, or even impossible. Downey then offered a solution to the problem: change the name, legally, to Rockhurst University, but keep referring to the school as Rockhurst College. Father Zuercher wrote back immediately, telling Downey he had read the comments and suggestions "with deep interest" and would take them up with

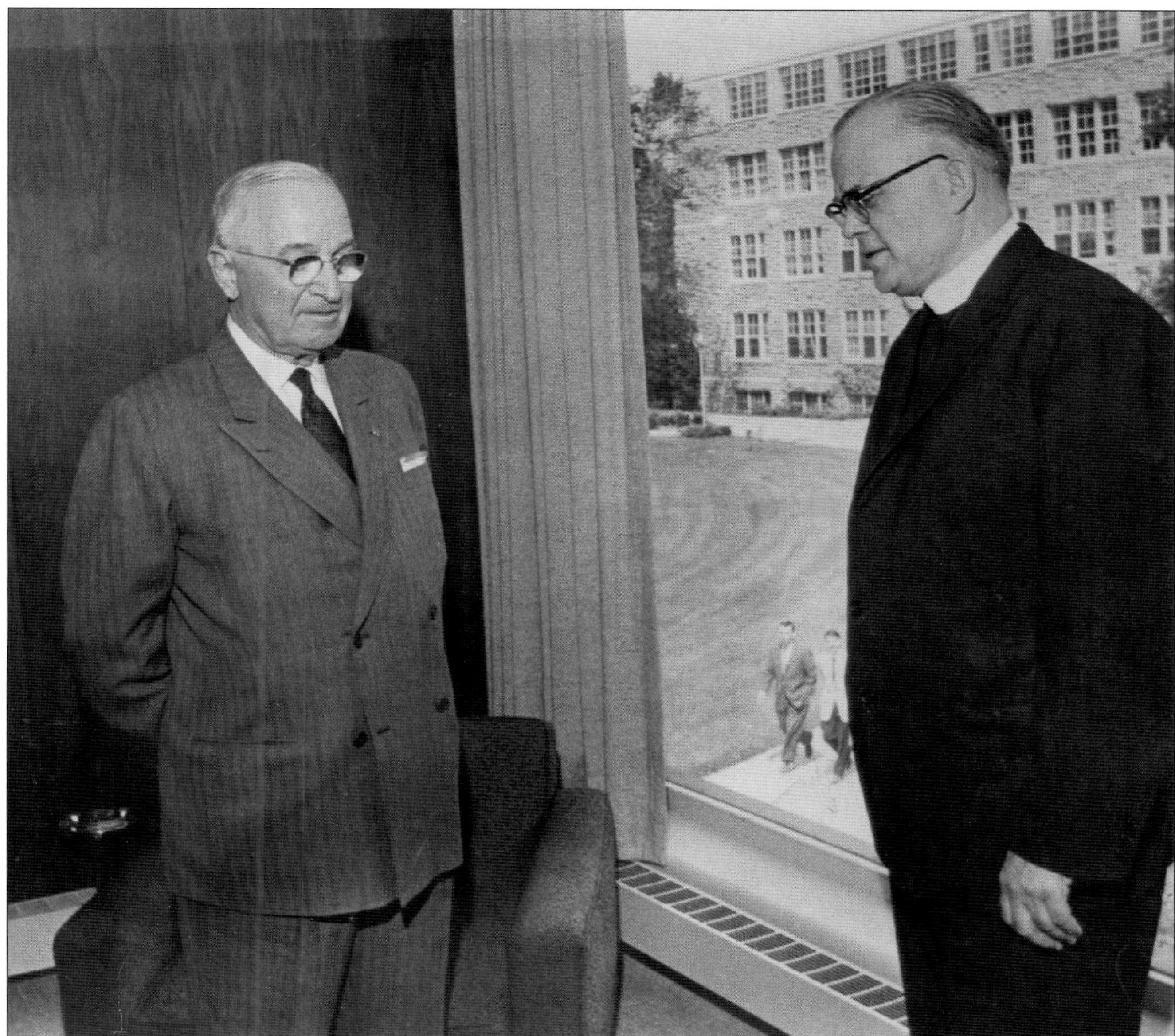

Former President Harry S. Truman and Father Maurice Van Ackeren, S.J. In May 1960, Truman received an honorary doctor of laws degree at the annual honors convocation. The former president addressed the students on the role of the presidency and the need for intelligent citizen participation in politics. Photo by Charles Brenneke. Courtesy of Rockhurst University Archives.

his advisers "in the very near future." He added that nothing would please him more than to expand Rockhurst into "a first class University," but the problem was a shortage of "Jesuit man power."[59]

Despite concerns, approval came a year later, in a letter from Zuercher dated March 29, 1950. "I have taken the matter up with my Consultors, and after carefully studying the document submitted by Mr. Downey, we give it our unanimous approval," the provincial wrote.[60] However, he added, the change of legal title "is not to be made public…We likewise stress and emphasize the fact that our approval, as given above, is in no way to be interpreted or construed as permission to expand Rockhurst College into a university. Rockhurst is to remain a college for an indefinite period of time." He again underlined his words for emphasis.

Despite Zuercher's insistence that the name change not be made public, it leaked out a year later when the necessary documents were filed at the Jackson County Courthouse. A story appeared in *The Kansas City Star* of March 7, 1951, announcing amendments to the Rockhurst charter—including the name change. "Files a Unique Decree," the headline read. The decree, painstakingly hand-lettered in sepia and gold on parchment imported from England, had been filed that very day in Jackson County Circuit Court, where it apparently was admired by clerks and declared to be "one of the most unusual documents ever filed with the circuit."[61] The reporter noted the major provision of the amended charter—the name change to Rockhurst University; but when he interviewed Hugh Downey, Downey played it down, saying the change "was prepared for future use" with an eye toward "any foreseeable growth and expansion which the institution may experience." He emphasized that the legal name did not mean

— OUR LADY OF THE SPRINGBOARD —

The grotto of the Blessed Virgin at the northeast corner of the quad has been a central feature of the campus for well over 50 years. It has been the venue of numerous graduation pictures, family portraits, and even a few marriage proposals. However, it has not always looked like it does now.

Begun in the 1950s as a class project, it was to be a stone cruciform with the statue of the Blessed Virgin perched at the top of the tree of the cross. However, the project cost proved to be greater than the total funds raised. As a result, the tree of the cross was built and the statue placed at its head. It remained that way for years, standing alone on a field of grass at the corner of the quad. As such—minus the evergreens that now provide an attractive backdrop, the benches for meditation and the enhancement of flowers and stone patio—it was a solitary edifice, visible from all angles and prominent in its state of incompletion.

Passing it daily, students being students decided it needed a name that would describe that architecture. The edifice soon became known as "Our Lady of the Springboard" due to its resemblance of someone standing on the end of a diving board. Of course, this title was uttered with all the solemnity that could be mustered by young men in the late 1950s and early 1960s (Rockhurst was all-male at the time), skating closely to but never crossing over into the sacrilegious.

It was not until 1963, when the Sodality raised funds for lighting, and later the installation of the arms of the cross, that the grotto began to look more like its present state, and the less-than-reverent moniker lost its significance.

Today, few people know about "Our Lady of the Springboard." In fact, due to the overgrowth of vines and crowding of evergreens, it is difficult to identify the cruciform on which the statue of the Blessed Virgin stands. But for some, it will always be "Our Lady of the Springboard," a testament to the creative, bridled mischief of young men looking for ways to bend but not break the societal and religious expectations of their Jesuit mentors.

— Jim Millard, Class of '64

To commemorate Rockhurst's Golden Jubilee, in October 1959, students for the first time entered a float in the American Royal Parade. Courtesy of Rockhurst University Archives.

the school "will occupy a university status at present." Again he emphasized that the change "was decided upon only on condition that the institution continue to operate as a college for an undetermined period of time."

Van Ackeren took over the presidency just days after the charter change made headlines, but he did not mention it. He did not mention it even as Rockhurst celebrated its Golden Jubilee that fall of 1959 and as the college worked steadily toward living up to its name, *university*. Events continued throughout the Jubilee year, highlighted on November 17, 1959, by the arrival on campus of poet Robert Frost, followed 2 days later by Brig. Gen. David Sarnoff, chairman of the board of the Radio Corporation of America. Sarnoff, who had had a direct hand in the development of radio and radio broadcasting, addressed the 28th annual dinner of the Rockhurst Honorary Directors. A parade of prominent scholars had followed that Jubilee year: author and history professor Anton C. Pegis on December 1; Harvard's Samuel Eliot Morison on March 29, 1960; and on May 2 and 3, William Albright, Old Testament scholar and professor emeritus of Semitic languages at Johns Hopkins University.

On a lighter note, Rockhurst students, for the first time, entered a float in the American Royal Parade. It was a 20-foot-long replica of the school crest—along with a rotating lollipop and 3-dimensional hawk. Tiles spelling AMDG for the Latin expression *ad majorem Dei gloriam*—"To the greater glory of God"—adorned the forward edge of the float, and on the rear was a papier-mâché stone wall and the words: "Rockhurst Salutes the American Royal." The sides carried the note, "Rockhurst Anniversary 1910-1960," and, a large, gold Styrofoam "50th."[62]

— Athletics —

With no football team, the Hawks concentrated on basketball. After a 10-year hiatus, they made it back to the National Association of Intercollegiate Athletics (NAIA) finals in the 1954-55 season, when they posted a

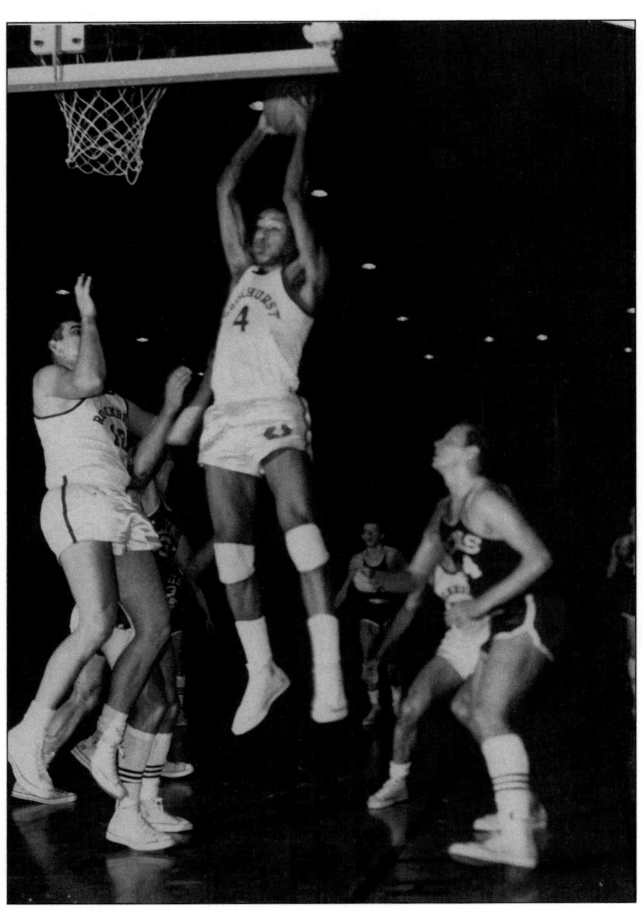

In the 1954-55 season, Ruell Tucker led Rockhurst to its best record in more than 20 years. Tucker was drafted in 1958 by Syracuse of the National Basketball Association. Courtesy of Rockhurst University Archives.

23-8 record, the best in Rockhurst history since Pat Mason's 1931-32 team went 17-3.[63] The Rockhurst cagers were averaging 79.1 points a game that winter of 1954-55, with 3 players scoring in double figures, Dolor Rehm, Jack McCloskey, and sophomore sensation Ruell Tucker—the only black player on the team. He was 6-foot-4, a native of Paris, Kentucky, and a brother of former All-American Jim Tucker of Duquesne University. It was not *The Hawk*, but Kansas City's black newspaper, *The Call,* which sang Tucker's praises that spring. "Rockhurst College's 1st Negro Quint Sparks K.C. School To Its Winningest Cage Season," *The Call* headlined in April 1955. "Tucker swept the boards with precision and frequently connected with his favorite jump shot to help Rockhurst open up a twelve-point lead in the first half," *The Call* wrote of the Blue and White's last game of the season against the Central College Eagles of Fayette, Missouri. The game against the Eagles, who were co-champions with Rockhurst in the MCAU conference, was a preliminary attraction before the annual East-West all-star game sponsored by the Ararat Shriners at Municipal Auditorium.[64]

Coach Joe Brehmer would again lead the Hawks to the NAIA tournament in March 1963, when they posted a final record of 27-4, only to lose in the quarterfinals to Fort Hayes State. Brehmer's team earned a berth again in March 1964 with a 22-6 record, and this time would go on to win the coveted championship, Rockhurst's first national title. The march to the finals in Municipal Auditorium had included 2 straight victories in the best-of-3 district playoffs against William Jewell College on a night when a capacity crowd of 2,200 watched the Hawks shoot 62 percent from the field, led by Dick Hennier and Al Payne on offense and Ralph Telken on defense. After that, opponents fell one after the other in the big tournament: Eastern Montana and Indiana Central in the early rounds, St. Mary's University of Texas in the quarterfinals, Emporia State in the semifinals, and Pan American College of Texas in the finals. Hawk fans had smelled victory as the 2-minute mark flashed on the clock. Sections 9 and 10 of Municipal Auditorium "vanished en mass down the ramps, seconds later to reappear floorside with an ear-splitting, 'We're Number One!'" *The Hawk* reported. Ralph Telken was selected for the NAIA All-Tournament Team and went on to become the eighth-round draft choice for the Detroit Pistons. The excitement had included the second "Dribble Derby," in which Hawk fans demonstrated their school spirit by marching the 7 miles from campus to Municipal Auditorium, dribbling a basketball as they went.[65]

The basketball Hawks advanced to the NAIA tourney again in March 1966 and March 1967, though the championship eluded them both times. The 1967 appearance was Rockhurst's fourth NAIA finals in 5 years and its

ROCKHURST
1964 N.A.I.A.
BASKETBALL CHAMPIONS

— NATIONAL CHAMPIONS —

At no time in the 100 year history of Rockhurst has the school and the Kansas City community embraced each other as much as they did the week of March 9 to 14, 1964. The magical week culminated in the Hawks winning the only national basketball championship in the school's history. By week's end local fans who had never seen a Hawks game were filling Municipal Auditorium each night to its capacity of 10,500.

As Rockhurst prepared to meet its first opponent on Monday night, a weeklong stay in the tournament seemed remote. The Hawks had looked forward to the 1963-64 season with great optimism. After all, they returned their top 6 scorers from a team that raced to a 27-4 record and a quarterfinal NAIA tournament finish in the previous year.

Prior to the tournament, the Hawks had already lost 6 games and were given only a number 10 seed. In their bracket were 2 future National Basketball Association all-stars—Willis Reed of Grambling and Lucius Jackson of Pan American. Moreover, to reach the championship game they would have to face arch-rival Emporia State, who had already defeated the Hawks twice during the regular season—once by 25 points.

Monday night, Rockhurst opened the tournament innocently enough with a 77-70 victory over Eastern Montana. Wednesday's second round game gave the first hint of what a magical week it could be. The opponent was seventh ranked Indiana Central. By early second half, the Greyhounds had raced ahead to a 57-46 lead. After a time-out, coach Joe Brehmer revamped the defensive assignments on Central's sharpshooter Tom Moran, virtually shutting him out. *The Kansas City Star* describes the ending.

"Deadly Dick Hennier brought Rockhurst back to life last night. Jumping from about 25 feet out and over four waving defensive hands, Hennier drilled home a basket with one second left to carry the Hawks to a 76-74 decision over torrid shooting Indiana Central and into the quarter-finals of the N.A.I.A. tournament."

1964 Rockhurst College national championship team. Back row from left: Joseph J. "Buddy" Brehmer, head coach; Joel Frisch; Harry Witte; Pat Caldwell; Al Payne; Jim Selzer, co-captain; Walter Tylicki; Patrick Campbell, manager; Joseph Dolor Rehm, assistant coach. Front row from left: Dennis Alieksaites, manager; Rich Grawer; Dick Hennier; Ralph Telken, co-captain; Chuck Dunlap; Tom Fisher; Dennis Rabbitt; Charles Plague, manager. Courtesy of Rockhurst University Archives.

Continued

ROCKHURST
1964 N.A.I.A.
BASKETBALL CHAMPIONS

Thursday night's quarterfinal match-up with the St. Mary's Rattlers was scheduled for 5:15 p.m. What unfolded before the game was, according to Kansas City police, the largest downtown traffic jam in Kansas City history. In an era prior to the interstate system, 10,000 fans were trying to get into downtown, and a far greater number of workers attempting to leave—all on normal city streets.

To make their Rattler nickname "audible," St. Mary's students invaded the auditorium armed with cricket noise-makers in their finger-tips. As the St. Mary's fans exited the game facing the long ride back to Texas, most of these cricket noise-makers found their way into the hands of Rockhurst students. By week's end the noise-makers escalated to include garbage can lids "borrowed" from the Rockhurst neighborhood.

The Friday night semifinal battle between rivals Emporia State and Rockhurst would be the tournament's stiffest test for the Hawks. As the auditorium gates opened hundreds of students from both schools poured into the arena. According to *The Star* Rockhurst fans were booming out organized cheers to the beat of a base drum an hour before the players even took the court. *The Star* story quoted a Rockhurst student (perhaps realizing that Pan American was lurking in the wings) saying, "Emporia beat us twice this season and we want this game. In fact, we want this game more than we want to win the tournament."

In the Emporia State game, the Rockhurst pressure defense, which seemed to gather momentum with each game, held the Hornets to a 33 percent shooting night in a 66-61 victory. Pat Caldwell drained 14 of 17 shots, leading to a 30 point night. The Saturday morning *Star* now carried the Rockhurst victory as the lead story on the front page.

After 4 hard-fought games that week, the stage was now set for Rockhurst to face Pan American, the defending national champions. Saturday afternoon, just hours before the Hawks were to take the court, Coach Joe Brehmer had his team on the Mason-Halpin Fieldhouse floor working on plays and the defense he was going to throw at the Broncos that evening.

As the teams took the court, Coach Brehmer's Saturday afternoon strategy became apparent. He inserted defensive specialists Jim Selzer and Joel Frisch into the starting line-up in place of Pat Caldwell and Harry Witte. The latter 2 would later come off the bench with fresh legs to make key offensive contributions.

The Rockhurst pressure defense had its finest moments in the championship game. Pan American, who had shot 60 percent from the field in their 2 prior tournaments, was held to 37 percent from the floor by the furious Hawk defense. Future NBA star Lucius Jackson was held to 11 points.

The final horn ended the game but was just the starting gun for the biggest party in Rockhurst's history. The dream had come true! The Hawks were national champions with a 66-55 victory—ironically their largest margin of victory for the week.

The victory celebration got off to a rocky start. The students, apparently thinking they had just witnessed a football championship, stormed the court and first tried to tear down the basketball goal themselves. When this failed they were content to merely cut down the nets—a rite usually reserved for the players themselves.

Continued

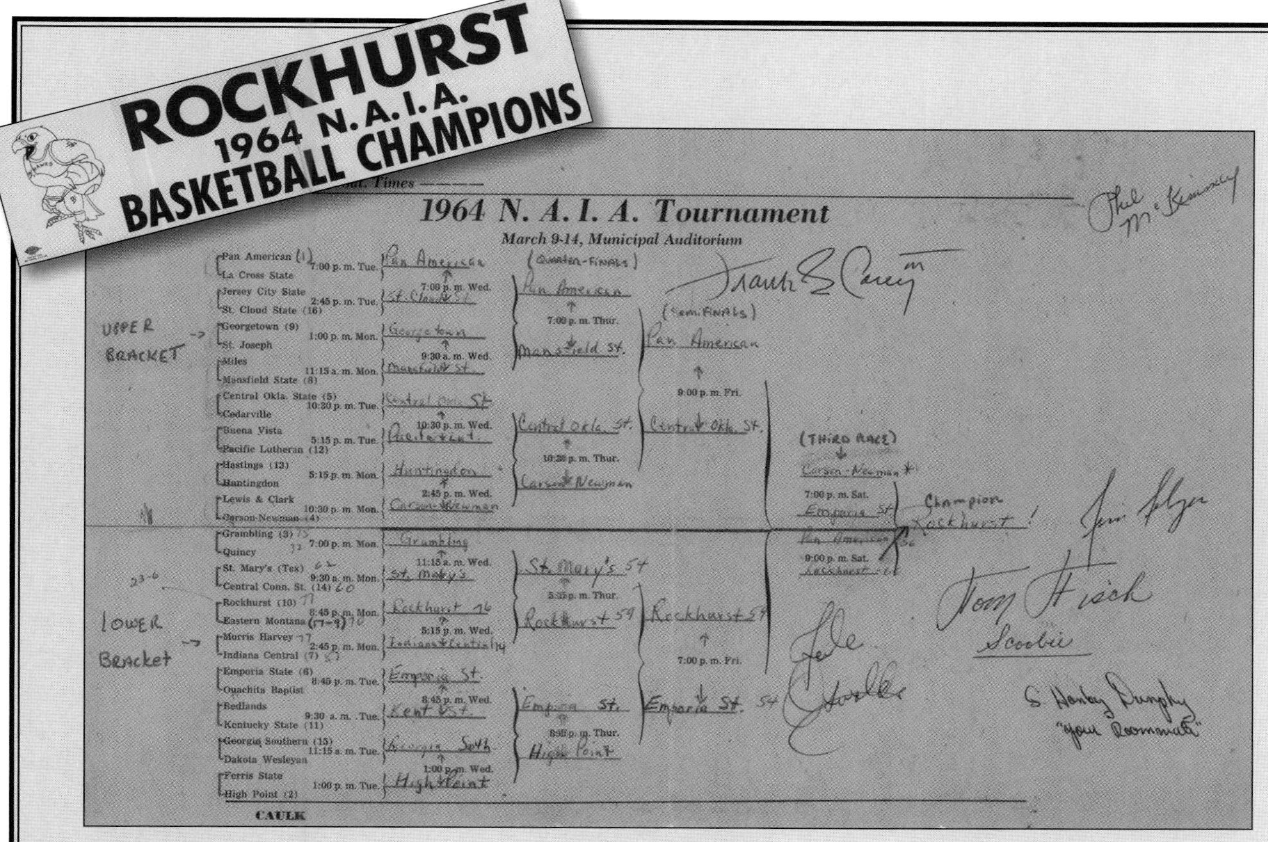

After the awards ceremony, the students formed a "conga-line" and snaked their way out of the auditorium and onto the auditorium plaza across the street, briefly blocking traffic on 12th Street. However, most drivers realized this was a special night for all of Kansas City and joined in by honking their horns. The line of students then weaved its way onto Baltimore Street, closing it down for a time. By midnight the parade had broken-up. The fans then dispersed to various parts of the city to party well into Sunday morning.

When the students returned to their quiet campus, a strange object had been dropped into the middle of the quadrangle—a brand new station wagon, a gift from a grateful school to its winning coach, Joe Brehmer!

— Mike Kleinman, Class of '63

sixth since 1946.[66] In 1968, Rockhurst standout Jim Healey was named to the NAIA All-American Team.

Rockhurst's less visible sports were not as successful. They were struggling enough in October 1963 that *The Hawk* ran an editorial lamenting the state of affairs. "Both the golf and tennis teams last year were coached and managed by students" who were given no help from the college, it said. The teams ended up with only 9 matches, a waste of talent, *The Hawk* wrote, considering that the tennis doubles team had suffered only one defeat in 4 years and the team had appeared in the NAIA playoffs.[67]

The bowling team, led by Ron Walleck, had a good schedule, but *The Hawk* blamed lack of financial support for its defeat in the regional tournament. Because members had to pay their own traveling expenses, they

Gene Hart, appointed athletic director in 1963, was responsible for adding soccer to the repertoire of Rockhurst sports. A 1950 graduate of the college, Hart played quarterback on the football team and was a 4-year letterman. He served as athletic director and taught math until his retirement in 1985. Courtesy of Rockhurst University Archives.

had decided against getting a hotel room and had driven all night to the regional roll-off in Omaha, where they arrived exhausted, then lost. "A mere $24 or $30 expense money would have remedied the situation and Rockhurst would not have been subjected to such an humiliating defeat," the newspaper editorialized, then called for some planning on behalf of the "minor" sports. "It is high time," *The Hawk* said, "that something was done to improve this situation before the 'minor' sports at Rockhurst become no sports at all." The bowlers did go on to capture the National Intercollegiate Bowling Association title in 1963-64, when Walleck was named the Number One College Bowler in the NIBA. There also had been honors for Rockhurst marksman Lew Hancock, who, in 1961, won the Distinguished Rifleman Medal, the highest junior rifle-shooting award in the nation.[68]

Sports were in the news that fall because Rockhurst's new athletic director, Gene Hart, had announced his intentions to form something new at Rockhurst—a club level soccer team. "Bolstered by several foreign students and those from the St. Louis area, the Rockhurst student body can field a team that will represent the school against such opponents as St. Benedict's and Park College," Hart said.[69] The very next fall, in its first year of intercollegiate competition, the Hawk soccer team compiled a perfect 8-0 record and was invited to the NAIA soccer championships in Montclair, New Jersey, where the team finished fourth.[70] In future years, Hawk kickers Terry Michler and Mike Murry would go on to sign contracts with the Kansas City Spurs, and Mike Barnstead, 1969 goalie, would be invited to try out for the 1972 U.S. Olympic soccer team.

On the academic side, the student newspaper continued to earn high marks for excellence, garnering Class A ratings in 1951-52 from the Associated College Press and in 1952-53 from the Missouri College Newspaper Association. *The Hawk* was recognized with the highest ranking again in 1964-65 and 1966-67, as well as receiving "All-Catholic" honors in 1961-62, 1964-65, and 1965-66. The Debate Society, reorganized as The Speakers, Inc., also continued to make a strong showing, including top honors at the National Jesuit Debate Tournament in 1960 and 1962.[71]

By the fall of 1966, Rockhurst had 3 social fraternities on campus, Alpha Delta Gamma, Sigma Upsilon Zeta, and Tau Kappa Epsilon, and one service fraternity, Alpha Phi Omega, which sponsored the annual Ugliest Man on Campus contest to raise money for the missions and other causes.[72] The Dramasquers continued to perform a variety of theatrical productions, from John Millington Synge's Irish comedy, *The Playboy of the Western World*, in 1951, to *Little Mary Sunshine* in 1963. Students had fun in the early 1960s with the Ratty Car Rally, in which drivers, helped by navigators, had to maintain an average speed of 18 miles an hour for the entire course, which started at Massman Hall and went to Mission Hills before turning back and ending at Swope Park.[73] A new freshman "orientation," sponsored by the Student Council and apparently meant to replace earlier forms of hazing, started in the fall of 1961. During a 3-week period, freshmen were required to wear a shirt and tie, green beanie, and a nametag. Each freshman was assigned a "big brother," who was to act as a friend, confidant, and occasional taskmaster. Freshmen were forbidden to walk on the college seal in the Massman lobby or enter the formal lounge.[74]

—A 10TH ANNIVERSARY —

As the 1960s got under way and Father Van marked his 10th anniversary at Rockhurst, there was much to admire—the new traditions, the new buildings.[75] There was praise for 21 graduating seniors in the Class of 1962 who had received fellowships for advanced studies at other universities. In 1963, the debate team reached the finals of the National Jesuit Tournament yet again, and a steadily rising enrollment—up 13 percent, to a record 864 day students in the fall of 1964—spoke to the future.

But the ironies and uncertainties of the time were there, as well. As the Dramasquers staged the happy *Little Mary Sunshine* in 1963, the homecoming float just the year before had replicated a bomb shelter.[76] The Cuban Missile Crisis that fall of 1962 would remind everyone of the grave danger of a world forever changed by nuclear weapons. And, as students put their penny in the jar and laughed over who would be the next Ugliest Man on Campus, there was a more serious contest going on just down the road, where a black man was trying to win the right to be served at a restaurant.

Rumblings of change could be heard in the Rock Room, where students got up a petition in March 1962 after a handful of men were disciplined for playing cards.[77] By November, students were demanding that dorm curfews be lifted, and *The Hawk* was editorializing on American foreign policy in a place called Laos. In 1960, Rockhurst issued its first student ID cards and by 1962 had opened a computer center with its $140,000 IBM 1620 data processing system.[78] Bigger changes were ahead, changes so dramatic and significant that historian David J. O'Brien refers to them as an "earthquake" so strong that it would shatter the once unquestioned identity of Catholic colleges and universities.[79]

By the early 1960s, Rockhurst had opened a computer center with a $140,000 IBM 1620 data processing system. Courtesy of Rockhurst University Archives.

Chapter Eleven

Turbulent Times and Years of Hope 1960–70

On February 1, 1960, at a local Woolworth's in Greensboro, North Carolina, 4 black college students took seats at the "whites only" lunch counter, determined to sit there until they were served. Although the 4 were arrested, their "sit-in" tactic worked and soon spread to other Southern cities. In Kansas City, a handful of students at Rockhurst took note in a time when most restaurants and lunch counters in Missouri, as in North Carolina, were segregated. A study by the Missouri Commission of Human Rights had found that black people were barred, as well, from the majority of Missouri's motels and resorts.[1] Undoubtedly inspired by reports of sit-ins emanating from the South, a group of about 40 Rockhurst students, in 1961, formed what they called the Kansas City Equal Rights Team. The most dedicated of the lot—13 students led by junior class president Al Botti and Sodality president Jim Steffen—decided to conduct a poll at nearby restaurants patronized by Rockhurst students. They wanted to know whether black people were served.

With that, they set out to the eating establishments within 2 blocks of campus: Eddie's Grill at 5315 Troost Avenue, the Southtown cafe at 5433 Troost, Probosco's tavern at 5424 Troost, and the Country Club Dairy at 5633 Troost, the only one of the 4 where they found black people allowed. "The regional condition of discrimination is prevalent in the Rockhurst college neighborhood," they reported back that February of 1961.[2] At Eddie's Grill, the owner had explained that if he served blacks he would lose most of his customers. "I did not refuse service," he had said. "I asked, as a favor, if they would leave. I am not prejudiced. But most of my customers would stop patronizing my place if I served Negroes."

The Hawk took an editorial stand that if an eatery served any Rockhurst students, it must serve them all, including the black student who, *The Hawk* reported, had to eat in his room because neighborhood cafes refused to serve him when he went out with his classmates. "It would only take occasional service to end the problem of our college students during vacations or during school when a group of them decides to eat out....If service is again refused to one of the college's students, we can only conclude that the owners' 'no personal prejudice' claim is false."[3]

During the next few years, as the civil rights movement grew, the Kansas City Council passed a public accommodations ordinance, which was forced on the ballot in a special election on April 7, 1964. Rockhurst got involved. Students handed out literature, and public relations director William

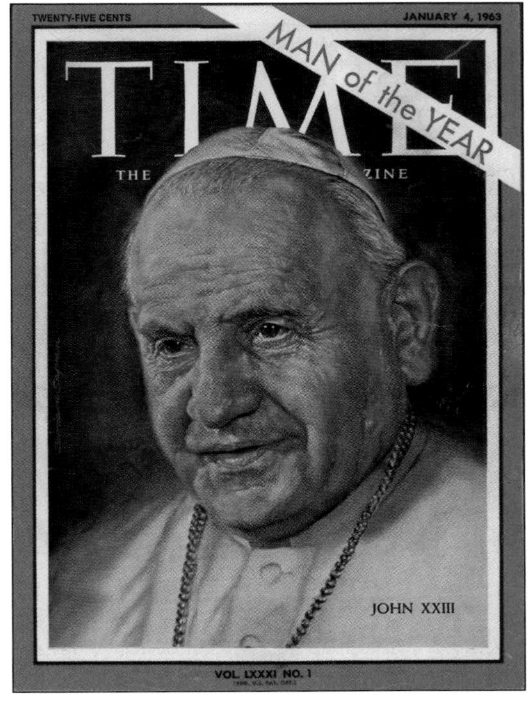

Shortly after ascending to the throne of St. Peter in 1958, Pope John XXIII surprised the world by announcing that he was going to convene a council of the world's bishops to update the church. The Second Vatican Council met in Rome each fall from 1962-65, and at the council's conclusion, the Roman Catholic Church emerged with a number of dramatic changes, the most noticeable being the Mass offered in the language of the people.

Bartholome represented the college on the mayor's special committee seeking passage of the ordinance, then engaged in a 3-hour radio discussion on WDAF with opposition leader Charles Genova. *The Hawk* kept an eye on events and urged passage of the measure, declaring that if voters defeated it, it would be a "severe setback to Kansas City's attempt to become a 'big league town.'" On election day, Rockhurst students went door to door, urging voters to go to the polls. When the ordinance passed by a mere 1,614 votes out of the 89,000 cast, *The Hawk* praised student efforts.[4]

— VATICAN II COUNCIL —

Even as the American civil rights movement intensified, other non-European people from around the world were calling for freedom from nineteenth century colonialism. Faced with these human rights issues and a host of global problems from the Cold War to the nuclear arms race, the Catholic Church, historian David J. O'Brien writes, "looked for a new image of itself"—and found it in Pope John XXIII. His Second Vatican Council, which met in Rome every autumn from 1962 to 1965, brought changes so dramatic that they rocked the Catholic world, including higher education at Jesuit colleges and universities.

Vatican II, unique for its inclusion of observers from Protestant and Eastern Orthodox churches, challenged the insular, hierarchical view of the Catholic Church that had reigned for centuries. The council looked outside of itself and directed the church in its tradition from a historically Western-dominated Catholicism to the embrace of a "world church" that would try to come to terms with an emerging global pluralism. The church, in the council's words, was "truly and intimately linked with mankind and its history." Collegiality, or what historian James Hennesey de-

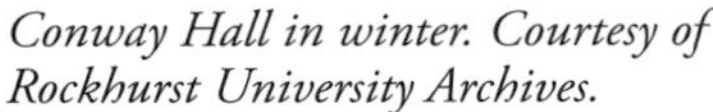
Conway Hall in winter. Courtesy of Rockhurst University Archives.

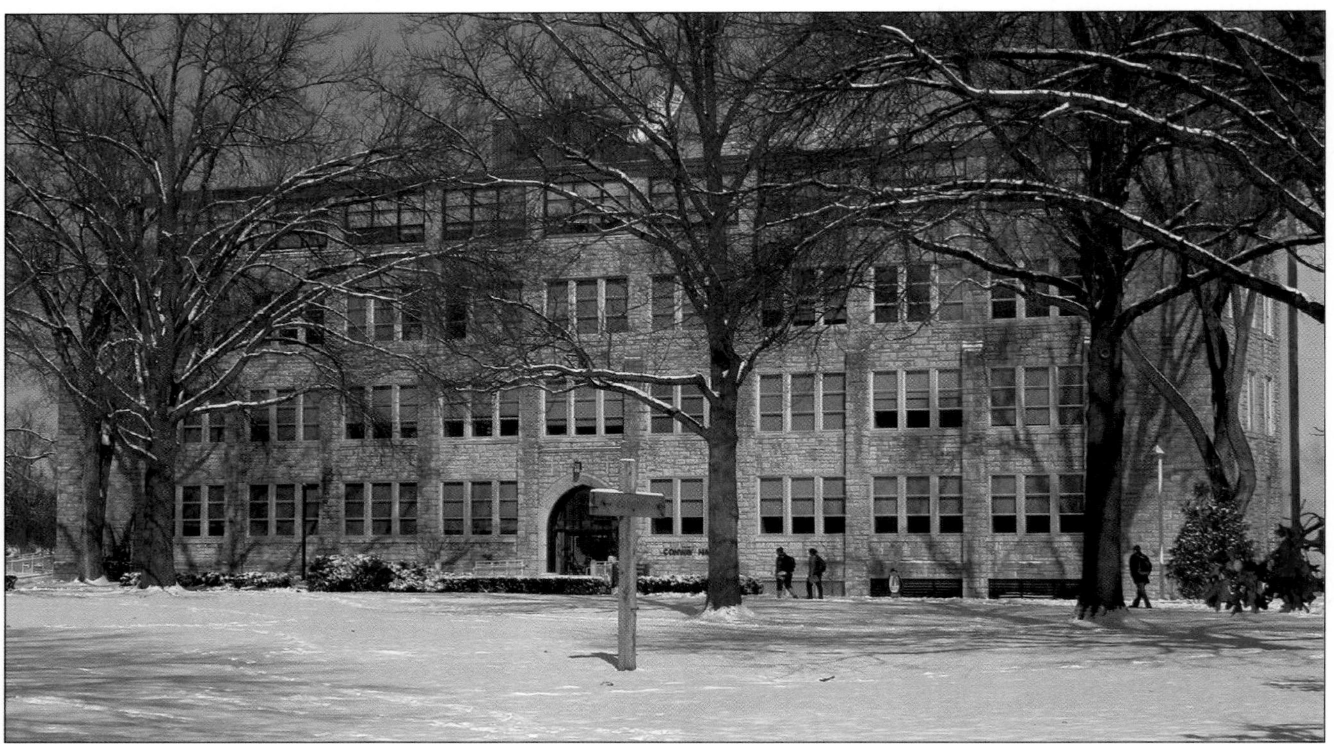

— EARLY LEADERS PASS ON —

Three pioneer Jesuits with a combined 86 years of service died in 1963. The Rev. George A. Deglman, S.J., a 25-year member of the faculty, was a professor of philosophy. Deglman arrived at Rockhurst in 1923, founded the Philosopher's Club, and worked closely with Fathers Weiand and Spillard in the early attempts to attain accreditation.

The Rev. Joseph Matoushek, S.J., also came to Rockhurst in 1923. For most of his years he was in charge of the material welfare of the Jesuit community and supervisor of buildings and grounds. In 1949 he was appointed treasurer of the college.

Hilke Gardens

The Rev. George C. Hilke, S.J., came to Rockhurst in 1940 and served as professor of economics and director of the Alumni Association. The Hilke Gardens, located between the Greenlease Gallery and Van Ackeren Hall, were established in memory of Fr. Hilke by Bob (Class of '49) and Pat Clune. Photos by Charles Brenneke and David Spaw.

George A. Deglman, S.J.

Joseph Matoushek, S.J.

George C. Hilke, S.J.

scribes as "the notion of shared responsibility," would temper the papacy's longstanding spiritual monarchy. Everyday people now would be called on to participate. The vernacular Mass, for example, was introduced in 1964 and mandated in 1970.[5]

These changes did not come without controversy and much discussion. No sooner did the council begin to meet than did the Sodality at Rockhurst take up the question: "Is Rockhurst a Catholic College?" Sodality members started with the premise that a Catholic college "ought to be different from a secular institution." What was its purpose "if not to instill in Catholic students a truly dynamic Catholic spirit?" That, the Sodality concluded, "should be the distinctive note of every Catholic college—a vital spirit of Catholicism which will manifest itself in every college activity." Students applied their premise to Rockhurst and spent months trying to determine whether this "Catholic spirit" existed on campus. In March 1963, they issued their findings.

"Search as we may," the Sodality said, this Catholic spirit "is difficult to discover. A few individuals possess it; a few activities manifest it. But where is that campus-wide atmosphere of Catholic spirituality which ought to set our college apart from the secular universities? Since the majority of Rockhurst students are Catholic, this question ought to be of vital importance."[6]

The Sodality found "systems of disorder" everywhere and listed them.

- Irreverence for the Mass as evidenced by late arrivals, early departures, reading books and magazines during Mass.
- Drunkenness at parties sponsored by campus organizations.
- Cheating on assignments and exams.
- Stealing in dormitories.
- Degrading and harmful pledge practices.
- Vile language and unsportsmanlike conduct at basketball games.
- Foul and profane language everywhere on campus.

Such "evils," the Sodality concluded, were "incompatible with the name and spirit of Catholicism which Rockhurst wants proudly to claim as the distinguishing norm on its campus. In many ways, Rockhurst College does not live up to the teachings of Christ and His Church." Apparently for the Sodality, Catholic identity was to be equated with the moral atmosphere on campus.

Joseph E. Gough, S.J., served as dean from 1950 until 1966. Courtesy of Missouri Valley Special Collections, Kansas City Public Library, Kansas City, Missouri.

The Sodality's concern for declining morality on campus went hand in hand with Catholic critics who contended that by immersing Catholic colleges and universities in the surrounding culture, Catholic higher education was on "the slippery slope" toward total secularization. And when that happened, critics said, the very mission that made Catholic education distinctive would disappear. Historically, Catholic colleges had served a mediating role between faith and life in a pluralistic, secular society. To that end, Rockhurst students were immersed in a humanistic and liberal education that required attendance at Mass and a yearly retreat, even as students learned science from a lay professor. If science won out over theology, how, critics asked, would a Catholic education be any different? What would become of the Catholic mission?

On the other hand, administrators at Jesuit colleges were striving for autonomy from ecclesiastical control. As the administration of individual schools became more complex, O'Brien writes, their presidents resented interference, even from their religious superiors.[7] Tellingly, in 1964, the Jesuit Education Association (JEA) revised its constitution to guarantee this freedom, and in 1966, issued a statement declaring that American Jesuits are engaged in higher education as "stewards of the public trust and must, as such, acknowledge a clear and direct obligation to the civil authority that gives their institutions civil existence." By 1970, Jesuit colleges would throw off provincial control, and the new Association of Jesuit

A more relaxed atmosphere reigned on campus in the 1960s, as evidenced by students sitting on the lawn of the quad for the annual Mass of the Holy Spirit. Courtesy of Rockhurst University Archives.

Colleges and Universities, which replaced the JEA, would be composed of presidents, not provincials.[8]

The convening of the Second Vatican Council put these deep questions into the public debate. At Rockhurst, *The Hawk* ran a series of articles saying the council had "perhaps stirred up more world-wide interest in the church than any event since the Crusades." From the council, Pope John XXIII hoped for "Christian unity," *The Hawk* explained, but the council's primary intent was to bring the church "into step with the modern world."[9] Already there were rumors that the council would abolish Friday abstinence and allow deacons to assist priests in their diocesan duties. Every Catholic needed to pay attention, *The Hawk* editorialized, because this "liberal trend" could affect their personal lives.

— A VOTE FOR KENNEDY —

Earlier rumblings of change were heard at Rockhurst as students took a strong interest in the election, in November 1960, of America's first Catholic president, John F. Kennedy. That month, when the sociology department took a presidential poll, Kennedy trounced Vice President Richard Nixon 4 to 1.[10] Programs such as Kennedy's Peace Corps spoke to the legions of idealistic "baby boomers" arriving on campus. Two graduates in the Class of 1962—Tom Gosebrink, a history major from St. Louis, and Harry Dunphy, an English major from Kansas City—joined the Peace Corps that spring and accepted an assignment in Africa. "Circumstances developed in such a way that I was able to do something about helping these people instead of just griping about the conditions in the world to-

Controversy over dress regulations came to a head in 1967 when senior Ray Townley arrived from summer vacation sporting a beard. Instructed by the dean of men to shave the beard or withdraw from school, the matter went all the way to the Board of Directors and President Van Ackeren, who declared that a well-kept beard would be allowed in classes. Courtesy of Rockhurst University Archives.

day," Gosebrink explained of his reasons for signing up.[11]

By 1970, the "baby boom" nearly doubled enrollment at Catholic colleges and universities in the United States. In the fall of 1970, 430,000 students were enrolled, compared with 220,000 in the fall of 1948 and only 92,000 in the last academic year of World War II. The record enrollment that Rockhurst set in the fall of 1964—864 students—would be broken again in the fall of 1966, the fall of 1967, and again in the fall of 1969, with a day enrollment of 1,043. Record enrollments continued into the early 1970s when nearly 85 percent of Rockhurst students were of the Catholic faith.[12]

As outspoken as they were idealistic, the new generation wasted no time in making its voice heard. When a few men were disciplined for playing cards in the Rock Room in 1962, they got up a petition, presented it to the dean through the Student Council, and got the rules changed. They also cleared it with the administration to invite women to the Rock and Aztec rooms.[13] When they didn't like the dormitory curfew at the new Corcoran Hall, they protested for a week and won a concession for upperclassmen, extending the weekday curfew from 11 p.m. to midnight.[14] Almost unanimously, dorm residents had refused to sign the code of conduct agreement, some explaining that they regarded it "as a personal insult." A major source of irritation, *The Hawk* reported, was a clause that read: "I take pride in the fact that I have the privilege of working, studying, and maturing in a college of the caliber of Rockhurst." Administrators acquiesced but shook their heads, saying the students "were making a mountain out of a mole hill." The clause, said Father Aloysius Rieckus, S.J., the school chaplain and a dorm prefect, "merely made explicit what had previously been implicit."

Before the decade was out, a Student Dress Regulation Committee, which included 2 faculty members, proposed a new dress policy on campus. While stipulating that students "should strive to be neat and clean and present the best possible appearance with regard to the current and local customs," the committee emphasized the importance of "freedom of choice" and bowed to the emerging trend of informality. The committee's 5-point recommendation:

- That students be allowed to wear shoes without socks in class.
- That sweatshirts be allowed in class as long as lettering, if any, is in good taste.
- That a well-kept beard be allowed in class.
- That shorts and blue jeans be allowed on upper campus and in class at the discretion of the teacher.
- T-shirts, colored or otherwise having lettering or a collar, be allowed in class.

Point three—on the right to wear a beard—created the biggest controversy. "The committee was divided," *The Hawk* said, "between the freedom of the student to keep a well-groomed beard and the possibility of a private institution like Rockhurst College turning into another Berkeley and losing the respect of the surrounding community and alumni."[15] On a 7-5 vote, the dress committee allowed beards, and the 5-point list was presented to the Student Welfare Board, chaired by Dean of Men Charles P. Cahill,

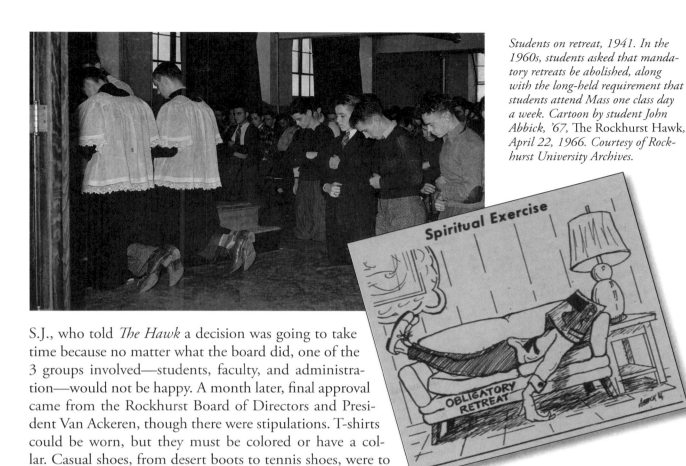

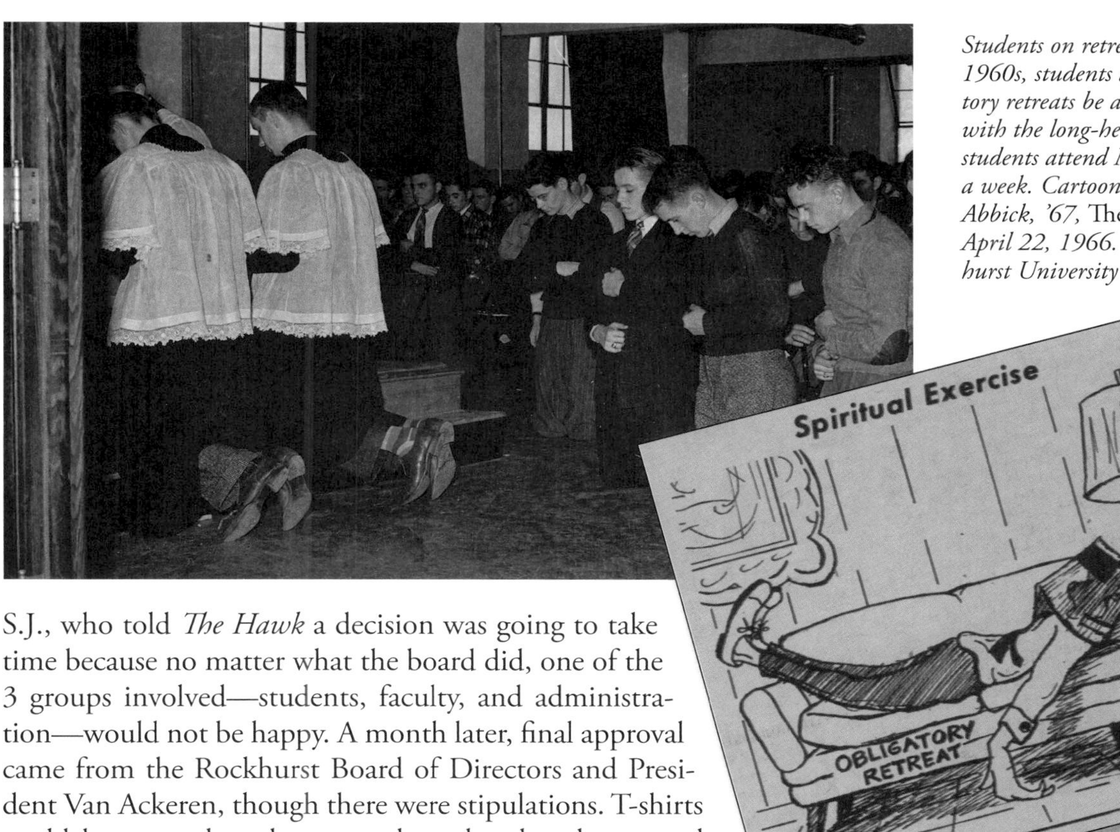

Students on retreat, 1941. In the 1960s, students asked that mandatory retreats be abolished, along with the long-held requirement that students attend Mass one class day a week. Cartoon by student John Abbick, '67, The Rockhurst Hawk, *April 22, 1966. Courtesy of Rockhurst University Archives.*

S.J., who told *The Hawk* a decision was going to take time because no matter what the board did, one of the 3 groups involved—students, faculty, and administration—would not be happy. A month later, final approval came from the Rockhurst Board of Directors and President Van Ackeren, though there were stipulations. T-shirts could be worn, but they must be colored or have a collar. Casual shoes, from desert boots to tennis shoes, were to be allowed on the upper campus, but no bedroom slippers, shower sandals, or "flip flops." "Upper campus," Dean Cahill explained, referred to all buildings other than the gymnasium and residence halls.

The outdated dress code was just one of a number of student gripes being aired. Rockhurst students never would become as radicalized as those who founded the Students for a Democratic Society and drew up their Port Huron manifesto rejecting Cold War ideology and emphasizing participatory politics; but in the same vein, the Rockhurst Student Council met behind closed doors and drew up its own "position paper." In it, members declared that Rockhurst students felt "frustration, bitterness and unrest" at the college's highly centralized authority structure, which they described as a "parental role." The prevailing standard for student life policies at Catholic colleges was indeed *in loco parentis*.

As an example, they cited an instance where the Student Council had to obtain the president's approval before installing a telephone. They wanted a more broad-based structure and called for student representation on policy boards and more freedom in spiritual matters. Specifically, they wanted mandatory retreats and mandatory theology courses abolished after the sophomore year, which, they argued, was in keeping with the spirit of Vatican II. They suggested a more "dynamic theology curriculum relevant to modern life" and a series of discussions dealing with contemporary theology.[16] The student position paper also called for an explanation of the Rockhurst activity and library fee, as well as reasons that a tuition increase was necessary. It went on to propose a policy of "faculty-before-buildings"

— KRC RADIO —

Radio programming was a part of Rockhurst for several decades of its history, both on campus and in the community. A number of students used their campus radio experience to enter broadcasting careers.

Community involvement began in 1943, when Professor Harry Kies represented Rockhurst College on the Radio Council of Greater Kansas City. This civic-minded group encouraged socially responsible radio programming and sponsored program production workshops toward that end. The Rev. Roswell Williams, S.J., chaired the production committee. His Rockhurst radio class produced programs for the RCGKC in 1945. During this time, script writing, production, and performance were directed by the English Department.

The first campus radio station was organized in 1949 by Charles Basgall and Joseph Flaherty as the Rockhurst College Amateur Radio Club, supervised by the Rev. John J. Higgins, S.J. It was a licensed amateur short wave station with call letters WØOPN.

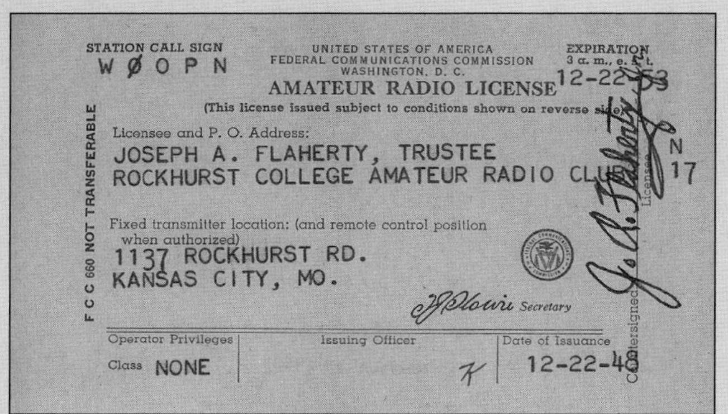

STATION CALL SIGN
WØOPN

UNITED STATES OF AMERICA
FEDERAL COMMUNICATIONS COMMISSION
WASHINGTON, D. C.
AMATEUR RADIO LICENSE
(This license issued subject to conditions shown on reverse side)

EXPIRATION
3 a. m., e. s. t.
12-22-53

FCC 660 NOT TRANSFERABLE

Licensee and P. O. Address:
JOSEPH A. FLAHERTY, TRUSTEE
ROCKHURST COLLEGE AMATEUR RADIO CLUB

N
17

Fixed transmitter location: (and remote control position when authorized)
1137 ROCKHURST RD.
KANSAS CITY, MO.

Secretary

Licensee
Countersigned

Operator Privileges	Issuing Officer	Date of Issuance
Class NONE	K	12-22-48

The original Amateur Radio License issued in 1948 to Rockhurst College. Courtesy of Rockhurst University Archives.

The Rev. James D. Wheeler, S.J., chemistry professor and a licensed amateur radio operator, became radio station advisor in the mid-1960s. As advisor to Alpha Phi Omega, the service fraternity, he encouraged APO to create radio programming to serve the college. Renamed KRC and no longer using an amateur license, the station operated as a carrier current system heard only on campus. Programming went from the studio over dedicated telephone lines to low-power transmitters in each dormitory. Electrical wiring in each building served as the transmitting antenna. KRC listeners tuned to 760 AM (later 660 AM) to hear student programs of music, DJ talk, interviews, and news.

In 1973, the Department of Communication assumed responsibility for KRC. Broadcasting instructor Harold Magariel became KRC faculty advisor. The station sold advertising and was organized with staff positions similar to a commercial radio station. William J. Ryan, a communication and journalism professor, succeeded Prof. Magariel in 1978.

Until 1980, studios were in various locations, such as third-floor Sedgwick Hall and Corcoran Hall basement. After two Corcoran burglaries (1977 and 1979), when virtually all equipment was stolen, President Weiss authorized Prof. Ryan to design space in Sedgwick Hall to provide a high-security, modern, state-of-the-art facility with programming studio, production studio, office, and supply room. The production studio would double as a lab for 4 academic courses in mass media and broadcast journalism. KRC moved to its new facilities in 1983.

KRC was not an FCC-licensed station, so could not broadcast beyond campus. However, noncommercial radio using a public access cable TV channel required no license. In 1983, station manager Ross Passantino asked Kansas City's cable TV franchise, American Cablevision, for 2 hours of programming on local access channel 29. This was approved, equipment was in-

Continued

KRC Radio student announcer Grace Whittle ('94). Courtesy of Rockhurst University Archives.

stalled, and advanced student announcers were selected. Call-in requests from area high school students were so numerous that an extra staffer was needed to answer the phone. KRC Cable Radio continued into 1991.

Special KRC programs included live debates by Student Senate presidential candidates, a weekly call-in show for students to talk with the college president, and an occasional basketball broadcast from the Mason-Halpin Fieldhouse. KRC facilities also were used to produce half-time shows aired during broadcast of men's basketball out-of-town games on a Kansas City commercial radio station. Prof. Ryan and Athletic Director Frank Diskin coordinated these broadcasts, acquired advertisers, and recruited alumni James Ryan and Ray Sonnenberg to announce the games.

KRC normally programmed 5 days a week, depending on the number of students on staff. In 1985, for example, 62 announcers worked Monday through Friday, noon-10 p.m. Students individually, or in pairs, had one- or 2-hour shifts, once or twice a week.

Annually, an elected station manager appointed a staff consisting of program director, music director, personnel manager, news director, and promotions manager. Students were free to develop their own programs, following student-developed guidelines. Technical maintenance was contracted to professional broadcast engineers. An annual awards banquet was a highlight for several years, honoring students who served KRC in numerous ways. Two KRC station managers were selected as Rockhurst Outstanding Student Leader of the Year, Ann Lockhart (1980-81) and DeAnn Dickens (1986-87).

Because students in any academic major were welcomed to be trained and participate, the Student Welfare Committee in 1987 approved KRC's request to change from a special interest club to a general interest organization. Funding came from student activity fees and periodic fund-raising activities. Music license fees to ASCAP and BMI were paid by the college.

In the 1990s, professor Ryan encouraged students to use the Internet to reach a broader audience and to achieve better reception. This was explored but not developed due to budget limitations. KRC ceased operation after Prof. Ryan's retirement in spring 2003.

— William J. Ryan, Professor Emeritus

and a program of paid sabbatical leaves for teachers. Students also complained about the ambiguity surrounding scholarship renewals.

The Student Council submitted its position paper to the administration on April 1, 1967. A meeting attended by 17 council members and 9 administrators, led by President Van Ackeren and Dean Robert F. Weiss, S.J., followed. Administrators responded to concerns point by point, but not before reminding students that they "sometimes were guilty of discourtesy." Federal regulations ruled scholarship renewals, they explained, and student rights to know college financial matters was under national study. As far as all the new buildings on campus went, they argued that competent faculty could not be recruited and retained without adequate facilities.

Where they felt they could, administrators acted. They agreed to allow student representatives to sit on administrative and faculty committees, except for the Rank and Tenure Committee and in discipline cases that came before the Student Welfare Committee. They said they were considering making the yearly retreat voluntary but were reluctant to do so until suitable alternatives could be presented. And they complimented the students "on their concern for a relevant, scholarly content in theology."[17] Rockhurst's Jesuits, however, were unwilling to concede to the 1960s notion that everything political was personal. A Catholic college was different, they argued. It simply was not acceptable for students to conclude that "all matters religious and spiritual are personal and private and not the domain of administrative control."

Yet, administrators did listen. In fact, they had been listening even before the Student Council presented its position paper. In March 1966, when the council proposed dumping the no-cut rule for classes, then-dean Joseph E. Gough, S.J., approved the idea on an experimental basis.[18] When the Student Council had suggested that the administration reconsider the long-held requirement that students attend Mass one class day a week, the administration also had bent. In February 1965, Rockhurst's compulsory Mass was limited to freshmen only, and a year later, in an open letter to students, Chaplain Aloysius Rieckus, S.J., announced "in the same spirit as Pope Paul" that obligatory Mass was being terminated for freshmen, as well.[19] Rieckus said the decision was made "not just to remove an obligation or make the Mass seem less important, but to make it appeal to all by virtue of its own value and its own importance."[20]

Charles P. Cahill, S.J., devoted over one-half of his life to administration at Rockhurst. He arrived in 1949, and by the time Cahill retired in 1986, he had served as dean of students, director of the evening division, director of summer school, and assistant academic dean. Courtesy of Rockhurst University Archives.

Two weeks later, the student-faculty committee on the liturgy sent a letter of concern to President Van Ackeren, asking to discuss "complex social, religious and intellectual difficulties on campus." Though few details were reported, Father Van set up discussions with several faculty committees, as well as the student-faculty committee, whose statement centered "on the need for relevance from the student's point of view in theology courses."

Theology courses had been at the center of debate since the first Student Council meeting the previous fall. Father Van had talked about the ideal that Jesuits held for college students, and Dean Gough had explained how courses at Rockhurst were directed at that ideal and how an understanding of theology was meant to give "a deeper understanding of faith" that would help the student throughout his life. Students apparently had

In the early years of the 1960s, Rockhurst students sponsored dances and concerts with many big-name groups, including the New Christy Minstrels and the Four Preps. By the mid-1960s, however, rock 'n' roll bands became the norm. Courtesy of Rockhurst University Archives.

listened closely but responded that theology classes focused too much on the history of the church and did not hold enough relevance to their everyday life or their future. Council vice president Jim Wirken also complained about retreats, saying they stressed things that students "already knew."[21]

In spite of student concerns, philosophy and theology requirements would remain the same for the next few years—15 semester hours in philosophy and 12 in theology. In 1971, philosophy requirements would be reduced to 12 hours, theology to 9. These requirements would hold steady until the curriculum revisions of the early 1990s, resulting in 6 hours required in each of the 2 disciplines, with an additional 3-hour elective in one or the other. Though the number of hours was reduced in each discipline, students were given more freedom over time to make choices among a wider range of courses.

— ROCK 'N' ROLL, VIETNAM AND ALCOHOL —

Not only Catholic students, but also the world seemed to be changing. When Rockhurst's sophomore class planned the annual fall dance in 1965, it broke tradition by bringing in a rock 'n' roll band from Lawrence, Kansas. In the past, dances had featured orchestra music. Enough protest was heard that Drew Shields, chairman of the sophomore class fall dance, felt compelled to write a letter to the editor of *The Hawk*. "Even though it may not be like it has been in the past with the traditional, conventional bands, it is what more people are going to enjoy and what our class wants to do," he wrote of the rock 'n' roll band. "Tradition is fine, but let's also let some new blood in and see what it produces."[22]

When Rockhurst presented its first endowed lecture in March 1965, the speaker was Pulitzer Prize-winning journalist Marguerite Higgins, a war correspondent in Vietnam, where the United States was getting ever more deeply involved. "America is her own worst enemy when it tries to force 'instant democracy' upon these people," Higgins told 500 people in the Rock Room. She did not blame John F. Kennedy but his "incompetent advisors" for getting America involved in what she described as "an internal political war."[23]

The war—and especially the draft—concerned Rockhurst men just as it did every other male student across the United States. "Are you in danger of being drafted?" *Hawk* writer Nick Hilger asked on March 25, 1966. Hilger's distrust of the United States government came through as he warned fellow students "to be careful." Although full-time students making satisfactory grades (at least a "C") were deferred, Hilger suggested that definitions always could change at the local draft board, which needed to fill quotas. When 2 draft card protesters who recently had burned draft files in Maryland and Wisconsin were allowed to set up an informal discussion in a Massman Hall lounge, threats poured in, according to *The Hawk*, from several alumni who said they were going to cancel their contributions to Rockhurst. One Kansas City high school also reportedly called, saying its counselors no longer would recommend Rockhurst. That day, Rockhurst students had passed in and out of the Massman lounge, some agreeing with what they heard, other's disagreeing, though the reception accorded the 2 protesters at the nearby University of Missouri-Kansas City was said to be much more responsive.[25] In March 1968, even as *The New York Times*' James Reston stood on a Rockhurst podium giving the Visiting Scholar Lecture, President Lyndon Baines Johnson was on national television, announcing his withdrawal from the November presidential race. When news of LBJ's announcement was relayed to Reston, he announced it to cheers and loud applause from the 2,000 people listening to him in Mason-Halpin Fieldhouse.[26]

With the explosion of issues that rocked the 1960s, The Rockhurst Hawk, *in its December 10, 1965 issue, argued that for the first time in years, Rockhurst students were making their voices heard. Courtesy of Rockhurst University Archives.*

When Robert F. Kennedy was assassinated that coming summer and anti-war candidate Eugene McCarthy defeated at the Democratic National Convention in Chicago, the party banner was left to Vice President Hubert H. Humphrey, who had supported Johnson's war policies. Just weeks before the November general election, Humphrey appeared at Rockhurst for a short address in the fieldhouse, followed by a question-and-answer session. There were scattered posters in the crowd proclaiming "Nixon's the one," but the great majority of the crowd, *The Hawk* reported, were Democrats who reciprocated with "All the way with H.H.H." or the occasional shout of "We want Gene."[27] Hubert Humphrey went on to defeat Republican candidate Richard Nixon 64 percent to 30 percent (with 6 percent for George Wallace) in a mock poll at Rockhurst, but

his mind again. Many colleges in the late 1960s and early 1970s were going coed as they faced rising costs and the prospect of a declining pool of students as the enrollment of "baby boomers" ebbed and the national birth rate declined. Van Ackeren was astutely aware of these issues, noting "the challenge" that growing enrollment at public colleges and universities, supported by public money, made for private colleges like Rockhurst. The public versus private enrollment ratio had gone from an even 50-50 in 1950 to 65-35 in favor of public colleges by the mid-1960s. Van Ackeren worried aloud in this Phase Two Blueprint report that the ratio was predicted to be 80-20 in favor of public colleges by 1975.

Although his report did not mention coeducation as a helpful remedy to the enrollment problem, the idea of opening Rockhurst to women was on the table by February 1968. That month, Van Ackeren appointed a committee, divided into 4 subcommittees, to study "the feasibility of co-education." The committees were an inclusive group, comprising representatives from the Board of Regents, the faculty, administration, alumni, parents, students, and diocesan education officers. As the committee first met on February 6, 1968, the Student Council took note, held discussions, and set up a poll to judge student attitudes toward opening Rockhurst to women. Results came back in the affirmative, 3 to 1, to admit women.[33] The feasibility committee also came back in favor, saying it found "overwhelming approval" for coeducation, not only among faculty and students, but also in every constituency except the alumni. A poll of 5,000 individuals had found faculty support at 96 percent, Board of Regents at 66 percent, parents of current students at 61 percent, members of the Priest Senates of the Kansas City-St. Joseph and Kansas City, Kansas, dioceses at 94 percent, and the Diocesan Lay Council at 83 percent. The alumni board was evenly split on the question.

The reasons women would be an asset to Rockhurst, the committee said, were the "different insights" they would bring, the "healthy sensitivity toward women as persons" that would be developed for male students, and the "needed spark" that women could provide to vitalize spiritual life on campus. Also, it thought coeducation would foster marriage between partners of equal education background, which would lead to more "marital happiness and to professional success."[34] Opponents, on the other hand, feared that academic standards might suffer and that women might come to dominate student government and activities. Most importantly, they argued that coeducation could destroy Rockhurst's identity, making the college "indistinguishable" from other small liberal arts colleges.

The committee also found that Rockhurst's physical facilities and programs were such that the college easily could accommodate an influx of

Women had been attending evening classes since 1933. When the evening division began to offer the bachelor of science degree in 1946, women were enrolled. In 1954, Margaret Joan McGraw, (upper photo), earned her B.S. in business administration after 6 years of night classes, becoming the first woman ever to receive a bachelor's degree from Rockhurst. At the same time McGraw was attending night school, Friederun Behrens was allowed to attend day classes, a decade and a half before the college went coed. Behrens graduated in 1956 with a double major in chemistry and biology, becoming the first woman to graduate from the Rockhurst day program. Friederun Behrens Boone, '56, (lower photo), returned to campus for a visit in 2006. Courtesy of Rockhurst University Public Relations and Marketing.

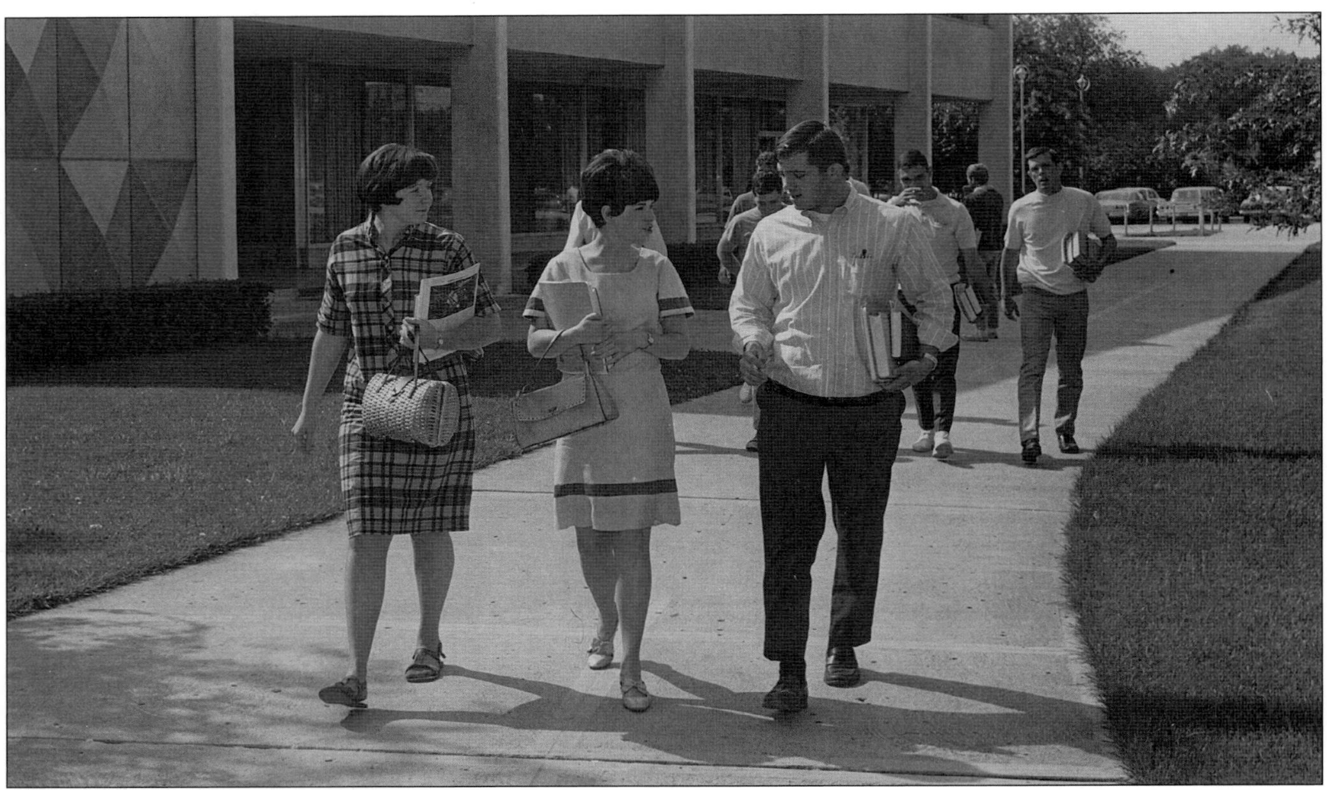

After a lengthy study to determine the feasibility of becoming coeducational, in the fall of 1969, 126 women enrolled as full-time students, marking a new era in Rockhurst's history. Courtesy of Rockhurst University Archives.

150 to 200, or possibly as many as 400, women. The committee estimated that male enrollment would peak at about 1,250 students in 1978. Because Rockhurst calculated that its operating costs would not appreciably increase for an enrollment of up to 1,500 (and possibly as many as 1,700 to 1,800), there was room to admit women. With a student body of 1,500, the report said, no new faculty would have to be hired, though the student-faculty ratio would increase from 12:1 to somewhere between 15:1 and 18:1.[35] To house women, the committee said, Rockhurst was looking at an additional $12,000 a year expenditure for residence hall staff and another $3,000 for renovation if women were admitted to the present dorms. The committee recommended that women be housed in 2 floors of the 4-story McGee Hall, built in 1966.

The beanie cap, donned by freshmen, disappeared with the arrival of women on campus. Courtesy of Rockhurst University Archives.

When Rockhurst surveyed 4 area Catholic colleges that might be affected by its decision to admit women, it met resistance from Avila College, which recently had moved to a new location in south Kansas City. Out of this, writes Ruth E. Cain, came the decision that both colleges would go coeducational and work on "a cooperative, on-going basis."[36] At a press conference on April 25, 1968, Father Van Ackeren and Sister Olive Louise Dallavis made the joint announcement that both colleges would "admit students of both sexes in September 1969." Van Ackeren emphasized that the announcement did not mean a merger was to occur and that both institutions would retain their separate identities.[37] "Our objective," he said, "is to find ways in which we can improve the quality of our programs by working and planning together with our faculties." He cited Avila's "excellent programs" in art, nursing, and elementary and special education, and Rockhurst's "broad range of degree curricula" in business, engineering, and the sciences.[38]

In the fall of 1969, 126 women enrolled as full-time students, marking a new era in Rockhurst's history. "It was more or less embarrassing, at first, walking around campus," new student Barb Pouyer told a reporter from the *Kansas City Times*.[39] "All the guys were looking us over—in the cafeteria, whole tables would turn around at one time and look at us." Pouyer, from St. Louis, was one of a number of women who came from out of town and took up residence on the top 2 floors of McGee Hall. Liz Tobin came from Oak Park, Illinois. "The first day," she told the *Times*, "they carried up our trunks and luggage—they were great. I never felt so nice." At the request of the Student Council, a dozen women started a pep club and "spread the word" for all women on campus to attend the next soccer game "as a cheering group." Dixie Kemp, a freshman from Sedalia, Missouri, served as ex-officio chairman of the group, explaining that one reason she decided to attend Rockhurst was that women were being encouraged to initiate activities. Pat Cherry, of Palisades Park, New Jersey, liked the challenge of Rockhurst. "We're sort of pioneers," she told the *Times*. "I think it gives us the chance to become more outgoing, by being interested enough in ourselves and the school to start clubs." Pat, whose brother, Tom Cherry, had just graduated from Rockhurst, enrolled with her twin sister, Kathy. Others said they chose Rockhurst because "it was near home" or it had "outstanding teachers" or "because of the favorable reputation of a department." Rockhurst was not alone as it moved to coeducation that fall. The Ivy League's

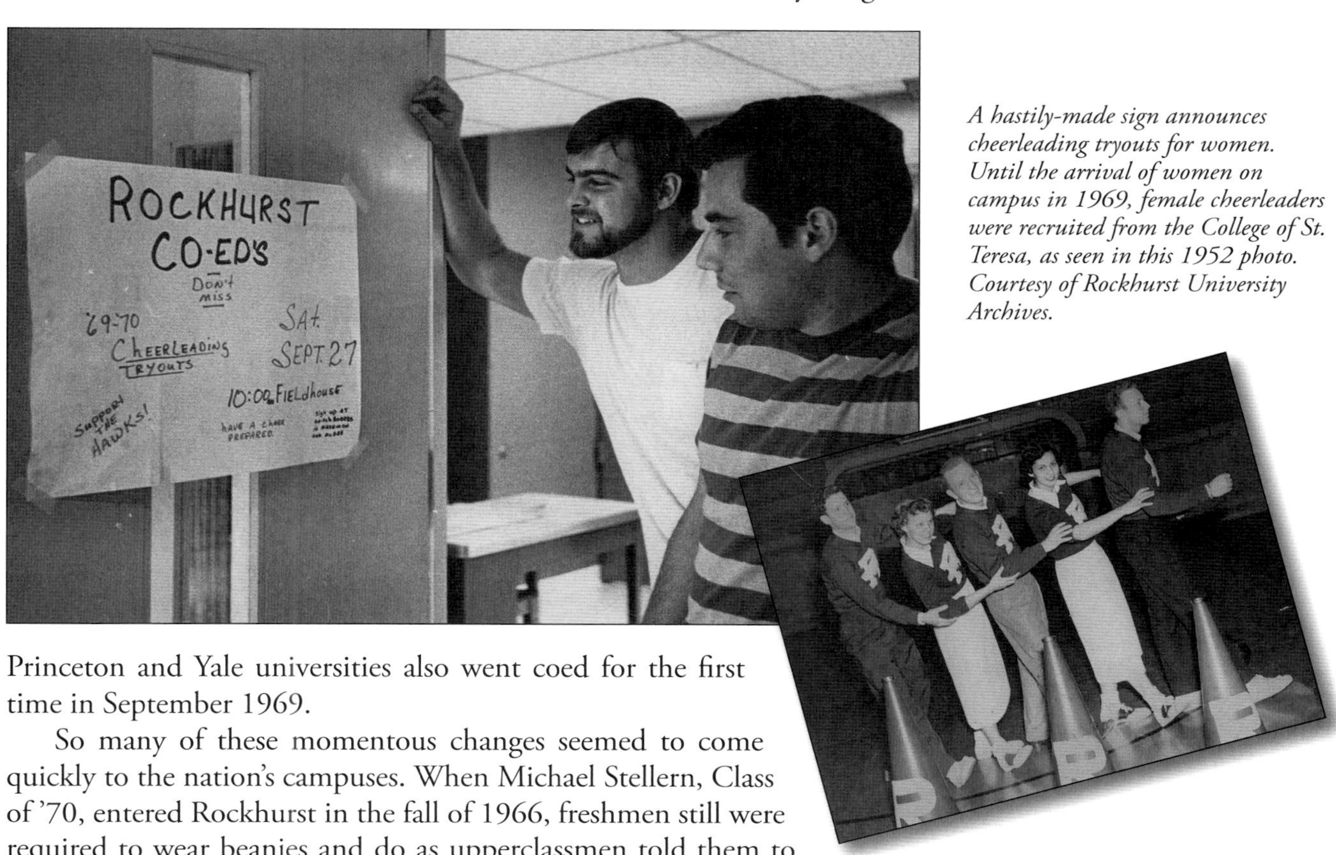

A hastily-made sign announces cheerleading tryouts for women. Until the arrival of women on campus in 1969, female cheerleaders were recruited from the College of St. Teresa, as seen in this 1952 photo. Courtesy of Rockhurst University Archives.

Princeton and Yale universities also went coed for the first time in September 1969.

So many of these momentous changes seemed to come quickly to the nation's campuses. When Michael Stellern, Class of '70, entered Rockhurst in the fall of 1966, freshmen still were required to wear beanies and do as upperclassmen told them to do. In a reminiscence published in 2005 in *Rockhurst: The Magazine of Rockhurst University*, Stellern recalled "freshmen students running around the pe-

— LOUIS B. MCGEE —

A civic leader and exemplary Catholic layman, Louie McGee was once described by Fr. Joseph Gough, S.J., as "the rare individual who could both organize and execute." His love for Rockhurst went all the way back to his days as a student. A 30-year member of the Rockhurst

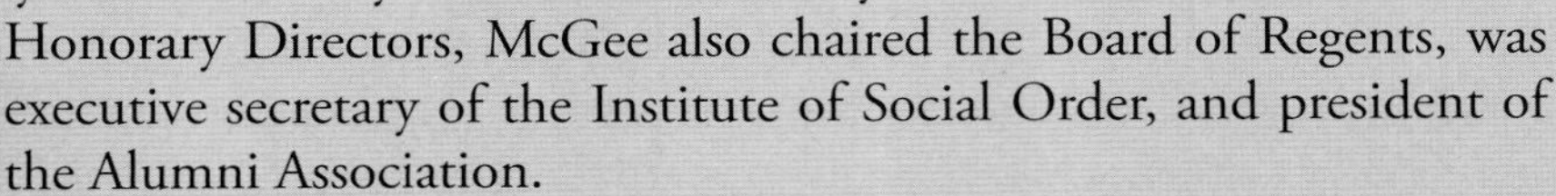

Honorary Directors, McGee also chaired the Board of Regents, was executive secretary of the Institute of Social Order, and president of the Alumni Association.

Before his death in 1964, McGee established a substantial endowment to provide scholarships named to honor Father Joseph Friedl, S.J., his own father, Thomas McGee, and his friend President Harry Truman. In 1966, Rockhurst prepared a special citation in recognition of McGee's "lifetime of distinguished service to his college and his fellow man and in special gratitude for generous scholarship endowments which perpetuate his memory and his high ideals."

The residence hall that opened in 1966 was named in Louis McGee's honor. Many members of the McGee family have continued the legacy of leadership and support of Rockhurst through the years. In 1977, Joseph J. McGee, Jr. was elected to the first lay Board of Trustees. That same year Rockhurst awarded him an honorary doctor of humanities degree. In 2001, the Anne and Joseph McGee Chair in Interpersonal Communication and Listening was established.

rimeter of the cafeteria quacking like ducks." There were no female students on campus then, only a handful of women teachers and many more Jesuits than there are today.[40] As a freshman and sophomore, Stellern was required to attend 2- and 3-day retreats, and dorm students had to abide by a 10 p.m. curfew. It was only during formal dances in the Rock and Aztec rooms that Stellern saw young women on campus. He watched the escalation of the Vietnam War and told how students were motivated to stay in college to avoid the draft. When Stellern was a senior, President Nixon introduced the lottery system to determine who would be drafted. "I remember that night because everyone was out drinking," he wrote, "whether to celebrate his high number or to forget the low number that meant he would be called up soon after graduation."

Women, Stellern wrote, arrived on campus "with very little interruption of normal activities," although the ratio of men to women that first fall of 1969 was 20:3. The number of women at Rockhurst would increase yearly, to 222 in 1970; 300 in 1971; and 337 in 1972, or 29 percent of the student body.[41]

— INTO THE 1970S —

As the turbulent 1960s stretched into the 1970s, questions of curriculum and college governance dominated headlines. Students continued to demand more authority and pressed Rockhurst to adopt a tripartite system of college government with equal representation among students, faculty, and administration. Students had complained that the college was overly centralized and too slow in decision-making. They wanted an outlet for their opinions to be heard.[42]

"Tired of taking the required 27 hours in philosophy and theology?" *The Hawk* had asked in the fall of 1968. Well, "there is hope," it said, because a newly formed Committee on the Study of Curriculum was looking into things and planning to hold a series of public forums where students and faculty could speak up. "This is not just something dreamed up by the administration to appease 'the mob,'" *The Hawk* said. "Things can and will be accomplished."[43] A curriculum questionnaire was handed out, and when they came back in favor of cutting theology and philosophy requirements in half and grading courses on a pass-fail system, it seemed as if the issues of the 1960s were not going to fade anytime soon.

Unlike more volatile campuses such as Columbia and San Francisco State, Rockhurst found a way, once again, for students and administrators to sit down and air their differences peaceably. In an editorial published February 11, 1970, *The Hawk* praised Father Van and members of the Board of Directors for their willingness to schedule meetings and discuss issues with students, and it praised the Student Council for working through proper channels. "Rockhurst is involved in the same kind of problems now that have caused buildings to be burned, students to carry guns and (stage) sit-ins on other campuses," *The Hawk* wrote. "This campus has been saved from this approach to problems by the fact that the student government has been willing to try every line of communication and by the fact that the college administration has seen that the students have a good issue in the problem of college governance."

In March 1970, President Van Ackeren appointed a committee, the Tripartite Committee, "to examine decision-making" within the college. After months of study, the committee, on June 15, 1971, issued an extensive report that favored adding students to a number of committees at Rockhurst.

Coeducation at Rockhurst. Students John Denny, Patty Tegeler, and Fran Siegel, 1969. Courtesy of Rockhurst University Archives.

It also called for developing accountability procedures for the college's vertical channels of decision-making. Recommendations included, for example, having the Board of Directors, which wielded final authority on all matters related to the college, appoint an executive committee that would meet, when the need arose, with appropriate groups of students and/or faculty. It called for the board to issue written explanations of its decisions and to place a time limit on any delay in its actions. The question of whether lay faculty and student representatives should serve on the all-Jesuit Board of Directors came up during committee discussions, but that emotionally charged issue would not be decided for another 10 years. In 1967, Saint Louis University had become the first Jesuit college to include lay members on its Board of Directors, which, in effect, took governing power over the college out of Jesuit hands, a revolutionary change that came out of the turbulent '60s and the new emphasis on the laity spawned by Vatican II.[44]

As the Tripartite Committee issued its report in 1971, Rockhurst students, for the past 4 years, had already been serving on 12 committees—from the Library Board and Student Welfare committees, to the Religious Activities and Visiting Scholar committees. While stipulating that the number of students on any committee should be decided on a case-by-case basis, the Tripartite Committee called for adding students to 5 other committees: Admissions, Teacher Preparation, Student Financial Aid, Athletic Council, and the new Curriculum Committee. Rockhurst went on to follow the recommendations and establish a tripartite committee system. The work of the Tripartite Committee met with high praise from President Van Ackeren, who said the college had taken "a real step forward in the direction of participation" in the making of college policies.[45]

Within months, the switch to a tripartite committee system was followed by another important change that spoke to the new era—this one

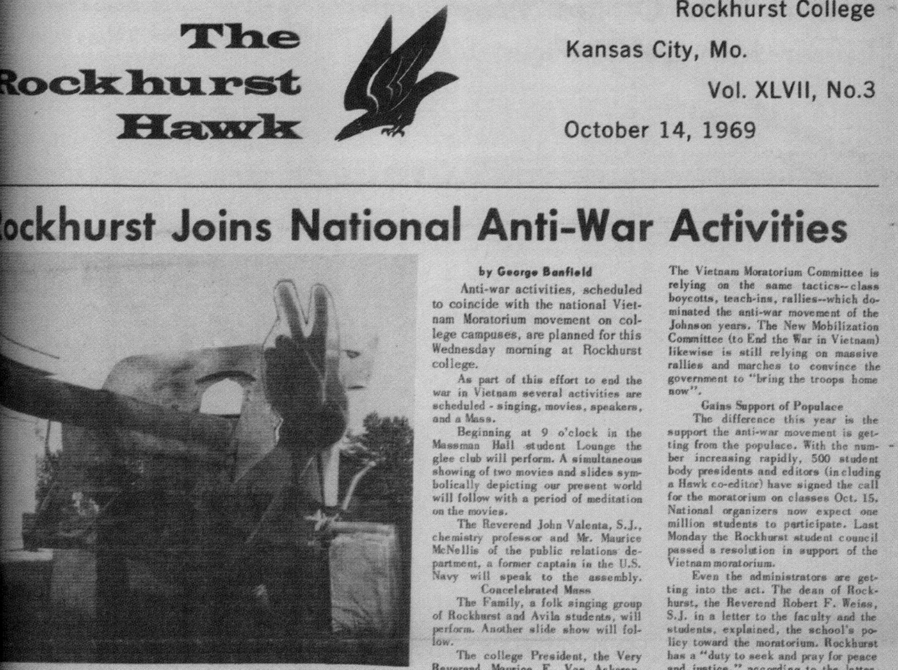

The Rockhurst Hawk

Rockhurst College
Kansas City, Mo.
Vol. XLVII, No.3
October 14, 1969

ockhurst Joins National Anti-War Activities

by George Banfield

Anti-war activities, scheduled to coincide with the national Vietnam Moratorium movement on college campuses, are planned for this Wednesday morning at Rockhurst college.

As part of this effort to end the war in Vietnam several activities are scheduled - singing, movies, speakers, and a Mass.

Beginning at 9 o'clock in the Massman Hall student Lounge the glee club will perform. A simultaneous showing of two movies and slides symbolically depicting our present world will follow with a period of meditation on the movies.

The Reverend John Valenta, S.J., chemistry professor and Mr. Maurice McNellis of the public relations department, a former captain in the U.S. Navy will speak to the assembly.

Concelebrated Mass

The Family, a folk singing group of Rockhurst and Avila students, will perform. Another slide show will follow.

The college President, the Very Reverend Maurice E. Van Ackeren,

The Vietnam Moratorium Committee is relying on the same tactics--class boycotts, teach-ins, rallies--which dominated the anti-war movement of the Johnson years. The New Mobilization Committee (to End the War in Vietnam) likewise is still relying on massive rallies and marches to convince the government to "bring the troops home now".

Gains Support of Populace

The difference this year is the support the anti-war movement is getting from the populace. With the number increasing rapidly, 500 student body presidents and editors (including a Hawk co-editor) have signed the call for the moratorium on classes Oct. 15. National organizers now expect one million students to participate. Last Monday the Rockhurst student council passed a resolution in support of the Vietnam moratorium.

Even the administrators are getting into the act. The dean of Rockhurst, the Reverend Robert F. Weiss, S.J. in a letter to the faculty and the students, explained, the school's policy toward the moratorium. Rockhurst has a "duty to seek and pray for peace and justice," according to the letter.

On October 15, 1969, Rockhurst students, faculty, and administrators joined in the national Vietnam moratorium, which called for a day of boycotts, to protest the war. As part of the changing attitudes toward war and symbols of war, the World War I cannon, which had been displayed on campus since 1921, was sold in 1972. Courtesy of Rockhurst University Archives.

— TRAGEDY HITS CAMPUS —

On October 30, 1971, the campus was shocked to learn that 4 athletes from the Rockhurst rugby team had been killed and another critically injured in a 2-car collision a few miles northwest of Platte City. The students were returning from Atchison after a game with Benedictine College. Witnesses stated that their car fishtailed coming down a hill and was broadsided by another car. Two persons in the other car were killed.

The Rockhurst victims were freshmen Michael Hardy and Michael Gronemeyer, sophomores John Mannion and Fred Wilkowski. Former Rockhurst student Stephen Cozzie also died in the wreck. Senior Craig Wakefield ('74), who survived the crash and was in a coma for almost 2 months, later returned to Rockhurst and completed his degree. To help defray the expenses of Wakefield's many operations, the Kansas City Chiefs and the Miami Dolphins staged a benefit basketball game between the two teams, played at Municipal Auditorium in March 1972. The Michael J. Hardy Memorial Scholarship was established by his family and friends in memory of Hardy.

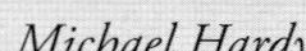

Michael Hardy

Michael Gronemeyer

John Mannion

Fred Wilkowski

Stephen Cozzie

involving the Rockhurst curriculum. A 16-member committee of faculty and administrators, known as the Committee on Study of the Curriculum, had been meeting for 2-1/2 years. On February 9, 1971, it released its recommendations.[46] The curriculum of Rockhurst College derived, the committee wrote, "from our nature as a Jesuit liberal arts college and from our involvement in an urban and secular environment." The college, it said, was "committed to the values of our Christian faith and our intellectual heritage," as well as, being "inevitably called upon to serve the community in which we live." These dual responsibilities meant that Rockhurst not only must provide the student with a "constellation of values" so that he might "relate all human culture eventually to the news of salvation," but also that the college must assist the student "in acquiring a reasonable competence in a specific field so that he may function effectively in a society which demands such competence of its college graduates."

The committee emphasized that Rockhurst was dedicated to "the aims of a liberal education," which constituted "a reaffirmation of our identity and a renewal of our dedication to the enduring principles which have guided those who came before us." For a liberal education to remain viable, "it must adapt," the report said, "to changes in both the intellectual sphere and the world surrounding the academy." Adaptability, it noted, was always

Right, Father Van Ackeren presents an honorary doctor of fine arts degree to artist Thomas Hart Benton at graduation in 1969. Above, the class of 1969, the final all-male graduating class, celebrated its 25-year reunion in 1994. Photo of Benton by Charles Brenneke. Courtesy of Rockhurst University Archives.

a distinguishing mark of a Jesuit liberal education, dating to the sixteenth century and the establishment of the Society's very first schools. And now, in the twentieth century, liberal education faced new challenges created by "extensive changes in the social order and in the realm of human knowledge." So many new disciplines now existed, the report said, "that it is now impossible for liberal education to extend its scope through simple addition to the curriculum." The sheer volume of new knowledge was so overwhelming that there needed to be a way to give it structure, which, paradoxically, the report stated, gives "still greater validity to liberal education."

The broad aims of liberal education sought by Rockhurst's curriculum could be addressed on 2 different fronts: what the report called the "outer breadth" of a "liberal core," and the "inner breadth" of an "area of concentration." A student's required 128 hours of course work would be divided 50-50 between the 2. The liberal core would require 16-17 hours in the natural sciences, social sciences, and mathematics; and 10-12 hours in the humanities, as well as composition, speech, and electives. Importantly, required courses in philosophy and theology were retained. Twelve hours were stipulated in philosophy, including 3 hours each in the Philosophy of Being, the Philosophy of Man, and Ethics. Nine hours were required in theology or religious studies. Requirements in a student's area of concentration called for a minimum of 18 and a maximum of 42 in the major field, as well as 30–54 hours in related fields, plus electives. New majors were added, including one in theology. Other majors were dropped, including those in Latin and the Classics. Rockhurst made the foreign language requirement optional; a student could replace it with computer science and statistics.[47]

These changes of the 1960s and 1970s occurred, historian David J. O'Brien explains, as 3 streams of historical change converged. First, the old

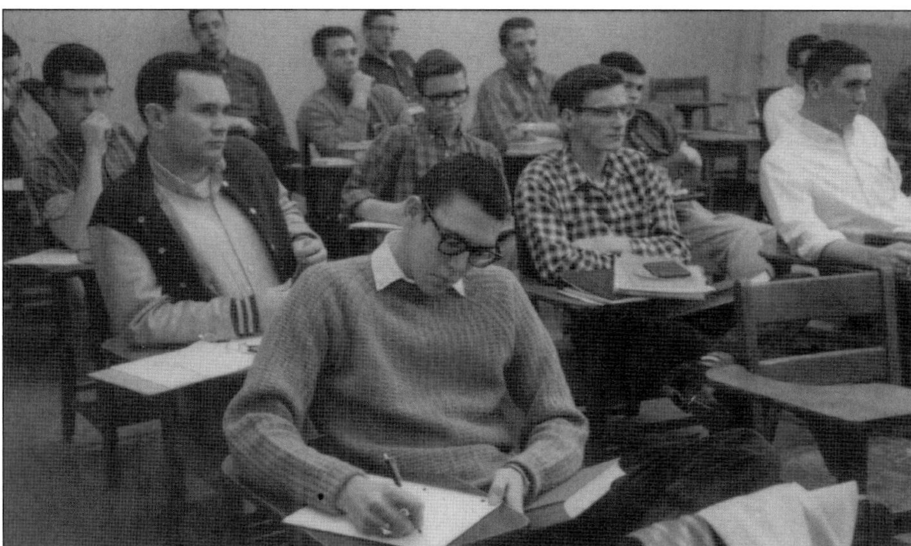

New student orientation, 1971 (photo above). The landscape of an all-male student body at Rockhurst (photo left) quickly changed after women were admitted in 1969. Courtesy of Rockhurst University Archives.

Catholic subculture found in blue-collar, ethnic neighborhoods waned as fewer Catholic immigrants entered the United States. Then, after World War II, using the GI Bill, more Catholics went to college and intermarried with non-Catholics, blurring the boundaries that separated Catholics from other Americans. Vatican II further erased differences by relaxing the authoritarianism that had marked the Catholic Church for centuries. In addition, O'Brien writes, Catholics found themselves divided, not only by the new religious pluralism spawned by the Vatican II Council, but also, like the rest of the nation, over the civil rights, women's, and anti-Vietnam War movements.[48]

In Kansas City, the civil rights movement, especially, would have far-reaching implications for the future of Rockhurst.

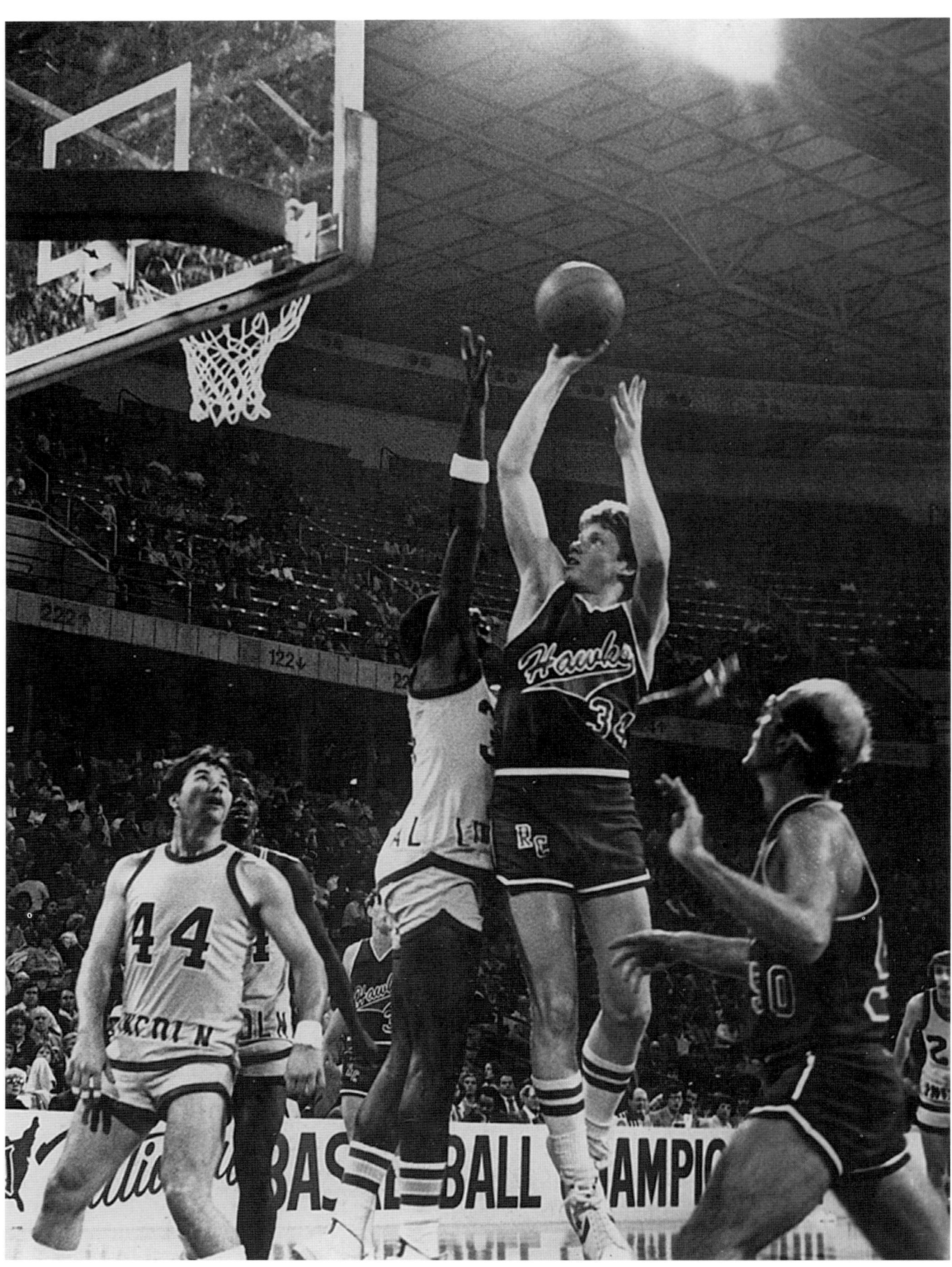

222
122
44
RC
50
BALL

Chapter Twelve

Focus on the Neighborhood 1970–85

By 1965, Rockhurst was hemmed in by a neighborhood of middle-class homes to the north, south, and east. On the west was a prospering commercial strip along Troost Avenue, including a U-Totem grocery store, which leased a Rockhurst-owned building on the southeast corner of 54th Street and Troost. The wide open farmlands surrounding the original campus that Father Dowling had purchased nearly 60 years before had been under development now for years. In fact, Father Dowling had envisioned a campus surrounded by residential homes when he filed the original 25-acre plat for Rockhurst Park. He had divided the plat into 2 distinct sections. One section, called Outlot No. 1, was reserved for the original Rockhurst campus. This outlot encompassed about 12 acres, which ran east to west from Tracy Avenue to Troost, and north to south from Rockhurst Road to 53rd Street.

Flanking the outlot to the north and east was the second section of Father Dowling's plat—another approximate 12 acres, divided into 62 individual lots, which Dowling intended to be sold as sites for houses, sales he hoped would help pay for his 25-acre purchase. To the east of campus, Lots 1 to 50 stretched east to Lydia Avenue, while Lots 51 to 62 hugged the north side of Rockhurst Road. Father Dowling's plan to sell these lots would not materialize, and the "lower campus," as it came to be called,

Hemmed in by houses to the north, south, and east, with the opening of McGee Hall in 1966, Rockhurst jumped the original campus boundary at 53rd Street. Courtesy of Rockhurst University Archives.

comprising these 50 unsold lots, had sat vacant for years except for a few World War II barracks and Mason-Halpin Fieldhouse, with its football field out back. An aerial photograph from the early 1950s captured this no-man's land on film. The photograph reveals signs of the old quarry where the limestone for Sedgwick Hall was dug. It also reveals a Rockhurst College surrounded by mature trees and row after row of single-family homes dating to the 1920s.

So hemmed in was the campus that in 1965, before the college could begin construction on McGee Hall—which jumped the original campus boundary at 53rd Street—houses sitting on the site were picked up and moved north and east of Dowling Hall, which still stood on the northeast corner of Troost Avenue and Rockhurst Road.[1] The expansion south to accommodate McGee Hall was a harbinger of things to come as Rockhurst's need to expand in the 1960s and 1970s coincided with racial issues so divisive in Kansas City that the college, in a moment of soul-searching, even considered whether it was wise to remain in the neighborhood.

The momentous changes to come began with the 1954 *Brown v. Board of Education of Topeka* ruling, which said that racial segregation in public schools was unconstitutional. At the time, Kansas City was a segregated city, where black children and white children attended separate schools, and where most of the city's black population—which had increased 25 percent during the World War II years—was squeezed into an area north of 27th Street and east of Troost Avenue. Black people were told not to cross 27th Street.[2] A letter written in 1950 by a Rockhurst neighbor reveals the intense racial feelings that marked the era. The writer, who was Caucasian but did not reveal his name, went straight to the top of the Jesuit province hierarchy, writing to the provincial in St. Louis to get something done about "a situation" that had arisen in the Rockhurst neighborhood. "Indignation of the people who live in the vicinity as well as people who have ever had any interest or connection with Rockhurst through the years is at a boiling point," he wrote. The problem centered on the Rockhurst football

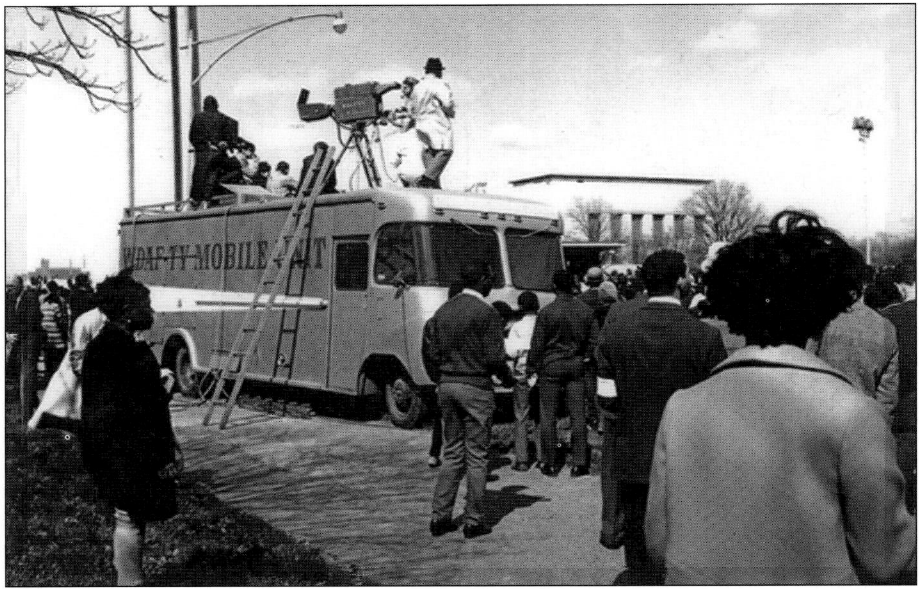

A mobile unit from WDAF-TV broadcasts a civil rights gathering from the Liberty Memorial. After the assassination of Dr. Martin Luther King, Jr., on April 4, 1968, riots occurred in cities nationwide, including Kansas City. Courtesy of WDAF-TV, Kansas City, Missouri.

field, which was "being made available to teams from colored schools... Please know that as a group, mostly Catholics, we are as tolerant as most people," the letter writer said. "We have raised no objection to the colored students being accepted in our Catholic schools, although we do feel that any colored student in Rockhurst High School has to come quite a distance out of his way unnecessarily."

He wrote that neighbors "found it hard to believe" that Rockhurst athletic director Paul Smith, S.J., was allowing the situation simply for the money gained from the contracts. "We don't like the remarks that have been made concerning the fine men of your Order since this has occurred and it is a bad thing for a group of religious to cause so much ill-feeling among their people." He pointed out that "most of the people in this vicinity" had attended Rockhurst themselves and sent their boys to the school. "It is quite a setback to these loyal supporters of Rockhurst, the builders of this community, to have a situation like this thrown at them," he continued. "The remark has even been made that for a price, the field would be rented to the Communists or anyone else willing to pay the price...."

The letter writer apologized for his presumptuousness in writing directly to the provincial (who was former Rockhurst President Daniel Conway), but explained that "since so many seem to think this is going to lead to trouble I hoped you might intervene with whomever at Rockhurst is responsible." He concluded: "Please do not regard this as a missive of intolerance—I have always been in sympathy with the colored people being treated fairly but we are not quite ready for a condition like this in our neighborhood and since there are other stadiums available to them why is it necessary to provoke this anger and ill-feeling?"[3]

Unready though the neighborhood was for change, it was fast on its way. In 1955, Rosa Parks refused to give up her seat on a Montgomery, Alabama, bus, and the civil rights movement accelerated from there. Sit-ins began in 1960 and freedom rides in 1961. The year 1963 brought the March on Washington and Martin Luther King, Jr.'s, "I Have a Dream" speech, as well as the assassination of President John F. Kennedy. Kennedy's vice president, Lyndon Johnson, set out to energize many of Kennedy's stalled programs and embarked on his own vision for what came to be known as the "Great Society." In 1964 the Civil Rights Act, with its keystone Title VII, outlawed discrimination in employment on the basis of race, religion, sex, or national origin. Another section barred discrimination in public accommodations. Armed with this law, integrationists could ask the U.S. attorney general to withhold federal funds from any government-run program that was not desegregated and could appeal discrimination in employment and public accommodations under the newly established Equal Employment Opportunity Commission.[4] These laws applied even to private colleges like Rockhurst, which felt pressure to comply as they increasingly depended on federal funds for things from student financial aid to building loans to special grant programs.

The country's racial divide had exploded into riots: New York City in 1964, the Watts section of Los Angeles in 1965, and in Newark, Detroit, and 20 other cities in 1967. When civil rights leader Martin Luther King,

Jr., was assassinated in Memphis on April 4, 1968, Kansas City exploded, as well. A protest march by high school students turned chaotic after police fired tear gas into a crowd gathered at city hall. Random violence descended into 5 days of looting and burning.[5]

At Rockhurst, a peaceful memorial service for the slain civil rights leader was held in Massman Hall on Monday, April 8. Efforts to address racial issues had been evident at Rockhurst since the early 1960s when students polled local restaurants and then canvassed the neighborhood in support of Kansas City's 1964 accommodations ordinance. Students had canvassed the neighborhood again in March 1966 as part of the nation's Fair Housing Campaign, when they requested residents to sign a Good Neighbor pledge.[6] In 1967, an Upward Bound program for disadvantaged high school students was established on campus and that same year the National Catholic Conference for Interracial Justice met in Greenlease Library. And now, at the King memorial service, the Rev. A. James Blumeyer, S.J., Rockhurst's coordinator of religious activities, declared that a fitting memorial to the slain civil rights leader would be to support another fair housing referendum coming up on the Kansas City ballot.[7]

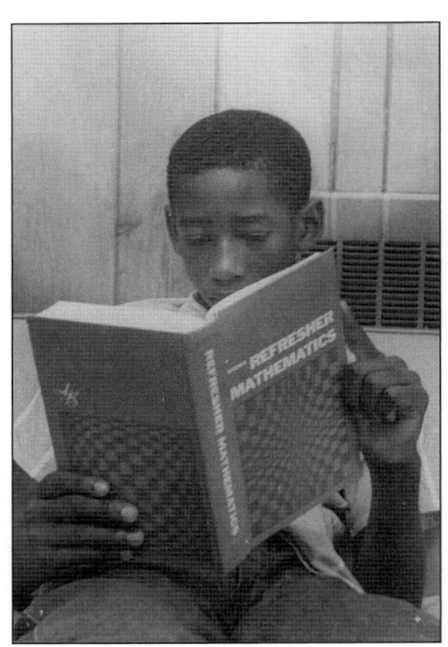

Designed to give disadvantaged high school students the confidence and motivation to succeed in college, Rockhurst established an Upward Bound program in 1967. Photo by Charles Brenneke. Courtesy of Rockhurst University Archives.

The measure, approved on April 30, 1968, had a tremendous impact on Kansas City and the Rockhurst neighborhood. It prohibited real estate brokers, their agents, and financiers from making any distinction in their sales based on race. It also prohibited any distinction in renting. The ordinance addressed the longstanding redlining policies that had kept black Kansas Citians confined to a small area in the northeastern part of the city. Kansas City's public schools had desegregated after the 1954 Brown ruling, but redlining and blockbusting had quickly re-segregated them and steered black people to one side of Troost Avenue and white people to the other. By 1966, nearby Paseo High School, nearly all white in 1955, was 68.7 percent black. Closer to downtown, at 11th Street and Prospect Avenue, the diocese closed St. Aloysius grade school. Within 5 years, as the Wayne Minor, East Attucks, and Independence Plaza urban renewal projects cut into the parish, nearly all the old buildings at St. Aloysius were demolished. A new church was dedicated in 1971.[8]

— THE 1970 CENSUS —

As urban renewal tore into older neighborhoods, construction of the new freeway loop demolished entire blocks of the city, and new highways, such as Interstate 35, provided easy access out of town, fueling flight to the suburbs. The 1970 census sent shock waves through the city when it revealed that, despite a series of annexations in the 1960s that had more than doubled the city's land base, the population had barely grown. Most troubling was the loss of population in the city's core. Almost 100,000 fewer white people lived within the old boundaries in 1970 than did in 1960. The black population, meanwhile, had increased by 20,000.

The changing neighborhood patterns were apparent around Rockhurst, which began to work with the newly formed 49/63 Neighborhood Coalition, which was working with real estate brokers to develop a "model, integrated community" in the north-south area from 49th to 63rd streets and

— ROBERT AND VIRGINIA GREENLEASE —

Robert C. and Virginia P. Greenlease were longtime benefactors and friends of the Kansas City Jesuits. In 1908, Robert Greenlease obtained a franchise for the Cadillac when it was a one-cylinder model priced at $800 with top speed of 30 miles per hour. After General Motors acquired Cadillac, Greenlease became its distributor for a 6-state area, and in 1967 was honored as the company's senior dealer in the U.S. In 1955, the Greenleases donated the land that eventually would become the site of Rockhurst High School. In 1967, the newly dedicated Greenlease Library was named in recognition of the couple's substantial contribution to the "Blueprint for 1970." Robert Greenlease was a 30-year member of the Honorary Directors at Rockhurst and a charter member of the Board of Regents. He died in 1969.

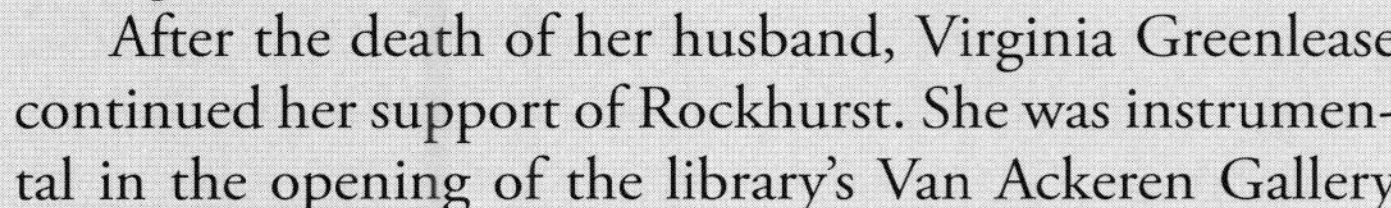

After the death of her husband, Virginia Greenlease continued her support of Rockhurst. She was instrumental in the opening of the library's Van Ackeren Gallery in 1975, which housed 20 pieces of Renaissance religious art, most of which were gifts from the Greenlease family. She was one of 6 lay persons elected to the previously all-Jesuit Board of Trustees in 1977, and the first woman elected to the Board. In 1978, Virginia was named a Foundress of the Missouri Province of the Society of Jesus for her many contributions to Rockhurst College. She also was a motivating force in the establishment of the Library Guild.

In 1986, President Robert Weiss, S.J., announced that Rockhurst, with financial help once again from Virginia Greenlease, had established its first endowed academic chair for a full-time faculty member in honor of Joseph Freeman, S.J., who had been teaching philosophy and theology at Rockhurst for 40 years and was a long-time friend to the Greenleases. In 2000, the newly constructed Greenlease Gallery of Art opened, named in honor of Virginia Greenlease. The gallery contains space for temporary exhibits, as well as the university's permanent collection. At her death in 2001, Virginia Greenlease bequeathed a large portion of her estate to Rockhurst University.

Photo courtesy of Rockhurst University Archives.

the east-west area from The Paseo to Oak Street.[9] As white residents fled to the suburbs, the 49/63 Coalition counted 71 "For Sale" signs posted in the neighborhood in June 1971. In the year and a half from January 1972 to June 1973, the federal Department of Housing and Urban Development had repossessed 41 subsidized houses in the Rockhurst neighborhood; by 1976, 39 structures were vacant. The closure of a nearby Mr. Steak restaurant on Troost Avenue only added to the perception of a declining neighborhood.[10]

Rockhurst was deeply concerned about the transitional nature of the neighborhood, and a perception that took root by mid-decade that "the area around Rockhurst College is not a safe place to be and is undesirable."[11] The college joined the 49/63 Coalition in taking action. Together, they pushed for an ordinance that rezoned almost all of the area for single-family residential use. Rockhurst provided rooms for coalition meetings and functions, as well as typing, printing, and duplicating services. The college also helped secure a federal Title I Aid to Higher Education grant that provided money to hire a part-time staff person who worked for improvements on Troost Avenue. Rockhurst, in fact, was so involved in neighborhood issues that Mary Service, Title I coordinator for the coalition's Business Renewal & Development Corporation, said the college's "interest and encouragement" had been "invaluable."[12]

— DEVELOPMENT —

In the midst of all these changes, Rockhurst President Van Ackeren continued to work on long-range planning. Phase Two of the Blueprint for 1970 had been completed in 1967 with construction of the $1 million Greenlease Library, a vast improvement over the old library, cramped on the second floor of Conway Hall. The new building, made of native ashlars and cut granite, featured a mezzanine, reading and study rooms, seating for 500 persons, and space for 143,000 volumes. It was dedicated on October 12, 1967, during ceremonies marking Rockhurst's 50th anniversary of the first college classes.[13] Just a year before, on October 21, 1966, the 6-story, 110-room McGee Hall dormitory was dedicated in honor of Louis B. McGee, a Kansas City civic leader and founder of the McGee Foundation, which supported a number of projects at Rockhurst.

After the opening of Greenlease Library, Rockhurst entered a period of evaluation and self-analysis. On May 17, 1969, a one-day planning conference convened at 9 a.m. in the Rock Room in Massman Hall, its stated purpose to examine the college's goals and programs, strengths, and weaknesses. Similar gatherings to exchange ideas would occur over the next few years as Rockhurst sought to broaden input from business and community leaders, as well as alumni, students, and faculty. The list of attendees would include prominent Kansas Citians such as R. Crosby Kemper, Sr., honorary chairman of the City National Bank and Trust Co.; Alfred E. Jordan, vice president of Trans World Airlines; George W. Miller, president of Mohawk Securities Company; Joseph A. Hoskins, an attorney with Hoskins, King, Springer & McGannon; and Herbert F. Tomasek, president of Chemagro Corporation. "All this increase in cooperative effort will certainly result in the development of a stronger college," Father Van stated.[14]

Groundbreaking, 1965, for the $1 million Greenlease Library. Left to right: Joseph Cardinal Ritter, Bishop Charles Helmsing, and Father Maurice Van Ackeren, S.J. Photo by Charles Brenneke. Courtesy of Rockhurst University Archives.

Following this conference, the Board of Directors, on June 28, 1969, approved another long-range plan for the college, the Values Program. It picked up where the Blueprint for 1970 left off by setting a new, 5-year target to raise $8 million by 1975. Of the money, $1 million was to go for financial aid for students, $1 million for faculty development, $1.925 million for programs and services, $2 million

In 1969, Library Guild member Helen Biersmith and her son Edward Biersmith III, Class of '63, donated this mural, which hangs on the west wall of Greenlease Library. The mural uses symbols and words to express Rockhurst's interests in science, the humanities, rhetoric, social sciences, athletics, and the fine arts. The artist, Eric J. Bransby of the University of Missouri-Kansas City, also included Saint Thomas More, patron of Rockhurst. Photo by Charles Brenneke. Courtesy of Rockhurst University Archives.

for the endowment fund, and $2.075 million for facilities, including an addition to Mason-Halpin Fieldhouse.

The Values campaign kicked off in October 1969 and raised $2 million in its first year. In January 1970, the college adopted its "principles and criteria for long-range planning," which noted the necessity of setting priorities and asking tough questions before proceeding. How essential, for instance, was a particular program to a college like Rockhurst, which was an urban liberal arts college, but also a Jesuit college that sought to cultivate Christian values and contribute to the community? Was there adequate space for the program? Was there sufficient staff to ensure its continued growth? Were there financial resources to support it? These kinds of questions would guide the college into the next decade, as the addition of new programs made Rockhurst a more comprehensive university.

As Father Van prepared his annual President's Report for the 1970-71 academic year, he sounded optimistic and reflective. He wrote with satisfaction of the 3,000 graduates who had passed through Rockhurst since his arrival 20 years before. "Today my files are bulging with news clips and correspondence verifying the progress and the contribution they are making in Kansas City and around the world," he wrote. Yes, there had been momentous changes at the college, he said, but there also were important constants. "The magnet which attracted young men to Rockhurst in 1951 is still the effective force today—their recognition that this campus offers a friendly climate in which to conduct their search for truth and value."[15]

Value, both cultural and economic, was the key word in a time of such great social and financial stress. Inflation and soaring energy prices strained economic resources in the early 1970s, even as colleges braced for the possible impact from a declining national birthrate. A study by the state of Missouri showed that enrollment in Missouri colleges and universities, both public and private, had grown by 269 percent between 1952 and 1971 (from 50,515 to 186,395). After 1968, however, enrollment had slowed; a 3.4 percent growth rate for the fall of 1971 was the lowest in the 20-year period (with the exception of 3.0 percent in 1959).[16] Rockhurst Vice President J. Barry McGannon, S.J., expressed concern that Rockhurst enrollment could drop by 20 percent or more as the 1980s neared.[17]

The new Values Program aimed to address cultural and economic concerns in one swoop by easing Rockhurst's financial burdens while simultaneously teaching personal responsibility and high moral values to its students. As the Values Program kicked off, it listed advances at Rockhurst during the past 10 years (from 1958 to 1968): an increase in total enrollment, from 1,749 to 3,039; an increase in faculty, from 73 to 141; an increase in the number of students receiving financial aid, from 91 to 298; and an endowment fund that stood at $748,098. Tuition, too, had risen, from $400 to $950.

At the 1971 convocation, CBS newsman and Kansas City native Walter Cronkite received a doctor of humane letters degree from Rockhurst. Courtesy of Rockhurst University Archives.

As Rockhurst held its 50th commencement on May 31, 1971, it graduated 252 men and women from the day and evening divisions. Bachelor's degrees were handed out in 19 major fields, and the college presented its 38th honorary doctorate to Missouri Sen. Thomas Eagleton. The college now was home to 30 Jesuits and employed 45 full-time and 64 part-time lay faculty, making for a faculty-student ratio of 14 to 1. Rockhurst's own Walter J. Ong, S.J., a nationally recognized scholar, delivered the annual Roy A. Roberts lecture, and Astronaut James A. Lovell, commander of the aborted Apollo XIII moon flight, delivered the first Charles M. Charroppin lecture. Two years later, in 1973, Rockhurst graduated the largest class in its history—295 students.[18]

That same year, the college opened the doors to what would be the last of its major construction projects for another decade—the new Physical Education and Convocation Center. Space for the athletic department had become more and more a priority as enrollment grew and Mason-Halpin Fieldhouse aged. Built in 1938 for a student body of 400, the fieldhouse hardly was suited to serve the anticipated college enrollment of 1,500 students by 1975. Space already was at a premium, not only for athletes on the men's basketball, baseball, soccer, bowling, tennis, and golf teams, but also for the nearly 50 percent of Rockhurst students, women included, who participated in at least one intramural sport, from badminton to weightlifting.[19] To accommodate the assortment of activities, construction began in the summer of 1972 on the 30,000-square-foot, self-standing addition to the fieldhouse. The new Physical Education and Convocation Center contained a 10,000-square-foot multipurpose room for intramurals and general physical education. With its integrated acoustical lighting and climate control system, the huge room also could serve as the setting for visiting scholar lectures, music and art programs, convocations, and adult education classes. The building also boasted a fully equipped gym, lockers and showers, a sauna, handball courts, offices, classroom space, and storage rooms. When it opened in the fall of 1973, 2 upper-level bridges connected it to the old fieldhouse.[20]

Astronaut James A. Lovell, commander of Apollo XIII, delivered a lecture for the sixteenth Rockhurst Day banquet and presented the college with a flag and patch that traveled on the 1970 flight to the moon. Courtesy of Rockhurst University Archives.

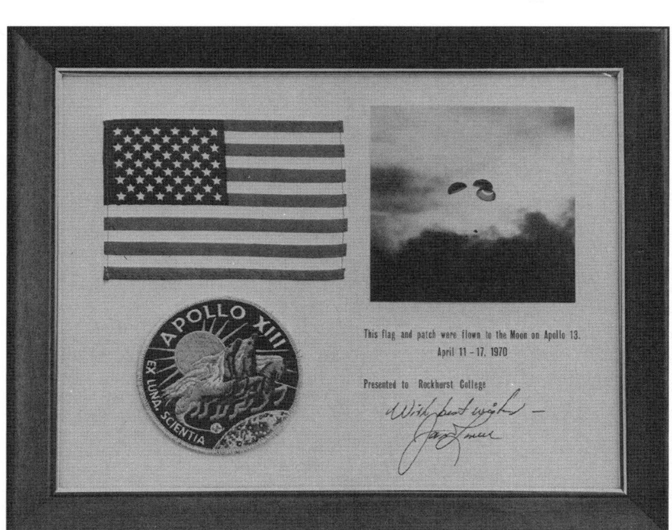

"Let's face it," Athletic Director Gene Hart had said as he stood in the center of the construction the previous April. "About the only thing you could use the other building for is basketball." Hart was enthusiastic as he talked of possibly adding wrestling, gymnastics, and volleyball to Rockhurst's intercollegiate lineup. "This could mean a lot to our enrollment," he told the *Kansas City Times*. "The trend I think is for enrollments to go down. We have to do things to keep our kids here. We're not K.U. or M.U. The difference in 20 or 30 kids means a lot to a school our size. With this building we also help make them active outside of the classroom, which I think is one of the things that makes for a happy community."[21]

Even as the Convocation Center went up, Rockhurst was under the gun to address deficiencies not only in its affirmative action programs, but also in Title IX of the Education Amendments Act of 1972, which broadened the 1964 Civil Rights Act to include educational institutions. Under the act, Congress prohibited colleges and universities that received federal funds from discriminating on the basis of sex, a change that particularly benefited women athletes.[22] By 1976, Rockhurst fielded women's teams in basketball, volleyball, tennis, and bowling, but "women's sports are still in a very shaky position," Hart wrote in a memo to the dean of students. With the exception of volleyball, he said, women's sports "are being given only token consideration." Women athletes had no full-time coach, no locker room or medical room of their own, an item, along with athletic grants, he said, that "leaves Rockhurst College very short when it comes to Title IX requirements, and I want to continue to alert the school that if the women athletes on this campus want to make an issue of it, they very well would have a strong talking point...."[23] Hart worried, too, that women athletes "could put greater pressure on the school for athletic scholarships," since Title IX required equity by 1978.

Women's bowling team, 1974. Top row, left to right: Debbie Doran, Connie Schmidt, Ellen Landgraf. Bottom row: Ginny Kenney, Jan Schultehenrich, Jean Dougherty, Mary Clevenger, Joseph Rydzel, coach. Bowling was the first women's intercollegiate sport at Rockhurst, and Jan Schultehenrich was the first woman to earn a varsity sports letter "R." Title IX of the Education Amendments Act of 1972 prohibited colleges and universities that received federal funds from discriminating on the basis of sex, a change that benefited women athletes. By 1976, Rockhurst fielded women's teams in basketball, volleyball, tennis, and bowling. Courtesy of Rockhurst University Archives.

The college also faced pressure to improve its affirmative action programs, which were designed to redress historical patterns of race discrimination in employment and education. Affirmative action programs began in 1965 in the Lyndon Johnson administration and by 1977 were credited with increasing to 1.1 million the number of black students in the nation's colleges and universities. That represented 9.3 percent of total student enrollment. Hispanics experienced similar gains.[24] In compliance with Title VII of the Civil Rights Act of 1964, as amended by the Equal Employment Opportunity Act of 1972, Rockhurst filled out an EEO form in May 1973 that revealed only 17 black employees at Rockhurst, 10 of whom were service workers. This was out of a total employment roll of 209.[25]

The college needed to do better and, in the summer of 1973, drafted a program restating its commitment "to equal opportunity according to the law for minorities and women in its employment practices and procedures, promotion, payment, etc." This called for adherence not only to Title VII, but also to Title IX, as well as the Equal Pay Act of 1963, which was amended for higher education in 1972. In its Affirmative Action Program, Rockhurst promised to set goals and analyze its workforce patterns annually, to hire the appropriate administrative personnel to implement the goals, and to set up procedures for monitoring and auditing the employee applicant flow and the final hiring disposition. It designated J. Barry

McGannon, S.J., college vice president, as Director of Affirmative Action Programs and set policy that demanded equal employment opportunity regardless of "race, sex, creed, color, age, place of origin, or family status," as well as the stated aim to "make every effort to include minorities and women in the workforce, particularly in those areas where such persons have not previously been employed."

The college policy made clear that it would recruit for staff positions in the Kansas City metropolitan area, which was 12.05 percent black. Kansas City, Missouri, proper was 22.32 percent black, compared with a national average of 11.1 percent.[26] In a June 19, 1973, letter to J.L. Thomas, regional branch chief, contract compliance for the Office of Civil Rights, McGannon enclosed a copy of the draft, stating that the college had put "a great deal of thought" into the policy. "In some areas we just don't have personnel policies," he explained. "We have just initiated a job classification effort which will cover all clerical and plant department employees.... We believe it is a step in the right direction, but it will take several months to complete. The same may be said for our personnel records which are far from efficient. Here, too, we have initiated changes which we hope will provide the necessary information."[27]

Still, 3 years later the college was chastised by EEO Specialist Elister Dewberry for "doing only what is minimally required by law." In an EEO Validation Review, the college had received an "inadequate" rating, not only in the "workforce pattern" category (for "upper jobs") but also in the "goals & timetables" category for its affirmative action program. When Rockhurst administrators explained that a lack of qualified minorities was a primary reason for not having minorities in full-time faculty or administrative positions, Dewberry suggested procedures that could help, such as contacting black colleges with M.B.A. or doctoral programs.[28]

The Rockhurst campus became more diverse in the 1970s as affirmative action programs sought to redress historical patterns of race discrimination in employment and education. Courtesy of Rockhurst University Archives.

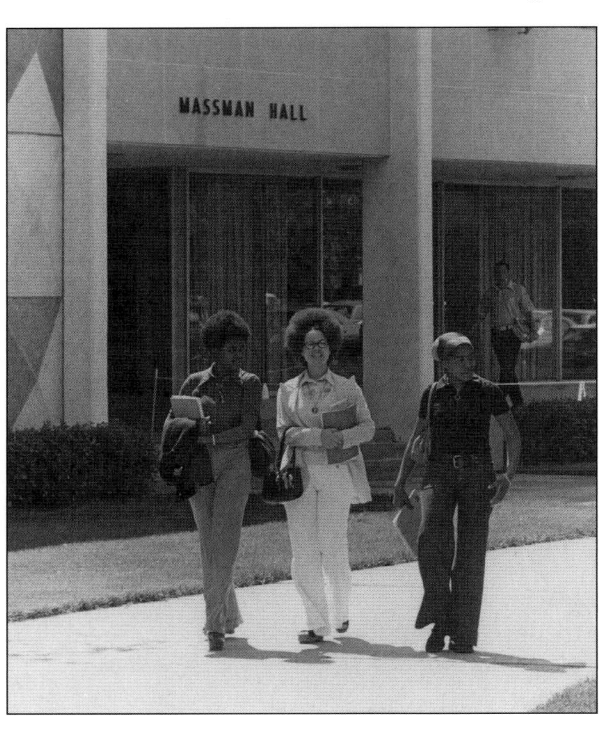

The plethora of federal regulations was a hallmark of the time as Rockhurst found itself dealing more with the federal government in academic areas, as well. In 1967-68, the college, for instance, received its first Title III monies under the U.S. Office of Education's Higher Education Act of 1965 for "developing institutions," a confusing term that actually centered on areas in which a college sought improvement, such as faculty-student ratio. By the 1973-74 academic year, Rockhurst had received more than $2.3 million under the program and used part of the money to establish its Tutoring Center.[29] The questionnaires and applications that Rockhurst filled out for federal grants reveal much about the college as it dealt in the 1970s with issues raised in the 1960s. For instance, the number of low-income students receiving federal aid at Rockhurst had increased from 67 in the fall of 1966 to 101 by the fall of 1972. Low-income students were considered those from families with an annual income of under $7,499. Rockhurst counted 201, or 17 percent, of its 1,171 students as low-income in the fall

— RESEARCH COLLEGE OF NURSING —

Research College of Nursing is a private college sponsored by Research Medical Center, located about a mile from the Rockhurst campus. Since 1905, Research College of Nursing has been providing nursing education. In 1979, Research College of Nursing forged a partnership with Rockhurst, and in 1980, admitted its first class of students studying for the Bachelor of Science in Nursing degree.

Faculty from both Rockhurst and Research have designed the nursing program to provide a consistent, integrated educational experience. Nursing students are enrolled at both institutions and take the same liberal arts courses as other Rockhurst students. Nursing students begin participating in clinical education at Research College in the second semester of their sophomore year.

In addition to the traditional undergraduate degree in nursing, an accelerated option is available for students with a previous non-nursing college degree. Additionally, Research offers a Master of Science in Nursing degree with four graduate tracks. In 2009, 121 undergraduate degrees and 18 graduate degrees in nursing were awarded.

Rosalinda Celeste Gomez, 1986 graduate of Research College of Nursing. Courtesy of Rockhurst University Archives.

of 1972. A total of 340 students, or 29 percent, came from high-income families with an annual income of more than $15,000.[30] Rockhurst also received three AIDP (Advanced Institutional Development Program) grants from the U.S. Department of Health, Education, and Welfare, Office of Education, to stimulate recruitment. Among other things, these funds were used to establish a Learning Center, a Career Center (both in 1975), and a Women's Center for Non-Traditional Careers.[31]

In the mid-1970s, the college looked to add enrollment as a way to reduce its operating deficit, which stood at an estimated $450,000 for 1973-74. (Sixty-five percent of operating income came from tuition and fees; 35 percent from gifts.) Day enrollment had leveled "at a plateau" of 1,150 to 1,200 students, although Rockhurst's goal was 1,500; the evening division stood at about 1,300, but aimed to enroll 1,800.

— THE "LIVEABLE" CITY —

These optimistic enrollment goals were right in step with a Kansas City that, despite its demographic problems, was touting itself in the early 1970s as "one of the few livable cities left." Downtown had been revital-

Jazz concert in the Massman "coffee house," 1975. Courtesy of Rockhurst University Archives.

ized with a new Federal Office Building at 601 E. 12th Street and a new Missouri State Office Building at 615 E. 13th Street. A new international airport had opened up north in Platte County and, out east, the baseball Royals and football Chiefs were playing on spotless artificial turf at the new Truman Sports Complex. Atop Signboard Hill, Hallmark's Crown Center had transformed an ugly forest of billboards into an architectural showcase, and in the West Bottoms, the new Kemper Arena was ready to host the 1976 Republican National Convention.

Rockhurst put another feather in the city's cap that year with its designation as an official Bicentennial Campus as the United States celebrated its 200th birthday anniversary. Ceremonies began on April 11, 1975, with the ringing of a bell that had hung in Kansas City's first log church in 1840—a Catholic church. It was a fitting reminder that the place that became Kansas City began as a tiny settlement of French Canadian fur traders—Catholics all.[32]

In 1975, Rockhurst was designated as a Bicentennial Campus, one of 4 colleges so recognized in Missouri. Celebrations included a Bicentennial series of Visiting Scholar lectures by such notables as historians Henry Steele Commager and Martin E. Marty. Courtesy of Rockhurst University Archives.

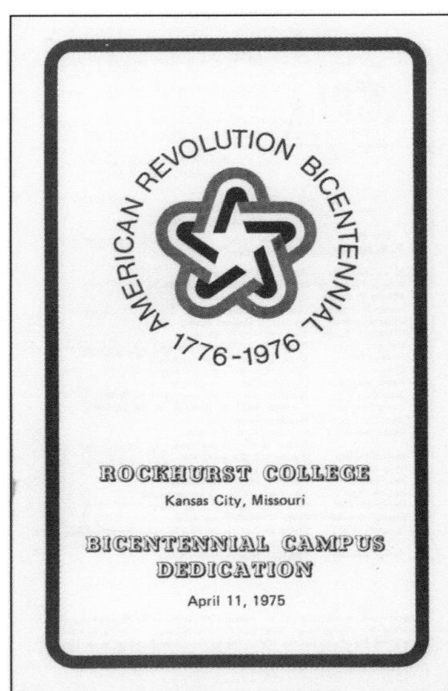

Many things were coming Rockhurst's way. In November 1976 came a $200,000 grant to establish the Helen G. Bonfils Endowment for the Fine and Performing Arts, and a $100,000 challenge grant from The Joyce Foundation of Chicago. The Bonfils Endowment would pay, among other things, for Rockhurst students to attend cultural events in the city and to meet visiting artists.[33] The Joyce Foundation grant was to be matched dollar-for-dollar with contributions to Rockhurst's latest fund drive, the Great Opportunities program, a 3-year, $4.7 million campaign that would pay for new classrooms and offices, new, energy-conserving windows for Sedgwick Hall, and an increase in scholarship funds and the college endowment. The campus would be landscaped and better-lit and the Thomas More Dining Room and kitchen renovated.[34] The Great Opportunities drive was launched on September 16, 1975, with a kick-off dinner in Massman Hall for 200 industrial, civic, and community leaders. The guest list spoke worlds about Father Van's great success in involving Kansas City movers and shakers in the college's fortunes. Former Kansas City Mayor Ilus W. Davis agreed to lead the fund drive, with assistants Gil P. Bourk, president of the First Mortgage Investment Company, and William P. Harsh, executive vice president of Hallmark Cards. Other committee leaders included Lester Milgram, chairman of the board of the Milgram Food Stores, Inc., and John G. Phillips, executive vice president of the Business Men's Assurance Company.[35]

As Father Van befriended these powerful men, he became involved in their hopes and plans for a Kansas City renaissance. Nothing proved this more than a most unusual gift that arrived in May 1976 from the Oppenstein Brothers Charitable Foundation, which turned over to Rockhurst the deed to the 20-story Phillips House hotel at 12th and Baltimore, in the heart of downtown. The Oppenstein Brothers, Michael, Harry, Samuel, and Louis, were jewelry retailers who had expanded into the downtown real estate business. The foundation liked President Van Ackeren's interest in downtown revival and his idea of developing a downtown center for Rockhurst's continuing education classes, and thus the gift was made. "It is difficult to put a dollar value on this gift, but I know that over $1 million was spent in refurbishing the hotel in the past two years," Father Van told *The Catholic Key*. "The college views the location as ideal with two or three floors readily suitable for its Evening Division courses…and for an educational and business conference center." With the Republican National Convention coming to town in a few months, Van Ackeren apparently saw Rockhurst continuing to operate part of the building as a hotel. "We think the future of downtown Kansas City holds tremendous promise and that there will be a growing need for a variety of enterprises catering to convention and expanding business requirements," Van Ackeren said.[36]

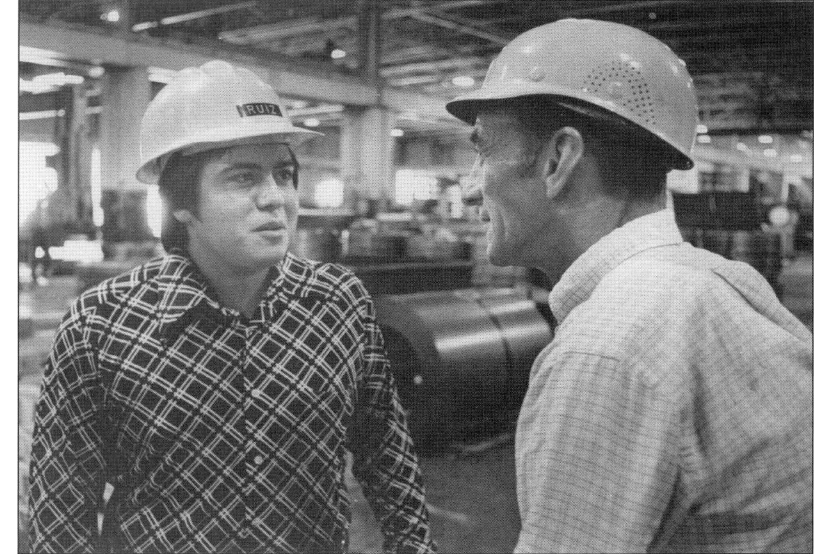

Arthur Ruiz, '76, was one of many students who participated in the Cooperative Education Program, an "earn while you learn" concept that allowed students to work for local companies while earning their Rockhurst degree. Photo by Charles Brenneke. Courtesy of Rockhurst University Archives.

His hopes for a downtown center did not materialize, however, and by the next summer, Rockhurst was trying to get out of the hotel business. Van Ackeren's assistant, Maurice M. McNellis, told the *Kansas City Times* that the 14 evening classes Rockhurst had offered downtown had drawn inadequate enrollment. The college had contracted with the Sunn Management Company to operate the hotel. Occupancy was averaging 35 percent, but there had been enough unexpected expenses and problems with personnel and management, in addition to a proposed tax increase, that the college wanted out.

"Rockhurst is in the business of providing a good education to young people at a reasonable price and is supported by more than 4,000 individuals and companies in achieving that purpose," McNellis told the newspaper. "To channel such funds to the operation of a hotel is not good stewardship."[37]

Jesuits from around the country came to Kansas City to celebrate Maurice Van Ackeren's 25th anniversary as president of Rockhurst. Before a crowd of 900 at Crown Center Hotel, Father Van (front row, second from left) announced that he was stepping down as president to assume the newly created office of chancellor. Photo by Mark Borserine. Courtesy of Rockhurst University Archives.

— FATHER VAN STEPS ASIDE —

As America celebrated its birthday in 1976, Rockhurst President Maurice Van Ackeren marked a milestone of his own that March—his 25th anniversary at Rockhurst. During a "Salute to Father Van" before a crowd of 900 at Crown Center Hotel, Van Ackeren announced that he was stepping down as president to assume the newly created office of chancellor, which would allow him to maintain his contacts and influence in Kansas City while focusing his energy on development. He was turning over the day-to-day internal operations of the college to a yet-to-be-named new president. "I feel it is time to lessen my responsibilities and pass along the presidency to a younger person," he wrote in a resignation letter addressed to faculty members.[38] In a personal letter to Pedro Arrupe, S.J., Father General of the Society, he spoke highly of the Crown Center celebration, which had brought together people of all faiths, a "real symbol," he said, of the "sincere friendship and cooperation" that had helped him in his efforts at Rockhurst.[39] "Some of these years have been very troublesome years," he confided to Father Arrupe, "but with the help of the good Lord and the guidance and support of our Jesuits and many loyal friends we have been able to maintain a Jesuit and Catholic college here in Kansas City." That summer, in honor of Father Van, the Jesuit Residence was renamed Van Ackeren Hall.

As the search committee began its quest for a new president, Rockhurst followed Saint Louis University's lead and expanded its legal governing body, the all-Jesuit Board of Directors, to include lay people. The new Board of Trustees, as it would be called, assumed responsibility for college finances and the formulation of policy. This was a gargantuan change in college governance that stemmed from many factors: the great influx of students and their demand for a greater variety of courses after World War

II; the professionalization of academic and financial planning boards in the 1950s; and, of course, the teachings of the Vatican II Council in the 1960s, which saw the need to broaden and intensify the apostolic role of the laity.[40] Jesuit-lay collaboration would become ever more important for the future of Jesuit education as the number of young men entering the Society of Jesus continued to diminish.

Among the lay persons elected to join the 8 Jesuits on the board were Ilus W. Davis; William H. Dunn, Sr.; Joseph J. McGee, Jr.; Richard W. Miller; Byron G. Thompson; and Virginia Greenlease, who would be honored in November 1978 as a Foundress of the Missouri Province of the Society of Jesus for her many contributions to Rockhurst College. Among them was her instrumental role in the opening of Van Ackeren Gallery in 1975 to house 20 pieces of Renaissance religious art, most of which were gifts from the Greenlease family. The collection had started with a single gift from the Greenlease family, a seventeenth-century wood carving of the crucifixion, which was placed in the Treasury Room of the brand new Greenlease Library the day after the library was dedicated in October 1967. A remodeled Treasury Room was dedicated as the Van Ackeren Gallery. All told, the Greenlease family had directed gifts of some $1.14 million to Rockhurst, as well as underwriting the expense of a variety of trips, including some to Europe, for members of the Jesuit community. Mrs. Greenlease also was a motivating force in the establishment of the Library Guild.[41]

— In the Rental Business —

In an attempt to stem the tide of vacant or deteriorating properties in the neighborhood, Rockhurst had begun, as early as the 1960s, to purchase houses within one block to the north, south, and east of campus. By the spring of 1977, the college owned 69 houses in the area and found itself in the rental business. Maurice McNellis, assistant to the president, turned to Miller Nichols of the J.C. Nichols Company for advice and found himself talking rent/price ratios and acquisition policy. He hired Thomas F. Lillis and Company to manage the properties and deal with a city code department that, in 1974-75, conducted an intensive code inspection program from 53rd to 55th, Troost to The Paseo, exactly the area where Rockhurst was buying up many properties.[42]

In 1977, Luke Byrne, Class of '22, returned to campus in celebration of the 55th year of his graduation from Rockhurst. Byrne was the first recipient of the Dowling Medal. Courtesy of Rockhurst University Archives.

Documents reveal that Rockhurst paid a low of $3,500 for a house at 5309 Tracy, purchased in December 1972, to a high of $18,000 for a house at 5301 Forest, purchased in April 1977. Rents ranged from $100 a month at 5308 Tracy to $150 at 5307 Forest and $200 at 5324 Virginia. In the first quarter of 1976, the college collected $24,637 in rent, leaving a cash flow of $2,446.66. College administrators established an acquisition policy, set up procedures for the trimming of grass and the making of repairs to meet city codes, and formed a Neighborhood Planning Committee, which was meeting weekly by the winter of 1979. The college's policy on property acquisition stated that "the College does not feel that it can allow houses so close to the campus to stand vacant or empty for a long period of time provided it has the resources to acquire them and to take care of them properly."[43]

In 1977, Rockhurst expanded its legal governing body, now called the Board of Trustees, to include lay members. Top row, left to right: Rev. Francis C. Brennan, S.J., Academic Vice President, Xavier University; Rev. J. Barry McGannon, S.J., Vice President, Rockhurst College; Rev. Richard C. Harrington, S.J., Professor of English, Creighton University; Rev. Maurice E. Van Ackeren, S.J., President, Rockhurst College; Rev. Thomas F. Denzer, S.J., Chairman and Associate Professor of Economics, Rockhurst College; Rev. Robert F. Weiss, S.J., President-elect, Rockhurst College; Rev. A. James Blumeyer, S.J., Academic Dean, Rockhurst College; Rev. Thomas J. Casey, S.J., Director at St. John's College Extension; Rev. John G. Valenta, S.J., Rector of the Jesuit Community, Rockhurst College. Joining the Jesuits on the board were (front row, left to right): Joseph J. McGee, Jr., insurance executive; Richard W. Miller, attorney; Byron G. Thompson, banker; Virginia Greenlease, Rockhurst benefactor; Ilus W. Davis, former mayor of Kansas City; and William H. Dunn, Sr., commercial builder. Courtesy of Rockhurst University Archives.

As Rockhurst looked to the future, it also hired a consulting firm, the Real Estate Research Corporation, to conduct a Neighborhood Impact Study, looking at Rockhurst's role in the neighborhood, its need for facility expansion, and the future course it should take. There had been trouble with neighbors over parking, rowdiness at the off-campus fraternity houses, and the high number of rental units owned by the college, which were seen to add to neighborhood instability. All of this needed to be dealt with, administrators realized, though the Neighborhood Impact Study would report that Rockhurst's image in the community at large and the immediate neighborhood was "good."[44]

Results of the study, released in November 1977, noted the changing economic and racial demographics of the neighborhood surrounding Rockhurst. It pointed to the aging and, in some cases, deteriorating housing stock, the shift to rental occupancy, and the poor property maintenance that injured the area's market potential. Rockhurst administrators listened carefully, especially James Blumeyer, S.J., chairman of the college's Neighborhood Planning Committee, who told *The Kansas City Star* that Rockhurst "realizes that it has a vital and important role in the stability and development of the surrounding residential neighborhood." While some people had raised the notion that the college save itself by moving out of the area, Blumeyer was adamant that Rockhurst was staying put. "This report has confirmed our view that the college's location provides unique advantages, due particularly to being a part of the cluster of educational, cultural and research institutions in the Country Club Plaza/Brush Creek Valley area," he said.[45]

Rockhurst followed the study's recommendations that the college focus on improvements in the area immediately surrounding the campus (an area bounded by Volker, 55th, Troost, and The Paseo) and that it monitor and support a larger area (bounded by 39th, State Line, Gregory, and Prospect) with programs designed to maintain and upgrade the neighborhood. "The stabilization of the Rockhurst neighborhood—especially the eastern 49/63 area—is paramount for protecting significant private and public invest-

— WALTER J. ONG, S.J. —

One of Rockhurst's most distinguished graduates was Rev. Walter J. Ong, S.J. An internationally respected scholar and literary theorist, Ong taught for most of his life at Saint Louis University. Born in Kansas City in 1912, he graduated from Rockhurst College in 1933 with a major in Latin. Ong entered the Society of Jesus in 1935 and was ordained in 1946. He earned a master's in English from SLU and a doctorate in English from Harvard.

A widely published author, Ong's most famous book, *Orality and Literacy: The Technologizing of the Word,* has been translated into a dozen languages. In 1968, Rockhurst awarded Ong a doctor of humane letters degree. To kick off Rockhurst's celebration of its 75th anniversary in 1985, a special symposium was held in tribute to Walter Ong and his work. More than 15 scholars presented papers and led discussions on topics related to Ong's scholarship.

Fr. Ong died August 12, 2003. That same year, the Walter Ong, S.J., Scholarship was established at Rockhurst. Rockhurst's English Club, the Walter J. Ong Society for Literary Study, is named in his honor.

ments in Kansas City," the report stated, and went on to laud recent efforts taken to stabilize and upgrade the area.

— A NEW PRESIDENT —

With the impact study completed, Rockhurst initiated long-term plans for campus acquisition and expansion. They would be led by new president Robert Weiss, S.J., who arrived in Kansas City from St. Louis, where he had been serving as president of Saint Louis University High School. Although he was a St. Louis native, Father Weiss arrived on campus in the fall of 1977 already possessing vast knowledge of Rockhurst. His first professional experience was teaching Latin and coaching the speech and debate teams at Rockhurst High School from 1953 to 1956. He came to Rockhurst College in the early 1960s and worked as an assistant professor and assistant dean until 1966, when he was named academic dean. He held the post for the next 6 years, during some of the most turbulent times in the history of Rockhurst, making him intimately familiar with the many recent changes at the college—from coeducation and the new curriculum, to the tripartite committee system and the altered face of the neighborhood. "Over half the faculty have served with him here, and he already is known by many of our friends in the Kansas City area," Father Van said of his successor. "He is a fine choice."[46]

Father Weiss' strong organizational abilities would come in handy as he set out to address Rockhurst's dire parking needs. A series of meetings was set up with neighborhood residents in the spring of 1978, and that summer Rockhurst representatives met with the City Planning Department to

PRESIDENTIAL PROFILE

— ROBERT F. WEISS, S.J. —

The Rev. Robert F. Weiss, S.J., became Rockhurst's tenth president in 1977. A native of St. Louis, Fr. Weiss entered the Society of Jesus in 1946 and was ordained in 1959. He earned B.A. and M.A. degrees from Saint Louis University in 1951 and 1953. Weiss taught Latin and coached speech and debate teams at Rockhurst High School from 1953-56. After earning a doctorate in education from the University of Minnesota in 1964, Fr. Weiss returned to Kansas City and Rockhurst College to serve as assistant professor of education and assistant dean. In 1966, he was named academic dean of the college, a position he held until 1973 when he was appointed president of Saint Louis University High School. From SLU High School he returned to Rockhurst to assume the presidency in 1977.

During Fr. Weiss' tenure as president, Rockhurst expanded its educational programs and completed a number of major renovations. A bachelor's degree in nursing was approved and accredited, the School of Management was established, and a bachelor's program in Physical Therapy was initiated. Renovations of Conway, Sedgwick, and Corcoran halls were completed, along with the addition of the conference center to Massman Hall. In 1984, Mabee Chapel was dedicated.

After leaving Rockhurst in 1988, Weiss returned to St. Louis where he has worked for the Missouri Province in the areas of higher education and advancement.

discuss college hopes to expand south from 53rd to 54th Street. A map of properties owned by the college in January 1979 indicates that Rockhurst, during the past few years, had purchased the entire east and west sides of Forest Avenue from 53rd to 54th streets and half of the lots on the Tracy Avenue block.[47] Rockhurst had been eyeing these lots, which sat directly south and east of McGee Hall, for the much-needed parking lot.

To the north and east of campus, along Troost, Forest, Tracy, Virginia, Lydia, and The Paseo, the map resembled a checkerboard of college-owned houses. Rockhurst attorney Thomas M. Sullivan of the Downey, Sullivan & Fitzgerald law offices pointed out difficulties faced to the planned southern expansion, primary among them that the houses acquired by Rockhurst—because they were separated by streets from campus—were not "on the same lot" as the college and, therefore, did not comply with city zoning requirements for expansion. To overcome this difficulty, Rockhurst sought (and received) a city variance to vacate 3 blocks of streets adjacent to campus—53rd Street from Troost Avenue to Tracy, and Forest Avenue from 53rd to 54th so Rockhurst could build a 160-car parking lot.[48]

The college continued to deal with a sometimes contentious 49/63 Neighborhood Coalition. After a series of 9 meetings in the fall and winter of 1978-79, the coalition finally gave its stamp of approval to the parking lot expansion after Rockhurst agreed to a 3-point compromise: the college would not expand anywhere else for 3 years, it would begin offering leases in nonexpansion areas, and it would begin to sell some houses more remote from campus.[49]

When President Weiss appeared before the Kansas City Plan Commission on April 3, 1979, to request the street vacations, as well as "an attractive entryway" at Troost and 53rd, he began his presentation with a brief history of the college, accompanied by a slide presentation.[50] "The site for Rockhurst College," he began, "was purchased in 1910 at a time when the improvements in the area were sparse indeed and the houses were few and far between." Early plans, he explained, had called for selling some of the 62 lots in the original campus plat as a way to pay for the overall purchase. "This development never came to pass, but homes did cluster around the college rather quickly," Father Weiss continued. In fact, Rockhurst was landlocked, hemmed in by homes and apartments, and streets now clogged with cars as an enrollment of 800 day and evening students in the early 1950s had mushroomed to 4,000 in the fall of 1978. The parking needs of the nearby University of Missouri-Kansas City didn't help matters. There was, Father Weiss said, an "urgent need for additional parking." With approval in hand, Rockhurst gave renters until May 31, 1979, to vacate, and that summer the college set about demolishing houses and abandoning utility lines for construction of what was being called the McGee Parking Lot.[51]

Dennis Luber, '83, shooting for the Hawks at the 1981 NAIA tournament at Kemper Arena. Luber was inducted into the Rockhurst Athletics Hall of Fame in 2000. Courtesy of Rockhurst University Archives.

— END TO THE "BABY BOOM" —

With the college's physical plant complete for the time being, concerns centered in other areas. Chief among "critical problems" was a declining pool of students as the "baby boom" generation graduated from college. Nationally, the number of 18-year-olds peaked in 1980 and was expected to drop 18 percent over the next 7 years. "Competition for a declining pool of students makes this problem one of survival itself," the new Long Range Planning Committee reported.[52] The committee identified negative factors working against Rockhurst enrollment, especially the need for close-in parking. With women now resident on campus and students attending evening school, safety was an issue, as the college, despite minimal crime, contended with the perception that the campus environment was unsafe. The committee identified 2 other "critical problems" in looking ahead to the 1980s: the threat to liberal arts departments as some students demanded a career-oriented education and the issue of faculty development and pay in a time of national economic woes. Between 1973 and the mid-1990s, most American workers saw their real incomes

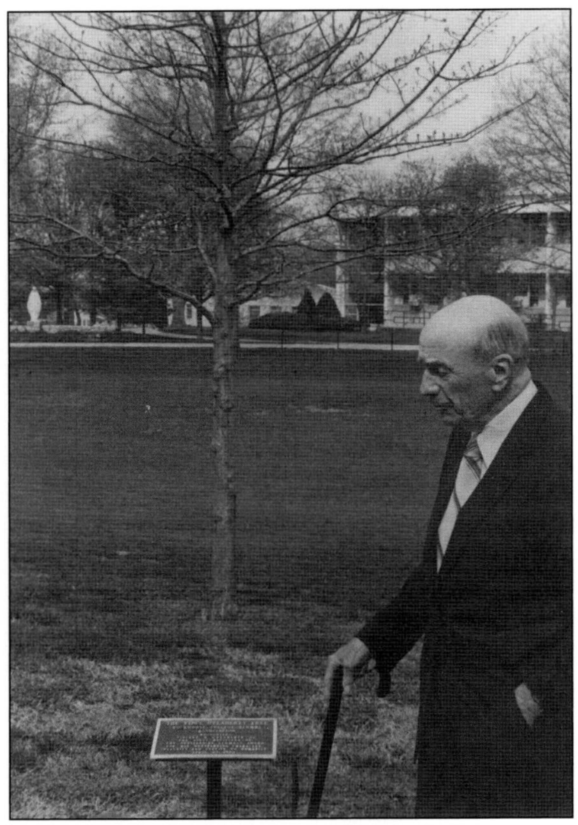

In 1982, Rockhurst honored Vincent J. O'Flaherty, who was in the first graduating class in 1921, with the planting of the "Vince O'Flaherty Tree" on the west side of the quad. Courtesy of Rockhurst University Archives.

drop as energy prices increased and inflation spiraled upward, reaching more than 13 percent in 1980.[53]

Rockhurst took steps to weather the times by trying to lure new students. By 1980, the college had added new academic majors in business economics, computer science, and business communication, as well as a new joint nursing degree program between Rockhurst and Research College of Nursing. The Evening Division had initiated new degree programs in real estate, savings and loan administration, and insurance, and a management center had been established to provide non-credit courses and workshops. Rockhurst had a new computer mainframe and was doing its best to keep up with campus maintenance. An underground sprinkler system had been installed for the intramural fields, and Mason-Halpin Fieldhouse had a new sound system. Dowling and Conway halls had new windows, and Xavier-Loyola had renovated rooms and corridors. Rockhurst also was remodeling the former U-Totem store at 54th and Troost for college offices.[54]

At a Board of Regents planning conference, Father Weiss stressed that Rockhurst "should not lose sight of promoting its image as the preeminent private institution in the area; an affordable alternative for the student who wants an extraordinary education." Rockhurst, he said, "must promote the distinctiveness of the institution's unique approach to education"—a liberal arts core that required not just knowledge, but wisdom...the ability to think and apply lessons learned. In January 1981, as Rockhurst prepared for its 10-year accreditation review by the North Central Association of Colleges and Schools, it reworked its mission statement, stating Rockhurst's first and foremost goal was "to strengthen our commitment to Judeo-Christian educational values in the Catholic and Jesuit tradition, respecting the pluralistic nature of our society and our student body."[55] The new mission statement spoke to the profound identity crisis that would continue to affect Catholic institutions into the new century. Many institutions, historian Philip Gleason writes, beginning with Notre Dame in 1973, drew up such statements as they looked at themselves anew after Vatican II.[56]

In the late spring of 1985, as Rockhurst approached its 75th anniversary, a 9-member committee comprising college deans, vice presidents, faculty, and the director of development, sat down to take a long look at Rockhurst's future. The committee met every other week that spring and by fall had written the draft of another comprehensive "Long Range Plan" for Rockhurst, this one for the years 1985-90. The report verified issues long discussed, chief among them the declining number of high school graduates. Indeed, in the fall of 1984, Rockhurst noted a 10 percent drop in the size of its freshman class—down to 375 freshmen from 417 in the fall of 1983. The number would fall another 5 percent (to 355) in the fall of 1985. "We will need," the committee wrote, "to make continuing and ever more creative efforts to reach new students and to retain those students who do enroll."[57] The committee set a goal of stabilizing freshman enrollment at 400 each fall, as well as boosting fall transfer enrollment to 150.

With globalization on the horizon, the committee also zeroed in on the core curriculum, reviewing it once again. Courses in the liberal arts, the committee stated, "should include a perspective which is less local, regional, and nationalistic." Rockhurst, it suggested, must look at courses focusing on cultures other than those of the West, put a greater emphasis on foreign languages, and make cross-cultural and/or global studies available to students in all areas, including business and the health fields. Special note was made of the new health science fields of medical technology, respiratory therapy, nursing, and physical therapy, which the committee said needed strengthening. In a departure from Rockhurst's long tradition of focusing on undergraduate education, the Long Range Planning Committee that spring of 1985 called on the college to begin offering post-baccalaureate summer courses for area teachers and to explore the establishment of a master of arts degree in the language arts and science. The only master's degree offered at the time was an M.B.A. through the School of Management. As the college made plans for these substantive changes from its liberal arts basis, it did so with its usual pragmatism and commitment to service to the region.

As it took stock, the committee noted gains in the professionalization of Rockhurst's faculty: in the College of Arts and Sciences, 75 percent now held a doctorate, and 55 percent in the School of Management. Rockhurst now employed 23 women faculty members (29 percent of the total), but only one full-time minority, a statistic the committee said Rockhurst had tried to improve "with little success." Alarmingly, the number of full-time Jesuits on the faculty continued to decline. In the 1984-85 academic year, there were only 15, 2 of whom already were older than 70 and 3 others fast

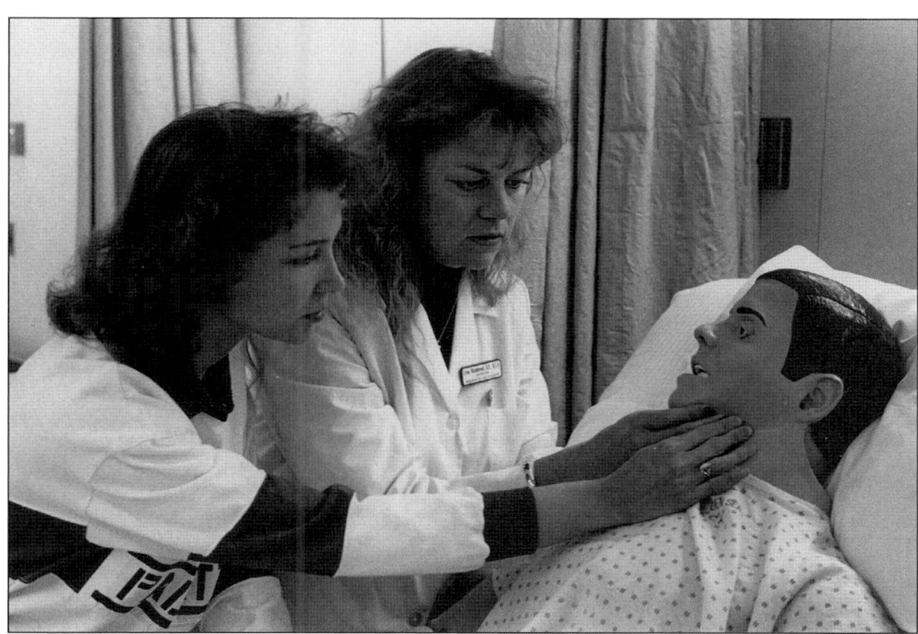

A joint nursing degree program between Rockhurst and Research College of Nursing began in 1980. Courtesy of Rockhurst University Archives.

— College Daze Reprised —

The student musical *College Daze* was originally produced by Jim Riley, '31, written by Jim McQueeny, '31, with music and lyrics by Frank Condon, '34. In 1980, to commemorate the 70th anniversary of the college, the Rockhurst College Players gave 3 performances of an updated version of the musical. Janet Watson Sheeran, then director of the theater program at Rockhurst, researched and reconstructed the script and music. Among other updates, the script substituted soccer for football and reflected the presence of women students on campus.

D. Frank Condon

The revival would have been impossible without the enthusiastic cooperation of the 3 men who originally wrote and produced the musical. The music and script had long disappeared from the Rockhurst archives, but Jim McQueeny still had a copy of the script, which he made available. In June 1980, Sheeran visited Frank Condon at his home in Louisiana. Condon, who had no formal training in music, recalled the tunes and played them on the piano for a tape-recording. From the recording, the songs were transcribed into sheet music. Condon died a short time later in August, and the 1980 production was dedicated to him.

Jim McQueeny (left) and Jim Riley (right) served as technical consultants for the revival of College Daze *in 1980.*

approaching, which intensified the committee's call to encourage interest in Rockhurst's Jesuit Apostolate. Rockhurst needed to "work closely with the appropriate Jesuit personnel directors," the committee said, and "obtain as soon as possible each year the list of Jesuits studying and the dates when they will be available."[58]

Though the future had yet to unfold, Rockhurst's planning committee recognized perhaps the 2 greatest trends of the coming decades—globalization and computer technology. In the recent past, Rockhurst had considered installing computers in the Learning Center, but the cost of hardware and the lack of adequate software had made it impractical. But now, as computer prices started to come down, the committee urged Rockhurst to explore the purchase of computers for the Learning Center, as well as a Computer Assisted Instruction (CAI) software program.

For all the many things that had changed during the years, Rockhurst's commitment to learning had not. In the appendix of the hefty report that looked ahead to the 1990s—and more immediately to Rockhurst's upcoming 75th anniversary—the committee reiterated the college's mission statement. Rockhurst was, No.1, it said, a learning community; No. 2, a liberal arts college; No. 3, a Catholic college; No. 4, a Jesuit college; and No. 5, a college involved in the city and the world.

— A SPECIAL ANNIVERSARY —

That the city and the world had much to learn from a Catholic college was the theme of Rockhurst's 75th Anniversary Convocation address, given on October 3, 1985, by Timothy Healy, S.J., president of the nation's oldest Jesuit university, Georgetown, founded in 1789. "Georgetown is standing proof, that there is life, lots of it, after 75," Healy began, undoubtedly with a smile.[59] The address that followed spoke to the tumultuous decades just passed and the important role played by the Catholic college. At 75, Rockhurst was a youngster, but it shared the same Catholic faith that works, Healy said, "to condition all learning, all teaching, all research." Rockhurst, like Georgetown, had responded to changing times, not by giving in to a secular society, but by adapting. Key was giving theology its rightful place in the curriculum, where, Healy said, it spoke "its wisdom to all other disciplines." Catholic colleges like Rockhurst were unique, he implied, because those other disciplines were free to speak back—imparting their own wisdom to theology. "In Catholic colleges theology leaves the seminary and the sacristy and moves into a mainstream of American intellectual discourse as a free citizen in a commonwealth of ideas, debate, challenge and investigation."

Nicholas Rashford, S.J., first dean of the School of Management, which was established in 1983. Rockhurst first began offering business classes in 1933 through its evening division. Within 6 years, the School of Commerce and Finance, as it was called, had enrolled over 500 students. Courtesy of Rockhurst University Archives.

Healy's address was one moment in a yearlong celebration during the 1985-86 academic year. Rockhurst's own Walter J. Ong, S.J., had delivered the "Homily for Mass on the Feast of St. Ignatius Loyola" the previous summer, and Kansas City businessman William E. Wall, chairman of the board and CEO of KPL Gas Service, in an address before the Kansas City Chamber of Commerce, had extolled Rockhurst's service to the business community.[60] There were faculty honors and colloquiums, student honors and student dances, a sports banquet, art exhibitions, concerts, and lectures by visiting scholars, including economist Jeremy Rifkin, Christian scholar Jaroslav Pelikan, and astronomer Owen Gingerich.

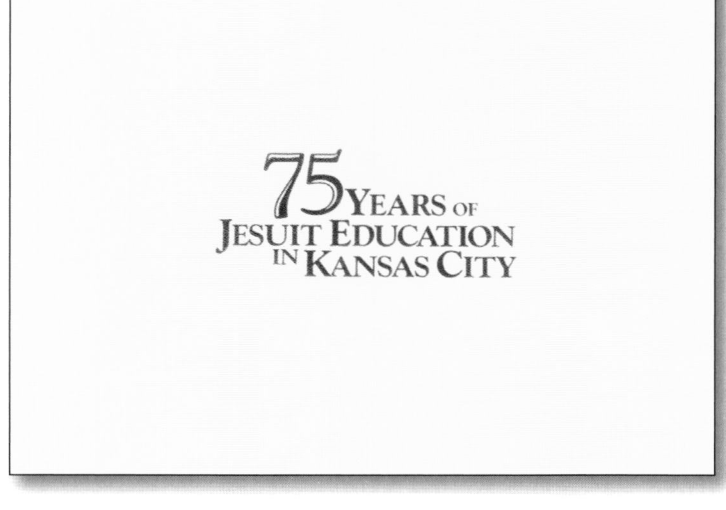

75 YEARS OF
JESUIT EDUCATION
IN KANSAS CITY

A highlight was the musical review *Best of Friends*, which hearkened back to that rollicking play, *College Daze*, first staged by students in 1929. The new playwright was Janet Watson Sheeran, professor of theater and later dean of the College of Arts and Sciences and interim president of the university. She had read Rockhurst history and hunted down every

— ROBERT J. IMBS, S.J. —

The Rev. Robert J. Imbs, S.J., was born November 1, 1916, and entered the Society of Jesus on September 1, 1938. He was ordained to the priesthood on June 14, 1949, and began his service at Rockhurst in 1952 as an instructor in history and speech. In addition to his service as a long-time history professor, Fr. Imbs was one of Rockhurst's first archivists, and served as the general chairman of the 50th anniversary celebration in 1960.

The dedication, imagination, and light-heartedness of Bob Imbs is captured in this resolution from the Senate of the state of Missouri: "Father Imbs who was known as a student's Professor, kind and generous to all who sought his counsel and advice, became one of the most popular professors ever to teach at Rockhurst College, and demonstrated to the entire Rockhurst college community and to everyone who met him wherever he went, the ability to address any problem, no matter who needed his help, not only with a scholarly and practical solution, but also with a smile and sense of humor that lightened the burdens of uncountable students and friends."

Characteristically, Fr. Imbs taught his class on the very day he passed away, September 21, 1985. The 1986 Rockhurst yearbook was dedicated to his memory.

Rockhurst song she could find.[61] She resurrected all the historical figures—Father Dowling and Bishop John Hogan as they tangled over the formation of St. Xavier Parish, Father Michael Ryan as he lived alone in the unfinished college building and labored in the quarry, and the mysterious Lee Sedgwick, wealthy businessman who seemed to come out of nowhere with the $25,000 Father Dowling needed to put the college building under roof. There was Brother Shaughnessy working single-handedly to level the college grounds, and here was Father Schwitalla unpacking boxes of chemistry equipment as he taught all of Rockhurst's first college classes. All the historical figures made an appearance: Rockhurst President John Weiand conferring an honorary degree on the World War I hero Marshal Ferdinand Foch, and presidents Spillard and Manion struggling unsuccessfully to gain college accreditation. Here were the ghosts of Pat Mason and Eddie Halpin, and President Daniel Conway dedicating a fieldhouse named in their honor. Here was John Friedl creating Rockhurst's Institute of Social Order and President Thomas Knapp hauling surplus War World II barracks to campus. Father Van arrived with a flourish and a song, intent on building Rockhurst into a university.

Watch out for Father Van
A most outstanding man
He's always on the town
He never lets us down
Friends nurtured, prayers attained
Plans launched for Rockhurst's fame
When Maurice Van Ackeren
Came to town.

Sheeran's play never missed a beat, taking the audience right up to the present, as President Robert Weiss spoke of Vatican II and the new age of self-direction. Here was the first women's basketball team at Rockhurst, the new Van Ackeren Gallery, and the hum of computers. How far Rockhurst had come since that first college curriculum focused on Latin and Greek. And how things had changed.

To mark Rockhurst's 75th anniversary, the *Jesuit Bulletin* interviewed Registrar Paul Arend, who had spent more than 40 years at Rockhurst. He had been at Rockhurst so long that he had watched argyles and baggy pants go out of style and then come back in. But some things had not changed, Arend said. "We haven't changed in the fact that we're Catholic," he said. "We haven't changed our emphasis on values. We haven't changed our interest in the personal educational growth of each student. We haven't changed our emphasis on philosophy and theology. We haven't changed our emphasis on community and thinking." What Rockhurst had done, Arend said, was to adjust.

That ability to adjust was evident from the earliest days when Rockhurst adopted an initial 4-year curriculum that offered modern subjects such as bookkeeping and chemistry, as well as the classics. It was, former student Sean Brennan argues in the *Missouri Historical Review*, a way to survive in a turn-of-the-century Kansas City that saw a university education as practical preparation for a future career.[62] Rockhurst had continued to adapt, whether that meant compromising with neighbors to get a parking lot built or establishing a new system of governance to embrace the ideals of the Vatican II Council and to keep in step with a changing culture.

Yes, 75 years was a long time. But there is life, lots of it, after 75.

As part of Rockhurst's 75th anniversary celebration, memorabilia were placed in a TimeBox in the wall of Massman Hall. Items in the TimeBox were reopened and displayed in 2010 for the 100th anniversary celebration. Photo by David Spaw.

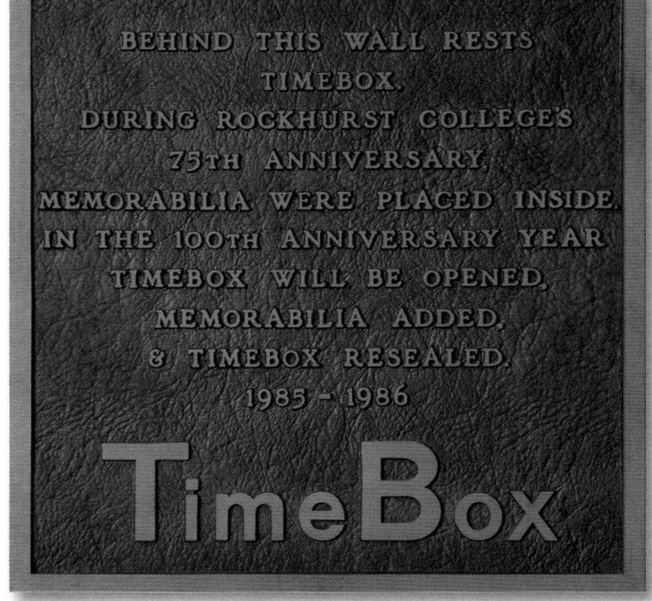

BEHIND THIS WALL RESTS
TIMEBOX.
DURING ROCKHURST COLLEGE'S
75TH ANNIVERSARY,
MEMORABILIA WERE PLACED INSIDE.
IN THE 100TH ANNIVERSARY YEAR
TIMEBOX WILL BE OPENED,
MEMORABILIA ADDED,
& TIMEBOX RESEALED.
1985 - 1986
TimeBox

ROCKHURST
UNIVERSITY

Chapter Thirteen

An Invitation to Excellence 1986–96

As Rockhurst President Robert Weiss, S.J., sat down in March 1986 to compose his annual letter to parents and students, he wrote on stationery stamped with a special letterhead: "75 Years of Jesuit Education in Kansas City: Rockhurst College." The yearlong anniversary celebration had caused him to reflect on the college's "great heritage" and brought home, he said, "how generously the Lord has blessed Rockhurst over the past three-quarters of a century." There was much to be proud of—not the least of which was inclusion in a recent book by *The New York Times* education editor Ed Fiske, listing Rockhurst as among the "best buys in college education."[1]

Affordability had become a major theme in higher education as spiraling costs for everything from health care to liability insurance forced colleges and universities across the nation to announce yearly increases in the price of tuition. To make matters worse, student financial aid seemed in jeopardy as the Reagan administration instituted widespread domestic budget reductions, forcing states and localities to cope with cuts in federal grants, including those for education. Complicating matters was a soaring federal deficit that would triple during the Reagan years, reaching $2.8 trillion by 1989.[2]

By May 1991, "tuition shock" was making headlines in *The Kansas City Star,* which reported that parents of a 5-year-old child that spring

President Robert Weiss, S.J., and students. The spiraling cost of education—accompanied by a declining pool of college-age youth—created competition for students. Enrollment concerns dominated talk at Rockhurst in the 1980s and beyond. Courtesy of Rockhurst University Archives.

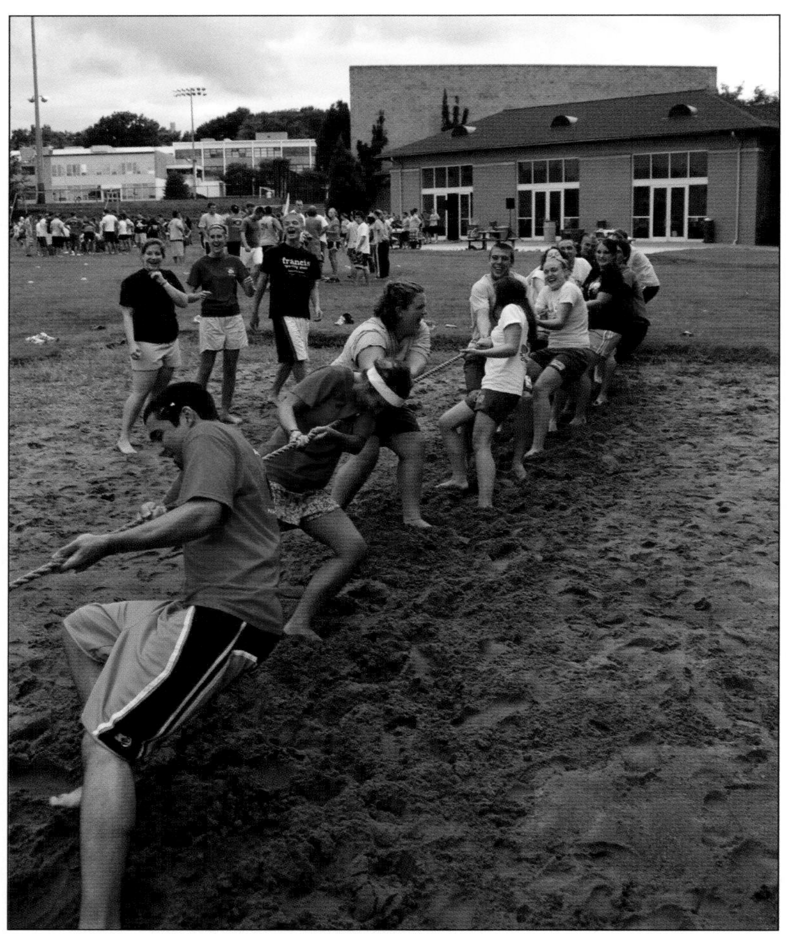

Freshman orientation. Courtesy of Rockhurst University Archives.

would have to save $164 a month during the next dozen years to be able to afford to send the child to an in-state public college. The story was direr for parents looking at private colleges, where tuition costs had more than tripled nationwide.[3] Rockhurst had not been spared. The college's premium for liability insurance alone had nearly tripled in the 1986-87 academic year, despite, President Weiss explained, "a sharp reduction in coverage." Health costs were up 60 percent and retirement benefits 20 percent. To cover expenses and preserve the quality of education, Father Weiss announced a tuition increase to $2,670 per semester for the 1986-87 academic year. Room and board charges would vary, but would increase an average of 7 percent, based on the individual student's accommodations and meal plan.[4]

Parents must have sighed at the news, seeing as they had not been spared a tuition increase during any academic year of the 1980s. Tuition had risen yearly—from $1,450 a semester in the 1980-81 academic year to $2,450 a semester by 1985-86. Throughout the 1980s, tuition would increase an average 10 percent every year. President Weiss acknowledged the sacrifices made by parents to keep their children at Rockhurst. "Your trust in us is gratifying and humbling," he wrote that spring of 1986. "I assure you that we will strive to be worthy of your confidence." There would be no letup in financial worries as Rockhurst watched the federal grants and loans received by its students drop from 48 percent of tuition costs in 1981 to 26 percent as the 1990s got under way.[5] By the 1989-90 academic year, tuition stood at $3,425 a semester and would continue to spiral upward, reaching $5,775 a semester by the fall of 1997.

The spiraling cost of education—accompanied by a declining pool of college-age youth—created a situation so serious that the National Association of Independent Colleges and Universities declared in 1992 that the very survival of institutions was at stake. Not since the Great Depression, it said, had demographic and economic factors put higher education at greater risk. It went on to list 4 "key challenges" facing schools: competition for students, the state fiscal crunch, student and faculty diversity, and federal policy malaise.[6]

Despite the ever-escalating costs, Rockhurst was affordable compared to many other private colleges, including other Jesuit institutions in the United States. This was a point of pride that would be noted repeatedly in the literature Rockhurst distributed to the public—and a key to the college's growing reputation. In his annual letter for 1987, for instance, President Weiss noted that Rockhurst's $2,670 tuition ranked "well below" the national average for independent colleges and universities and was one of the least expensive of the nation's 28 Jesuit institutions. Specifically, he compared Rockhurst to non-Jesuit Notre Dame, where tuition was $4,300; Boston College at $5,160; and Saint Louis University at $3,060. Rockhurst charged less than Denver's Regis, at $3,468, and Omaha's Creighton, at $2,787.[7]

— LOOKING FOR STUDENTS —

Enrollment concerns dominated talk at Rockhurst, just as it did at other colleges across the country. "The concern is real and should head our list of the issues we face at Rockhurst," then President Thomas Savage, S.J., wrote in his mid-summer report of 1991. Nationwide, the number of high school graduates had been declining for 15 years running (except for a slight respite in 1988 and 1989) and wasn't expected to let up until 1994.[8] Preliminary figures at the University of Missouri-Columbia showed an enrollment decline of 4.7 percent for the fall of 1993. At the University of Kansas, the decline came in at 1.5 percent, which KU Chancellor Gene Budig blamed on "the fragile economy." Continuing education students, he said, had dropped out to get jobs, with the idea of returning to their studies when possible.

But then, the job market for college graduates, *The Kansas City Star* reported, was "in the midst of its worst slump in 50 years." At the University of Missouri-Kansas City, where preliminary enrollment was down 6 percent, spokeswoman Barbara Smith noted that more students seemed to be choosing community colleges for 2 years before transferring to 4-year programs. She also attributed the decline to enrollment caps in business and education programs—a statement surely noted at nearby Rockhurst, where the business program had long been a strength. Just months before, in fact, Rockhurst had received a $2.5 million grant from the Hall Family Foundation to help its School of Management, founded in 1983, achieve national recognition. Plans already were under way to add faculty, develop programs, upgrade classrooms, and renovate Conway Hall, the school's home.[9]

The grant said much about Rockhurst's ongoing efforts to raise funds and, as it always had done, survive troubled times. "These are the lean years," President Savage wrote in the summer of 1991 as the college ended its fiscal year with no surplus funds. But always a man of action, Father Savage seemed to thrive on the challenge. He set to work instituting what was being called "enrollment management." He pushed to get students from overseas and to incorporate part-time and evening students into campus life. He set retention of students as a goal, hired a new multicultural affairs specialist, and succeeded in getting the Board of Trustees to create the Rockhurst College Continuing Education Center, which would focus on offering non-credit continuing education courses, which he was certain would extend Rockhurst's mission and identity.[10]

Tellingly, even as Rockhurst's neighbors—public institutions at that—reported enrollment declines in the fall of 1993, Rockhurst spokesman Bob Jacobi told the press that Rockhurst was expecting an increase of 200

Paul Arend, Class of '42, began working at Rockhurst in 1947. In 1951, he was appointed registrar, a position he held until his retirement in 1986. Arend died in 1992. Courtesy of Rockhurst University Archives.

1986 men's soccer team at the national tournament in Wichita Falls, Texas. Front row, left to right: Tim Dockery, Dan DuFour, Dan Mueth, Andrew Janson, Dan Anglim, Rick Pearce, Jim Mosquedo, Dan Janson, John Ross. Back row, left to right: Tony Tocco, coach, John Knox, John Makowski, Mark Visconti, Mike Cucchi, Rick Schaeffer, John Hungerford, Kevin Koetters, Paul Martin, Steve Nikodem, Kurt Schoen, Kevin Eleeson, Brian McChessney. Courtesy of Rockhurst University Archives.

students. He attributed the gain "mostly to increased recruiting efforts." Student numbers were extremely important at Rockhurst, which, unlike its neighbors, received no taxpayer subsidy. As a private college, it counted on tuition to fund nearly three-quarters of its budget.[11]

Rockhurst's efforts to hold down tuition and find ways to increase the in-house financial aid it offered certainly played a role in the enrollment jump as well. In the 1984-85 academic year, Rockhurst budgeted $726,278 for financial aid. During the next 5 years, the Board of Trustees budgeted more and more money to help students finance their education, until, by the 1989-90 academic year, the money had more than doubled—to $1.5 million. That year, the college also offered more loans at lower interest rates, higher work study wages, and a 10 percent tuition reduction for families with more than one child attending Rockhurst simultaneously.[12]

As Rockhurst worked to attract students, it also kept its eye on the quality of those students and on its own resolve for excellence. As early as January 1981, with a worsening economy, students banked on finding a job by majoring in business. As they swelled Rockhurst's Business Division and as the Kansas City business community funneled money into the School of Management, the Board of Trustees was concerned enough about the college's liberal arts and sciences program that it requested a study intended to safeguard and promote Rockhurst's identity as a liberal arts institution.

A committee of 4 professors and Arts and Sciences Dean Raymond A. Schroth, S.J., met during the course of the second semester of 1981 to begin what they called "an intellectual and practical dialogue" to deal honestly with Rockhurst's strengths and weaknesses. It was, the committee wrote, "an invitation to excellence," a recognition that "good as we are, we are not as good as we can be."[13] This willingness to look at itself honestly had become a hallmark of the college. Hadn't Father Conway looked square in the eye at Rockhurst's deficiencies as he struggled to gain accreditation? And hadn't Father Van Ackeren listened patiently, and then responded, to student criticisms in the 1960s? These many years later, Rockhurst continued to look within, to reassess, and to ask itself how it could improve.

The 5-member committee came back that year of 1981 with a startling conclusion—Rockhurst was "at a critical point in its history," and unless it made a strong effort to bolster arts and sciences, it would become, one consultant said, "primarily a business and pre-professional or professional school." The challenge was clear to John W. Padberg, S.J., president of Weston College of Theology and a professor of church history there. "Rockhurst," he told the committee, "is a good college poised at the edge of being other." It stood on a plateau and faced the danger of remaining there unless action was taken to tip the scale back to one of Rockhurst's greatest and most long-standing strengths: its ability to maintain a balance between liberal and career-oriented education. Bottom line, the balance had tipped toward the Business Division, and Rockhurst must, the committee concluded, improve the strength and quality of its liberal arts college. The committee urged the faculty to renew its commitment to teaching and to find ways to increase its scholarly activity, a call that would require a greater commitment of time and money from the administration and Board of Trustees. Research grants, travel grants, teaching improvement grants, and money to support faculty development projects would be needed. The committee called for items as big as curriculum revision and as small as an expanded faculty lounge or college-owned house set aside as a faculty club.

A 5-member committee of 4 professors and Arts and Sciences dean, Raymond A. Schroth, S.J., met during the course of the second semester of 1981 to take an honest look at Rockhurst's strengths and weaknesses. Among other recommendations, the committee urged faculty to find ways to increase its scholarly output, something that would require a greater commitment of time and money. In 1987, as a result of the generosity of Daniel Brenner (pictured), longtime regent and friend of the college, the Daniel L. Brenner award for outstanding scholarship was established to support and recognize faculty scholarly achievements. Courtesy of Rockhurst University Archives.

The Rockhurst administration apparently took the evaluation seriously because a recommendation that the college establish an endowed chair for a distinguished visiting scholar was answered as early as January 1986 when President Weiss announced that retiring U.S. Senator Thomas Eagleton, a Missouri Democrat, had accepted an offer to teach political science seminars at Rockhurst, starting in January 1987. Eagleton, who had served in the Senate for nearly 20 years, was a graduate of Harvard Law School. A committee led by Kansas City businessman Morton I. Sosland got busy raising money to build an endowment for the new visiting professorship.[14] Just a month later came word that Rockhurst, with financial help once again from Mrs. Virginia Greenlease, had established its first endowed academic chair for a full-time faculty member in honor of Joseph Freeman, S.J., who had been teaching philosophy and theology at Rockhurst for 40 years. Father Freeman held the chair for the next dozen years. The School of Management also established its first endowed chair in 1986—the George and Gladys Miller Chair in Business Administration, which was unveiled at the annual Honorary Directors dinner. Accounting professor Anthony Tocco was the first to hold this chair.[15]

Retiring U.S. Senator Thomas Eagleton, a Missouri Democrat, accepted an offer in 1986 to teach political science seminars at Rockhurst as a visiting professor. Courtesy of Rockhurst University Archives.

— CORE QUESTIONS —

Before the 1980s were over, Rockhurst took up other committee recommendations, including an examination of the core curriculum. Not to be left out of the discussion was the evening division, where a review would recommend bringing evening division course requirements in line with those of the day division. Specifically, it was recommended that students in the evening division be required to complete the same coursework in theology and natural science as day students—courses not required as late as the spring of 1989. The change was deemed necessary if Rockhurst were to remain true to its mission and purpose and to the college's claim that a bachelor's degree earned by an adult student in the evening was no different from a bachelor's degree earned in traditional day classes.[16]

Rockhurst continued to study its core curriculum into the summer of 1989 and beyond. Faculty discussion centered on the purposes of undergraduate education and the distinctions between general education and liberal education. How, members of a review task force asked in the summer of 1989, should the curriculum reflect the mission—or identity—of a Catholic institution like Rockhurst? Was there any conflict in expressing Rockhurst's Jesuit character and at the same time fulfilling the goals and standards of contemporary American higher education? These were weighty questions, as was understanding and implementing a particular approach to curriculum—should it take an "outcomes/assessment" perspective (in which student achievement was measured and assessed in some way); a "canon" approach (which emphasized a major body of knowledge and the great works); or a "critical issues" approach (which sought to prepare students for the contemporary world)?

Debate over the right core curriculum for Rockhurst continued well into the 1990s, creating heated discussion as the faculty tried to reach consensus. In the Jesuit tradition, some viewed the college's purpose as furthering the development of human beings in the pursuit of knowledge and truth. They believed strongly that the core curriculum must, therefore, require extensive study in theology and philosophy. This requirement, in fact, was identified as the very thing that set Rockhurst apart from other colleges. Rockhurst had made that clear for years, and certainly since the times of Vatican II and the turbulent years of the 1960s. But the issue seemed unresolved as some faculty members called on Rockhurst to adapt to changing times. They wanted fewer required courses in the core—particularly when it came to theology and philosophy. As a professional school, the Research College of Nursing, in partnership with Rockhurst since 1979, had long been granted core curriculum exceptions, and it, especially, was upset that this might change under curriculum revisions. Other faculty members wanted more emphasis in the curriculum on contemporary issues they regarded as critical, such as racism, sexism, and other types of social injustice.

Appalachia service project, 1987. For several years prior to his death in 1993, William Finucane, S.J., director of campus ministry, took students to work in Appalachia over their spring break. Since 1993, the Finucane Service Project has been a highlight of the freshman orientation experience. Courtesy of Rockhurst University Archives.

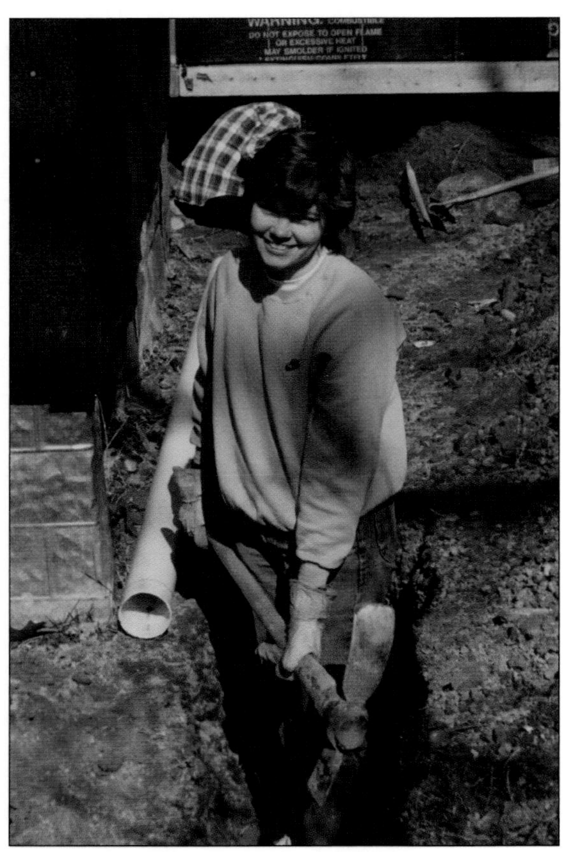

On December 8, 1992, when the Faculty General Assembly voted on the core curriculum, it came out in support of what was being called the "baseline model." The existing core was built around "ways of knowing." The new "baseline model" was essentially a modification of the old core with a new rationale—"ways of knowing" became "modes of inquiry" with new distribution requirements. Also, students were required to demonstrate proficiency in oral and written communication and in mathematics.

— J. Ernest Dunn —

The Rev. Joseph E. Gough, S.J., once called Ernie Dunn "one of God's most great and humble servants." In his lifetime, Rockhurst made many attempts to confer honors on Dunn, but each time he refused the recognition. One year after his death in 1965, he received, posthumously, Rockhurst's Pro Meritis Award.

The J.E. Dunn Construction Company, founded by Ernie in 1924, is today the largest general contractor in Kansas City and one of the largest in the United States. Typical of Ernie's philanthropic spirit, during World War II he refused to accept any profits on a number of government projects. Always one to accept and carry out responsibilities with distinction, Dunn served as the second chairman of the Board of Regents. His legacy, however, is mostly associated with 5 major buildings on campus and Rockhurst High School, all of which are tributes to his leadership and generosity.

The Dunn family has continued the legacy of leadership and support for Rockhurst. Ernie's son William (Bill) H. Dunn, Sr., Class of '46, served on the first lay Board of Trustees at Rockhurst and is currently an Honorary Trustee. All of Bill Dunn's 5 sons have attended Rockhurst University. His son Terrence (Terry) P. Dunn, Class of '71, is currently a member of the Rockhurst Board of Trustees and his daughter Mary Ellen Daly, whose life was also shaped by Rockhurst, has remained supportive of the university, both in honor of her father and her husband Roy Daly, Class of '42.

The new curriculum reduced the number of required core courses in theology and philosophy. The meeting that day had been contentious, with faculty members so divided and feelings so raw that theology professor Donald J. Murphy, S.J., who had been at Rockhurst since 1978, was upset enough to write a long letter to the Rockhurst president. He stated that the meeting was so tense that he had felt "around me a kind of coldness and absence of communication that I have seldom experienced in my life."[17] Feelings were so strong, perhaps most decidedly for Jesuits like Father Murphy, because calls to reduce the number of hours from the core curriculum in theology and philosophy put at stake the very identity of Rockhurst as a Jesuit institution. "After what happened during the first semester of this year," Father Murphy wrote, "I am less sanguine than I had been about the future Jesuit identity of Rockhurst."

Upset as Father Murphy was, he could, perhaps, take comfort in knowing that the issue was not just a Rockhurst one, but one shared by institutions nationwide as colleges and universities tried to maintain strength in the liberal arts while at the same time recognizing that more and more students were majoring in professional disciplines. When Father Murphy poured out his concerns to fellow Jesuit George F. Lundy, who had served for 6 years as academic vice president at Loyola University in New Orleans, he found a man of like mind who agreed that it was important that

In 1986, Kansas City artist Frank Szasz donated a mural-size portrait of Mother Teresa to Rockhurst. Szasz taught at Rockhurst in the 1960s, and a number of his works can be seen on campus, including portraits of Mark Twain, Albert Schweitzer, Albert Einstein, and Pedro Aruppe, S.J. The Mother Teresa portrait hangs on the north wall of Greenlease Library. Photo by David Spaw.

Rockhurst's liberal arts core apply equally to all students. Although the "baseline model" did not appeal to Father Murphy, Lundy pointed out that the Rockhurst faculty had at least been able to decide on a core that applied to all—School of Nursing, School of Management, and College of Arts and Sciences alike. This, he wrote, was not the case with every other Jesuit college. "I believe the faculty of Rockhurst have done much," Lundy wrote, "to advance the commitment to the College's mission by working out, albeit painfully, a core that will apply to all of its undergraduate majors." The new core curriculum was implemented in 1994.[18]

As these important academic and philosophical decisions took place internally, Rockhurst, externally, continued to focus on its physical needs—from buying up property for future expansion to adding and improving its buildings. The Conference Center addition to Massman Hall, with its improved dining areas and beautiful Mabee Chapel, had been dedicated in October 1984, and Mason-Halpin Fieldhouse was renovated in 1986, the same year that local artist Frank Szasz donated his mural-size portrait of Mother Teresa to Rockhurst. It was installed on the north wall of Greenlease Library that spring.[19]

— A Tradition of Arts and Letters —

Greenlease Library had been a home to art ever since it opened in 1967, when what was known as the Treasury Room held a collection of religious art from the fifteenth through eighteenth centuries, much of it donated to the college by Robert and Virginia Greenlease. As the collection grew in museum quality pieces, the Treasury Room was transformed (by the same architects who designed the fourth floor of the Nelson Art Gallery) into what was named the Van Ackeren Gallery, in honor of Father Van. It formally opened on May 23, 1975, with 14 artworks, including paintings, a baroque silver chalice, a velvet half-chasuble circa 1450, a pieta, and an ornately carved Italian prie-dieu.[20] By 1980, the collection comprised 22 pieces of religious art, including Tiepolo's *St. Mark the Evangelist,* Crespi's *The Holy Family,* and Il Bacchiacca's *Madonna and Child with the Infant Saint John*. Rockhurst turned to the gallery in the holiday season, reproducing 2 pieces on Christmas cards. A local TV station also came by at Christmastime and telecast the religious art into Kansas City living rooms.[21]

As early as 1970, with the hiring of artist Robert Bailey as a faculty member, Rockhurst could boast an artist-in-residence. Bailey's paintings and drawings would be featured in the gallery in Massman Hall.[22] That same year of 1970, when London Grafica Arts stopped at Rockhurst on its tour of U.S. campuses, it was in Massman Hall that it set up its collection of 500 original graphics—from the old masters to the modern, as well as a wide range of contemporary prints, offered for sale from $10 to $3,000.[23]

Massman Hall was the scene of ongoing cultural events at Rockhurst. In the spring semester of 1986 alone, as part of the 75th anniversary celebration, Massman hosted 5 art exhibitions, the first hosted by faculty from sister school Creighton University.[24] The paintings of local artist Marijana Grisnik went on display the following fall as part of a springboard for discussion of immigration, family, religion, neighborhoods, and "becoming American." The discussions were part of a symposium held that November on the nearby University of Missouri-Kansas City campus.[25] Rockhurst also joined that same fall with William Jewell College to sponsor "Ceremonies in Dark Old Men," a presentation at the Folly Theater downtown by the nationally recognized Negro Ensemble Company.[26]

The Van Ackeren Gallery formally opened on May 23, 1975, with 14 works of art, including this baroque silver chalice. Courtesy of Greenlease Gallery.

While the Massman Gallery displayed works of art, Massman Hall also hosted the ongoing Midwest Poets Series, which celebrated its twenty-fifth anniversary in 2008. Over the years, the series brought top fiction writers, poets, and essayists to campus, from Kansas City's own David Ray, past editor of Kansas City's *New Letters* magazine and host of KCUR-FM's "New Letters on the Air," to writer Jane Smiley and poet Grace Paley (1990-91), to Pulitzer Prize-winning poets W.S. Merwin and Henry Taylor (1999), to Poets Laureate of the United States, including Billy Collins (2002) and Charles Simic (2009).[27]

Rockhurst formed a Committee on the Arts, which kicked off its "Season of the Arts," in September 1985 with the 12-member New American Ragtime Ensemble, which brought its brass, flutes, and percussion to Mabee Theater and recreated the time when Scott Joplin was all the rage.[28] The Season of the Arts, founded in 1977 by English professor Robert R. Burke, S.J., became a Rockhurst tradition, which, over the years, would aim to highlight cultural diversity by bringing a series of events to campus each year. In the spring of 1995, for instance, the series brought the Harlem Spiritual Ensemble and the Athol Rugard play, *My Children! My Africa!*, to campus, as well as 3 Native American sisters who composed the Spiderwoman Theater.[29]

In 1992, Billy Collins, Poet Laureate of the United States, appeared at Rockhurst as part of the Midwest Poets Series, which celebrated its 25th anniversary in 2008. Photo by Joann Carney. Courtesy of Rockhurst University Archives.

Rockhurst's own drama group, the Rockhurst Players, performed as well, staging plays such as Paul Zindel's *The Effect of Gamma Rays on Man-in-the-Moon Marigolds* to the classic *Our Town*.[30] As early as the 1975-76 academic year, Father Burke invited English majors and other interested students to join him on a trip to New York City to see live theater productions.[31] The cultural scene on campus that year included a visit by the Royal Lichtenstein Circus, run by Nick Weber, S.J., and a presentation of American Indian dancing, singing, and crafts by students from Haskell Indian Junior College in nearby Lawrence, Kansas.[32] Rockhurst also offered on-campus films for students. In the mid-1970s, they included the popular *Deliver-*

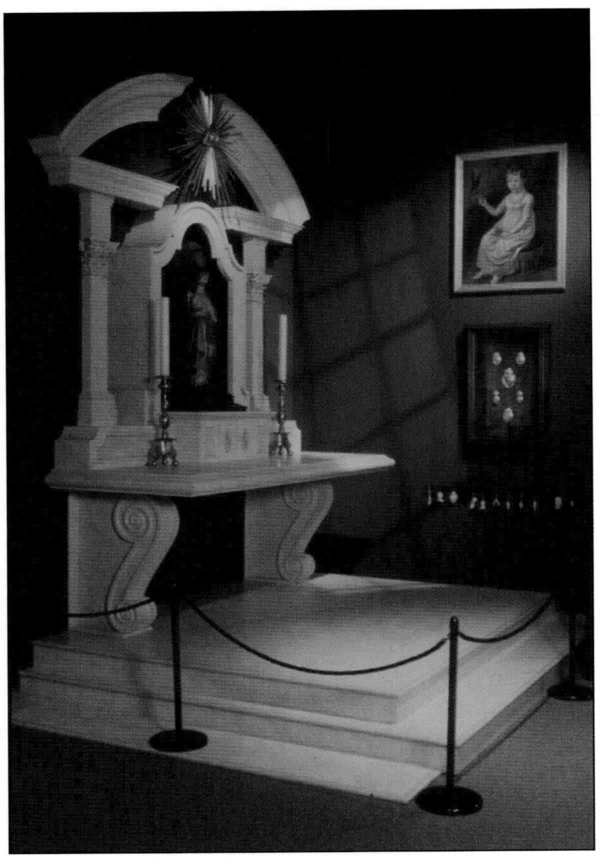

Sacred Encounters, a multimedia traveling exhibit, opened at Rockhurst's south campus on April 23, 1994, and remained for 4 months. The exhibit featured drawings by Nicholas Point, the Jesuit who, in 1840, had ministered to the people at Kawsmouth and to the traders and merchants in the town of Westport. Photo by Roy Inman. Courtesy of Rockhurst University Archives.

ance and *Jeremiah Johnson*, as well as a series of assertiveness training films for women.

Popular exhibits of the 1990s included the highly acclaimed *Sacred Encounters: An Exhibit of Father De-Smet and the Indians of the Rocky Mountains,* a $1.7 million, 7,000-square-foot multimedia traveling exhibit that opened on Rockhurst's south campus on April 23, 1994, and remained for 4 months. The exhibit featured maps drawn by Peter DeSmet, S.J., and drawings by the Jesuit Nicholas Point, who accompanied DeSmet on his journey in 1841 to the Salish, Coeur d'Alene, Kalispell, Spokane, Sanpoil, and Kootenai peoples, who welcomed Jesuit missionaries to their homes in the northern Rocky Mountains. Nicholas Point, the year before joining Father DeSmet, had ministered to the mixed-race people at Kawsmouth and to the traders and merchants in the budding town of Westport. In addition to maps and drawings, visitors to the *Sacred Encounters* exhibit saw objects such as Father DeSmet's crucifix and a native American ceremonial pipe—2 different expressions of the holy, a sacred encounter.

Rockhurst President Thom Savage, S.J., was there for the opening ceremonies, as were Kansas City-St. Joseph Bishop Raymond Boland and Salish tribal member Myrna Adams, who gave the opening Native American blessing. Fittingly, it was a Rockhurst Jesuit, professor emeritus Vincent Daues, S.J., who gave the opening Catholic blessing. After all, it had been Jesuits—from Nicholas Point to Michael Dowling—who had worked so hard to bring the Catholic message to Kansas City, be it to the Indian people at Kawsmouth or the Irish in the West Bottoms. And it was the Jesuit Rockhurst College that had sponsored, jointly with the Kansas City Museum, the *Sacred Encounters'* visit to Kansas City. The Missouri Province's Midwest Jesuit Archives in St. Louis had played an instrumental role as well. It was there that historian and exhibit creator Jacqueline Peterson had been inspired by the archives' collection of DeSmet maps.[33] When another popular exhibit, *Treasures of the Czars,* set up in Topeka, Kansas the following year, Rockhurst's Center for Arts and Letters, founded in 1989, sponsored a tour.[34]

The Rockhurst campus always seemed alive with activities, be it the annual President's holiday party, with refreshments, music, and dancing in the Rock Room,[35] or a science camp that brought schoolchildren to campus. In June of 1990, the quad bustled with little scientists who tested their rockets there. The K-8 students were part of a camp sponsored by Rockhurst and SHARE in Science Education Inc.[36] Additionally, Rockhurst biology professor Richard E. Wilson, who in 1993 would be named Missouri Professor of the Year, founded Rockhurst's Science Knowledge Bowl, which by 1996 was drawing as many as 900 high school students to campus to compete based on their knowledge of science. Winners went on to the national competition held in Washington, D.C.[37]

Rockhurst's Department of Mathematics and Computer Science also reached out to area students. In May 1985, teams from 6 area high schools arrived on campus to compete in a computer-programming contest using the PASCAL language. Shawnee Mission West emerged victorious in the 3-hour contest to solve 10 programming problems.[38] The PASCAL language had gone through a number of revisions by 1995 when the Rockhurst faculty launched its first Computer Fair for middle and high school students. On Saturday, March 11, 1995, the Convocation Center buzzed with computers as more than 50 teams from area schools demonstrated their computer knowledge, from programming to graphics.[39]

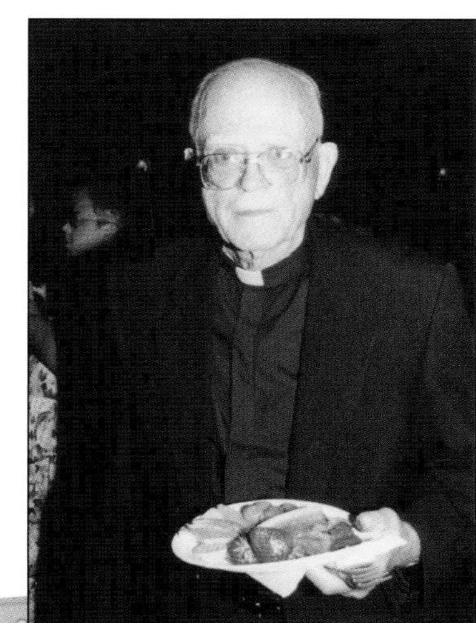

Father Maurice Van Ackeren, S.J., on the occasion of his 60th year as a Jesuit, September, 1992. Courtesy of Rockhurst University Archives.

Events on campus were ongoing through the years, from an Alcohol Awareness Week in 1986, which found faculty members and staff driving golf carts around cones, to a Galileo symposium, to the semi-annual Robert W. Miller speech competition for members of the introductory communication class. The competition, won that December of 1986 by student Sean Phelan, was held in honor of longtime Rockhurst speech teacher, Robert Miller.[40]

Through the 1990s, Rockhurst would sponsored annual events such as the holiday Ceremony of Lessons and Carols concert at St. Francis Xavier Church and the Safe Trick-or-Treat Halloween party and haunted house for neighborhood and employee families. In 1997, the party was held in the Security Department parking lot at 5401 Troost Avenue and featured a visit from McGruff the Dog, a fortune-teller, and Dracula, plus candy, food, drinks, and prizes.[41]

A highlight of every year was the annual Rockhurst University Gala, first held on February 24, 1996, in the Count Basie Ballroom of the downtown Marriott. The black-tie event, which featured a gourmet dinner and ballroom dancing, was organized by Rockhurst's Volunteer Council, which comprised representatives from all of the university's volunteer groups, such as the Alumni Association, Library Guild, and Honorary Directors. Former Rockhurst professor Ursula Pfahl and her husband, Kurt Pfahl, a retired executive for Hallmark Cards, took on responsibility as the gala's first co-chairs, along with Patty and Charles Garney. Mrs. Garney was a prominent civic leader in Kansas City North, and Mr. Garney was the head of construction and development companies. The 2 couples and their more than 40 volunteers enlisted corporate sponsors such as Sprint and Western Resources Inc., which contributed $5,000 each, and a number of other corporations, including Hallmark, Deloitte & Touche LLP, the Andrews & McMeel Founda-

Thomas F. Denzer, S.J., professor of economics, visits with students on the quad. Fr. Denzer served more than 40 years at Rockhurst, retiring in 2002. Courtesy of Rockhurst University Archives.

Paul O. Smith, S.J., had two stints of service at Rockhurst, for a total of 39 years. From 1941-62, he served as athletic director. He returned to Rockhurst in 1968 to work in admissions and campus ministry. Nicknamed "Stoney" by students, Smith later lived in McGee Hall. When he retired to St. Louis at age 83, a 5-story high sign made of bed sheets hung from McGee, which read, "We Love You, Stoney." Fr. Smith was one of the founders of the National Association of Intercollegiate Athletics (NAIA), a member of the NAIA Hall of Fame, and a charter inductee in Rockhurst's Athletics Hall of Fame. He died in 1993. Courtesy of Rockhurst University Archives.

tion, and Helzberg Diamond Shops, to sponsor corporate tables at $2,000 each. Another 36 individuals, couples, and companies paid $1,000 each for a personal table. The first gala was a huge success, raising $82,300 for Greenlease Library and launching an annual event that by 2002 had raised more than $1 million, not only for the library, but also for funding scholarships and student service trips to Guatemala, Mexico, and Belize.[42]

— SOURCES OF STRENGTH —

Rockhurst organizations—from the Honorary Directors to the Rockhurst Circle, Sanctuary Guild, and Library Guild—continued to be a source of strength to the college, and, as the years advanced, Rockhurst traditions posted milestones. In 1975-76, the Visiting Scholar Program celebrated its twentieth year with a photography display of outstanding scholars from the past. The exhibit was provided through the courtesy of photographer Charles Brenneke, a 1939 Rockhurst graduate.[43] That same year, the Honorary Directors Association, which had announced its 1,000th member (Leo D. Mullin, Class of '38) 15 years earlier, funded $64,480 in scholarships to 295 students. During its 4 decades at Rockhurst, the association had provided more than $1 million in financial aid to students.[44]

The Rockhurst Circle continued its monthly luncheons and card parties, placing the proceeds into its Rockhurst Circle Scholarship Fund, which assisted talented students who could not otherwise go to college. In 1972-73, the circle's activities included sponsorship of the world premiere of *Rain for a Dusty Summer,* starring Ernest Borgnine and actor-priest Padre Humberto.[45] In 1976-77, the Jesuit Sanctuary Guild marked its fiftieth anniversary of continued support to Rockhurst's Jesuit community. The College Library Guild continued to sponsor lectures and its annual Critique and Brunch, which in 1975-76 featured Saul Bellow's novel, *Humboldt's Gift.* That year, with Mrs. John A. Roach as president, the guild boasted 200 members and a $10,545 contribution the previous year in support of Greenlease Library.[46] The Parents' Association, led that year by Mr. and Mrs. Jerry Sullivan, organized a number of events, including a Parents' Day orientation to Rockhurst and a reception for graduates and their families. The Ambassadors and Senior Ambassadors, meanwhile, continued to represent Rockhurst to corporations and area businesses.[47]

The Rockhurst Alumni Association was increasingly active, scheduling events to rekindle friendships and keep the Hawk spirit alive. In 1986, for instance, alums could join in on a Rockhurst Night at Royals Stadium, a trip to Ak-Sar-Ben race track in Omaha, or an Alumni Golf Tournament at River Oaks Golf Course. The alumni Business Breakfast was an ongoing gathering.[48] The majority of Rockhurst alumni continued to live in the 4-state Rockhurst area after graduation, but those who moved away returned to campus occasionally. In the winter of 1986, for instance, Ruth and Vincent Murphy, Class of '59, came from their home in San Diego, California. They admired the brand new addition to Massman Hall and told how they had hosted Rockhurst alumni parties in California.[49] Similar gatherings of Hawk alumni were occurring in many cities, often spurred by a visit of the college president.[50]

Alumni who had not been on campus for a few years surely enjoyed the latest news from a Rockhurst that had changed so much in recent years: the new Greenlease Library had replaced the old, cramped quarters in Conway Hall, and Sedgwick Hall was now air-conditioned. Just the year before, the Class of '71 had given the college a new sign that illuminated at night. It had been erected between Sedgwick Hall and the library, announcing "Rockhurst College" to all who passed by on Troost Avenue.[51] The high school boys were gone and in their place were college women, who, Father Van remarked, had "brought great advantages to the overall educational program." The "girls," he said, "are strong competitors in their classes and liven up the campus in many ways. They are fine students, taking an active part in all the college organizations." In fact, that June of 1972, a woman, for the first time in Rockhurst history, received the Senior Class Medal. She was Elizabeth Ann Thurlow, daughter of Mr. and Mrs. R.H. Thurlow, 4216 Holly. Elizabeth was a Latin major who graduated summa cum laude with a 3.97 grade point average.[52]

During the 1970s Rockhurst began to make a concerted effort to encourage alumni clubs and gatherings in cities across the country. Alumni met for dinner at the Stockyards Restaurant in New York City and the 181 Grill in Chicago. They met for a cookout at the home of Harry Bonfils (Class of '49) in Gaithersburg, Maryland, for cocktails and hors d'oeuvres at the Marriott Hotel North in Dallas and the Houston Country Club in Houston. Alumni would meet in San Francisco, Phoenix, Omaha, and, of course, in St. Louis and Kansas City. Alums from many eras stepped up to help organize the meetings—William Conwell, Class of '48, in San Francisco; Joe Flaherty, '52, and Mike Frick, '68, in New York; Edward Cahill, '38, in Washington, D.C.; James Beckley, '62, and Al Botti, '63, in Chicago; and Dan Breen, '50, in Houston. When Father Van showed up for these gatherings in the 1970s, he often would have a slide projector in tow and be eager to offer an update on Rockhurst's progress and enlist a promise that alumni would talk up the school in their respective cities. His visits usually coincided with a business trip as he traveled the country to contact companies, foundations, and businesses on Rockhurst's behalf. "The alumni working in their various companies are the best salesmen for Rockhurst as they live and work...in accord with things they have learned at Rockhurst," a report from one alumni meeting explained.[53]

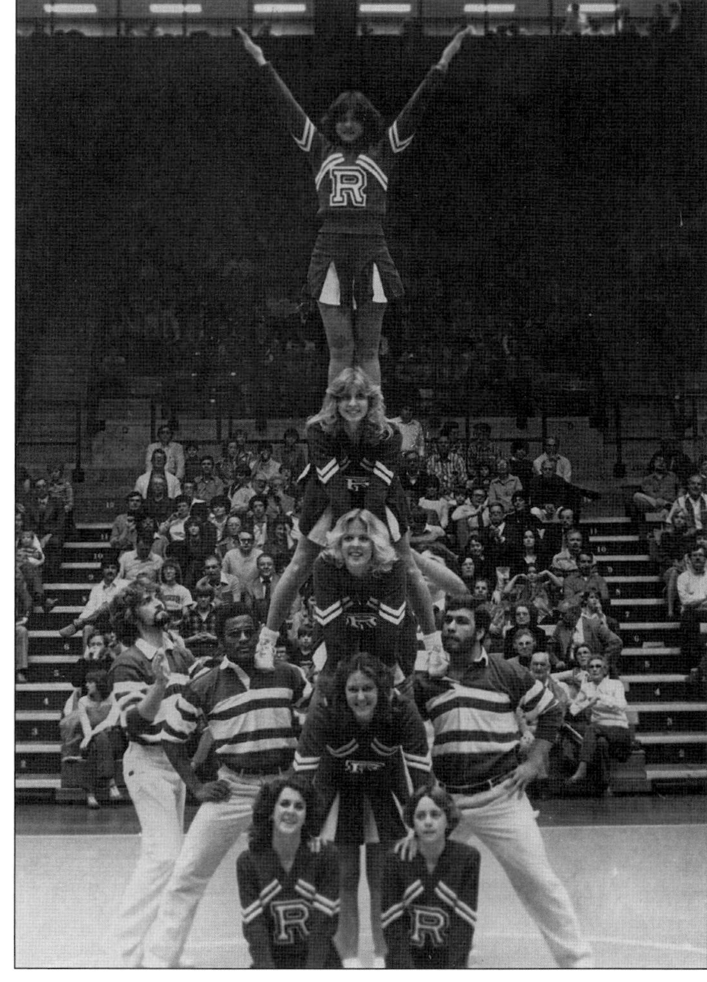

Rockhurst cheerleaders form a pyramid, 1982. Courtesy of Rockhurst University Archives.

Alumni who had gone into business surely were interested to hear about Rockhurst's new Cooperative Business Program. It was attract-

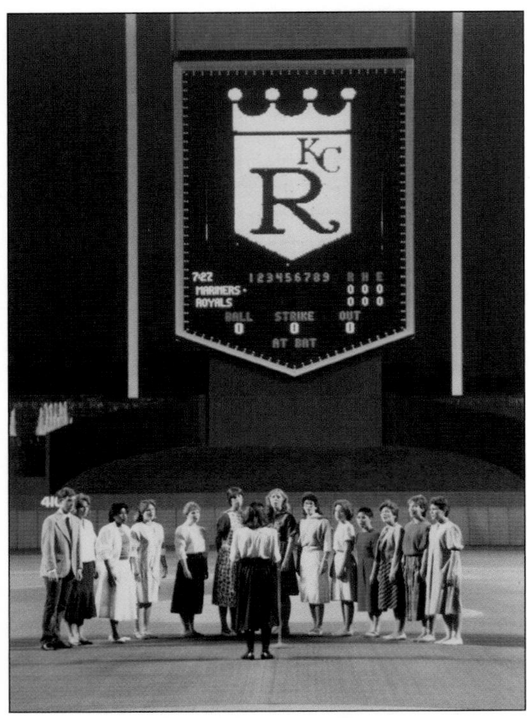

Chorus at Rockhurst night at Royals Stadium. Courtesy of Rockhurst University Archives.

ing a lot of attention in Kansas City, where 30 companies had opened their doors to students, who, over a 2-year period, could spend 2 semesters and a summer, gaining on-the-job experience. Rockhurst had added majors in Elementary Education and Medical Technology and was cooperating with area hospitals. By the spring of 1972, Rockhurst's science program had grown strong, counting 19 teachers all-told in chemistry, biology, physics, engineering science, and mathematics. "This," alumni were told, "is a long cry from the days when Dr. Ryan, Dr. Hamptil, Father Doyle and Dr. Meulemans held forth on the fourth floor of Conway Hall."[54]

Such alumni gatherings—off campus and on—continue to the present. In 2006, Dan and Melinda Hinkson, Class of '78, opened their home in Scottsdale for the Arizona Alumni Gathering, while Clifford Alexander, '66, hosted the Washington, D.C., Alumni Gathering at his law offices, Kirkpatrick & Lockhart LLP.[55] On campus, special alumni events that year of 2006 included a benefit Casino Night in the Rock Room and a "Dinner With 10 Strangers," in which area alums, in an effort to promote communication, volunteered to invite current students to their home or a restaurant for dinner.[56] Alumni also come back to campus for the annual Alumni Homecoming/ Reunion weekend. Those marking the fiftieth year since graduation are inducted as Golden Hawks, an honor conferred on longtime Missouri State Sen. Harry Wiggins, Class of '53, in 2003. Reunion weekend events have included Mass in Mabee Chapel, Hawk basketball games, and a postgame party by the Booster Club, a group of alumni and friends who assisted in every phase of the development of student athletes—from recruiting quality athletes to helping athletes secure jobs after graduation. It was the Booster Club that helped finance the electronic scoreboard on the Bourke soccer field.[57]

In 1995, the World War II veterans of Rockhurst gathered for their 50th reunion. Courtesy of Rockhurst University Archives.

— The Center for Arts and Letters —

The Center for Arts and Letters was formed in 1989 to create a partnership of participation, involvement, and interaction among the university's cultural programs. Programs include:

- Rockhurst Film Series.
- Greenlease Gallery, composed of both the Permanent Collection/Van Ackeren Collection of Religious Art and the Contemporary Exhibit Series.
- Midwest Poets Series, featuring internationally prominent writers including readings by Poets Laureate of the United States and Pulitzer Prize winners.
- Musica Sacra Chorus and Orchestra, performing 4 annual concerts of sacred masterworks for chorus, vocal soloists, and orchestra.
- Plays-in-Progress Workshop, which sponsors a bi-annual playwriting contest.
- Return to the Classics, a great books discussion.
- Rockhurst Chorus, Chamber Singers, and Women's Chorale, student groups that perform two annual concerts of sacred and secular music.
- *Rockhurst Review*, a fine arts journal published annually.
- Rockhurst Theatre, which presents 3 major productions and performances of student-directed, one-act plays yearly by Rockhurst students.
- Visiting Scholar Lecture Series, which enriches the intellectual life of the university and provides free public lectures for the Kansas City community.

Photo by David Spaw.

A highlight of the Alumni Homecoming/Reunion is the Alumni Awards Dinner, when outstanding alums are recognized. These awards began in 1981 with creation of the Rockhurst Athletics Hall of Fame. Among the first inductees were coach Patrick W. Mason, Class of '21; longtime athletic director Paul O. Smith, S.J.; Ralph Telken, a star on the 1964 national champion basketball team; and James Gleeson, Class of '33, who went on to play major league baseball for the Cleveland Indians, Cincinnati Reds, and Chicago Cubs. As a right fielder for the Cubs in 1940, Gleeson was one of the leading hitters in the National League with a .313 batting average.[58]

Actor George Wendt, Class of '71, was presented with the first-ever alumni award for Outstanding Artistic Performance in 1996. Wendt, of "Cheers" fame, chats with his former professor, Fr. Joseph Freeman, S.J. Courtesy of Rockhurst University Archives.

Beginning in 1982, Rockhurst created an Outstanding Alumnus award, the first of which went to a member of the college's first graduating class—Vincent J. O'Flaherty, Jr., Class of '21. This award was replaced, beginning in 1991, by the Alumnus/a of the Year for Outstanding Service award, the first going that year to Joseph J. McGee, Jr., '41, the first lay person to serve as chairman of the Rockhurst Board of Trustees. Two new awards also were created: Alumnus/a of the Year for Outstanding Achievement and Honorary Alumnus. A special award—for Outstanding Artistic Performance—was given to George Wendt, Class of '71, an economics major who went on to become a popular actor, starring as Norm Peterson in the hit television sitcom, "Cheers."[59]

— A DYNAMIC NEW PRESIDENT —

Rockhurst's growing reputation—and its visibility—gained new heights during the 1990s with the inauguration of a dynamic new president, Thomas J. Savage, S.J. He arrived on campus in 1988 with a vita that spoke of a man of energy and many interests—from his Catholic faith to health care and architecture, urban planning and governance, to counseling and neighborhood outreach. Only 40 years old, he held a doctorate in education from Harvard University and, in addition to his graduate theological training, two master's degrees—one in public planning from Harvard's John F. Kennedy School of Government and another in city and regional planning from the University of California-Berkeley. He had studied architecture at Catholic University of America before entering the Society of Jesus in 1967, then went on to earn his bachelor's degree in philosophy and sociology from Boston College, graduating summa cum laude in 1971. He was ordained in June 1979.[60]

Father "Thom," as he spelled his name, had been at Rockhurst for only a few months when he distributed his "Report on the First 100 Days," in which he spelled out his priorities for the college. At the top of the list was his "Strategic Plan," copies of which he already had handed out to faculty and administrators and discussed in a number of formal and informal sessions. His enthusiasm came through as he stated his primary goal: to make Rockhurst *the best* independent comprehensive college in all of Kansas City and the entire metropolitan region. He wanted *every* student to count and *every* faculty member to make a difference. He believed that a liberal education in the arts and sciences, including philosophy and theology, defined Rockhurst and that liberal arts core courses must be required of every undergraduate. He challenged students by exhorting them to "examine not only what you want, but why; come here to learn how to live as well as how to earn a living." Father Thom spoke of values, diversity, inclusion, and something new at Rockhurst—a "big picture" view that called for innovative ways to reach out to the larger community through partnerships and cooperative ventures. He spoke of the bold leadership it would take to "bind together values, vision and voice" and of the largest capital campaign ever to get Rockhurst to where he wanted it to be.[61]

By April 1990, President Savage had outlined 10 goals for Rockhurst, including a doubling of the college endowment and a 4-phase, $45 million Campus Master Plan prepared by the Kansas City design firm of Howard, Needles, Tammen & Bergendoff.[62] It was an impressive plan, intended to guide campus development to the year 2010. Many of the capital improvements it proposed would become important parts of today's campus, including a new residence for the Jesuit community, renovation of Van Ackeren Hall for academic use, an extended Campus Center for student activities, and a new building to house the science and math departments. The projected cost of the physical improvements alone was $20–$25 million.

PRESIDENTIAL PROFILE

— THOMAS J. SAVAGE, S.J. —

The Rev. Thomas J. Savage, S.J., was appointed Rockhurst's eleventh president in 1988. At age 40, Savage was Rockhurst's youngest president ever. After having entered the Jesuit novitiate in 1967, Fr. Thom earned a bachelor's degree from Boston College and, in addition to his graduate theological training, held two master's degrees—one in public planning from Harvard University and another in city and regional planning from the University of California-Berkeley. He also earned a doctorate in education from Harvard. Fr. Savage was ordained in June 1979.

Prior to his arrival at Rockhurst, Fr. Thom had served at the Cheswick Center in Boston, the Institutional Strategy Association in Massachusetts, the Management Program at the University of California-Berkeley, the Boston College School of Education, the Lesley College Graduate School Management Division, and, immediately prior to his arrival at Rockhurst, he was assistant academic vice president at Fairfield University.

Fr. Thom was deeply involved in the life of Kansas City, providing civic leadership to the community. Kansas City's *Ingram's* magazine called him a "local hero." Under Savage's leadership, a number of campus improvements were accomplished including a new residence for the Jesuit community, renovation of Van Ackeren Hall for academic use, and the construction of the Town House Village and the Science Center.

Savage died on May 10, 1999, at age 51. Father Edward Kinerk, S.J., who later became Rockhurst's thirteenth president, described Fr. Savage as a "meteor that burned itself out in the service of others."

Ingram's quote from Robin Silverman and Frederic Hron, "Local Heroes," *Ingram's*, December 1991.

Savage was clear on what he saw as the role of a university and its president: a university was a builder of society and a president the university's provocateur.[63] "It is equally incumbent upon him to prod the foot-dragger and encourage the less confident to action," he stated in his inaugural address. And that is exactly what he did, not just for the university, but the city itself, which he surmised was suffering from something of an inferiority complex. In a column titled "Straight Talk" in *Kansas City Live!* magazine, he spoke of Kansas City as a city "in the middle"—a middle-sized city in the middle of the country with many of its businesses of a middle size. The trouble, Father Savage wrote, "is we are not always happy about being in the middle." Being in the middle could make one feel vulnerable or unsure about one's identity. "We are not first or last, biggest or smallest, newest or oldest, the fastest growing or the slowest. So what are we? Always being in the middle can lead to a perpetual identity crisis."

The indomitable Father Thom called on Rockhurst and Kansas City to not hang their heads, but to celebrate their "in-the-middleness" by taking advantage of its many opportunities, not the least of which was physical location. Rockhurst, he pointed out, was in the middle of the city, which brought together people of diverse ethnic, racial, religious, and economic backgrounds, and Kansas City was in the middle of the nation, which presented tremendous opportunities for economic development. Father Thom had been in town for only 3 years when Kansas City's *Ingram's* magazine called him a "local hero."[64]

The magazine embraced him for the way he bicycled about the city or took long walks, praying along the way and talking to people he met.

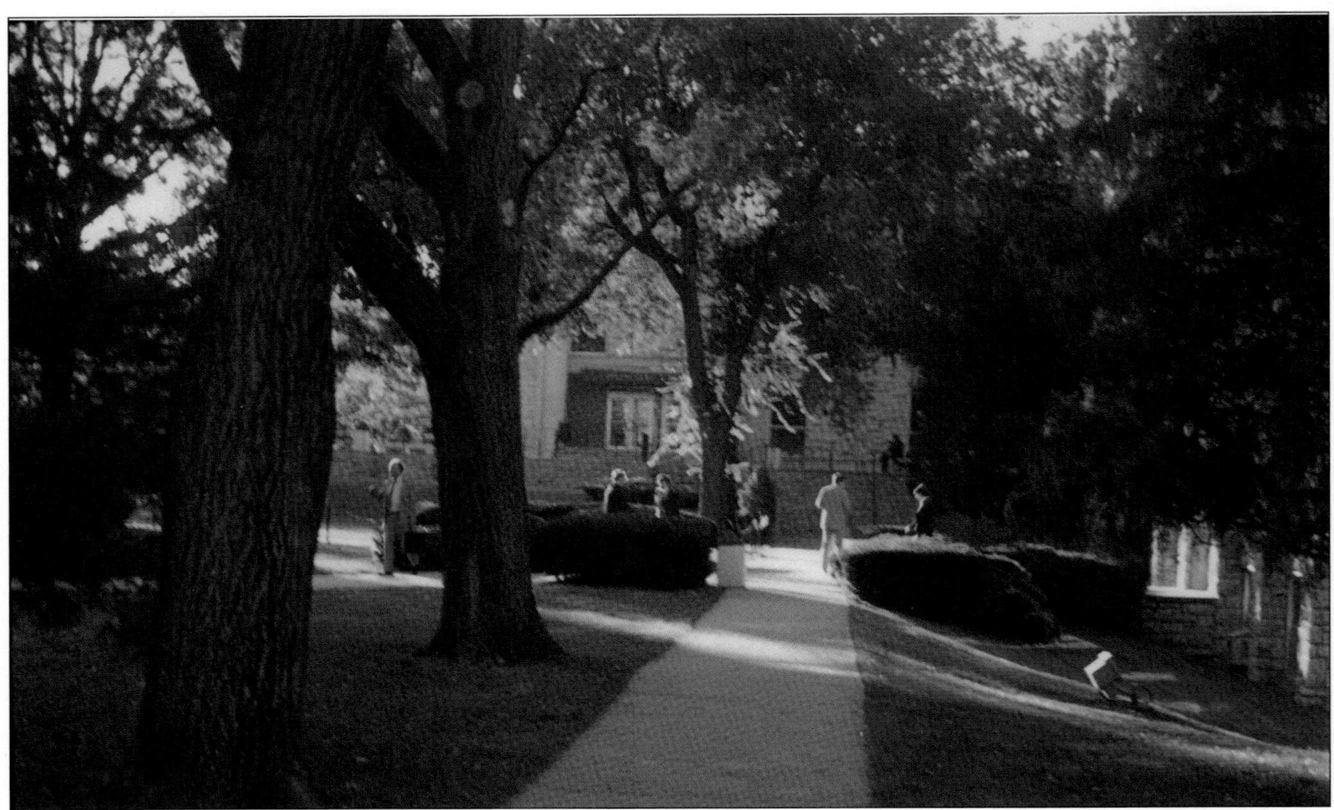

Fr. Thom Savage (left) as King Arthur and James Owens, '94 as Merlyn in the Rockhurst production of Camelot. Courtesy of Rockhurst University Department of Communication and Fine Arts.

It liked the way he encouraged dialogue among diverse people and the way he celebrated, rather than bemoaned, Rockhurst's location along Troost Avenue. "If we cannot make Troost a symbol of the bridge instead of a dividing line, there is no future for greater Kansas City," he told the magazine. "And if Kansas City can't do it, I'm very skeptical of whether this nation can do it." He called on Kansas City to be a model for the rest of the nation and for the Rockhurst community to get involved in neighborhood and city projects. "The challenge for all of us," he would say, "is to discover through action and reflection the priceless gift of service above self and becoming men and women for others."[65]

— A CALL FOR ACCOUNTABILITY —

Even as the laudatory *Ingram's* article appeared, Father Savage's aspirations to make Rockhurst "the best" were creating some tension on campus. This was the conclusion of the Atlanta-based education consultant, Communicorp, which had visited campus and submitted its *Review and Reflection Paper* that very month.[66] The consultants, apparently hired to find ways to increase admissions, had been impressed with Rockhurst's methods of teaching—where "knowing some of the questions was better than knowing all the answers." They praised highly what they called the "radiant corona of supportiveness" they found on campus. But they worried that the re-evaluation under Savage, especially in difficult economic times that drove budget priorities, had created unease and some divisions. "Paradoxically," the consultants said, "Rockhurst's struggle to forge a new identity might be difficult precisely *because* the college has such a strong self-concept." As Rockhurst moved forward, the report said, "it must ask itself how it can best move away from the past without devaluing its history." The word *accountability* came up as the best way to build a better esprit de corps. There needed to be accountability in the admissions office, for example, where the enrollment goal of 315 freshmen for fall 1991 had been revised downward to 285. And then, only 234 actually enrolled, a situation that created a sizable budget deficit.

One of Rockhurst's most successful advertising campaigns compared Rockhurst to other famous "rocks," including Elvis Presley, the King of Rock 'n' Roll. Courtesy of Rockhurst University Archives.

Difficult demographics and inadequate financial aid lay at the heart of the problem. As everyone knew, the "baby boom" tide had ebbed, and the United States had fewer college-age students. But there was something else—a new trend that saw increasing numbers of transfer and nontraditional students. These trends had "crept up" on Rockhurst, and the college had failed in its short- and long-range planning to address them, the consultants said. And even though the college had increased the amount of financial aid in its budget—to more than $1 million—it was not enough.

"No one faces the fact that we're in trouble," one longtime admissions officer told the consultants.

In keeping with the vision of Father Thom, Rockhurst needed to market itself, and Communicorp had the plan. It called on Rockhurst to do a number of things. No. 1 was to position itself as committed to a strong liberal arts curriculum, empowered by 450 years of Jesuit thought and tradition. Rockhurst should emphasize its commitment to teaching students *how* to learn as well as *what* to learn. Then, rather than *comparing* itself to other Jesuit colleges, it should present itself in contrast to them and emphasize the opportunities it offered students to serve as volunteers locally and nationally. Rockhurst also should position itself, Communicorp said, as an "educational beacon in the Midwest and in the life of Kansas City," make an effort to increase the diversity of its student body, including Hispanic students, and tout the way it was central to the lives of its students—even after graduation.

During his time as president of Rockhurst, Fr. Savage co-hosted a weekly radio talk show titled "Religion on the Line" with Protestant minister Rev. Robert Lee Hill of Community Christian Church (left) and Rabbi Michael Zedek of Temple B'nai Jehudah (right). Courtesy of Robert Lee Hill.

That the administration took these suggestions to heart was evident by 1994, most tellingly, perhaps, with a new enrollment plan that included improved recruitment brochures and a clever new advertising campaign that promoted Rockhurst by positioning it with other "Famous Rocks." Here was Rockhurst and there was the Rock of Gibraltar. Here was Rockhurst and there was that movie star boxer, Rocky Balboa. Rockhurst and Rockefeller Center, Rockhurst and that infamous rock, Alcatraz. Rockhurst and that storied rock of the Pilgrims, Plymouth Rock. And here was that "Solid Rock" Rockhurst, and the King of Rock 'n' Roll, Elvis Presley. The ad campaign, created by Kansas City's Fleishman-Hillard, was so successful that it ran for a number of years and received gold and bronze awards from the Council for the Advancement and Support of Education, District VI.[67]

Rockhurst also advertised in 1994 for an Executive Director and Dean of Enrollment Services, a new position that spoke to the No. 1 goal in President Savage's 8-point "Strategic Plan for 1995–2000"—an increased student enrollment, with an emphasis on nontraditional students. The No. 2 goal, surely fashioned according to Communicorp recommendations, called on Rockhurst to emphasize its distinctive Jesuit mission and values, and its reputation for student-centeredness.

Also in 1994, *The Jesuit Bulletin* put Sedgwick Hall on its cover, declaring "A New Era Taking Shape" at Rockhurst. The story inside led with a photograph of Father Savage walking on campus with 2 students. He had, the magazine declared, given a "facelift" to the small college, which, since his arrival, "had emerged as a leader in private higher education, not just in Kansas City, but in the region."[68] *Money* magazine had just ranked Rockhurst as one of the top 20 "Best College Buys" in the Midwest and among the top 100 in the nation. *U.S. News and World Report* also had ranked Rockhurst—as 18th among colleges and universities in the Midwest.

"Savage's outgoing, charismatic style has earned him the praise and respect of Kansas City's top civic and business leaders," *The Jesuit Bulletin* reported, noting that this was quite a feat since "a newcomer from Boston doesn't easily break into Kansas City's established power circles." Father Savage had done it by getting involved. He had co-chaired FOCUS, a strategic planning effort in Kansas City, and served as a consultant on numerous governing boards, from health care to public agencies. And he had co-hosted a weekly radio talk show, sitting side by side with a prominent rabbi and a Protestant minister.

Dorm life. In 1994, Rockhurst expanded its student housing with the construction of the Town House Village, increasing on-campus housing by more than a third. Courtesy of Rockhurst University Archives.

Some pointed to Father Savage's bold initiatives as his most significant contribution to Rockhurst. In June 1991, for instance, he was instrumental in establishing the nonprofit Rockhurst College Continuing Education Center Inc. (RCCEC), which soon acquired National Seminars Inc., an Overland Park, Kansas, firm that had put more than 2 million people through its seminars since its founding in 1984. The firm's Mark and Gary Truitt would continue operating the day-to-day business, but Rockhurst would own it. The idea for the Truitts, explained the *Kansas City Business Journal,* was to cut expenses. For Rockhurst, the deal was a way to meet its commitment to "lifelong learning" and to make continuing education

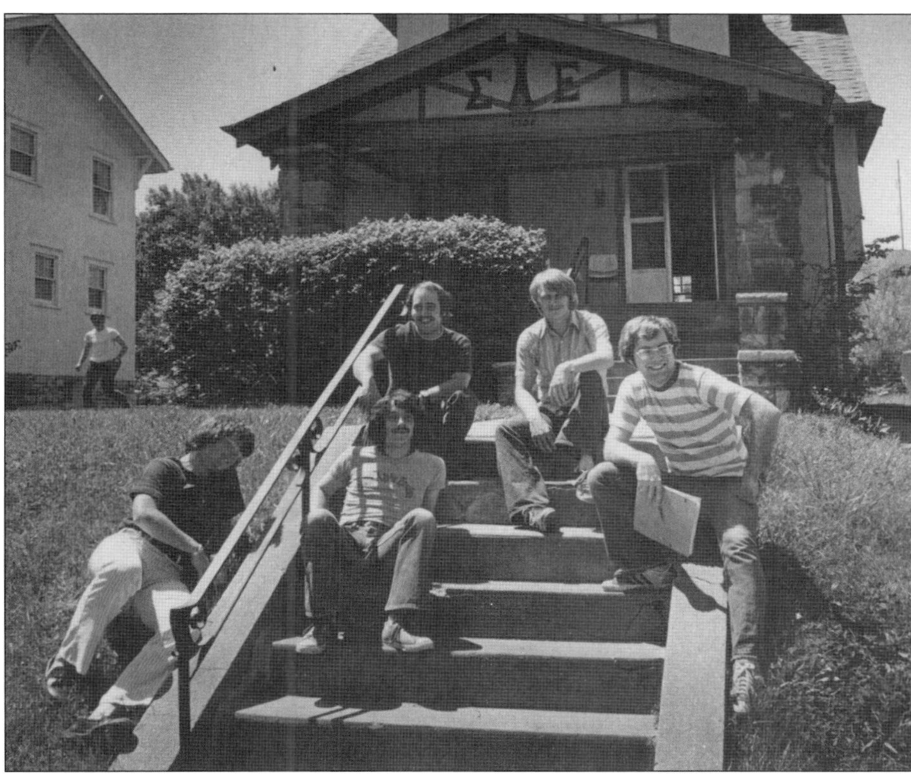

To make way for the Science Center and a new entrance at 54th Street and Troost Avenue, Rockhurst razed numerous houses and buildings, including fraternity houses. Photo by Ron Sherman. Courtesy of Rockhurst University Archives.

— CURA PERSONALIS: A FAMILY AFFAIR —

A hallmark of Jesuit spirituality, *cura personalis* is a Latin phrase that can be translated as "care for the whole person." While many in the Rockhurst family have exemplified that principle, few have done so spanning the generations. The Miller family's love and support for Rockhurst began with Robert W. Miller, a Kansas City attorney, who taught public speaking part time at Rockhurst from 1936-1941 and from 1946-1966. Among his many services to the community, Miller created an organization called "Orphan Sponsors," which mentored orphans through school and life. More importantly, he instilled in his children the same commitment to care for others.

Miller's two sons, Robert (Bob) E. Miller, '49, and Richard (Dick) W. Miller, '52, have continued this legacy of service established by their father. Beginning in 1953 and continuing for 33 years, Bob, like his father, also taught public speaking part time at Rockhurst. Bob Miller's service to others has literally taken him around the world. Additionally, he has been president of the Rockhurst Alumni Association and, since 1977, has been a Rockhurst regent.

Co-founder of the highly successful Christmas In October program, Dick Miller has also continued his father's tradition of giving back to others. Among the many boards and foundations in the community that have benefited from Dick's generosity of time and resources, he served on the first lay Board of Trustees at Rockhurst and as president of the Rockhurst Alumni Association.

courses more applicable to people in the workplace. At the same time, the acquisition would enable RCCEC to become self-supporting and require no use of college funds. The *Business Journal* praised the acquisition as a "smart move" sure to boost Rockhurst's already strong business program, though the newspaper wondered whether National Seminars' competitors would view the move kindly.[69]

— AN EXPANDING CAMPUS —

New initiatives were taking place on campus as well. Underground fiber-optic cable was installed in the summer of 1992 to connect campus buildings, and a contract had been signed for a new, $4.1 million Town House Village. Its 2-bedroom town homes for 180 students would increase on-campus housing by more than a third.[70] The summer before, plans were proceeding to move the Jesuit living quarters out of Van Ackeren Hall and remodel the building for academic use. The renovated building, dedicated on August 24, 1992, would house the dean of the College of Arts and Sciences, as well as the departments of psychology, political science, global studies, sociology, education, and continuing education. Rockhurst's physical and occupational therapy programs also would be housed there. Rockhurst's 30 resident Jesuits, meanwhile, were preparing to move into 2 newly-constructed quarters across Rockhurst Road on Tracy Avenue. The twin projects were being helped along by a $1 million challenge grant from the Tulsa, Oklahoma-based Mabee Foundation, bringing to $2.3 million the money the foundation had given to Rockhurst during the past dozen years.

As part of a 5-year, $35 million Comprehensive Campaign to get work going on the Campus Master Plan, the Kemper Foundation gave $300,000 toward planning and construction of the Town House Village.[71]

To make way for what would become the Science Center, as well as a new entrance on 54th Street, Rockhurst set to work razing numerous houses and buildings along Troost Avenue. One victim was the college's Goppert Center, a remodeled convenience store that housed Rockhurst's career center. Two blocks east, at 53rd Street and Tracy Avenue, crews were tearing down 11 houses to make room for visitor and faculty parking. Based on newspaper accounts, the uproar that had greeted Rockhurst expansion into the neighborhood in the 1960s had died down. In fact, city officials, at least, seemed pleased with Rockhurst expansion along the Troost corridor, which, from 53rd to 63rd streets, had recently been designated an urban renewal area. By the mid-1990s, Rockhurst's campus expanded to 35 acres.[72]

Vincent F. Daues, S.J., began his teaching career at Rockhurst in 1950. In 1954, he established Rockhurst's chapter of Alpha Sigma Nu, the Jesuit Honor Society. One year later, Fr. Daues founded the Visiting Scholar Lecture Series, which he directed for more than 30 years. In 1968, Fr. Daues received the Pro Meritis Award, one of only 2 Jesuits who have ever received that award. Daues was named Emeritus Professor of Philosophy in 1986. He died in 1998.

— A Strong Sports Tradition —

The college's athletic programs were not to be overlooked. A new, coed cross-country team had been established in 1985, and, in the fall of 1994, Rockhurst added baseball and men's and women's tennis to its programs, bringing to 8 its number of NAIA intercollegiate sports.[73] Actually, baseball was not new at Rockhurst, but was being revived after an absence of nearly 20 years. Baseball was being reinstated, Athletic Director Frank Diskin explained, thanks to a $100,000 donation from alumnus John Sullivan. Taking on what promised to be a difficult coaching job for the new baseball team was 34-year-old Gary Burns, a former assistant baseball coach at Vanderbilt and Clemson. "He does not yet have a bat, ball, uniform, staff or home field but already has a fast start on a schedule," *The Kansas City Star* columnist Jonathan Rand wrote. It seemed that Kansas City area schools were so eager to take on the fledgling Rockhurst team that rival coaches had wasted no time phoning Burns to schedule games. Burn's team turned out, however, to be no easy-pickings. It would top .500 in its first year, with a 28-24 record, including 23-8 in NAIA competition.[74]

The women's volleyball team, under coach Tracy Rietzke, who has been at the helm since 1988, has been nationally ranked each season since joining the NCAA in 1998. In 1996, the Lady Hawks competed in the NAIA Final Four. Courtesy of Rockhurst University Archives.

Rockhurst always was a strong competitor no matter the sport. The previous winter, in February 1993, Rockhurst's women's basketball team with a 30-1 record—tied for best in the nation—had advanced to the NAIA Division I nationals. As the team entered the season of 1994-95, coach Tracy Rietzke boasted a 156-35 record and had been named "District 16 Coach of the Year" 4 times.[75] In 1999, under new coach Maryann Mitts, a 1992 Rockhurst alum, the Lady Hawks, now part of the NCAA, distinguished themselves by being named the No. 1 academic team in the nation in NCAA Division II. Overall, the players racked up a combined 3.744 grade-point average. Two freshmen, Laura Crowley and Katie Losbaker, achieved a perfect 4.0 GPA.[76] In the 1980s, the Lady Hawks had been to the District 16 finals 3 years running, as had the men's basketball team, which claimed the district championship in 1984-85 with a 21-8 record.

The women's volleyball team, coached since 1988 by Tracy Rietzke, claimed 3 straight District 16 championships, in 1989, 1990, and 1991. The Lady Hawks held a No. 2 national ranking during most of the 1993 season, posted its best-ever 57-5 record, and went on to nationals. The team repeated the feat the next year with a record of 47-5, and, in 1996, went on to compete in the NAIA Final Four. In 2005, with Rietzke still at the helm and Rockhurst playing its first season in the Great Lakes Valley Conference, the volleyball team captured the conference title. During the year, Rietzke reached his 900th career victory and was named Coach of the Year in the GLVC.[77]

The men's soccer team had had a rich history since its inception, including 2 national tournament appearances in the 1980s. As the 1994-95 season began, head coach Tony Tocco, who also was a professor of accounting at Rockhurst, held a phenomenal 356-77-25 record and had been named NAIA Soccer Coach of the Year 3 times. In 1996, Rockhurst sophomore Thomas Andreasen was selected as one of 11 members of the NAIA All-American first team. Blair Quinn, a senior, and Kevin Schoen, a junior, made the second team. In that same year, Diego Gutierrez was drafted by the Kansas City Wizards and went on to a successful career as a midfielder for the Wizards and later for the Chicago Fire. The strong tradition would continue, with the men's soccer team ranking sixth in the national poll during the 1998, 2003, and 2008 seasons. On November 13, 2007, Rockhurst's Tony Tocco was inducted into the National Association of Intercollegiate Athletics Hall of Fame in Olathe, Kansas. During the soccer team's years in the NAIA under Tocco—from 1973 to 1997—the Hawks played in 17 national championship tournaments, advanced to the Final Four 10 times, and finished as national runner-up 4 times.[78]

Women's soccer began as an intramural sport in 1981, moved to club level in 1989, and became a varsity sport

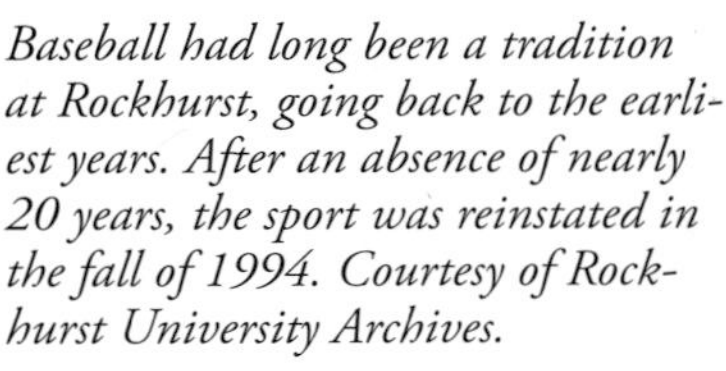

Baseball had long been a tradition at Rockhurst, going back to the earliest years. After an absence of nearly 20 years, the sport was reinstated in the fall of 1994. Courtesy of Rockhurst University Archives.

— TONY TOCCO —

In 2009, Anthony (Tony) L. Tocco celebrated his 40th year as as an accounting professor and men's soccer coach. Few coaches in all of college athletics can boast a more impressive record than Tony Tocco. His 574 career victories ranks first among active intercollegiate coaches and third on the all-time coaching list.

The Hawks were a perennial power in the NAIA from 1973-97 under Tocco. Rockhurst played in 17 national tournaments, advancing to the Final Four 10 times and finishing national runner-up 4 times in 1973, 1976, 1979, and 1997. Tocco, who was inducted into the NAIA Hall of Fame in 2007, was the winningest coach in the NAIA with 437 victories prior to the 2008 season. He was named the NAIA National Coach of the Year three times (1974, '76, and '86). His teams won 20 or more games 8 times, including his last 4 teams that competed in the NAIA. Since joining the NCAA in 1998, the Hawks have posted a 118-48-21 record and advanced to the national tournament in 2002, '03, '05 and '08. The Hawks rose to fourth in the nation in Division II in 2008 and were the No. 1 seeded team in the NCAA Midwest Regional.

The National Soccer Coaches Association of America (NSCAA) named Tocco the 2002 Coach of the Year for senior college men Division II Central. He was also named National Coach of the Year for senior colleges in 1986 by the NSCAA and was a three-time NSCAA Midwest Region Coach of the Year. He was also named the Great Lakes Valley Conference Coach of the Year in 2008.

A 1967 graduate of Saint Louis University, Tocco played on the only undefeated and untied soccer team in Saint Louis University history in 1964 and pitched in the College Baseball World Series in 1965. He also received his master's degree and Ph.D. from SLU.

— *John Dodderidge*

in 1991. By 1996, in only its sixth varsity season, the women's team was ranked nationally and advanced to the regional finals.[79] The quick success of Rockhurst teams and athletes was demonstrated as well by the coed cross-country team, which, in its first year (1985) qualified 2 runners—Matt Lewis and Steve Schmid—for the NAIA meet in Kenosha, Wisconsin.[80]

Women's softball and men's and women's golf would not be added for another decade, but by 1994, a total of 214 Rockhurst students, men

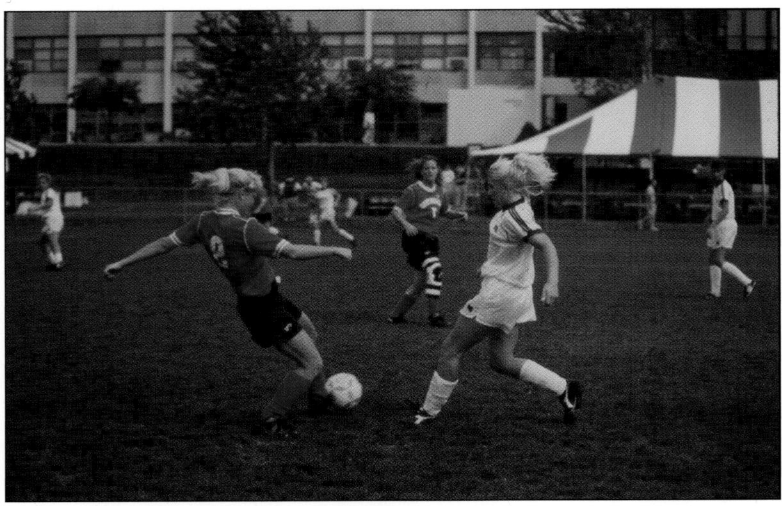

Women's soccer became a varsity sport in 1991. Courtesy of Rockhurst University Archives.

and women, were participating in intercollegiate athletics—up from just 70 in 1985.[81]

— A PLANNING GUIDE —

Rockhurst viewed its expanded sports program as a boon in its effort to get more students on campus in these times of declining enrollment and escalating costs. So critical were student numbers that in late 1992 Rockhurst's Office of Institutional Research & Planning published a fact book titled "Planning Guide," in which it took a hard look at enrollment, from profiling its entering classes, to dissecting its distribution of majors, to comparing itself to other Jesuit colleges and universities. The statistics revealed a Rockhurst much-changed from "the little school on the hill" of even 25 years before. Freshman women now outnumbered freshman men and composed 58 percent of the class (190 women to 137 men). Of the first-time, full-time students entering Rockhurst that fall of 1992, fewer than half—46.5 percent—had come from Catholic high schools, although, as always, most came from Missouri (65 percent), and another 19 percent from Kansas. Statistics also revealed the popularity of Rockhurst's School of Management, which awarded 169 M.B.A.s in the 1991-92 academic year—or 34 percent of the total degrees granted. It was only 15 years before that Rockhurst had conferred its first M.B.A.s—a total of 2 in 1976-77.

A retention study, which followed in 1993, found that Rockhurst had done "remarkably well in retaining students through to graduation" despite a host of issues—from an increased number of students with financial needs, to professional programs, such as physical therapy and nursing, which had such rigorous requirements that some students became discouraged and dropped out. According to the Office of the Registrar, the retention rate for first-time college freshmen (who graduated within 3 to 6 years) stood at 58 percent from 1979 to 1987, up 7 percentage points from that of the preceding 9 years.[83] The retention rate likely got a boost from Rockhurst's efforts during the Weiss and Savage eras to increase scholarship aid, which accounted for 33.5 percent of endowment disbursements by the fall of 1992.

"We think higher education is at a crossroad," Father Savage told *The Kansas City Star* in December 1994.[84] Faced with another tight budget, he said the college was expecting its greatest growth to be in its continuing education seminars. He was hoping for a full-time undergraduate enrollment of 1,400 to 1,500 by the year 2000. He could point optimistically to a 9.6 percent jump in full-time undergraduate enrollment that very fall.

There were many positives. The college had gotten itself hooked up to the Internet in the fall of 1994 and, 2 years later, would establish the Office of Information and Technology, a sign of Rockhurst's commitment to the growing role of technology in achieving its academic goals and mission.[85] Signs of progress were everywhere evident as the campus transformation

Rockhurst soccer player Diego Gutierrez was drafted by the Kansas City Wizards in 1996 and went on to a successful career as a midfielder for the Chicago Fire. In 2009, he was inducted into the World Sports Humanitarian Hall of Fame for his efforts to prevent malaria-related deaths in Africa through his work with Nothing But Nets. Courtesy of Rockhurst University Athletic Department.

— The Science Hall of Fame —

A few months after the dedication of the Science Center in 1996, Rockhurst honored 6 graduates by inducting them into the new Science Hall of Fame. Inducted were James E. Monahan, '48, Joseph A. Flaherty, Jr., '52, A. Donald Goedeke, '56, Joseph Glas, '60, Joseph M. Jaklevic, '62, and William G. Bartholome, '65. Over the years, others have been inducted including James B. Kring, '47, William J. Haggerty, Jr., '54, Henry N. Wellman, '56, Robert C. Jaklevic, '56, Paul C. Wheeler, '63, Salvatore J. Enna, '65, and Lawrence J. Marnett, '69. The accomplishments of these Rockhurst graduates are many and span multiple fields in science and technology. Even though any one of these illustrious alumni could be featured, James Monahan serves as a representative of them all.

Dr. James E. Monahan

Jim Monahan's career at Rockhurst was interrupted by his service in the U.S. Army during World War II. He returned to Rockhurst after the war and graduated in 1948 with a major in physics and a minor in mathematics. He earned the M.S. and Ph.D. degrees in physics from Saint Louis University. After graduating from SLU, Monahan joined the Argonne National Laboratory, retiring as senior physicist in 1985. In 1996, the James Emmett and Elizabeth Ann Monahan Student-Faculty Research Laboratory was established in the college's new Science Center in honor of Jim and his wife, Betty.

continued. Students now were living in Town House Village, classes were being held in the renovated Van Ackeren Hall, and work was progressing on the new Science Center.

— An Unexpected Resignation —

In another of Father Thom's bold moves, Rockhurst, in conjunction with Saint Louis University, had opened a south campus at the former Marillac Center at Wornall Road and 106th Street. Offered there were continuing education courses, as well as an undergraduate degree in sociology and a 2-year accelerated M.B.A. program. "This is more than a satellite campus," Savage told the *Kansas City Business Journal.* "It's a symbol of what's happening."[86] The *Business Journal* lauded Savage's efforts to, as its headline said, move Rockhurst "onto the fast track." A Ewing Marion Kauffman Foundation executive compared Father Thom to Father Van in his success in lining up "influential people" and in his tireless efforts to stay involved. He had worked on the Civic Council's new education program, helped prepare a "report card" on Kansas City area children, raised money for the United Way, and even helped create a new master plan for the city. Father Savage was, after all, the *Business*

With more than half of incoming freshmen expressing an interest in majoring in science or a health-related field, construction began in 1994 on the $7 million Science Center. Photo by Roy Inman. Courtesy of Rockhurst University Archives.

Journal explained, the CEO of a major institution. "You grow a business by building from within, by acquisitions and by joint ventures," Savage had said in the interview. "We are doing all three." He told the *Business Journal* of a national survey he once read in which business leaders said the only time they ever saw the president of the local college was when he was asking for money. "I was determined that would not be said about me or Rockhurst," he was quoted. "I want to be able to ask for support because I can honestly say we are making a difference."

It was exactly because Father Thom seemed to be making a difference that the news of his resignation came as a surprise to many. It came on October 10, 1995, when he told his staff that the Board of Trustees had agreed to begin searching for his replacement. He announced the news formally during a Faculty General Assembly meeting, sent an e-mail to all employees, and instructed his staff to post his letter of resignation on the Massman Hall bulletin board at 4 p.m. It wasn't 10 minutes later that the news was related to WDAF-TV. In an interview with *The Kansas City Star* the next day, Father Savage said his 8-year tenure was long enough for a college president and that he wanted to focus on new initiatives involving lifelong learning; thus, he would remain chairman of the Rockhurst College Continuing Education Center and stay on as president until a successor could be found, which he thought could take a year or 2.[87]

It was just months later, however, in the summer of 1996, that Rockhurst's twelfth president, Peter B. Ely, S.J., arrived. He was 57 years old, the current academic vice president and associate professor of religious studies at Gonzaga University in Spokane, Washington. "He brings a strong record

PRESIDENTIAL PROFILE

— PETER B. ELY, S.J. —

The Rev. Peter B. Ely, S.J., was appointed Rockhurst's twelfth president in the summer of 1996. Born in 1938, Ely entered the Society of Jesus in 1956 and was ordained a priest in 1969. From 1963-66, he taught at the Jesuit High School in Portland, Oregon. He joined the faculty of Gonzaga in 1973 in the religious studies department and in 1978 became academic vice president. Fr. Ely holds a bachelor's in divinity from Regis College, Ontario, and bachelor's and master's degrees in philosophy from Gonzaga University. He earned a Ph.D. in theology from Fordham University.

Ely served as president of Rockhurst less than a year, resigning at the end of the 1996-97 academic year. He is currently vice president for Mission and Ministry at Seattle University.

Four Rockhurst presidents, left to right: Robert F. Weiss, S.J., Maurice E. Van Ackeren, S.J., Peter B. Ely, S.J., Thomas J. Savage, S.J. The photo was taken on November 1, 1996, at the inauguration of Fr. Peter Ely as president. Photo by Roy Inman. Courtesy of Rockhurst University Archives.

of experience and achievement to his new position," Father Savage said of his successor. "He will continue to strengthen Rockhurst's distinctive educational mission for the whole Kansas City community."[88] An in-house newsletter reported in June that as soon as Father Ely began his presidency, Father Savage would take a short sabbatical and then receive his next assignment from his religious superior, the provincial of the New England Province of the Society of Jesus. Savage remained on campus all summer, saying his goodbyes to Rockhurst in a letter published in the campus newsletter that August. In his usual inclusive style, he spoke of the "unique contribution" each member of the Rockhurst community—whether in a visible or behind-the-scenes role—made to the college every day. "We all share in the mission of this very special place called Rockhurst," he wrote.[89]

President Savage's last public achievement at Rockhurst was the dedication, on May 2, 1996, of the $7 million Science Center, an important addition to the landscape and revitalization of Troost Avenue as it was to the campus, where more than half of incoming freshmen now expressed an interest in majoring in science or a health-related field.[90] Father Thom addressed the gathering that day, his words echoing Pope John Paul II, who had declared in his *Ex Corde Ecclesia* that universities, Catholic or not, had always been recognized as a center "of creativity and knowledge for the good of humanity." The pope had written of the joy of searching for, discovering, and communicating truth in every field of knowledge—even the field of science, though it had caused so much controversy in Christian circles.[91]

Father Thom agreed with the pope saying that the Jesuit tradition had always viewed science and learning as pathways to understanding God and helping people. How sad it was, then, that science would not be able to help Father Thom. If he knew that spring day of 1996 that he was infected with the virus that causes AIDS, there was no hint of it.

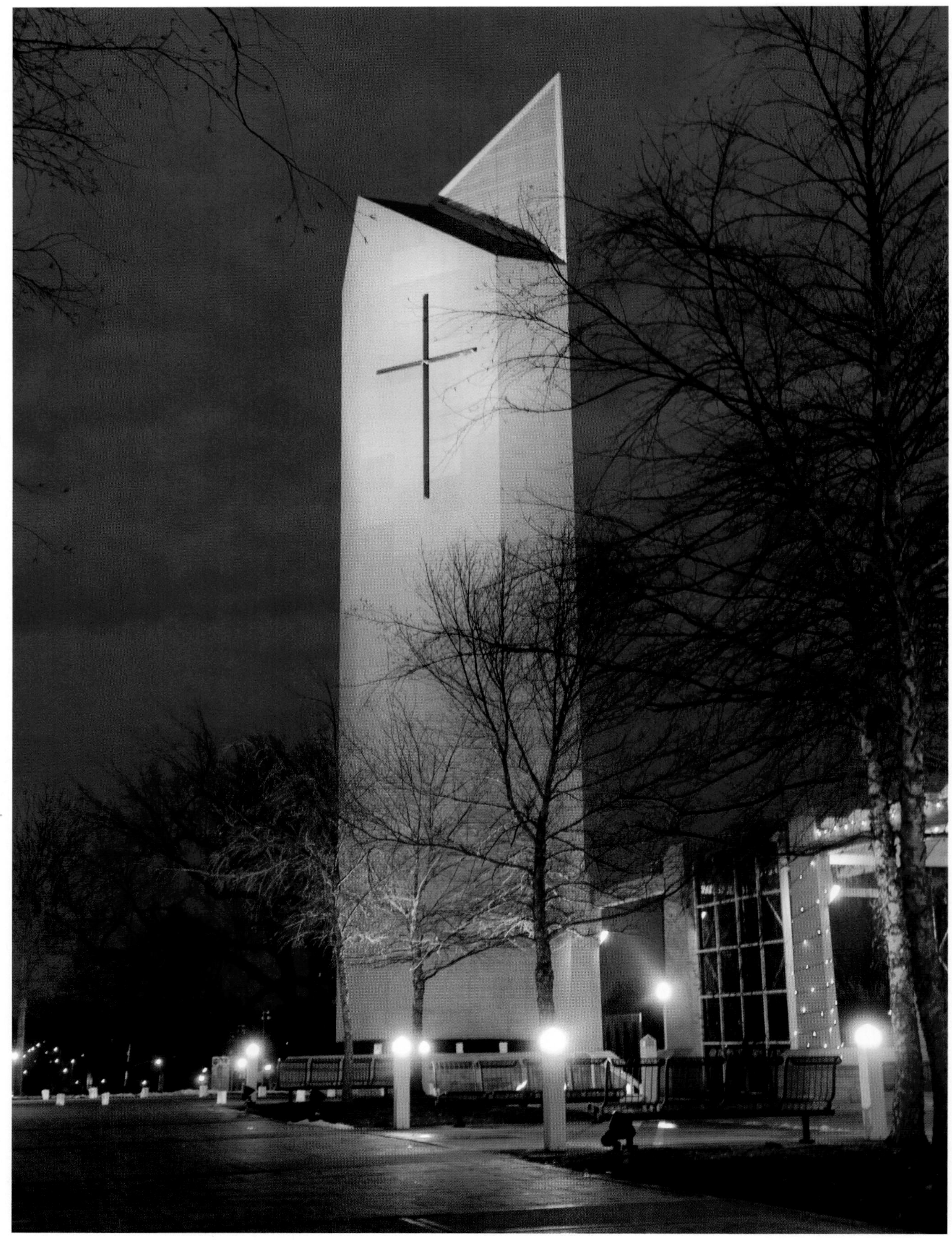

Chapter Fourteen

Keeping the Vision Alive 1997–2010

In the summer of 1999, Mary Anne Beck marked her twentieth year as a Rockhurst employee. She had arrived on campus August 13, 1979, and walked into the old dean's office in Massman 104. Twenty years later, as assistant to the president, she looked back on her years at Rockhurst in an article she wrote for the faculty and staff newsletter. Hers was one in a series of articles titled "Rockhurst Reflections" that ran periodically in the newsletter, the aptly named *Rockhurst Community*. For it was the *community* she found on campus that went straight to Mary Anne Beck's heart.

"I had never been on the inside of an educational institution," she wrote, "and quickly found that everything was different—for the first year it felt like a ride on the Mamba without a seat belt—and that people, problems and ideas are just more interesting here than in most places."[1] She loved to walk across the quad, where, she wrote, "you're liable to overhear a discussion about the bones of the foot, a burst of song from the music practice rooms, or an argument about ethics in business." She found much to learn on the Rockhurst campus. "It's hard not to learn," she wrote, "when intriguing ideas and creativity simply teem around you." She loved walking to work amid the trees and the landscaping that made Rockhurst feel like a park, and she enjoyed dealing with most everyone—students, faculty, administrators, and volunteers. "Our student body is growing and diversifying," she noted as the academic year of 1999-2000 got set to begin. "Our faculty, always a source of pride, is undertaking initiatives that will keep excellent teaching in the forefront of our activities here. Our community volunteers are distinguished and enthusiastic Rockhurst supporters...." To Mary Anne Beck, Rockhurst felt "a lot like a family." It was a place where "you will be supported and appreciated," she wrote, but a place where you also better be prepared to be "stretched to develop new talents and interests."

From 1997-1998, Janet Watson Sheeran served as interim president of Rockhurst, the first woman and lay person to hold that position. Sheeran began her career at Rockhurst in 1977, first in the Communication and Fine Arts department, where she directed the theater program, and later as dean of the College of Arts and Sciences, from 1991-97. After leaving Rockhurst in 1998, Sheeran went on to become the Provost/Vice-President for Academic Affairs at Saint Michael's College, Vermont. Since 2005, she has been a higher education consultant. Courtesy of Rockhurst University Archives.

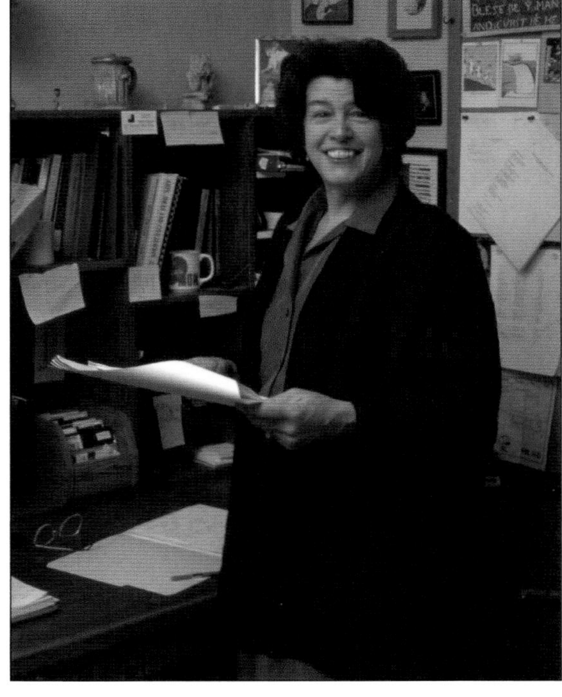

There was no mistaking the pride and enthusiasm in Mary Anne Beck's words as she mentioned the "dirt and hammering" going on around campus that summer of 1999. In fact, the campus was awash in a sea of construction mud as a new president—Edward Kinerk, S.J., had arrived and wasted no time in beginning the initial stages of a capital campaign that would enhance the master plan begun a decade before under President Savage. Father Kinerk, Rockhurst's thirteenth president, officially succeeded Peter Ely, S.J., on June 1, 1998. Father Ely had served only 10 months when he announced his resignation at the end of the 1996-

PRESIDENTIAL PROFILE

— E. EDWARD KINERK, S.J. —

Elected thirteenth president of Rockhurst, Father Edward Kinerk, S.J., was the first and only alumnus to serve as president. A native of Kansas City, Kinerk attended St. Francis Xavier School, crossed the street to attend Rockhurst High School, graduating in 1960, then stayed on for his college work, receiving a bachelor's in mathematics from Rockhurst College in 1964. He joined the Society of Jesus in 1966, earned a master's in theology from Saint Louis University in 1970, and a doctorate in spiritual theology from the Gregorian University in Rome in 1975. Ordained in 1972, Fr. Kinerk's first assignment was to Sacred Heart Jesuit Retreat House in 1975. In subsequent years he served as novice director, provincial of the Missouri Province of Jesuits, and, from 1998 until 2006, as president of Rockhurst University. Currently, Fr. Kinerk is administrator at Sacred Heart Jesuit Retreat House, Sedalia, Colorado.

Under Fr. Kinerk's 8-year tenure as president, the campus was transformed through a number of construction projects and renovations including a pedestrian mall with a pergola, fountain, and 93-foot bell tower, the renovation of Xavier-Loyola dorms and Conway Hall, the opening of the Rockhurst Community Center, the construction of Greenlease Gallery, and the dedication of the Loyola Park Athletic Complex. Though Rockhurst had officially changed its charter in 1951 to become a university, it was under Kinerk's leadership that use of the name "Rockhurst University" was approved by the Board of Trustees. In 2006, the campus quadrangle was named Kinerk Commons in honor of Fr. Kinerk.

97 academic year, saying that the Rockhurst presidency "was just not a good fit for me."[2] Janet Watson Sheeran, dean of the College of Arts and Sciences, had stepped in as interim president while the university searched for a permanent replacement.

With the overwhelming support of trustees, faculty, and staff, they found an ideal replacement in Edward Kinerk, who recently had served as provincial of the Missouri Province of the Society of Jesus and already was serving on the Board of Trustees.[3] He was a Kansas City native who, as a child, had attended St. Francis Xavier grade school, crossed the street to attend Rockhurst High School, which at the time still shared space with the college, and then graduated in 1964 from Rockhurst College with a degree in mathematics. He went on to join the Society of Jesus and earn a master's degree in theology from Saint Louis University and a doctorate in spiritual theology from the Gregorian University in Rome. Ordained in 1972, Father Kinerk was the first Rockhurst alum ever to serve as university president.

"This is my home. I owe a huge debt to Rockhurst College," he said in the campus newsletter. "I cannot think of a better way of being a priest and Jesuit than in serving as president of Rockhurst College." He said he would work to continue "the welcoming environment so characteristic of Rockhurst." He spoke of Rockhurst's location on the border of the city's black and white sections as "a gift" and promised to strengthen the institution's Jesuit mission and to further develop its academic facilities.[4]

By the summer of 1999, the Xavier-Loyola dorms were being overhauled in what had become a "race to the finish" to beat the arrival of students that fall, and, nearby, a new Student Activities Center, commonly called the "Party Barn," was under construction even as the basement of Corcoran Hall was being remodeled for student use.[5] After years of delay, a new art gallery also was under construction. Named the Greenlease Gallery of Art in honor of longtime benefactor Virginia Greenlease, it was going up between Sedgwick and Van Ackeren halls. The new gallery included space for temporary exhibits, as well as the university's permanent collection, then housed in the library's Van Ackeren Gallery.[6]

When the new gallery was completed in 2000, the permanent collection was moved in and, over the years, would share space with temporary exhibitions. In 2003, for example, "Kansas Roots" showcased drawings, paintings, and mixed media by artist Susi Lulaki.[7] The gallery's 2005-06 Contemporary Exhibitions Series opened with a group show, "Once Upon a Time," with guest curators Barry Anderson of the University of Missouri-Kansas City and Sarah Mote of the Kansas City Art Institute. Featured artists came not only from Kansas City, but also from Bloomington, Indiana; Fort Worth, Texas; Wooster, Ohio; and New York City for a show that used painting, photography, mixed media, performance, and video to explore how stories shape our experience and how meaning is negotiated.[8]

Far more pedestrian was Rockhurst's need for additional parking, which led to the demolition of old Dowling Hall. Named for Rockhurst founder Michael Dowling, the 2-story building at the northeast corner of Troost Avenue and Rockhurst Road dated to 1922, when it had served an important role as the first building set aside for college use. As the old gave way to the new, Rockhurst added security cameras, security phones, and increased lighting as the number of young people now living on campus topped 700 students.[9]

As Rockhurst moved toward a more residential campus, the university explored new housing options. In the summer of 1990, 4 duplexes on Lydia Avenue were made available for students in their senior year; they quickly filled. In time, university-owned houses on other neighborhood streets, such as Forest Avenue, also were renovated and offered for student living. Also in 1990, Rockhurst tested its first "theme house," which it opened for students interested in technology. As part of their living/learning experience, the students were to staff a computer lab for other students to use.[10] Town House Village, with its 4-person town homes, opened in 1994.

As Rockhurst enrollment increased, housing became a pressing issue. By 2006, the campus housing situation was dire enough that the student newspaper ran an editorial urging the administration to build new dormi-

Reva R. Servoss taught chemistry at Rockhurst for 33 years. A native of Belgium, Servoss fled the Nazis during World War II. At one point she was sheltered by the Belgium underground in a Catholic convent where she masqueraded as a novice, following the routine of the sisters and wearing their habit. When Servoss began teaching at Rockhurst in 1963, she was one of the few women on faculty. She retired in 1996 and died in 2007. The Reva R. Servoss Endowed Prize is awarded to Rockhurst women who have declared a major in chemistry.

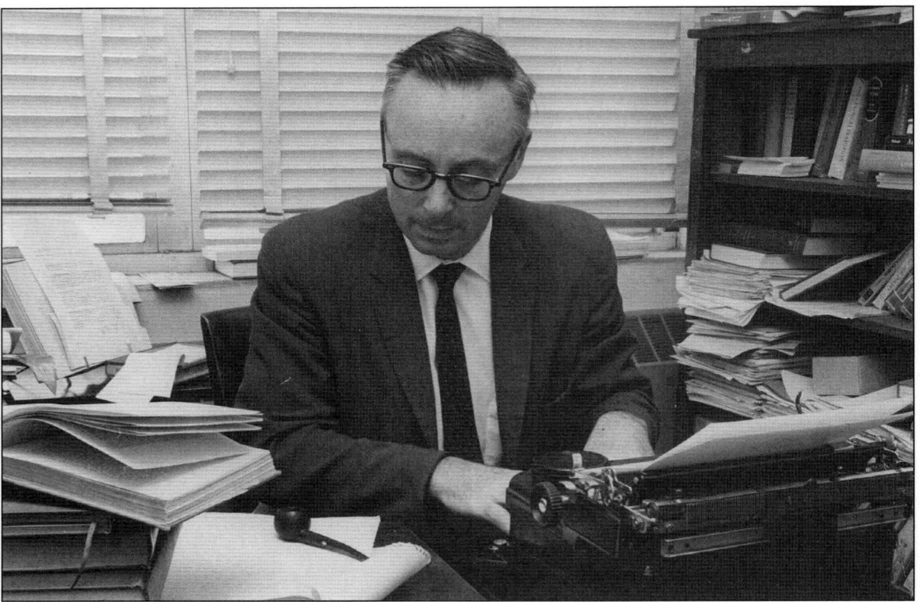

For 53 years, M. Robert Knickerbocker taught English to several generations of students. He arrived at Rockhurst in 1950 when Fr. Thomas Knapp, S.J., was president, retiring in 2003 under the presidency of Fr. Edward Kinerk, S.J. In addition to his duties in the English department, "Knick" was active in matters of faculty governance and sat on a number of important committees and boards for the college. Photo by Charles Brenneke. Courtesy of Rockhurst University Archives.

tories or more town homes. Xavier-Loyola, Corcoran, and McGee dorms "seem filled to their breaking point," the newspaper wrote, "as do the townhouses."[11] This was no "minor issue," the newspaper editorialized, because "it is quite likely that single rooms in dorms are going to be a thing of the past for the immediate future." And already, the editorial said, "there appears to be a great deal of discussion about turning 4 person townhouses into 6 person townhouses."[12]

— Just a Darn Good School —

Rockhurst's increasing enrollment reflected its gains in respectability and reputation for affordability. While the price tag to attend Rockhurst would continue to go up, the college still compared well to other private colleges and universities. For the academic year 1996-97, for example, the cost to send a child to Rockhurst was $15,410. That included tuition and fees, a double-dorm room, and the weekly 19-meal food plan. Expensive as it was, Rockhurst's tuition and fees still were $2,740 less expensive than those at Saint Louis University and $970 less than those at Creighton. When compared to the larger and more renowned Jesuit institutions, such as Georgetown (tuition and fees of $20,388) and Boston College (tuition and fees of $19,298), Rockhurst shone. Rockhurst's tuition and fees for that academic year of 1996-97 were, in fact, the least of any of the 28 Jesuit institutions in the United States.[13]

National publications like *Money* magazine and *U.S. News and World Report* took note in their annual college rankings, listing Rockhurst as among the "best values" in higher education. By the summer of 1998, Rockhurst had broken into the top 15 of *U.S. News'* rankings for regional colleges in the Midwest. The ranking made headlines in *The Kansas City Star*, which explained that the ranking was based on academic reputation, graduation and retention rates, faculty resources, financial aid for students, alumni giving, and student selectivity, which measured how hard it was for a student to get accepted.[14]

Rockhurst's reputation had gone up another notch in the spring of 1997 when President Bill Clinton lauded the school for its commitment to service and volunteerism. The praise, noted by the local media, came during the President's Summit for America's Future, held in Washington, D.C.[15] That same year, Rockhurst also made the fourteenth edition of *Rugg's Recommendations on the Colleges*. Editor Frederick E. Rugg placed Rockhurst in his list of 100 colleges that were "Just Darn Good Schools." Rockhurst's business administration and chemistry programs received special mention based on the caliber of their students, who tended to hold a B average and register high scores on the SAT (between 1100 and 1200) and ACT (24 to 26) exams.[16]

Rockhurst had always attracted talented young people, and the high caliber of students admitted to Rockhurst would continue into the new century. A profile of just-admitted, full-time undergraduates compiled by the Office of Admissions in 2002 revealed that the Class of 2006 entered Rockhurst with an average ACT score of 23.88 and an average high school grade point average of 3.31—and included 14 valedictorians. The proportion of women to men had climbed to about two-thirds/one-third, though it had been half and half just the year before. The number of Catholics entering Rockhurst was on the rise: from 59.4 percent in 1998 to 71 percent in 2002, though racial diversity had held fairly steady at 15 percent. As it always had, Rockhurst drew the greatest number of its freshmen that fall of 2002 from the Kansas City area, followed by St. Louis, Omaha, and the state of Kansas.[17] Rockhurst was justly proud, as well, of its 13:1 student-faculty ratio and its average class size of 24 students. In 2006, the university was recognized by the prestigious Carnegie Foundation for its initiatives to improve teaching in higher education.[18]

That same year, Rockhurst also received accolades from that most important of constituents—its students, who made such glowing remarks about the university in an anonymous survey conducted by the *Princeton Review* that the review designated Rockhurst a 2007 Best Midwestern College.[19] "So what did Rockhurst students have to say behind the University's back?" the campus newsletter asked in an article published in December 2006. Well, they had noted the "widely diverse population of racial backgrounds and interests," they found at Rockhurst, as well as the "strong involvement of the student body in University activities and affairs." They had praised the access to faculty members and the quality of their teaching. They liked Rockhurst's "tight-knit, involved community," its service opportunities, and its convenient, urban location.[20]

Members of the Rockhurst community work in Anapra, México. Since the 1980s, when former director of campus ministry William Finucane, S.J., took students to Appalachia during spring break, hundreds of Rockhurst students, staff, and faculty have participated in spring break service trips both inside and outside the United States. Courtesy of Rockhurst University Public Relations and Marketing.

— A COMMITMENT TO SERVICE —

As young people always had, Rockhurst students brought their enthusiasm and idealism to campus. Some spent their spring break on service missions to foreign countries, while others took on service projects at home,

Alumna Mary Pimmel's ('06) paintings of the 6 Jesuits martyred in El Salvador in 1989 are displayed in Sedgwick Hall. Pictured is Fr. Joaquín López y López ("Lolo"). Though quiet and timid, Fr. Lolo worked passionately for the people of El Salvador. To symbolize his calm, unassuming presence, the portrait is painted in blue. Photo by David Spaw.

from building houses for Habitat for Humanity and tutoring children at the city's Boys and Girls Clubs, to planting tulips on Troost Avenue and working with 'tweens and teens at St. Monica School.[21] At Christmastime, 1996, members of Tri-Beta, the national biology honor society, sold ornaments to help children in need, while the next year, Rockhurst's JUSTICE group sponsored a Giving Tree Project in which ornaments containing gift requests for area residents were hung on Christmas trees in Massman Hall. Anyone at Rockhurst could select an ornament, buy the requested gift, and place it under one of the trees. "Gifts needed are items like shoes, sweaters, clothing, toys, and other things that can brighten Christmas for those less fortunate," explained senior Mark Costaldi.[22]

It was Rockhurst senior Maureen Krueger, Class of 2000, who spearheaded a project for Habitat for Humanity. Krueger organized a fall fundraiser, wrote a successful grant application, and recruited volunteers—more than 120 of them—students, alumni, faculty, and staff—who spent the spring break of 2000 as construction workers on a Habitat house.[23] As a sophomore, Allison Rank went on mission to Juárez, México, where she helped build a cinderblock house for a family that had no running water.[24] Junior Ana Cimino partnered with the organization, Foundation of Sustainable Development, and served an 8-week summer internship living in a mud hut in Lubao, Kenya.[25] Rockhurst junior David LeFebvre spent his summer much closer to home—in a downtown Kansas City office building, busy coordinating a 3-day conference to be held later by American Humanics, a national alliance dedicated to preparing the next generation of leaders in the nonprofit sector.[26] Senior Pat Sommer came up with the idea of forming a Hawks Service Corps, open to any student willing to commit to an hour or 2 of volunteer work every week during the semester. In the spring of 2005, Sommer was working with the Center for Service Learning to get the program off the ground.[27]

A commitment to service was such an important part of the Rockhurst mission that graduating seniors received 2 transcripts–one for academic work and another for their service. Each year, Rockhurst's Center for Service Learning matched student volunteers with more than 100 local organizations in need. In the academic year of 1999-2000 alone, as part of President Kinerk's call for "Learning, Leadership, and Service"—which became a Rockhurst hallmark—students gave 25,000 hours of public service to Kansas City.[28]

For several years prior to his death in 1993, William Finucane, S.J., director of campus ministries, had taken students to work in Appalachia over their spring break.[29] In 1997, Brother E. Glenn Kerfoot, S.J., was hired as assistant campus minister, in part, to revitalize student service opportunities. Kerfoot befriended Ross Beaudoin, deacon at St. Mark's Parish in Independence, Missouri, who directed a parish program that sent volunteers to work in Juárez, México. When Beaudoin and Kerfoot offered Rockhurst students the chance to join the project over the 10-day spring break, 9 students applied for what were only 6 positions. The students flew to El Paso, Texas, took a bus to the border, and crossed into México, where they stayed in La Colonia del Rancho de la Puerto de Anapra, which Kerfoot described in an article for the *Jesuit Bulletin* as a shantytown on the outskirts of Juárez.[30] There, that first group of Rockhurst students to serve in México worked on building an adobe house for María Teresa, a *maquiladora*, and her 2 children, Marisol and Raulito. They had moved from the south of México so María could find work in one of the shops or factories set up on the border by international companies looking for cheap labor.

In the second year of Kerfoot's program, more than 40 students applied to serve and 28 were selected for 2 projects—one in Juárez and Anapra, the other in Guatemala. On a third trip, in May 2000, all but one of the women who went to Juárez belonged to the same sorority, Zeta Tau Alpha.[31] They were students in pre-med, nursing, and occupational and physical therapy majors. One of the Zetas, Sara Wisch, Kerfoot wrote, led the group in developing a health screening project for kindergarten and grade school children in the clinic that St. Mark's Parish helped support and maintain in Juárez.[32]

— GREEK LIFE —

Many members of Rockhurst sororities and fraternities were deeply involved in service projects, giving nearly 6,000 hours of service in 1999 alone, from assisting at the Ronald McDonald House and the Special Olympics to pitching in on a clean streets project.[33] That same year—the seventy-fifth of Greek life at Rockhurst—Brian Hesse, director of Greek Affairs, wrote a brief history of the Greek community at Rockhurst as part of the "Rockhurst Reflections" series in the faculty/staff newsletter. Greeks, Hesse wrote, had been a part of life at Rockhurst since 1924 with formation of the college's first fraternity, the local Beta Kappa Sigma, which was dedicated to academic fellowship and service to others. In 1932, Beta Kappa Sigma went national as the Zeta Chapter of Alpha Delta Gamma.[34] It wasn't until 1966 that a second fraternity, Tau Kappa Epsilon, was founded, followed by Sigma Alpha Epsilon in 1972 and Pi Kappa Alpha in 1993. The next year, 1994, the first sororities arrived on campus, Alpha Sigma Alpha and Zeta Tau Alpha. Two others followed, Delta Xi Phi in 2006 and Theta Phi Alpha in 2007.[35] The Greeks' healthy overall grade point average (3.34 GPA for spring 2006) and high retention rate (100 percent from freshman to sophomore year) was a plus for attracting new members. In the spring of 2006, Rockhurst counted 303 students who belonged to a sorority or fraternity, and Greek Week had become a yearly highlight on campus.[36]

Greek games. Photo by Roy Inman. Courtesy of Rockhurst University Archives.

As Rockhurst's first multicultural sorority, the formation

in May 2006 of Delta Xi Phi was especially notable. A handful of young women from different racial and ethnic backgrounds, had launched what they called the Women's Society of Sisterhood and Diversity, then sought and achieved affiliation with the national multicultural sorority. "When I first transferred to Rockhurst, I felt like a fish out of water," Brandie Morris, '07, president of the group, told *Rockhurst Magazine*. "The university is not as diverse as it could be, and our eyes are not as open as they should be." Morris, an African-American, said she hoped to help break down stereotypes and open people's minds to diversity and multiculturalism.[37]

— AIMING FOR DIVERSITY —

Diversity had been a concern at Rockhurst since the early 1970s when it first struggled to attract minority students and faculty. By the late 1980s, the catchall term "multiculturalism" was in vogue in the United States and other Western countries. By the spring of 1991, Rockhurst had formed a Multicultural Affairs Committee, which presented the college's first Multicultural Awareness Series. It kicked off with a symposium in Massman Gallery on April 11, 1991. Five prominent Kansas City leaders were invited to campus to sit on a panel and address various "myth vs. facts" involving the African-American, Hispanic, and Islamic communities, as well as welfare and homelessness, and the women's movement.[38] Events continued into the next week with a special class on the Middle East, an "ethnic cuisine" evening meal featuring Italian, Mexican, Chinese, Spanish, and American dishes, a debate on the desegregation of Kansas City schools, and a concert for Peace and Justice in the Rock Room on Saturday, April 20. Closing ceremonies featured musical performances by various ethnic groups.[39]

Study abroad. Courtesy of Rockhurst University Archives.

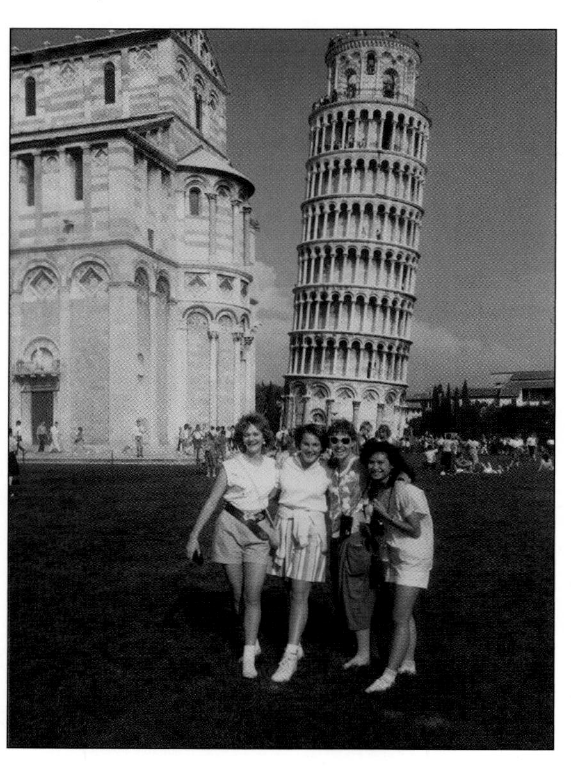

In March 1997, President Peter Ely, S.J., formed a Presidential Task Force on Diversity, chaired by Rosita Elizalde-McCoy, director of public relations and marketing. "I consider creating a more supportive environment for diversity to be one of the most important institution-wide issues for Rockhurst College," Father Ely wrote that March.[40] The task force, comprising faculty, students, and staff from minority and majority populations, set out to address complex issues, asking such questions as: "What does it take to become an educated and culturally literate person today?" and "How are diversity issues related to the college's Catholic, Jesuit mission and values?" As it began to meet, the task force listed 5 goals: increasing diversity among students; developing a plan to make diversity an integral part of student life; developing a comprehensive, ongoing cultural enrichment program on campus; increasing diversity among faculty and administrators; and recommending effective ways to develop a more culturally diverse curriculum.[41]

The previous summer, a study conducted by human resource administrators at Rockhurst had concluded that "a respect for and ability to work with colleagues from diverse backgrounds" was essential for successful employment.[42]

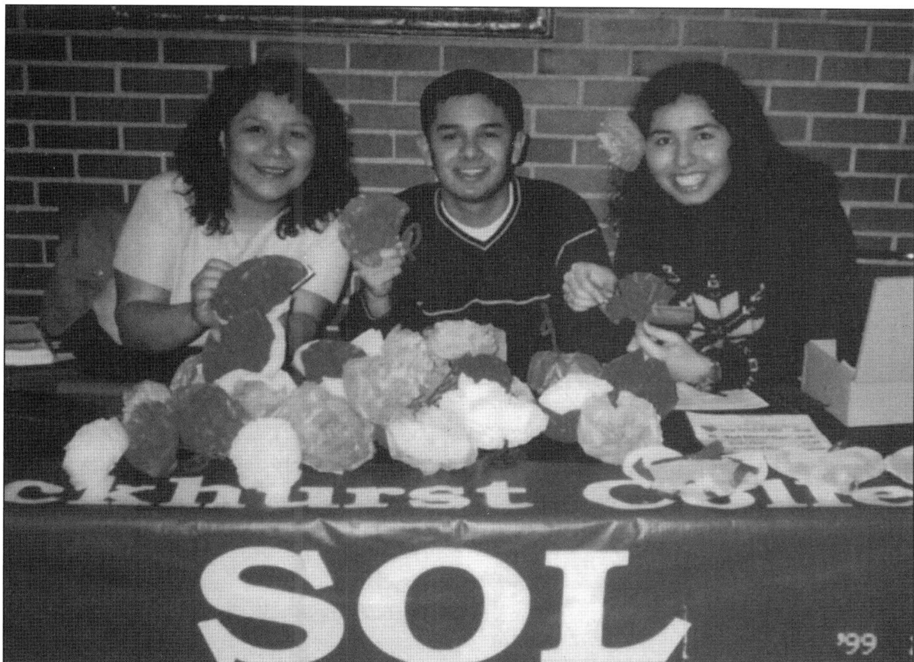

The Student Organization of Latinos was one of many organizations that sought to promote diversity, while providing support for minority students at Rockhurst. Pictured in this 1999 photo are (from left) Rocio Duncan, faculty moderator; Danny Melgoza, SOL president; and Katherine Williams, SOL member. Courtesy of Rockhurst University Archives.

That same summer, the Diversity Task Force invited the nationally recognized scholar Ronald Takaki to campus. Takaki, an ethics studies professor at the University of California-Berkeley, helped introduce, in 1989, multicultural studies as a graduation requirement at Berkeley. In a speech in Mabee Theater on August 25, 1997, he encouraged Rockhurst professors to rethink their approach to American history and to introduce a dialogue on multiculturalism in their classrooms.[43] "Intellectually, it's our duty to give an accurate portrayal of American history to all students," he said. "And morally it's the right thing to do, especially at a Jesuit institution that cares about social justice."[44]

Rockhurst now had an Office of Multicultural and International Affairs, which sponsored open forums and programs using interactive exercises, videos, and discussions to educate students about diversity.[45] Over the years, new Rockhurst organizations had formed: the Asian and Eastern Group, the Black Student Union, the Black Alumni Club, and the Student Organization of Latinos, which, in 1990, began hosting a yearly Hispanics of Today conference.[46] In the spring of 1995, the organization was expecting 300 students from throughout the Midwest to arrive on campus to attend workshops, a career fair, and a dinner-dance. Attorney José Gutiérrez, a professor at the University of Texas-Arlington, was invited to speak, as was Lena López, executive director of the Denver Hispanic Institute.[47]

Rockhurst began to reach out and welcome to campus young people from troubled spots in the world, be it Kosovo or America's own hurricane-ravaged New Orleans. In the fall of 1998, several students arrived from Botswana and 9 others from Kosovo. In the fall of 2005, following Hurricane Katrina, Rockhurst accepted, at no cost, 27 students from New Orleans, most from Loyola University, a sister Jesuit school.[48]

It was for Black History Month in 2005 that *Rockhurst Sentinel* staffer Caroline English thumbed through old yearbooks, looking for information about black students at Rockhurst. In an article published in *The Sentinel* on February 4, 2005, English named William Blake, Class of '51, as Rockhurst's first black graduate. She picked up the college yearbook from 1963 and reported that "young men in black suits and ties with cigarettes hanging form their mouths are prominent, but black students are not." She counted only a couple of photographs of the 4 black students attending Rockhurst that year. "It was not so much a financial situation that kept students away but intimidation," she wrote. "The black students that did attend Rockhurst were usually athletes or veterans using their G.I. Bill."[49]

English tracked down Charles Shumate, a black graduate, Class of '61, who told her that the majority of black people attending Rockhurst at the time went to night school. "The racial climate of the Kansas City area was reflective of the time," he said, though he added that he did not remember facing any discrimination at Rockhurst. When English talked to former student Mike Kleimann he agreed that black students were treated no differently from white students. "The Jesuits would not have allowed it," he said. English talked to another former student, Thomas Audley, '61, who told her "it was more noticeable when women started attending rather than when blacks started coming." Audley, she wrote, "remembers the few black students in his class being very personable and admired." Integrating Rockhurst, English argued, "was an easy transition," though "blacks did not flood to the university."[50] By 2009, Rockhurst counted 149 black students among its 3,029-member student body.

When a disturbing outbreak of racial graffiti hit campus in 1997, students placed hundreds of blue balloons in the shape of a ribbon on the quad to symbolize the signatures of more than 850 students, faculty, administration, and staff who signed petitions and wore ribbons against racism. Pictured are Jessica Stolz ('99) and Chris Tallent ('01). Courtesy of Rockhurst University Archives.

Rockhurst's concern for Kansas City's minority community found expression as early as 1970 in a weeklong celebration of black culture, heralded as Rockhurst's first Black Renaissance Fine Arts Festival. Sponsored in part by the Rockhurst Association for Black Collegiality, it opened on Sunday, October 12, 1970, with the Charlie Parker Memorial Concert, led by Clarence Rivers, a priest from Cincinnati who had composed an acclaimed American "Folk Mass." An audience of 3,000 attended the Mass, which included singing by Kansas City's own Lincoln High School chorus.[51]

The week that followed included a 5-hour jazz concert featuring popular local musicians Bettye Miller and Milt Abel, as well as swing and bop trumpeter Clark Terry, who had played with the Count Basie and Duke Ellington orchestras, then went on to television fame as a spotlighted player in the "Tonight Show" band.[52] There had been a lecture by artist Hank Smith, who had his own gallery at 30th and Main streets; a performance by a new drama group, the Black Contemporary Players of Kansas City; and poetry readings by the Black Writers Workshop of Kansas City. A performance in Mason-Halpin Fieldhouse by the Haitian dance troupe, the Leon Destiné Company from New York City, drew an audience of 2,000 people. Rockhurst student Ann Bartholome was there and published a detailed report in the *Jesuit Bulletin* the following February.

The festival had ended with a midnight "black and white Mass for peace and brotherhood" in St. Francis Xavier Church. Bartholome had watched as 18 priests, including Rockhurst President Maurice Van Ackeren, walked into the church to the slow, soft blues of "Nobody Knows the Trouble I've Seen." There had been hymns, readings from the *Autobiography of Malcolm*

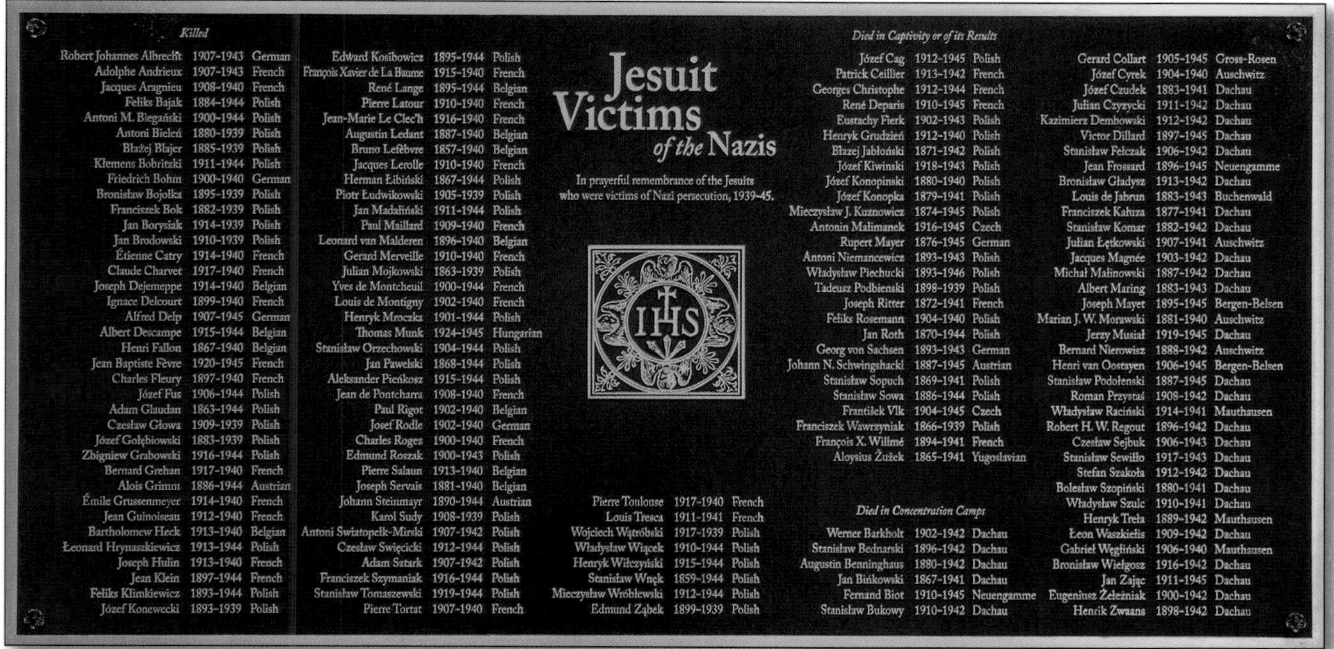

In 2007, a bronze plaque was dedicated to Jesuit victims of the Nazis, the only such memorial in the world. The plaque is located on the Rockhurst campus in the courtyard of the Finucane Jesuit Center. Photo by David Spaw.

X, black and white banners, and a rousing recessional to strains of the "Battle Hymn of the Republic." The church had been so full that 4 rows of people had banked the walls and stood during the entire service.[53]

"As the crowds surged out after the Mass," Bartholome reported, "they were still singing the 'Battle Hymn of the Republic,' many of them in tears, and all seemingly grateful for the shared experience of the week which saw ten thousand people, black and white, becoming more aware of the black man's rich heritage and powerful future potential." Rockhurst's own Robert R. Lakas, S.J., had helped coordinate the festival and supplied the closing remarks. "He visualized an optimistic spirit issuing from the festival and urged the need for action," Bartholome wrote, "especially action towards better understanding of all peoples' cultures."[54]

— THE MANY FACES OF ROCKHURST —

The words fit Father Robert Lakas to a tee. He had joined the Rockhurst faculty in 1955, an animated professor of English literature who might be found standing atop his desk delivering in Greek some tragedy or other, or giving an extemporaneous prayer or *avant-garde* liturgical presentation in the old chapel in Conway Hall, where he celebrated the afternoon Mass.[55] Father Lakas had produced a 2-hour television production, "The History of the Mass," and hosted a weekly TV show, "The Thomas More Show" on which he was so outspoken about classical and contemporary cultural issues that Harry Adamson said his comments became "the gist for much cocktail party chatter and more than an occasional letter to the editor."[56] Lakas also established the Men's Guild of the Kansas City Philharmonic and a book club that met monthly at the homes of members, who included such distinguished couples as *The Kansas City Star* editor Roy Roberts and his wife, Virginia and Robert Greenlease, Cecelia and Harry Massman, and Lena and Benjamin Sosland.[57]

A characteristic pose of Robert R. Lakas, S.J., as he celebrated Mass. After earning a Ph.D. in English from Yale, Fr. Lakas joined the faculty of Rockhurst in 1955. Rockhurst was immediately enriched by his work in academics, religion, and cultural affairs. He founded the Honors Program at Rockhurst and established the Thomas More Centre, which promoted fine and performing arts. Fr. Lakas served on the boards of many civic organizations and wrote and hosted a weekly television show that focused on cultural affairs and events in the community. He died of a heart attack in 1974 while greeting parishioners before the start of Mass at St. Francis Xavier Church. He was 57 years old. Painting by Louis Marak, 47½" x 72 ½", oil on linen. Photo of painting by Anne Pearce.

Robert Lakas was one of the many faces of Rockhurst Jesuits etched in memory. It was during the Second World War that economics professor George C. Hilke, S.J., was appointed alumni director and soon opened the first Rockhurst Alumni Office, in Conway Hall. After serving as director for 17 years, Father Hilke was honored at a dinner attended by 300 alumni on November 9, 1961. That night in Massman Hall, alumni president Gil P. Bourk had presented a bronze plaque and an engraved desk set to Father Hilke. As Hilke stood to thank the association, he turned to Kathleen Milburn, who was sitting at the head guest table, and gave her credit for the association's growth. "When Miss Milburn and I opened the office," Father

Hilke said, "they gave us an office and a box of plain 3x5 cards and nothing else. Not even a pencil. Miss Milburn had to bring her own pen and pencils from home." But over the years, they had watched the association mushroom from 200 members to nearly 4,000 by 1961.[58]

There were many memories: the twenty-fifth anniversary dinner in 1951 for chemistry professor Vanston H. Ryan and Jesuit Joseph Matoushek, and the all-Jesuit alumni dinner in 1952, when Jesuits from throughout the Kansas City area and administrators from across the country met in Kansas City for the National Catholic Educational Association. "We had 633 people in the fieldhouse for the dinner," Father Hilke recalled.[59] As Hilke retired from the alumni office, Rockhurst history instructor Hugh M. Owens, S.J., Class of '43, stepped into the job. Owens had joined the Navy and served 4 years in the South Pacific during World War II before entering the Society of Jesus and earning a master's degree from Saint Louis University, where his thesis, a history of the first 25 years of Rockhurst College, has stood the test of time.[60]

Father Hilke went on to serve as superior of the Rockhurst Jesuit community until his death, at age 66, on September 16, 1963.[61] Just days later, word came of the death of Joseph D. Horigan, the first boy to register on that long ago rainy day when Father Dowling opened the doors to a school that was then a college in name only. Mr. Horigan, 65 years old, had died in the Veterans Hospital in Biloxi, Mississippi. He had served in France with the 129th field artillery unit during World War I and left Kansas City soon after the war ended. He had worked as a salesman in Oklahoma City and left a son, James E. Horigan, of Denver, and 3 sisters, including one who had become a nun, Sister M. Inez Horigan of the Loretto Academy.[62]

Bernard Hale, a member of the high school's first graduating class in 1917, died on April 18, 1951.[63] As a young man, the popular Hale had been a star pitcher for the Kansas City Athletic Club and played in the minor leagues at Omaha for 2 years before giving up baseball to become a priest. He was ordained in 1923 and went on to serve several churches in Kansas City, culminating in 1940 with his appointment as pastor of St. Catherine of Siena Parish in Hickman Mills. Father Hale, who also served as the first director of Kansas City's Catholic Youth Council, was one of the best-known priests in the diocese. In 1948, on the twenty-fifth anniversary of his ordination, an estimated 375 people turned out at the Hotel President to help him celebrate. Tributes had come from President Harry S. Truman, big league manager Connie Mack, and Notre Dame football coach Frank Leahy, who once had served as Father Hale's batboy.[64]

Thomas J. Audley, '61, is currently the longest serving staff-member at Rockhurst. From 1974-90, he was director of admission, and since 1990, has worked in the university's advancement office. Audley was awarded the Harry B. Kies Award for Distinguished Service in 2005.

The names and faces of Rockhurst's dedicated priests cascaded through the years: English professor Louis Oldani, S.J., editing books on Jesuit theater; theology professor Martin J. Bredeck, S.J., presenting papers at the national meetings of the American Academy of Religion and the College Theology Society; English professor Robert R. Burke, S.J., accompanying students and friends for a week of theater in New York; college vice president J. Barry McGannon, S.J., named to a committee of the Association of American Colleges; and Maurice Van Ackeren, S.J., receiving an honorary doctor of laws degree from Benedictine College.[65] Here was Frank Mur-

Hugh Owens, Class of '43, returned to Rockhurst in 1959 to teach history and serve in the alumni office. He retired in 1992. The topic of Owens' master's thesis was a history of the first 25 years of Rockhurst, the first comprehensive history of the college to that point. The Hugh M. Owens' Prize in History, given annually to a Rockhurst student, is named in his honor. Courtesy of Rockhurst University Archives.

phy, S.J., longtime professor of industrial relations at Rockhurst, being recognized with the Harry B. Kies Award for Distinguished Service[66] and a $500,000 fund for the philosophy and theology departments in honor of professor Wilfred LaCroix, S.J., who, in 2010, marked his thirty-ninth year at Rockhurst.[67] Here was Jack Callahan, S.J., a Jesuit for 4 decades, coming on board in 1998 to serve as Rockhurst's director of mission and values and setting up a "Retreat in Everyday Life" to help those at Rockhurst set aside time to reflect and meditate according to the Spiritual Exercises of St. Ignatius.[68] And here were Joseph Gough, S.J., Francis Carey, S.J., and Joseph Freeman, S.J., celebrating their diamond jubilee as Jesuits.[69] After 52 years as a member of the Rockhurst philosophy department, Father Freeman retired from active teaching in the spring of 1998.

Amazing as was Father Freeman's long service at Rockhurst, another Jesuit would surpass him in longevity. He was the much-loved James D. Wheeler, S.J., who, in the fall of 2009, began his fifty-fourth year of teaching chemistry at Rockhurst. In the fall of 2005, when Father Wheeler was 82, *Rockhurst Magazine* featured him in an article headlined: "Solid Gold: Rockhurst icon celebrates 50 years of teaching chemistry."[70] Writer Katherine Frohoff didn't take long to marvel at Father Wheeler's amazing network of contacts, a network he kept up through his twice-yearly *Chemistry Newsletter*, which she described as "a no-frills publication written in a stream-of-consciousness style that defies editing." In it, Wheeler compiled the many e-mails he received from former students and added stories about those who had phoned or dropped in to see him. That fall, his most recent newsletter, No. 36, had gone out to 943 people. "It's a formula that has charmed alumni into contacting him just to get their names and stories included in the pages," Philip Colombo, Class of '91, who now taught alongside Wheeler, told Frohoff.[71]

Father Wheeler was indeed an icon at Rockhurst, where students might see him in shorts, walking from the Jesuit residence to the weight room, where he worked out. Testaments came in that fall of 2005, how Father Wheeler had been "a 'rock' of wisdom and faith" and a "wonderful mentor," and how he had made you "work like a dog" whether it was in the classroom or the gym. Bill Oulvey, S.J., Class of '74 and now rector-elect of the Rockhurst Jesuit community, wrote in with his recollections: "I signed up for chemistry because I thought I wanted to be a doctor," Oulvey wrote. "I was assigned to General Chemistry with 80 other freshmen in the basement lecture hall of Conway....

"At 11 a.m., in walks this short gentleman, with a flat-top haircut, desert boots, white socks, powder-blue pants, orange tie, glasses and a nondescript suit coat, and he says, 'Good morning, my name is Fr. Wheeler, this is General Chemistry, take out a half-sheet of paper, question number one.' The entire class was in shock and stunned silence," Oulvey recalled. "Who was this person who had invaded our lives? We soon learned however that looks can be deceiving. Fr. Wheeler is a terrific teacher, a very pastoral priest and a dear friend. He led me into the Jesuits."[72]

Father Wheeler had been at Rockhurst for so long that college president and alum Edward Kinerk, '64, had once sat in his class. By 2010, Wheeler

— JOSEPH M. FREEMAN, S.J. —

Much beloved by generations of students, the Rev. Joseph M. Freeman, S.J., began teaching philosophy and theology at Rockhurst in 1946. For 52 years, Freeman was a legend on campus.

He was noted for never missing class, attending all athletic events, and a memory for the names of the thousands of people he met. Alumnus Jim Millard ('64) remembered, "His classes were never lectures, they were thought-provoking. He taught us to dissect thoughts, to search for the truth in all things."

Fr. Freeman could frequently be seen walking about campus praying the Rosary. It was Fr. Freeman who initiated the campaign to raise money for the statue of the Virgin Mary that graces the campus. In 1986, Virginia Greenlease established the Rev. Joseph M. Freeman, S.J., Chair in Philosophy at Rockhurst to honor her longtime friend. Fr. Freeman retired from teaching after the spring 1998 semester, though he reminded people that he did not "give up being a Jesuit." By the time of his retirement, he had worked under 6 Rockhurst presidents and, from the time the first college classes were offered in 1917, had taught for all but 31 years of the college's existence. Fr. Freeman died in 2002 at the age of 91.

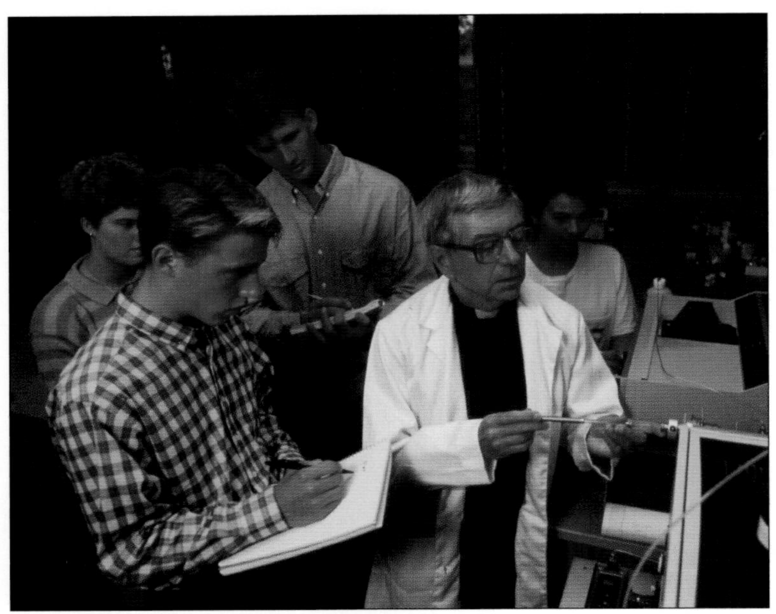

In the fall of 2009, James D. Wheeler, S.J., began his fifty-fourth year of teaching chemistry at Rockhurst. Having joined the faculty in 1955, Wheeler has worked under 6 college presidents, and one of those presidents, Edward Kinerk, '64, once sat in Wheeler's class. Photo by A.S. Weiner. Courtesy of Rockhurst University Archives.

had taught countless numbers of students and worked under 6 college presidents, including the one with the longest tenure—Maurice Van Ackeren, S.J., who had been at the helm when Father Wheeler joined the Rockhurst faculty in 1955.[73] In those days, there was not yet a Massman Hall or a Greenlease Library, and World War II surplus buildings still dotted the campus. Father Wheeler had watched the great changes on campus over the years; he had been there through the happy times and the sad, which seemed to come ever more frequently as old friends passed away. It was in May 1997, that he joined Rockhurst in mourning the death of Father Van.

— DEATHS IN THE FAMILY —

Maurice Van Ackeren, S.J., the man who, like Father Wheeler, had served Rockhurst for so long, died on May 12, 1997. He had served as president for 26 years, from 1951 to 1977, and then continued on as chancellor. "There are few institutions which are marked by the life of one man in the way that Rockhurst has been marked by Father Van Ackeren," Rockhurst President Peter Ely, S.J., told *The Kansas City Star*.[74] "It is the end of an era." It was Father Van, 85 years old, the newspaper said, who was credited with changing Rockhurst's image "from a seminary and junior college to a nationally recognized liberal arts school." Many people noted Father Van's fund-raising skills, including Donald Hall, chairman of the board of Hallmark Cards. "He'd come in modestly and chat and after a while you knew he'd gotten you," Hall said, describing Father Van as "a wonderfully kind and friendly man, who enjoyed people. Everyone who knew him loved him."[75]

It was the Rev. Edward Kinerk, S.J., still serving as provincial of the Missouri Province of the Society of Jesus, who gave the homily during Father Van's funeral that May 16. "I don't know of any human being who had less ego," Father Kinerk had said, calling Van Ackeren a "builder" of connections with people. He was a man, Kinerk said, "who brought forth generosity, humor, selflessness and determination of purpose in all he met."[76] Bishop George K. Fitzsimons of Salina, Kansas, a 1948 Rockhurst College alumnus, concelebrated the funeral Mass at St. Francis Xavier Church. A total of 37 priests attended, with Father Van's fellow Jesuits strongly represented.

It was on another day in May, 2 years later, that word came that former Rockhurst president Thomas Savage, S.J., was gravely ill. "He is experiencing severe respiratory complications with pneumonia and asthma," Father Kinerk informed the Rockhurst community on May 10, 1999. Father Thom had been working with Mercer Consultants and living in California until his health had worsened to the point that he was taken back to a

Jesuit infirmary in his home province of New England. Just hours later on that same day of May 10, President Kinerk sent out another communiqué to the Rockhurst community, this one saying that Father Thom had just died, at 2:25 p.m. Kansas City time, in Weston, Massachusetts.[77] He was only 51 years old.

Rockhurst held a memorial service at St. Francis Xavier Church on May 18. The ecumenical reflections—by the Rev. Emanuel Cleaver of St. James United Methodist Church, Rabbi Michael Zedek of Temple B'nai Jehudah, and the Rev. Robert L. Hill of Community Christian Church—spoke to the inclusiveness that had been so much a part of Father Thom's tenure at Rockhurst. Like Father Van, he had been a people person. "Father Thom was one of the most extraordinarily talented people I've ever known," President Kinerk told *The Catholic Key*. "He reached out to the greater Kansas City community and brought Rockhurst College with him. All of us at this institution and in this city owe him a great deal."[78]

Praise of Father Thom poured in, from the city of Westwood, Kansas, to the Council of Independent Colleges in Washington, D.C., to the

James Wheeler, S.J.

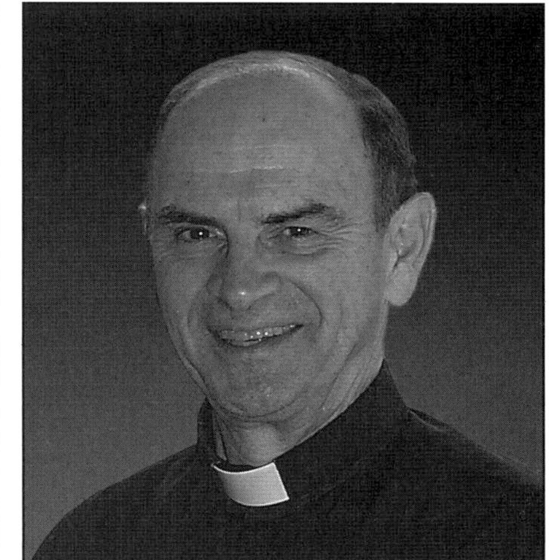
Wilfred LaCroix, S.J.

Louis Oldani, S.J.

Martin Bredeck, S.J.

At the 100th anniversary of Rockhurst, only 4 teaching Jesuits remained. James D. Wheeler, S.J. (chemistry), Louis J. Oldani, S.J. (English), Wilfred L. LaCroix, S.J. (philosophy), and Martin J. Bredeck, S.J. (theology and religious studies). At the conclusion of the 2009-10 academic year, these 4 Jesuits had provided 164 years of classroom instruction to Rockhurst students. Courtesy of Rockhurst University Archives.

Spiritual Care Department of St. Joseph's Health Center, to the president of Kansas City's Historic Garment District Group.[79] Father Kinerk and others from Rockhurst made plans to attend his funeral services, to be held on May 13 in the Jesuit Health and Renewal Center in Weston, Massachusetts. Rockhurst sent flowers, and the Public Relations Department prepared a large card for those on campus to sign. Father Kinerk planned to take it with him to Massachusetts.[80]

Then, on February 1, 2000, as part of a series on "AIDS in the Priesthood," *The Kansas City Star* reported that Father Thom, who had kept his battle with AIDS private, was among priests who had died from complications of the disease. The series and its blatant inferences made headlines nationwide, including a response that November in *The Catholic World* by the Jesuit Paul J. Shaughnessey, who decried the "ugly and indisputable fact" of gay men in the priesthood. Shaughnessey wrote with disgust of the sin and "moral delinquency" of the priests involved, blamed the situation on a lack of accountability at the highest levels and on the "liberal agenda" of many in the Church. He wrote of the "shame" of the faithful and expressed astonishment at the response of Rockhurst's Father Kinerk, who, unlike the Rev. Shaughnessey, did not condemn.[81]

"As a Jesuit, I cannot feel anything but pride and gratitude for a meteor that burned itself out in the service of others," Father Kinerk had told the writer of *The Kansas City Star* series, Judy Thomas. "On May 10, 1999, God took the gift back. Thom is with God. As Jesuits, we rejoice. He has done what God sent him to do." Not only did President Kinerk embrace Father Thom in death as in life, but also the university celebrated his life by adding a panel in his honor to the national AIDS Memorial Quilt. "We will remember him for his vision, energy and love of Rockhurst and Kansas City," Father Kinerk would say. "He dedicated his life to making our community a better place to live. We should all be proud to have his name associated with Rockhurst University, where he left an indelible mark."[82]

In 1961, Edward S. Kos joined the Rockhurst faculty in biology. He retired from full-time teaching in 1998, but has continued teaching part-time, while serving as the university archivist. In 2010, Kos began his 50th year at Rockhurst. Courtesy of Rockhurst University Archives.

To commemorate the life of Fr. Thomas Savage, S.J., a group of faculty, staff, and students created a panel for the AIDS Memorial Quilt. The panel displays a drawing of Fr. Savage, the Rockhurst logo, and a shooting star—reminiscent of Fr. Edward Kinerk's description of Fr. Savage as "a meteor that burned itself out in the service of others." Pictured holding the quilt are (from left) Janet Cooper, Marie Pickard, and Nina Marsh. Courtesy of Rockhurst University Public Relations and Marketing.

A NEW, HIGH-TECH WORLD —

As he had done since he was named president, Father Kinerk continued to work to complete the master plan drawn during Father Savage's tenure. That summer of 1999, as one construction crew worked feverishly to renovate the Xavier-Loyola dorms, another was building a new 54th Street campus entrance. The old, longtime main entrance—at 53rd Street and Troost Avenue—was being closed to make way for an exciting new project—a pedestrian mall that would include a pergola, fountain, and bell tower at the south end of the quadrangle. By the spring of 2000, there was talk of another exciting project—a new baseball field, tennis courts, and jogging paths, made possible with an anonymous challenge gift of $500,000 and the completed purchase of all the property between 53rd and 54th streets.[83]

Less visible was Rockhurst's first and only interactive classroom in Conway Hall, which was up and running by the fall of 1998. Its TV cameras, monitors, VCR, and voice-activated cameras were so cutting edge that an open house was scheduled that October to show them off. The new IT age moved so fast, however, that it would be in just a few years, thanks to generous gifts from Barnett and Shirley Helzberg, Thomas A. McDonnell, '66, and others, that all of Conway Hall would be renovated to include new computer labs and more "smart classrooms" with multimedia capabilities.[84] The renovated Conway, reopened in 2002, was so well received that it led to the technological upgrade of classrooms throughout the campus.

With the budding technological age came new innovations. In the summer of 1995, a new campus phone system, featuring voice mail, video conferencing, and caller ID, was installed,[85] followed by an updated home

A new, high-tech world of computers and wireless Internet stood in stark contrast to this vintage Monroe Calculating Machine, on display in the Science Center. Photo by David Spaw.

The first graduating class from the School of Professional Studies, 1998-99. From left, President Edward Kinerk, S.J., David Rasmussen, Kim Roberts, Bill Clark, Jim Millerschultz, Steve Bean, Michael Cooney, Patricia Mallory, Gary Varner, Dean Nan Tonjes. Three others not pictured also made up the initial graduating class.

page on what was being called the World Wide Web. The Public Relations and Marketing Department, with help from the Computer Services staff, was working hard by the spring of 1996 to add more information, graphics, and links between the main home page and departmental home pages. A wireless network that provided Internet and network access from anywhere on campus was up and ready to go as the academic year of 2005 began. That fall, the Student Senate provided free USB flash drives to all full-time undergraduates. Small enough to fit on a keychain, the drives provided 128 MB of portable storage space, allowing students to plug into their laptop and check e-mail or write a paper anywhere on campus.[86]

"If you have a laptop, you have a computer lab," Matt Heinrich, associate vice president of administration, told *Rockhurst Magazine*.[87] Students who didn't own a laptop still could use the flash drive to transfer files between any of the hundreds of state-of-the-art personal computers throughout campus, many available 24 hours a day. The new generation of tech savvy students had come to expect—and depend—on such things. "Students look at technological capabilities when making their decisions on what school to attend," Heinrich explained. "Most schools have wireless hot spots but don't have complete coverage."[88]

Rockhurst, in fact, was so up-to-date that it was ranked No. 26 in the nation on Intel's 2005 list of top wireless campuses in the United States.[89] It was the only institution in the Kansas City region and the only Jesuit school to make the list. Rockhurst's smaller size, Heinrich explained, made it easier to stretch a wireless network across the entire campus.

— OLD TRADITIONS, NEW NAME —

Much would be accomplished during Father Kinerk's administration. There had been significant grants and gifts as part of the Excellence in the City capital campaign, including $695,000 from the Kauffman Foundation, $350,000 from the Francis Family Foundation, and $150,000 from the Rose Tiecher estate. In 1999, John Hayes, '59, former chair of the Board of Trustees, and his wife Jean, donated $1 million for scholarships, and the U.S. Department of Education designated a $1.7 million Title III grant to Rockhurst for technology and faculty development. In addition, the annual gala continued to be well attended, netting hundreds of thousands of dollars for the university.[90]

Yes, *university*. Although Rockhurst officially had changed its charter to become a university in 1951, use of the term had been discouraged and, for all intents and purposes, kept under wraps for nearly 50 years. It wasn't until Father's Kinerk's tenure, in the fall of 1998, that the name change came before the Board of Trustees. That September, Father Kinerk sought faculty opinions and outlined, as he saw them, the pros and cons of the name change. By calling itself a *college*, he said, Rockhurst exuded connotations of a close-knit community with a caring, student-centered education—exactly the characteristics so essential to Rockhurst's self-understanding. On the other hand, based on an image study conducted in 1997, the term *college* led to a perception by prospective students that Rockhurst had limited academic offerings. In addition, many community colleges across the nation were dropping the "community" from their name, further confusing the public's perception.[91]

"In many ways we already function as a university," Kinerk wrote. "We have the College of Arts and Sciences, the School of Management, and the School of Professional Studies; and we are partnered with Research College of Nursing. Each of these schools or colleges has its own dean, budget, and programs. We offer four master's degrees with a fifth on line for next year,

— Barnett and Shirley Helzberg —

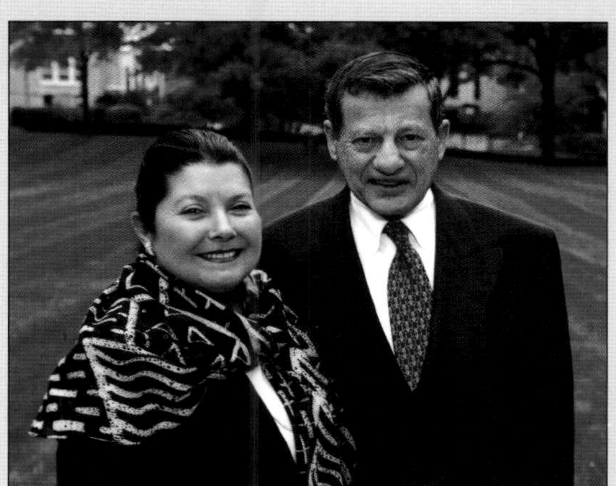

In honor of Shirley and Barnett Helzberg's generosity to the Rockhurst University School of Management, in 2001 the school was renamed the Helzberg School of Management. Barnett Helzberg was chairman of the national jewelry chain, Helzberg Diamond Shops, Inc., and his wife, Shirley, was one of the co-chairs of Rockhurst's "Excellence in the City" capital campaign.

Both Shirley and Barnett have been longtime friends of the university, sharing a special connection with past president Rev. Thomas Savage, S.J. Barnett's relationship with Rockhurst took a new turn in the late 1980s when he began teaching M.B.A. classes in management and entrepreneurship at Rockhurst. In 2006, the Helzberg School of Management was accredited by the Association to Advance Collegiate Schools of Business, the highest rating given for business schools.

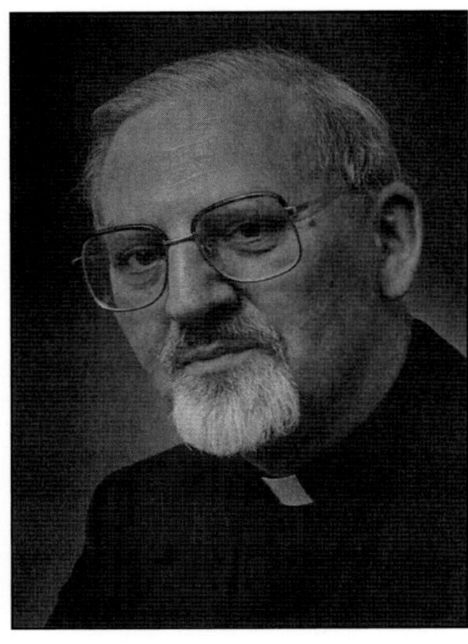

On October 17, 2002, the Very Rev. Peter-Hans Kolvenbach, S.J., Superior General of the Society of Jesus, celebrated Mass at St. Francis Xavier Church, followed by a reception on Rockhurst's campus.

In 2002, Rockhurst opened a Community Center to serve the unmet needs of residents in the university's immediate neighborhood. In addition to extending free recreational and educational opportunities, the Community Center seeks to develop working partnerships with neighborhood residents. Courtesy of Rockhurst University Public Relations and Marketing.

and we are contemplating more."[92] At a meeting of the Board of Trustees on December 5, 1998, the board approved the change to *Rockhurst University*, effective July 1, 1999.[93]

A number of new degree programs were established, including a master's of integrated humanities and education (MIHE), a master's in communication science and disorders, a bachelor's in biochemistry, and, in the fall of 2004, Rockhurst's first doctoral program—in physical therapy.[94] In October 2001, the School of Management was renamed the Helzberg School of Management in honor of the Kansas City Helzberg family. Barnett Helzberg, the retired chairman of Helzberg Diamond Shops, Inc., was an adjunct professor at the school, and Shirley Helzberg was co-chair of Father Kinerk's Excellence in the City capital campaign.[95] In 2006, the Helzberg School of Management was accredited by the Association to Advance Collegiate Schools of Business, the highest given for schools of business. As it had sought to attain AACSB accreditation, Rockhurst consolidated all its business courses on the main campus and sold its south campus to a Methodist church.[96]

Changes were apparent everywhere. A new Community Center opened in 2002 in a renovated Kroger grocery store at the corner of 54th and Troost Avenue, and the university's new Campus Ministry House opened at 5134 Forest Avenue in late 2005. By then, fund-raising was under way for a new Health and Wellness Complex. The innovative design plan called for a bridge to connect the Convocation Center and Massman Hall; the area between would be transformed into a pedestrian mall,[97] an idea that complemented the existing pedestrian walkway, which was dedicated under beautiful blue skies on October 17, 2000.

Bells rang and water flowed that day as the new fountain and carillon tower were blessed and dedicated. Father Kinerk and the Board of Trustees had sent out invitations for a ceremony that Kinerk described as "brief and successful." The new tower, pergola, and fountain, together with the

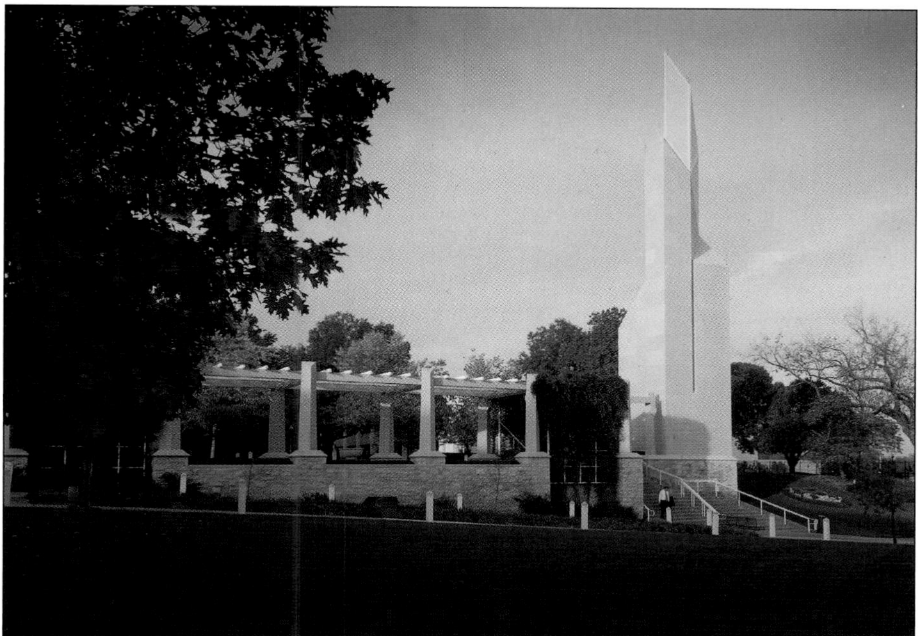

The new millennium brought a major improvement to the campus landscape with the addition of a pedestrian mall, pergola, fountain, and bell tower. Photo by David Spaw.

pedestrian walkway that had replaced the old 53rd Street campus entrance had, he said, "transformed the campus." Indeed, it was even more beautiful when illuminated at night.[98] The inscription chiseled into the side of the tower quoted Peter-Hans Kolvenbach, twenty-ninth Superior General of the Society of Jesus. During a visit to Rockhurst in October 2002, Father Kolvenbach walked the expanded quad and undoubtedly read his own words inscribed on the tower.[99]

Adding to the space was the "Generations Walkway," which gave everyone a chance to participate. For $100, those loyal to Rockhurst could have their name or a loved one's name engraved, along with the Rockhurst logo, on a 4-inch by 8-inch brick that would be added to the pedestrian walkway with hundreds of others.[100]

Topping off construction was the new Loyola Park athletic complex, with its new tennis courts, softball field, and baseball diamond, with home plate gracing the spot where houses once stood at Tracy Avenue and 54th Street. The diamond was completed in the fall of 2003 with a big boost from DST Systems CEO and Board of Trustees Chairman Tom McDonnell and his wife, Jean, who donated $2.3 million. Their gift came close to putting Father Kinerk's 2-year, $50 million Excellence in the City capital campaign over the top.[101]

Softball was inaugurated in 2004 as Rockhurst's eleventh varsity sport—and the new softball field completed in time for the home opener on March 15, 2005.[102] Loyola Park's new tennis courts had opened in the fall of 2004, but plans for a new soccer field were not realized. The amount of dirt that needed to be removed turned out to be cost prohibitive.[103] Instead, Rockhurst widened the existing Bourke Field soccer grid to meet NCAA requirements, a necessity because Rockhurst, in 1998, had left the NAIA and joined Division II of the National Collegiate Athletic Association. In the fall of 2005, Rockhurst joined the 14-team, 2-division, Great Lakes Valley Conference. The Hawks would compete in the Western Divi-

"Shaw's Brickyard." The Rockhurst Generations Walkway, located near the bell tower, pergola, and fountain, consists of personalized bricks that donors have purchased for themselves or others. Over the years, Dick and Daffy Shaw have purchased hundreds of bricks in honor of family, former teachers and colleagues, and people of importance in their lives and to Rockhurst. Dick ('60) taught marketing at Rockhurst for 22 years. Daffy worked in admissions at Rockhurst for 15 years.

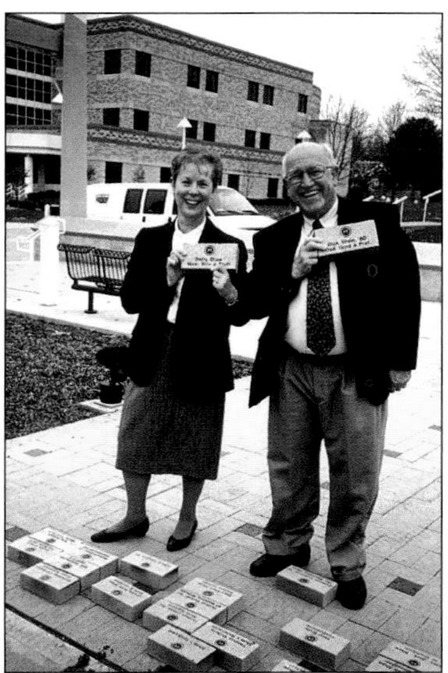

sion with Drury and Quincy universities, Southern Illinois-Edwardsville, Missouri University of Science and Technology, the University of Missouri-St. Louis, and the University of Southern Indiana.[104]

The new baseball diamond was completed just in time to host the re-introduction of a Rockhurst tradition that had fallen by the wayside—the annual Rockhurst Day celebration, begun by Father Van Ackeren in 1953. Only about 500 people turned out for the 2003 revival, but Rockhurst Day grew stronger year by year as fun events were added. On Friday, September 30, 2005, the rejuvenated Rockhurst Day included carnival games, concessions, a beer garden, and the Great Baby Race, held during halftime of the Rockhurst women's soccer match. The Homecoming Court took the field during halftime of the men's soccer game, which was followed by fireworks.[105]

Other traditions, old and new, took hold. The annual Golf Classic raised money for the athletic department, while the Polar Walk was a benefit for local charities.[106]

The Gift and Bequest Council, founded in 1956 by President Van Ackeren, marked its fiftieth year in 2006. Now called the Planned Giving Committee, the council over the years had assisted donors in giving more than $26 million to the university.[107] The Visiting Scholar Lecture Series celebrated its fiftieth anniversary in October 2004, counting more than 270 guest speakers who had visited campus to lecture and talk to students and the Rockhurst and Kansas City communities—from poet Robert Frost and presidential adviser Henry Kissinger to Archbishop Joseph Cardinal Bernardin. "Whenever you have the opportunity not only to listen to but to have a conversation with the person who has written the book in your philosophy class, for example, that's exciting," said Rockhurst English pro-

The Loyola Park athletic complex includes tennis courts and softball and baseball fields. Courtesy of Rockhurst University Public Relations and Marketing.

Softball was inaugurated as a varsity sport in 2004. Pictured is the 2008 women's softball team. Courtesy of Rockhurst University Public Relations and Marketing.

fessor Joseph Cirincione, who had directed the series for 15 years. He had followed in the footsteps of Rockhurst's Vincent Daues, S.J., who founded the lecture series and directed it for more than 30 years.[108]

Rockhurst's Midwest Poet Series also continued to bring noted people to campus. The Greenlease Gallery of Art hosted exhibitions, and the Rockhurst Players performed in Mabee Theater, staging classics such as *The Glass Menagerie* in 2003 and the more recent *Dead Man Walking* in 2004.[109] In support of the student drama group, Rockhurst seniors, in August of 2006, transformed the Convocation Center into a Southern beauty parlor for a dinner theater production of the popular *Steel Magnolias*. A portion of the $25 ticket price supported the Rockhurst theater program.[110]

Rockhurst activities now included the autumn Foreign Language Film Series on campus and the springtime Rockstock, an outdoor music concert and festival, which was part of Hawkwild Week. In April 2006 students were buzzing about the headliner, punk band Sugarcult. The weeklong festival featured bands from around the Kansas City area, as well as a paintball event and Casino Night, put on in the "Party Barn" by the Student Senate.[111]

The new generation of students shook their heads at a Rock Room that seemed "stuck in a time warp" with its brown-and-orange retro feel. "Soon the groovy '70s-style décor will be renovated," the *Rockhurst Community* reported in May 2003.[112] That summer, modern flooring, wall coverings, and lighting were to be installed and an outdoor patio added to the Pub. By the summer of 2006, the Rock Room seemed totally twenty-first century with the addition of a Starbucks coffee shop and Planet Sub.[113]

The Great Baby Race was one of many fun events at Rockhurst Day, 2007. The celebration of Rockhurst Day was a tradition begun by Maurice Van Ackeren, S.J., in 1953. After an absence of many years, the annual event was revived in 2003. Courtesy of Rockhurst University Public Relations and Marketing.

In April 2008, Rockhurst alumni gathered to watch the Chicago Cubs from Beyond the Ivy, a rooftop venue overlooking the stadium. Pictured are (front, center) Pete Kammerer, '06, (from left, front row) Mary Landers, alumni director, Deanna Johnson, '06, Lauren Cardwell, '06, '07 (M.Ed.), Michelle Gartner, '07, Christy Still, '00, Chris Gaubatz, '98, Diego Gutierrez, '05, (from left, top row), Rev. Thomas Curran, O.S.F.S., Carl Jansen, '65, Joel Sobanski, '00, Dan Brunnert, '00, Ted Toczylowski, '99, Ward Condon, '83, and David Kramer, '86. Courtesy of Rockhurst University Public Relations and Marketing.

— A CHANGING WORLD —

On the eve of the twenty-first century, Americans braced for Y2K, fearing that the digital switch to the year 2000 would crash computers worldwide. At Rockhurst, the university took precautions by shutting down its system for 24 hours, which, to everyone's relief, proved to have been unnecessary.[114] The century's smooth beginning would not last. The previous April of 1999, 2 young men had murdered fellow students at Columbine High School in Colorado, a scenario that would be repeated at other schools, in other places. If the world seemed to have gone crazy, the events of September 11, 2001, cemented the feeling. The horrific terrorist attacks on the World Trade Center and Pentagon created deep angst and led America into a war that seemed to have no end. Closer to home, a gunmen shot and killed 2 monks at Missouri's Conception Abbey in June 2002, and Rockhurst hadn't forgotten its own Chrisha Siebert, the 28-year-old technical director of Mabee Theater who had been lost in the unexplained explosion of TWA Flight 800.[115] When Hurricane Katrina broke the levees and flooded New Orleans, Americans talked of global warming and the widening gap between rich and poor. As if things weren't bad enough, Catholics were shaken by another scandal, this one accusing scores of priests of sexually abusing children.

Nearly a decade before any of these disturbing events, Pope John Paul II had recognized a modern world in desperate need. In his *Ex Corde Ecclesiae*, issued in Rome on August 15, 1990, he had claimed for the Catholic university a central role in the mission of the Church as it faced the staggering challenges of the future.[116] The Catholic university, distinguished "by its free search for the whole truth about nature, man and God," gave him, the pope said, "a well-founded hope for a new flowering of Christian culture." In a world characterized by such rapid developments in science and technology, the pope believed that the tasks of a Catholic university assumed an ever-greater importance and urgency. What good, he asked, were scientific and technological discoveries unless they be used "for the authentic good of individuals and of human society as a whole?" Because those of faith believed this outcome required a corresponding "search for meaning," the Catholic university—with its inclusion of the moral, spiritual, and religious dimension of research—was called upon to respond.

Chrisha Siebert was one of 230 people killed in the explosion of TWA Flight 800 on July 17, 1996. In addition to teaching classes in theater, Siebert was technical director for Mabee Theater.

John Paul's *Ex Corde Ecclesiae* addressed the still burning question of identity and mission that had confronted Catholic universities since the 1960s. His message centered on a call for integration—the integration of knowledge, pursued through a dialogue between faith and reason, a pervasive "ethical concern" and vigorous "theological perspective."[117] The basic mission of a university, he declared, was "a continuous quest for truth through its research, and the preservation and communication of knowledge for the good of society." John Paul concluded by asserting his "deep conviction that a Catholic University is without any doubt one of the best instruments that the Church offers to our age which is searching for certainty and wisdom."

So important was the Catholic tradition on which Rockhurst was founded that in the spring of 1999 Father Kinerk formed a task force to explore ways to enrich the study of Catholicism at Rockhurst. Out of this came the establishment of the Thomas More Center for the Study of Catholic Thought and Culture, directed by Richard Janet, a professor of history. "As a Catholic university, we are heirs to 2000 years of cultural and intellectual tradition, yet we sometimes ignore that tradition in our quest to learn new perspectives and escape our 'ghetto mentality,'" Janet wrote as the new center took hold. "We fail to appreciate that our tradition is actually an encouragement to growth and development."[118]

The Thomas More Center for the Study of Catholic Thought and Culture was established in 1999. Directed by Richard Janet, a professor of history, the Center offered its first course in 2000, "Catholicism at the Millennium," out of which came a book of essays published in 2001 by the newly established Rockhurst University Press. Today, the Thomas More Center sponsors lectures, manages a grant program to assist faculty in research on Catholic topics, and offers courses leading to a minor in Catholic studies.

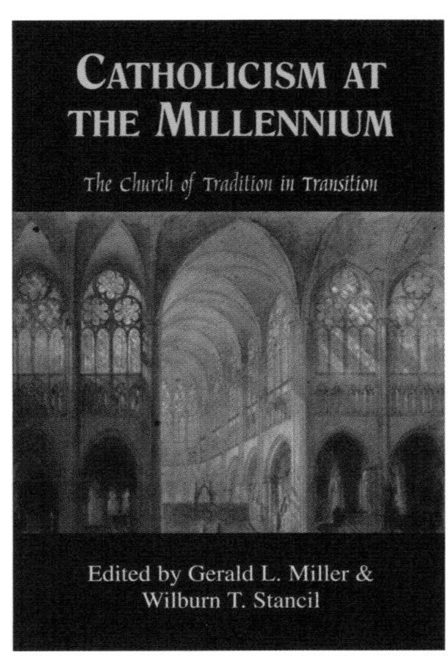

In the spring of 2000, the Thomas More Center offered its first course, "Catholicism at the Millennium," out of which came a book of essays published in 2001 by the newly established Rockhurst University Press. The second course offered by the center, "Catholic Biographies," highlighted a variety of famous Catholics—from St. Paul and Erasmus to Thomas Merton and Dorothy Day—and explored their impact on the development of the church. Lectures, offered one day a week, were led by faculty members and yielded yet another book of essays on the nature of Catholic culture.[119]

Other efforts to renew the focus on Rockhurst's Jesuit mission and values led to the creation, in August 2007, of the Office of Mission and Ministry and the hiring of Kevin Cullen, S.J. Father Cullen, who had served previously as the Missouri provincial's assistant for social and international ministries, was named Rockhurst vice president for mission and ministry and set out to provide leadership and direction.[120]

Catholic scholars could point to the new Office of Mission and Ministry and the Thomas More Center as evidence at Rockhurst that Catholic higher education was prospering as the twenty-first century began.[121] It

PRESIDENTIAL PROFILE

— THOMAS B. CURRAN, O.S.F.S. —

The Rev. Thomas Curran, O.S.F.S., was appointed Rockhurst's fourteenth president in June 2006. Born in 1955 in Philadelphia, Fr. Curran holds a bachelor's degree from DeSales University and three master's degrees—an M.A. in theology from DeSales School of Theology, an M.A. in liberal studies, public policy and government from Georgetown University, and an M.B.A. from St. Joseph's University. He also earned a law degree from the Catholic University of America.

In 1977, Curran became a professed member of the Oblates of St. Francis de Sales (O.S.F.S.) and was ordained to the priesthood in 1984. Among his wide-ranging experiences are the presidency of the Northeast Catholic High School for Boys in Philadelphia from 1993-1997, the presidency of Salesianum School in Wilmington, Delaware from 1997-2004, and founder and director of Nativity Preparatory School in Wilmington, a tuition-free middle school for boys. Immediately prior to his arrival at Rockhurst, Fr. Curran served as Associate Vice President for University Relations and Assistant to the President of Regis University, Denver.

Fr. Curran is the first non-Jesuit to serve as Rockhurst president. His impact at Rockhurst was immediate, putting into motion long-range planning for greater financial stability. It will be his task to lead the university into its next 100 years.

prospered even as the number of Jesuits, who had once dominated Catholic higher education, declined. In 1970, there were 7,775 Jesuits in the United States, more than 4,000 of them involved in education. By 1992 the number of Jesuits in the U.S. had dropped to 4,484, and by the year 2000 to 3,172. The number was expected to bottom out at 2,411 by 2010. Alarmingly, the number of seminarians had plummeted from 3,559 in 1965 to only 389 in 2000.[122] Rockhurst University, in the spring of 2004, considered itself fortunate to count 24 Jesuits in its community, although many worked at Rockhurst High School or in positions not directly related to the university.

That spring, *Rockhurst: The Magazine of Rockhurst University* ran an article titled "The Changing Face of Jesuits at Rockhurst," in which it featured the community's younger Jesuits. They were men like 45-year-old John Vowells, S.J., campus minister, who told the magazine that he had entered the Society of Jesus after being inspired by the Jesuits he met at Rockhurst High School. "They seemed like they really enjoyed what they were doing, they were real friendly with each other, and they took an interest in me," Father Vowells said. Matthew Ruhl, a 45-year-old Jesuit who was pastor of St. Francis Xavier Church, said he liked the ability of Jesuits "to be very serious and then turn right around and be very silly—their humanity was attractive to me."

As Rockhurst prepared to celebrate its one hundredth anniversary, the university catalog listed only 4 teaching Jesuits: fathers Wheeler (chemistry), Oldani (English), LaCroix (philosophy), and Bredeck (theology and religious studies).[123] As Jesuit numbers had declined, their positions on the faculty, in the administration, and even on the governing Board of Trustees were filled more and more by lay people, including many non-Catholics. But still, Catholic higher education prospered. In the summer of 2006, as freshmen in the Rockhurst University Class of 2010 arrived on campus, they numbered an even 400 students—the largest class in 23 years and a 30 percent increase in enrollment in just 2 years.[124]

It was that very spring of 2006 that *Rockhurst Magazine* introduced Father Kinerk's successor. He was the Rev. Thomas B. Curran, a Philadelphia native, the fifth of 6 children who had, like every other Rockhurst president, chosen the religious life. There was, however, no S.J. after Father Curran's name. He was a Salesian, an O.S.F.S., meaning a member of the Oblates of St. Francis de Sales, founded in 1875. At age 50, Father Curran had come to Rockhurst with a law degree and an M.B.A., as well as a master's in theology and another master's in public policy and government from Georgetown University. He had spent the greater part of his life working with young people, from the presidency of a struggling high school for boys in northeast Philadelphia, to an associate vice presidency at the Jesuit Regis University in Denver. As president of Salesianum School in Wilmington, Delaware, Father Curran had created a strategic plan for the school's one hundredth anniversary, a celebration that he had taken beyond campus to include all of the city.

That was the kind of president in keeping with a Rockhurst University that always had fashioned itself as part of the greater Kansas City area. It had been that way from the first, when Father Michael Dowling, faced with establishing a college in a city with a small Catholic population, had chosen a name that would not offend. It had been that way in 1933, when Rockhurst established its night school of commerce to reach out to older, working adults. And it had been that way in the 1960s and 1970s, as Rockhurst worked with city officials and the 49/63 Coalition to stabilize a neighborhood that seemed on the verge of decline. Rockhurst's presidents, as well, had always looked beyond the campus gates, be it Daniel Conway reaching out to the city's business community by forming the Honorary Directors, or Maurice Van Ackeren engaging in the city's hopes for downtown revival by making Rockhurst a part of the answer, or Thomas Savage creating the Rockhurst College Continuing Education Center to extend Rockhurst's mission and identity.

"Francis de Sales encourages us with these words," Father Curran said in his inaugural address in Mason-Halpin Fieldhouse: "Be who you are and be it well."[125] Though de Sales was speaking of the life of a religious, the words could apply equally to Rockhurst University. The little school on the

When they arrived on campus as freshmen in 2006, one of the first activities of the Class of 2010 was to form the numbers representing their graduation year, which is also the 100th anniversary of Rockhurst. Courtesy of Rockhurst University Public Relations and Marketing.

hill had always been what it is—Catholic and Jesuit, a place committed to a liberal education of learning, leadership, service, and the pursuit of justice. As Rockhurst looks ahead to the next 100 years, no one doubts that it will continue in that tradition—and continue to do it well.

Presidents of Rockhurst University

1910-1915
Rev. Michael P. Dowling, S.J.

1915-1918
Rev. Aloysius A. Breen, S.J.

1918-1924
Rev. John A. Weiand, S.J.

1924-1928
Rev. Arthur D. Spillard, S.J.

1928-1933
Rev. William P. Manion, S.J.

1933-1940
Rev. Daniel H. Conway, S.J.

1940-1945
Rev. William H. McCabe, S.J.

1945-1951
Rev. Thomas M. Knapp, S.J.

1951-1977
Rev. Maurice E. Van Ackeren, S.J.

1977-1988
Rev. Robert F. Weiss, S.J.

1988-1996
Rev. Thomas J. Savage, S.J.

1996-1997
Rev. Peter B. Ely, S.J.

1997-1998
Janet Watson Sheeran, Ph.D. (Interim)

1998-2006
Rev. E. Edward Kinerk, S.J., '64

2006-
Rev. Thomas B. Curran, O.S.F.S.

— Honors and Awards —

— The Visiting Scholars —

1955-1956
André Mercier
Rev. Paul Henry, S.J.
Rev. Josef Nuttin

1956-1957
Rev. John Courtney Murray, S.J.
Rev. John C. Ford, S.J.
Rev. Joseph Owens, C.Ss.R.
Rev. John L. Thomas, S.J.

1957-1958
Saul S. Weinberg
Lt. Gen. James H. Doolittle
Col. Thomas G. Lanphier Jr.
Senator Stuart Symington
Edward Teller
Sister M. Madeleva, C.S.C.
Clarence K. Streit
Rev. Henri Renard, S.J.

1958-1959
Erik Ritter von Kuehnelt-Leddihn
Rev. Bruce Vawter, C.M.
Rev. Gerald B. Phelan
Rev. Thurston N. Davis, S.J.

1959-1960
Robert Frost
Anton Charles Pegis
Samuel Eliot Morison
William F. Albright

1960-1961
Rev. Joseph M. Bochenski, O.P.
Francis J. Braceland
Harlow M. Shapley
Allan Nevins
Etienne Gilson

1961-1962
Cleanth Brooks
Jerome Gregory Kerwin
Henry A. Kissinger
Dexter Perkins
Barbara Ward
R. Buckminster Fuller
André Girard
Hans Schwieger
Rev. C.J. McNaspy, S.J.

1962-1963
Rev. Clifford Howell, S.J.
Clinton Rossiter
Roger D. Reid
George Bagshawe Harrison

1963-1964
Peter J.W. DeBye
Douglas Hyde
Paul Engle
James D. Collins

1964-1965
Marguerite Higgins
Harold Clurman
Rev. Virgil C. Blum, S.J.
Hon. Charles Malik
Rev. Roland de Vaux, O.P.
Bernard Cardinal Alfrink

1965-1966
Samuel John Hazo
Ferenc Nagy
Ruth Mary Fox
Rev. Francis X. Murphy,C.Ss.R.
John Canaday

1966-1967
Rev. Hans Kung
Cornelius Ryan
Edward Albee
Alan Lomax

1967-1968
Maynard Mack
Rev. Edward Schillebeeckx, O.P.
Robert C. Weaver
Constantinos Doxiadis
Ian L. McHarg
James B. Reston
Walter W. Heller

1968-1969
Rev. Bernard J. Lonergan, S.J.
Haynes Johnson
Rollo May
Sir Tyrone Guthrie

1969-1970
John A. McLaughlin
Victor C. Ferkiss
Rev. Walter J. Ong, S.J.
James A. Lovell

1970-1971
Harry A. Schwartz
George Marek
Fernando Belaunde-Terry
Michael Harrington

1971-1972
Edwin O. Reischauer
James M. Gustafson
John Kenneth Galbraith

1972-1973
Gail and Thomas Parker
George Romney
Arthur Schlesinger Jr.
Nathan A. Scott Jr.

1973-1974
Rev. Robert North, S.J.
Nila Magidoff
Cornelio Fabro
Paul Ramsey

1974-1975
Bill Schustik
John Hope Franklin
Howard James
Hon. Floyd R. Gibson
Russell Millin
Willard Bunch
Hon. Harold Holliday Sr.
Ralph Martin
Robert Sigman
Austin Van Buskirk
John F. Mee

1975-1976
Elizabeth Janeway
Martin E. Marty
Anthony Burgess
Daniel Bell
Henry Steele Commager

1976-1977
Louis L'Amour
John T. Noonan Jr.
Claire Hollingworth
Herbert Baumel
Alfonzo Ortiz

1977-1978
Frank Manley
Rev. David Tracy
Clarence C. Walton
Captain Grace Murry Hopper, U.S.N.
L'Abbé Germain Marc'hadour

1978-1979
Rev. Walter J. Burghardt, S.J.
David S. Broder
Jack Reynolds
Thomas Hoving

1979-1980
John Macquarrie
Wayne Clayson Booth
Lerone Bennett Jr.
Garry Wills
Rev. William Sloane Coffin, Jr.
Admiral Elmo R. Zumwalt, Jr.

1980-1981
Anthony Lewis
Ralph McInerny
Rev. Robert Drinan, S.J.
Lester Carl Thurow
Paul Craig Roberts
Natalie Hinderas
Yale Brozen

1981-1982
Rev. Joseph A. Fitzmyer, S.J.
David D. Burns
Fritjof Capra
Robert E. White

1982-1983
Mortimer J. Adler
Stanley Siegel
Erik Ritter von Kuehnelt-Leddihn
Malcolm Toon
James MacGregor Burns
Alfred Kahn

1983-1984
Rev. Jared Wicks, S.J.
Rev. Ladislas Orsy, S.J.
Jonathan D. Spence
Jerry Lee Jordan
Ernest L. Boyer
Edmund S. Wehrle

1984-1985
Vernon J. Bourke
Rev. David Gill, S.J.
Jean-Michel Cousteau
Robert Farris Thompson
Stanton Samenow
William Poole

1985-1986
Col. John Cottell
Jeremy Rifkin
Rev. Avery Dulles, S.J.
Jaroslav Pelikan
Rabbi Marc H. Tanenbaum
Rev. William Byron, S.J.
Jean Dietz Moss
Rev. William Wallace, O.P.
Owen Gingerich
Malcolm Miller
Leif Olsen

1986-1987
Amb. Philip Habib
Rev. Piet Schoonenberg, S.J.
Rev. Robert C. Baumiller, S.J.
Bert Hornback
Malcolm Miller
Rev. W. Norris Clarke, S.J.

1987-1988
Loret Miller Ruppe
Guido Fernandez
James F. Scott
Rev. James Hennesey, S.J.
Rev. Leo Sweeney, S.O.
John T. Noonan, Jr.

1988-1989
Rev. Richard Neuhaus
Rev. Martin McCarthy, S.J.
Fred Barnes
Thomas Flanagan
Rev. Theodore M. Hesburgh, C.S.C.

1989-1990
Rev. Peter Milward, S.J.
Monika Hellwig
Arthur L. Caplan
Robert Jay Lifton
John M. Merriman
Harry Edwards
Rev. Jon Sobrino, S.J.

1990-1991
Rev. Marvin R. O'Connell
Julie Roy Jeffrey
Robert Collier
Rev. Robert Brungs, S.J.
Charles E. Rice
Rev. John Powell, S.J.
Rev. George Hunt, S.J.

1991-1992
Sr. Mary Clark, R.S.C.J.
Adele Dutton Terrell
Marion Montgomery

Rev. Richard P. McBrien
Sidney Callahan
Eoin McKiernan

1992-1993
Clarence Page
Catharine Stimpson
Theodore Hamerow
James Shenton
Mary Jo Nye
Rev. Gerald McCool, S.J.
Rev. Carl Starkloff, S.J.

1993-1994
Rev. Robert Barth, S.J.
Rev. Stanley Jaki
Bel Kaufman
Al Eaton
Joseph Pappin
Jacob Neusner

1994-1995
Zev Kedem
Rev. Richard Blake, S.J.
Christina Hoff Sommers
Rev. Brian Davies, O.P.
Paula Rothenberg
Joseph Cardinal Bernardin
Rev. J. Bryan Hehir

1995-1996
Paul Lombardo
H. James Birx
Rev. John Kavanaugh, S.J.
William Eckhardt
Toinette Eugene
Roger Cardinal Mahony
Rev. Michael Himes

1996-1997
Michael Medved
Timothy McDermott
Rev. Leonid Kishkovsky
James Q. Wilson

1997-1998
Stanley Fish
Rev. Raymond Brown
Dallas Willard
Gertrude Himmelfarb

1998-1999
Joseph E. Persico
Peter Awn
Leroy Hood
David Lehman
Rev. Robert Sokolowski

1999-2000
Helen Thomas
Richard Bernstein
Jody Williams
Rev. Cyprian Davis, O.S.B.
Maxine Greene
Linda Zagzebski

2000-2001
Rev. Kevin Burke, S.J.
Mary E. Shaw
Rigoberta Menchú Tum
Steven Benson
Jean B. Elshtain
David J. O'Brien
Rev. Robert J. Schreiter
Daniel Callahan

2001-2002
Edmund Pellegrino
Mairead Corrigan Maguire
Kenneth Goodpaster
Rev. Terrence Dempsey, S.J.
Rev. James V. Schall, S.J.
J. Matthew Ashley

2002-2003
Garry Wills
Oscar Arias
Daniel Dombrowski
R. Scott Appleby
John L. Esposito
Bill Kurtis

2003-2004
Chris Hedges
Corey Flintoff
Adolfo Pérez Esquival
Tom Fox
Jorge Gracia
Michael Cuneo

2004-2005
John Foreyt
Terrence Roberts
Mark Nanos
José Ramos-Horta
Rev. Ronald Rolheiser, O.M.I.
Dava Sobel
Jude Dougherty
Kathleen Mahoney

2005-2006
David A. Prentice
Kevin Willmott
Sen. George J. Mitchell
Rev. Charles M. Shelton, S.J.

2006-2007
Rev. Joseph Koterski, S.J.
Carolyn Maher
Christina Chan
Rev. George Coyne, S. J.
Robert L. Wilken
Gerald Coles

2007-2008
Paul G. Schervish
Ralph McInerny
Kevin Fox Gotham
Lt. Cmdr. Charles D. Swift (Ret.)
Rev. Jan Michael Joncas
Deborah Burger
Diana L. Hayes

2008-2009
James Sterba
Jon Coleman
Leonard Krishtalka
Richard Lindzen
Rev. James Profit, S.J.
Tissa Hami

2009-2010
Andrew Card
Thomas Hibbs
Jon Lee Anderson
Rev. Greg Boyle, S.J.
Lisa Wagner

OUTSTANDING ALUMNUS AWARD

1982 Vincent J. O'Flaherty, Jr. '21
1983 James Spellman '30
1984 William H. Dunn '46
1985 John Harry Wiggins '53
1986 Gil P. Bourk '48
1987 John J. Sullivan, Jr. '39
1988 John H. Bolin, Jr. '48
1989 Louis DeFeo, Jr. '57

**In 1991, the Outstanding Alumnus Award was divided into two categories: Alumnus/a of the Year for Outstanding Achievement, and Alumnus/a of the Year for Outstanding Service.*

OUTSTANDING ACHIEVEMENT AWARD

1991 Joseph P. Glas '60
1992 Godfrey S. Kobets '39
1993 Salvatore J. Enna '65
1994 Joseph A. Flaherty, Jr. '52
1995 Thomas A. McDonnell '66
1996 Rev. George K. Fitzsimons '48
1997 Dr. Veron Rice '57
1998 Mr. Louis W. Smith '80
1999 Mr. Blake B. Mulvany '57
2000 Mark C. Lamping '80
2001 James Castellano '73
2002 Hector V. Barreto, Jr. '83
2003 Thomas M. Downs '64
2004 Richard T. Sullivan, Jr. '73
2005 Daniel C. Prefontaine, QC, '61

OUTSTANDING SERVICE AWARD

1991 Joseph McGee, Jr. '41
1992 Robert E. Miller '49
Richard W. Miller '52
1993 Gerard Meiners '59
1994 Robert Cunningham '49
1995 D. Eugene (Gene) Hart '50
1996 Raymond W. Sonnenberg '69
1997 John E. Hayes, Jr. '59
1998 Rev. Thomas F. Denzer, S.J. '48
1999 Maurice M. McNellis '49
2000 Michael Bahlinger '85
2001 Jerry Haake '70
2002 G. Lawrence Blankinship, Jr. '83
2003 Michael A. Kleinman '63
2004 Kathleen A. and P. Scott Hummel '85
2005 Richard A. Ruiz '92

HONORARY ALUMNUS

1991 Samuel J. Kennedy
1992 Ilus W. Davis
1993 Byron G. Thompson
1994 Rev. Maurice Van Ackeren, S.J.
1995 Robert J. Dineen
1996 Joseph S. Rydzel
1997 Adolph Heine
1998 Rev. Joseph M. Freeman, S.J.
1999 Rev. Jules M. Brady, S.J.
2000 Mary Sue Karl
2003 Reva R. Servoss
2005 Larry Moore

HONORARY DEGREES

1921 LL.D. Marshal Ferdinand Foch
1942 LL.D. Bernard J. Muller-Thym
1942 Sc.D. Charles F. Schnabel
1948 LL.D. Robert Woods Johnson
1948 LL.D. Henry J. Massman, Sr.
1948 LL.D. Rev. Bernard Joseph Hale
1952 LL.D. Jack P. Whitaker
1953 Litt.D. Francis Cardinal Spellman
1954 LL.D. Carlos P. Romulo
1955 LL.D. Lewis Strauss
1956 LL.D. Sen. John F. Kennedy
1957 LL.D. Ricardo Arias
1958 LL.D. Alfred M. Gruenther
1959 LL.D. Sen. Stuart Symington
1959 LL.D. John A. McCone
1959 LL.D. Roy A. Roberts
1960 LL.D. President Harry S. Truman
1960 LL.D. Charles H. Kellstadt
1961 LL.D. Charles E. Bohlen
1961 Litt.D. John C. H. Wu
1962 LL.D. Frederick H. Boland
1964 L.H.D Bishop Charles H. Helmsing
1964 LL.D. Sen. Abraham Ribicoff
1965 L.H.D. Joseph Cardinal Ritter
1965 LL.D. Thomas Joseph Dodd
1966 LL.D. Robert D. Murphy
1966 LL.D. Herbert H. Wilson
1966 LL.D. Edwin G. Borserine
1967 LL.D. Arthur S. Fleming
1967 LL.D. Edward V. Long
1967 Litt.D. Jaroslav Pelikan
1967 HH.D. Bishop Harold R. Perry
1967 LL.D. Gov. Warren Hearnes
1968 L.H.D. John R. Cauley
1968 L.H.D. Rev. Walter J. Ong, S.J.
1969 D.F.A. Thomas Hart Benton
1969 Mus.D. Hans Schwieger
1970 Sc.D. James A. Lovell
1970 LL.D. Sen. Thomas F. Eagleton
1971 LL.D. Richard Bolling
1971 L.H.D. Walter Cronkite
1971 LL.D. Thomas H. Eliot
1972 D.H. H. Roe Bartle
1972 D.F.A. Laurence Sickman
1972 D.H.L. Msgr. Arthur M. Tighe
1973 D.H.L. Rev. John Bannon, S.J.
1973 Sc.D. A. Donald Goedeke
1973 LL.D. Leonor K. Sullivan
1974 LL.D. Sen. John C. Danforth
1974 D.P.S. Charles Newton Kimball
1974 Sc.D. Joseph Collins Shipman
1975 Mus.D. Grace Melzia Bumbry
1975 Sc.D. Richard Marlin Perkins
1975 D.H. James Berton Rhoades
1976 LL.D. Rev. Robert J. Henle, S.J.
1976 HH.D. Margaret Truman Daniel
1977 D.H. Joseph J. McGee, Jr.
1979 Sc.D. Arthur Burns
1979 L.H.D. Rev. Frederick C. Copleston, S.J.
1980 D.H. Rev. Cesar Jerez, S.J.
1980 Mus.D. Mary Lou Williams
1981 Sc.D. Thomas Michael Donahue
1981 D.B.A. William P. Harsh
1981 LL.D. Msgr. George Gilmary Higgins
1982 D.H. Rev. Joseph H. Fichter, S.J.
1982 D.H. Clarence H. Goppert

1982 D.H. Vita M. Goppert
1982 LL.D. Harry B. Kies
1983 D.H. Virginia Pollock Greenlease
1983 D.H. Bishop John J. Sullivan
1984 D.H.L. Rev. Joseph A. O'Hare, S.J.
1984 D.L. Bishop George K. Fitzsimons
1985 D.H. Adele Coryell Hall
1985 D.B.A. Donald J. Hall
1985 D.H. Rev. Timothy S. Healy, S.J.
1986 LL.D. Donald P. Moyers
1986 D.H.L. Rev. George E. Ganss, S.J.
1987 D.H.L. Rev. Vincent F. Daues, S.J.
1988 D.H.L. Rev. John L. May
1988 LL.D. Hon. William H. Webster
1988 D.H.L. Rev. Theodore Hesburgh, C.S.C.
1989 D.H.L. Clarence H. Miller
1989 D.H.L. Rev. Raymond E. Brown, S.S.
1989 D.S. Joseph A. Flaherty
1990 D.H.L. Rev. William J. Byron, S.J.
1990 D.H. Donald C. Bakely
1990 D.H.L Rev. Christopher F. Mooney, S. J.
1990 L.L.D. Charles E. Rice
1991 D.H.L. Mortimer Adler
1991 D.H. Rev. Harold C. Bradley, S.J.
1991 LL.D. Elliot Richardson
1992 LL.D. Alvin Brooks
1992 D.H.L. Georgie Anne Geyer
1992 D.H.L. Rev. Maurice McNamee, S.J.
1993 D.F.A. Nikki Giovanni
1993 D.H.L. Rev.William B. Faherty, S.J.
1994 D.P.S. Sr. Mary Rose McGeady, D.C.
1994 D.H.L. Rev. Lawrence Biondi, S.J.
1994 D.H.L. Michael Novak
1995 D.P.P. Rev. Bryan Hehir, D.P.P.
1995 LL.D. Susan M. Stanton
1995 D.H. Virginia Stowers
1995 D.B.A. James E. Stowers, Jr.
1996 D.F.A. Gwendolyn Brooks
1996 D.H.L. Joseph T. McGuff
1997 D.A. William McGlaughlin
1997 D.H.L. William McSweeney, Jr.
1998 D.P.S. Sen. Thomas Eagleton
1999 D.H. Monika K. Hellwig
1999 D.P.S. Ferdinand Mahfood
2001 D.H. Máiread Corrigan Maguire
2002 D.H. Oscar Arias
2003 D.P.S. Adolfo Pérez Esquivel
2004 D.M. Bishop Raymond J. Boland
2006 D.H.L. Robert A. Long
2010 D.H.L. Rev. Charles L. Currie, S.J.

ATHLETICS HALL OF FAME

1981 James J. Gleeson '33
1981 Patrick W. Mason '21
1981 Paul O. Smith
1981 Raymond J. Sonnenberg, Sr. '34
1981 John S. Sullivan '30
1981 Ralph Telken '64
1982 Patrick J. Caldwell '66
1982 Godfrey S. Kobets '39
1982 Raymond T. McKee '29
1982 Terry M. Michler '69
1982 John M. Mitchell '46
1982 Victor H. Zahner '31
1983 James F. Healey, Jr. '69
1983 Owen F. Murphy '36
1984 Paul J. Martel '48
1985 John P. Scanlon, Sr. '42
1986 D. Eugene Hart '50
1987 John W. Malinee '78
1986 John J. Reichmeier '53
1987 James J. Ryan, Jr. '49
1988 Robert Castaneda '60
1989 1964 N.A.I.A. National Championship Basketball Team: Pat Caldwell, Chuck Dunlap, Tom Fisher, Joel Frisch, Rich Grawer, Dick Hennier, Al Payne, Dennis Rabbitt, Jim Selzer, Ralph Telken, Walt Tylicki, Harry Witte
Coaches: Joe Brehmer and Dolor Rehm
Managers: Dennis Alieksaites, Pat Campbell, Chuck Plague
1990 James E. Kopp '72
1990 George W. Richter, Jr. '48
1990 Robert J. Williams '53
1991 Amos H. Hutchin '40
1992 Thomas F. Callahan '43
1992 James F. Karl '57
1992 Donald J. Klein '58
1993 Joseph F. Keirnan '47
1993 Dennis C. Lee '77
1994 John A. Steck, Jr. '46
1994 Richard A. Suit '74
1995 Kathryn R. Anderson '89
1996 Francis Muckenthaler '47
1996 Michael G. Powers '80
1997 Maureen Walsh Herrmann '82
1997 Mark R. Teahan '82
1998 Richard E. Donahue '53
1999 Craig A. Stahl '81
1999 Anthony L. Tocco
2000 Dennis Luber '83
2001 Doug Wemhoff, '89
2002 John Sanderson '49
2002 John Stapler '50
2002 Larry Fitzgerald '51
2002 Thomas Holton '50
2002 William Spurck '36
2002 Robert Aylward '50
2002 Barney Byard '50
2002 Bishop George Fitzsimons '48
2002 Clarence Deitchman '49
2002 Thomas O'Brien '50
2002 Joseph Mallon '51
2003 Susan Konop Malisch '86
2003 Joseph M. Grantham '56
2004 Kristine Rehm Nusbaum '91
2004 Sid E. Bordman '54
2005 John Williams '54
2006 Keith Gehling '77
2006 Jack McCloskey '56
2007 Frank Diskin

2007 Andrea Tinsley '93

Science Hall of Fame

1996 William G. Bartholome, M.D. '65
1996 Joseph A. Flaherty, Ph.D. '52
1996 Joseph M. Jaklevic, Ph.D. '62
1996 Joseph P. Glas, Ph.D. '60
1996 A. Donald Goedeke, Ph.D. '56
1996 James Emmett Monahan, Ph.D. '48
1997 James B. Kring, Ph.D. '47
1997 Henry N. Wellman, M.D. '56
1998 Lawrence J. Marnett, Ph.D. '69
1999 Robert C. Jaklevic, Ph.D. '56
2001 Salvatore Enna, Ph.D. '65
Paul Wheeler, Ph.D. '63
2005 William Haggerty, Ph.D. '54

St. Thomas More Academy of Scholars

1992 Rev. Walter Ong, S.J. '33
1994 Daniel Ferritor, Ph.D. '62
2000 Mark Curran, Ph.D. '63
2000 Robert T. Crossley '67
2003 Dr. Edward A. Purcell, Jr. '62

Daniel L. Brenner Scholarly Achievement Award

1988 William F. McInerny, Ph.D.
1990 Frank J. Smist Jr., Ph.D.
1991 Don E. Gibbs, Ph.D.
1992 Curtis L. Hancock, Ph.D.
1993 Richard G. Newman, Ph.D.
1994 Patricia Cleary Miller, Ph.D.
1995 Steven W. Brown, Ph.D.
1996 Jean M. Hiebert, Ph.D.
1997 Jules M. Brady, S.J., Ph.D.
1998 Timothy L. McDonald, Ph.D.
1999 Don E. Gibbs, Ph.D.
2000 Sudhakar S. Raju, Ph.D.
2001 Risa J. Stein, Ph.D.
2002 Thomas Ward, Ph.D.
2003 Daniel F. Stramara, Jr., Ph.D.
2004 Craig Prentiss, Ph.D.
2005 Paula Shorter, Ph.D.
2006 Charlotte K. Shelton, Ed.D.
2007 Laura Janusik, Ph.D.
2009 Craig Prentiss, Ph.D.
2010 Margaret Wye, Ph.D.

Hall Family Foundation Chair

1987-89 Bryce J. Jones, Ph.D.
1989-91 Rev. E. Eugene Arthur, S.J., D.B.A.
1991-92 Cheryl A. McConnell
1992-95 Richard G. Newman, D.B.A.
1995-96 Richard Hunt, Ph.D.
1996-98 Gail A. Hoover, Ed.D.
1998-99 Randolph R. Schwering, Ph.D.
1999-00 Peter D. Nugent, Ph.D.
2000-02 Brian D. Fitzpatrick, Ph.D.; Sudhakar S. Raju, Ph.D.
2002-04 Charlotte K. Shelton, Ed.D.
2006-09 Myles P. Gartland II, Ph.D.
2009-10 Laura Fitzpatrick, Ph.D.

Harry B. Kies Award for Distinguished Service

1985 Paul D. Arend
Rev. Charles P. Cahill, S.J.
Rev. Thomas F. Denzer, S.J.
M. Robert Knickerbocker
1987 Bryce J. Jones
Reva R. Servoss
1988 Thomas L. Lyon
Marilyn K. Rigby
Joyce A. Smith
1989 Richard E. Wilson
Rev. Francis J. Murphy, S.J.
1990 Janet Watson Sheeran
Sr. Rosemary Flanigan, C.S.J.
1991 Anthony L. Tocco
Rev. Vincent Daues, S.J.
1992 Delores J. Curry
1993 Edward S. Kos
1994 Marilyn N. Carroll
1995 Weslynn S. Martin
1996 Anita Salem
1997 Adolphine C. Shaw
Richard D. Shaw
1998 Gerald L. Miller
1999 John G. Koelzer
2000 Mary Anne Beck
2001 Marian Nigro
2002 Rev. James Wheeler, S.J.
2003 James and Margaret Millard
2004 Charlie F. Morris
2005 Thomas J. Audley
2006 Ellen Spake
2007 Jeanne Langdon
2008 Timothy L. McDonald
2009 Charles Kovich
2010 Paula M. Shorter

Anne and Joseph McGee Chair in Interpersonal Communication and Listening

2001-03 Weslynn S. Martin
2004-10 Laura A. Janusik, Ph.D.

George and Gladys Miller chair in Business Administration

1988-91 Anthony L. Tocco, Ph.D.
1991-92 Marlene S. Donahue, Ph.D.
1992-93 James E. Puetz, Ph.D.
1993-95 Gerald L. Miller, Ph.D.
1995-96 Keith B. Myles, Ph.D.
1996-97 Faye S. McIntyre, Ph.D.
1997-98 Sudhakar Satyanarayan, Ph.D.
2000-02 Randolph E. Schwering, Ph.D.
2002-05 Cheryl McConnell, M.P.A./C.P.A.;
David B. Vicknair, Ph.D.
2005-10 Martin Stack, Ph.D.

Teaching Excellence Award

1990 Anita Salem
1991 Marshall Andersen, Ph.D.
1992 Weslynn S. Martin
1993 Will Valk
1994 Gerald L. Miller, Ph.D.
1995 Donna J. Calvert, Ph.D.

1996 Judith C. Richards, Ph.D.
1997 Edward S. Kos, Ph.D.
1998 Rev. W. L. LaCroix, S.J.
1999 Cheryl A. McConnell
2000 William J. Ryan
2001 Paula M. Shorter, Ph.D.
2002 Robert Hegarty, Ph.D.
2003 Joseph A. Cirincione, Ph.D.
2005 Rev. Robert J. Mahoney, Ph.D.
2006 Jean Hiebert, Ph.D.
2007 Jane Rues, Ed.D.
2008 Brian D. Fitzpatrick, Ph.D.
2009 John Kerrigan, Ph.D.
2010 Daniel J. Martin, Ph.D.

JOSEPH M. FREEMAN, S.J. CHAIR IN PHILOSOPHY

1986-98 Rev. Joseph M. Freeman, S.J.
1998- Curtis L. Hancock, Ph.D.

JOHN J. AND LAURA J. SULLIVAN CHAIR IN ETHICS

1992-96 Rev. Wilfred L. LaCroix, S.J.
1996-99 Rev. E. Eugene Arthur, S.J.
2000-02 Gerald L. Miller, Ph.D.
2003-05 Randolph E. Schwering, Ph.D.
2006-10 John Meyers, Ph.D.

BREEN INTERNATIONAL FELLOWSHIP

1995 Gerald L. Miller, Ph.D.
1996 Thomas L. Lyon, Ph.D.
2000 Thomas L. Lyon, Ph.D.
2000-02 Sudhakar S. Raju, Ph.D.
2000-04 Brian D. Fitzpatrick, Ph.D.

UNIVERSITY FACULTY SENATE CHAIR

2000-02 William Sturgill, Ph.D.
2002-04 Marshall Andersen, Ph.D.
2004-06 Michael Stellern, Ph.D.
2006-08 Timothy McDonald, Ph.D.
2008-10 Ellen Spake, Ph.D.

THE CHANCELLOR'S AWARD

1959 Harry B. Kies
Vanston H. Ryan
David Sarnoff
Robert Frost
1960 Samuel Eliot Morison
1961 Etienne Gilson
1966 Rev. Paul C. Reinert, S.J.
1971 Joyce Hall
1978 L'Abbé Germain Marc'hadour
1981 Ilus W. Davis
1986 Rev. William Byron, S.J.
1988 Rev. Robert F. Weiss, S.J.
1996 Rev. Thomas J. Savage, S.J.
1998 Rev. Thomas F. Denzer, S.J.
1999 M. Robert Knickerbocker

EXCELLENCE IN TEACHING AWARD FROM MISSOURI GOVERNOR'S CONFERENCE ON HIGHER EDUCATION

1992 Anita Salem
1993 Richard D. Shaw
1994 Weslynn Martin
1995 William F. Haefele
1996 Robin E. Bowen
1997 Curtis L. Hancock
1998 Cheryl A. McConnell
1999 Joseph A. Cirincione
2000 Anthony L. Tocco
2001 Donna J. Calvert
2002 Rev. Wilfred LaCroix, S.J.
2003 Sudhakar Raju
2004 Renee Michael

PRO MERITIS AWARD

Aug. 27, 1959
James Hazlett
Dr. Elmer Ellis
Sister Rose Carmel, S.C.L.
Mar. 24, 1960
Edwin G. Borserine
Willard J. Breidenthal
Mrs. Ethel B. Francisco
Mrs. Clarence Kivett
Arthur Mag
Albert A. Ridge
Herbert H. Wilson
Mar. 29, 1960
Dr. Floyd Shoemaker
April 25, 1960
John R. Cauley
Louis B. McGee
Vincent J. O'Flaherty, Jr.
June 4, 1966
Charles L. Aylward
Lathrop G. Backstrom
J. Frank Hudson
Henry J. Massman, Sr.
Robert J. Muntzel
J. Ernest Dunn
May 10, 1967
Nathan J. Stark
1968 J.F. Hughes
J.E. Couture
Oct. 4, 1968
Rev. Vincent F. Daues, S.J.
May 14, 1970
Lester Milgram
Jerome A. Smith
Homer C. Wadsworth
Rev. John W. Williams
May 17, 1973
Thomas Hart Benton
Frederick James
Wiktor Labunski
Patricia McIlrath
July 11, 1978
Roy K. Dietrich
Jan. 11, 1979
Dr. C. Kermit Phelps
May 13, 1979
John Herman Tietze
May 14, 1980
Mary McGuirk
May 16, 1982
Rev. Patrick Tobin
Sept. 22, 1982
Dr. Elbert C. Cole
May 15, 1983
Godfrey S. Kobets
Oct. 3, 1985
Aubrey E. Richardson
Mar. 12, 1987
Maurice E. McNellis
May 17, 1987
Stuart L. Simmons
Blake B. Mulvany

May 15, 1988
Sr. Mary Margaret Sneddon, M.M.B.
April 29, 1990
Charles W. Gusewelle
Betty Taliaferro
May 5, 1991
Sr. Barbara Moore, C.S.J.
Cynthia Siebert
May 2, 1993
James T. Nunnelly
May 1, 1994
Scott and Kathleen Hummel
May 15, 1994
Lem T. Jones Jr.
May 7, 1995
Rabbi Michael R. Zedek
May 5, 1996
Miyo Wagner
May 4, 1997
John J. Sullivan, Jr.
May 3, 1998
Michael V. Meyer
May 2, 1999
Sr. Rosemary Flanigan, C.S.J.
Bryce J. Jones
April 30, 2000
Rev. James Wheeler, S.J.
William Bartholome
May 13, 2001
Larry Moore

Chapter One – CATHOLIC BEGINNINGS

1. "In 15 Days, 14.2 Inches: Rainfall This Month Smashes All Other Records," *The Kansas City Star*, September 15, 1914. *The Star* reported that 3.65 inches of rain fell within about 3 hours on the morning of September 15.
2. Rev. Patrick F. Harvey, S.J., *History of Rockhurst College*, n.d., p. 10, Rockhurst University Archives.
3. *Woodstock Letters* 43 (1914): 418.
4. Of the remaining 28 Jesuit colleges in the United States, Rockhurst was the twenty-third established.
5. David J. O'Brien, *From the Heart of the American Church: Catholic Higher Education and American Culture* (Maryknoll, New York: Orbis Books, 1994), p. 37.
6. John J. Callahan, S.J., *First Principles: The Jesuit Tradition in Higher Education*, (1999), p. 7, Rockhurst University Archives.
7. David R. Contosta, *Saint Joseph's: Philadelphia's Jesuit University, 150 Years* (Philadelphia: Saint Joseph's University Press, 2000), p. 3, 22. Other Jesuit colleges up to 1851 were the following: Spring Hill in Mobile, Alabama (1830); St. Charles in Grand Coteau, Louisiana, (1837, now closed); Immaculate Conception in New Orleans (1847, now closed); Holy Cross in Worcester, Massachusetts (1843), Santa Clara in Santa Clara, California (1851).
8. See Gilbert J. Garraghan, S.J., *Catholic Beginnings in Kansas City, Missouri: An Historical Sketch* (Chicago: Loyola University Press, 1920), p. 28; and John E. Rothensteiner, *History of the Archdiocese of St. Louis: In Its Various Stages of Development from A.D. 1673 to A.D. 1928* , vol. 1 (St. Louis: Blackwell Wielandy, 1928), p. 452-454.
9. Garraghan, *Catholic Beginnings*, p. 15. Lutz set out from St. Louis on July 30, 1828.
10. James A. Henretta et al., eds., *America's History: Volume 1: To 1877* (Boston: Bedford/St. Martin's Press, 2000), p. 46.
11. See Garraghan, *Catholic Beginnings*, p. 28-31; and Lutz to Rosati, November 12, 1828. Copies of Lutz's letters are in the archives of the Diocese of Kansas City-St. Joseph. The letters, addressed "From the area at the Kansas River," provide one of the earliest descriptions of the place that in years hence would become Kansas City.
12. Garraghan, *Catholic Beginnings*, p. 32.
13. Though documentation is lacking, tradition says the first priest to visit Kawsmouth was Charles De La Croix, a parish priest at Florissant, near St. Louis, who traveled west in the spring and again in the summer of 1822 to visit the Osage near present-day Papinville, in Bates County. See Garraghan, *Catholic Beginnings*, p. 22-26.
14. Ibid., p. 35-65.
15. Ibid., p. 56.
16. Ibid., p. 59.
17. Ibid., p. 44, 61, 81.
18. The name of founder Joseph Smith's church between 1830 and 1834 was Church of Christ, and between 1834 and 1838, Church of the Latter-day Saints. Then, it acquired the current name, The Church of Jesus Christ of Latter-day Saints.
19. Samuel A. Burgess, "The Regions Round about Jackson County and Missouri," (Mormon Church) *Journal of History*, 17:3 (July 1924), p. 305-308. Burgess quotes founder Joseph Smith's *Doctrine and Covenants* 98:9 as ordering the purchase of "all lands by money, which can be purchased for money … in Jackson County, and the counties round about…." The article states: "How far the 'regions round about' may have extended is a matter of opinion. But Zion evidently included a large part, if not all, of Missouri, probably southern Iowa and eastern Nebraska, Kansas, and a corner of Oklahoma." Because the first settlers built on the wooded hillsides, Partridge bought up county land on the prairie, much of which (46,000 acres) had been set aside as "seminary lands" for a future college and had come on the market only recently.
20. See O.B. and Joanne Chiles Eakin, *Records of Original Entries to Lands in Jackson County Missouri* (Independence, Mo., 1985), p. 21; and U.S. Bureau of the Census, *Fifth and Sixth Census of the United States, Jackson County, Missouri.*
21. Ron Romig in Elizabeth Raymond, *Morman Mormon? Settlement and Expulsion From Jackson County Missouri, 1832-1834* (April 2, 1975) Jackson County Historical Society Archives, A264, 3F6; and Joseph A. Geddes, *The United Order Among the Mormons (Missouri Phase): An Unfinished Experiment in Economic Organization* (Salt Lake City: The Deseret News Press, 1924), 36-39. As bishop, Partridge served as both spiritual and financial leader of the colony in Missouri.
22. See Eakin, *Records*, p. 112; and *Journal of History*, 16:1 (January 1923), p. 255. The second purchase occurred on August 17, 1832.
23. See note 18 above for the various names of Joseph Smith's church.
24. See James West Davidson, et al, *Nation of Nations: A Narrative History of the American Republic*, 4th ed., vol. 1 (New York: McGraw Hill, 1995), p. 362-63, 374-75; and H.H. Smith, "Edward Partridge," *Journal of History*, 1:4 (October, 1908), p. 411-22. See Larry C. Porter, "The Colesville Branch in Kaw Township, Jackson County, Missouri, 1831-1833" in Arnold K. Garr and Clark V. Johnson, eds. *Regional Studies in Latter-day Saints Church History (Missouri)* (Provo, Utah: Brigham Young University, 1994), p. 286. The Temple Lot in Independence was dedicated just days later, on August 3, 1831. Joshua Lewis and his family would be among those forced to flee Jackson County in 1833. Joshua Lewis died in Clay County on October 28, 1835. See Porter, "The Colesville Branch," p. 291. Special thanks is due Ron Romig, an archivist for the Community of Christ Church, for his assistance in this section on Mormon history.
25. Eleanor Moliere Johnson, "The Gathering of the Mormons in Jackson County, Missouri" (M.A. thesis, University of Nebraska, 1927).
26. See *Evening and Morning Star*, December 1, 1831; and Paul C. Nagel, *Missouri: A Bicentennial History* (New York: W.W. Norton & Company, Inc., 1977), p. 121.
27. See Joseph A. Geddes, *The United Order Among the Mormons (Missouri Phase)*, p. 113; and H.H. Smith, "Edward Partridge," *Journal of History*, 1:4 (October, 1908), p. 418-19.
28. Geddes, *The United Order Among the Mormons (Missouri Phase)*, p. 36-39, 105. Geddes states that it was Joseph Smith's intent to purchase the holdings of all the old settlers and as much government land as possible in Jackson County, especially to the west, all the way to the Kansas border.
29. See *Jackson County, Missouri, Deeds, 1827-1845*, vol. 1 (Independence, Mo.: Jackson County Genealogical Society), p. 78; and Mrs. Pearl Wilcox, "Original Research," Library and Archives, Community of Christ, Independence, Missouri. In 1839, the saints purchased land in what then was the town of Commerce, Illinois, (renamed Nauvoo). Edward Partridge relocated with his family, and it was there he died of pleurisy on May 27, 1840. He was 46 years old.

30. See U.S. Bureau of the Census, *Eighth and Tenth United States Census, 1860, 1880, Jackson County;* and marriage records, http://www.ancestry.com.
31. Ibid.
32. Deed Book 50, vol. A20, p. 43. Jackson County Courthouse, Kansas City.
33. Leonard Dinnerstein and David M. Reimers, *Ethnic Americans: A History of Immigration*, 3rd ed. (New York: Harper Collins Publishers, 1988), p. 16.
34. See Garraghan, *The Jesuits of the Middle United States*, vol. 1 (New York: America Press, 1938), p. 266-68; Dorothy Brandt Marra, *This Far by Faith: A Popular History of the Catholic People of West and Northwest Missouri,* vol. 1 (Kansas City, Mo.: Diocese of Kansas City-St. Joseph, 1992), p. 21-24, 35; and City of St. Joseph, www.ci.st-joseph.mo.us/history/history.cfm.
35. Garraghan, *The Jesuits of the Middle United States*, vol. 1, p. 266.
36. Mildred Cecile Cox, "Medley of Beginnings at Kawsmouth," copy of speech to The Kansas City Corral, The Westerners, Hotel Bellerive, December 10, 1957, p. 6.
37. See Garraghan, *Catholic Beginnings*, p. 103-06; and Joseph P. Donnelly, S.J., ed., *Wilderness Kingdom: Indian Life in the Rocky Mountains: 1840-1847. The Journals & Paintings of Nicolas Point, S.J.* (New York: Holt, Rinehart and Winston, 1967), p. 20.
38. See Eakin, *Record of Original Entries,* p. 99; James J. Schlafly, "Birth of Kansas City's Pioneer Church," *Missouri Historical Review* 44:4 (July 1950), p. 364-72; and Garraghan, *The Jesuits of the Middle United States,* vol. 1, p. 260. The tract where the log church stood, Garraghan writes, ran along the west line of Broadway, from 9th to 12th streets and a 100 feet west of Jefferson Street. Though the log church originally was called "Chouteau's Church," by the fall of 1839 Father Herman Aelen, superior at Sugar Creek Mission, was calling it St. Francis Regis. Based on a letter from Father Charles Van Quickenborne, who stopped at Kawsmouth in the summer of 1835, the church had been built by then. The log church was replaced in 1856 by a new brick church. (William J. Dalton, *Life of Father Bernard Donnelly,* p. 59-60.) The part that Father Roux sold went to Francis Mumbleau for $700 on October 20, 1838.
39. Ibid., p. 11-14. The town company purchased the Prudhomme property on November 14, 1838, for $4,220, but it would be 1846 before legal issues were settled and the company replatted the land and got down to business. The Town of Kansas became an official municipality in 1850 when it was chartered by the County Court. It was chartered again in 1853 by a special act of the Missouri legislature, this time as the "City of Kansas." In 1889 it became, formally, Kansas City. (Cox, "Medley of Beginnings at Kawsmouth," p. 21.)
40. See Jami Parkison, *Path to Glory: A Pictorial Celebration of the Santa Fe Trail* (Kansas City, Mo.: Highwater Editions, 1996), p. 31; Shirl Kasper and Rick Montgomery, *Kansas City: An American Story* (Kansas City, Mo.: Kansas City Star Books, 1999), p. 27-32; and Garraghan, *Catholic Beginnings,* p. 103.
41. See William F. Dalton, *Historical Sketches of Kansas City, Souvenir of Silver Jubilee of Annunciation Parish,* June 30, 1897, p. 8; Pat O'Neill, *From the Bottom Up: The Story of the Irish in Kansas City* (Kansas City, Mo.: Seat O' the Pants Publishing, 1999), p. 16, 22; Sherry Lamb Schirmer, *Historical Overview of the Ethnic Communities of Kansas City* (Independence, Mo.: Pan-Educational Institute, 1976); "History of the Diocese of Kansas City," *Kansas City Register*, October 30, 1955; *Kansas City Times,* January, 17, 30, February 2, 1894; and Father Donnelly's journal, Native Sons Collection, and "Foreigners" vertical file, Kansas City Public Library.
42. O'Neill, *From the Bottom Up,* p. 14, 18.
43. Ibid., p. 35. The 1900 United States Census suggests that Henry Soden's family was far from poor. Although Henry's mother was a widow at age 39, she employed 2 American-born servants, Cora Schuman and Mary Mullen.
44. See Dalton, *Historical Sketches,* p. 8; and Marra, *This Far by Faith,* vol. 2, p. 259. The German church was served originally by the German-speaking Father Reusse, who moved from Henry County, Missouri, to take the Kansas City church.
45. Charles N. Glaab, *Kansas City and the Railroads: Community Policy in the Growth of a Regional Metropolis* (Lawrence: University of Kansas Press, 1993), p. 40-41, 94.
46. Marra, *This Far by Faith,* vol. 1, p. 28-29.
47. *The Official Catholic Directory, 1817-2004* (P.J. Kennedy & Son, 2004), p. 594.
48. Garraghan, *The Jesuits of the Middle United States,* vol. 2, p. 170. The most important case was the conviction of Father John Cummings in Pike County. The case was appealed to the U.S. Supreme Court, which ruled the test oath null and void.
49. Marra, *This Far By Faith,* vol. 1, p. 61.
50. William Dalton obituary, *Missouri Democrat,* February 23, 1927. He was born in 1847.
51. See Dalton, *Historical Sketches;* Marra, *This Far by Faith,* vol. 1, p. 69; and Schirmer, *Historical Overview,* p. 3. Schirmer says that 500 Irish families had settled in the West Bottoms by 1880.
52. See Kasper and Montgomery, *Kansas City: An American Story*, p. 118; and Dalton, *Historical Sketches.*
53. Charles Dudley Warner, "Studies in the Great West," *Harper's New Monthly Magazine,* October 1888, p. 761. The U.S. Census reported a population of 32,000 in 1870; 55,000 in 1880; and 132,000 by 1890.
54. Emma Abbott Gage, *Western Wanderings and Summer Saunterings Through Picturesque Colorado* (Baltimore: Lord Baltimore Press), quoted in Kasper and Montgomery, *Kansas City,* p. 122.
55. Dinnerstein and Reimers, *Ethnic Americans,* p. 28.
56. See Marra, *This Far By Faith,* vol. 1, p. 82; and Schlafly, "Birth of Kansas City's Pioneer Church."

Chapter Two – A JESUIT PARISH

1. Dorothy Brandt Marra, *This Far by Faith: A Popular History of the Catholic People of West and Northwest Missouri,* vol. 2 (Kansas City, Mo.: Diocese of Kansas City-St. Joseph, 1992), p. 198.
2. See "Diocese of Kansas City," in *Catholic Encyclopedia,* www.newadvent.org; *The Official Catholic Directory, 1817-2004* (P.J. Kennedy & Son, 2004), p. 594; "The Catholic Church," *The Kansas City Star,* June 4, 1950; Marra, *This Far by Faith,* vol. 1, p. 82, 91. Hogan's dual jurisdiction continued until June 19, 1893, when the separate jurisdiction of the Diocese of St. Joseph was established. *The Kansas City Star* of June 4, 1950, said Kansas City had a Catholic population of 9,000 (or 16.3

percent) in 1880, with 5 Catholic churches, 4 schools, one hospital, and one academy.

3. See Marra, *This Far by Faith,* vol. 2, p. 184-85; *Kansas City Journal of Commerce,* May 26, 1878; "Redemptorists," in *Catholic Encyclopedia,* http://www.newadvent.org; and Dalton, *Historical Sketches,* p. 19.
4. Marra, *This Far by Faith,* vol. 2, p. 149-50.
5. Ibid., p. 286-87; and Rev. William J. Stack, C.M., *The Fifty Years of St. Vincent's Parish* (Kansas City, Mo.: St. Vincent's Parish, 1939), p. 30.
6. Bishop John Hogan to Father Leopold Bushart, August 31, 1885, Folder III, Kansas City, Midwest Jesuit Archives, St. Louis.
7. *Souvenir Album of Jesuit Colleges.*
8. See *History of St. Aloysius Parish, August 31, 1885-August 20, 1920,* p. 1-2; Rev. Alexander Leutkemeyer, O.S.B., *History of St. Aloysius Parish: On the Occasion of the Centennial Celebration of St. Aloysius Parish* (Kansas City, Mo.: June 21, 1986), p. 1-2; Hugh M. Owens, *History of Rockhurst College: The First Quarter Century (1914-1939),* p. 3; and "Map of the City of Kansas: Plan Showing Streets Paved," January 1, 1888, Kansas City Public Library.
9. See "Map of the City of Kansas: Plan Showing Streets Paved"; *History of St. Aloysius Parish, August 31, 1885-August 20, 1920,* p. 1; and Box III, Kansas City, "Deeds" folder, Midwest Jesuit Archives. In about 1910, Michael Dowling, S.J., made a list of property owned by St. Aloysius as follows: St. Aloysius church and residence: Lots 8, 9, 10, Block 3, South Winfield Place; St. Aloysius school: property purchased before the area was platted and described by metes and bounds as "Fifty-five (55) feet front, on the north line of Peery Avenue, by the west of and adjacent to the west line of Graham Place and running north one-hundred and twenty (120) feet, in the southwest quarter of the northwest section of Section 3, Township 49, Range 33; St. Aloysius playground and Sisters' residence: Lots 1,2,3,4 Graham Place; and land at the northwest corner of 11th Street and Prospect Avenue, running one hundred (100) feet on 11th Street by one hundred thirty-two (132) feet on Prospect Avenue, Lots 47 and 48 of Clouser & Cole's Addition." The title to this piece of land was in the name of Saint Louis University, while the title to the other holdings was in the name of Bishop John J. Hogan. (Document filed with St. Aloysius papers, Rockhurst University Archives.)
10. William T. Doran, "Biography of James A. Dowling," Midwest Jesuit Archives. James Dowling would serve St. Aloysius Parish until October 3, 1895.
11. *History of St. Aloysius Parish, 1885-1920,* p. 4.
12. Jay P. Dolan, *The American Catholic Experience: A History from Colonial Times to the Present* (New York: Doubleday & Company, Inc., 1985), p. 262-66.
13. Ibid., p. 268-70.
14. James Hennesey, S.J., *American Catholics: A History of the Roman Catholic Community in the United States* (New York: Oxford University Press, 1981), p. 121.
15. Dolan, *The American Catholic Experience,* p. 202.
16. George Brown Tindall and David E. Shi, *America: A Narrative History,* vol. 2, 4th ed. (New York: W.W. Norton & Company, 1996), p. 893.
17. *The Kansas City Star,* April 4, 1894, p. 1.
18. *Memorials Left by the Missouri Provincial for the Church and Residence at Kansas City, Mo.,* 1894-1919. Rockhurst University Archives.
19. Ibid.
20. *History of St. Aloysius Parish, 1885-1920,* p. 5.
21. See Ibid., p. 6, 7; and *History of St. Aloysius Parish: On the Occasion of the Centennial,* p. 9.
22. Michael Dowling, S.J., list of property, Rockhurst University Archives. When St. Aloysius Church was demolished in 1969, during the feverish days of urban renewal, the bells were reinstalled at the Benedictine Monastery in Pevely, Missouri (now dissolved). They were moved a second time, to the Benedictine Sisters of Columbia in Columbia, Missouri. (Leutkemeyer, O.S.B., *History of St. Aloysius Parish,* supplement.)
23. Ibid.
24. Giovanni Schiavo, *The Italians in Missouri* (Chicago: Italian American Publishing Company, 1929), p. 159-78.
25. Ibid. After a fire, the present brick church was constructed in 1903.
26. Rothensteiner, *History of the Archdiocese of St. Louis,* p. 278-81.
27. Marra, *This Far By Faith,* vol. 2, p. 134-35, 518-20.
28. See "Father Michael P. Dowling," *Woodstock Letters,* vol. 44, 1915, p. 228-35; and Father William T. Doran, "St. Mary's College," Midwest Jesuit Archives. Dowling would remain at Detroit College until December 28, 1893. Creighton College was founded on September 2, 1878.
29. See biographical sketch, May 1911, Rev. M.P. Dowling, Rockhurst University Archives; "Rev. Michael P. Dowling," in *Men of Affairs in Greater Kansas City, 1912: A Newspaper Reference Work* (Kansas City, Mo.: Kansas City Press Club, April 1912), p. 35; and "Father Michael P. Dowling," *Woodstock Letters,* 44 (1915), p. 228-35.
30. See "Creighton University," in *Catholic Encyclopedia,* http://www.newadvent.org; and Creighton University Web site: www.creighton.edu. It would take about $32.7 million in today's money to equal the purchasing power of $1.5 million in 1900, according to the Economic History Services Web site: http://eh.net/hmit.
31. *Woodstock Letters.*
32. Ibid.
33. Ibid.
34. Ibid.
35. See Harvey, *History of Rockhurst College,* p.5.
36. Leutkemeyer, *History of St. Aloysius Parish,* p. 24.
37. *History of St. Aloysius Parish, 1885-1920,* p. 17-18.
38. Michael Dowling to Father Provincial, March 18, 1909.
39. Marra, *This Far By Faith,* vol. 2, p. 518-20; and "The Catholic Church," *The Kansas City Star,* June 4, 1950. Joseph Benoist's will was contested, in the end leaving only $30,000 for De La Salle. In its first year, De La Salle drew 141 students, including freshmen and sophomores. In 1915, the academy was accredited by the University of Missouri.
40. Michael Dowling to Father Provincial, December 20, 1913.

Chapter Three – A WELL-CHOSEN NAME

1. D.M. Bone, ed., *Annual Review of Greater Kansas City, Illustrated 1908* (Kansas City: Business Men's League), p. 29-30.
2. Lawrence Larsen, "Kansas City: 100 Years of Business," *Kansas City Business Journal,* Fall 1991, p. 14-15.
3. *Kansas City Times,* October 2, 1905. At the time, priests were taught at St. Benedictine in Atchison, Kan., and Conception College in Conception, Mo.
4. Bone, *Annual Review,* p. 31.
5. *Report of the Board of Park Commissioners of Kansas City, Mo.,* April 18, 1910.
6. W.A. Satterlee, "Fifteen Miles for 5 Cents," *Greater Kansas City Official Yearbook, 1904-05* (Kansas City: E.L. Gates, 1905), p. 106-08.
7. See "G.W. Sedgwick Dies Suddenly," *The Kansas City Star,* May 4, 1899; "His A Peaceful End," *Kansas City Journal,* May 4, 6, 1899; Paul W. Gates, "The Railroads of Missouri, 1850-1870," *Missouri Historical Review,* 26:1 (October 1931): 129-141; Charles N. Glaab, *Kansas City and the Railroads: Community Policy in the Growth of a Regional Metropolis* (University of Kansas Press, 1993), p. 38-41; U.S. Bureau of the Census, Ninth, Tenth, and Twelfth United States Census, 1870, 1880, 1900, Jackson County, Mo.; and Daniel F. Stramara, Jr. census research, Rockhurst University Archives.
8. See *Kansas City Directory 1884,* p. 443; "E.A. Phillips," in Theodore S. Case, *History of Kansas City* (Syracuse, N.Y.: D. Mason & Co. Publishers, 1888), p. 591; and "Transcript of Register of Baptism of Mr. Lee Massachusetts John Sedgwick," August 14, 1908, Rockhurst University Archives.
9. *Kansas City Directory 1888,* p. 614.
10. See "Transcript of Register of Baptism of Mr. Lee Massachusetts John Sedgwick"; and "George W. Sedgwick's Funeral," *Kansas City Journal,* May 6, 1899. George Sedgwick's funeral service was held at Westminster Presbyterian Church.
11. *M.J. Boyle Diary 1871,* St. Mary's Mission, Box 1, Folder Ch2, Midwest Jesuit Archives, St. Louis.
12. William S. Worley, *J.C. Nichols and the Shaping of Kansas City: Innovation in Planned Residential Communities* (Columbia: University of Missouri Press, 1990), p. 68-70, 77, 128.
13. *Kansas City, Mo., Sanborn Co. Map 1906-1917,* vol. 4, 1909, Sheets 548, 551, 552.
14. Dowling to Meyer, January 8, 1909.
15. Rev. Michael P. Dowling, *Prospectus of a College in Kansas City* (May 1909), Rockhurst University Archives.
16. See ibid.; Harvey, *History of Rockhurst College,* p. 2-3 and Meyer to Dowling, February 5, 1909.
17. Meyer to Dowling, January 11, February 5, 1909.
18. The college's publicity department noted: "The immediate question which strangers to Rockhurst College ask is 'Where did such a name come from?' This query is entirely justified in that the name is unusual."
19. Dowling to Meyer, January 8, 1909.
20. Michael P. Dowling, *Report of the Rev. Fr. Dowling in 1908 to His Superiors on the Advisability of Locating a High School and College at Kansas City, Mo.* (1908), p. 5, Rockhurst University Archives.
21. http://www.stonyhurst.ac.uk. Stonyhurst College was founded in France in 1593, but after the French Revolution it was moved to England, eventually locating, in 1794, on the Stonyhurst estate of a former pupil, Thomas Weld. Dowling, *Report ... to His Superiors,* p. 5.
22. Dowling, *Report ... to His Superiors,* p. 5.
23. See ibid., and Meyer to Dowling, January 26, 1909.
24. Rock-Dowling correspondence, January 4, 11, 20, 1909; March 24, 1909; April 1, 1909. Mother Rock loaned $3,000 to Dowling, at 4 percent interest for 2 years, and sent him a gold coin for good luck.
25. See "Modernism," *Catholic Encyclopedia,* http://www.newadvent.org; Philip Gleason, *Contending With Modernity: Catholic Higher Education in the Twentieth Century* (New York: Oxford University Press, 1995), p. 21, 31, 35; and Jay P. Dolan, *The American Catholic Experience: A History from Colonial Times to the Present* (Garden City, New York: Doubleday & Company, Inc., 1985), p. 290.
26. See Dolan, *The American Catholic Experience,* p. 292-93; Gleason, *Contending With Modernity,* p. 26-29; and James Hennesey, S.J., *American Catholics: A History of the Roman Catholic Community in the United States* (New York: Oxford University Press, 1981), p. 187.
27. See Dolan, *The American Catholic Experience,* p. 262, 266-67, 272, 276, 286-87; and John J. Callahan, S.J., *Coming to Terms With the Mission: The Catholic and Jesuit University in America* (n.p., 1998), p. 3.
28. Gleason, *Contending With Modernity,* p. 40.
29. Ibid., p. 5.
30. Ibid., p. 47.
31. Ibid., p. 50.
32. Ibid., p. 51.
33. Ibid., p. 23-25.
34. J. Gordon Kingsley, *'Tiding Up Harvard Yard': Foundations of Higher Education in Kansas City, 1849-1933,* Midcontinent Perspectives lecture series, April 14, 1974.
35. See *The Kansas City Star,* May 30, 1909; and *Kansas City Times,* May 31, 1909, November 17, 1939. While the Jesuits' St. Aloysius Parish also had a high school, it was for girls only because the nuns who taught there were not allowed to teach boys beyond the elementary years. See Michael Dowling, *Prospectus for a College at Kansas City.*
36. "Ours at the Second Annual Conference of Catholic Colleges," *Woodstock Letters,* vol. 29, 1900, p. 343.
37. Gleason, *Contending With Modernity,* p. 56-57.
38. See *The Kansas City Star,* March 22, 1909; and Dowling, *Prospectus of a College in Kansas City.*
39. Dowling to Meyer, March 18, 1909.
40. See ibid.; and Dowling, *Prospectus of a College.*
41. Dowling to Hogan, April 26, 1909.
42. Dowling to Meyer, May 11, 1909. Thomas E. Lillis was appointed coadjutor to Bishop John J. Hogan, with the right to succession, in March 1910. Lillis, a native of Lexington, Missouri, was ordained by Hogan in 1885 and consecrated as bishop of Leavenworth on December 27, 1904. While serving as Hogan's coadjutor, Lillis retained his responsibilities for the Diocese of Leavenworth. He lived in Kansas City, Kansas, so he could fulfill his duties to both dioceses. See: Albert de Zutter, "Bishop John J. Hogan," *Catholic Key.* http://catholickey.org/index.php3?archive=1&gif=news.gif&mode=view&issue=19990905&article_id=422

43. Dowling to Meyer, May 11, 1909.
44. Ibid.
45. Dowling to Meyer, March 18, 1909.
46. Dowling to Meyer, April 10, 1909.
47. Hogan to Dowling, May 4, 1909.
48. Dowling to Meyer, May 11, 1909.
49. Dowling to Meyer, June 1, 1909.
50. Ibid.
51. Dorothy Brandt Marra, *This Far by Faith: A Popular History of the Catholic People of West and Northwest Missouri* vol. 2 (Kansas City, Mo.: Diocese of Kansas City-St. Joseph, 1992), p. 150, 184-186.
52. Dowling to Meyer, June 1, 1909.
53. Dowling to Meyer, June 25, 1909.
54. Ibid.
55. "Father Michael J. Ryan," *The Province News-Letter* (February 1936).
56. See Dowling to Hogan, July 23, 1909; Dowling memorandum, September 1909, Rockhurst University Archives; and Hugh M. Owens, *History of Rockhurst College: The First Quarter Century (1914-1939),* p. 14.
57. See Owens, *History of Rockhurst College,* p. 14; Rev. Patrick F. Harvey, S.J., "History of Rockhurst College," n.d., p. 4, 8; and *Jesuit Bulletin* (April 1934), p. 1. Of the mud, Harvey writes that Father Hoffend had tried to start a Sodality in the new parish, but the roads to Rockhurst were so muddy, people couldn't make it. Harvey also writes that Father Dowling had wanted to name the new church St. Ignatius, "but when Fr. Ryan called upon Bishop Hogan to learn his pleasure in the matter, the bishop expressed the wish that it be called St. Francis Xavier, for he said, 'That was the title of the first church in Kansas City,'" though actually the name of the first church was St. Francis Regis. According to Harvey, those in attendance at the first Mass were Mr. and Mrs. H.P. Stewart, Agnes Stewart, Duke Stewart, H.P. Stewart Jr., James Green, Marion Green, Ella Collins, Carrie Britain, Nora McChesney, K. Fisher, Mr. and Mrs. J.H. Hedding, L.J. Schwager, Mr. and Mrs. T. Kelly and their five children, Douglas, Claud, and Lillian Sullivan, Mrs. George Muehlebach, Mrs. Frank Walsh, Louise Walsh, Cecelia Walsh, Marie Walsh, Teresa Ryan, Kate Ryan, John Bolan, Belle McGonegal, Angelina Kennedy, Mrs. J. Cahill, Hattie Jewel, Brother Charles, Frank McLaughlin, W. Dobel, E. Caffrey, Ed. Coffey, M. Sheron, Helen, Emma, Hedwig, Louise, Henry George, Arthur and Tony Forster, Dr. T.E. Flannigan, Clarence Reardon, Eugene Dobel, Francis Brannon, Mr. and Mrs. T.J. Noone, Mrs. J. E. McMellen, Mr. and Mrs. James Donahue, and Adali Donahue.

Chapter Four – A COLLEGE BUILDING 1909–1914

1. See Dowling memorandum, September 15, 1909; and Rockhurst College Building Association to Architect, 1909, Rockhurst University Archives.
2. Dowling to Lillis, September 17, 1909.
3. Ibid.
4. See Harvey, *History of Rockhurst College,* p. 4-5. According to Harvey, the chapel with schoolroom attached was erected during the fall of 1909 and was dedicated by the Rev. Lillis in the summer of 1910. The parochial school opened on September 6, 1910.
5. See Dowling to Meyer, January 13, 20, 1910; and Rockhurst College Building Association to Architect, 1909.
6. Dowling to Meyer, March 16, 1910.
7. See Harvey, *History of Rockhurst College,* p. 4; and Owens, *History of Rockhurst College,* p. 17.
8. Dowling to Meyer, May 6, 1910.
9. Dowling to Meyer, January 13, May 6, 1910. According to Harvey, *History of Rockhurst College,* p. 4, Father Ryan had officiated at the Rockhurst chapel through September 1909, when he returned to St. Mary's College. Father Eugene C. Kieffer, S.J., then took charge of the congregation.
10. Harvey, *History of Rockhurst College,* p. 7.
11. See ibid., p. 5; and Owens, *History of Rockhurst College,* 15-16, 21. Harvey puts the date of incorporation as September 2, 1910, but Owens notes that September 2 was the date the court clerk certified the Pro Forma decree. Rockhurst, in the eyes of the state, Owens writes, would have been established on August 30. The incorporation papers were filed in Jefferson City on September 13, 1910.
12. *The Kansas City Star,* August 12, 1910.
13. Philip Gleason, *Contending With Modernity: Catholic Higher Education in the Twentieth Century* (New York: Oxford University Press, 1995), p. 96-97.
14. Ibid., p. 101.
15. Dowling quoted in Gleason, ibid., p. 101-02.
16. See Dowling to Meyer, November 16, 1910; and Harvey, *History of Rockhurst College,* p. 5. It must have been well known that the old quarry was on the Rockhurst site because, according to Harvey, houses in the neighborhood had been built from the rock mined there. He mentions specifically "Mrs. Lyon's house, 53rd and Virginia; Mr. Williamson's house on Tracy; and the home of Dr. Horrigan, 53rd and Troost...."
17. See *The Kansas City Star,* August 12, 1910; Owens, *History of Rockhurst College,* p. 17; and Harvey, *History of Rockhurst College,* p. 5, 6. For a list of men on the Board of Trustees, see Harvey, p. 6.
18. Dowling to Meyer, May 19, 1911.
19. See "Boys Hotel" and "Girls Hotel," local history files, Kansas City Public Library.
20. Dowling to Meyer, May 19, 1911.
21. Ibid.
22. Ibid.
23. Ibid.
24. Ibid.
25. "A Word to the Committees," n.d., Rockhurst University Archives.
26. See Mayor Darus Brown to Secretary John McQueeny, June 29, 1911, and various letters, committees to businesses, Rockhurst University Archives.
27. Dr. Owen Krueger to John McQueeny, June 28, 1911.

28. Ibid., July 25, 1911.
29. Michael Dowling, August 8, 1911.
30. John McQueeny to R.S. Latshaw, June 8, 1911.
31. John McQueeny to H.P. Stewart, July 11, 1911.
32. Rockhurst College to Mrs. John R. Foran, September 28, 1911.
33. John McQueeny to various men, July 31, 1911.
34. See Harvey, *History of Rockhurst College,* p. 6; and Owens, *History of Rockhurst College,* p. 18.
35. See letters, The Committee of 100, Rockhurst University Archives.
36. See Harvey, *History of Rockhurst College,* p. 7; Owens, *History of Rockhurst College,* p. 18; and Dowling to Meyer, June 7, 1911. Harvey writes that work resumed on one or two occasions, only to be abandoned shortly afterwards for lack of funds. Also apparently holding up the project was a request from the man who owned the 15 acres directly north of Rockhurst "to plat with him the part of our property which we intend to sell; and make an attractive addition, with the college as the center." The man, who probably was Robert Jones, already had laid out another addition to the city that impressed Dowling with its "winding roads and beautiful landscape," so Dowling wanted to concur if possible. He hired a landscape engineer and planned to go with Jones if it was not too costly.
37. See *The Kansas City Star,* September 20, 1911, and Harvey, *History of Rockhurst College,* p. 6.
38. *The Kansas City Star,* January 26, 1912.
39. See the *Kansas City Times,* February 16, 1912; and Dowling to Burrowes, January 2, 1914.
40. Owens, *History of Rockhurst College,* p. 16. Owens writes that fathers Kieffer and Sullivan had been in charge of the parish before Father Ryan's return. Unlike Father Ryan, both priests had lived in the Jesuit residence at St. Aloysius. Owens writes that Father Ryan was able to live at Rockhurst without a salary thanks to the generosity of a Miss M. Ryan of Chicago, and H.P. Stewart, Mrs. E. Reardon, and Mr. C. Bombeck of Kansas City.
41. *The Kansas City Star,* March 23, 1913.
42. Ibid.
43. Hoffend, January 21, 1914, quoted in Harvey, *History of Rockhurst College,* p. 8.
44. See Owens, *History of Rockhurst College,* p. 19; and Dowling to Burrowes, May 8, 1913.
45. See Burrowes to Dowling, May 13, 1913; and Dowling to Burrowes, May 19, 1913.
46. Dowling to Burrowes, December 20, 1913.
47. Ibid.
48. See Matoushek to McCabe, March 1941; and Conway to McCabe, April 7, 1941.
49. Breen to McCabe, week of March 11, 1941.
50. Ibid., March 19, 1941. Breen told how he once received a letter from Sedgwick postmarked in Patna, India. Sedgwick was on a trip around the world and had had Christmas dinner with Father William Eline, who was at the mission in Bettiah or possibly another mission in India, Breen said.
51. See "Transcript of Register of Baptism," Sedgwick folder, Rockhurst University Archives; and Thomas S. Bowden, S.J., to Father B. McG (incomplete salutation), May 14, 1915.
52. McQueeny to Sedgwick, August 5, 1911.
53. Bowden to McG, May 14, 1915.
54. "First Declaration," Sedgwick folder, Rockhurst University Archives.
55. Ibid.
56. Sedgwick to Dowling, February 16, 1913.
57. Dowling to Burrowes, May 8, 1913.
58. Ibid.
59. Dowling to Burrowes, December 16, 1913.
60. Ibid.
61. Ibid.
62. Dowling to Burrowes, January 2, 1914.
63. *The Kansas City Star,* April 30, 1914.
64. Harvey, *History of Rockhurst College,* p. 8, 9.

Chapter Five – FIRST YEARS AT ROCKHURST 1914–17

1. "Father Patrick F. Harvey," *Missouri Province News-Letter* (May 1941), p. 360. Harvey had spent a year as a secular priest before entering the Jesuits' novitiate at Florissant on September 7, 1903, when he was 24 years old. He was born on February 5, 1879.
2. Rev. Patrick F. Harvey, S.J., *History of Rockhurst College*, n.d., p. 9.
3. Ibid., p. 14.
4. Ibid., p. 12.
5. James Hennesey, S.J., *American Catholics: A History of the Roman Catholic Community in the United States* (New York: Oxford University Press, 1981), p. 207. Bishop Thomas Lillis' father, for example, was an Irish immigrant, born in County Claire. He became a successful contractor in Kansas City and, in 1885, built the city's first street railway. See Sherry Lamb Schirmer, "Overview of the Irish Community," in *Historic Overview of the Ethnic Communities in Kansas City* (Kansas City: Pan-Educational Institute, 1976), p. 6.
6. Hennesey, *American Catholics,* p. 220.
7. See Schirmer, "Overview of the Irish Community"; and Sherry Lamb Schirmer and Richard D. McKinzie, *At the River's Bend: An Illustrated History of Kansas City, Independence & Jackson County* (Woodland Hills, Calif.: Windsor Publications Inc. in association with the Jackson County Historical Society, 1982), p. 12.
8. Harvey, *History of Rockhurst College,* p. 10, 13.
9. See *The Kansas City Star,* December 9, 1934.
10. Ibid.
11. Ibid.
12. Harvey, *History of Rockhurst College,* p. 15.
13. *Memorial Book,* 1917, Rockhurst University Archives.
14. Harvey, *History of Rockhurst College,* p. 12.
15. See "Walter A. Roemer, S.J., 1890-1971," in Midwest Jesuit Archives, St. Louis; and "Brother Patrick Kehoe, S.J.," *The Dial* (March 1919), p. 115.
16. *The Kansas City Star,* December 9, 1934.
17. Hugh M. Owens, *History of Rockhurst College: The First Quarter Century (1914-1939),* p. 46.
18. *The Kansas City Star,* December 9, 1934.
19. See Harvey, *History of Rockhurst College,* p. 12; and *Jesuit Bulletin* (October 1935), p. 4.

20. Harvey, *History of Rockhurst College,* p. 16.
21. Ibid., p. 19, 25.
22. John Jennings, *History of Rockhurst College,* (Ph.B. thesis, Rockhurst College, 1938), p. 6.
23. Owens, *History of Rockhurst College,* p. 44.
24. Sean Brennan, "The Little School on the Hill: The Founding of Rockhurst," *Missouri Historical Review,* vol. 96, no. 1 (October 2001), p. 32-33.
25. W.F. Bartholome, "Jesuit Series," *Fairfield University STAG* (February 20, 1952), Rockhurst University Archives.
26. See, George Brown Tindall and David E. Shi, *America: A Narrative History,* 4th ed. vol. 2 (New York: W.W. Norton & Company, 1996), p. 1113; and Paul S. Boyer, et al., *The Enduring People: A History of the American People,* 3rd ed., vol. 2 (New York: Houghton Mifflin Company, 1998), p. 482.
27. Philip Gleason, *Contending With Modernity: Catholic Higher Education in the Twentieth Century* (New York: Oxford University Press, 1995), p. 78-80. Following World War I, college enrollments in the United States soared with the country's new leadership position in the world. Previously, Gleason writes, students in the nineteenth century had flocked to German universities.
28. Brennan, "The Little School on the Hill," p. 43-45.
29. "Prospectus of Rockhurst College," quoted in Owens, *History of Rockhurst College,* p. 38-39, 45.
30. See *Rockhurst College Catalog for 1932-43;* Richard Janet, "A Story of Perseverance & Faith: Rockhurst's Early History," *Rockhurst: The Magazine of Rockhurst University* (Fall 2004), p. 15; and "General Statement," Public Relations Department, 1952, Rockhurst University Archives.
31. Schwitalla interview, quoted in Owens, *History of Rockhurst College,* p. 45.
32. "Prospectus," quoted in Owens, *History of Rockhurst College,* p. 45.
33. *Rockhurst College Annual Catalog,* June 1920, quoted in Owens, *History of Rockhurst College,* p. 59.
34. See "Obituary," Midwest Jesuit Archives; Who's Who in America, 1950-51; and Father Knipscher to Dr. V.H. Ryan, February 1, 1938.
35. Harvey, *History of Rockhurst College,* p. 24, 31.
36. See Knipscher to Ryan, February 1, 1938; and Harvey, *History of Rockhurst College,* p. 27, 29. According to Owens, *History of Rockhurst College,* p. 44, Bernard Muller-Thym, Joseph Z. Miller, III, V.J. Flaherty, Sr., and Dr. Thomas E. Purcell were the men who donated much of the $5,000 demanded by the provincial to open the college in the first place. Much of this money, Owens writes, was spent on scientific apparatus that Schwitalla bought in Chicago.
37. See *The Rockhurst Sentinel,* February 17, November 6, December 11, 1919; and Harvey, *History of Rockhurst College,* p. 16.
38. Owens, *History of Rockhurst College,* p. 46.
39. Ibid.
40. See Harvey, *History of Rockhurst College,* p. 16-17; and Owens, *History of Rockhurst College,* p. 44.
41. "The College Bell," *The Rockhurst Sentinel,* April 11, 1919.
42. *Year Book of Benefactors,* Rockhurst University Archives.
43. See Knipscher to Ryan, February 1, 1938; *Province News-Letter* (September 1922); and "Stocks presented by J.Z. Miller III for Sodality," miscellaneous document, Rockhurst University Archives. The handwritten document notes receipt of a letter from Miller to Father Henry R. Ehrhard dated November 13, 1915. The same document states that on August 8, 1924, the shares were worth $8.35 each.
44. *Year Book of Benefactors,* Rockhurst University Archives.
45. Breen to Burrowes, October 31, 1916. With his letter, Breen included "the agreement" the college had signed with Sedgwick. According to Harvey, *History of Rockhurst College,* p. 22, Breen paid his visit to Sedgwick while Provincial Burrowes was in town for the Visitation. "Before Fr. Provincial went away, Mr. Sedgwick had dinner with the community at St. Aloysius."
46. See Harvey, *History of Rockhurst College,* p. 19, 22, 25, 29, 33; and *The Province News-Letter,* vol. 2, (November 1920), p. 15.
47. See Harvey, *History of Rockhurst College,* p. 23, 28; and *The Kansas City Star,* May 21, 1916. *The Star* reported that 10 contractors bid for the project, which was awarded to Adam E. Madorie, who began work on May 24.
48. Harvey, *History of Rockhurst College,* p. 24.
49. See ibid., p. 34-35, 36; Owens, *History of Rockhurst College,* p. 50; and *The Rockhurst Sentinel,* April 11, 1919, December 22, 1921.
50. *The Rockhurst Sentinel,* October 9, 1919; October 13, 1920.
51. See ibid., October 7, 1918, January 20, February 17, 1919, November 15, 1920; and Harvey, *The History of Rockhurst College,* p. 33, 37.
52. See Harvey, *History of Rockhurst College,* p. 30; *Jesuit Bulletin* (April 1934); and *The Province News-Letter,* vol. 5 (September 1923), p. 12.
53. Harvey, *History of Rockhurst College,* p. 29.
54. "Neighborhood Expansion," *The Rockhurst Sentinel,* December 22, 1921.
55. Ibid.
56. Dowling to provincial, December 20, 1913. Dowling described his illness as "tubercular ulceration of the peritoneum and carcinoma."
57. Dowling to provincial, March 22, 1914.
58. See *Woodstock Letters,* vol. 44, 1915, p. 234; and *The Kansas City Star,* February 13, 1915.
59. *Woodstock Letters,* vol. 44, 1916, p. 386-38. James Dowling was on the pastoral staff of Holy Family Church at 12th and May streets in Chicago. Hearing that his brother Michael was near death, James had visited Michael in Kansas City just 6 weeks before his own death. He apparently was in good health during his visit to Kansas City, but upon his return to Chicago "became aware that he was suffering from some insidious malady." He underwent an operation at St. Anthony's Hospital and died there 4 hours afterward, on February 6, 1915.
60. *Woodstock Letters,* vol. 44, 1915, p. 234.
61. "Father Dowling Called By Death," *Omaha Sunday Herald,* February 14, 1915.
62. *Woodstock Letters,* vol. 44, 1915, p. 234.
63. Weiand to Breen, January 21, 1921; Breen to Weiand, January 25, 1921.
64. Ryan to Weiand, January 28, 1921. Father Dowling's sister was married to Joseph Hempfling, of Kansas City.
65. Breen to Weiand, January 25, 1921.
66. "The Dowling Medal," miscellaneous document, Rockhurst University Archives.
67. Jennings, *History of Rockhurst College,* p. 7.

Chapter Six – THE YOUNG SCHOOL MOVES FORWARD 1917–24

1. Rev. Patrick F. Harvey, S.J., *History of Rockhurst College,* n.d., p. 28.
2. See "Roll of Honor," *The Rockhurst Sentinel,* February 17, 1919, p. 4; and Harvey, *History of Rockhurst College,* p. 31.
3. See *The Junior Sentinel,* January 11, March 11, April 8, 1918; and *The Rockhurst Sentinel,* October 7, 1918.
4. See "Conservation of Coal," *The Junior Sentinel,* January 18, 1918. It took 16 Thrift Stamps, purchased for 25 cents each, to fill one Thrift Card. Once filled, the card could be exchanged at the U.S. Post Office, a bank or other authorized place for $5 on January 1, 1923.
5. See *The Junior Sentinel,* March 11, March 25, April 15, May 27, 1918.
6. John Jennings, *History of Rockhurst College,* (Ph.B. thesis, Rockhurst College, 1938), p. 7.
7. Philip Gleason, *Contending With Modernity: Catholic Higher Education in the Twentieth Century* (New York: Oxford University Press, 1995), p. 73-74.
8. Ibid., p. 74, 342.
9. See *The Kansas City Star,* December 9, 1934; and *The Rockhurst Sentinel,* April 11, 1919. *The Star* article, based on an interview with President Daniel Conway, said that Weiand, "when president of Rockhurst College, built with his own hands the platforms in the school rooms on which the teachers sit, and he also did other carpentry work."
10. "Rockhurst Students Join S.A.T.C.," *The Rockhurst Sentinel,* September 30, 1918.
11. "Rockhurst Alumni Association, Minutes of Meetings," September 7, 1918.
12. Ibid., September 23, 1918.
13. *The Rockhurst Sentinel,* October 7, 1918.
14. *The Rockhurst Sentinel,* November 25, 1918.
15. See ibid., December 4, 1921; and Weiand to J.Z. Miller, Jr., November 6, 1921.
16. James A. Henretta, et al., *America's History,* vol. 2 (Boston, New York: Bedford/St. Martin's), 4th ed., p. 705-65.
17. See Hennesey, *American Catholics,* p. 235; Jay P. Dolan, *The American Catholic Experience: A History from Colonial Times to the Present* (Garden City, New York: Doubleday & Company, Inc., 1985), p. 390; Shirl Kasper and Rick Montgomery, *Kansas City: An American Story* (Kansas City, Mo.: Kansas City Star Books, 1999), p. 205; and Liberty Memorial Web site, www.libertymemorialmuseum.org. The site for the Liberty Memorial was dedicated on November 1, 1921; the monument itself, except for the north frieze wall, opened on November 11, 1926.
18. "Marshal Foch Receives Degree at Rockhurst College," *The Rockhurst Sentinel,* November 11, 1921.
19. Ibid.
20. *The Province News-Letter,* December 1921, p. 28.
21. Jay P. Dolan, *The American Catholic Experience: A History from Colonial Times to the Present* (Garden City, New York: Doubleday & Company, Inc., 1985), p. 384-86.
22. See *The Rockhurst Sentinel,* March 29, 1920, and "A Short Diary of the College," October 8, 1925, in Rockhurst University Archives.
23. Dorothy Brandt Marra, *This Far by Faith: A Popular History of the Catholic People of West and Northwest Missouri,* vol. 1 (Kansas City, Mo.: Diocese of Kansas City-St. Joseph, 1992), p. 117. A $1,000 contribution from Bernard Corrigan helped St. Monica Parish survive. The Sisters of the Blessed Sacrament for Indians and Colored People also gave $8,000 to buy land at 17th Street and Lydia Avenue, where a combined church and school were built.
24. Dolan, *The American Catholic Experience,* p. 246.
25. Ibid., p. 351, 400. By 1950, Jesuits would operate 42 percent of the Catholic colleges in the United States.
26. Ledóchowski to Rockhurst College, June 7, 1928.
27. Ibid.
28. See *Rockhurst College Catalog,* 1932-33, p. 8-9; an undated note from the dean on college enrollment, Rockhurst University Archives. The note lists estimated enrollment for the academic years 1921-22 through 1930-31 and goes on to say, "We had no record of the religion of the students before this year. But by consulting former teachers, I found, that at times no non-Catholics, and sometimes up to three or five were present. This year we have ten. All are protestants."
29. See undated letter from the Rockhurst president, Rockhurst University Archives. Probably written in 1924 by Arthur Spillard, S.J., as he assumed the college presidency, the letter goes into detail about Rockhurst's finances and needs.
30. A dispute over past tuition for students from St. Francis Xavier Parish would lead to a heated "domestic Jesuit dispute" in the 1940s, when Rockhurst tried to buy back a 150-foot by 300-foot piece of land it had sold to the SFX parish in 1926 for St. Francis Xavier to build a new church. The dispute centered on an agreement made between Rockhurst President Manion (1928–33) and SFX pastor McDonnell during the early years of the Depression. According to Manion, St. Francis Xavier had agreed to pay $10 a month, or the full tuition bill of $100 a year, for every boy from St. Francis Xavier Parish who agreed to attend Rockhurst High School. When Father Manion left office on February 2, 1933, McDonnell met with the new rector, Daniel Conway, S.J., and apparently reduced the figure to $7.50 a month, or $75 a year for each boy. This, Rockhurst President William H. McCabe (1940–45) later would conclude, looked "very much like a cheerful Irish railroading, achieved at a strategic moment." Because the early 1930s were difficult years, Rockhurst needed any money it could get, which explained why Manion did not feel he could protest McDonnell's shenanigans, McCabe concluded in the 1940s. "There is no doubt," McCabe wrote, "that he (Manion), as his successor (Conway) was on the spot, because this student attendance, even at $7.50, was a lifesaver for the school in hard times." The touchy subject was exacerbated because the consultors had ruled that SFX boys should not be given a break on tuition, lest other parishes cry discrimination. Documents show that on July 31, 1932, Manion and McDonnell entered into the $10-a-month agreement that "the boys of St. Francis Xavier parish of high school age are to be sent to Rockhurst High School each year. The parish is responsible to the Treasurer for the tuition of each boy, $100 for each boy for the ten-month year or $10 per month." The document goes on to say that "in view of the fact that hard times are with us it may be impossible for Fr. McDonnell to collect the full amount for each boy during the current year (of 1932)." A decade later, in 1943, then-Rockhurst President McCabe determined that St. Francis Xavier owed Rockhurst $4,572.50. The agreement between Manion and McDonnell, and McCabe's notes, dated October 8, 1943, are in the Rockhurst University Archives.

31. See *The Rockhurst Sentinel,* June 1, 1927; and annual enrollment figures in *The Province News-Letter.* In 1927, for example, Rockhurst had only 8 college graduates. Expanding enrollment in Jesuit colleges across the United States is recorded in *The Province News-Letter* of June 1931. Total students in 1910—14,668; in 1920—36,377; and in 1930—60,125.

32. *The Jesuit Bulletin,* October 1935, p. 8. According to *The Province News-Letter* of November 1929, 50 percent of Rockhurst's freshman class comprised "graduates from the city's public high schools." As late as 1935 most of Rockhurst's students came from Kansas City and its suburbs, especially the city's 2 Catholic high schools.

33. See Hugh M. Owens, *History of Rockhurst College: The First Quarter Century (1914-1939),* p. 62; *The Province News-Letter,* September 1922, p. 27; "The New Building," *The Rockhurst Sentinel,* October 30, 1922; and *Woodstock Letters,* vol. 52, 1923. "I am gathering friends and so far have been quite successful," Weiand wrote to Provincial McMenamy on May 7, 1924. But in September 1925, his work for a new building was suspended because of lack of accreditation.

34. *The Province News-Letter,* June 1923, p. 78; and September 1923, p. 12.

35. See *The Kansas City Star,* December 9, 1934; Owens, *History of Rockhurst College,* p. 55; and notes of a special meeting of the Board of Directors, September 15, 1921, August 12, 1923, Rockhurst University Archives. The directors agreed to sell Lot 57 for $1,325 and Lot 56 for $1,400.

36. See *The Rockhurst Sentinel,* October 30, 1922; Owens, *History of Rockhurst College,* p. 55, 61; and Daniel Conway to Zacheus Maher, March 11, 1937. "A new building has been erected and is now occupied by the college department which fills it nearly to capacity," *The Sentinel* reported. "This building, however, is merely temporary and is so constructed that it can be converted without great trouble or expense into a dormitory."

37. See "A Short History of the College," 1923-24, Rockhurst University Archives, and *The Rockhurst Sentinel,* December 13, 1929.

38. See Spillard to McMenamy, April 2, 1926; *The Province News-Letter,* September 1922, p. 27; *The Rockhurst Sentinel,* June 14, 1922; and "A Short Diary of the College," 1925.

39. Harvey, *History of Rockhurst College,* p. 38-39.

40. William S. Worley, *J.C. Nichols and the Shaping of Kansas City: Innovation in Planned Residential Communities* (Columbia: University of Missouri Press, 1990), p. 211, 217, 221.

41. See Gleason, *Contending With Modernity,* p. 35-37; Alphonse M. Schwitalla, S.J., "Rockhurst Golden Anniversary," Rockhurst University Archives; and David J. O'Brien, *From the Heart of the American Church: Catholic Higher Education and American Culture* (Maryknoll, New York: Orbis Books, 1994), p. 41.

42. Gleason, *Contending With Modernity,* p. 50-51. According to the Web site of the National Catholic Educational Association, the NCEA traces its official beginning to a meeting held in St. Louis, July 12-14, 1904. At that meeting the separate Catholic education organizations, the Education Conference of Catholic Seminary Faculties (1898), the Association of Catholic Colleges (1899), and the Parish School Conference (1902) agreed to unite as the Catholic Educational Association (CEA). See http://www.ncea.org/about/index.asp.

43. Gleason, *Contending With Modernity,* p. 51-53.

44. Ibid., p. 39-40, 43, 57-58. Gleason also explains the difficulty Catholics faced in coordinating all the elements of Catholic education. On one hand, the chain of command rested in the bishop of the local diocese, who oversaw parochial schools. On the other hand, religious communities at the turn of the twentieth century ran all but about a half dozen of the 188 Catholic men's colleges in the United States. Because most of these Catholic colleges were top heavy with prep students, as was Rockhurst, the religious knew they needed the goodwill of the bishop, though they were not under his immediate jurisdiction. For Catholics leaving parochial school, the choice was to go to a public high school or to upgrade aspirations by shifting to the "college" track at a school like Rockhurst. Adding to difficulties was the "we-go-our-own-way" attitude of many Jesuits, understandable since every Jesuit college had to support itself.

45. "Contemplated Program of Rockhurst College," Rockhurst University Archives.

46. "A Short History of the College."

47. "A Kansas City Priest Has Been Fifty Years in Jesuit Order," *Kansas City Times,* May 31, 1934. Rockhurst's Father Patrick Harvey temporarily had taken over St. Francis Xavier Parish duties in the fall of 1921. Rockhurst Jesuit Edward Coppinger would become Leary's first, full-time assistant.

48. *The Province News-Letter,* June 1923, p. 78.

49. See *The Kansas City Star,* September 19, 1925; and *The Province News-Letter,* November 1925, p. 18.

50. See McMenamy to Spillard, January 16, 1926; and Owens, *History of Rockhurst College,* p. 63.

51. McCabe to father provincial, April 17, 1945. A letter in the Rockhurst University Archives, signed by Spillard, April 2, 1926, states that Spillard had given the deed to the property to Father Leary.

52. *The Jesuit Bulletin,* April 1934.

53. "A Short History of the College."

54. *The Rockhurst Sentinel,* October 23, 1919, March 19, 1920.

55. Ibid., April 23, May 19, 1920; December 21, 1922.

56. *The Rockhurst Sentinel,* October 30, 1923.

57. Weiand to provincial, July 9, 1924.

58. See "Minutes of meetings," Rockhurst Alumni Association, November 14, 1922.

59. See Ibid.; and April 10, May 24, October 12, December 10, 1923; February 13, March 24, 1924 in the Rockhurst University Archives; and *The Rockhurst Sentinel,* January 29, 1923.

60. "A Short History of the College," September 13, 14, 1924; January 5, 1925.

61. Weiand to McMenamy, May 7, 1924, quoted in Owens, *History of Rockhurst College,* p. 62.

62. Spillard to provincial, September 2, 1924.

63. "A Short History of the College," October 29-31, November 13, 1924. The *Rockhurst Magazine Jubilee Issue,* October 1959, says this daybook of the college was kept by Father George Deglman.

64. See Spillard to provincial, November 17, 1924; and "A Short History of the College," November 17, 1924. Spillard was hoping for a Junior Rating for the first 2 years of the college and now seemed amendable to keeping the last 2 years without credits.

65. Owens, *History of Rockhurst College,* p. 62.

Chapter Seven – INVENTING TRADITIONS 1923–29

1. See *The Rockhurst Sentinel,* October 30, 1923, April 30, 1924, October 21, 1927; "A Short Diary of the College," October 25, 1923, April 28, 1924; *The Kansas City Star,* September 30, 1927; and Hugh M. Owens, *History of Rockhurst College: The First Quarter Century (1914-1939),* p 56.
2. See *The Province News-Letter,* November 1926, p. 19; "A Short Diary of the College," November 13, 1923, March 6, 7, 10, 1924; *Rockhurst Sentinel Magazine,* Spring 1937, p. 18; and *The Rockhurst Sentinel,* December 21, 1922, January 25, 1929.
3. See *The Rockhurst Sentinel,* October 30, 1922; "A Short History of the College," October 11, 1923; John Jennings, *History of Rockhurst College,* (Ph.B. thesis, Rockhurst College, 1938), p. 41; and Sandra Scott Wilks, *Rockhurst College: 75 Years of Jesuit Education in Kansas City, 1910-1985* (Kansas City: The Lowell Press, 1985), p. 11.
4. "Wasn't It Some Picnic?" *The Rockhurst Sentinel,* June 16, 1920.
5. Ibid., "College Outing Held at Hickman Mills," May 11, 1927; and "Collegians Carefree at Annual Picnic," May 29, 1928.
6. See ibid., March 30, May 16, 1928; and Jennings, *History of Rockhurst College*, p. 36.
7. Owens, *History of Rockhurst College,* p. 45.
8. See *The Rockhurst Sentinel,* February 17, October 23, 1919, February 17, March 19, 1920; and Rev. Patrick F. Harvey, S.J., *History of Rockhurst College,* n.d., p. 28.
9. See Thomas F. Divine, S.J., "Memories of Early Days of Rockhurst," *The Jesuit Bulletin,* 39:2 (April 1960), p. 17-18.
10. See ibid., and "Rockhurst in Intercollegiate Debate," *The Rockhurst Sentinel,* November 27, 1922. The newspaper did not report the results of the first debate, but did name the debaters selected: Frank Meyer, Earl Hapke, and Carl Brady.
11. See Owens, *History of Rockhurst College,* p. 56, 63, 65-66, 89; "Father Victor F. Gettleman Diary," Rockhurst University Archives, March 25, 1927; Wilks, *Rockhurst College: 75 Years of Jesuit Education in Kansas City,* p. 11; *Rockhurst Magazine Jubilee Issue,* October 7, 1959, p. 7; *The Province News-Letter,* February, March 1933; and *The Rockhurst Sentinel,* November 27, 1922, April 27, 1932. Owens says the Campion Society was for freshman, while the Dowling Literary Society was restricted to upper classmen.
12. *The Province News-Letter,* November 1934, p. 230.
13. See "The Oratorical Contest Was Excellent," *The Junior Sentinel,* May 20, 1918; "College Orators in Contest," *The Rockhurst Sentinel,* May 19, 1920; and *The Province News-Letter,* June 1927, p. 76.
14. See *The Province News-Letter,* June 1927, p. 76; and "Rockhurst Song," *The Rockhurst Sentinel,* May 11, 1927. Divine was a 1917 graduate of the high school.
15. *The Rockhurst Sentinel*, October 28, 1920.
16. Ibid., December 21, 1923.
17. Ibid., May 19, 1920.
18. Ibid., December 16, 1926.
19. *The Junior Sentinel,* December 21, 1917. *The Sentinel* is available in Greenlease Library beginning with its fourth issue, December 21, 1917. The first 3 issues apparently are missing.
20. See Jennings, *History of Rockhurst College*, p. 30; and *The Rockhurst Sentinel,* September 18, 1924, December 16, 1926.
21. See *The Province News-Letter,* April, June 1933; *The Rockhurst Sentinel,* April 26, 1933; Jennings, *History of Rockhurst College*, p. 30; and Owens, *History of Rockhurst College,* p. 88-89.
22. *The Province News-Letter,* June 1934, p. 27.
23. See *The Junior Sentinel,* December 21, 1917; *The Rockhurst Sentinel,* January 29, March 31, 1919, January 21, 1921; and Owens, *History of Rockhurst College,* p. 45.
24. See "Who's Who in the Clubs," *The Rockhurst Sentinel,* April 15, 1924; and Owens, *History of Rockhurst College,* p. 83.
25. *The Rockhurst Sentinel,* April 15, 1924.
26. See "Constitution of the Philosophers' Club," Rockhurst University Archives; "A Short Diary of the College," which says the club was organized on September 28, 1923; *The Rockhurst Sentinel,* April 30, 1924; Owens, *History of Rockhurst College,* p. 88-90; Wilks, *Rockhurst College: 75 Years of Jesuit Education in Kansas City,* p. 11; and "President's Report, 1931," Rockhurst University Archives.
27. Harvey, *History of Rockhurst College,* p. 27.
28. See Jennings, *History of Rockhurst College,* p. 32, and "College Team Victorious in Initial Clash," *The Rockhurst Sentinel,* January 29, 1919.
29. See Harvey, *History of Rockhurst College,* p. 27-28; and "High School Stars Will Have Trouble Beating Catholics," n.p., n.d., 1917 Scrapbook, Rockhurst University Archives. Rockhurst lost the games: 58-26; 66-20; 52-23.
30. *The Rockhurst Sentinel,* February 11, March 19, 1920.
31. Ibid., January 19, 1920.
32. Ibid., December 23, 1920, January 21, 1921, December 16, 1926. The first college-alumni game featured alums Brooks Hale, Martin Crowe, Louis McGee, George Korty, Martin Mangan, James Walsh, and Mason O'Brien.
33. See Wilks, *Rockhurst College: 75 Years of Jesuit Education in Kansas City,* p. 11.
34. "Athletic Store Opens," *The Rockhurst Sentinel,* November 17, 1919.
35. The track team competed in the KU Relays in April 1924 and 1926, and Rockhurst held its own field day on May 31, 1924, but the track team apparently struggled to gain interest and was discontinued by 1928. See "Gettleman Diary," Rockhurst University Archives; "A Short Diary of the College," March 13, 1925; *The Rockhurst Sentinel,* March 15, April 30, 1924; and Mary T. Mattione, *The History of Rockhurst College,* p. 17.
36. "1927-28 Banner Season in Rockhurst Sports History," *The Rockhurst Sentinel,* May 29, 1928. The loss came to St. Benedict's College, 6-0, and the tie with Chillicothe Business College.
37. See ibid., and Owens, *History of Rockhurst College,* p. 70.
38. *The Rockhurst Sentinel,* November 12, 1927.
39. See *The Rockhurst Sentinel,* June 14, 1922, November 12, 1927; *The Province News-Letter,* November 1927, p. 13; and Owens, *History of Rockhurst College,* p. 66. Brother Shaughnessy was so enthusiastic about gardening work that he apparently had requested President Manion to purchase a lawnmower for the college. In a letter to Manion from Provincial Matthew Germing, dated March 25, 1929, Germing advised Manion: "I certainly would not allow Bro. Shaughnessy to buy that thousand dollar lawnmower. You may say that you need the Provincial's

permission for such an expense, which is correct. This will delay things, and then I can write to you about it and you read him my letter."

40. See *The Rockhurst Sentinel,* October 10, 1928; *The Province News-Letter,* October 1928, p. 5; "Gettleman Diary"; and Owens, *History of Rockhurst College,* p. 66.
41. See *The Rockhurst Sentinel,* February 22, 1928; and Owens, *History of Rockhurst College,* p. 51.
42. *The Rockhurst Sentinel,* October 13, 1920, November 12, 1927.
43. Harvey, *History of Rockhurst College,* p. 20. "As the boys had never played before, the season was not a success," Harvey writes.
44. See ibid., p. 26-7; and "Rockhurst Plans Big Sport Year in 1918, War Will Not Stop Activities at Catholic Institution," n.p., n.d., 1918 Scrapbook, Rockhurst University Archives; *The Kansas City Journal,* October 12, 1916; *The Kansas City Star,* November 25, 1916; and *The Kansas City Post,* n.d., 1916 Scrapbook, Rockhurst University Archives.
45. Harvey, *History of Rockhurst College,* p. 27.
46. See *The Kansas City Post,* October 6, 21, 1916; and "Rockhurst Plans Big Sport Year in 1918, War Will Not Stop Activities at Catholic Institution," n.p., n.d., 1918 Scrapbook. *The Rockhurst Sentinel,* February 22, 1928, wrote that one of Rockhurst's early baseball teams was so good it played a game against the professional Kansas City Blues, but lost.
47. See Philip A. Dynan, "Football at Rockhurst," Rockhurst University Archives; "Rockhurst College to Play Kansas City University," *The Rockhurst Sentinel,* November 6, 1919; and "College Team Wins: Kansas City University defeated, Score 28-6," November 17, 1919.
48. Dynan, "Football at Rockhurst."
49. See ibid., and Owens, *History of Rockhurst College,* p. 63. According to the college daybook, the "first real college football game with only college men on the team" was played against the alumni on November 3, 1923, a rainy day with a wet field. Another game was played a week later, on November 8, 1923, against the Olathe Mutes, Rockhurst losing, 25-0. Dynan, however, writes that the first college game was played on October 8, 1921, when the Rockhurst team beat the alumni, 13-0. In one other game that year, on October 22, 1921, Dynan says Rockhurst lost to St. Benedict's College, 35-0.
50. "Hawks Win M.S.C. Grid Title Again," *The Rockhurst Sentinel,* December 5, 1928.
51. See Dynan, "Football at Rockhurst"; *The Kansas City Journal-Post,* n.d.; "Pep Organization to be Formed in College," *The Rockhurst Sentinel,* October 10, 1928; and Wilks, *Rockhurst College: 75 Years of Jesuit Education in Kansas City,* p. 12.
52. Dynan, "Football at Rockhurst."
53. See *The Rockhurst Sentinel,* March 9, 1932, and *The Kansas City Star,* October 17, 1939.
54. See "The Athletic Cups at Rockhurst Bring Reminiscences of Past Great Teams," *The Rockhurst Sentinel,* February 22, 1928; and "Hawk Tennis Men Retain Singles Cup," May 20, 1927.
55. See ibid., "Hawks New Name for College Teams," March 23, 1927, "'R' Club Formed By Winners of College Letters," April 6, 1927; and 1927 Scrapbook, Rockhurst University Archives.
56. *The Rockhurst Sentinel,* April 6, May 11, 1927. Within a year of the founding of the Rockhurst Circle, another group of women organized the Rockhurst Sanctuary Society, later known as the Sanctuary Guild, to assist Rockhurst. These women had sons, brothers, or other relatives in the Society of Jesus. Hugh Owens, *A History of Rockhurst College,* p. 66, says the first meeting was held in the home of Mrs. Joseph Sheehy on February 6, 1928.
57. See ibid.; Lela Shortle Bannon, "A Short History, Rockhurst Circle," 1951, Rockhurst University Archives; and "Founding of Group 25 Years Ago is Observed," *The Kansas City Star,* April 21, 1952.
58. Rockhurst College Annual Catalogue, 1918, quoted in Owens, *History of Rockhurst College,* p. 67; *The Junior Sentinel,* May 13, 1918; and "A Short Diary of the College," April 14, 1925, Rockhurst University Archives.
59. For a sampling of Rockhurst Circle activities, see *The Rockhurst Sentinel,* May 11, 20, June 1, October 7, 21, November 3, 30, 1927; February 8, March 30, April 18, October 10, December 5, 1928; January 25, February 8, May 3, 1929; and *The Province News-Letter,* June 1927, p. 77, February 1928, p. 38, December 1929, p. 1, February 1933, p. 108.
60. See "Constitution and By-Laws, Rockhurst Circle," 1927, "A Tabulation of Gifts Received, Excluding Building and Endowment Funds," and "The Account of 'Rockhurst Circle,'" Rockhurst University Archives. In 1927 membership dues were $1 a year, as they were, as well, in 1939 for an active membership; $5 a year for a sustaining membership; or $25 for a life membership or a memorial membership. By 1977 dues were $5 a year; $25 for a life membership; or $10 for a scholarship donation.
61. See "Stars of College Daze Offer Miniature Show," *The Rockhurst Sentinel,* April 19, 1929; and Jennings, *History of Rockhurst College,* p. 37-39.
62. *The Rockhurst Sentinel,* May 15, 1929.
63. See ibid., January 29, March 3, December 11, 1919; April 6, 1923; Divine, "Memories of Early Days of Rockhurst"; and Harvey, *History of Rockhurst College,* p. 28.
64. See *The Rockhurst Sentinel,* March 30, 1928, April 19, 1929; and provincial to Manion, July 14, 1932. Based on an interview with Daniel Conway, S.J., in *The Kansas City Star,* December 9, 1934, there was indeed one radio in the Jesuit living quarters. "One of us, Father Leary, is paralyzed and we have him with us so we can the better care for him. He is the only priest of the 29 who has a radio in his room, a luxury," Conway is quoted as saying. Father Michael Leary was the longtime pastor at St. Francis Xavier Church. In another letter from the provincial, September 29, 1932, complaints about the radio continued, the provincial stating that "you have been caught belittling the regulations," and that the information had gone "to Rome."
65. See *The Rockhurst Sentinel,* May 31, 1929; and *The Province News-Letter,* November 1942, p. 10, and November 1928, p. 10.

Chapter Eight – STRUGGLE FOR ACCREDITATION 1924–39

1. See *The Catholic Register,* February 2, 1933; and *Kansas City Times,* August 1, 1928. Father Manion was born on August 4, 1887.
2. Lillis to Manion, July 23, 1929. Lillis told Manion that when he got the second 99 pledges, he would give another subscription. "In other words," Lillis explained, "I want to be a subscriber for each one hundred people you find." He added: "Let us try to get some substantial assurance that a dignified sum of money will be given to Rockhurst for educational purposes and let me assure you that when I can be of any help to you, you are at full liberty to call me."
3. Hugh M. Owens, *History of Rockhurst College: The First Quarter Century (1914-1939),* p. 67. Spillard had written to the provincial on April 27, 1926, saying that he had met with Lillis the previous week and had succeeded in getting his support "in raising a sum of $750,000 which minimum amount we consider a necessity if Rockhurst College is to reach the proportions of a first-class four-year college."
4. Spillard to F.X. McMenamy, February 16, March 31, 1925.
5. See Aylward to Spillard, February 17, 1927; Spillard to McMenamy, June 24, 1926; and "Rockhurst College Endowment Fund," Rockhurst University Archives. The endowment fund apparently did not get going until the administration of Daniel H. Conway (1933–40). A book in the Rockhurst University Archives even then lists only two initial donors, $25,000 from H.J. Massman, Sr. and $4,500 from Miss Agnes Corrigan.
6. See the *Woodstock Letters,* vol. 58, 1929; Owens, *History of Rockhurst College,* p. 70-73; and *The Rockhurst Sentinel,* October 2, 1929. According to *The Sentinel* of February 17, 1919, the physics laboratory originally had occupied the main part of Sedgwick's third floor, and chemistry classes were held on the top floor of the north wing. The newspaper also reported that the library had subscriptions to these newspapers: *Catholic Daily Tribune, Denver Catholic Register, United States Daily, The New York Times, Chicago Tribune,* and *The Kansas City Journal-Post.*
7. Owens, *History of Rockhurst College,* p. 70.
8. See ibid., p. 71; *The Jesuit Bulletin,* October 1935; *The Province News-Letter,* November 1932; John Jennings, *History of Rockhurst College,* (Ph.B. thesis, Rockhurst College, 1938), p. 9; Mary Mattione, *The History of Rockhurst College,* p. 19; and *Kansas City Journal,* October 19, 1939.
9. See Owens, *History of Rockhurst College,* p. 73; and Manion to provincial, July 31, 1930, March 31, 1931.
10. Horine to Manion, September 2, 1931.
11. Philip Gleason, *Contending With Modernity: Catholic Higher Education in the Twentieth Century* (New York: Oxford University Press, 1995), p. 184-87. The professional competence of faculty members, rated in terms of the graduate training they had received, was a problem for Catholic colleges because so many faculty members at Catholic colleges took their graduate degrees from other Catholic institutions, while the NCA wanted to see at least some of the graduate work done at non-sectarian colleges. The "living endowment"—meaning the services provided free by priests, sisters and brothers at Catholic colleges—also was a problem for the NCA, and in 1930, it stipulated that "the amount Catholic schools could claim as living endowment had to be reduced by the net cost of noncontributed faculty services." This issue, however, would be absorbed into another revision of accreditation standards in the early years of the decade.
12. See James Hennesey, S.J., *American Catholics: A History of the Roman Catholic Community in the United States* (New York: Oxford University Press, 1981), p. 254; Shirl Kasper and Rick Montgomery, *Kansas City: An American Story* (Kansas City, Mo.: Kansas City Star Books, 1999), p. 216, 225-26, 231; and *The New York Times,* December 6, 1935, filed in Scrapbook C5, Rockhurst University Archives.
13. See Germing to Manion, November 8, 14, 1929; Horine to procurator, June 29, 1932; *Rockhurst Magazine Golden Jubilee,* October 1959, p. 8; and Owens, *History of Rockhurst College,* p. 74. According to a letter from the Rockhurst auditor to Conrad Mann, dated June 23, 1926, Spillard had said "that a little better than 10 percent of the student-body regardless of their individual religious affiliations are free of tuition."
14. See Horine to Manion, September 10, 1932; and Manion, "A Special Announcement," May 15, 1931.
15. See Germing to Manion, February 10, 1931; Manion to Horine, May 22, 1932; Owens, *History of Rockhurst College,* p. 74; and Jennings, *History of Rockhurst College,* p. 35.
16. *The Rockhurst Sentinel,* March 30, April 13, 1932. The reason for the pink sheets, Collins explained, was so newsboys couldn't palm off a first edition for the last, and for its advertising effect.
17. See "The Civic Value of Rockhurst College: A Series of Three Radio Broadcasts Delivered by William J. Moore," 1932, Rockhurst University Archives; and "Ex-Editor Boosts Rockhurst on Air," *The Rockhurst Sentinel,* May 11, 1932. The talks were arranged by Maurice J. McNellis, president of the South Side Bank at 39th and Main streets. According to the *Sentinel,* McNellis had a standing invitation to deliver a weekly address over KWKC and had donated his time to Rockhurst.
18. Minister's Diary quoted in Owens, *History of Rockhurst College,* p. 75-76.
19. See ibid.; and Horine to Manion, September 29, 1932.
20. See *The Province News-Letter,* November 1932, p. 82; December 1932, p. 92; and "The Rockhurst Club" constitution, Rockhurst University Archives.
21. "Rockhurst Loses Father Manion," *The Catholic Register,* February 2, 1933.
22. See Owens, *History of Rockhurst College,* p. 81; W. F. Bartholome, Conway obituary, November 26, 1956, Rockhurst University Archives; and "The Builder of Rockhurst," *The Kansas City Star,* November 3, 1956.
23. See "A Rockhurst Appeal," *The Kansas City Star,* September 28, 1933; and *Rockhurst Magazine Jubilee Issue,* October 1959, p. 8.
24. See *Rockhurst College, Catalog,* 1935-36, p. 42-43; and *Rockhurst Sentinel Magazine,* Spring 1937, p. 30.
25. See *Rockhurst College, Catalog,* 1935-36, p. 22; and *The Province News-Letter,* October 1934, p. 223; *Kansas City Times,* November 20, 1933; Owens, *History of Rockhurst College,* p. 83; Jennings, *History of Rockhurst College,* p. 13; and *The Jesuit Bulletin,* October 1935.
26. See *The Province News-Letter,* April 1934, June 1934, p. 213; *The Kansas City Star,* December 9, 1934; and Owens, *History of Rockhurst College,* p. 81-82.
27. Conway to Zacheus Maher, March 11, 1937.
28. Owens, *History of Rockhurst College,* p. 85.
29. Conway to Maher, March 11, 1937.
30. *The Province News-Letter,* October 1936, p. 9-10; November 1937, p. 84-85.

31. Conway to Maher, March 11, 1937.
32. Ibid.
33. Rockhurst building program, Rockhurst University Archives.
34. "Rockhurst College 5 Year $500,000 Expansion Plan," Rockhurst University Archives.
35. Owens, *History of Rockhurst College,* p. 86.
36. *The Kansas City Star,* April 28, 1937.
37. Owens, *History of Rockhurst College,* p. 86-87.
38. *Kansas City Times,* September 13, 1937.
39. Ibid.
40. Mattione, *A History of Rockhurst College,* p. 23.
41. Ibid., p. 24; and Owens, *History of Rockhurst College,* p. 87.
42. *The Province News-Letter,* November 1937, p. 81.
43. *The Jesuit Bulletin,* December 1937, p. 4.
44. See *The Kansas City Star,* April 24, 1938; *The Rockhurst Sentinel,* May 11, 1938; and Jennings, *History of Rockhurst College,* p. 10. According to Jennings, before classes moved into the new building, a midweek retreat was held first, from January 25 to 27.
45. See *The Kansas City Star,* August 1, 1937; and *The Jesuit Bulletin,* December 1937, p. 7.
46. *The Rockhurst Sentinel,* October 11, 1938.
47. Ibid.
48. "Pat Mason's Contribution," *The Kansas City Star,* n.d.
49. See "Pat Mason is Dead," *The Kansas City Star,* October 10, 1938; and Parke Carroll, n.p., October 11, 1938.
50. "Pat Mason's Boys His Pallbearers," *The Kansas City Star,* October 10, 1938; and interview with Virginia Mason Waters, 2008.
51. See *The Kansas City Star,* "Halpin Is Near Death," July 28, 1936, "The Halpin Rites Friday," July 29,1936, "His a Zestful Sojourn," July 31,1936; and "Death to Eddie Halpin," *Kansas City Times,* July 29, 1936.
52. "To a Hospital by Plane," *The Kansas City Star,* July 27, 1936.
53. "His a Zestful Sojourn," *The Kansas City Star,* July 31, 1936.
54. Ibid., December 25, 1938; and Owens, *History of Rockhurst College,* p. 88.
55. See Conway to Provincial Peter A. Brooks, October, 15, 1938, quoted in Owens, *History of Rockhurst College,* p. 90; *The Province News-Letter,* November 1937, p. 84-85; and *The Rockhurst Sentinel,* April 18, 1934. Rockhurst's hopes for accreditation may have gotten a boost when former Rockhurst teacher Alphonse Schwitalla, S.J., served as president of the North Central Association in 1936. See "Rev. Alphonse Mary Schwitalla," *Who's Who in America, 1950-51,* C5 Scrapbook, Rockhurst University Archives. Schwitalla, Dean of the School of Nursing at Saint Louis University, was the first Catholic priest to lead the 41-year-old association.
56. See *The Province News-Letter,* October 1939, p. 222; and Owens, *History of Rockhurst College,* p. 90.
57. "Report to the Board of Review of the Commission on Institutions of Higher Education, North Central Association of Colleges and Secondary Schools, Rockhurst College," quoted in Owens, *History of Rockhurst College,* p. 91.
58. See *The Province News-Letter,* May 1939, p. 205; and *Kansas City Times,* March 31, 1939.
59. See ibid., October 1939, p. 222; and "First Rockhurst Air Student," *The Kansas City Star,* December 2, 1939.
60. Father Edward B. Rooney, S.J., "Report of Rockhurst College and High School," quoted in Owens, *History of Rockhurst College,* p. 92.

Chapter Nine – THE WAR YEARS AND AFTERWARDS 1940–50

1. See William H. McCabe, S.J., to Zacheus J. Maher, S.J., August 12, 1940; and Peter Brooks, S.J., to McCabe, September 21, 1940.
2. See *Kansas City Times,* April 3, 4, 1940; and *The* (Catholic) *Register*, n.d., scrapbook, Rockhurst University Archives.
3. *The Kansas City Star,* April 14, 1940.
4. "Rush for Air Training," n.p., n.d., scrapbook, Rockhurst University Archives.
5. *The Kansas City Star,* August 16, 1940.
6. Wayne G. Miller, *History of the 73rd College Training Detachment (Aircrew), Rockhurst College,* Kansas City, Missouri, p. 3, Rockhurst University Archives.
7. McCabe to Brooks, July 23, 1941. McCabe told the provincial that Rockhurst did not have a yearbook, but expressed his opinion about proper decorum for yearbook photographs.
8. See Brooks to McCabe, August 8, 1940; and "First peacetime draft," www.historylink.org. Only those in critical professions and those mentally or physically unfit for service were given deferments.
9. Association of American Colleges to Rockhurst College, September 14, 1940.
10. See McCabe to The Major General Commandant, U.S. Marine Corps Headquarters, September 20, 1940; T. Holcomb to McCabe, September 25, 1940; McCabe to The Commandant Ninth Naval District, September 20, 1940; Capt. F.A. Braisted to McCabe, November 22, 1940; McCabe to Lt. Comdr. Ross F. Collins, August 25, 1941; and Collins to McCabe, September 3, 1941. After the war started, McCabe continued to correspond with the Navy, hoping to land a naval training unit for Rockhurst. "We undisguisedly prefer cooperation with the Navy" to any other branch of the service, he wrote on December 26, 1942, "because our relations with the Navy are already established locally." By 1942, he also was able to say that 34 percent of the Rockhurst student body was enlisted in the Navy's V-1, V-5, or V-7 programs.
11. *The Kansas City Star,* September 12, 13, 1940.
12. See "President's Report at Commencement," May 31, 1942, Rockhurst University Archives; and Miller, *History of the 73rd College Training Detachment,* p. 3. In his report, McCabe said his most recent count found that 89 Rockhurst men were serving as commissioned officers. "For the size of the College," Miller wrote, "Rockhurst has an unusually large percentage of its alumni as officers in the air forces, as well as in all other branches of the armed services."
13. See "Rockhurst Will Join Accelerated Education Plan," n.p., January, 1942, scrapbook, Rockhurst University Archives; and *Historia Domus,* June 22, 1943. According to Miller, *History of the 73rd College Training Detachment,* Rockhurst College was an accredited member of the North Central Association of Colleges and Secondary Schools and held memberships in the Jesuit Educational Association, the National Catholic Educa-

tional Association, the Association of American Colleges, the American Council on Education, the Missouri College Union, and the American Association of Collegiate Registrars, as well as other national and state associations in various fields of knowledge. The war conference in Baltimore was sponsored by the Committee on Military Affairs of the National Committee on Education and Defense and the U.S. Office of Education.

14. See Philip Gleason, *Contending With Modernity: Catholic Higher Education in the Twentieth Century* (New York: Oxford University Press, 1995), p. 209-12; *Historia Domus,* January 16, 1943; and Miller, *History of the 73rd College Training Detachment,* p. i. The Navy's V programs included V-7, which allowed male college graduates to enlist in the Navy as reserves, and later, when called to service, to enter officer's training. After Pearl Harbor, V-7 was modified to include college juniors and seniors, and V-1 was created for freshmen and sophomores. A V-5 program was set up for prospective naval aviators.

15. The 5-story hotel was erected in 1918 and 1919 as the Brookside Investment Company. The hotel was purchased for $335,000 on February 2, 1943, from the Southland Life Insurance Company of Dallas by three Chicago investors, Philip Pekow and Robert S. Levy, each with three-eighths interest, and J.A. Bisno with one-quarter. See "To Vacate Brookside," n.p., n.d., scrapbook, Rockhurst University Archives; and Miller, *History of the 73rd College Training Detachment,* p. 5. Interestingly, Father McCabe, in a letter to the War Relocation Authority dated February 26, 1943, offered to let reliable American citizens of Japanese descent, then held in relocation camps, to come to Kansas City and work at the Brookside Hotel. "Since our maintenance work has been in the past largely given to needy students to enable them to attend college, and since their call to arms is fast reducing their number, there are places open here for men suitable for this work," he wrote, stipulating that they would be needed only for as long as Rockhurst retained its contract with the Army Air Forces. "The College," he said, "would be willing to employ eight men at once for the purpose mentioned, provided the Department of Labor and other governmental authorities concerned would fully approve." Documents do not say whether the men ever arrived, but a telegram from a Mr. E.H. Leker, supervisor with the War Relocation Authority in Kansas City, approved the request, though adding that McCabe also should seek approval from the commanding officer in charge of the Army program at Rockhurst.

16. *The* (Catholic) *Register,* March 14, 1943. On May 18, 1943, Rockhurst President William McCabe recommended that Lt. Priesmeyer be promoted to captain. He cited his "exceptional qualities" and the "smooth inception and progress" of the Army program at Rockhurst. The promotion occurred at some point before the program ended at Rockhurst. See McCabe to The Commanding General, Gulf Coast Training Center, Randolph Field, Texas, May 18, 1943.

17. Miller, *History of the 73rd College Training Detachment,* p. 30.

18. See McCabe to Zacheus J. Maher, S.J., February 4, 1944; McCabe to provincial, February 19, July 28, 1943; and "The Story of Rockhurst College," press release, n.d., Rockhurst University Archives.

19. Gleason, *Contending With Modernity,* p. 214-15. In the report, Rooney argued that members of religious orders teaching in the Army's ASTP or Navy's V-12 program performed a service worth a salary and what the religious did with the money was no business of the government's. He argued, according to Gleason, that "not to pay them for value received would, in effect, compel them to give to the government what they had freely agreed to give to their religious communities."

20. Annual salaries ranged from $2,400 to $3,600. See "Memorandum on College Teachers' Salaries from March 1, 1943, opening date of the Army Air Force College Training Program at Rockhurst College" and "Schedule of Faculty Salaries in Rockhurst College," Rockhurst University Archives.

21. McCabe to provincial, May 11, 1942, February 4, 1944.

22. See *Historia Domus,* December 8, 14, 1942, August 26, 1943, March 14, 1944; *The Rockhurst Sentinel,* February 12, 19, April 1, 1942; "Rockhurst Scholarship Club," January 28, 1942, Rockhurst University Archives; and "Zip Into Rush Orders," *Kansas City Times,* December 22, 1944.

23. See *Historia Domus,* July 4, 1943; "No Hawk Team," "First Home Game," n.p., n.d, scrapbook, Rockhurst University Archives; "Hawks on Court," *The Kansas City Star,* November 26, 1944; and "There's Something in the Name Sedgwick," *Rockhurst Prep News,* December 1943, which noted that Lee Sedgwick had died on August 26, 1935. His remains were taken to the chapel of the Sister Servants of Mary in Kansas City, Kansas, to whom he had given the money to build a convent there, as well as in Los Angeles and New Orleans. He was buried in Forest Hills Cemetery in Kansas City, Missouri.

24. See McCabe to Miller, April 28, 1942; and Miller to McCabe, June 15, 1942.

25. "Tardy Honor to Flier," n.p., n.d, scrapbook, Rockhurst University Archives.

26. "Eager For Air Battle," n.p., February 20, 1943, scrapbook, Rockhurst University Archives.

27. "Honor Missouri Fliers," n.p., n.d., scrapbook, Rockhurst University Archives.

28. "He Was in Wake Saga," n.p., n.d., scrapbook, Rockhurst University Archives.

29. See "On Wings of Service," n.p., n.d, scrapbook, Rockhurst University Archives; and "She Flies For Britain," *The Kansas City Star,* March 29, 1942.

30. See "15th Gold Star Added to Honor Roll of Rockhurst," *The* (Catholic) *Register,* n.d., scrapbook, Rockhurst University Archives; "Dies in a Crash in Air," *The Kansas City Star,* October 28, 1943; and "Griffin is Lost in Plane Over Latin America," n.p., n.d., scrapbook, Rockhurst University Archives.

31. See "Lieut. Charles E. Epp Lost," "Coughlin Dies in Crash Over Mexican Gulf," n.p., n.d., scrapbook, Rockhurst University Archives; Rockhurst Newsletter, July 1944, which lists the names of 26 "Rockhurst Gold Stars"; and *Historia Domus,* March 15, November 30, 1945, and October 3, 1945, which quotes the Rockhurst High School newspaper, naming 58 high school and college Gold Star men.

32. See "Lieut. A.F. Monaco Missing," "Roy G. Sanders, Jr., Killed," n.p., n.d, scrapbook, Rockhurst University Archives; "Rockhurst Grad Has Downed 5 Japanese Planes," *The* (Catholic) *Register,* July 23, 1944; "Rockhurst Grad Who Was a Pacific Ace is Missing," *The* (Catholic) *Register,* August 6, 1944; "Fighter Pilot Is Missing," *The Kansas City Star,* March 25, 1945.

33. See "Marine Wounded on Saipan," *The Kansas City Star,* July 15, 1944; "Richard Dillon Wounded," *Kansas City Times,* November 29, 1944; "Medal to Joseph Phillips," *Kansas City Times,* April 14, 1945; "Former Student in Rockhurst Is Sicily War Hero," and *The* (Catholic) *Register,* n.d., scrapbook, Rockhurst University Archives.

34. "Hero From Rockhurst," *Kansas City Times,* July 1, 1942.

35. See *Historia Domus,* November 29, 1943; McCabe to John LaFarge, S.J., May 16, 1942; McCabe to Daprato Studios, Chicago, May 20, 1942; and "School Has A 'Soul,'" n.d., n.p.,

scrapbook, Rockhurst University Archives. On October 22, 1945, Father Driscoll wrote in the *Historia Domus:* "Today Oct. 22 we are celebrating for the first time, Rockhurst Founder's day & it will be repeated each year.... To celebrate the occasion we had a 1st class feast in our refectory at which Ours & the lay faculty were present. After the dinner we all met for recreation in the H School study hall, & the new Rockhurst Anthem, "A Song of Wisdom" was sung. It is our official song or Anthem & honors our Patron St. Thomas More." "Rockhurst Twenty-Fourth Commencement" program, June 11, 1944. The graduates were Donald Martin Flaherty, B.A., major in English; George Vincent Aylward, B.S., philosophy; Joseph Camille Azar, B.S., economics; Richard Louis Boegner, B.S., chemistry; and Robert Charles Downey, B.S., physics.

36. "Rockhurst Has A 'Soul,'" n.p., n.d, scrapbook, Rockhurst University Archives. Prior to adopting the new seal, Rockhurst historian Sandra Wilks writes, Rockhurst's motto was simply "Sigillum Collegii Rockhurstensis Kansanurbe" or "The Seal of Rockhurst College, Kansas City." Its face had shown a half side of bars for St. Ignatius and a half side with a picture of two wolves stirring a pot, a Jesuit symbol.
37. McCabe to Peter Brooks, July 23, 1941.
38. Ibid., October 18, 1941.
39. Ibid., March 4, 1942.
40. Brooks to McCabe, April 6, 1942. On June 12, 1942, just days after St. Aloysius Church had been turned over to the diocese, McCabe received a letter from Aloysius A. Breen, S.J., Rockhurst's second president. Breen wrote: "Somehow or other I felt rather disappointed when I heard that you had to give up St. Aloysius Church; but, of course, the transfer did not surprise me. Many years ago, by mutual agreement between Bishop John Hogan and Father Michael Dowling, we promised to hand over the parish to the diocese in 1919. When that time came Father McMenamy and I called on Bishop Lillis and offered to carry out our part of the contract but he strenuously objected and said he wanted the Jesuits to carry on in that field indefinitely."
41. McCabe to Brooks, June 9, 1942. Father Gerst became assistant pastor at St. Francis Xavier Church.
42. *Historia Domus,* July 21, 22, 1944. Driscoll added: "He (Roosevelt) is not, however, a Catholic, but honors our Holy Father Pius the XII by sending a special envoy to his Roman court, though Protestant bigots objected."
43. "In the Fifth Century," *Time* magazine, December 28, 1942.
44. Zacheus J. Maher, S.J., to "the rectors and superiors of the American Assistancy," January 3, 1943.
45. McCabe to Maher, January 7, 1943.
46. McCabe to Brooks, September 12, 1942.
47. "Letter of Intent," Army Air Forces, February 19, 1943. Rockhurst's quota later was increased to 400 cadets.
48. "Rockhurst College Endowment Fund," July 9, 1943. The document was signed by McCabe and directors Arthur Evans, S.J.; John J. Higgins, S.J.; Thomas J. Smith, S.J.; and Joseph Matoushek, S.J. In addition to Henry Massman, Sr., the earliest and largest contributors to the fund were Miss Agnes Corrigan, $5,000, and Nell Quinlan Reed, $2,000.
49. Former Rockhurst President Daniel Conway, S.J., was now rector at St. Mary's Theological School in St. Marys, Kansas. The former St. Mary's College had been forced to close during the Great Depression.
50. See Rockhurst Newsletter, July 1944; "A Suggestion," December 1, 1944; and *The* (Catholic) *Register,* December 3, 1944.
51. Gleason, *Contending With Modernity,* p. 213.
52. "About Rockhurst," Rockhurst Newsletter, July 1944.
53. Ibid.
54. See McCabe to Paul V. McNutt, Office for Emergency Management, War Manpower Commission, December 6, 1943; *Historia Domus,* October 25, 1944; and *The* (Catholic) *Register,* n.d., scrapbook, Rockhurst University Archives. Col. George W. Mundy, personal representative of Brig. Gen. Walter K. Kraus, commanding general of the Army Air Forces Central Flying Training Command, headquartered in Fort Worth, Texas, made the presentation.
55. Gleason, *Contending With Modernity,* p. 215.
56. "Minutes of the Regional Directors of Education and Deans of the Central Regional Group of the J.E.A." Loyola University, Chicago, November 22, 23, 1941.
57. *The* (Catholic) *Register,* April 1, May 7, 1945.
58. *The Kansas City Star,* March 25, 1945.
59. See "Only 3 in Class of 128 Graduated at Rockhurst," *The* (Catholic) *Register,* June 10, 1945; and *Historia Domus,* June 10, 1945.
60. Jay P. Dolan, *The American Catholic Experience: A History from Colonial Times to the Present* (Garden City, New York: Doubleday & Company, Inc., 1985), p. 399-400. The number of colleges for men actually declined in this period, Dolan writes, but Catholic women's colleges increased, from 19 in 1915 to 116 in 1950, composing 66 percent of the number (175) of Catholic colleges in the United States.
61. U.S. Department of Veterans Affairs, www.gibill.va.gov/GI Bill Info/history.htm. Millions also took advantage of the GI Bill's home loan guaranty. From 1944 to 1952, the VA backed nearly 2.4 million home loans for World War II veterans.
62. *Historia Domus,* August 28, 1945. Enrollment for the 1945-46 school year was 461, according to "School Lists Near End," n.p., n.d., scrapbook, Rockhurst University Archives.
63. *The* (Catholic) *Register,* September 24, 1944.
64. See "School Lists Near End" and "Rockhurst Roll of 750," n.p., n.d., scrapbook, Rockhurst University Archives.
65. "School Lists Near End," n.p., n.d., scrapbook, Rockhurst University Archives.
66. Ibid.
67. *Historia Domus,* January 18, 1947.
68. N.p., January 30, February 3, 1947, scrapbook, Rockhurst University Archives. Summer school enrollment also soared. "Record Enrollment at Rockhurst," *Kansas City Times,* June 12, 1948, put first-session summer enrollment at 383. That outpaced the previous record of 378, set just the summer before in the first session, June 16 to July 19, 1947. (*Kansas City Times,* June 14, 1947.)
69. "McCabe to Creighton U.," *Kansas City Times,* December 26, 1945. McCabe's appointment to Creighton came a week after he was succeeded by Knapp.
70. *The Kansas City Star,* September 8, 1946, June 6, 1948. *The Star* described SLU's corporate colleges as independent financially, but welded into the university scholastically. They were all women's colleges, Fontbonne, Maryville and Webster, all in St. Louis.
71. Ibid., June 6, 1948.
72. Ibid., September 8, 1946.

73. Untitled press release, n.d., Rockhurst University Archives. An official public relations office did not open until 1951. "Public Relations Office Will Open at Rockhurst College on Sept. 1," *The* (Catholic) *Register*, August 5, 1951.
74. www.b-westerns.com.
75. See untitled press release, n.d., Rockhurst University Archives; and *Historia Domus*, April 24, 1947.
76. See "To Add to Rockhurst," n.p., September 21, 1946, scrapbook, Rockhurst University Archives; "Get 70 Campus Homes," *The Kansas City Star*, n.d., scrapbook, Rockhurst University Archives; and Knapp to Provincial Joseph P. Zuercher, December 30, 1946. The 8 buildings were: 3 to house single veterans; 2 to house married students and their families; one for the cafeteria; a 2-story structure for classrooms and administrative offices; and one structure as a general maintenance and storage building.
77. Sandra Scott Wilks, *Rockhurst College: 75 Years of Jesuit Education in Kansas City*, p. 21.
78. See *The Kansas City Star*, May 28, 1946; "Rockhurst in a Gain," *Kansas City Times*, n.d., scrapbook, Rockhurst University Archives; and *Historia Domus*, October 29, 1946.
79. The faculty members were Dr. and Mrs. Charles N. Hamtil and their two children, and Mr. and Mrs. Ralph Cormany, who were newlyweds. Hamtil was head of the college physics department; Cormany was the high school coach and an assistant at the college. *Kansas City Times*, December 25, 1946.
80. *The Kansas City Star*, May 23, 1947.
81. Gleason, *Contending With Modernity*, p. 244.
82. Ibid., p. 245.
83. See "Sees a Threat to Faith," *Kansas City Times*, June 2, 1947; and *The* (Catholic) *Register*, n.d., scrapbook, Rockhurst University Archives.
84. Dolan, *The American Catholic Experience*, p. 394-95. The papal encyclical, *Casti Connubii*, had voiced concerns about the family and the "moral gangrene" of American society as early as 1930.
85. "Warns Students of Reds," n.p., n.d, scrapbook, Rockhurst University Archives.
86. See "Dramatic Radio Program Series to Open Oct. 17," *The* (Catholic) *Register*, October 12, 1943; and *Historia Domus*, February 27, October 9, 1945. Programs, often written by Rockhurst students, included, for instance, a sketch of George Gershwin and another of Bishop Edwin O'Hara. The first of the 1943 season was titled "Highlights in Literature and History."
87. *The* (Catholic) *Register*, August 27, September 24, 1944.
88. "Hawks' Spirit Is High," *Kansas City Times*, October 25, 1946.
89. *Historia Domus*, August 24, 1947, July 6, 1949.
90. See "Rockhurst Cancels Football Program," *St. Louis Globe-Democrat*, September 2, 1950; "Rockhurst Is In," *The Kansas City Star*, May 16, 1948; "Rockhurst Is Out," *The Kansas City Star*, December 5, 1950; and "Due to Player Loss," n.p., n.d., scrapbook, Rockhurst University Archives. Rockhurst College had been a member of the league since May 1948. The league included St. Benedict's, Emporia State, Fort Hayes State, Pittsburg State, Southwestern, Washburn, Warrensburg State, and Chillicothe Business College.
91. See "Cagers Are TV Stars," and "K.U. Takes It Easy," n.p., n.d, scrapbook, Rockhurst University Archives.
92. See *The Kansas City Star*, June 6, 1949; and *Kansas City Times*, June 27, 1949. The number of graduates in 1949 was double that of the Class of 1948, which had 76 graduates. According to *Historia Domus*, February 23, 1948, a large house on the church property was in the process of being torn down to make way for the new church. On March 14, 1948, Kansas City Bishop O'Hara broke ground for the new church.

Chapter Ten – GROWTH AND EXPANSION 1951–63

1. See Robert Murray Davis, *A Lower-Middle-Class Education* (Norman: University of Oklahoma Press, 1996), p. 15; and James Hennesey, S.J., *American Catholics: A History of the Roman Catholic Community in the United States* (New York: Oxford University Press, 1981), p. 283.
2. An article in *The Rockhurst Hawk*, May 1, 1953, stated that 48 students had taken the Selective Service's college qualification test on April 23. "The test," *The Hawk* wrote, "allows students who are pursuing a college degree to postpone their time until the draft affects them. There is one more test date left for this school year." In a letter to Missouri Provincial Daniel H. Conway, January 31, 1951, Rockhurst Dean Charles P. Cahill, S.J., had said Rockhurst's enrollment had "stood up much better than I had thought for the second semester of this year. No doubt the new draft registrations kept many of the lads in college now that they can pick their branch of the service."
3. Davis, *A Lower-Middle-Class Education*, p. 28, 33.
4. See Hennesey, *American Catholics*, p. 287, 296; and David J. O'Brien, *From the Heart of the American Church: Catholic Higher Education and American Culture* (Maryknoll, N.Y.: Orbis Books, 1994), p. 71.
5. "God & Man at Notre Dame," *Time*, February 9, 1962.
6. Hennesey, *American Catholics*, p. 301. John Tracy Ellis' speech would later be published as "American Catholics and the Intellectual Life" in the journal *Thought*, *XXX* (Autumn 1955), p. 351-88.
7. See *Kansas City Times*, March 19, 1971, and *The* (Catholic) *Register*, March 25, 1951. Van Ackeren had returned to Saint Louis University for a year of graduate study in the field of education in 1945, and also took a final year of spiritual training at Manresa Hall in Port Townsend, Washington.
8. *The Squire*, March 25, 1976.
9. *The Sun Herald*, April 12, 1951.
10. See *The Kansas City Star*, April 19, 1951; and *The* (Catholic) *Register*, May 6, 1951.
11. *The* (Catholic) *Register*, August 5, 1951.
12. The "Inventory of the Physical Facilities and Human Resources of Rockhurst College" was prepared January 15, 1951, along the lines suggested by the Federal Security Agency's Office of Education. According to a letter from Rockhurst Dean Charles P. Cahill, S.J., to Provincial Daniel H. Conway, January 31, 1951, the inventory was taken and mailed to the Federal Security Agency "in connection with possible procurement of some sort of an Army or Navy program here at Rockhurst in the event that such government contracts are given out." The inventory lists 3 "veterans barracks" at 1316-22, 1328-34, and

1340-46 E. 53rd Street; married veterans barracks at 1323-29 and 1335-41 Rockhurst Road; and the Thomas More Cafeteria on the quad.

13. Davis, *A Lower-Middle-Class Education*, p. 28.
14. Ibid., p. 72.
15. "Inventory of the Physical Facilities and Human Resources," Part 2, p. 5. While the Rockhurst faculty included only 4 full professors, it also had 4 associate professors and 8 assistant professors.
16. Davis, *A Lower-Middle-Class Education*, p. 74, 76.
17. See ibid., p. 36; *The Rockhurst Hawk*, April 25, 1952; and *Kansas City Times*, March 19, 1951. A fact sheet, "Twenty Facts About Rockhurst College and the 1953 Development Program," states that there were 37 Jesuit priests and 51 laymen on the teaching staff.
18. "Big School Step," *The Kansas City Star*, December 14, 1952.
19. See "College Bid to Future," *The Kansas City Star*, January 28, 1953; and *The* (Catholic) *Register*, April 2, 10, 1955. The $675,000 Faculty Residence price tag included money to remodel and modernize Sedgwick Hall.
20. See Van Ackeren to Friends of Rockhurst, Eastertide, 1953; and "Progress on College Hall," *The Kansas City Star*, March 24, 1953.
21. *Kansas City Times*, April 21, 1953.
22. Hennesey, *American Catholics*, p. 293-94.
23. *Kansas City Times*, April 21, 1953.
24. See "A Full Rockhurst Day," *The Kansas City Star*, May 16, 1954; *Kansas City Times*, May 17, 1954; and Kansas City *News-Press*, May 23, 1954. Gen. Romulo was introduced by former president Harry Truman. In 1943, with a contribution of $25,000, Henry Massman, Sr., had been instrumental in establishing a Rockhurst endowment fund. On June 1, 1952, Rockhurst had conferred its seventh honorary doctorate to Jack P. Whitaker, a Kansas City industrial and civic leader and a national figure in the Boy Scouts. The first honorary degree, in 1921, had gone to Marshal Ferdinand Foch. Others had followed: in 1942, to Dr. Bernard J. Muller-Thym, a scholar and Rockhurst alum, and Charles F. Schnabel, a research pioneer in the chemistry of grasses. In 1948, degrees had been given to Gen. Robert Woods Johnson, president of Johnson & Johnson Co., to Rockhurst benefactor Henry J. Massman, Sr., and to Rockhurst alum Bernard Joseph Hale. See *Kansas City Times*, April 21, 1953; and *The Kansas City Star*, May 18, 1952.
25. *Kansas City Times*, May 3, 1954.
26. The Rockhurst Jesuit community had the services of a Jesuit father minister until March 2, 2005, when a layperson designated as house manager was hired as a replacement. As provided in the Constitutions of the Society of Jesus ([88], [431], [432], [434]), the father minister is an official in each Jesuit community. His array of duties are authorized by the community's rector or superior. Father minister's duties address the community's common good by providing for material necessities and physical needs. These include overseeing upkeep and cleaning of the Jesuit house, repairs, food service, bookkeeping, members' health care, etc. The father minister also takes the place of the rector or superior when the latter is absent or ill.
27. *The Kansas City Star*, May 1, 2, 1954.
28. See *The* (Catholic) *Register*, June 28, 1953; *The Kansas City Star*, May 2, 1954; *The Kansas Citian*, May 4, 1954; *Kansas City Times*, June 1, 1954; and "This is Your Opportunity To Gain A Spiritual Share In An Unusual Program," Midwest Jesuit Archives.
29. See *The* (Catholic) *Register*, June 28, 1953, April 10, 1955; *Kansas City Times*, June 8, 1954; *The Kansas City Star*, July 20, 1954; April 2, May 25, 1955; and *The Rockhurst Hawk*, May 13, 1955. The college continued its Rockhurst Day tradition of inviting prominent guests of honor. In 1955 it was Adm. Lewis L. Strauss, chairman of the Atomic Energy Commission, who received an honorary doctor of laws degree during the afternoon ceremonies and spoke that night at the annual banquet at the Hotel Muehlebach.
30. "New Dorms Are Next Rockhurst College Project," *The Rockhurst Hawk*, November 18, 1955. The sale of $750,000 in dormitory bonds was approved by the Board of Directors at a special meeting on December 18, 1956.
31. Ibid.
32. See "Likable Senator Kennedy to Speak Here Saturday," *The Kansas City Star*, May 27, 1956; and *The* (Catholic) *Register*, June 3, 1956.
33. *The Rockhurst Hawk*, November 18, 1955, December 13, 1957. According to *The* (Catholic) *Register*, February 10, 1957, Massman Hall was first occupied over the Christmas holidays of 1956 and the surplus buildings removed between then and February. *The Rockhurst Hawk* said the administration allowed the senior class to hold its Christmas dance in the Massman lounge on December 14, even though the building was not yet finished.
34. See "Massman Hall Open House," *The* (Catholic) *Register*, February 10, 1957; and "Hall Fete Is Here," *The Kansas City Star*, February 3, 1957.
35. *The Rockhurst Hawk*, May 6, September 22, 1957.
36. See ibid., October 27, 1955; and "See Rockhurst Surge," *The Kansas City Star*, November 8, 1955.
37. After Robert Greenlease died in 1969, Mrs. Virginia Greenlease and Mrs. Sam Roberts were elected, in 1971, to the Rockhurst Board of Regents as its first women members. Father Robert Krause to *Jesuit Bulletin*, n.d., Midwest Jesuit Archives.
38. *The Rockhurst Hawk*, March 17, 1961, October 5, 1962.
39. "West Side Dorm Opens; Completion Set for November 1," *The Rockhurst Hawk*, October 12, 1962, and "Dads Here, Dorm Will Be Dedicated," *The Rockhurst Hawk*, December 7, 1962. Ground was broken for Corcoran Hall on the ninth annual Rockhurst Day, May 23, 1961. According to Jim Millard, '64, the delay in the arrival of the wooden doors was due to a carpenters' strike.
40. Ibid., March 17, 1961; December 14, 1962.
41. "A Big Rockhurst Plan," *The Kansas City Star*, May 9, 1962.
42. "Rock President Outlines New Expansion Program," *The Rockhurst Hawk*, December 19, 1958.
43. See *The Kansas City Star*, May 9, 1962, and "The Rockhurst Mid-Century Program" pamphlet, Rockhurst University Archives.
44. "School Adds a Study," *The Kansas City Star*, May 31, 1953.
45. "Engineering Science" brochure, Midwest Jesuit Archives.
46. See "The Student, the Employer, and the Cooperative Plan," brochure, Midwest Jesuit Archives; and *The Kansas City Star*, n.d., scrapbooks, Rockhurst University Archives.
47. See "Night Study List Open," *The Kansas City Star*, September 9, 1953; "Rockhurst Reports on Seven Years of Business Administration Program," *The Kansas Citian*, August 4, 1953; and "Division of Business Administration," public relations, Rockhurst University Archives.
48. See *The Rockhurst Hawk*, October 25, 1963; and "Rockhurst Moves Ahead," *The Kansas Citian*, August 1967, p 32.

49. "President's Annual Report to Shareholders," March 1963.

50. See "Rockhurst College Planning Conference," May 17, 1969; *House History of Rockhurst College 1967*; and Sandra Scott Wilks, *Rockhurst College: 75 Years of Jesuit Education in Kansas City*, p. 27. Wilks writes that the Honors Program, under the direction of Robert R. Lakas, S.J., was open to students with at least a "B" average. Rockhurst offered a 46-day tour of Europe for students, faculty, alumni, and friends of Rockhurst, escorted by Robert J. Imbs, S.J., in the summer of 1964. "Chance to Tour Europe 46 Days This Summer," *The Rockhurst Hawk*, March 20, 1964.

51. See Susan L. Poulson and Loretta P. Higgins, "Gender, Coeducation, and the Transformation of Catholic Identity in American Catholic Higher Education," *Catholic Historical Review* 89 (3): 2003, p. 496; and O'Brien, *From the Heart of the American Church*, p. 211-12.

52. "New Board of Regents Will Assist in Development Plans," *The Rockhurst Hawk*, October 27, 1955.

53. "See Rockhurst Surge," *The Kansas City Star*, November 8, 1955. Currently, there are approximately 110 Rockhurst University Regents.

54. See W. F. Bartholome, "A Brief Historic Summary," Rockhurst University Archives, circa 1957; and Honorary Directors 20th anniversary dinner. Among those who received 20-year certificates were Jim Pendergast, Roy Roberts, William Kemper, Dr. T.S. Bourke, and Lewis McGee.

55. "College Celebrates Golden Jubilee," *The Rockhurst Magazine Jubilee* issue, October 1959.

56. "College's President Interviewed on TV," *The Rockhurst Hawk*, October 9, 1959.

57. Wilfred M. Mallon to Joseph Zuercher, January 18, 1946.

58. Ibid.

59. Zuercher, to Hugh B. Downey, April 14, 1949.

60. Zuercher to Thomas Knapp, S.J., March 29, 1950.

61. *The Kansas City Star*, March 7, 1951, reported that the hand-lettered decree was crafted by a nun, now at Our Lady of Mercy home, 918 E. 9th Street, who had studied art in Spain. The amended charter also included a provision that allowed Rockhurst "to affiliate, merge or consolidate" with other schools, much as the University of Kansas City had done when it entered compacts with the Kansas City Dental College and the Kansas City Law School.

62. *The Rockhurst Hawk*, October 9, 1959.

63. *The Kansas City Star*, December 26, 1954. *The Rockhurst Hawk* of March 4, 1966, reported that Rockhurst's first trip to the NAIA was in 1946, when the Hawks were eliminated in the first round by Arizona State.

64. See *The Call*, April, 1955; Kansas City *News-Press*, January 23, 1955; and *The Kansas City Star*, January 5, 1955. Rockhurst had resigned its membership in the old Missouri State Conference in 1932 and did not return to conference play until 1948, when it joined the Central Intercollegiate Conference. It dropped out of the C.I.C., effective June 1, 1951, after ending its football program the previous year. In commenting on its resignation from the C.I.C., athletic director Paul O. Smith, S.J., said Rockhurst was dropping out because a conference rule required members to compete in both football and basketball. Smith told the media that Rockhurst would continue its athletic program in all sports but football and would do so for the time being as an independent. By 1955, the school had joined the Missouri College Athletic Union. See *The Kansas City Star*, May 16, 1948, December 5, 1950.

65. See *The Rockhurst Hawk*, March 6, 20, 1964, March 4, 1966; and Wilks, *Rockhurst College*, p. 30.

66. See "Rockhurst Returns to N.A.I.A," *The Rockhurst Hawk*, March 4, 1966; and "Area Cagers Chosen," *The Kansas City Star*, March 27, 1968.

67. Ned Holland, *The Rockhurst Hawk*, October 11, 1963. According to *The Hawk*, May 22, 1959, the golf team posted an undefeated season in 1958-59 and advanced to the NAIA meet.

68. Wilks, *Rockhurst College* draft manuscript, Rockhurst University Archives, says the bowling team won the conference again in 1968-69.

69. "Kickball Starts, On Club Basis," *The Rockhurst Hawk*, September 27, 1963.

70. See "Rockhurst Eyes Soccer Crown," *The Rockhurst Hawk*, November 20, 1964, and Wilks, *Rockhurst College*, draft manuscript. The team went back to the tournament in 1967 and took second place, followed by the championship of the Missouri-Kansas League in 1968. Rockhurst members on the NAIA All-Tournament Team for the decade were Mike Morell, Geoff Melchoir, Mike Tucker, Cesar Castro, and Mike Kavanaugh.

71. Wilks, *Rockhurst College*, p. 24-25, 29.

72. See *The Rockhurst Hawk*, March 10, April 14, 1961; March 22, 1965, September 23, 1966; and Wilks, *Rockhurst College*, p. 35. In 1953, a Rockhurst chapter of Alpha Sigma Nu, the national Jesuit honor fraternity, was recognized, and in 1954, Rockhurst established Gamma Rho, a chapter of Alpha Kappa Psi, a fraternity for students interested in pursing a career in business or industry.

73. See "Dramasquers to Present Irish Comedy," *The* (Catholic) *Register*, March 31, 1951; and "Students Had Fun in the Early 1960s With the Ratty Car Rally," *The Rockhurst Hawk*, April 21, 28, 1961; April 26, 1963.

74. See "Enlightened Initiation Program Going Strong," *The Rockhurst Hawk*, September 22, 1961; and "Rock Frosh Are Initiated and Orientated," September 28, 1962.

75. Ibid., March 17, 1961.

76. Ibid., February 16, 1962.

77. Ibid., March 16, May 4, 1962.

78. See ibid., November 2, 1962; and Mary T. Mattione, *The History of Rockhurst College,* draft manuscript, Rockhurst University Archives.

79. O'Brien, *From the Heart of the American Church*, p. 6.

Chapter Eleven – TURBULENT TIMES AND YEARS OF HOPE 1960–70

1. See James A. Henretta, et al., *America's History*, vol. 2, 4th ed. (New York: Bedford/St. Martin's, 2000), p. 927; and *The Rockhurst Hawk*, February 10, 1961.

2. "Neighborhood Survey Shows Restaurants Discriminate," *The Rockhurst Hawk*, February 10, 1961.

3. Ibid., February 17, March 10, 24, 1961.

4. See ibid., March 20, April 10, 1964; and Shirl Kasper and Rick Montgomery, *Kansas City: An American Story* (Kansas City, Mo.: Kansas City Star Books, 1999), p. 292.

5. See David J. O'Brien, *From the Heart of the American Church: Catholic Higher Education and American Culture* (Maryknoll, New York: Orbis Books, 1994), p. 28-29; and James Hennesey,

S.J., *American Catholics: A History of the Roman Catholic Community in the United States* (New York: Oxford University Press, 1981), p. 301-302, 309, 312.

6. "Catholic Spirit Not Evident on Campus, Report States," *The Rockhurst Hawk*, March 22, 1963.
7. O'Brien, *From the Heart of the American Church*, p. 29-30, 51.
8. See ibid.; and Ruth E. Cain, "Responding to a Changing World: The Transition to Co-education at Rockhurst College," December 13, 2000, p. 3, Rockhurst University Archives.
9. "Vatican Council Attempts Church Modernization" and "Ecumenical Council," *The Rockhurst Hawk*, March 22, 1963.
10. Ibid., "In Presidential Poll, Big Vote to Kennedy," November 18, 1960. Of the 413 votes cast, Kennedy garnered 333 to Nixon's 80—a winning margin of 80.6 percent.
11. Ibid., "Two Seniors Join Peace Corps," May 22, 1962. According to *The Rockhurst Hawk*, January 12, 1962, Rockhurst graduate Jim Gilbreth, Class of '58, was the first Rockhurst man to join the Peace Corps. He was in training that January for an assignment to Carmarines Norte in the Philippines.
12. See ibid., September 28, 1964, September 23, 1966; September 30, 1968; "The President's Report 1970"; and O'Brien, *From the Heart of the American Church*, p. 52-53. *The Rockhurst Report*, October 26, 1971, placed day enrollment in the fall of 1971 at 1,147 (847 men and 300 women). In the fall of 1970 it was 1,145. The profile that October of 1971 showed 631 students from Missouri, 264 from Kansas, 209 from 31 other states and 24 countries. Of the total, 15.3 percent were not of the Catholic faith.
13. *The Rockhurst Hawk*, February 23, March 16, May 4, 1962.
14. Ibid., "Rule Concessions in New Dormitory Following Protest," November 2, 1962. With the discretion of the dorm prefect, residents also could get the weekend curfew extended to 3 a.m. Without permission, it remained at 2 a.m.
15. Ibid., "New Dress Policy Drafted," November 6, 1967; "Dress Policy Question Tabled," November 20, 1967; and "Dress Regulations Are Approved," December 18, 1967.
16. Ibid., "Council Airs Student Gripes," April 7, 1967.
17. Ibid., "Council Indicates Major Campus Problems," May 5, 1967.
18. Ibid., February 18, March 4, 1966. The unlimited cut system was to be used at the discretion of individual faculty members. Student Council meetings with President Van Ackeren had started as early as 1965. Ibid., "Path to Administration Open," October 1, 1965.
19. Ibid., February 5, 1965, March 4, 1966.
20. "Chaplain Removes Mass Requirement for Freshmen," *The Rockhurst Hawk*, March 4, 1966.
21. Ibid., November 12, 1965. Sandra Scott Wilks, *Rockhurst College: 75 Years of Jesuit Education in Kansas City*, p. 29, says mandatory retreats were eliminated in 1968.
22. "Sophomores Defend Band Choice," *The Rockhurst Hawk*, October 15, 1965.
23. Ibid., "Rush Costs America in Viet Nam," March 22, 1965. Higgins spoke at the first Henry A. Bundschu Visiting Scholar lecture on March 16, 1965. The Visiting Scholar Lecture Series was established in 1955-56, but endowed later by Henry Bundschu and others.
24. Ibid., "Quotas Determine Chances In Draft," March 22, 1966.
25. Ibid., "Rockhurst Response," December 9, 1968. One of the draft protesters who spoke on campus was David Darst, a Christian Brother who, in May 1968, had participated in the Catonsville Nine action in which 9 peace activists entered draft offices in Catonsville, a suburb of Baltimore, and demanded the draft records from the frightened employees and then took the records out of the building and burned them with a "napalm-like" substance. http://www.brdaviddarstcenter.org/david_darst.html. According to *The Rockhurst Hawk*, March 25, 1968, Rockhurst student Raymond Townley had turned in his draft card and left college to work with a group known as CADRE, the Chicago area draft resisters.
26. Ibid., "Reston Assails LBJ's Secrecy," April 8, 1968.
27. Ibid., "Politics Frustrating for Vice-President," October 22, 1968.
28. Ibid., "Beer Ban Comes to a Head," February 25, 1969, and "Disciplinary Committee Letter," April 1, 1969.
29. "An Avila Link to Rockhurst," *The Kansas City Star*, April 25, 1968.
30. See "Three Brothers and Girl in Rockhurst Class," *Kansas City Times*, June 1, 1954; and "Joan McGraw is First Woman Graduate at Rockhurst," *The Kansas City Star*, May 30, 1954.
31. Susan L. Poulson and Loretta P. Higgins, "Gender, Coeducation, and the Transformation of Catholic Identity in American Catholic Higher Education," *Catholic Historical Review* 89 (3): 2003, p. 490-91.
32. Cain, "Responding to a Changing World," p. 6.
33. "Student Co-education Poll Scheduled," *The Rockhurst Hawk*, February 26, 1968, and "Co-education Favored by 3-1 Vote," March 11, 1968. The vote was in the majority, 76.5 percent, but only 451 students voted, or about 44 percent of the student body.
34. Cain, "Responding to a Changing World," p. 11, 13.
35. Ibid., p. 8, 14.
36. Ibid., p. 16. The three colleges in addition to Avila were Mount St. Scholastica in Atchison, Kansas; Donnelly Junior College in Kansas City, Kansas; and St. Mary's College in Leavenworth, Kansas.
37. *The Kansas City Star*, April 25, 1968.
38. Cain, "Responding to a Changing World," p. 18, writes that this cooperative venture "did not seem to attract large numbers of students."
39. See ibid., p. 19; and *Kansas City Times*, September 25, 1969.
40. According to *The Rockhurst Hawk*, February 12, 1968, Rockhurst had 8 women faculty in the second semester of the 1967-68 academic year. "Rockhurst College," a fact sheet in the Rockhurst University Archives, states that Rockhurst had 30 Jesuits on its staff in 1968-69. See Michael Stellern, "A Different Time," *Rockhurst: The Magazine of Rockhurst University*, Fall 2005, p. 10-11.
41. *Rockhurst Report*, October 26, 1971; Cain, "Responding to a Changing World," p. 19; and AIDP grant sheet, October 1973, Rockhurst University Archives. Michael Stellern, a professor of economics in the Helzberg School of Management, began teaching at Rockhurst in 1979.
42. "Final Report of the Tri-Partite Committee to the President of Rockhurst College," June 15, 1971.
43. "Curriculum Changes Studied by Committee," *The Rockhurst Hawk,* November 4, 1968; "Student-Teacher Interviews Indicate Upcoming Feud Over Requirements," February 25, 1969; and "Curriculum Committee—Past and Present," September 16, 1969.
44. O'Brien, *From the Heart of the American Church*, p. 20-21. The Tripartite Committee recommended that Rockhurst create a new administrative position to lighten the burden on the president's duties. This was done.

45. Van Ackeren to Members of the Rockhurst Community, September 13, 1971.
46. "Report and Recommendations of the Committee on Study of the Curriculum," February 9, 1971.
47. Ibid.
48. O'Brien, *From the Heart of the American Church*, p. 19-20.

Chapter Twelve – FOCUS ON THE NEIGHBORHOOD 1970–85

1. "Presentation to the Plans and Zoning Committee of the Kansas City, Missouri, City Council," May 24, 1979.
2. See Shirl Kasper and Rick Montgomery, *Kansas City: An American Story* (Kansas City, Mo.: Kansas City Star Books, 1999), p. 297; Sherry Lamb Schirmer, *Historical Overview of the Ethnic Communities of Kansas City* (Kansas City: Pan-Educational Institute), 1976; and Kevin Fox Gotham, "Constructing the Segregated City," University of Kansas doctoral dissertation, 1997.
3. A Rockhurst neighbor to Rev. Daniel Conway, October 31, 1950, Rockhurst University Archives.
4. James A. Henretta, et al., *America's History*, vol. 2, 4th ed. (New York: Bedford/St. Martin's, 2000), p. 928-31.
5. Kasper and Montgomery, *Kansas City: An American Story*, p. 298.
6. *The Rockhurst Hawk*, March 4, 1966.
7. See ibid., May 19, 1967; *The New People*, December 22, 1967; and *Kansas City Times*, April 9, 1968.
8. See Kasper and Montgomery, *Kansas City: An American Story*, p. 285; and Rev. Alexander Leutkemeyer, O.S.B., *History of St. Aloysius Parish: On the Occasion of the Centennial Celebration of St. Aloysius Parish* (Kansas City, Mo.: June 21, 1986), p. 35-39.
9. See "Novel Neighborhood Pact," *The Kansas City Star*, February 6, 1972; and *The University News*, October 24, 1974. According to *The Star*, the coalition was formed in October 1970.
10. See *The Kansas City Star*, February 6, 1972; and "Neighborhood Impact Evaluation," Rockhurst University Archives.
11. "Administrative Council Minutes of Liberty Planning Session," June 14-15, 1976.
12. See *The Kansas City Star*, September 20, 1972; "Report to the Long Range Planning Committee," March 7, 1977; and Mary B. Service, coordinator, Title I, report for the 49/63 Business Renewal & Development Corporation, n.d., Rockhurst University Archives.
13. See *The Rockhurst Hawk*, April 30, 1965; *The Kansas City Star*, May 9, 1962, October 11, 1967; *Kansas Citian*, August 1966; "Rockhurst College: Long Range Plan, 1985-1990"; and Sandra Scott Wilks, *Rockhurst College: 75 Years of Jesuit Education in Kansas City* (Kansas City: The Lowell Press, 1985), p. 26. In 1967, the Library Guild was founded and would work to add holdings through membership dues, a commemorative book fund, and special events.
14. *Rockhurst Report*, June 10, 1969.
15. "The President's Report 1970," Rockhurst University Archives.
16. Missouri Commission on Higher Education, "The Second Plan for the Coordination of Higher Education in Missouri," September 1972.
17. J. Barry McGannon, S.J., to Members of the Faculty and Administration, April 21, 1976.
18. "Degree Day at Rockhurst," *Kansas City Times*, May 14, 1973; and "The President's Report 1970." The lecture series mentioned are now part of the Visiting Scholar Lecture Series.
19. "Annual Report for 1974-75, Intramurals."
20. *The Kansas City Star*, April 29, July 1, September 6, 1973.
21. *Kansas City Times*, April 20, 1973.
22. Henretta, *America's History*, p. 990.
23. Gene Hart to Paul O'Connell, "Annual Report to the President and Board of Directors on Intercollegiate Athletics, 1976-77."
24. Henretta, *America's History*, p. 994.
25. EEO Employer Information Report EEO-1, mailed May 16, 1973, Rockhurst University Archives.
26. "Affirmative Action Program to Achieve Equal Opportunity in Employment for Rockhurst College, Kansas City, Missouri," draft, June 19, 1973.
27. J. Barry McGannon, S.J., to J.L. Thomas, June 19, 1973.
28. "Project Equality EEO Validation Review Report," May 27, 1976.
29. "Rockhurst College Long Range Plan, 1985-90."
30. U.S. General Accounting Office, "Developing Institutions Program Questionnaire."
31. "Rockhurst College Long Range Plan, 1985-90." The Women's Center for Non-Traditional Careers was established in the fall of 1975, providing academic or career guidance for women, including those looking to enter professional fields or higher level management positions.
32. "Official Bicentennial Dedication Ceremony," Office of News and Publications, Rockhurst College.
33. See *Kansas City Times*, September 17, 1975; and *The Catholic Key*, November 21, 1976.
34. "President's Report 1976-77," Rockhurst University Archives.
35. *The Catholic Key*, September 21, 1975.
36. Ibid., "Rockhurst College Is New Owner of Phillips House," May 9, 1976.
37. See ibid., "Rockhurst College at the Phillips House: Early Evening Classes Begin August 31," August 29, 1976; "Rockhurst to Sell Phillips House," *Kansas City Times*, July 8, 1977; "College Classes Planned," *The Sun Newspaper*, August 31, 1976.
38. Van Ackeren to faculty members, May 17, 1976.
39. Van Ackeren to Pedro Arrupe, S.J., January 27, 1977.
40. "Continuing Vitality in Jesuit Apostolate of Higher Education," *Jesuit Bulletin* 45: 1 (Spring 1986), p. 10. The establishment of lay boards of trustees had been an ongoing discussion among Catholic educators, particularly reflected in the Land O' Lakes declaration of 1967: "The evolving nature of the Catholic university will necessitate basic reorganizations of structure in order not only to achieve a greater internal cooperation and participation, but also to share the responsibility of direction more broadly and to enlist wider support. A great deal of study and experimentation will be necessary to carry out these changes, but changes of this kind are essential for the future of the Catholic university."

41. See "Father Robert Krause to *Jesuit Bulletin*," n.d., Midwest Jesuit Archives; Van Ackeren to Rev. Leo F. Weber, S.J., March 30, 1977; and "Program: Dinner to Honor the First Kansas Citian as Foundress of the Missouri Province of the Society of Jesus," November 22, 1978, Midwest Jesuit Archives.
42. Maurice M. McNellis to Miller Nichols, January 3, 1975.
43. See McNellis to Van Ackeren, April 27, 1976; "Report to the Long Range Planning Committee: Rockhurst's Role in the Neighborhood," March 7, 1977; "Rockhurst College Properties," March 31, 1977; "Policy on Property Acquisition," draft, November 22, 1978; "Sub-Area No. 1" policies; and "Rockhurst College Long Range Plan, 1985-1990," Rockhurst University Archives. Rockhurst had begun buying properties as early as 1960 but the majority of purchases occurred between 1971 and 1977. Rockhurst also joined the Brush Creek Planning Group, an informal organization including Rockhurst, UMKC, the Nelson Gallery, Kansas City Art Institute, Menorah Hospital, St. Luke's Hospital, and the Plaza business interests, represented by the J.C. Nichols Co. and the Plaza Bank of Commerce. The group was organized in early 1976, its discussions focusing on strengthening and planning for the institutional zone formed by the land controlled by the member institutions. An offshoot was the Troost Corridor Committee, which concerned itself with improving the business climate from Brush Creek to 87th Street, and Main Street to Prospect Avenue.
44. Real Estate Research Corporation, "Neighborhood Impact Evaluation," April 22, 1977.
45. "Study Points Way to Stable Rockhurst Area," *The Kansas City Star*, November 13, 1977.
46. See *The Catholic Key*, January 9, 1977; and *Eastern Kansas Register*, January 21, 1977. Wilks, *Rockhurst History*, says Weiss assumed duties October 1, 1977, but was not officially inaugurated until October 30.
47. That Rockhurst needed to acquire more land on Forest and Tracy avenues between 53rd and 54th streets for parking, recreation, and future development was already a stated goal. See "Planning Conference, Program and Background Data," May 17, 1969, Rockhurst University Archives; "Values: America's Great Challenge, A Comprehensive Program to Generate $8,000,000 in Support for Achievement of the Highest Priority Goals, 1969-1975"; and *Rockhurst Report*, June 10, 1969.
48. See John Sweeney to Robert Weiss, January 18, 1979; Thomas M. Sullivan to Weiss, July 25, 1978; Weiss to Council members, March 8, 1979; and "A summary of college-neighborhood interaction," March 8, 1979, Rockhurst University Archives. Rockhurst's first request, on June 27, 1978, for an off-street parking lot was rejected by the Board of Zoning Adjustment, which suggested that the college submit a complete campus development plan.
49. See "Minutes of the Neighborhood Planning Committee," February 23, March 2, June 1, 8, 1979; and Weiss to Michael Balmuth, February 28, 1979.
50. "Presentation to the City Plan Commission," April 3, 1979.
51. See John Sweeney of John F. Sweeney & Associates, a brokerage, appraisal and consulting firm, to NPC Committee members, December 18, 1978; and Sweeney to Francois Moseby of 5319 Forest, "Notice to Vacate," April 24, 1979.
52. See "Long Range Planning, Prologue," May 5, 1978; and "Board of Regents Planning Conference," March 8, 1980.
53. Henretta, *America's History*, p. 981-84.
54. "Board of Regents Planning Conference," March 8, 1980. A letter from McNellis to Van Ackeren, May 12, 1976, said Rockhurst held a lease, beginning January 1, 1969, and terminating December 31, 1984, on the U-Totem building. The college also received 2 percent of sales in excess of $200,000 annually.
55. "A Plan for the 80's," January 1981.
56. Philip Gleason, *Contending With Modernity: Catholic Higher Education in the Twentieth Century* (New York: Oxford University Press, 1995), p. 321.
57. "Rockhurst College Long Range Plan, 1985-1990." The college counted 113 transfer students in 1984 and 116 in 1985.
58. Ibid. The number of minorities on the faculty increased in the 1985-86 academic year to 3 full-time and one part-time.
59. Thomas Healy, S.J., "Address at the Rockhurst 75th Convocation," October 3, 1985," in "The Rockhurst Occasional Papers," no. 1, Summer 1986. The 2 most important things the Catholic university had to teach the world, Healy said, were the ideal of contemplation and the gift of sacramental imagination, which enabled one to find beauty, power and intricacy with all creation.
60. See Walter J. Ong, "Homily for Mass on the Feast of St. Ignatius Loyola," July 31, 1985; and William E. Wall, "Rockhurst College: A Businessman's Perspective," October 1, 1985, in "The Rockhurst Occasional Papers," no. 1, Summer 1986.
61. See Janet Watson Sheeran, *Best of Friends*; and Sheeran to Joseph Gough, S.J., December 22, 1992.
62. See Sean Brennan, "The Little School on the Hill: The Founding of Rockhurst," *Missouri Historical Review*, vol. 96, no. 1 (October 2001), p. 37-38; and Charles M. Coleman, J.C.L., *This Far by Faith*, vol. 2, p. 557. Brennan also writes that Rockhurst adapted by using nonsectarian rhetoric to appeal to a city of few Catholics.

Chapter Thirteen – AN INVITATION TO EXCELLENCE 1986–96

1. Robert F. Weiss, S.J., to Rockhurst parents and students, March 4, 1986.
2. James A. Henretta, et al., eds., *America's History Volume 2: Since 1865* (Boston: Bedford/St. Martin's Press, 2000), p. 1006-1008.
3. "Tuition Shock: The Cost of College Soars," *The Kansas City Star*, May 26, 1991.
4. Weiss to parents and students, March 4, 1986, February 1987.
5. See ibid.; and Thomas Savage, S.J., to Business & Education Partnership Commission, January 3, 1991; and Savage to students and families, March 1992.
6. National Summit of Independent Higher Education report, 1992. In the article, "Demographics of Higher Education: Redefining the Problem," published in the summer 1990 issue of the *Harvard Graduate School of Education Alumni Bulletin*, Arthur Levine wrote that the number of traditional college-age students (18-22) dropped 14 percent between 1979 and 1989 and was expected to drop another 17 percent by 1992. Levine called for a new focus on underserved populations—those who lacked educational opportunity—black people, poor white people, and Hispanics. That, he argued, could buoy the population of 18-year-old potential college students to 616,009 by the year 1998.
7. Weiss to parents and students, February 1987.

8. Savage, "Mid-Summer Report," July 26, 1991.
9. See "President's Report, 1986"; "Rockhurst Gets $2.5 Million Grant," *The Kansas City Star*, February 21, 1993; and "Fewer Enroll at Colleges," *The Kansas City Star*, August 26, 1993.
10. Savage, "Mid-Summer Report," July 26, 1991.
11. See Savage to students, March 1989; and *The Kansas City Star*, August 26, 1993.
12. See Rockhurst College Proposed 1989-90 Budget; Board of Trustees Finance Committee minutes, February 17, 1989; and Savage to students, March 1989.
13. "An Invitation to Excellence: Report of the Committee on the Liberal Arts and Sciences," 1981, Rockhurst University Archives.
14. *Rockhurst Report*, February 14, March 28, 1986.
15. "President's Report, 1986."
16. Larry Padberg to Anita Salem, chairperson, Curriculum Committee, May 8, 1989. This recommendation by Padberg's ad hoc committee came about as President Thomas Savage announced an administrative restructuring that would eliminate a separate evening division office and director.
17. Donald J. Murphy, S.J., to Thomas Savage, S.J., January 6, 1993.
18. George F. Lundy, S.J., to Donald J. Murphy, S.J., February 26, 1993.
19. See Weiss to parents and students, March 5, 1985, October 31, 1986; and *Rockhurst Report*, July 31, 1986. The "Finance Committee Report" of March 2, 1990, stated that Rockhurst spent approximately $1.2 million in the 1989-90 fiscal year to buy property near campus.
20. "The Van Ackeren Gallery," *Jesuit Bulletin*, January 1980.
21. Ibid.
22. *Rockhurst Report*, March 28, 1986.
23. "One-day Exhibit-Sale By London Grafica Arts," *Rockhurst Report*, October 13, 1970.
24. Ibid., January 3, 1986.
25. Ibid., October 31, 1986.
26. Ibid.
27. See ibid.; "President's Report, 1990-91"; *Rockhurst Community*, February 11, 2000; and "The Year in Review," *Rockhurst: The Magazine of Rockhurst University*, Spring 2003.
28. *Rockhurst Report*, August 23, 1985.
29. See ibid., Spring 1995; and *Rockhurst Community*, November 2003.
30. Ibid., September 19, October 31, 1986.
31. "President's Report, 1975-76."
32. Ibid.
33. See ibid., March, Mid-April 1994; and "Sacred Encounters," *Jesuit Bulletin*, Summer 1993.
34. *Rockhurst Community*, October 1995, November 2003.
35. Ibid., December 1994.
36. Ibid., July 10, 1990.
37. See ibid., Mid-September, October 1993, May 1997; *Rockhurst Report*, January 24, 1986; and "President's Report, 1996." The Professor of the Year for Missouri award was presented by the Council for Advancement and Support of Education. In 1997, Wilson also was honored with the Louis W. Smith Citation for Outstanding Support of Science Education.
38. *Rockhurst Report*, May 17, 1985.
39. *Rockhurst Community*, March 1995.
40. *Rockhurst Report*, March 7, November 21, 1986, January 9, 1987.
41. See *Rockhurst Community*, Mid-October 1996, October 24, 1997, October 2003, and November 2005.
42. Ibid., Summer 1996 and August 2002.
43. "President's Report, 1975-76."
44. See ibid.; and *Rockhurst* magazine, March 1960.
45. "President's Report, 1972."
46. "President's Report, 1975-76."
47. Ibid.
48. *Rockhurst Report*, May 9, 1986.
49. Ibid., January 24, 1986.
50. Hugh M. Owens, S.J., to Alumnus, February 11, March 23, 1972.
51. *Alumni Report*, June 8, 1971.
52. See Owens to Alumnus, March 23, 1972; and "Mark At Rockhurst By Senior Woman," *Kansas City Times*, June 24, 1972.
53. "Report on the Rockhurst Alumni Meeting," New York City, Stockyards Restaurant, 423 Madison Avenue, January 17, 1971.
54. Owens to Alumnus, March 23, 1972.
55. Alumni Gather Across the Nation," *Alumni News & Events*, Spring 2006.
56. Ibid.
57. See *Rockhurst Report*, November 15, 1985; and "Wiggins Wraps Up Impressive Political Career," *Rockhurst: The Magazine of Rockhurst University*, Fall 2002.
58. See Rockhurst University Catalog; and *The Kansas City Star*, January 22, 1939, September 14, 1940. Also among the first inductees were Raymond J. Sonnenberg, Sr., '34, and John S. Sullivan, '30.
59. See *Rockhurst Report*, July 5, 1985, January 9, 1987; "Alumni Awards Program," October 24, 1998, Rockhurst University Archives; and *Rockhurst Community*, August 2002. Joseph P. Glas received the first Outstanding Achievement award, and Samuel J. Kennedy the first Honorary Alumnus.
60. Vita, Rockhurst University Archives.
61. Thomas J. Savage, S.J., "A Report of the First 100 Days to the Rockhurst College Community," January 1989.
62. See Savage to college community, April 6, 1990; and Howard Needles Tammen & Bergendoff Architects Engineers Planners, "Rockhurst College Campus Master Plan," 1990.
63. He had learned this, he said in his inaugural speech, from his mentor, the Rev. Seavey Joyce, S.J., the former president of Boston College who had been instrumental in the resurgence of Boston in the 1960s.
64. Robin Silverman and Frederic Hron, "Local Heroes," *Ingram's*, December 1991.
65. *KCRCHE News*, 1989.
66. Communicorp: The Education Group, Atlanta, Georgia, *Rockhurst College Review and Reflection Paper*, December 2, 1991.
67. See "Rockhurst Ads Get the King of Rock," *The Kansas City Star*, August 17, 1993; and *Rockhurst Community*, January/February 2004.
68. Rosita McCoy, "A New Era Taking Shape," *Jesuit Bulletin*, Fall/Winter 1994.
69. See *Kansas City Business Journal*, October 4-10, 11-17, 1991; and Savage to college community, October 1, 1991.

70. See Board of Trustees minutes, June 13, December 12, 1992; and Finance Committee, March 12, 1992. Prior to the construction of Town House Village, the 1990 Campus Master Plan said a total of 565 students lived in Rockhurst's 3 dormitories—Xavier-Loyola, Corcoran, and McGee. Another 10 students lived in 3 single-family houses on Forest Avenue that had been converted by the college to Global Study Houses.
71. See Joyce A. Smith to department chairs, May 7, 1991; "Rockhurst College Receives $1 Million Grant," Rockhurst press release, April 17, 1991; and "Kemper Foundation Unloads Grant," *Kansas City Business Journal*, March 13, 1992.
72. See Campus Master Plan, 1990; and Board of Trustees minutes, September 16, 1995.
73. See "Rockhurst to Add Baseball and Tennis to Athletic Program," *The Kansas City Star*, April 7, 1993; and *Rockhurst Report*, August 23, 1985.
74. See "Dream Job No Place to Sleep," *The Kansas City Star*, May 31, 1993; and "All Sports Program, 1994-95," Rockhurst University Archives.
75. "Rockhurst Women Win, Advance to Nationals," *The Kansas City Star*, February 27, 1993; and "All Sports Program, 1994-95." The women basketball team's record of 30-1 tied for best record in the nation with Hastings, Nebraska.
76. See *Rockhurst Community*, October 8, 1999. Also with impressive grade point averages were freshmen Katie Cramer, Laura Rhodes, and Rachel Farmer, and the only senior on the team, Tammy Pryor, each with a 3.8 GPA.
77. See "Rietzke Reaches 900-Win Milestone," *Rockhurst: The Magazine of Rockhurst University*, Spring 2006; *The Kansas City Star*, November 10, 1991, November 30, 1994; "All Sports Program, 1994-95"; and "Sports Stats," 1980-81 to 1987-88, Rockhurst University Archives.
78. See "Tocco Receives NAIA's Highest Honor," *Rockhurst: The Magazine of Rockhurst University*, Winter 2007; "Rockhurst Adds to District Title String," *The Kansas City Star*, November 7, 1993; "President's Report 1996"; and www.rockhurst.edu/ru_athletics.
79. See "All Sports Program, 1994-95"; and "1996-97 Records," Rockhurst College Athletic Department, Rockhurst University Archives.
80. *Rockhurst Report*, August 23, 1985; August 29, 1986.
81. "All Sports Program, 1994-95."
82. *Rockhurst Community*, February 1995.
83. "Retention at Rockhurst College," Office of the Registrar, July 22, 1993, Rockhurst University Archives.
84. "Rockhurst College Plans for Growth on a Tight Budget," *The Kansas City Star*, December 17, 1994.
85. See *Rockhurst Community*, September 1994; and "President's Report, 1996."
86. See "Savage Moves Rockhurst onto Fast Track," *Kansas City Business Journal*, October 30-November 5, 1992; "Southside Campus to Open," *The Kansas City Star*, September 19, 1992; and "Open House Set for Rockhurst College's South Campus," *College Boulevard News*, December 8, 1992.
87. See *Rockhurst Community*, Mid-October 1995; and "Rockhurst's Leader Planning to Resign," *The Kansas City Star*, October 11, 1995.
88. *Rockhurst Community*, June 1996.
89. Ibid., August 1996.
90. "President's Report, 1996." In recognition of the new Science Center, Rockhurst received its fifth Cornerstone Award from the Economic Development Corp. of Kansas City. The awards recognized projects that invested in and benefited the city.
91. *Ex Corde Ecclesia*, available at www.vatican.va/.

Chapter Fourteen – KEEPING THE VISION ALIVE 1997–2010

1. Mary Anne Beck, "Rockhurst Reflections," *Rockhurst Community*, September 10, 1999.
2. See *Rockhurst Report*, Fall 1997; and *Rockhurst Community*, December 17, 1997, Winter 1997-98.
3. *Rockhurst Community*, December 17, 1997.
4. Ibid.
5. Kinerk to friends, April 8, July 7, 1999.
6. In 1986, the mezzanine in Greenlease Library was closed in and 6 new study group rooms created. The library also was remodeled to accommodate persons with disabilities with an entrance ramp and renovated restrooms. *Rockhurst Report*, June 27, 1986.
7. *Rockhurst Community*, September 2003.
8. Ibid., September 2005.
9. See Kinerk e-mail to the campus, April 6, 1999; Kinerk to friends, February 15, March 29, April 8, August 23, 1999. By 2008, about 850 students were living on campus.
10. *Rockhurst Community*, July 10, 1990, Mid-April 1994.
11. "Questioning the Issue of Dorm Space," *The Rockhurst Sentinel*, April 27, 2006.
12. Ibid.
13. *Chronicle of Higher Education*, October 4, 1996, cited by Rockhurst Finance Committee, November 21, 1996. Creighton was the second least expensive Jesuit institution.
14. "Rockhurst Wins High Marks," *The Kansas City Star*, August 21, 1998. The term "regional" referred to colleges that offered bachelor's degrees and some master's degrees, but few, if any, doctorates.
15. *Rockhurst Report*, Summer 1997.
16. *Rockhurst Community*, May 1997.
17. Of the 214 freshman in the fall of 2002, 77 came from Kansas City, 61 from St. Louis, 21 from Omaha, and 15 from Kansas; "2002 FTC Profile," Office of Admissions, Rockhurst University Archives.
18. http://www.rockhurst.edu.
19. *Rockhurst Community*, December 2006.
20. Ibid.
21. See ibid., December 1996; and *Rockhurst: The Magazine of Rockhurst University*, Spring 2006.
22. *Rockhurst Community*, November 25, 1997, December 1996. JUSTICE, or Jesuit University and College Students Concerned with Empowerment, was a student group that aimed to preserve

and promote the Jesuit tradition as established by St. Ignatius of Loyola.

23. *Rockhurst: The Magazine of Rockhurst University*, Spring 2000.
24. Ibid., Winter 2007.
25. Ibid.
26. Ibid.
27. "Serving Up a Sizzling Idea for Students," *The Rockhurst Sentinel*, February 4, 2005.
28. See Edward Kinerk, S.J., to friends, April 4, 2000; "The Center for Service Learning Newsletter," October 23, 2006; and www.rockhurst.edu.
29. Brother E. Glenn Kerfoot, "Will You Build Me a House? Rockhurst University Students Give Up Their Spring Break to Do Service Projects," *Jesuit Bulletin*, Fall 2000.
30. Ibid.
31. Ibid.
32. Ibid.
33. Brian Hesse, "Rockhurst Reflections," *Rockhurst Community*, October 22, 1999.
34. Ibid.
35. www.rockhurst.edu/studentlife.greeklife/index.asp.
36. Ibid.
37. "Students Launch Multicultural Sorority," *Rockhurst: The Magazine of Rockhurst University*, Spring 2006.
38. *Rockhurst Community*, April 9, 1991.
39. Ibid.
40. See Peter Ely, S.J., to Rockhurst College community, March 13, 1997; and *Rockhurst Report*, Fall 1997. Father Ely thanked Alexandra Gregory, "who suggested the formation of this group to me."
41. *Rockhurst Community*, September 12, 1997.
42. *Rockhurst Report*, Fall 1997.
43. Ibid.
44. Ibid. In 2008, Rockhurst added a "global perspectives" requirement to its core curriculum. Additionally, the university celebrates an annual World Cultures Day.
45. *Rockhurst Community*, February 25, September 11, 1998.
46. Ibid., March 1995, February 25, 1998.
47. Ibid., March 1995.
48. See ibid., September 11, 1998; Campus e-mail, August 17, 1999; and Kinerk to friends, September 26, 2005.
49. Caroline English, "Changing the Tradition: Rockhurst Ahead of the Times," *The Rockhurst Sentinel*, February 4, 2005.
50. Ibid.
51. Ann Bartholome, "Black Renaissance Festival at Rockhurst," *Jesuit Bulletin*, February 1970.
52. www.riverwalkjazz.org.
53. Bartholome, "Black Renaissance Festival."
54. Ibid.
55. Harry Adamson, "Biography of Robert R. Lakas, S.J.," Rockhurst University Archives.
56. Ibid.
57. Ibid.
58. See Maurice E. Van Ackeren to J. Russ Gramlich, June 26, 1961; "Alumni fete retiring director, Fr. Hilke," n.p., Rockhurst University Archives; "Fr. Hilke Leaves Alumni Job to Concentrate on Teaching," *The Rockhurst Magazine*, n.d., Rockhurst University Archives; and "Rev. George C. Hilke: Jesuit Superior Dies at Age 66," *The Kansas City Star*, September 16, 1963. Although Father Hilke spoke as if Kathleen Milburn had been part of the operation from the beginning, *The Rockhurst Magazine* says she served as secretary from 1947 to 1958. Hilke was appointed director in 1944.
59. *The Rockhurst Magazine*, July 1961, Rockhurst University Archives.
60. Ibid.
61. "Rev. George C. Hilke, S.J.," *The Kansas City Star*, September 16, 1963.
62. *Kansas City Times*, October 16, 1963.
63. See "Father Hale is Dead," *The Kansas City Star*, April 18, 1951; and "Father B.J. Hale Dies in St. Joseph's," *The Catholic Register*, April 29, 1951.
64. See ibid.; and "Join in Bow to Priest," *The Kansas City Star*, n.d., Rockhurst University Archives.
65. See "President's Report, 1975-76," Rockhurst University Archives; and *Rockhurst Community*, November 2003.
66. *Rockhurst Magazine*, Fall 1989.
67. "President's Report, 1996." The $500,000 gift to establish the Rev. Wilfred LaCroix, S.J., Philosophy Fund came from a trust established in Father LaCroix's name by his mother, Elizabeth LaCroix, who died in 1995. The fund would support continued improvement in faculty resources in the college's philosophy and theology departments.
68. Rev. Jack Callahan, S.J., "Rockhurst Reflections," *Rockhurst Community*, October 8, 1999.
69. "President's Report, 1990-91," Rockhurst University Archives. Freeman and Gough marked their anniversaries in September 1990; Carey in September 1991.
70. Katherine Frohoff, "Solid Gold: Rockhurst icon celebrates 50 years of teaching chemistry," *Rockhurst: The Magazine of Rockhurst University*, Fall 2005. Father Wheeler was born July 19, 1923.
71. Ibid.
72. Ibid.
73. Ibid.
74. "Rockhurst's 'Father Van' Is Dead at 85," *The Kansas City Star*, May 13, 1997.
75. Ibid.
76. *Rockhurst Report*, Summer 1997.
77. Kinerk to friends, May 10, 1999.
78. "Rockhurst Ex-president Praised for Achievement," *The Catholic Key*, May 16, 1999.
79. See Allen P. Splete, president, The Council of Independent Colleges, to Edward Kinerk, May 14, 1999; William L. Kostar, Westwood mayor, to Kinerk, May 12, 1999; Kinerk to Spiritual Care Department, St. Joseph's Health Center, June 1, 1999; and Harvey J. Fried, president, Historic Garment District Group, to Kinerk, February 14, 2000.
80. Kinerk to friends, May 11, 1999.
81. See Judy L. Thomas, "Vibrant Leader Kept AIDS Secret," *The Kansas City Star*, February 1, 2000; Paul J. Shaughnessy, S.J.,

"The Gay Priest Problem," *The Catholic World*, November 2000; and "Survey of AIDS Infection Among Priests Shocks U.S. Catholics," *Ecumenical News International*, February 1, 2000.

82. See *The Kansas City Star*, February 1, 2000; *Rockhurst: The Magazine of Rockhurst University*, Spring 2000; and *Rockhurst Community*, February 11, 2000.
83. Kinerk to friends, April 14, 2000.
84. See "Conway Hall Sports Complete Makeover," *Rockhurst: The Magazine of Rockhurst University*, Fall 2002; and *Rockhurst Community*, October 30, 1998, October 2002.
85. *Rockhurst Community*, June 1995.
86. "Students Connect With Technology," *Rockhurst: The Magazine of Rockhurst University*, Fall 2005.
87. Ibid.
88. See ibid.; *Rockhurst Community*, November 2005; and "Rockhurst Traditions," *Rockhurst University 2008-2010 Catalog*, p. 342.
89. *Rockhurst Community*, November 2005.
90. See Kinerk to friends, November 1999, March 13, 2001; and *Rockhurst Community*, October 16, 1998.
91. Kinerk to faculty, September 2, 1998.
92. Ibid.
93. *Rockhurst Community*, December 18, 1998.
94. See Kinerk to friends, Summer 1998; *Rockhurst Community*, August 2003; "Articulation Agreement," January 26, 2004, Rockhurst University Archives; and "Rockhurst Traditions," *Rockhurst University 2008-2010 Catalog*, p. 342-44. The MIHE program was discontinued in 2002.
95. See *Rockhurst Community*, October 30, 1998; Kinerk to friends, August 17, 2001; "School of Management Renamed in Honor of Helzbergs," *Rockhurst: The Magazine of Rockhurst University*, Fall 2001; and "The Year in Review," *Rockhurst: The Magazine of Rockhurst University*, Spring 2003.
96. See Kinerk to friends, January 15, May 1, 2002, March 2006. In his March 2006 letter, Kinerk wrote that Rockhurst had acquired the property "jointly with St. Louis University in 1996 with the thought that the two schools would run joint programs there. The hope never materialized and about five years ago St. Louis University sold its share in the facility to Rockhurst."
97. See "Strengthening Community," *Rockhurst: The Magazine of Rockhurst University*, Spring 2002; "There's No Place Like Home" and "Health and Wellness Complex," *Rockhurst: The Magazine of Rockhurst University*, Spring 2006. This project was later postponed.
98. See "Quadrangle Beautification Dedication" flier, October 17, 2000; and Kinerk to friends, October 19, 26, 2000. The new campus entrance at 54th Street and Troost Avenue opened on January 21, 2000.
99. "The Year in Review," *Rockhurst: The Magazine of Rockhurst University*, Spring 2003.
100. Ibid., "Pathway Paves the Way to Rockhurst's Future," Winter 2001.
101. See *Rockhurst Community*, March 2003; and "Rockhurst Gets Gift for Sports Park," *The Kansas City Star*, February 13, 2003. The capital campaign, begun in June 2001 and scheduled to end in June 2003, reached $48.6 million with the McDonnell gift. It ended with $50.5 million.
102. See Kinerk to friends, Spring 2005; "Rockhurst Traditions," *Rockhurst University 2008-2010 Catalog*, p. 342-44; *Rockhurst: The Magazine of Rockhurst University*, Spring 2004.
103. See Kinerk to campus community, November 25, 2003; and Kinerk to friends, November 2004.
104. See "Rockhurst Seeks NCAA Division II Membership," *The Kansas City Star*, August 27, 1993; Kinerk to friends, Summer 2005; *Rockhurst: The Magazine of Rockhurst University*, Fall 1999.
105. *Rockhurst Community*, September 2005.
106. See ibid., January/February 2004, December 2006; and "Hit the Links With a Pro," *Rockhurst: The Magazine of Rockhurst University*, Spring 2006.
107. "Gift and Bequest Council Celebrates 50 Years," *Rockhurst: The Magazine of Rockhurst University*, Spring 2006.
108. *Rockhurst Community*, October 2004.
109. Ibid., October 2003, August 2004.
110. Ibid., August 2006.
111. See ibid., September 2003; and *The Rockhurst Sentinel*, April 27, 2006.
112. *Rockhurst Community*, May, September 2003.
113. Ibid., August 2006.
114. Kinerk to friends, January 12, 2000.
115. See *Rockhurst Community*, September 1996, November 2001; "President's Report, 1996"; and Kinerk to Right Rev. Gregory Polan, OSB, June 12, 2002. In addition to working as technical theater director, Siebert also taught 2 classes, supervised an independent study program, and was set and lighting designer for Rockhurst College Players' productions. Following the September 11 terrorist attacks, Rockhurst students sent a "banner of support" to students at Fordham College, a sister Jesuit school with a campus at Lincoln Center, in the heart of New York City.
116. David J. O'Brien, *From the Heart of the American Church: Catholic Higher Education and American Culture* (Maryknoll, N.Y.: Orbis Books, 1994), p. 63-68.
117. Ibid., p. 64.
118. Rick Janet, "Rockhurst Reflections—Why Catholic Studies?" *Rockhurst Community*, January 2001.
119. See ibid.; Kinerk to students, February 18, 2002; Gerald L. Miller and Wilburn T. Stancil, eds. *Catholicism at the Millennium: the Church of Tradition in Transition*. Kansas City: Rockhurst University Press, 2001; Joseph A. Cirincione, ed. *Deep Down Things: Essays on Catholic Culture*. Lanham, Maryland: Lexington Books, 2008.
120. "Rockhurst Strengthens Its Focus on Mission," *Rockhurst: The Magazine of Rockhurst University*, Winter 2007.
121. O'Brien, *From the Heart of the American Church*, p. 69.
122. See ibid., p. 71; and "Not Your Father's Jesuits," *Rockhurst: The Magazine of Rockhurst University*, Spring 2004.
123. *Rockhurst University, 2008-2010 Catalog*, p. 324-330.
124. *Rockhurst Community*, August 2004, September 2005, August 2006.
125. Thomas B. Curran, O.S.F.S., "Inaugural Speech," October 27, 2006.

Index

— D —

— E —

— F —

— N —

— O —

— P —

— Q —

— R —

— S —

— T —

— U —